Experimental Psychology

NINTH EDITION

Barry. H. Kantowitz
University of Michigan

Henry L. Roediger III
Washington University in St. Louis

David G. Elmes
Washington and Lee University

WADSWORTH
CENGAGE Learning

Australia • Brazil • Japan • Korea • Mexico •
Singapore • Spain • United Kingdom • United States

WADSWORTH
CENGAGE Learning™

Experimental Psychology, Ninth Edition
Barry H. Kantowitz, Henry L. Roediger III,
David G. Elmes

Publisher: Michele Sordi

Assistant Editor: Rebecca Rosenberg

Technology Project Manager: Lauren Keyes

Marketing Manager: Michelle Williams

Marketing Assistant: Melanie Cregger

Marketing Communications Manager:
Linda Yip

Project Manager, Editorial Production:
Pat Waldo

Creative Director: Rob Hugel

Art Director: Vernon Boes

Text Designer: Cheryl Carrington

Print Buyer: Paula Vang

Text/Art Permissions Editor:
Margaret Chamberlain-Gaston

Image Permissions Editor: Deanna Ettinger

Production Service: Carol O'Connell, Graphic
World Publishing Services

Photo Researcher: Susan Van Etten

Illustrator: Lori Heckleman

Cover Designer: Bill Stanton

Cover Image: © Ryuichi Okano/Getty Images
(main image) and © Akira Inoue/Getty
Images (inset image)

Compositor: Graphic World Inc.

For product information and technology assistance, contact us at
Cengage Learning Customer & Sales Support, 1-800-354-9706
For permission to use material from this text or product,
submit all requests online at **cengage.com/permissions**
Further permissions questions can be e-mailed to
permissionrequest@cengage.com

Library of Congress Control Number: 2008920142

ISBN- 13: 978-0-495-59533-5

ISBN- 10: 0-495-59533-0

Wadsworth
10 Davis Drive
Belmont, CA 94002-3098
USA

Cengage Learning is a leading provider of customized learning solutions with office locations around the globe, including Singapore, the United Kingdom, Australia, Mexico, Brazil, and Japan. Locate your local office at **international.cengage.com/region.**

Cengage Learning products are represented in Canada by Nelson Education, Ltd.

For your course and learning solutions, visit **academic.cengage.com.**

Purchase any of our products at your local college store or at our preferred online store **www.ichapters.com.**

Printed in the United States of America
1   2   3   4   5   6   7   12   11   10   09   08

To three outstanding psychologists who shared the fun
and excitement of experimental psychology with us,
David A. Grant, William M. Hinton, and L. Starling Reid

ABOUT THE AUTHORS

BARRY H. KANTOWITZ is Professor of Psychology, Professor of Industrial and Operational Engineering, and former Director of the Transportation Research Institute at the University of Michigan. Prior to that, he was Chief Scientist of the Human Factors Transportation Center of the Battelle Memorial Institute in Seattle. He received the Ph.D. degree in experimental psychol-  ogy from the University of Wisconsin in 1969. From 1969 to 1987 he held positions as Assistant, Associate, and Professor of Psychological Sciences at Purdue University, West Lafayette, Indiana. Dr. Kantowitz was elected a Fellow of the American Psychological Association in 1974. He has been a National Institute of Mental Health Postdoctoral Fellow at the University of Oregon, a Senior Lecturer in Ergonomics at the Norwegian Institute of Technology, Trondheim, Norway, and a Visiting Professor of Technical Psychology at the University of Lulea, Sweden. He has written and edited more than one dozen books. His research on human attention, mental workload, reaction time, human-machine interaction, and human factors has been supported by the Office of Education, the National Institute of Mental Health, the National Aeronautics and Space Administration, the Air Force Office of Scientific Research, and the Federal Highway Administration. He has served as editor of the *Transportation Human Factors Journal,* Associate Editor of *Human Factors,* and edits the book series *Human Factors in Transportation.*

HENRY L. ROEDIGER III is the James S. McDonnell University Distinguished University Professor of Psychology and Dean of Academic Planning at Washington University in St. Louis, where he has taught since 1996. He received a B.A. degree in psychology from Washington and Lee University in 1969 and a Ph.D. in cog-  nitive psychology from Yale University in 1973. He has taught at Rice University (1988–1996) and Purdue University (1973–1988) and spent 3 years as a visiting professor at the University of Toronto. His research interests lie in cognitive psychology, particularly in human learning and memory. Dr. Roediger has published over 180 articles, chapters, and reviews, as well as two other textbooks: *Psychology* (coauthored with E. D. Capaldi, S. G. Paris, J. Polivy, and P. Herman) and *Research Methods in Psychology* (with D. G. Elmes and B. H. Kantowitz). He also co-edited *Varieties of Memory and Consciousness: Essays in Honour of Endel Tulving* (1989) and *The Science of Memory: Concepts* (2007), as well as several other books. Dr. Roediger has served as editor of the *Journal of Experimental Psychology: Learning, Memory and Cognition* (1984–1989) and was the founding editor of *Psychonomic Bulletin & Review* (1994-1997). He is a consulting editor for nine journals, including *Psychological Science,* the *Journal of Experimental Psychology: Learning, Memory, and Cognition,* the *Journal of Memory and Language,* and *Memory,* among others. He has served as President of the American Psychological Society, the Midwest Psychological Association, and the Experimental Psychology Division of the American Psychological Association. He was a member of the Governing Board of the Psychonomic Society for 5 years and its Chair in 1989–1990. He has been named a Highly Cited Researcher by the Institute of Scientific Information and also received a Guggenheim Fellowship. Roediger has been elected to membership in the Society of Experimental Psychologists and the American Academy of Arts and Sciences, as well as being elected Fellow of the American Association for the Advancement of Science, the American Psychological Association, the Association for Psychological Science, and the Canadian Psychological Association.

DAVID G. ELMES is Professor Emeritus of Psychology at Washington and Lee University, where he taught for 40 years. He earned his B.A. with high honors from the University of Virginia and completed the M.A. and Ph.D. degrees in psychology there. Dr. Elmes was an adjunct professor at Hampden-Sydney College, was a research associate for a year in the Human Performance Center of the University of Michigan, and was a Visiting Fellow of University College at the University of Oxford. At Washington and Lee, he codirected the Cognitive Science Program for 14 years and chaired the Department of Psychology for ten years. Pro-fessor Elmes edited *Readings in Experimental Psychology, Directory of Research in Psychology at Primarily Undergraduate Institutions,* and is coauthor of the eighth edition of *Research Methods in Psychology* (2006, with B. H. Kantowitz and H. L. Roediger III). Dr. Elmes has published numerous articles concerned with human and animal learning, memory, and the sense of smell. The smell research has been supported by the National Institute of Environmental Health Sciences. He frequently referees papers submitted to technical journals and was a consulting editor for the *Journal of Experimental Psychology: Learning, Memory and Cognition* for several years. Professor Elmes is passionate about the educational value of undergraduate research. For a number of years he was active in the Council of Undergraduate Research, for which he has served as Psychology Councilor, Psychology Division Chair, and President. Dr. Elmes is a fellow of the Association for Psychological Science.

CONTENTS IN BRIEF

CONTENTS

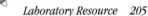

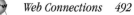

PREFACE

The term *experimental psychology* used to denote only a few selected topics in psychology. In, say, 1930, experiments were conducted to understand sensation, perception, learning, memory, and a few other topics. The situation is quite different today: Experimental methods are used to investigate social psychology, developmental psychology, individual differences, and many other topics (such as environmental psychology) that were not considered in psychology's vision eighty years ago. The use of experimental methods has expanded to include most topics in the field. Writing a textbook aimed at this topic has therefore become an increasing challenge.

This textbook is the ninth edition of a book first published in 1978. Each edition has seen both major and minor changes in response to students' and professors' comments, and this edition is no exception. Readers familiar with the previous edition will find changes in every chapter. We have tried to blend the best aspects of the previous eight editions with new features to make the book even more appealing. (We describe the changes in more detail below.) We are pleased that the continued popularity of this text has permitted us to produce this new edition, because we think we have been able to improve it, and we have enjoyed working on it again.

The title *Experimental Psychology* has appeared on many textbooks that have become classics, beginning with E. B. Titchener's pair in the early 1900s, through Woodworth's 1928 text and its revision (Woodworth & Schlossberg, 1954), and finally to those books by Osgood (1953) and Underwood (1966). All these books provided an introduction to research methodology, but they did so in the context of fundamental research in experimental psychology. The books were primarily about the content of experimental psychology, with an emphasis on the research methods used to acquire the knowledge. We see our textbook as firmly within this tradition, even if much less encyclopedic than the great books mentioned above.

Today this approach is unique; during the 1970s and the 1980s, many "research methods" texts appeared that organize the subject matter quite differently. Instead of providing methodology in the context in which it is used, these books treat methodological topics (e.g., between-subjects designs, small-*n* designs) as chapter titles and introduce content examples to flesh out the discussion of the methods. This is also an excellent approach, and we have produced another text that embodies this method (*Research Methods in Psychology,* by Elmes, Kantowitz, and Roediger, also published by Wadsworth). However, *Experimental Psychology* seeks to provide an integrated blend of content and methodology, with methods discussed in the context of actual research. Primary differences between our text and those of our predecessors in this tradition are that our approach is to select particular examples that best illustrate the methodological point under consideration and that our book is intended mostly for an undergraduate audience with only a first course in psychology as a background.

We should note one point about terms in our book. In 1994, the *Publication Manual of the American Psychological Association* recommended that the traditional term *subjects,* which had been used for over a century to refer to people who were tested in psychological research, be changed to *participants.* This change received a mixed reaction in the research community, and some other organizations that publish psychology journals did not go along. For example, the Psychonomic Society permits use of either term in papers published in their journals. In addition, the copyeditors of the American Psychological Association journals do not insist that participants be used as the favored term, but rather encourage its use. Because the situation is unsettled, we have followed the convention of using both *subjects* and *participants* when referring to people in psychological research. We tend to use *subjects* when referring to non-human animals in research, but we use both terms when referring to humans. The usage in our text therefore reflects current practice in the field at large.

▼ TEXT ORGANIZATION

The philosophy of the text remains unchanged. As with the first eight editions, we have striven to achieve an integrated treatment of experimental psychology with a seamless link binding methodology and content. The book includes two main parts. The first five chapters constitute Part One, Fundamentals of Research, and discuss some basic methodological preliminaries that students need. In these chapters we describe some general aspects of science and theory construction; the features of (and differences among) observational, correlational, and experimental methods (with an emphasis on the last); ethical issues in research; and how to read and write research reports.

In the remaining ten chapters, which make up Part Two, Principles and Practices of Research, we flesh out the bare bones provided in Part One by illustrating methodological topics in the context of actual research problems. The chapters are provided with content titles (for example, Perception), and some content is covered in its own right, but the main purpose of the chapters is to present methodological topics in the context of actual research. This organization reflects our belief that the best way to provide students with an understanding of methodology is to embed it in the context of real problems that occur in conducting research. Methodology does not exist in a vacuum, but is devised to solve concrete research problems. We hope that presenting methods in the context of important content issues will help students to see the importance of considering research methods.

Chapter Format

The chapters in Part Two all share a common format. This parallel structure should help orient students to important features of the text that facilitate learning.

Chapter Opening The chapters begin with an outline and quotation. Following a brief orientation to the content area explored in the chapter, the student will come across the first of several boxed inserts, which readers of the previous editions have found to be helpful and which have therefore been carried over to the ninth edition.

Introducing the Variables This feature quickly orients the student to those independent, dependent, and control variables commonly used in particular research areas. Our coverage of these variables does not exhaust the possibilities, but does include some of the most common ones.

Experimental Topics and Research Illustrations This feature represents the main part of the chapter, in which two or three methodology issues are presented in the context of an actual research problem. Thus, for example, in Chapter 10 we discuss the difficulty of ceiling and floor effects in the context of a memory experiment in which this problem actually arose. Many of these experimental topics have been introduced in Part One and are covered in more detail in Part Two. Some crucial topics are discussed more than once in Part Two to ensure better comprehension. The content topics were chosen to be good vehicles for discussing the particular methodological point under consideration. Thus, the content topics may not represent the most important topics in the subject under discussion, nor do we intend our chapters to represent a complete summary of contemporary work in the area. Our intent is to illustrate issues of methods in the context of actual research problems that are of interest. Two other unique features appear toward the end of each chapter in Part Two.

From Problem To Experiment: The Nuts and Bolts In this section, we present the rationale behind experimental design decisions—how many subjects should be used, why variable X is selected instead of variable Y, and so on—when hypotheses are taken from a general form to the specifics of an experiment. These decisions are the "nuts and bolts" of experimental research. They are second nature to practicing experimenters and hence seldom articulated in journal articles, but they may represent puzzles to those new to research.

Psychology in Action This feature suggests safe and simple experimental demonstrations that require little or no equipment and that can be used in or out of class. For example, Chapter 7 includes a demonstration of the Stroop effect and Chapter 14 presents methods to measure the effects of noise on memory.

End-of-Chapter Features Finally each chapter contains a summary in which the main points of the chapter are reviewed, a set of key terms for review and study, and several discussion questions.

Chapter Sequence

Although students will be best served by reading Part One in correct serial order (especially the first three chapters), those professors and students more interested in methodology than in content can ignore the chapter numbers in Part Two. The table that cross-lists chapter numbers and experimental topics (to be found after the Preface) can be used to determine the order in which chapters in Part Two are assigned. Thus, the instructor has the option of following a more- or less-traditional order or of creating a unique ordering better suited to his or her educational goals. Two lesser-used chapters that, however, may be quite necessary for some, are located in appendixes. Appendix A provides a brief sketch of the history of experimental psychology, and Appendix B contains a review of basic statistics.

Ancillaries

Ancillaries for this edition include the following:

Instructor's Manual with Test Bank Resources for instructors include chapter outlines, key terms, answers to discussion questions, lecture suggestions, demonstration suggestions, and "experimental dilemmas." The test bank contains multiple-choice, true-false, and essay questions for each chapter. The test bank is also available electronically in the ExamView® format for the instructors to create their own tests/answers.

Electronic Transparencies Many of the figures from the text are available as Power-Point® slides that can be downloaded and used in the classroom.

Book Companion Website academic.cengage.com/psychology/kantowitz The website contains several helpful features for both instructors and students. Instructors will be able to find teaching activities, chapter outlines, and chapters summaries. To aid students, the website contains a glossary, flashcards, crossword puzzles to help learn key terms, and web links to Wadsworth Online Research Methods workshops, as well as other useful web links; suggestions for using Infotrac College Edition; and multiple-choice, matching, fill-in-the-blank, and essay tutorial quizzes that can be printed out or emailed directly to instructors.

Changes in the Ninth Edition

Users of the previous edition will discover many changes in the current edition. Web references have been updated for all chapters; while these were working in January 2008, some will undoubtedly change during the life of this edition. These references guide readers to relevant discussions online, including the Wadsworth Online at The Wadsworth Psychology Study Center. In addition, instructors in North America who have specified that InfoTrac College Edition be packaged with this text have been provided 4 months of free access to this extensive virtual library for their students.

New coverage and more recent references have been added in every chapter, and some chapters have been rebuilt to reflect the most recent findings and topics, even though this meant removing substantial amounts of text dearly cherished by the authors. Chapter 1 adds new research on the dangers of using a cell phone while driving, and the section on relationships between applied and basic research has been updated to cover recent developments in the push to translate basic findings into applications at NIH. Chapter 2 contains new data in Table 2-1 and new discussion that media violence is a threat to public health, and the chapter now discusses the attitudes of voters toward the appearance of presidential candidates on late-night comedy shows. Chapter 3 has a new and more interesting example, relating belief in God to aggression, which illustrates the importance of interactions. Chapter 4 has additional description of the IRB process and problems associated with perceived unfairness. Chapter 5 has a new sample journal article and also refers to a recent list of tips for authors of journal articles. In Chapter 6 we replaced a 1952 chapter-opening example with a 2007 example, even though the author really liked the old example. In Chapter 7 the discussion of perceptual defense was replaced by a discussion of explicit awareness research. Chapter 8 has a new discussion of cognitive control. Chapter 9 has a new discussion of changing-criterion design as used in therapy. Chapter 10 has new examples of flash-bulb memory and the savings method. Chapter 11 now includes mention of recent neuroimaging research. Chapter 12 also adds current work on brain imaging as well as recent work on motivation and intellectual performance. Chapter 13 includes new research on social contagion of memory, obedience, and implicit attitudes and behavior. Chapter 14 adds new work that challenges the classical animal model of crowding and also research that improves a measure of density in a train car. Chapter 15 adds a new study on dynamic visual acuity and a brief discussion on the use of models to explain mental workload. Please continue to let the authors know how you and your students react to these substantial changes.

▼ ACKNOWLEDGMENTS

It takes many more people than authors to create a text that has endured for nine editions, and the authors are pleased to acknowledge with gratitude the assistance of numerous others. Our greatest debt is to the readers of previous editions who continue to offer many useful comments. Without their helpful suggestions, this new edition would not exist.

Mila Sugovic provided excellent editorial help, especially with the art work in Chapters 2, 7, and 9, and Keith Lyle and Jane McConnell provided valuable assistance in manuscript preparation and proofreading among other things, and we thank them all. We also thank Erik Evans, Rebecca Rosenberg, and Pat Waldo at Cengage and Carol O'Connell at Graphic World Publishing Services for their substantial efforts guiding our book through the production process.

We would like to thank the following reviewers, who provided feedback to help us with this revision: Jeffrey M. Zacks, Washington University; Sandra Sego, American International College; Hallie Stephens, Southeastern Oklahoma State University; and Paul Thuras, St. Mary's University of Minnesota.

ORGANIZATION OF THE BOOK

Experimental Topics	6	7	8	9	10	11	12	13	14	15
Choosing the dependent variable								X		
Confounding			X							
Converging operations		X								
Counterbalancing				X						
Demand characteristics								X		
Ethical issues									X	
Experimental control/ extraneous variables						X		X		
Field research								X		X
Generalization of results					X				X	
Interaction effects			X		X					
Measurement scales	X									
Operational definition	X						X			
Quasi-experiments									X	
Regression artifacts							X			
Reliability of measures						X	X			
Scale attenuation					X					
Selection of dependent variable			X					X		X
Small-n design	X			X						X
Verbal report		X				X				
Within- and between-subjects designs				X						

FUNDAMENTALS OF RESEARCH

CHAPTER 1

EXPLANATION IN SCIENTIFIC PSYCHOLOGY

Ask any scientist what he conceives the scientific method to be, and he will adopt an expression that is at once solemn and shifty-eyed; solemn, because he feels he ought to declare an opinion, shifty-eyed because he is wondering how to conceal the fact that he has no opinion to declare. If taunted he would probably mumble something about "Induction" and "Establishing the Laws of Nature," but if anyone working in a laboratory professed to be trying to establish Laws of Nature by induction, we should begin to think he was overdue for leave. (P. B. MEDAWAR)

The goal of scientific psychology is to understand why people think and act as they do. In contrast to nonscientists, who rely on informal and secondary sources of knowledge, psychologists use a variety of well-developed techniques to gather information and develop theoretical explanations. As one example of this scientific approach to understanding, consider the following case study of the research process.

▼ MAKING SENSE OF THE WORLD

Social Loafing

A common observation—one you probably have made yourself on many occasions—is that people working in a group often seem to "slack off" in their effort. Many people in groups seem willing to let a few do the work. Bibb Latané, a social psychologist, noticed this tendency and decided to study it experimentally. Initially, Latané examined the research literature for evidence of this phenomenon of people working less hard in groups, which he named **social loafing.** One of the earliest studies of social loafing was conducted by a French agricultural engineer (Ringelmann, 1913; Kravitz & Martin, 1986) who asked people to pull on a rope as hard as they could. The subjects pulled by themselves or with one, two, or seven others. A sensitive gauge was used to measure how hard they pulled the rope. If people exert the same amount of effort in groups as when alone, then the group performance should be the sum of the efforts of all individuals. Ringelmann discovered that groups of two pulled at only 95 percent of their capacity, and groups of three and eight sank to 85 percent and 49 percent, respectively. So, it is probably not just our imaginations when we notice others (and ourselves?) seeming to put forth less effort when working in groups: Ringelmann's research provides us with a good example of social loafing.

Latané and his colleagues went on to perform a systematic series of experiments on the phenomenon of social loafing (Latané, 1981; Latané, Williams, & Harkins, 1979). They first showed that the phenomenon could be obtained in other experimental situations besides that of rope pulling. They also demonstrated that social loafing occurs in several different cultures (Gabrenya, Latané, & Wang, 1983) and even holds for young children. Thus, social loafing seems to be a pervasive characteristic of working in groups.

Latané has related this work to a more general theory of human social behavior (Latané, 1981). The evidence from the experimental studies points to **diffusion of responsibility** as a possible reason for social loafing. People working by themselves think they are responsible for completing the task; when they work in groups, however, this feeling of responsibility diffuses to others. The same idea accounts for behavior in other group situations: If one of your professors asks a question in a class containing only two other people, you would probably feel responsible for trying to answer. However, if there were two hundred other people in the class, you would likely feel much less responsible for answering. Similarly, people are more likely to help in an emergency when they feel the burden of responsibility than when there are several others about who could help.

One possible benefit of such basic research into a phenomenon is that the findings may be applied later to solve some practical problem. A great problem in American society is the difficulty of keeping worker productivity high. Although social loafing is, at best, only one factor involved in this complicated issue, Marriott (1949) showed that factory workers working in large groups produce less per individual than do those working in small groups. Thus, basic research that would show a way to overcome the problem of social loafing may be of great practical import. In fact, Williams, Harkins, and Latané (1981) found conditions that eliminated the effect of social loafing. When individual performance (rather than just performance of the entire group) could be monitored within the group situation, the individuals worked just as hard as they did when they worked alone. Certainly more research must be done, but it may be that simply measuring individual performance in group situations could help eliminate social loafing and increase productivity. The proposed solution may seem simple, but in many jobs only group performance is measured and individual performance is ignored.

We have discussed Latané's studies of social loafing as an example of psychological research to illustrate how an interesting problem can be brought into a laboratory setting and studied in a controlled manner. The experiments performed will, when carefully conducted, promote a better understanding of the phenomenon of interest than will simple observation of events and reflection about them. This book is largely about the proper conduct of such experimental studies—how to develop hypotheses, arrange experimental conditions to test the hypotheses, collect observations (data) within an experiment, and then analyze and interpret the data collected. In short, in this book we try to cover the fundamentals of scientific inquiry as applied to psychology.

Before examining the specifics of research, we discuss some general issues in the remainder of this chapter. The research on social loafing is used to illustrate several aspects of psychological science—its purposes, its sources, and its nature.

Curiosity: The Wellspring of Science

A scientist wants to discover how and why things work. In this desire, he or she is not different from a child or anyone else who is curious about the world we inhabit. The casual observer may not feel terribly frustrated if some observation (for example, that water always goes down a sink drain counterclockwise or that individual effort in a group is low) cannot be explained. However, the professional scientist has a strong desire to pursue an observation until an explanation is at hand or a problem is solved. It is not so much that scientists are more curious than other people as it is that they are willing to go to much greater lengths to satisfy their curiosity than are nonscientists. This unwillingness to tolerate unanswered questions and unsolved problems has led science to develop several techniques for obtaining relief from curiosity. It is the careful application of these techniques that distinguishes scientific curiosity from everyday curiosity.

The common denominator for many of these scientific techniques is skepticism. Skepticism is the philosophical belief that the truth of all knowledge is questionable. Therefore, all inquiry must be accompanied by reasonable doubt. No scientific fact can be known with 100 percent certainty. For example, bridge engineering is a practical discipline derived from a scientific foundation in such fields as physics and metallurgy. Most people, when they drive a car across a bridge, do not actively consider that the bridge might collapse. It is a known fact that well-maintained bridges are safe. Yet in the summer of 2007, a bridge in Minneapolis–St. Paul, Minnesota, collapsed. This event will lead to further research, to result in safer bridges being built. Many of the tools, such as statistics, discussed in this text allow the skeptical scientist to measure reasonable doubt.

Of what use is scientific curiosity? What purpose does it serve? We have stated that psychologists try to determine why people think and act as they do. Let us explore what this means in more detail.

▼ SOURCES OF KNOWLEDGE

Fixation of Belief

The scientific method is a valid way to acquire knowledge about the world around us. What characteristics of the scientific approach make it a desirable way to learn about and arrive at beliefs about the nature of things? Perhaps the best way to answer this question is to contrast science with other modes of fixing belief, since science is only one way in which beliefs are formed.

More than one hundred years ago, the American philosopher Charles Sanders Peirce (1877) compared the scientific way of knowing with three other methods of developing beliefs. He called these the **authority, tenacity,** and *a priori* **methods.** According to Peirce, the simplest way of fixing belief is to take someone else's word on faith. A trusted authority tells you what is true and what is false. Young children believe what their parents tell them simply because Mommy and Daddy are always right. As children get older, they may discover, unhappily, that Mom and Dad are not always correct when it comes to astrophysics, macroeconomics, computer technology, and other specialized fields of knowledge. Although this may cause children to doubt some of their parents' earlier proclamations, it may not result in utter rejection of this method of fixing belief. Instead, some other authority may be sought.

Religious beliefs are formed by the method of authority. Long after Catholic children have rejected their parents as the source of all knowledge, particularly about religious doctrine, they may still believe that the pope is infallible. Believing the news you see on television means that you accept CNN or some other news network as an authority. You may believe your professors because they are authorities. Since people lack the resources to investigate everything they learn, much knowledge and many beliefs are fixed by the method of authority. Provided nothing happens to raise doubts about the competence of the authority setting the beliefs, this method offers the great advantages of minimum effort and substantial security. It is most pleasant in a troubled world to have complete faith in beliefs handed down to you.

Another method of fixing belief is one in which a person steadfastly refuses to alter acquired knowledge, regardless of evidence to the contrary. The **method of tenacity,** as it was termed by Peirce, is commonly seen in racial bigots who rigidly cling to a stereotype even in the presence of a good counterexample. Although this method of maintaining a belief may not be entirely rational, we cannot say it is completely without value. The method of tenacity allows people to maintain a uniform and constant outlook on things, so it may relieve them from a certain amount of stress and psychological discomfort.

The third nonscientific method discussed by Peirce fixes belief *a priori*. In this context, the term *a priori* refers to something that is believed without prior study or examination. Propositions that seem reasonable are believed. This is an extension of the method of authority. However, there is no one particular authority being followed blindly in this method. The general cultural outlook is what seems to fix belief *a priori*. People once believed the world was flat, and it did seem reasonable to suppose that the sun revolved around the earth as does the moon. Indeed, the world does look flat if you are not in a spacecraft.

The tenacity and *a priori* methods are similar in that they minimize the possibility of being influenced by conflicting opinion. In the method of tenacity, other points of view, although noticed, are completely discounted. Thus, a racial stereotype is preserved despite other evidence, such as the good qualities of a person of a different race who lives next door. In the *a priori* method, other points of view go unnoticed. For example, the sight of a ship disappearing from bottom to top, instead of all at once, as it leaves port may seem irrelevant if you already know the world is flat.

The last of Peirce's methods, the **scientific method,** fixes belief on the basis of experience. Science is based on the assumption that events have causes and that we can discover those causes through controlled observation. This belief, that observable causes determine events, is known as **determinism.** If we define scientific psychology (as well as science in general) as a repeatable, self-correcting undertaking that seeks to understand phenomena on the basis of empirical observation, then we can see several advantages to the scientific method over the methods just outlined. Let us see what we mean by **empirical** and **self-correcting** and examine the advantages associated with those aspects of science.

The first advantage of the scientific method is its emphasis on empirical observation. None of those other methods relies on data (observations of the world) obtained by systematic observation. In other words, there is no empirical basis for fixing belief. The word *empirical* is derived from an old Greek word meaning "experience." Having an empirical basis for beliefs means that experience rather than faith is the source of knowledge. Having one's beliefs fixed by authority carries no guarantee that the authority obtained data before forming an opinion. By definition, the method of tenacity refuses to consider data, as does the *a priori* method. Facts that are considered in these other modes of fixing belief are not ordinarily obtained by systematic procedures. For example, casual observation was the "method" that led to the ideas that the world was flat and that frogs spontaneously generated from the mud each spring, as Aristotle believed.

The second advantage of science is that it offers procedures for establishing the superiority of one belief over another. Persons holding different beliefs will find it difficult to reconcile their opinions. Science overcomes this problem. In principle, anyone can make an empirical observation, which means that scientific data can be public and can be repeatedly obtained. Through public observations, new beliefs are compared with old beliefs, and old beliefs are discarded if they do not fit the empirical facts. This does not imply that each and every scientist instantaneously drops outmoded beliefs in favor of new opinions. Changing scientific beliefs is usually a slow process, but eventually incorrect ideas are weeded out. Empirical, public observations are the cornerstone of the scientific method, because they make science a *self-correcting* endeavor.

▼ THE NATURE OF THE SCIENTIFIC EXPLANATION

What Is a Theory?

A theory can be crudely defined as a set of related statements that explains a variety of occurrences. The more the occurrences and the fewer the statements, the better the theory. The law of gravity explains falling apples, the behavior of roller coasters, and the position of bodies within the solar system. With a small number of statements about the mutual attraction of bodies, it explains a large number of events. It is therefore a powerful theory. (This does not necessarily mean it is a correct theory, since there are some events it cannot explain.)

Theory in psychology performs two major functions. First, it provides a framework for the systematic and orderly display of data—that is, it serves as a convenient way for the scientist to *organize* data. Even the most dedicated inductive scientist will eventually have difficulty remembering the outcomes of dozens of experiments. Theory can be used as a kind of filing system to help experimenters organize results. Second, it allows the scientist to generate *predictions* for situations in which no data have been obtained. The greater the degree of precision of these predictions, the better the theory. With the best of intentions, scientists who claim to be testing the same theory often derive from the theory different predictions about the same situation. This unfortunate circumstance is relatively more common in psychology, where many theories are stated in a loose verbal fashion, than in physics, where theories are more formal and better quantified through the use of mathematics. Although psychologists are rapidly becoming equipped to state their theories more precisely through such formal mechanisms as mathematics and computer simulations, the typical psychological theory is still not as precise as theories in more established, older sciences.

Let us see how the theory devised by Latané to account for social loafing stacks up with regard to organization and prediction. The theory of diffusion of responsibility organizes a substantial amount of data about social loafing. More important, the theory seems to account for a remarkable variety of other observations. For example, Latané (1981) notes that the size of a tip left at a restaurant table is inversely related to the number of people in the dinner party. Likewise, proportionately more people committed themselves to Christ at smaller Billy Graham crusades than at larger ones. Finally, work by Latané and Darley (1970), which is discussed in detail later in this book, shows that the willingness of people to help in a crisis is inversely related to the number of other bystanders present. The entire pattern of results can be subsumed under the notion of diffusion of responsibility, which asserts that people feel less responsibility for their own actions when they are in a group than when they are alone—so they are less likely to help in an emergency, they are less likely to leave a large tip, and so on. Latané's theory also makes rather precise predictions about the impact of the presence of other people on a person's actions. In fact, one version of the theory (Latané, 1981) presents its major assumptions in terms of mathematical equations.

Theories are devised to organize concepts and facts into a coherent pattern and to predict additional observations. Sometimes the two functions of theory—organization and prediction—are called **description** and **explanation,** respectively. Unfortunately, formulating the roles of theory in this manner often leads to an argument about the relative superiority of deductive or inductive approaches to science—a discussion the following section concludes is fruitless. According to the deductive scientist, the inductive scientist is concerned only with description. The inductive scientist defends against this charge by retorting that description is explanation—if a psychologist could correctly predict and control all behavior by referring to properly organized sets of results, then that psychologist would also be explaining behavior. The argument is futile because both views are correct. If all the necessary data were properly organized, predictions could be made without recourse to a formal body of theoretical statements. Since all the data are not properly organized as yet, and perhaps never will be, theories are required to bridge the gap between knowledge and ignorance. Remember, however, that theories will never be complete, because *all* the data will never be available. So, we have merely recast the argument between inductive and deductive views about which approach will more quickly and surely lead to truth. Ultimately, description and explanation may be equivalent. The two terms describe the path taken more than they describe the eventual theoretical outcome. To avoid this pitfall, we shall refer to the two major functions of theory as **organization** and **prediction** rather than as description and explanation.

Induction and Deduction

Certain basic elements are shared by all approaches to science. The most important of these are **data** (empirical observations) and **theory** (organization of concepts that permit prediction of data). Science needs and uses both data and theory, and our outline of research on social loafing indicates that they can be interlinked in a complex way. However, in the history of science, individual scientists have differed about which is more important and which comes first. Trying to decide this is a little like trying to decide whether the chicken or the egg comes first. Science attempts to understand why things work the way they do, and, as we will argue, understanding involves both data and theory.

Although Bacon recognized the importance of both data and theory, he believed in the primacy of empirical observations; modern scientists also emphasize data and view progress in science as working from data to theory. Such an approach is an example of **induction,** in which reasoning proceeds from particular data to a general theory. The converse approach, which emphasizes theory predicting data, is called **deduction;** here, reasoning proceeds from a general theory to particular data (Figure 1.1). Because many scientists and philosophers of science have argued for the primacy of one form of reasoning over the other, we will examine induction and deduction in some detail. Because empirical **observations** distinguish science from other modes of fixing belief, many have argued that induction must be the way that science should work. As Harré (1983) states it, "observations and the results of experiments are said to be 'data,' which provide a sound and solid base for the erection of the fragile edifice of scientific thought"

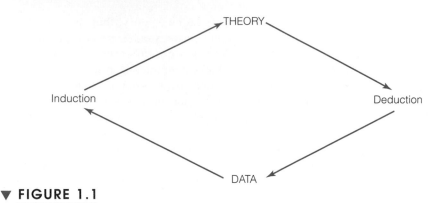

▼ **FIGURE 1.1**

A Theory Organizes and Predicts Data. By means of deduction, particular observations (data) may be predicted. By means of induction, the data suggest organizing principles (theories). This circular relationship indicates that theories are tentative pictures of how data are organized.

(p. 6). In the case of social loafing, the argument would be that the facts of social loafing derived from **experimentation** produced the theory of diffusion of responsibility.

One problem with a purely inductive approach has to do with the finality of empirical observations. Scientific observations are tied to the circumstances under which they are made, which means that the laws or theories that are induced from them must also be limited in scope. Subsequent experiments in different contexts may suggest another theory or modifications to an existing one, so our theories that are induced on the basis of particular observations can (and usually do) change when other observations are made. This, of course, is a problem only if one takes an authoritarian view of ideas and believes in clinging tenaciously to a particular theory. Thus, theories induced from observations are tentative ideas, not final truths, and the theoretical changes that occur as a result of continued empirical work exemplify the self-correcting nature of science.

According to the deductive view, which emphasizes the primacy of theory, the important scientific aspect of the social loafing research is the empirical guidance provided by the formal theory of social loafing. Furthermore, the more general theory, diffusion of responsibility, provides an understanding of social loafing. The deductive approach holds well-developed theories in high regard. Casual observations, informal theories, and data take second place to broad theories that describe and predict a substantial number of observations.

From the standpoint of the deductive approach, scientific understanding means, in part, that a theory will predict that certain kinds of empirical observations should occur. In the case of social loafing, the theory of diffusion of responsibility suggests that monitoring individual performance in a group should reduce the diffusion of responsibility, which in turn will reduce the amount of social loafing that is observed. This prediction, as we have seen, proves to be correct.

But what do correct predictions reveal? If a theory is verified by the results of experiments, a deductive scientist might have increased confidence in the veracity of the theory. However, since empirical observations are not final and can change, something other than verification may be essential for acceptance or rejection of a theory. Popper

(1961), a philosopher of science, has suggested that good theories must be fallible; that is, the empirical predictions must be capable of tests that could show them to be false. This suggestion of Popper's has been called the **falsifiability view.** According to the falsifiability view, the temporary nature of induction makes negative evidence more important than positive support. If a prediction is supported by data, one cannot say that the theory is true. However, if a theory leads to a prediction that is not supported by the data, then Popper would argue that the theory must be false, and it should be rejected. According to Popper, a theory can never be proven; it can only be disproven.

Popper's view about the difficulty of proving a theory can be illustrated by thinking about a specific theory; for example, does a bag of marbles contain only black marbles? One good way to test this theory would be to reach into the bag and draw out a marble. The marble is black. What can you conclude about the theory that all the marbles are black? While the datum (one black marble) is consistent with the theory, it does not prove it. There might still be a white marble inside the bag. So pull out another marble; indeed, pull out ten more marbles. All ten are black. Is the theory now proved? No, there still might be a single white marble lurking in the bag. You would have to remove every marble to ensure that there were no white marbles. It is easy to prove the theory wrong if a white marble gets drawn. Proving the theory to be correct depends on the size of the bag. If the bag is infinitely large, the theory can never be proven because the next marble you examine might be white.

Proctor and Capaldi (2001) have noted two kinds of objections to Popper's approach. First, there is a logical problem (Salmon, 1988). Since a theory potentially can always be disconfirmed by the next experiment, the number of accomplished experiments consistent with the theory is irrelevant. So logically a well-collaborated theory is not more valuable and does not necessarily make better predictions than a theory that has never been tested. This logical view conflicts with the practical view that scientists tend to be more comfortable with theories that have passed several experimental tests. This practical view (Kuhn, 1970) is what Proctor and Capaldi (2001) offer as the second, empirical, objection to falsification: Theories tend to be accepted, at least initially, on the basis of their ability to explain (organize) existing phenomena more than on their ability to predict new results.

One problem with the deductive approach has to do with the theories themselves. Most theories include many assumptions about the world that are difficult to test and that may be wrong. In Latané's work, one assumption underlying the general theory is that measuring a person's behavior in an experimental context does not change the behavior in question. Although this often is a reasonable assumption, we will show later that people can react to being observed in unusual ways, which means that this assumption is sometimes wrong. If the untested assumptions are wrong, then a particular experiment that falsifies a theory may have falsified it for the wrong reasons. That is, the test of the theory may not have been fair or appropriate. It can be concluded, therefore, that the deductive approach by itself cannot lead to scientific understanding.

At this point, you may be wondering whether scientific understanding is possible if both induction and deduction are not infallible. Do not despair. Science is self-correcting, and it can provide answers to problems, however temporary those answers may be. Scientific understanding changes as scientists ply their trade. We have a better understanding of social loafing now than we did before Latané and his coworkers undertook their research. Through a combination of induction and deduction (see Figure 1.1), science progresses toward a more thorough understanding of its problems.

By way of concluding this section, we reexamine social loafing. Initially, positive experimental results bolstered our confidence in the general notion of social loafing. These results, in turn, suggested hypotheses about the nature of social loafing. Is it a general phenomenon that would influence even group-oriented individuals? Does it occur in the workplace as well as the laboratory? Positive answers to these questions are consistent with a diffusion-of-responsibility interpretation of social loafing.

In the next phase of the research, Latané and his colleagues attempted to eliminate other explanations of social loafing by falsifying predictions made by these alternative theories. In their earlier work, Latané and his colleagues tested a particular person's effort both when alone and when in a group. They subsequently reasoned that under these conditions, a person might rest during the group test so that greater effort could be allocated to the task when he or she was tested alone. To eliminate the possibility that allocation of effort rather than diffusion of responsibility accounted for social loafing, they conducted additional experiments in which a person was tested either alone or in a group—but not in both situations. Contrary to the allocation-of-effort hypothesis, the results indicated that social loafing occurred when a person was tested in just that one condition of being in a group (Harkins, Latané, & Williams, 1980). Therefore, it was concluded that diffusion of responsibility was a more appropriate account of social loafing than was allocation of effort.

Note the course of events here. Successive experiments pitted two possible outcomes against each other with the hope that one possibility would be eliminated and one supported by the outcome of the research. Of course, subsequent tests of the diffusion-of-responsibility theory probably will contradict it or add to it in some way. Thus, the theory might be revised or, with enough contradictions, rejected for an alternative explanation, itself supported by empirical observations. In any event, where we stand now is that we have constructed a reasonable view of what social loafing entails and what seems to cause it. It is the mixture of hypotheses induced from data and experimental tests deduced from theory that resulted in the theory that diffusion of responsibility leads to social loafing.

From Theory to Hypothesis

Theories cannot be tested directly. There is no single magical experiment that will prove a theory to be correct or incorrect. Instead, scientists perform experiments to test hypotheses that are derived from a theory. But exactly what are scientific hypotheses and where do they come from?

It is important to distinguish between hypotheses and generalizations (Kluger & Tikochinsky, 2001). A **hypothesis** is a very specific testable statement that can be evaluated from observable data. For example, we might hypothesize that drivers older than sixty-five years would have a higher frequency of accidents involving left turns across oncoming traffic when driving at night than do younger drivers. By looking at police records of accident data, we could determine, with the help of some statistics (see Appendix B), if this hypothesis is incorrect. A **generalization** is a broader statement that cannot be tested directly. For example, we might generalize that older drivers are unsafe at any speed and should have restrictions, such as not being able to drive at night, on their driver's license. Since "unsafe at any speed" is not clearly defined, this is not a testable statement. Similarly, the generalization does not define an age range for older drivers. However, it can be used to derive several testable hypotheses.

Figure 1.2 illustrates this process. Each generalization can produce more than one hypothesis. Only two are illustrated in the figure to keep it simple, but a good generalization can produce a horde of hypotheses. For example, the older-driver generalization could produce many hypotheses about different kinds of accidents and behaviors that befall aging drivers: crashing into stopped vehicles, failing to signal for turns, driving on the sidewalk, backing up into objects, not keeping within their lane, and so on. These hypotheses could be tested by making observations in traffic, on closed test tracks (safer for the driving public if the generalization is true), or in driving simulators (safest for the driving public).

Now that we have explained that hypotheses come from generalizations, we can go on to the next question: Where do generalizations come from? Figure 1.2 shows there are two sources for generalizations. They can come from theory or from experience. While only three generalizations are shown in Figure 1.2, a good theory will produce a gaggle of generalizations. You may think that the aging-driver generalization comes from experience rather than from theory. You may have firsthand experience being a passenger in a car driven by a grandparent, and that experience may have caused you to agree with the generalization. This is an inductive process (see Figure 1.1) based upon data, namely casual observation of the driving behavior of elderly citizens. Hypotheses derived from this inductive process are called common-sense hypotheses. While testing common-sense hypotheses was once frowned upon in experimental psychology as being inferior to testing hypotheses derived from theory, there is currently a new appreciation of the value of common-sense hypotheses (Kluger & Tikochinsky, 2001).

Nevertheless, most psychologists prefer testing hypotheses based upon theory. In this case, the generalization is formed deductively (see Figure 1.1) from the theory. The aging-driver generalization could also be derived from theories of attention, perception, and decision making (Kantowitz, 2001). As we age, our ability to attend to multiple tasks decreases and our decision making becomes more conservative, often requiring more time to accomplish. So an elderly driver might (a) have trouble seeing oncoming traffic at night, (b) have trouble attending to oncoming traffic while paying attention to a radio or a passenger, and (c) take a long time to decide if a left-hand turn across traffic is safe, so

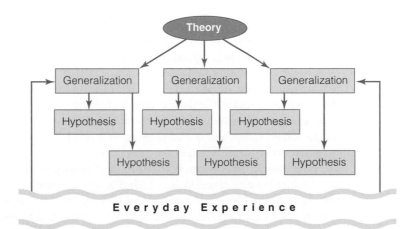

▼ FIGURE 1.2

Gaggles of Generalizations Produce Hordes of Hypotheses.

that when he or she finally makes the turn it is too late and oncoming traffic cannot avoid an accident. The advantage of a good theory is that it produces many generalizations. Theories of attention not only deal with aging drivers but make generalizations about many other practical situations such as operating airplanes and nuclear power plants, to say nothing of more abstract predictions to be tested in laboratories. For example, many theories of attention would predict that talking on your cell phone while you are driving would be dangerous, and indeed laboratory research suggests that it is (Steayer & Drew, 2007). However, common-sense generalizations are not productive because, even if they are correct, they do not create new generalizations. So theories are more efficient in advancing scientific inquiry.

While hypothesis testing is the dominant methodology used in experimental psychology, there are other points of view. Most theories in psychology are verbal and qualitative so that mathematical predictions are hard to come by. However, if a formal model can be generated either mathematically or by computer simulation, then it becomes possible to estimate parameters of the model. Parameter estimation is superior to hypothesis testing and curve fitting (Kantowitz & Fujita, 1990), and as psychology evolves as a science, estimation will supplement, and perhaps eventually replace, hypothesis testing. Indeed, there is a new movement in the philosophy of science, called naturalism, that criticizes current methodologies such as hypothesis testing, and its tentacles have reached the shores of psychological science (Proctor & Capaldi, 2001). Naturalism suggests that methodological criteria are not fixed for eternity based on logical premises, but can change and evolve (just like theories) on pragmatic grounds.

Evaluating Theories

The sophisticated scientist does not try to determine if a particular theory is true or false in an absolute sense. There is no black-and-white approach to theory evaluation. A theory may be known to be incorrect in some portion and yet continue to be used. In modern physics, light is represented, according to the theory chosen, either as discrete particles called quanta or as continuous waves. Logically, light cannot be both at the same time. Thus, you might think that at least one of these two theoretical views must necessarily be false. The physicist tolerates this ambiguity (although perhaps not cheerfully) and uses whichever representation—quantum or wave—is more appropriate. Instead of flatly stating that a theory is true, the scientist is much more likely to state that it is supported substantially by data, thereby leaving open the possibility that new data may not support the theory. Although scientists do not state that a theory is true, they must often decide which of several theories is best. As noted earlier, explanations are tentative; nevertheless, the scientist still needs to decide which theory is best for now. To do so, explicit criteria are needed for evaluating a theory. Four such criteria are **parsimony, precision, testability,** and **ability to fit data.**

One important criterion was hinted at earlier when we stated that the fewer the statements in a theory, the better the theory. This criterion is called parsimony, or sometimes Occam's razor, after William of Occam. If a theory needs a separate statement for every result it must explain, clearly no economy has been gained by the theory. Theories gain power when they can explain many results with few explanatory concepts. Thus, if two theories have the same number of concepts, the one that can explain more results is a better theory. If two theories can explain the same number of results, the one with fewer explanatory concepts is preferred.

Precision is another important criterion, especially in psychology (where it is often lacking). Theories that involve mathematical equations or computer problems are generally more precise, and hence better, than those that use loose verbal statements (all other things being equal, of course). Unless a theory is so precise that different investigators can agree about its predictions, it is for all intents and purposes useless.

Testability goes beyond precision. A theory can be very precise and yet not able to be tested. For example, when Einstein proposed the equivalence of matter and energy ($E = mc^2$), nuclear technology was not able to test this relationship directly. The scientist places a very high value on the criterion of testability, because a theory that cannot be tested can never be disproved. At first you might think this would be a good quality since it would be impossible to demonstrate that such a theory was incorrect. The scientist takes the opposite view. For example, consider ESP (extrasensory perception). Some believers in ESP claim that the presence of a disbeliever is sufficient to prevent a person gifted with ESP from performing, because the disbeliever puts out "bad vibes" that disrupt ESP. This means that ESP cannot be evaluated, because only believers can be present when it is demonstrated. The scientist takes a dim view of this logic, and most scientists, especially psychologists, are skeptical about ESP. Belief in a theory increases as it survives tests that could reject it. Since it is logically possible that some future test may find a flaw, belief in a theory is never absolute. If it is not logically possible to test a theory, it cannot be evaluated; hence, it is useless to the scientist. If it is logically possible but not yet technically feasible, as was once the case with Einstein's theory, then evaluation of a theory is deferred.

Finally, a theory must fit the data it explains. While goodness of fit is not a sufficient criterion for accepting a theory (Roberts & Pashler, 2000), there is little point in pursuing a theory that fails to fit the data (Rodgers & Rowe, 2002).

Intervening Variables

Theories often use constructs that summarize the effects of several variables. Variables are discussed at greater length in Chapter 3. For now, we briefly describe two different kinds of variables. Independent variables are those manipulated by the experimenter. For example, not allowing rats to have any water for several hours would create an independent variable called hours of deprivation. Dependent variables are those observed by the experimenter. For example, one could observe how much water a rat drinks.

Science tries to explain the world by relating independent and dependent variables. **Intervening variables** are abstract concepts that link independent variables to dependent variables. Gravity is a familiar construct that accomplishes this goal. It can relate an independent variable, the feet of height from which an object is dropped, to a dependent variable, the speed of the object when it hits the ground. Gravity also summarizes the effects of height on speed for all manner of objects. Gravity explains falling apples as well as falling baseballs. Science progresses when a single construct, such as gravity, explains outcomes in many different environments.

Miller (1959) has explained how a single intervening variable, thirst, organizes experimental results efficiently. Figure 1.3 shows a direct and an indirect way to relate an independent variable, hours of deprivation, to a dependent variable, rate of bar

Independent Variable	Intervening Variable	Dependent Variable
Hours of deprivation ⟶		Rate of bar pressing
Hours of deprivation ⟶	Thirst ⟶	Rate of bar pressing

▼ **FIGURE 1.3**

One Set of Variables.

pressing. The dependent variable is obtained by placing a rat into a small chamber where it can press a bar to obtain drinking water. The experimenter observes the rate (how many presses per minute) at which the rat presses the bar to get water. The direct relationship uses only one arrow to link hours of deprivation to rate of bar pressing. After doing the experiment, we could build a mathematical formula that directly relates hours of deprivation to rate of bar pressing. The indirect method in Figure 1.3 uses two arrows. The first arrow relates hours of deprivation to thirst, an intervening variable. The second arrow relates the intervening variable, thirst, to the rate of bar pressing. Since the indirect method is more complicated, requiring an extra arrow, you might expect the scientist to prefer the direct method of explanation. Indeed, if the only scientific goal were to relate hours of deprivation to rate of bar pressing, you would be correct because science prefers simple explanations to complex explanations. However, as we shall explain, the scientific goal is more general.

Figure 1.4 relates two independent variables, hours of deprivation and feeding dry food, to two dependent variables, rate of bar pressing and volume of water drunk. Again, both direct and indirect explanations are shown. In Figure 1.4, direct and indirect explanations are equally complex. Each requires four distinct arrows.

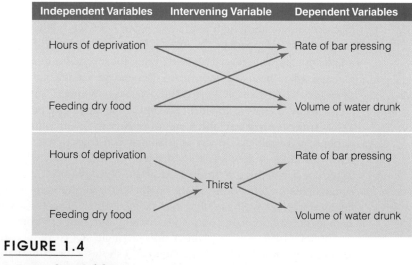

▼ **FIGURE 1.4**

Two Sets of Variables.

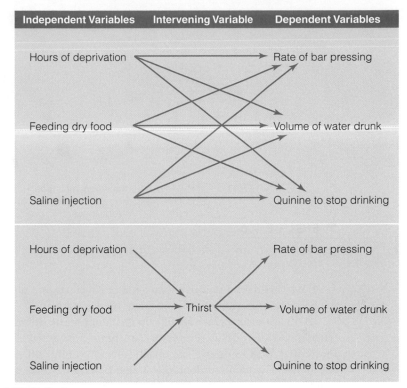

▼ **FIGURE 1.5**

Three Sets of Variables.

Figure 1.5 relates three independent variables, hours of deprivation, feeding dry food, and saline injection (giving a rat saltwater through a tube inserted in its stomach), to three dependent variables, rate of bar pressing, volume of water drunk, and amount of quinine required to stop the rat from drinking. Again, both direct and indirect explanations are shown. Now, it is obvious that the indirect method is less complicated. It requires six distinct arrows, whereas the direct method requires nine arrows. So as science tries to relate more independent and dependent variables, intervening variables become more efficient.

There is yet another advantage of intervening variables. Thirst, regardless of how it is produced, should have the same effect on all dependent variables. This can be tested in experiments. If it is not true, we can reject the idea of a single intervening variable. Later chapters discuss this issue under the topic of converging operations.

Foxes and Hedgehogs Roaming through Psychological Theory

Research in experimental psychology tends to be organized by sub-fields; indeed, Part Two of this textbook presents chapters for such sub-fields as perception, memory, and social influence. This approach is the way of the fox who knows many paths (Figure 1.6). Such was not always the case in the history of psychology. There were psychologists (e.g., James,

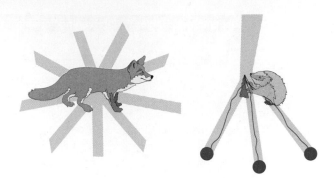

"The fox knows many things,
but the hedgehog knows one big thing."
–Archilocus

▼ FIGURE 1.6

Segmented (fox) and unified (hedgehog) approaches to psychological theory.

1890) who tried for a unified explanation of psychological phenomena. This is the way of the hedgehog who knows one big thing (see Figure 1.6).

Both approaches face significant challenges. The dominant approach builds strong barriers between fields. Professors are hired within a field and tend to have offices located by field of specialization, the better to fend off territorial thrusts from other sub-fields. Graduate students get trained by field, with appropriate course requirements, and this perpetuates the division. Even panels that evaluate grant proposals are organized by specialties. The new Ph.D. who takes a job in industry is ill prepared for the cooperation across fields necessary to solve any important practical problem.

Recently, sympathy has been growing for a more unified (hedgehog) approach to psychology (Sternberg, Grigorenko, & Kalmar, 2001). These theorists try to knit competing theories together, stressing that the explanation role of theory is more crucial than the predictive role. Theory knitting is a worthy goal if it can be accomplished. However, the present divided system arose because earlier integrated theories were unable to span all the sub-fields of psychology. Will the new hedgehogs knit better than the old hedgehogs?

▼ THE SCIENCE OF PSYCHOLOGY

Some students find it difficult to think of psychology as a science in the same sense that physics and chemistry are sciences. They believe that there are aspects of human experience, such as the arts, literature, and religion, that defy scientific analysis. How can the beauty of a Klee lithograph, a Beethoven sonata, or a Cartier-Bresson photograph be reduced to cold scientific equations? How can the tender feelings of a first romance, the thrill of driving a sports car at 100 miles per hour, or the agony of a defeated football team be captured in the objective, disinterested fashion required by science?

Some psychologists, known as humanists, would answer these questions in the negative. These humanists, most often clinical and counseling psychologists, claim that it is impossible to evaluate and test objectively much of human feelings and experience by traditional scientific methods. Even tough, "brass-instrument" experimental psychologists concur that the domain of science is limited. We cannot establish or refute the existence of God by scientific means any more than we could test gravity by theological methods. Science operates where its tools are appropriate (see Chapter 14). This does not imply that knowledge cannot be gained wherever science fears to tread—that is, by nonscientific means. Many important fields of human endeavor have yet to benefit from extensive scientific analysis—ethics, morals, and law, to name but a few.

However, most scientists would hold out the hope that scientific analysis eventually might be usefully applied to many such areas. Much of contemporary psychology was regarded as the sole property of philosophy at one time. As psychological techniques improved, these aspects of human expertise and behavior moved into the realm of science. And now most psychologists believe that virtually all facets of human experience are fair game for the science of psychology. Deriding scientific progress in psychology, as did one U.S. senator who criticized the National Science Foundation for supporting research on romantic love, will not halt efforts to expand psychological knowledge. Although concern for the proper and ethical use of such knowledge is valid and important, ignorance is no solution.

Psychology and the Real World

Scientists, in general, and psychologists, in particular, have many reasons for pursuing their profession. Although we think it rather easy to prove that psychological research does serve humanity, we would like to stress that we do not find this the only, or necessarily the major, justification for a career as a research psychologist. Many scientists investigate certain problems simply because they find them interesting. We have complete sympathy with a colleague who might state that he or she studies gerbils just because gerbils provoke his or her curiosity. It is true that certain studies are performed on animals because they are unethical or impractical to perform on humans—for example, studies of long-term crowding, punishment, drugs, and so on—but it is equally true that the behavior of animals is interesting in its own right.

Scientific research is often divided into two categories: basic and applied. **Applied research** aims at solving a specific problem—such as how to cure bedwetting—whereas **basic research** has no immediate practical goal. Basic research establishes a reservoir of data, theoretical explanations, and concepts that can be tapped by the applied researcher. Without this source, applied research would soon dry up and sputter to a halt, unless applied researchers became of necessity basic researchers. It takes quite a while for a concept developed by basic research to find some useful application in society. Adams (1972) traced five socially important products to discover the impact, if any, of basic research. Although basic research accounted for 70 percent of the significant events, the research occurred twenty to thirty years before the ultimate use of the product. This long time lag obscures the crucial role of basic research so that many persons incorrectly believe that basic research is not very useful to society. It is quite difficult to tell what basic research being done today will have an impact thirty years from now. But this inability to predict hardly means that we should stop doing basic research.

Although most experimental psychologists are content with a scientist–practitioner model where applied research is based on the fruits of basic research, more recently there has been a push for a two-track system (Fishman & Neigher, 1982; Howell, 1994) where basic and applied research diverge. From a historical perspective (Bevan, 1980) these two approaches to science can be traced to René Descartes and Francis Bacon. In the Cartesian model, science is a basic good whose aim is to understand nature. The Baconian model promotes the goal of science as improving human welfare, which places useful results ahead of increasing knowledge. However, a number of researchers argue that the basic/applied research dichotomy either has been oversimplified or represents a false distinction (Pedhazur & Pedhazur Schmelkin, 1991). For example, definitions of basic and applied research differ considerably among researchers. Furthermore, all scientific research is conducted with the goal of obtaining knowledge. In this sense, all research can be considered basic to some extent. Likewise, most research has some practical value. For example, the *European Journal of Cognitive Psychology* (2007) recently dedicated an entire special issue to research on memory (see Chapter 10) in educationally relevant settings. Some of this research may be viewed as basic, in that it tests whether principles of memory discovered using relatively simple laboratory materials (e.g., word lists) hold true for more complex classroom-type materials, but it may also be seen as applied, in that the results suggest ways to maximize student learning. Thus, the basic/applied distinction may be better thought of in less discrete terms, or as forming a continuum.

The decrease in government funding for research that started during the administration of President Reagan (Fishman & Neigher, 1982) and the more recent cutback of industrial research funds (Yeager, 1996) suggest that American society has turned toward the Baconian model. Scientists, who of course benefit from research funding, have tried to explain the advantages of research in both governmental and private sectors. Of necessity, behavioral scientists have become more active in promoting government research (National Advisory Mental Health Council Behavioral Science Task Force, 1995). Yeager (1996) has argued that, in the private sector, while industry can easily calculate the short-term costs of research, it has not fully appreciated the long-term benefits. Failure to perform industrial research can cripple major industries. Well-known examples are the decline of the U.S. automobile and steel industries due to their inability to compete with Japanese advanced technology in the 1980s.

Human factors (see Chapter 15) is an applied area that has been growing rapidly. The majority of members of the Human Factors and Ergonomics Society have been trained as psychologists. Yet a past editor of their journal, *Human Factors,* himself a psychologist, believes that the discipline of human factors in 10 years will be "more a profession and less a science, particularly a *psychological* science. It will continue to produce research, but of an increasingly problem-specific nature. . . . What continues to worry me, however, is how an increasingly professional discipline is going to bridge the gap between science and practice as the scope of the science becomes wider and the number of true scientists in that discipline becomes smaller" (Howell, 1994, p. 5). In the domain of medical research, there is similar concern about bridging the gap between basic and applied research. Therefore, in 2006 the National Institutes of Health launched a new program to promote research aimed at translating basic laboratory discoveries into practical applications.

The choice between Cartesian and Baconian approaches to science is one that ultimately will not be decided by scientists. It will be decided by funding decisions made in the private and public sectors as to what criteria are most appropriate for evaluating scientific work. But all of us, scientists and nonscientists alike, will be profoundly affected by this choice.

Although the division of research into basic and applied categories is common, a far more important distinction is between good and bad research. The principles and practices covered in this text apply with equal force to basic and applied research. You can and should use them to evaluate all the psychological research you encounter, whether as a student, a professional psychologist, or an educated person reading the daily newspaper.

Are Experiments Too Far from Real Life? Students of psychology typically demand a higher level of relevance in their psychology courses than they expect from other sciences. Students who are not at all dismayed that their course in introductory physics did not enable them to repair their automobile are often disturbed that their course in introductory psychology did not give them a better insight into their own motivations, did not cure their neuroses, and failed to show them how to gain eternal happiness. If you did not find such information in introductory psychology, we doubt that you will find it in this text either. If this seems unfair, read on.

The data that psychologists gather may at first seem unimportant, because an immediate relationship between basic psychological research and pressing social or personal problems may be difficult to establish. It is natural then to doubt the importance of certain types of research and to wonder why the federal government, through various agencies, is funding researchers to watch rats press bars or run through mazes.

The difficulty, however, is not with the research but with the expectations as to how "useful" research should be conducted. As noted by Sidman (1960), people expect progress to occur by the establishment of laboratory situations that are analogous to real-life situations: "In order to study psychosis in animals we must learn how to make animals psychotic." This is off the mark. The psychologist tries to understand the underlying *processes* rather than the physical situations that produce these processes. The physical situations in the real world and the laboratory need not be at all similar, provided that the same processes are occurring.

Suppose we would like to know why airplane accidents occur or, more specifically, what the relationship is between airplane accidents and failure of attention on the part of the pilot and/or the air traffic controller. A basic researcher might approach this problem by having college sophomores sit in front of several lights that turn on in rapid succession. The sophomore has to press a key as each light is illuminated. This probably seems somewhat removed from midair collisions of aircraft. Yet although the physical situations are quite different, the processes are similar. Pressing a key is an index of attention (see Chapter 8). Psychologists can overload the human operator by presenting lights that blink faster than he or she can respond. Thus, this simple physical situation in a laboratory allows the psychologist to study failure of attention in a carefully controlled environment. In addition to the obvious safety benefits of studying attention without having to crash airplanes, there are many scientific advantages to the laboratory environment (see Chapter 3). Because failures of attention are responsible for many kinds of industrial accidents (DeGreene, 1970, Chapters 7 and 15), studies of attention by use of lights and buttons can lead to improvements outside the laboratory.

By the same token, establishing similar physical situations does not guarantee similarity of processes. One can easily train a rat to pick up coins in its mouth and bury them in its cage. But this does not necessarily mean that the "miserly" rat and the miserly human who keeps coins under his or her mattress do so because the same psychological processes are controlling their behaviors.

We should not only be concerned with the psychological processes that may generalize from the laboratory to an application but also be aware of two important reasons for doing research, the purpose of which (at least initially) may not be directly related to practical affairs (Mook, 1983). One reason that basic research aids understanding is that it often demonstrates what *can* happen. Thus, under controlled conditions, scientists can determine whether social loafing does occur. Furthermore, the laboratory affords an opportunity to determine the characteristics of social loafing more clearly than does the workplace, where a number of uncontrolled factors, such as salary and job security, could mask or alter the effects of social loafing (see Chapter 3).

A second reason for the value of basic research is that the findings from a controlled, laboratory setting may have more force than similar findings obtained in a real-life setting. Showing that the human operator can be overloaded in a relatively nonstressful laboratory task suggests that attentional factors are crucial for performance; individuals could be even more likely to be overloaded under the stressful conditions of piloting large passenger planes in crowded airspaces.

Of course, if a researcher wants to test a theoretical prediction or apply a laboratory result in an applied setting, then real-life tests will be necessary. Installing a way of assessing individual performance to reduce social loafing in a group manufacturing situation without first testing its applicability in that setting would be foolhardy. The moral, then, is that the researcher needs to be concerned with the goal of the experiments. The researcher or the evaluator of a piece of research should consider well that goal.

Neither the practice nor the use of science is easy. The benefits that can be derived from scientific knowledge and understanding depend on critical and well-informed citizens and scientists. Your involvement with a career, a family, and social affairs will be determined partially by scientific findings. You must be in a position to evaluate those findings accurately and accept those that seem most reliable and valid. Unless you plan to hibernate or drop out of society in some other way, you are going to be affected by psychological research. As a citizen, you will be a consumer of the results of psychological research, and we hope that the material discussed in this book will help to make you an intelligent consumer.

Some of you, we hope, will become scientists. We also hope that some of you budding scientists will focus on why people think and act as they do. We wish you future scientists good fortune. Your scientific career will be exciting, and we hope that your endeavors will be positively influenced by the principles of psychological research presented herein.

▼ Summary

1. Scientific psychology is concerned with the methods and techniques used to understand why people think and act as they do. This curiosity may be satisfied by basic or applied research, which usually go hand in hand to provide understanding.

2. Our beliefs are often established by the method of authority, the method of tenacity, or the a priori method. The scientific method offers advantages over these other methods because it relies on systematic observation and is self-correcting.

3. Scientists use both inductive and deductive reasoning to arrive at explanations of thought and action.

4. Gaggles of generalizations produce hordes of hypotheses.

5. A theory organizes sets of data and generates predictions for new situations in which data have not been obtained. A good theory is parsimonious, precise, testable, and fits the data it explains.

6. Laboratory research is concerned with the processes that govern behavior and with showing the conditions under which certain psychological processes can be observed.

▼ KEY TERMS

a priori method
applied research
authority
basic research
data
deduction
description
determinism
diffusion of responsibility
empirical approach
experimentation
explanation
falsifiability view
generalization
hypothesis

induction
intervening variables
method of authority
method of tenacity
observation
organization
parsimony
precision
prediction
scientific method
self-correcting
social loafing
tenacity
testability
theory

▼ DISCUSSION QUESTIONS

1. Make a list of five statements that might be considered true. Include some controversial statements (for example, men have lower IQs than women), as well as some you are sure are correct. Survey some of your friends by asking if they agree with these statements. Then, ask their justifications for their opinions. Classify their justifications into one of the methods of fixing beliefs discussed in this chapter.

2. Compare and contrast inductive and deductive approaches to science. Clarify your answers by referring to at least one branch of science outside of experimental psychology.

3. Discuss social loafing research from the standpoint of falsifiability of theory.

4. Is it necessary (or even desirable) for experimental psychologists to justify their research in terms of applied benefits to society?

5. Read this article: Skinner, B. F. (1956). A case history in scientific method. *American Psychologist,* 11, 221–233. Analyze Skinner's views from the standpoint of the issues discussed in this chapter.

WEB CONNECTIONS

Explore the step-by-step presentation of **"What is Science? Ways of Thinking about the World"** on The Wadsworth Psychology Resource Center, Statistics and Research Methods activities at:

http://academic.cengage.com/psychology/workshops

Two excellent general purpose websites are:

http://www.apa.org

http://www.psychologicalscience.org

CHAPTER 2

RESEARCH TECHNIQUES: OBSERVATION AND CORRELATION

Scientific observation does not differ from everyday observation by being infallible although it is quantitatively less fallible than ordinary observation. Rather, it differs from everyday observation in that the scientist gradually uncovers his previous errors and corrects them. . . . Indeed, the history of psychology as a science has been the development of procedural and instrumental aids that gradually eliminate or correct for biases and distortions in making observations. (RAY HYMAN)

Science is perhaps the only intellectual enterprise that builds cumulatively. From a scientific perspective, we know more about the world today than people have known at any other time in history. On the other hand, literature, art, and philosophy may be different today than they were in ancient Greece, but we probably cannot say that these disciplines are in a better state or more accurately represent the world.

One primary reason that science cumulates is the fact that scientists strive for the most accurate observation possible of the world. Science is self-correcting in that theories and hypotheses are put forward that allow prediction about what should happen under specified conditions, and then these ideas are tested` by comparing the predictions to carefully collected observations. When the facts differ consistently and drastically from the predictions, it is necessary to modify or abandon our theoretical conceptions. Much of the scientific enterprise is concerned with observation: the collection of data on some particular aspect of the world.

In this chapter, we discuss several nonexperimental methods of gathering psychological data. One such method is **naturalistic observation,** which is the most obvious and perhaps the most venerable way of gathering data. Many people, such as birdwatchers, are amateur naturalists, but scientific naturalists, as we will see, are more systematic in their observations. For example, male blue-throated hummingbirds have songs that consist of notes organized into five song units; males in a particular area tend to sing the same song units (Ficken et al., 2000).

Another way of gathering information is a **case study,** which usually involves the detailed examination of one individual, but it may also involve a comparison of a small number of individuals. One recent case revealed that when K. R., a thirty-year-old mother of four, came to therapy, she had various counting rituals that severely hampered daily activities (Oltmanns et al., 2006). During grocery shopping, for example, K. R. believed that if she selected one of the initial four items on a shelf, then one of her children would suffer dire consequences. She believed that selecting the second box of cereal would result in a disaster happening to her second child, selecting the third box would hurt her third child, and so on.

Similar to the case study is the **survey.** Instead of small numbers of people, surveys gather detailed, self-reported information from a large number of individuals. An interesting example of a large-scale sample is the 2000 National Annenberg Election Survey (Waldman, 2004), which is based on detailed telephone interviews of a random sample of 58,373 people. In an analysis of a portion of the survey data, Moy, Xenos, and Hess (2005) found that the appearance of political candidates on late-night television affected the attitudes of the viewers toward the candidates. Following George W. Bush's appearance on the *Late Show with David Letterman,* for example, Moy and her associates found that viewers of Letterman had higher ratings of how much Bush cares for "people just like me" than did nonviewers of late-night television.

The descriptive information gathered by the procedures just outlined are often combined in various ways so that predictions about a person's activities are possible. This attempt at prediction is a **correlational technique.** One example of that procedure reveals that a person's confidence in his or her ability to identify a criminal correctly does not predict how well she or he can pick the criminal out of a police lineup (Cutler & Penrod, 1989).

As the preceding results indicate, the observational and correlational methods can yield interesting data about interesting phenomena. We examine these methods in some detail, showing both their strengths and weaknesses as ways of determining why people and animals think and act as they do.

▼ NATURALISTIC OBSERVATION

As we all know, observers are fallible. Seeing should not be believing—at least not always. Often our perceptions fool us, as seen by the way we perceive the optical illusion in Figure 2.1. We have all seen magicians perform seemingly impossible feats before our eyes that we knew were being accomplished by natural means. Such tricks

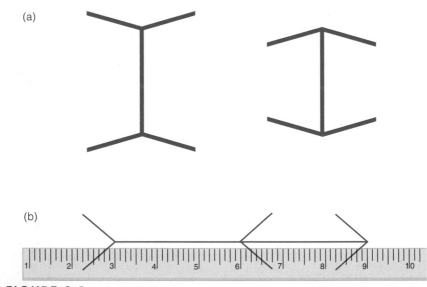

▼ FIGURE 2.1

A Visual Illusion. (a) The Müller-Lyer illusion. The vertical lines are the same length but appear unequal due to the different directions of the fins in the two cases. (b) The illusion apparently distorts even an objective measuring device, the ruler. But close examination indicates that the ruler is not really distorted and that the lines are of equal length. (Taken from R. L. Gregory, 1970, pp. 80–81.)

demonstrate that direct perceptions can be inaccurate if we are not careful, and sometimes even if we are.

Scientists, being human, also commit errors of observation. Essentially, the research techniques employed by scientists—including logic, use of complicated apparatus, controlled conditions, and so on—attempt to guard against errors of perception and to ensure that observations reflect the state of nature as accurately as possible. Even with our best methods and most careful techniques of observation, however, we can only approximate this ideal. Nevertheless, naturalistic observation as a research method differs from casual observation of the world. The work of Ginsburg and Miller (1982) on risk taking in boys and girls shows how prolonged careful unobtrusive observations can pay off. Most people would agree that young boys seem to be more daring than girls.

Is this an accurate observation, or are casual observers merely confirming general stereotypes? Ginsburg and Miller naturally observed nearly five hundred children up to eleven years old in a zoo as they fed animals, petted them, had an opportunity to ride an elephant, and so on. Two independent observers noted the frequency with which boys and girls engaged in these challenging ("risky") activities. Boys, especially the older ones, were more likely to engage in the risky activities than girls. Getting frequency counts of specific behaviors in specific situations by two observers bolsters the conclusion from casual observation that boys are more daring than girls. This research, however, does not provide information as to why this is the case.

Miller (1977) enumerated several important roles that naturalistic observation can play in psychology. Miller suggests that observation provides a major part of the database that can lead to subsequent, more highly controlled research. Naturalistic observation describes the thoughts and behaviors of organisms, which is a necessary first step in understanding. A familiar example is Harlow's (1958) work on mother love in infants, which Blum (2002) describes in detail. Prior to his experiments, Harlow needed to know what behaviors infant monkeys exhibited; he also needed to know some of the things infant monkeys seemed to like (their soft blankets) and dislike (the wire floor of the cage). With this background information, Harlow could attempt to explain the behavior through experimentation. Likewise, Pytte, Rusch, and Ficken (2003) followed up their earlier observations of hummingbird songs. They varied the background noise present in the environment of blue-throated hummingbirds, and the experiments showed that the loudness of the birds' songs increases with the loudness of the background. Since such experiments would have been unlikely without the prior observational work of Ficken and her associates, we should not view observation as somehow secondary or subordinate to experimentation because it lacks control. As the previous examples illustrate, observation can provide the basis for experimentation.

In making scientific observations, we confront two basic problems that threaten the validity or soundness of the observations. (These problems can plague experimentation as well, which we examine later.) One problem has to do with **delimiting** the choice of behaviors to observe. Human observers have a finite capacity to perceive and think about events. Although most of us can walk and chew gum at the same time, most of us cannot attend to and remember twenty different behaviors occurring over short periods. Thus, some boundary on the range of behaviors must determine what we plan to observe. We must choose the behaviors critical to the problem we study. The second problem concerns the participant's reaction to being observed. This problem, called **reactivity,** presents problems in conducting any sort of psychological research.

What Do We Observe?

How do we delimit the range of behaviors to be studied? Part of this answer seems straightforward. If we are interested in human nonverbal communication, we observe human nonverbal communication. However, this is not necessarily easy to do. In the first place, nonverbal communication is highly complex, which means that we observers are faced with the same problem we started out trying to avoid: Which nonverbal behaviors do we observe? In the second place, examining nonverbal behaviors presupposes that we already know some of the behaviors to observe. Obviously, we do not enter a research project devoid of all knowledge, but neither do we start out with all the answers. We usually begin a series of observational studies with some behaviors in mind, and then successive projects rely on previous data to refine and delimit the field of inquiry. Some examples will illustrate the refinement procedure.

An Ethogram   Naturalistic research of interest to psychologists seems most prevalent in the area of **ethology,** the study of naturally occurring behavior (often in the wild). Simply observing the behavior of animals or humans permits a global impression of the characteristics and range of behavior. However, one may soon desire more systematic observation. One way ethologists make more systematic observations is by identifying different categories of experience for the organism under study and then recording the number of times the organism engages in each behavior. These behaviors can be divided into large units, such as mating, grooming, sleeping, fighting, eating, and so on, or into much smaller units. For example, an **ethogram** of the various behaviors involved in the courtship pattern of a fish, the orange chromide, is shown in Figure 2.2. (An ethogram is a relatively complete inventory of the specific behaviors performed by one species of animal.) By counting the number of times that any specific behavior occurs, ethologists can begin to get some idea of the significance of the behavior.

Ficken and associates (2000) characterized the songs of blue-throated hummingbirds. They also developed an ethogram of when hummingbirds would sing. Clearly, the researchers had to be able to record and analyze the songs. This is not a trivial undertaking.

Obtaining accurate records in a natural habitat is difficult. For example, continuous vigilance usually is impossible, even with automatic recording apparatus. Additionally, both the apparatus and the observers may result in reactivity, which would spoil the measures. These are just a few of the challenges associated with naturalistic observation of animals.

Applying similar techniques to human behavior can be even more difficult, because people do not usually appreciate having their every action noted by a curious scientist. Barker and his associates (for example, Barker & Wright, 1951; Barker, 1968) pioneered the application of naturalistic observation to humans in a number of settings, and the work by Ginsburg and Miller (1982) on risk taking can be considered an example of human ethology. Additional examples of naturalistic observations of humans follow.

Flashing Eyebrows   The famous ethologist of human behavior Eibl-Eibesfeldt (for example, 1970, 1972) has done a substantial amount of field research on human facial expressions. He and his colleagues traveled around the world taking pictures of facial

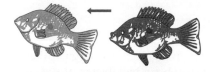

(a) *Charging*: An accelerated swim of one fish toward another.

(d) *Nipping*: An O-shaped mouth action that cleans out the (presumptive) spawning bed.

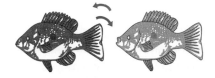

(b) *Tail Beating*: An emphatic beating of the tail toward another fish.

(c) *Quivering*: A rapid, lateral, shivering movement that starts at the head and dies out as it passes posteriorly through the body.

(e) *Skimming*: The actual spawning movement whereby the fish places its ventral surface against the spawning site and meanders along it for a few seconds.

▼ **FIGURE 2.2**

Ethogram Showing Courtship Pattern in Orange Chromide. An ethogram can be compiled for all behaviors of a species or for only selected aspects of behavior. (From *Animal Behavior: Concepts, Processes, and Methods,* p. 28, by L. C. Drickamer and S. H. Vesey, 1982, Boston: Willard Grant Press. Reprinted by permission of McGraw-Hill Companies.)

expressions in a variety of contexts. Careful examination of the expressions indicated that many are similar across cultures and some are not. In the process of examining facial expressions associated with people greeting each other, Eibl-Eibesfeldt discovered that most humans give a brief eyebrow flash. He went on to examine this phenomenon in detail.

The eyebrow flash is a brief (one-sixth of a second) raising of the eyebrows, accompanied by a slight smile and a quick nod of the head. The flash has been observed in people of many cultures, including Bushmen, Balinese, and Europeans, but some cultures differ in how they use it. The Japanese do not use the flash, because in Japan it is considered suggestive or indecent. Furthermore, Eibl-Eibesfeldt found that the flash occurred in other circumstances, such as in flirting and acknowledging a gift or service (that is, as a kind of thank you), in addition to greeting.

We can see from his work that previous observations suggested additional ones for Eibl-Eibesfeldt, and by delimiting his range of inquiry to flashing eyebrows, he could gather substantial information about a common human behavior.

Reactivity

Two general methods are available to try to guard against the participants' reactions ruining observations: (1) **unobtrusive observations** and (2) **unobtrusive measures** (Webb et al., 1966). We consider these in turn.

Unobtrusive Observations Imagine you are walking down a street in your hometown.

Occasionally you greet a friend (perhaps with a handshake, perhaps with an eyebrow flash). As your walk continues, a man with a large camera approaches and proceeds to take a moving picture of you every time you greet one of your friends. How are you likely to react to this attention? Quite likely, your mode of greeting people will change dramatically. (Have you ever noticed how spectators behave at sporting events when they know the television camera is on them?) Eibl-Eibesfeldt guarded against participant reactivity in his research by using a camera with a special sideways lens. This lens permitted him to aim the camera away from the subject 90 degrees; presumably, the subject would think that Eibl-Eibesfeldt was photographing something else. Thus, the subject would not react abnormally to the presence of the observer and his camera; instead, the subject would act naturally, which is what Eibl-Eibesfeldt intended. The special camera lens allowed the researcher to observe without intruding on the subject. We say that Eibl-Eibesfeldt used an unobtrusive observation technique.

In general, unobtrusive observations of subjects are likely to reveal more natural behavior than those in which the subjects are aware of being observed. In studying animals, researchers use unobtrusive observations whenever possible. Sometimes, however, either the subjects themselves, the terrain, or some other aspect of the project demands close contact. In these situations, **participant observation** often provides a solution. As the phrase suggests, the observer becomes an active (and intrusive) participant in the lives of the subjects being observed. For example, Fossey (1972) spent a great amount of time observing the mountain gorilla. The mountain gorilla lives in central Africa, and its habitat is threatened by human beings who are moving into that area. The mountain gorilla's natural habitat is the mountainous rainforest; this makes long-range, unobtrusive spying out of the question. Fossey was particularly concerned with the free-ranging behavior of the gorillas, so she decided to become a participant observer. This was difficult, because the gorillas are not tame. She had to act like a gorilla in front of the gorillas so that they would become accustomed to her presence. She mimicked aspects of the animal's behavior, such as eating, grooming, and making weird gorilla-like vocalizations. As she said, "One feels like a fool thumping one's chest rhythmically or sitting about pretending to munch on a stalk of wild celery as though it were the most delectable morsel in the world. But the gorillas have responded favorably" (p. 211). It took several months for Fossey to gain the confidence of the gorillas, and she continued to live with and study the gorillas until her death in 1986. How would you like to act like a gorilla for ten or fifteen years?

Reactivity does not always result from observation, because not all forms of observation seem to result in reactivity. Substantial observations of daily family interaction by means of audiotape recorders indicates that the families respond the same whether or not they know the audio recorder has been activated (Jacob et al., 1994). One could imagine, however, that a more intrusive observational procedure that combined both audio and video recording would likely cause the families to react unnaturally.

Unobtrusive Measures Unobtrusive measures, in contrast to unobtrusive observations, consist of indirect "observations" of behavior. Unobtrusive measures are indirect because it is the result of behavior, not the behavior itself, that is being studied. Thus, instead of observing behavior directly, we examine it after the fact by looking at what the behavior has accomplished. Instead of observing a student's studying activities, we examine his or her transcript. Instead of living with the gorillas, we look at their effect on the environment. The critical difference, then, between unobtrusive observation and unobtrusive measures rests on whether the subject and the observer are in the same place at the same time. When the researcher is present, he or she attempts to observe unobtrusively the subject's behavior. When absent, he or she studies the product or result of the behavior.

Obviously, unobtrusive measures are not suitable for all questions being investigated (an unobtrusive measure of an eyebrow flash might be difficult), but for some research problems, these measures are not merely good—they are the only ones that are feasible. Consider the question of graffiti in public restrooms. Who does it? What is the usual subject area? A number of serious ethical questions (ethics are discussed in Chapter 4) would be raised if a researcher stood around in restrooms observing the patrons.

However, the graffiti itself can be examined and can provide substantial information. Kinsey, Pomeroy, and Martin (1953) discovered that graffiti in men's restrooms was more erotic than graffiti in women's restrooms. Furthermore, they found more graffiti in men's rooms than in women's rooms.

The Case Study

One of the most venerable forms of inquiry in psychology is the case study. Freud's psychoanalytic theory arose from his observations and reflections on individual cases. In general, a case study is the intensive investigation of a single case of some sort, whether of a neurotic patient, a spiritual medium, or a group awaiting the end of the world. An interesting case study of this last instance was provided by Festinger, Riecken, and Schachter (1956), who infiltrated a small group of persons who were indeed awaiting the end of the world. The members thought themselves to be in contact with beings from another planet, who had communicated to one member that the destruction of the earth was near. The group was expecting to be rescued by spacecraft before the catastrophe. Festinger and his colleagues were especially interested in the reactions of the group when the calamity did not occur. They observed that for many of the members of the group, belief in its delusional system actually increased rather than decreased after the predicted date of catastrophe had passed.

The case study is a type of naturalistic observation and is subject to the advantages and disadvantages of that method. One chief disadvantage is that case studies usually do not allow firm inferences to be made about what causes what. Typically, all one can do is describe the course of events. Often, however, case studies provide implicit comparisons that allow the researcher to make some reasonable guesses as to what causes what. The case study of K. R., the compulsive counter who was described earlier, revealed an exceptionally stern upbringing that involved rigid orderliness and severe punishments for supposed sins and misdeeds. K. R.'s current family life seemed beyond her control—her children were unruly, and her husband suffered from a disabling illness. The therapist concluded that her rituals were an attempt to gain control and to be orderly (Oltmanns et al., 2006). We should be cautious about the therapist's assertion, however, because we do not know what kind of person K. R. would have become had she had a more permissive childhood and a less stressful family situation.

A type of case study that best attempts to minimize the difficulties of making inferences is the **deviant-case analysis.** Here, the researcher considers two cases that bear a number of similarities and yet differ in outcome. For example, one twin brother might become schizophrenic and the other not. The researcher attempts to pinpoint, through a careful comparison of the two cases, the factors that are responsible for the difference in outcome. Such comparisons usually cannot be made because comparable cases that differ in only one factor are rare. Furthermore, any conclusions, even from this method, cannot really be considered firm or well established because the researcher can never be certain that he or she has identified the critical causes in the differing outcomes.

These cautions notwithstanding, let us consider a case study reported by Butters and Cermak (1986) that illustrates how judicious use of the procedure can provide valuable information. The study is about P. Z., a world-famous scientist who suffered from severe memory loss (amnesia) in 1981 after long-term alcohol abuse resulted in a disease called Korsakoff's syndrome. He had extreme difficulty both in remembering new information and in recollecting past events and people. The latter memory deficit was easy to determine, because two years prior to the onset of amnesia, P. Z. had written his autobiography. When he was queried about the names and events mentioned in his autobiography, he showed a drastic memory deficit. P. Z.'s memory for these events was compared with the retention of a colleague of similar age (the comparison person for deviant-case analysis) who did not have a history of alcohol abuse. Since the comparison case did not show a memory deficit as serious as P. Z.'s, Butters and Cermak reasoned that the long-term alcohol abuse was an important causal factor in P. Z.'s amnesia. Furthermore, P. Z.'s memory deficit for new information was very similar to that shown by other people with Korsakoff's syndrome. This latter technique of comparing the case's behavior with that of others is essentially an experimental one, and it will be illustrated again in Chapter 6.

Survey Research

Case studies usually involve only a few subjects, and often these individuals are not at all representative of the population at large. P. Z., for example, was both a brilliant scientist and an amnesiac. Often researchers want to obtain information on a large random sample of people in a large geographic area (such as the survey about late-night TV viewing at the beginning of the chapter), even though the amount of information obtained from any one person is necessarily limited. Survey research is much more common in some areas of psychology than in others. For example, this technique is used quite frequently in industrial/organizational, clinical, and social psychology but almost never in cognitive psychology. One advantage of survey research is that, given the precise sampling procedures now available, a researcher can survey a relatively small number of people to generalize well to the population at large.

Because the survey leads to results that are generally descriptive in nature, this technique is not particularly popular with psychologists in areas with a strong experimental orientation, such as cognitive psychology or psychophysics. Nevertheless, clever use of the method may allow contributions to almost all areas of psychology. For example, Lovelace and Twohig (1990) surveyed healthy elderly Americans and found that 68 percent claimed that an inability to remember names was a vexing memory problem. However, the majority reported that memory problems have little effect on their daily functioning. The respondents reported that they relied very strongly on notes, lists, and other external memory aids to help them remember to do things. Further, the elderly respondents claimed not to rely on various memory "tricks," such as mnemonic devices. The results reported by Lovelace and Twohig agree with other survey data (Moscovitch, 1982) that show that compared with younger people, the elderly are much more likely to make lists and use date books and are less likely to resort to internal memory procedures, such as mnemonic devices. These results are provocative, because they suggest that the elderly are aware that they may have some memory limitations, which they try to minimize by relying on external memory aids. Given the converging evidence from Lovelace and Twohig (1990) and Moscovitch (1982), this seems like a plausible hypothesis. Information gained from these surveys can provide the framework for more controlled research to test this hypothesis.

Because a researcher has to intrude on a person to obtain survey data, the possibility of reactivity by the respondents is always present. Sussman and associates (1993) used naturalistic observation to study adolescent tobacco use. Their observations led them to conclusions different from those they derived from results of an earlier survey. The survey indicated that tobacco use takes place in small groups, and nearly half of those surveyed reported that group members offered them tobacco (Hahn et al., 1990). These sorts of findings led to educational programs that encourage teens to "Just Say 'No.'" In the naturalistic observation research, which was conducted unobtrusively, Sussman and associates noted that the adolescents frequently requested cigarettes, but they were rarely offered. Furthermore, cigarettes were rarely offered to nonusers who were in the groups. Thus, the possibility that tobacco use results from peer pressure, as indicated by survey results, is contradicted in this unobtrusive observation study. From these results Sussman and his colleagues suggested that alternatives to the "Just Say 'No'" program ought to be explored.

Finally, recall that the survey work by Moy and her associates (2005) following George W. Bush's appearance on the *Late Show with David Letterman* found that viewers of Letterman had higher ratings of how much Bush cares for "people just like me" than did nonviewers. This comparison technique is very similar to the case study work on P. Z.'s memory, and this survey technique also provides a comparison similar to an experiment. However, people were not assigned to be viewers or nonviewers, which means that, as was true of the case of P. Z., the comparison is not as solid as that used in experimentation (see below).

Advantages and Disadvantages of Naturalistic Observations

As noted earlier, naturalistic observation is extremely useful in the early stages of research, when one desires simply to gain some idea of the breadth and range of the problem of interest (Miller, 1977). It is primarily descriptive, however, and does not allow one to infer how factors may be related. In some cases, there is no way to employ more controlled methods of observation; therefore, only naturalistic ones are available. If you want to know how penguins behave in their natural habitat, you simply have to observe them there. Still, for most psychological problems, naturalistic observation is useful primarily in defining the problem area and raising interesting questions for more controlled study by other means, especially experimental ones. For example, the work described earlier of Lovelace and Twohig (1990) and Moscovitch (1982) could be followed up by more controlled methods of investigation comparing different methods of using external memory aids in elderly subjects. Which aids work best? Another example is the case study by Festinger and his colleagues of the group that predicted the end of the earth. This case study helped lead to Festinger's (1957) cognitive dissonance theory of attitude change, which has been quite important in guiding social psychological research.

The primary problem unique to naturalistic observation is that it is simply descriptive in nature and does not allow us to assess relationships among events. An investigator might note that grooming behavior in free-ranging monkeys occurs at certain times, following five different conditions (such as eating). If one is interested in finding out which antecedent conditions are necessary to produce grooming, naturalistic observation cannot provide an answer, since it is not possible to manipulate these antecedent conditions. For this, one needs an experiment.

Naturalistic observation sometimes produces data that are deficient in other ways, too. Scientific data should be easy to reproduce by other people using standardized procedures if these people doubt the observations or are interested in repeating them. Many naturalistic methods, such as the case study, do not allow reproducibility; they are thus open to question by other investigators.

Another problem in naturalistic approaches is that of maintaining as strictly as possible a descriptive rather than an interpretive level of observation. In the study of animals, the problem is often one of **anthropomorphizing,** or attributing human characteristics to animals. When you come home and your dog wags its tail and moves about excitedly, it seems perfectly natural to say that it is happy to see you. But this is anthropomorphizing, and if one were engaged in naturalistic observation of the scene, it would be inappropriate. Instead, one should record the overt behaviors of the dog with the least possible attribution of underlying motives, such as happiness, sadness, or hunger.

Of course, the case studies of Freud are based entirely on just such interpretations of the facts. Besides being nonreproducible, critics charge that such cases suffer from the possibility that if we are allowed to (1) select our data from case studies and answers people give to the questions we ask and then (2) weave these "facts" into a previous conceptual system of our own devising, case studies could probably be used to "prove" any theory. (This is not to detract from the creative flair and genius evident in Freud's system; he is, however, certainly open to criticism in terms of the evidence he used as a basis of his theory.)

Pavlov reports another instance of this interpretive problem that is closer to scientific psychology in his early research on the conditioned reflex (see Chapter 9). When they began to study the dog's psychological processes, he and his coworkers discovered they had a problem that had not been apparent when they had previously been concerned only with the digestive system. The problem was severe, for they could not agree on the observations they were making. Pavlov describes the problem of studying conditioned reflexes:

But how is this to be studied? Taking the dog when he eats rapidly, snatches something in his mouth, chews for a long time, it seems clear that at such a time the animal strongly desires to eat, and so rushes to the food, seizes it, and falls to eating. He longs to eat. . . . When he eats, you see the work of the muscles alone, striving in every way to seize the food in the mouth, to chew and to swallow it. From all this we can say that he derives pleasure from it. . . . Now when we proceeded to explain and analyze this, we readily adopted this trite point of view. We had to deal with the feelings, wishes, conceptions, etc., of our animal. The results were astounding, extraordinary; I and one of my colleagues came to irreconcilable opinions. We could not agree, could not prove to one another which was right. . . . After this we had to deliberate carefully. It seemed probable we were not on the right track. The more we thought about the matter, the greater grew our conviction that it was necessary to choose another exit. The first steps were very difficult, but along the way of persistent, intense, concentrated thinking I finally reached the firm ground of pure objectivity. We absolutely prohibited ourselves (in the laboratory there was an actual fine imposed) the use of such psychological expressions as the dog guessed, wanted, wished, etc. (Pavlov, reprinted 1963, pp. 263–264)

One further problem is discussed here, although it is relevant to all types of observation in all types of research. This is the issue of how much our conceptual schemes determine and bias what we "see" as the facts. Pavlov's statement is eloquent testimony of how difficult it is to establish objective methods so that we can all see the facts in the same way. He had found it initially "astounding" and "extraordinary" that this was so and was surprised at the elaborate precautions needed to ensure objectivity. Philosophers of science have pointed out that our observations are always influenced by our conceptions of the world—if in no other way, at least by the particular observations we make (see, for example, Hanson, 1958, Chapter 2). "Pure objectivity," to use Pavlov's phrase, is quite elusive, if not impossible. One illustration Hanson uses is that of two trained microbiologists viewing a stained and prepared slide through a microscope and "seeing" different things. (As is well known, the primary thing a novice typically reports seeing in a microscope is his or her own eyeball.) Objective and repeatable observation in science is an ideal to be approximated, but we may never be completely confident that we have achieved it. Certainly, however, we must make every possible step toward this ideal, which is what much of the technical paraphernalia of science is concerned with.

The problem of observations being unduly influenced by expectations is not automatically overcome by the use of the technical equipment of hard science, however, as is evident in an illustration cited by Hyman (1964, p. 38). In 1902, shortly after X rays were discovered, the eminent French physicist R. P. Blondlot reported the discovery of "N rays." Other French scientists quickly repeated and confirmed Blondlot's discovery; in 1904, no fewer than seventy-seven publications appeared on the topic. However, the discovery became controversial when American, German, and Italian scientists failed to replicate Blondlot's findings.

The American physicist R. W. Wood, failing to find N rays in his own lab at Johns Hopkins University, visited Blondlot. Blondlot displayed a card to Wood with luminous circles painted on it. Then he turned down the room light, fixed N rays on the card, and pointed out to Wood that the circles increased in luminosity. When Wood said he could see no change, Blondlot argued that this must be because Wood's eyes were too insensitive. Next, Wood asked if he could perform some simple tests, to which Blondlot consented. In one case, Wood moved a lead screen repeatedly between the N rays and the cards, while Blondlot reported the corresponding changes in luminosity of the circles on the card. (The lead shield was to prevent passage of the N rays.) Blondlot was consistently in error, and often reported a change in luminosity when the screen had not been moved! This and other tests clearly indicated that there was no evidence for the existence of N rays, despite their "confirmation" by other French scientists.

After 1909 there were no further publications on N rays. The mistake was too much for Blondlot. He never recovered and died in disgrace some years later. We can see from this dramatic example that even with the sophisticated apparatus of physicists, errors of observation are possible and must be guarded against.

▼ THE RELATIONAL APPROACH

Scientists describe, relate, and experiment. **Relational research** attempts to determine how two (usually) or more variables are related to each other. A **variable** is something that can be measured or manipulated. Typically, relational research does not involve manipulation of variables, so the data that are related are called **ex post facto** data, which means "after the fact." The data that are related come from naturally occurring events and do not result from direct manipulation by the researcher. The researcher categorizes or assess the data and probes for relationships.

Contingency Research

Contingency research is one sort of relational research in which data on two variables are compared to see whether the values of one variable depend on the values of the other. Suppose that you want to determine the distribution of men and women in various major programs at your college. To examine this, you assess the frequencies with which women and men declare major programs and enter the outcome of your results in a contingency table. A *contingency table* is a tabular presentation of all combinations of categories of two variables, which allows the relationships between the two to be examined. An example of the development of a contingency table appears in Table 2.1.

Panel A of Table 2.1 shows the number of women majoring in various departments. More women are majoring in journalism than in any of the other departments listed. History has the fewest women majors. The number of men majors in the five departments appears in panel B. Note that more men major in history than in any other department. Psychology has the fewest men. Panel C illustrates the entire contingency table and adds some important information—the relative frequency of men and women majors. The relative frequencies for each cell in the table show the percentage of men and women in each major program. The contingency table illustrated in panel C is referred to as a 2 × 5 contingency table, because it has two rows and five columns (not including the totals). Contingency tables require at least two rows and at least two columns. The convention is to present the number of rows and then the number of columns in the description. A particular row–column combination is called a *cell;* for example, the cell entry indicating the percentage of women psychology majors is 74.2 percent.

The percentages in the table clearly indicate that there is a relationship between a person's gender and his or her choice of major at this particular college: History has

▼ **TABLE 2.1**

Development of a Contingency Table Indicating Some of the Major Programs Chosen by Men and Women at a Small Liberal Arts College

Panel A: Number of Women Majoring in Five Departments				
Major Program				
Biology	English	History	Journalism	Psychology
36	50	22	57	49

Panel B: Number of Men Majoring in Five Departments				
Major Program				
Biology	English	History	Journalism	Psychology
29	18	66	23	17

Panel C: Contingency Table of Frequency and Relative Frequency in Percentage of Women and Men Majoring in the Five Departments						
	Major Program					
Gender	Biology	English	History	Journalism	Psychology	Total
Women	36	50	22	57	49	214
	55.4%	73.5%	25.0%	71.3%	74.2%	58.3%
Men	29	18	66	23	17	153
	44.6%	26.5%	75.0%	28.7%	25.8%	41.7%
Total	65	68	88	80	66	367
	100.0%	100.0%	100.0%	100.0%	100.0%	100.0%

proportionately more men than women majors, and the reverse is true for the other major programs. This kind of relationship indicates a lack of independence between gender and choice of major. If you wanted to statistically analyze the data in the table, you would probably use a χ^2 **test for independence,** which is a statistical test often used to determine whether the data in a contingency table are statistically significant. Calculation of this statistic is illustrated in Appendix B.

Participant reactivity can be a problem in contingency research, especially when the participants have been interviewed or surveyed. However, not all contingency research is subject to reactivity. The data presented in Table 2.1 are completely ex post facto, so that the people who declared a particular major do not know that they have appeared in a particular cell of a contingency table. This at first may seem to be a big factor in favor of such research. However, you should be aware that the participants' reactivity is unknown in this particular example. The real problem is that they could have chosen a particular major for reactive reasons ("Mom wants me to be an English major"). There is no simple way to determine that sort of reactivity if you collate the data from statistics prepared by someone who simply notes who majors in a particular program. So, what often occurs in ex post facto research is that there is participant reactivity of an unknown magnitude and an unknown source. When researchers assess rather than manipulate, they often remain in the dark with regard to such possible confounding as participant reactivity.

Correlational Research

The second sort of relational research we consider is called **correlational research,** which allows the researcher to determine simultaneously the degree and direction of a relationship with a single statistic. As is true of most contingency research, correlational research examines variables ex post facto.

One typical example of the correlational approach is the exploration of the relationship between cigarette smoking and lung cancer. Studies in the 1950s and early 1960s consistently found a moderately high positive correlation between cigarette smoking and lung cancer: The greater the number of cigarettes a person smoked, the more likely that person was to have lung cancer. Knowledge of this relationship allows predictions to be made. From the knowledge of how much someone smokes, we can predict (though not perfectly) how likely that person is to contract cancer and vice versa. The U.S. Surgeon General's report in 1964, which concluded that smoking was dangerous to health, was based almost entirely on correlational evidence. We examine some problems in interpreting correlational evidence; but first, let us consider the properties of the correlation coefficient itself.

The Correlation Coefficient

A **correlation coefficient** measures the degree and direction of the relationship between two variables. There are several different types of correlation coefficients, but almost all have in common the property that they can vary from -1.00 through 0.00 to $+1.00$. Commonly, they will not be one of these three figures, but something in between, such as $+.72$ or $-.39$. The magnitude of the correlation coefficient indicates the degree of relationship (larger numbers reflecting greater relationships), and the sign indicates the direction of the relationship, positive or negative. It is important to put the appropriate sign in front of the correlation coefficient, otherwise one cannot know which way the two variables are related, positively or negatively. It is common practice, though, to omit the plus sign before positive correlations so that a correlation of .55 would be interpreted as $+.55$. It is a better practice always to include the sign. An example of a **positive correlation** is the relationship between lung cancer and smoking. As one variable increases, so does the other (though not perfectly—that is, the correlation coefficient is less than $+1.00$). There is also a documented **negative correlation** between smoking and another variable, namely, grades in college. People who smoke a lot have tended to have lower grades than those who smoke less (Huff, 1954, p. 87).

As mentioned, several different types of correlation coefficients exist, and which type is used depends on the characteristics of the variables being correlated. We consider one commonly used by psychologists: **Pearson's product-moment correlation**

coefficient, or **Pearson r.** The calculation formula for Pearson *r* is presented in Appendix B. Remember that this is only one of several methods; if you actually need to compute a correlation on some data, consult a statistics text (such as Howell, 2008) to determine which method is appropriate for your particular case.

Imagine that we are among the bevy of psychologists who devote their careers to the study of human memory. One of these psychologists hits on a simple, intuitive idea concerning head size and memory, which goes like this. Information from the outside world enters the head through the senses and is stored there. An analogy can be made between the head (where information is stored) and other physical vessels, such as boxes, where all kinds of things can be stored. On the basis of such analogical reasoning, which is common in science, the psychologist makes the following prediction from his or her knowledge of the properties of physical containers: As the head size of a person increases, so should the person's memory. More things can be stored in bigger boxes than in smaller, and similarly more information should be stored in larger heads than in smaller ones.

This "theory" proposes a simple relationship: that as head size increases, so should memory. A positive correlation between these two variables is predicted. A random sample of the local population could be taken. The persons chosen could be measured on two dimensions: head size and the number of words they can recall from a list of thirty, presented to them once, at the rate of one word every three seconds. Three hypothetical sets of results from ten subjects are presented in Table 2.2. For each individual, there are two measures, one of head size and the other of number of words recalled. Also, the two types of measures need not be similar in any way to be correlated. They do not have to be on the same scale. Just as one can correlate head size with number of words recalled, one could also correlate IQ with street-address number or any two sets of numbers.

The graphical representations of the data in the three panels of Table 2.2 are presented in the three panels of Figure 2.3; head size is plotted along the horizontal *X*-axis (the abscissa), and number of words recalled is plotted along the vertical *Y*-axis (the

▼ **TABLE 2.2**

Three Hypothetical Examples of Data Taken on Head Size and Recall. The examples represent (a) a positive correlation, (b) a low (near-zero) correlation, and (c) a negative correlation.

Subject	(a) Head Size (cm)	Recall (words)	Subject	(b) Head Size (cm)	Recall (words)	Subject	(c) Head Size (cm)	Recall (words)
1	50.8	17	1	50.8	23	1	50.8	12
2	63.5	21	2	63.5	12	2	63.5	9
3	45.7	16	3	45.7	13	3	45.7	13
4	25.4	11	4	25.4	21	4	25.4	23
5	29.2	9	5	29.2	9	5	29.2	21
6	49.5	15	6	49.5	14	6	49.5	16
7	38.1	13	7	38.1	16	7	38.1	14
8	30.5	12	8	30.5	15	8	30.5	17
9	35.6	14	9	35.6	11	9	35.6	15
10	58.4	23	10	58.4	16	10	58.4	11
	r = +.93			*r* = −.07			*r* = −.89	

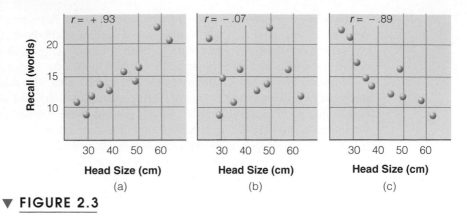

▼ **FIGURE 2.3**

Graphical Representation of the Data in Table 2.2. These graphs show the characteristic pattern of (a) a high positive correlation, (b) an essentially zero correlation, and (c) a strong negative correlation.

ordinate). The high positive correlation between head size and number of words recalled in the (a) panel in Table 2.2 is translated into a visual representation that tilts upward to the right, whereas the negative correlation in (c) is depicted as sloping downward to the right. Thus, you can see how knowing a person's score on one variable helps predict (though not perfectly in these cases) the level of performance on the other. So, knowing a person's head size in the hypothetical data in (a) and (c) helps predict recall and vice versa. This is the primary reason correlations are useful: They specify the amount of relationship and allow predictions to be made. This last statement cannot be made about the data in (b), where there is essentially a zero correlation. The points are scattered about, and there is no consistent relationship, which is just what a low Pearson r reflects. Even in the cases where the size of the correlation is rather large, it will not be possible to predict perfectly an individual's score on one variable given his or her position on the other. Even with a high correlation ($+.93$) between head size and number of words recalled, it is still quite possible for a person with a large head size to recall few words and vice versa. Unless the correlation is perfect ($+1.00$ or -1.00), prediction of one score when given the other will not be perfect either.

What do you think the real correlation would be between head size and recall for a random sample of the population at large? Although we have not actually done such a study, we think it quite likely that it would be positive. Willerman and associates (1991) conducted research on a related topic, the relation between brain size and intelligence, or IQ. They found a correlation of $+.51$ between brain size and IQ in a sample of forty right-handed, Caucasian introductory psychology students. The results of recent brain volume studies by Haier and associates (Haier, Jung, Yeo, Head & Alkire, 2004; Colom, Jung, & Haier, 2006) demonstrate that larger volumes of brain areas are positively correlated with IQ, and these areas are distributed throughout the brain. Do the brain size data mean that brain size causes differences in cognitive ability? In the next section, we address the issue of correlation and causation.

Interpreting Correlation Coefficients An important warning is always given in any discussion of correlation: The existence of even a sizable correlation implies nothing about the existence of a causal relationship between the two variables under consideration. Correlation does not prove causation. On the basis of a correlation alone, one cannot say whether factor X causes factor Y, factor Y causes factor X, or some underlying third factor causes both. Let us consider some examples. Suppose we have found a correlation of $+.70$ between head size and recall of words in children. This is in general agreement with our theory that larger heads hold more information, but certainly there are other interpretations of this relationship. It could be argued that the high positive correlation between head size and recall is mediated or produced by some third factor underlying both, such as age. We know that children's heads grow as they age and that recall also improves with age. Therefore, age (or one of its correlates) might actually be responsible for the large positive correlation we have found between head size and number of words recalled.

In correlational studies, we cannot conclude that any one factor produces or causes another, because there are likely to be a number of factors that vary simultaneously with the one of interest. In an experiment, we attempt to avoid this problem by directly manipulating one factor while holding all the others constant. If we are successful in holding other factors constant, which is very difficult to do, then the influence of the manipulated factor on whatever we are measuring can be directly attributed to the factor of interest. **Confounding** occurs when two (or more) factors are varied at the same time, so we cannot know whether one factor, the other factor, or both operating together produce some effect. Confounding is inherent in correlational research and leads to the interpretational difficulties with such research. In the example of the correlation between head size and recall, we cannot say that variations in head size produced or caused differences in recall, since head size was confounded with at least one other factor: age.

In other cases, the relationship between two factors may seem to allow a causal interpretation, but again this is not strictly permitted. Some studies have shown a positive correlation between the number of handguns in a geographic area and the number of murders in that area. Proponents of gun control might use this evidence to support the contention that an increased number of guns leads to (causes, produces) more murders, but this is not the only plausible interpretation. People in high-crime neighborhoods might be buying handguns to protect themselves. Finally, a third factor, such as socioeconomic class, could mediate both. We can see, therefore, that no causal conclusion is justified simply on the basis of a moderate or even a high correlation.

Because correlations can be calculated between any two sets of scores, even very high correlations can be accidental and not linked to one another at all. There may be a very high correlation between the number of preachers and the number of pornographic movies produced each year since 1950, with both being on the increase. It would take an unusual theory to relate these two in a causal manner.

A high degree of correlation is given greater weight in cases in which obvious competing explanations (from confounding factors) seem less plausible. Also, more weight is given to a high correlation when there is converging evidence from a number of independent studies, an underlying mechanism is identified, and the consequences of the decision are great. The interpretation of the evidence linking cigarette smoking to lung cancer provides a good example of these points. The early evidence regarding this link was correlational; yet the conclusion was drawn (over the protests of cigarette manufacturers) in the 1964 U.S. Surgeon General's report that cigarettes were likely to lead to or cause cancer. This eventually led to warnings on cigarette packages and a ban on advertising cigarettes on television, among other things. The correlation was taken as indicative of a causal relationship, probably because competing hypotheses seemed implausible. It seems unlikely, for example, that having lung cancer causes one to smoke more cigarettes (to soothe the lungs?). Furthermore, the smoking–cancer correlation was demonstrated in a number of independent studies (converging evidence), and the consequences of declaring a causal relationship between the two were great (prevention of additional deaths due to lung cancer). Finally, the mechanism underlying the smoking–cancer correlation was fairly obvious and straightforward (malignant cell production from long-term inhalation of a noxious substance).

All these arguments notwithstanding, the possibility remains that some underlying third factor (such as anxiety) produces the relationship. In fact, Eysenck and Eaves (1981) have argued that the correlation between lung cancer and smoking in humans is produced by personality differences. Certain personality types, according to Eysenck and Eaves, are more likely to smoke and also to get lung cancer. Thus, they argue that the smoking–cancer correlation does not imply causation. Because the link between cigarette smoking and lung cancer has now been established by experimental studies with nonhuman animals, most scientists disagree with the view of Eysenck and Eaves.

As a final example of the pitfalls of the correlational approach, consider the negative relationship mentioned previously between cigarette smoking and grades. More smoking has been related to poorer grades. Does smoking cause poorer grades? This seems unlikely, and certainly there are ready alternative interpretations. Students with poor grades may be more anxious and thus smoke more, or more sociable students may smoke more and study less, and so on. As is true for the observational method, the correlational method is very useful for suggesting possible relationships and directing further inquiry, but it is not useful for establishing direct causal relationships.

The correlational method is superior to the observational method, because the degree of relation between two variables can be precisely stated and thus predictions can be made about the (approximate) value of one variable if the value of the other is known.

Low Correlations: A Caution If high correlations cannot be interpreted as evidence for some sort of causal relationship, one might think it should at least be possible to rule out a causative relationship between two variables if their correlation is very low, approaching zero. If the correlation between head size and recall had been −.02, would this have ruled out our theory that greater head size leads to better recall? Or if the correlation between smoking and lung cancer had been +.08, should we have abandoned the idea that they are causally related? The answer is sometimes, under certain conditions. Other factors can cause low or zero correlations and may mask an actual relationship.

One common problem is that of **restriction of range.** For a meaningful correlation coefficient to be calculated, there must be rather great differences among the scores in each of the variables of interest; there must be a certain amount of spread or variability in the numbers. If all the head sizes were the same in the panels of Table 2.2 and the recall scores varied, the correlation between the two would be zero. (You can work it out yourself using Equation B.5 in Appendix B.) If we looked only at the correlation between head size and recall in college students, it might be quite low, because the differences in head size and recall among college students might not be very great, compared with the population at large. This could happen even though there might be a positive (or negative) correlation between the two variables if head size were sampled over a wider range. The problem of restricted range can produce a low correlation, even when there is an actual correlation present between two variables.

The problem of restricted range can arise in unexpected places. Consider the problem of predicting success in college from SAT I scores at a college with strict admission standards. Subtest scores can range from 200 to 800, with a mean (average) performance slightly below 500. Imagine the mean scores at our hypothetical college are 800 on each subtest. The admissions officer computes a correlation between combined SAT scores and freshman grades and finds one of +.00. Her conclusion is that SAT scores should not be used to predict grades in college. The problem, however, is that the SAT scores are from a very restricted range, specifically all the same. Since people with low scores are not admitted to the college, the restricted range problem is probably a factor here, or in any situation involving a limited sample of participants with homogeneous characteristics.

This example, in which all the scores on one variable are the same, is obviously fictional. Let us look at a real example. Bridgeman, McCamley-Jenkins, and Ervin (2000) looked at the correlation between SAT I scores and freshman grades both collectively and individually at twenty-three colleges. When they adjusted scores for restrictions in range, they found higher average SAT I scores predicted freshman grades somewhat better than lower average SAT I scores. The reason for this result is difficult to determine, but it might arise from the fact that grades receive higher emphasis at the more selective schools. Because psychologists often use homogeneous populations such as college students, the restricted-range problems must be carefully considered in interpreting correlations.

A final problem in interpreting low correlations is that one must be certain that the assumptions underlying the use of a particular correlation coefficient have been met. Otherwise, its use may well be inappropriate and lead to spuriously low estimates of relationship. These have not been discussed here, but it is imperative to check on these assumptions in a statistics book before employing Pearson r or any other correlation coefficient. For example, one assumption underlying Pearson r is that the relationship between the two variables is linear (can be described by a straight line) rather than curvilinear, as in the hypothetical (but plausible) relationship in Figure 2.4 between age and long-term memory. At very young ages, the line is flat; then it increases between

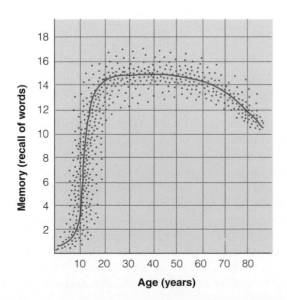

▼ **FIGURE 2.4**

A Hypothetical Figure Depicting a Curvilinear Relationship Between Long-Term Memory and Age. Although memory is related to age in a systematic fashion and one could predict recall by knowing age, Pearson r would be quite low, since the relationship is not linear.

ages three and sixteen, where it again levels off until late middle age, where it drops slightly, until very old age, where it decreases at a greater rate (Howard & Wiggs, 1993). Thus, one can predict recall of words from a person's age fairly well, but Pearson r will be rather low, since the relationship between the two variables is not linear. This could, of course, always be checked by plotting a scatter diagram, as in Figure 2.4. Low correlations, then, may not reflect that a relationship is absent but only that the assumptions of the particular coefficient employed have not been met.

Complex Correlational Procedures

"Media violence poses a threat to public health inasmuch as it leads to an increase in real-world violence and aggression" (Huesmann & Taylor, 2006, p. 393). How do we determine whether viewing violent media causes aggressive behavior? Eron and associates (1972) measured children's preferences for violent TV programs and the children's aggressiveness as rated by their peers. For these third-graders, Eron and coworkers found a moderate positive correlation, $r = +.21$, indicating that children who were more aggressive tended to watch more violent TV (and less aggressive children tended to watch less violent programs). How are we to interpret this positive correlation? Can we say that watching violent programs causes aggressiveness? The answer is no. To see why this is the case, all we have to do is to turn our causal statement around and assert that being aggressive causes a preference for violent TV. We have no reasonable way to decide on the direction of causality, based on this one correlation coefficient. Causal statements are difficult, if not impossible, to make on the basis of a single correlational study. Instead, researchers typically view correlational evidence as tentative until there is converging evidence from independent studies and a compelling underlying mechanism is identified.

The explanatory power of correlational research may be enhanced by examining patterns of correlations. One technique is call the **cross-lagged panel correlation** procedure, and Eron and coworkers used it in a ten-year follow-up study of the same children in the "thirteenth" grade, as well as in a recent project that examined aggression in adults who were initially interviewed in the mid-1970s (Huesmann et al., 2003). The designs of the two studies are summarized in the two panels of Figure 2.5.

The logic of the cross-lagged procedure is that the correlations along the diagonals will help us understand the direction of causation between the variables. Do aggressive people watch violent TV, or does watching violent TV produce aggression? If watching violent TV produces aggressive behavior, we would expect a small or null relationship between early aggression and later preference for violent TV (the dashed diagonals) and a positive correlation between an early preference for violent TV and later aggression (the thick, solid diagonal). The underlying assumption is that if one variable causes the other, the first (watching violent TV programs) should be more strongly related to the second (aggressiveness) later in time than when the second (effect) variable is measured at the same time as the first cause. The remaining correlations are of interest and may permit predictions, but they suffer from the inability to determine causation. In the 1972 project, 211 males were studied. Both males (152) and females (176) provided data for the 2003 report. For the 1972 study, the correlation between a preference for violent TV and aggression was essentially zero ($r = -.05$) in the thirteenth grade. Similarly, they found a negligible relation between preference for violent TV in the third and thirteenth grade ($r = +.05$). They did obtain a relation between aggressiveness in the two grades

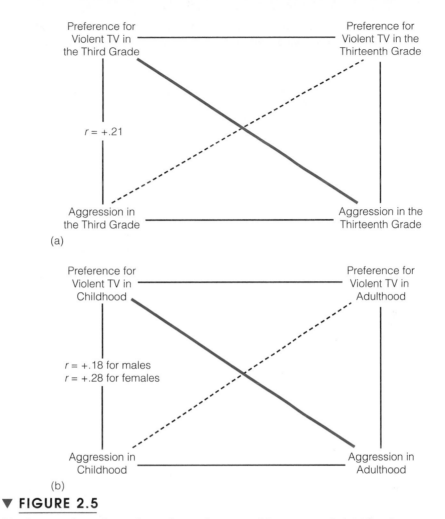

▼ FIGURE 2.5

(a) The cross-lagged panel correlation design used by Eron et al. (1972), who examined the correlations between a preference for violent TV programs and aggression as rated by peers. The diagonals indicate important cross-lagged correlations. The dashed correlation should be small, the solid one is expected to be positive and large. (b) The design used by Huesmann et al. (2003). Preference for violent TV programs was correlated with aggression. Participants were first examined at ages six to ten and then about fifteen years later. Adult aggression was measured by self-reported incidents, ratings by another person (including spouses), and arrest records. The aggression measure is a composite one that includes physical violence as well as verbal aggression.

($r = +.38$), indicating that it is a somewhat stable trait. The cross-lagged correlation between aggressiveness in the third grade and preference for violent TV in the thirteenth was very small ($r = +.01$). On the other hand, the crucial cross-lagged correlation between early watching of violent TV and aggression in the thirteenth grade was positive and statistically significant, $r = +.31$. Similar results appeared in the 2003 report. The important cross-lagged correlation between watching violent TV in childhood and adult aggression was positive and significant for both males ($r = +.21$) and females

($r = +.19$). The cross-lagged correlation between childhood aggression and adult TV violence viewing was small for both males ($r = +.08$) and females ($r = +.10$).

The cross-lagged panel correlations in these studies, along with other complex analyses, led Eron and colleagues to conclude that childhood exposure to violent TV increases later aggression (also see Eron, 1982; and Huesmann et al., 1973). Of course, many other factors contribute to aggressiveness; this is just one example of how cross-lagged panel correlations can aid in arriving at an explanation from correlational research. However, causal statements cannot be as strong as those that come from experiments, because the variables have not been manipulated by the researcher. Nevertheless, short-term increases in aggressive behavior can be produced by watching violent videos and playing violent video games (for a review, see Bushman & Huesmann, 2006).

The general strategy of the cross-lagged procedure, then, is to obtain several correlations over time and, on the basis of the size and direction of the rs, determine what leads to what. The cross-lagged technique has the obvious drawback that the research project may be very time consuming. Nevertheless, this method for trying to determine causation has been used with some success in several problem areas.

Consider the work of Corrigan and associates (1994) on burnout of staff members in a psychiatric hospital. In earlier work they had shown a significant positive correlation between anxiety and burnout, but they correctly noted that this correlation did not indicate the direction of the relationship: Are anxious workers more likely to burn out, or does worker burnout lead to anxiety? To try to answer this, they used the cross-lagged procedure, getting measurements of anxiety and several components of burnout eight months apart. The cross-lagged correlations indicated that burnout resulted in the workers being more anxious, rather than the other way around. For these same workers, other measures submitted to the cross-lagged procedure indicated that some of the effects of burnout could be attributed to lack of collegial support.

In addition to cross-lagged panel correlations, several other statistical procedures are used to try to gain a better understanding of causation in correlational research. Some of these include partial correlation, multiple-regression analysis, and path analysis. These other techniques also involve an examination of several relationships, not just a single correlation, and are described in numerous texts (see especially Cook & Campbell, 1979).

Cause: A Note

We have repeatedly cautioned you about incorrectly concluding that a correlation means causation. Causation is a controversial subject in science and philosophy, and we now consider some of the issues. Owing to the influence of some philosophers of science, it has become unpopular among contemporary scientists to use the term ***cause,*** because the philosophical implications become frightfully complicated. Thinking too long about the cause of even a very simple event leads to an infinite regress of causes for that event. For this and other reasons, the term *cause* has dropped out of use in some circles. In this book we muddle through using the term *cause,* since its meaning is always limited; experiments lead to causal inferences because one factor is varied while all others are, in the ideal case, held constant. Thus, we can say that whatever effect occurs in such cases has been caused by the factor that varied.

A more interesting point is that many factors that are experimentally varied are themselves quite complicated sets of independent events, any one of which could be the cause of an experimental effect. Time is a good example of such a variable. If we are interested in the effects of the length of time a person studies a persuasive communication on the amount the person's attitude changes toward the communication, we vary the amount of time people spend studying the message. Suppose we find an increase in attitude change with increases in study time when other factors are held constant. Can we say that time has caused an increase in attitude change? In a sense, this is true, but in a more fundamental sense, it is not. Presumably, it is some psychological process, acting over time, that causes the attitude change. It is something correlated with time but not time itself, because time is not a causative agent. If we leave a bicycle out in the rain and it rusts, we do not say that time caused the rust; chemical processes acting over time caused it.

A manipulated variable is usually composed of a number of complex and interacting parts, any one or set of which may actually cause some effect. For this reason, it is sometimes said that experiments are only controlled correlations, since the variable manipulated is actually composed of a number of confounded parts. This is certainly an accurate characterization in at least some cases; even so, we are far ahead of having a simple correlation, because we know the direction of effect. Take the example of how the amount of time spent studying a persuasive communication affects attitude change. We could simply give the message to a number of people and let them read it for as long as they desired. We could time this for each person and then see how much the person's attitude changed. If we found a positive correlation, we would not know whether the time people spent studying the passage caused more attitude change or whether the more that people decided to change their attitudes, the more they studied the passage to make sure they knew the facts. There are other possible reasons for the relationship, too. At least in the experiment on study time, we, as researchers, can manipulate the variable of study time (rather than leaving it to the discretion of our subjects) and hold other factors constant; therefore, we can say that more study time leads to (determines, produces, causes) more attitude change. Because of the complex nature of a variable such as study time, we cannot be absolutely certain that study time per se is the causal factor. For example, it may be that individuals who were allowed more time to study the persuasive communication became more involved in the experiment, and it is this difference in personal involvement that produces the attitude change.

Since the true causal factor (personal involvement) may be embedded within the manipulated variable (study time), we must consider that possibility carefully in conducting experiments. Nonetheless, the advantage of experiments over correlational studies resides in the fact that we know the direction of the relationship between two variables. Experiments also inform us (which a correlation does not) that the causal factor is at least embedded in the independent variable and not in some third, extraneous factor. It is in this sense that experiments tell us about causes.

Before turning to the next chapter, let us conclude this discussion by pointing out that there is no single research technique that is generally superior to all others. The key to conducting good research is to choose the technique that is best suited to the hypothesis being tested. If the hypothesis centers around behavior as it occurs naturally (whether it is the grooming activity of primates in the jungle or graffiti penned by humans in public restrooms), then naturalistic observation would be more appropriate than would a highly controlled experiment. In contrast, if the hypothesis is one that can be reasonably investigated by conducting either a correlational study or an experiment, an experiment would provide a more conclusive test of the hypothesis for all the reasons that we have discussed in this chapter. We turn to this important scientific tool—the experiment—in the next chapter.

▼ SUMMARY

1. Much of science is concerned with careful observation and study of the natural world. Two basic techniques discussed in this chapter are naturalistic observation and the correlational approach. Both of these are useful scientific methods, but they do not allow statements about what factors cause what effects. They are very useful in the early stages of exploration of a topic and in studying topics that cannot practically or ethically be studied by experimental means.

2. After delimiting the range of events to be studied, naturalistic observation typically involves the unobtrusive (nonreactive) observation or unobtrusive measurement of events naturally occurring in the environment. Of more use to psychologists are two reactive variants of naturalistic observation: case studies and surveys. However, these methods of observation have the disadvantage of not allowing statements about how factors are related to one another.

3. Relational research attempts to show how variables are related to one another. Relational research is typically ex post facto in that variables are not manipulated, but measured.

4. Contingency research tries to determine whether the value of one variable depends on the value of another. A typical question might be to try to determine whether the choice of a major program is related to a person's gender. A statistical test used to determine whether two variables are independent is the test of independence.

5. The correlational approach allows statements of relationship, of what goes with what. Correlations can vary from −1.00 to +1.00, with the magnitude of the number reflecting the strength of the relationship and the sign indicating the direction. For example, height is positively correlated with weight, and mean yearly temperature is negatively correlated with distance of location from the equator. There are several measures of correlation, but the one most commonly used by psychologists is the Pearson product-moment correlation coefficient, or Pearson r.

6. The correlational approach allows one to establish the amount of relation between two variables, which is useful for prediction. However, its primary drawback is that it cannot establish the direction of relationship. Even if two variables, X and Y, are strongly related, we cannot say whether the relation is accidental, X caused Y, Y caused X, or some third factor caused both.

7. In correlational studies, a number of factors usually vary together, so that the results are confounded. But correlational research is quite appropriate in situations where it is impossible to perform experiments—for example, in studying conditions related to race riots.

8. When researchers discover that the correlation between two measures is near zero, they will often conclude that there is no relation between the measures. Before drawing such a conclusion, even though it often is correct, researchers must determine if assumptions underlying the use of the correlational measure have been met. One common problem is restriction of range, or a lack of variation in the distribution of one set of scores. If all the measures on one variable are about the same, the correlation coefficient will approach zero, even if there is a true relation between the measures when a wider sampling of scores is taken.

9. Much research attempts to introduce a measure of control into correlational studies to better determine cause-and-effect relations. In some cases, statistical techniques, such as the cross-lagged correlational procedure, can be used to try to determine causes in correlational studies.

KEY TERMS

anthropomorphizing
case study
cause
confounding
contingency research
correlation coefficient
correlational research
correlational technique
cross-lagged panel correlation procedure
delimiting observations
deviant-case analysis
ethogram
ethology
ex post facto research

naturalistic observation
negative correlation
participant observation
Pearson's product-moment correlation coefficient, or Pearson r
positive correlation
reactivity
relational research
restriction of range
survey
unobtrusive measures
unobtrusive observations
variable
χ^2 test for independence

DISCUSSION QUESTIONS

1. Imagine you are a researcher just beginning a study of how mothers interact with their babies. You want to gain some idea as to the frequency (1) of the mother's performance of some act regarding the baby that is relatively independent of the baby's immediate needs, (2) of the baby's acting in various ways when the mother is not attending to it, and (3) of the mother's and child's actions when they are interacting. Make a list of all the behaviors that you think might occur with relatively great frequency in the three categories. This would be a type of ethogram, as discussed in this chapter. If you observed mothers and babies for five hours a day over a period of weeks, what kinds of conclusions could you draw? What kinds of information would you want to know but not be able to obtain from this sort of naturalistic observation?

2. One of the first pieces of evidence that linked lung cancer with cigarette smoking was published by Doll (1955). He tabulated the average number of cigarettes consumed by the people of eleven countries in 1930 and the number of deaths from lung cancer among men in 1950. The measure of deaths was taken twenty years after the measure of cigarette consumption, since it seems natural that it would take years for a cause-and-effect relation to

be seen if one were there. Since very few women smoked in 1930, it also seemed best to relate the smoking rates to male deaths. The table is an adaptation of Doll's important results.

(a) Examine the results. What do the two columns of numbers seem to show?

(b) Plot a graph relating the two measures, such as the one shown in Figure 2.3. What does it show?

Doll's Results

Country	1930 Cigarette Consumption	1950 Deaths per million*
Australia	480	180
Canada	500	150
Denmark	380	170
Finland	1,100	350
Great Britain	1,100	460
Holland	490	240
Iceland	230	60
Norway	250	90
Sweden	300	110
Switzerland	510	250
United States	1,300	200

*From lung cancer.

(c) Now calculate the exact relation between the two variables by using the formula for Pearson *r* given in Appendix B. What is the exact magnitude and sign of the correlation coefficient you have obtained?

3. Do the analyses you performed in Question 2(c) permit the conclusion that smoking causes lung cancer? If the correlation coefficient were higher, say, +.95, would you be more certain of the cause-and-effect relation? If you think these data do not argue that smoking causes lung cancer, how else might you explain the results?

4. Make a list of pairs of variables that you believe are highly correlated (either positively or negatively) but between which you think there is little chance of a causal connection. How could you determine whether the correlation does indicate a cause-and-effect relation?

WEB CONNECTIONS

Explore the step-by-step presentation of **"Nonexperimental approaches to research—The Survey Method"** on the Wadsworth Psychology Resource Center, Statistics and Research Methods activities at:

http://academic.cengage.com/psychology/workshops

▼ LABORATORY RESOURCE

Chapters 1 and 2 in Langston's manual discuss naturalistic observation and survey research, respectively. The naturalistic observation research concerns humans defending parking spaces, and the survey research focuses on grade inflation in college.

Langston's manual (2002) discusses relational research in Chapter 3. The major issue examined by Langston is the relationship between pet ownership and health.

Langston, W. (2002). *Research methods laboratory manual for psychology.* Pacific Grove, CA: Wadsworth Group.

CHAPTER 3

RESEARCH TECHNIQUES: EXPERIMENTS

No one believes an hypothesis except its originator, but everyone believes an experiment except the experimenter. (W. I. B. BEVERIDGE)

Imagine you are a student in a class in environmental psychology and have received the following assignment: Go to the library and "defend" a table by preventing anyone else from sitting down for as long as you can. You must use only nonverbal and non-violent means to accomplish this. To carry out this task, you might wait in the crowded library until a table is vacant, quickly sit down, and proceed to strew your books, clothing, and other belongings all over the table in hopes that this disarray might keep others away. After some time, say, fifteen minutes or so, someone finally does sit down at your table, ending your assignment. Have you performed an experiment?

Before answering this question, let us sketch out the major criteria for an experiment, which were briefly discussed in the preceding chapters. An experiment occurs when the environment is systematically manipulated so that the causal effect of this manipulation on some behavior can be observed. Aspects of the environment that are not of interest, and hence not manipulated, are held constant, so as not to influence the outcome of the experiment. We can then conclude that the behavior resulted from the manipulation. We must explain two special terms briefly introduced in Chapter 1—*independent* and *dependent* variables—to describe how the environment is manipulated and how behavior is observed.

▼ WHAT IS AN EXPERIMENT?

Many students are surprised to discover that the actions described in our library table exercise do not constitute an experiment. All experiments require at least these two special features, the independent and dependent variables just mentioned. The **dependent variable** is the response measure of an experiment that is *dependent* on the subject. In this case, the time that elapsed until someone else sits down at the table is the dependent variable or response measure. The **independent variable** is a manipulation of the environment controlled by the experimenter: In this case, it is the strewing of articles on the table.

But an experiment must have at least two values, or **levels,** of the environment. These levels may differ in a quantitative sense (items strewn across only a portion of the table versus items strewn across the entire table), or the levels may reflect a qualitative difference (the person defending the table assumes a friendly, inviting expression as opposed to a stern, forbidding expression). The point is that at least two conditions must be compared with each other to determine if the independent variable (portion of table covered or facial expression) produces a change in a behavior or outcome. Sometimes, these two levels might simply be the presence or absence of a manipulation. The library example fails to meet this criterion, since it involves only one level of the independent variable.

How might we change the procedure to obtain an experiment? The simplest way would be to sit down again, this time without scattering anything. Then our independent variable would have the necessary two levels: the table with items strewn about and the bare table with no items strewn about. Now we have something to compare with the first condition.

This experiment has three possible outcomes: (1) Strewing articles on the table results in a longer time before the table is invaded by another person; (2) the time until invasion is the same, whether or not articles are strewn about; and (3) scattering articles results in a shorter time until invasion. Without the second level of the independent variable (the table with no articles strewn about), these three outcomes cannot be formulated. Indeed, it is impossible to say anything about how effective articles strewn about are in defending library tables until two levels of the independent variable are tested.

When this library experiment is performed properly, the first possible outcome is obtained. A table can be better protected by a person plus assorted articles than by a person alone.

We can see, then, that experiments must have at least independent and dependent variables. The research techniques discussed in the preceding chapter do not allow or require manipulation of the environment; but before an **experiment** can be established, independent variables with at least two levels are necessary.

Advantages of Experiments

The main advantage of experiments over the techniques discussed in Chapter 2 is better control of extraneous variation. In the ideal experiment, no factors (variables) except the one being studied are permitted to influence the outcome; in the jargon of experimental psychology, we say that these other factors are *controlled*. If, as in the ideal experiment, all factors but one (that under investigation) are held constant, we can logically conclude that any differences in outcome must be caused by manipulation of that one independent variable. As the levels of the independent variable are changed, the resulting differences in the dependent variable can occur only because the independent variable has changed. In other words, changes in the independent variable cause the observed changes in the dependent variable. In the library example, we might want to manipulate the facial expression of the person "defending" the table. To control for extraneous variation, we would need to give careful consideration to other factors that might compromise our ability to make statements about causation. In this case, we might want to hire only one assistant to defend the table during the duration of the experiment or else establish objectively that our assistants are, for example, equally attractive. We might also decide to *control* for gender by either incorporating it as an additional independent variable or by using only female (or male) research assistants. Designing experiments so that there can be only one explanation of the results is at the heart of the experimental method. Whereas nonexperimental research techniques are limited to statements about description and correlation, experiments permit statements about causation—that is, independent variable A (facial expression) causes variable B (time elapsed until someone else sits down) to change. In this experiment, we would expect the time elapsed to be shorter when the assistant assumes a friendly and inviting expression than when the assistant's expression is stern and forbidding.

Thus, in principle, experiments lead to statements about causation. In practice, these statements are not always true. No experiment is 100 percent successful in eliminating or holding constant all other sources of variation but the one being studied.

However, experiments eliminate more extraneous variation than do other research techniques. Later in this chapter, we discuss specific ways in which experiments limit extraneous variation.

Another advantage of experiments is economy. Using the technique of naturalistic observation requires that the scientist wait patiently until the conditions of interest occur. If you lived in Trondheim, Norway—near the Arctic Circle—and wanted to study how heat affects aggression, relying on the sun to produce high temperatures would require great patience and lots of time. The experimenter controls the situation by creating the conditions of interest (various levels of heat in a laboratory setting), thus obtaining data quickly and efficiently.

Why Experiments Are Conducted

The same general reasons that apply to the conduct of any research also explain why psychologists perform experiments. In basic research, experiments are performed to test theories and to provide a database for explanations of behavior. These kinds of experiments are typically well planned, with the investigator having a clear idea of the anticipated outcome. So-called **critical experiments** try to pit against each other two theories that make different predictions. One outcome favors theory A; the other, theory B. Thus, in principle, the experiment will determine which theory to reject and which to keep. In practice, these critical experiments do not work out so well, because supporters of the rejected theory are ingenious in thinking up explanations to discredit the unfavorable interpretation of the experiment. One example of such an explanation is found in a study of how people forget. Two major explanations of forgetting are that (1) items decay or fade out over time, just the way an incandescent light bulb fades when the electricity is turned off (this explanation is called "trace decay") or that (2) items never fade, but because of this, they interfere with each other, causing confusion. A simple critical experiment would vary the time between introduction into memory of successive items, holding the number of items constant (Waugh & Norman, 1965). Memory should be worse with longer times, according to trace-decay theorists, because there is more time for items to fade out. But because the number of items remains the same regardless of the time at which they are introduced, interference theory predicts no differences in forgetting. When this experiment is performed, there is no difference in memory; this would seem to nullify the trace-decay explanation. The rejoinder by trace-decay theorists, however, is that the extra time given between items allows people to rehearse—that is, repeat the item to themselves—which prevents forgetting.

Less often, researchers perform an experiment in the absence of a compelling theory just to see what happens; we can call this a **what-if experiment.** Students often come up with what-if experiments, since these experiments require no knowledge of theory or the existing database and can be formulated on the basis of personal experience and observations. Some scientists frown on what-if experiments; the main objection to them is their inefficiency. If, as is often the case, nothing much happens in a what-if experiment—say, the independent variable has no effect—nothing is gained from the experiment. By contrast, if nothing much happens in a careful experiment for which a theory predicts something will happen, the finding of no difference can be useful. We must admit to having tried what-if experiments. Most of them did not work, but they were fun. Our advice is to check with your instructor before trying a what-if experiment. He or she probably can give you an estimate of the odds of your coming up with anything or may even know the results of a similar experiment that has already been performed.

This brings us to the last major reason for doing experiments in basic research, which is to repeat or replicate a previous finding. A single experiment by itself is far less convincing than a series of related experiments. The simplest replication is the direct repetition of an existing experiment, with no change in procedures. Direct replications are especially useful when the original experiment was quite novel. Generally, however, a better way to replicate is to *extend* the previous procedure by adding something new while retaining something old. Thus, part of the replication is a literal repetition, but the novel part adds to scientific knowledge. This kind of repetition demonstrates the generality of a result by showing how it is (or is not) maintained over different independent variables. The concept of replication and its various forms are discussed at greater length in Chapter 11.

▼ VARIABLES

Variables are the gears and cogs that make experiments run. Effective selection and manipulation of variables make the difference between a good experiment and a poor one. This section covers the three kinds of variables that must be carefully considered before starting an experiment: *independent, dependent,* and *control variables.* We conclude by discussing experiments that have more than one independent or dependent variable.

Independent Variables

In true experiments, independent variables are those *manipulated* by the experimenter. The brightness of a light, the loudness of a tone, the temperature of a room, the number of food pellets given to a rat—all are independent variables, since the experimenter determines their quality and quantity. Independent variables are selected because an experimenter believes they will cause changes in behavior. Increasing the intensity of a tone should increase the speed with which people respond to the tone. Increasing the number of pellets given to a rat for pressing a bar should increase the number of times the bar is pressed. When a change in the level (amount) of an independent variable causes a change in behavior, we say that the behavior is under control of the independent variable.

Failure of an independent variable to control behavior, often called **null results,** can have more than one interpretation. First, the experimenter may have guessed incorrectly that the independent variable was important: The null results may be correct. Most scientists will accept this interpretation only reluctantly, and so the following alternate explanations of null results are common. The experimenter may not have created a valid manipulation of the independent variable. Let us say you are conducting an experiment on second-grade children and your independent variable is the number of small candies (M&Ms, jelly beans) they get after each correct response. Some children get only one, whereas others get two. You find no difference in behavior. However, if your independent variable had involved a greater range—that is, from one piece of candy to ten pieces of candy—perhaps you would have obtained a difference. Your manipulation might not have been sufficient to reveal an effect of the independent variable. Or perhaps, unknown to you, the children had a birthday party just before the experiment started and their little tummies were filled with ice cream and cake. In this case, maybe even ten pieces of candy would not show any effect. This is why, in studies of animal learning with food as a reward, the animals are deprived of food before the experiment starts.

We can see that experimenters must be careful to produce a strong manipulation of the independent variable. Failure to do so is a common cause of null results. Because there is no way to determine if the manipulation failed or the null results are correct, experimenters cannot reach any conclusions regarding the effect of the independent variable on the dependent variable. Other common causes of null results are related to dependent and control variables, to which we now turn.

Dependent Variables

The *dependent variable* is the response measure of an experiment that is *dependent* on the subject's response to our manipulation of the environment. In other words, the subject's behavior is observed and recorded by the experimenter and is dependent on the independent variable. Time elapsed before a subject sits down at a table defended by a research assistant, the speed of a worm crawling through a maze, the number of times a rat presses a bar—all are dependent variables, because they are dependent on the way in which the experimenter manipulates the environment. In the library example, we might predict that a subject would be more reluctant to sit down at a table that is defended by an assistant who displays a forbidding expression than if the assistant assumes a congenial expression. In this instance, the subject's behavior is *dependent* on the expression that we instruct the assistant to adopt. The time that elapses until the subject sits down at the table is the dependent variable of interest.

One criterion for a good dependent variable is **stability.** When an experiment is repeated exactly—same subject, same levels of independent variable, and so on—the dependent variable should yield the same score as it did previously. Instability can occur because of some deficit in the way we measure some dependent variable. Assume that we wish to measure the weight in grams of an object—say, a candle—before and after it is lit for 15 minutes. We use a scale that works by having a spring move a pointer. The spring contracts when it is cold and expands when it is hot. As long as our weight measurements are taken at constant temperatures, they will be reliable. But if temperature varies while objects are being weighed, the same object will yield different readings. Our dependent variable lacks stability.

Null results can often be caused by inadequacies in the dependent variable, even if it is stable. The most common cause is a restricted or limited range of the dependent variable, so that it gets "stuck" at the top or bottom of its scale. Imagine that you are teaching a rather uncoordinated friend how to bowl for the first time. Since you know from introductory psychology that reward improves performance, you offer to buy your friend a beer every time he or she gets a strike. Your friend gets all gutter balls, so you drink the beer yourself. Thus, you can no longer offer a reward; you therefore expect a decrement in performance. But since it is impossible to do any worse than all gutter balls, you cannot observe any decrement. Your friend is already at the bottom of the scale. This is called a **floor effect.** The opposite problem, getting 100 percent correct, is called a **ceiling effect.** Ceiling and floor effects (see Chapter 10) prevent the influence of an independent variable from being accurately reflected in a dependent variable.

Control Variables

A **control variable** is a potential independent variable that is held constant during an experiment because it is controlled by the experimenter. For any one experiment, the list of relevant control variables is quite large, far larger than can ever be accomplished in practice. In even a relatively simple experiment—for example, requiring people to memorize three-letter syllables—many variables should be controlled. Time of day changes your efficiency; ideally, this should be controlled. Temperature could be important, because you might fall asleep if the testing room were too warm. Time since your last meal might also affect memory performance. Intelligence is also related. The list could be extended. In practice, an experimenter tries to control as many salient variables as possible, hoping that the effect of uncontrolled factors will be small relative to the effect of the independent variable. Although it is always important to exercise strict control over extraneous factors, it is even more critical when the independent variable produces a small effect on the dependent variable. Holding a variable constant is not the only way to remove extraneous variation. Statistical techniques (discussed later in the chapter) also control extraneous variables. However, holding a variable constant is the most direct experimental technique for controlling extraneous factors, so we limit our definition of control variables to only this technique. Null results often occur in an experiment because there is insufficient control of these other factors—that is, they have been left to vary systematically with the independent variable. Depending on the relationship between an extraneous variable and an independent variable, this uncontrolled variation can either obscure or inflate the effect of the independent variable on the dependent variable of interest. The problem of extraneous variation occurs more often in studies that are conducted outside of laboratories, where the ability to hold control variables constant is greatly decreased.

INDEPENDENT variable is MANIPULATED
DEPENDENT variable is OBSERVED
CONTROL variable is held CONSTANT

Name the Variables

Because understanding independent, dependent, and control variables is so important, we have included some examples for your use in checking your understanding. For each situation, name the three kinds of variables. The answers follow the examples. No peeking!

1. An automobile manufacturer wants to know how bright brake lights should be to minimize the time required for the driver of a following car to realize that the car in front is stopping. An experiment is conducted to answer this. Name the variables.

2. A pigeon is trained to peck a key if a green light is illuminated but not if a red light is on. Correct pecks are rewarded by access to grain. Name the variables.

3. A therapist tries to improve a patient's image of himself. Every time the patient says something positive about himself, the therapist rewards this by nodding, smiling, and being extra-attentive. Name the variables.

4. A social psychologist does an experiment to discover whether men or women give lower ratings of discomfort when six people are crowded into a telephone booth. Name the variables.

ANSWERS

1. Independent (manipulated) variable: Intensity (brightness) of brake lights

   Dependent (observed) variable: Time from onset of brake lights until depression of brake pedal by following driver

   Control (constant) variables: Color of brake lights, shape of brake pedal, force needed to depress brake pedal, external illumination, etc.

2. Independent variable: Color of light (red or green)
   Dependent variable: Number of key pecks
   Control variables: Hours of food deprivation, size of key, intensity of red and green lights, etc.

3. Independent variable: Actually, this is not an experiment, because there is only one level of the independent variable. To make this an experiment, we need another level— say, rewarding positive statements about the patient's mother-in-law and ignoring negative ones. Then the independent variable would be: Kind of statement rewarded.

   Dependent variable: Number (or frequency) of statements
   Control variables: Office setting, therapist

4. Independent variable: Gender of participant[1]
   Dependent variable: Rating of discomfort
   Control variables: Size of telephone booth, number of persons (six) crowded into booth, size of individuals, etc.

[1] Gender is a special type of independent variable called a subject variable, discussed later in this chapter.

More Than One Independent Variable

It is unusual to find an experiment reported in a psychological journal in which only one independent (manipulated) variable is used; the typical experiment manipulates from two to four independent variables simultaneously. This procedure has several advantages. First, it is often more efficient to conduct one experiment with, say, three independent variables than to conduct three separate experiments. Second, experimental control is often better, since with a single experiment, some control variables—time of day, temperature, humidity, and so on—are more likely to be held constant than with three separate experiments. Third, and most important, is that results generalized—that is, shown to be valid in several situations—across several independent variables are more valuable than data that have yet to be generalized. Just as it is important to establish generality of results across different types of experimental subjects (see Chapter 12), experimenters also need to discover if some result is valid across levels of independent variables. Fourth, this allows us to study interactions, the relationships among independent variables. We illustrate these advantages with some examples.

Let us say we wish to find out which of two kinds of rewards facilitates the learning of geometry by high school students. The first reward is an outright cash payment for problems correctly solved; the second reward is early dismissal from class—that is, each correct solution entitles the student to leave class five minutes early. Assume that the results of this (hypothetical) experiment show early dismissal to be the better reward. Before we make early dismissal a universal rule in high school, we should first establish its generality by comparing the two kinds of reward in other classes, such as history or biology. Here, subject matter of the class would be a second independent variable. It would be better to put these two variables into a single experiment than to conduct two successive experiments. This would avoid problems of control, such as one class being tested the week of the big football game (when no reward would improve learning) and the other class being tested the week after the game is won (when students felt better about learning).

When the effects produced by one independent variable are different at each level of a second independent variable, we have an **interaction.** The search for interactions is a major reason for using more than one independent variable per experiment. This can best be demonstrated by example.

In a research report titled "When God Sanctions Killing," Bushman, Ridge, Da, Key, and Busath (2007) described a laboratory study of aggression. Participants read a violent passage that purportedly came from either the Bible or an ancient scroll. Following that, they performed an additional task that allowed them to present loud sounds to another subject in the experiment. They controlled the intensity of this sound, and higher intensities were interpreted as revealing greater aggression. The dependent variable was the number of times participants selected the highest noise levels in a set of 25 trials. Therefore, aggression scores could range from a low of 0 to a high of 25.

There were two independent variables. The first was the source of the violent passage: either the Bible or an ancient scroll. The second independent variable was whether or not the subject believed in God; this is a special type of independent variable, called a subject variable, which is discussed later in this chapter.

Results from this experiment are shown in Figure 3.1, with each independent variable plotted by itself. Reading a passage from the Bible produced greater aggression. Subjects who believed in God also acted more aggressively.

Figure 3.2 shows that this simple interpretation of the results, while correct, is incomplete. Here both independent variables are plotted on the same graph, making some relationships easier to see. If there was no mention of God because the passage came from an ancient scroll, subjects who believe in God and subjects who do not believe in God exhibited similar levels of aggression. But when God sanctioned violence because the passage came from the Bible, greater levels of aggression were exhibited by those subjects who believe in God.

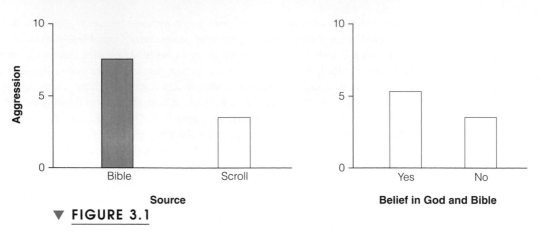

▼ **FIGURE 3.1**

Effects of Two Independent Variables on Aggression. (Data from Bushman et al., 2007.)

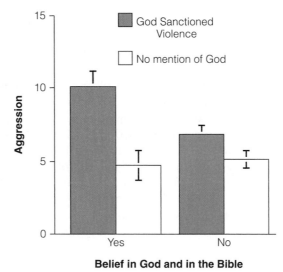

▼ **FIGURE 3.2**

Effect of Belief in God and in the Bible on Aggression Levels after Reading a Violent Passage in Which Either God Sanctioned the Violence or God Was Not Mentioned. The Measure of Aggression Was the Number of Trials (Out of 25) on Which Participants Chose to Deliver the Highest Noise Levels (i.e., 9 and 10) to their Ostensible Partners. Thus, Aggression Scores Could Range from 0 to 25. Gapped Vertical Bars Denote $\pm 1\ SE$. (From Bushman et al., 2007 with permission.)

Remember, an interaction between two independent variables indicates that effects produced by one independent variable (belief in God) are not the same at each level of a second independent variable (source of the passage). When the passage contains no mention of God, belief in God has no effect upon aggression. But when the passage comes from the Bible, the increase in aggression is greater for subjects who believe in God than for subjects who do not believe in God. This is an interaction.

Figure 3.3 shows hypothetical data we invented to illustrate how these results might look if there were no interaction. The effect of one independent variable is the same at each level of the other independent variable. The dotted lines in Figure 3.3 are parallel, which is an easy way to detect the lack of an interaction. If similar lines were drawn in Figure 3.2., they would not be parallel because that figure shows an interaction of two independent variables.

Many experiments include two or more independent variables; this means that the results may contain an interaction. Because of the frequency with which you are likely to encounter interactions, we present another example of a two-variable experiment to help you practice interpreting the results of complex experiments.

In the experiment on social loafing (see Chapter 1) by Brickner, Harkins, and Ostrom (1986), the authors wanted to determine the effect of personal involvement in a task on the amount of social loafing shown on that task. Brickner and her associates noted that low-involvement tasks, such as clapping and generating uses for a knife, had been used in earlier research on social loafing. The authors reasoned that the effort devoted to a task should be related to the intrinsic importance or personal significance that the task has for the individual. High personal involvement in a task should reduce social loafing, because individuals should put forth a substantial amount of effort on such tasks, regardless of whether their individual performance is monitored. So, the researchers varied the subjects' involvement in the task and also varied the amount that individual effort could be assessed. If their reasoning was correct, there should be an interaction: Low involvement should lead to social loafing (reduced effort when the individual's effort cannot be assessed), but high involvement should lead to about the same amount of effort, whether or not individual effort could be identified.

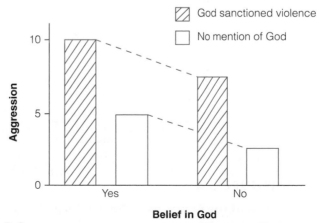

▼ FIGURE 3.3

Hypothetical Data with No Interaction. Note Parallel Lines.

Brickner and associates had college students generate as many thoughts as they could in a 12-minute period about a proposal to implement senior comprehensive exams, which a student would have to pass in order to graduate. In the high-involvement condition, the students were led to believe that the proposal would be instituted at their college prior to their graduation.

Thus, the addition of comprehensive exams as one prerequisite to graduation should have high personal relevance. In the low personal-involvement condition, the students were led to believe that the exams would be instituted later, at another college. The possible identifiability of individual effort was also manipulated by instructions. Subjects wrote each of their thoughts about comprehensives on an individual slip of paper. In the low-identifiability condition, the subjects were told that their thoughts would be collected together with those of other subjects, because the committee evaluating the thoughts wanted to assess the range of opinions for the group as a whole. In the high-identifiability condition, the subjects were told that their opinions would be considered separately from those of others, because the committee in charge wanted to assess individual responses.

To summarize, the dependent variable was the number of thoughts generated in the four conditions: low identifiability and low involvement; low identifiability and high involvement; high identifiability and low involvement; and high identifiability and high involvement.

The results are shown in Figure 3.4, which plots the number of thoughts generated against identifiability for the two involvement conditions. Earlier social loafing research is replicated in the low-involvement condition: Fewer thoughts were generated when

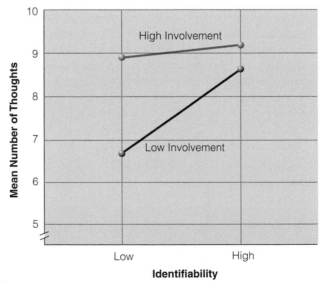

▼ **FIGURE 3.4**

Results of the Experiment by Brickner, Harkins, and Ostrom (1986), Showing an Interaction. Social loafing (low numbers of thoughts generated with low as opposed to high identifiability) occurs with a low-involvement task but not with a high-involvement one.

the subjects believed that their individual performance was not being assessed. Now examine the results when there was high involvement: The number of thoughts was about the same, regardless of identifiability. Thus, the variables interact: The effects of identifiability depend on the level of task involvement. Put another way, social loafing, and therefore diffusion of responsibility, is less likely to occur when a person is confronted with a personally involving task than when the task does not have much intrinsic interest.

In summary, an interaction occurs when the levels of one independent variable are differentially affected by the levels of other independent variables. When interactions are present, it does not make sense to discuss the effects of each independent variable separately. Because the effects of one variable also depend on the levels of the other variables, we are forced to discuss interacting variables together.

More Than One Dependent Variable

The dependent (observed) variable is used as an index of behavior. It indicates how well or poorly the subject is performing. It permits the experimenter to score behavior. The experimenter must decide which aspects of behavior are relevant to the experiment at hand. Although some variables traditionally have been used, this does not mean that they are the only, or even the best, indexes of behavior. Take, for example, the behavior of a rat pressing a bar or a pigeon pecking a key, responses that are used in studies of animal learning. The most common dependent variable is the number of presses or pecks observed. But the force with which a key is pecked can also lead to interesting findings (see Neuringer 2002, p. 680; Notterman & Mintz, 1965), as can the latency (the time taken to respond). Researchers can usually come up with several dependent variables that may be appropriate. Let us say we wish to study the legibility of the typeface that you are now reading. We cannot observe "legibility," of course. What dependent variables might we observe? Here are some that have been used in the past: retention of meaningful information after reading text, time needed to read a fixed number of words, number of errors in recognizing single letters, speed in transcribing or retyping text, heart rate during reading, and muscular tension during reading—and this list is far from exhaustive.

Reasons of economy argue for obtaining as many dependent measures at the same time as is feasible. Despite this, the typical experiment uses only one, or at the most, two dependent variables simultaneously. This is unfortunate: Just as the generality of an experiment is expanded by having more than one independent variable, it is also expanded with several dependent variables. The reason why more dependent variables are not used is probably because it is statistically difficult to analyze several dependent variables at once. Although modern computer techniques make the calculations quite feasible, many experimental psychologists have not been well trained in these multivariate statistical procedures and thus hesitate to use them. Separate analyses could be conducted for each dependent variable by itself, but this loses information in much the same way that a separate analysis of independent variables ignores interactions. Multivariate analysis is complex; nevertheless, you should be aware that it is often advantageous to use more than one dependent variable in an experiment.

▼ EXPERIMENTAL DESIGNS

The purpose of experimental design is to minimize extraneous or uncontrolled variation, thereby increasing the likelihood that an experiment will produce valid, consistent results. Entire books have been written about experimental design. Here, we cover a sample of some common techniques used to improve the design of experiments.

One of the first design decisions an experimenter must make is how to assign subjects to the various levels of independent variables. The two main possibilities are to assign only some subjects to each level or to assign each subject to every level. The first possibility is called a **between-subjects design** and the second, a **within-subjects design.** The difference can be shown with a simple example. Thirty students in introductory psychology have signed up for an experiment that you are conducting to test ability to remember nonsense words. Your independent variable is the number of times you will say each item: one time or five times. You expect that an item presented five times will be learned better than an item presented only once. The between-subjects design calls for you to divide your subjects by halves—that is, into two groups of 15 students each—with one group receiving five repetitions and the other, one repetition. (How to select which subjects to put in each group is discussed shortly.) The within-subjects design has all 30 subjects learning with both levels of the independent variable—that is, each is tested with one repetition and again with five repetitions. (How to determine the order in which each subject gets these two treatments is also discussed later.) Which design should you use?

Between-Subjects Designs

The between-subjects (two groups) design is conservative. There is no chance that one treatment will continue to contaminate the other, because each person receives only one treatment (one repetition or five repetitions, but not both). One drawback, however, is that the between-subjects design must deal with differences among people, and this decreases its efficiency—that is, its ability to detect real differences between one and five repetitions of the memory items.

In any between-subjects design, the experimenter must try to minimize differences among the subjects in the two or more treatment groups. Clearly, if we took the five best memorizers and deliberately placed them in the one-repetition group, and put the five worst in the five-repetition group, we might wind up with no difference in results—even, perhaps, with the one-repetition group doing better. To prevent this outcome, the experimenter must ensure that both groups are equivalent at the start of the experiment.

Equivalent Groups One way to ensure equivalence would be to administer a memory test to all 30 subjects before the regular experiment started, to obtain a **baseline** measure of the subjects' ability to memorize nonsense words. Subjects' baseline scores could then be used to form pairs of subjects that had equal or very similar scores. One member of each pair would be randomly assigned to one group and the other member to the second group. This technique is called **matching**. One difficulty with matching is that an experimenter cannot match subjects on every possible characteristic. Thus, there is always the possibility that the groups, even though matched on some characteristic(s), differ on some other characteristic that may be relevant (matching is discussed in greater detail later in this chapter).

A more common technique used to ensure that equivalent groups are formed is **randomization.** Randomization means that each person participating in an experiment has an equal chance of being assigned to any particular group. In our repetition experiment, one way to form two groups by randomization would be to draw names out of a hat. Or we could ask each person to step forward and then throw a die. Even throws would be assigned to one group and odd throws to the other. If we did not have any dice, a table of random numbers could be used to generate even and odd digits. This method of assigning subjects to experimental conditions has no bias, since it ignores all characteristics of the subjects; we expect that the groups so created would be equivalent on any and all relevant dimensions. However, randomization does not guarantee that groups will always be equal. By chance, a greater number of better memorizers might be assigned to one of the groups. The odds of this occurring can be calculated by the methods of probability theory as applied to statistics (see Appendix B). This is one reason why experimental designs and statistics are often treated as the same topic. However, design is concerned with the logic of arranging experiments, whereas statistics deals with calculating odds, probabilities, and other mathematical quantities.

If we are sure that all relevant dimensions have been dealt with, matching is preferable to randomization. But because we seldom are sure, randomization is used more often.

Within-Subjects Designs

Many experimental psychologists would prefer the within-subjects (one group) design in which all 30 subjects were tested with one repetition and again with five repetitions (or vice versa). It is more efficient, since each subject is compared with himself or herself. Any differences resulting from one versus five repetitions cannot be the result of differences between the people in the two groups, as might be the case for the between-subjects design.

General Practice Effects   There is a risk, however, in the more-efficient within-subjects design. Imagine that all 30 subjects first learn a large number of items with five repetitions and then learn with one repetition. By the time subjects begin the one-repetition treatment, they might have become more proficient in learning nonsense words, or they might be experiencing some boredom or fatigue with the task. Both these possibilities are termed **general practice effects.** These effects are usually assumed to be the same for all treatment conditions so that it does not matter whether subjects learned with one repetition followed by five repetitions or five followed by one repetition. Because general practice effects are the same for all treatment conditions, they can be controlled largely through **counterbalancing.** With counterbalancing, the experimenter faces the difficulty of determining the order in which treatments should be given to subjects. Again, one solution is to use randomization by drawing the treatment titles out of a hat, using a random-number table, or using a computer to order conditions randomly. The logic behind this was discussed earlier. However, although counterbalancing treatments through randomization produces equivalent orders in the long run, it is less likely to be suitable when there are only a small number of treatments. In most experiments, the number of subjects exceeds the number of treatments, so randomization is a good technique for assigning subjects to treatments.

Complete counterbalancing makes sure that all possible treatment orders are used. In the repetition experiment, this is easy because there are only two orders: one and five repetitions, five and one repetitions. Half the subjects would receive one repetition followed by five repetitions, and the other half would get the opposite order. As the number of treatments increases, the number of orders becomes large indeed. Three treatments have 6 different orders; four treatments have 24 different orders; five treatments have 120 different orders; and so on. As the levels of an independent variable increase, complete counterbalancing soon becomes impractical.

Counterbalancing does not eliminate the effects of order. It does allow experimenters to evaluate possible order effects. If such effects are present, and especially if they form interactions with other, more important independent variables, steps need to be taken to correct the design. The experimenter might decide to repeat the experiment, using a between-subjects design to avoid order effects. Alternatively, the original experiment could be reanalyzed as a between-subjects one, by examining behavior in just the initial condition experienced by each subject.

Differential Carryover Effects   Differential carryover effects pose a more serious problem than do general practice effects. In the case of **differential carryover effects,** the effect of the early part of the experiment on the later part of the experiment varies depending on which treatment comes first. Imagine that all 30 subjects first learn items with five repetitions and then learn with one repetition. As a result of their earlier experience with five repetitions, they might decide to repeat to themselves four more times the item that was only presented once. This would destroy any differences between the two levels of the independent variable. This is an example of a differential carryover effect given that the effect of the first treatment on the second treatment differs depending on which treatment came first. This was not the case with general practice effects in which subjects approached the second treatment in the same way (i.e., with greater skill, boredom, or fatigue), regardless of the treatment they received in the first phase of the experiment. Differential carryover effects can be diminished somewhat through counterbalancing, but counterbalancing cannot eliminate these effects entirely. If there is reason to expect differential carryover effects, we can do one of two things in addition to counterbalancing: use the between-subjects design or build in a sufficient time delay between the two treatments. Because the between-subjects design is less efficient, it will require that many more subjects be tested; but this is preferable to conducting a seriously flawed experiment. If we decide to insert a time delay between the two treatments, we must identify a duration of time that is sufficient to eliminate the possibility of differential carryover effects.

Small-*n* Designs

Before turning to a discussion of mixed designs, we would like to mention a variant on the traditional within-subjects design—the **small-*n* design.** Small-*n* designs present the levels of the independent variable or treatments to a small number of subjects or a single subject. Because few subjects are tested, a substantial number of observations are recorded for each subject, resulting in a very economical and highly controlled experiment. Small-*n* experiments are common in psychophysical, clinical, and operant-conditioning research. Just as with the within-subjects design, the experimenter must be careful to counterbalance treatments and anticipate any problems associated with administering multiple treatments to individual subjects. Small-n designs are discussed at length in Chapter 9 of this text and in Chapter 9 of Elmes, Kantowitz, and Roediger (2003).

Mixed Designs

Experiments need not be exclusively of within-subjects or between-subjects design. It is often convenient and prudent to have some independent variables treated as between-subjects and others as within-subjects in the same experiment (assuming the experiment has more than one independent variable, of course). If one variable—for example, the administration of a drug—seems likely to affect others, it can be made a between-subjects variable, while the rest of the variables are varied within subjects. When trials or repeated practice on a task are of interest, it is of necessity a within-subjects variable. Frequently, a mixed design is used, in which some variable is imposed between subjects to see its effect across a second, within-subjects variable. This type of compromise design (**mixed design**) is not as efficient or economical as a pure within-subjects design, but it is often safer.

Control Conditions

Independent variables must be varied (or manipulated) by the experimenter. This implies that each and every independent variable must vary either in amount (quantitative variation) or in kind (qualitative variation) within the experiment. For example, if the amount of reward given to a rat is an independent variable, the amounts chosen by the experimenter might be one and four pellets of food. Alternatively, we could offer different kinds of rewards, such as food and water. The technical term for a single treatment or condition of an independent variable is level. We would state that the levels of the independent variable are one and four food pellets in the first example and food and water in the second example.

Many experiments contain, in addition to independent variables, some **control group** (between-subjects design) or **control condition** (within-subjects design). In its simplest form, the control group does not receive the levels of interest of the independent variable. In the reward example just described, a control group of rats would receive no reward. Or say an experimenter is interested in the effect of noise on studying. Using a between-subjects design, the experimenter would expose one group of subjects to loud noise for half an hour while they were studying; this is the level of interest of the independent variable. A control group would study the same material for half an hour in a quiet setting (a very low level of noise). Then both groups would be tested on the material. Any obtained difference on the test between the two groups would be attributed to the effect of noise.

The important characteristic of a control condition is the fact that it provides a baseline against which some variable of interest can be compared. Sometimes the best baseline is no treatment, but often the best baseline requires some activity. A frequent example occurs in memory research, where a group of subjects is required to learn two different lists of words. The experimenter is interested in how learning one list interferes with

Experimental Group	Learn List A	Learn List B	Test List A
Control Group	Learn List A	Do Arithmetic	Test List A

▼ **FIGURE 3.5**

Examples of Experimental and Control Groups for List Learning.

learning the other. The experimental group (receiving the level of interest of the independent variable) first learns list A, then learns list B, and then is tested again on list A. The experimenter would like to show that learning list B interferes with retaining list A. But before any conclusion of this sort can be reached, a comparison control condition is required. Merely comparing the final test of list A with the first test is insufficient, because subjects might do worse on the last list A test simply because they are tired, or they might do better because they have had extra practice. A control condition with no treatment would have a control group learn list A, then sit around for the time it took the experimental group to learn list B, and then be tested again on list A. But this would be a poor control condition, because subjects might practice or rehearse list A while they were sitting around. This would improve their final performance on the last list A test and incorrectly make it appear that in the experimental group, list B interfered more than it really did with list A. A proper baseline condition would occupy the control group during the time the experimental group was learning list B; perhaps the experimenter would have them do arithmetic or some other "busy work" that would prevent rehearsal (Figure 3.5).

Sometimes the control condition is contained implicitly within the experiment. Recall the memory experiment discussed earlier, in which the independent variable was the number of repetitions of an item: one or five. No experimenter would bother to include a control group or condition with zero repetitions, since no learning could occur under this odd circumstance. The control condition is implicit, in that five repetitions can be compared with one, and vice versa. Since the experimenter might well be as interested in the effects of a single repetition as in five repetitions, we probably would not explicitly call the one-repetition level a control condition. But it does provide a baseline for comparison—and so, for that matter, does the five-repetition condition, since the one-repetition results can be compared with it.

Many types of experiments require more than one baseline. In physiological and drug research, for example, a control for surgical or injection trauma is needed. So, a subject might receive a sham operation or the injection of an inert substance (a placebo) in the control condition; those would also be compared with other controls that received no operation or no injection.

Pitfalls

Unfortunately, it is quite easy to formulate an inadequate experimental design; most experimental psychologists have hidden away mistakes of this kind in a dusty file cabinet. In this section, we discuss only a small sample of errors in design, those that are so common you should be aware of them.

Demand Characteristics Laboratory experiments attempt to capture behavior as it really is influenced by the independent variable. Sometimes the laboratory setting itself or the knowledge that an experiment is under way may alter patterns of behavior. Many times, research participants spontaneously form hypotheses or assumptions about the experimenter's purpose in conducting the experiment and then behave or respond in a way that will satisfy this "purpose." Try this simple demonstration to convince yourself that such effects occur. Tell five of your friends that you are conducting an experiment for your psychology class and would like their cooperation as subjects. If they agree, ask them to hold three ice cubes in their bare hands. Note how many hold the ice cubes until they melt. Now ask five other friends to hold the ice cubes, without mentioning anything about an experiment. Instead of holding the ice cubes until they melt, they will consider your request somewhat strange and soon so inform you. There is something unusual about the ready compliance of those friends who knew they were participating in an experiment: More of them were willing to hold the ice cubes for a longer period. Psychologists call the cues available to subjects that allow them to determine the purpose of the experiment, or what is expected by the experimenter, **demand characteristics.** To the extent that the behavior of research participants is controlled by demand characteristics instead of by independent variables, experiments are invalid and cannot be generalized beyond the test situation.

A well-known example of a demand characteristic is the **Hawthorne effect,** named after the Western Electric Company plant where it was first observed. The company was interested in improving worker morale and productivity and conducted several experiments (such as improving lighting) to better the workers' environment. No matter what experimental manipulation was tried, worker productivity improved. The workers knew they were in a "special" group, and therefore tried to do their best at all times. (See Bramel & Friend, 1981, and Parsons, 1974, for alternate interpretations of these results.) The demand characteristics were more important in determining the workers' productivity than were the experimental manipulations. Although the term *Hawthorne effect* is widely used to describe field experiments where productivity increased due to participation in the study, there have been several detailed reviews of the original Hawthorne experiment that suggest the original conclusion was based upon weak evidence (Brannigan & Zwerman, 2001; Wickström & Bendix, 2000). Nevertheless, the term remains in wide use.

Demand characteristics, and the Hawthorne effect, must be carefully evaluated. A recent study (Fostervold, Buckmann, & Lie, 2001) contained special control conditions for evaluating the effects of visual display unit (VDU) filters on computer screens. In the first part of the study one group of participants had filters (filter group) and another control group did not. Comparing the two groups' results showed various benefits for the filter group. However, the researchers also included a second phase where the control group was given a filter while the filter group continued with the same filter. Only minor changes were observed for the initial control group. Furthermore, initial benefits for the filter group declined during the second phase. Thus, results in the first phase were due to demand characteristics and not to benefits associated with VDU filters. Had the experimenters conducted only the first phase of their study, a false benefit of filters, actually due to demand characteristics, might have been claimed incorrectly.

Experimenter Effects A pitfall closely related to demand characteristics is the **experimenter effect,** which influences the outcome accidentally by providing participants with slight cues as to the experimenter's expectations. For example, an experimenter might not be aware that he or she nods approvingly when a correct response is given and frowns after errors. The gender, race, and ethnicity of the experimenter are also potential experimenter effects. Experimenter characteristics are more likely to bias the results of an experiment in research that focuses on issues related to these characteristics—for example, the race of an experimenter who is conducting an experiment concerning the effect of skin color on work performance ratings.

These effects are not limited to experiments with humans. The experimenter effect can also occur in seemingly objective experiments with animal subjects. Rosenthal and Fode (1963) told student experimenters that the rats they were to test in a maze were from special strains: either maze-bright or maze-dull. Actually, the rats came from the same population. Nevertheless, the rats that were labeled maze-bright had fewer errors than those labeled maze-dull, and this difference was statistically reliable. The student experimenters were observed while they tested the rats: They did not cheat or do anything overt to bias the results. It seems reasonable that the lucky students who got supposedly bright rats were more motivated to perform the experiment than those unfortunates who had to teach stupid rats to go through the maze. Somehow, this affected the results of the experiment—perhaps because experimenters handled the two groups of rats differently.

The best way to eliminate this kind of experimenter effect is to hide the experimental condition from the experimenter on the premise that experimenters cannot communicate what they do not know. This procedure is termed a **double-blind experiment** because neither the experimenter nor the research participant knows which subjects are in which treatment conditions. Such a procedure was, for instance, used in a study of behavioral effects of air pollution. Subjects breathed either pure air or air taken from a busy roadway. The air was contained in tanks; the experimenter did not know which tank held pure air and which tank held polluted air. The subjects' poorer performance in polluted air cannot, then, be attributed to the experimenter inadvertently disclosing the air quality to subjects or treating them differently.

Experimenter effects are not always this subtle. One of the authors was once involved in an experiment concerning the human eye-blink response. Several experimenters helped conduct the same experiment, and it was soon noticed that one of them obtained results that were quite different from those of the rest of us. His subjects started out experimental sessions with massive flurries of frenzied blinking. The cause of this odd behavior was easily discovered. To record eye blinks, the experimenter must attach a tiny metal rod to the subject's eyelid with special tape—ordinarily a painless procedure. However, the experimenter in question had a very heavy thumb and was unable to attach the rod without irritating the eye, causing the strange flurries of blinking.

When an experimenter suspects that some aspect of his or her appearance or manner (e.g., gender, race, ethnicity) may alter the pattern of subjects' behavior, then a possible solution is to incorporate this as an additional independent variable or control variable in the experimental design. If an African-American experimenter is conducting research on skin color and work performance ratings, he or she could ask a white colleague or research assistant to test half the subjects and then compare the effects of skin color in the two experimenter race conditions.

Automation of Experiments   Experimenter effects can be eliminated or greatly reduced by having computers or other equipment conduct the experiment so that the subject is untouched by human hands. In many laboratories, a subject enters a testing booth and sees a message on a screen that tells her or him to push a button to begin. Pushing the button causes instructions for the experiment to appear on the screen. The entire experiment is then conducted by a computer. The experimenter appears at the end of the data collection to debrief the participant, giving the aims of the study and explaining how the subject has helped advance science. Until then, the experimenter simply monitors the equipment and the subject to ensure that the subject is following instructions and that nothing untoward happens. Such automation obviously reduces the dangers of experimenter bias.

Quasi-Experiments

For one reason or another, many variables cannot be manipulated directly. One deterrent to manipulation of variables in experiments is the ethical considerations all scientists must have (see Chapter 4). It is ethical to survey or otherwise observe the use of drugs by college students as long as permission is obtained. By no stretch of the imagination, however, would it be ethical to create a group of drug abusers and compare their activities with a nonabusing group that we also created. A second barrier to manipulation is Mother Nature. Some variables, such as the sex of our subjects, cannot be varied by the experimenter (except in very rare and controversial circumstances); other variables, such as natural disasters (tornadoes, hurricanes) or unnatural disasters (wars, airplane crashes), are both physically and morally difficult to implement. Can we do experiments that concern these phenomena? After all, such variables and others like them are fascinating and may play an important part in human experience.

The answer to the question (assuming you are an ethical scientist) is this: You can and you cannot. We are not being silly here; rather, we are emphasizing the fact that you cannot do real experiments on phenomena such as the ones just listed. You can, however, conduct **quasi-experiments.** The technique here is similar to the ex post facto examination in correlational research, except that two or more levels of the variable of interest are examined rather than correlated. We wait for Mother Nature to do her work, and then we compare the effects of that "independent variable" with the effects that occur when that variable is not present or differs in some way. If we compare the reading ability of men with that of women, or that of speed readers with that of average adults, we have conducted a quasi-experiment.

The advantages of quasi-experiments are obvious: They use naturally occurring independent variables, most of which have a high degree of intrinsic interest and important practical implications. In a quasi-experiment, we take advantage of observational and correlational procedures and combine them with the power of experimentation. The typical quasi-experiment has a **subject variable** as an independent variable. If we want to find out about almost any inherent subject variable (age, sex, race, ethnic group), socially caused subject attribute (social class, region of residence), or disease- and illness-related subject attribute (limb loss, mental illness, brain damage, effects of disasters), we are going to have to select rather than vary our independent variables, unless it is possible to do the experiment directly on infrahuman organisms. Although quasi-experiments are interesting and can contribute very important research, we should caution you here that the advantages of quasi-experiments are gained at the expense of control. When the researcher has to take what is given, what is given may include several important confounding variables.

Because much research in psychology is concerned with subject variables and because quasi-experiments using subject variables are likely to be confounded, we now examine the problems and possible solutions.

An experimenter cannot manipulate a subject variable while holding other factors constant; she or he can only select subjects who already have the characteristic in some varying degree and then compare them based on the behavior of interest. If the subjects in the different groups (say, high, medium, and low IQ) differ on the behavior, we cannot conclude that the subject-variable difference has produced or is responsible for the difference in behavior. The reason is that other factors may be covariant and confounded with the subject variable. If high-IQ subjects perform some task better than low-IQ subjects, we cannot say that IQ produced or caused the difference, because the different groups of subjects are likely to vary on other relevant dimensions, such as motivation, education, and so forth. When subject variables are investigated, we cannot safely attribute differences in behavior to this variable, as we can with true experimental variables. Such designs, then, essentially produce correlations between variables. We can say that the variables are related, but we cannot say that one variable produces or causes the effect in the other variable.

This is a very important point; let us consider an example. Suppose an investigator is interested in the intellectual functioning (or lack thereof) of people suffering from schizophrenia. People diagnosed as belonging to this group are given numerous tests that are meant to measure various mental abilities. The researcher also gives these tests to another group of people, so-called normals. He or she discovers that schizophrenics do especially poorly relative to normals in tests involving semantic aspects of language, such as those that involve understanding the meanings of words or comprehending prose passages. The investigator concludes that the schizophrenics perform these tests more poorly *because* they are schizophrenics and that their inability to use language well in communication is a likely contributing cause of schizophrenia.

Studies such as this are common in some areas of psychology. Despite the fact that conclusions similar to this are often drawn from such studies, they are completely unwarranted. Both conclusions are based on correlations, and other factors could well be the critical ones. Schizophrenics may do more poorly than normals for any number of reasons. They may not be as intelligent, as motivated, as educated, or as wise at taking tests. It may simply be that they have been institutionalized for a long time, with a resulting poverty of social and intellectual intercourse. So we cannot conclude that the reason that the two groups differ on verbal tests is schizophrenia or its absence in the two groups. Even if we could conclude this, it would certainly not imply the other conclusion, that language problems are involved in causing schizophrenia. Again, all we would have is a correlation between these two variables, with no idea of whether or how the two are causally related.

Use of subject variables is very common in all psychological research, but it is absolutely crucial in such areas as clinical and developmental psychology. Therefore, the problems with making inferences from such research should be carefully considered. A primary variable in developmental psychology is age, a subject variable; this means that much research in this field is correlational in nature. In general, the problem of individual differences among subjects in psychology is one that is often ignored, though there are often appeals to consider this problem as crucial (see Underwood, 1975). We devote a chapter later in the book to individual differences (Chapter 12). Let us consider here one way of attempting more sound inferences from experiments employing subject variables.

Matching Again The basic problem in the investigation of subject variables and in other ex post facto research is the fact that whatever differences are observed in behavior may be caused by their confounded variables. One way to try to avoid this problem is by matching subjects on the other relevant variables. In the comparison of schizophrenic and normal subjects, we noted that the two groups were also likely to differ on other characteristics, such as IQ, education, motivation, institutionalization, and perhaps even age. Rather than simply comparing the schizophrenic subjects with normal subjects, we might try to compare them with another group more closely matched on these other dimensions, so that, we hope, the main difference between the groups would be the presence or absence of schizophrenia. For example, we might use a group of patients who, on the average, are similar to the schizophrenics in terms of age, IQ, length of time institutionalized, gender, and some measure of motivation. When the two groups have been matched on all these characteristics, then we can more confidently attribute any difference in performance between them to the factor of interest, namely, schizophrenia. By matching, investigators attempt to introduce the crucial characteristic of experimentation—being able to hold constant extraneous factors to avoid confoundings—into what is essentially a correlational observation. The desire is to allow one to infer that the variable of interest (schizophrenia) produces the observed effect.

Several rather severe problems are associated with matching. For one thing, it often requires a great deal of effort, because some of the relevant variables may be quite difficult to measure. Even when one goes to the trouble of taking the needed additional measures, it may still be impossible to match the groups, especially if few subjects are involved before matching is attempted. Even when matching is successful, it often greatly reduces the size of the sample on which the observations are made. We then have less confidence in our observations, because they may not be stable and repeatable.

Matching is often difficult because crucial differences among subjects may have subtle effects. In addition, the effects of one difference may interact with another. Thus, *subtle interactions* among matched variables may confound the results. To illustrate these difficulties, let us consider some of the work done by Lester and Brazelton (1982) on neonatal behavior.

Brazelton's primary interest is in cultural differences in neonatal behavior, as measured by the Brazelton Neonatal Behavioral Assessment Scale. The general strategy is to compare neonates from various cultures and ethnic groups with neonates from the United States. In these quasi-experiments, culture or ethnic group, which is a subject variable, is the quasi-independent variable. Attempts are usually made to match the babies from different cultures along various dimensions, such as birth weight, birth length, and obstetrical risk (including whether the mother received medication during birth, whether the baby was premature, and so on). Lester and Brazelton show that there is a synergistic relationship among these factors. **Synergism** in a medical context means that the combined effects of two or more variables are not additive: The combined effect is greater than the sum of the individual components. This means that the variables interact.

The way in which neonatal characteristics and obstetrical risk interact is as follows. Studies have shown that the behavior (as measured by the Brazelton scale) of slightly underweight infants is more strongly influenced (negatively) by small amounts of medication taken by the mother than is the behavior of neonates who are closer to the average in weight. Even though the neonates are carefully selected, subtle and interactive effects of the matched variables can influence the results. This is an especially difficult problem in Brazelton's work, because much of his research has examined neonates from impoverished cultures, where birth weight is low and obstetrical risk is very high. Generally, you should remember that matched variables are rarely under direct control, which means that the possibility of confounding is always present.

Another problem with matching involves the introduction of the dreaded **regression artifact.** This is discussed in Chapter 12, but we explain it briefly here. Under certain conditions in many types of measurements, a statistical phenomenon occurs known as **regression to the mean.** The mean of a group of scores is what most people think of as the average: the total of all observations divided by the number of observations. For example, mean height in a sample of 60 people is the sum of all their heights divided by 60. Typically, if people who received extreme scores (i.e., very high or very low) on some characteristic are retested, their second scores will be closer to the mean of the entire group than were their original scores. Consider an example. We give 200 people a standard test of mathematical reasoning for which there are two equivalent forms, or two versions of the test that we know to be equivalent. The average (mean) score on the test is 60 of 100 possible points. We take the 15 people who score highest and the 15 who score lowest. The mean of these groups is, say 95 and 30, respectively. Then we test them again on the other version of the test. Now we might find that the means of the two groups are 87 and 35. On the second test, the scores of these two extreme groups regress toward the mean; the high-scoring group scores more poorly, and the low-scoring group does somewhat better. Basically, this happens for the high-scoring group because some people whose "true scores" are somewhat lower than actually tested lucked out and scored higher than they should have on the test. When retested, people with extremely high scores tend to score lower, near their true score. The situation is reversed for the low-scoring group. That is, some of them scored below their "true scores" on the first test; retesting leads to their scoring higher or nearer the true score.

This regression toward the mean is always observed under conditions when there is a less-than-perfect correlation between the two measures. The more extreme the selection of scores, the greater the regression toward the mean. It also occurs in all types of measurement situations. If abnormally tall or short parents have a child, it will likely be closer to the population mean than the height of the parents. As with most statistical phenomena, regression to the mean is true of groups of observations and is probabilistic (i.e., it may not occur every time). For example, a few individual subjects may move away from the mean in the second test of mathematical reasoning, but the group tendency will be toward the mean.

How does regression toward the mean affect quasi-experiments, in which subjects have been matched on some variable? Again, consider an example. This one, like much ex post facto research done on applied societal problems, has important implications. Let us assume that we have an educational program that we believe will be especially advantageous for increasing the reading scores of African-American children. This is especially important because African-American children's scores are typically lower than those of whites, presumably because of different cultural environments. We take two groups of children, one African-American and one white, and match them on several criteria, including age, sex, and, most important, initial reading performance. We give both groups of children the reading improvement program and then test their reading scores after the program. We find, much to our surprise, that the African-American children actually perform worse after the reading program than before it, and the white children improve. We conclude, of course, that the program helped white children but actually hurt African-American children, despite the fact that it was especially designed for the latter.

This conclusion, even though it may seem reasonable to you, is almost surely erroneous in this case, because of regression artifacts. Consider what happened when the African-American and white children were matched on initial reading scores. Since the populations differed initially, with African-Americans scoring lower than whites, in order to match two samples it was necessary to select the African-American students having higher scores than the mean for their group and the white students having lower scores than their group mean. Having picked these extreme groups, we would predict (because of regression to the mean) that when retested, the African-American children would have poorer scores and the white children would have better ones, on the average, even if the reading improvement program had no effect at all! The exceptionally high-scoring African-American children would tend to regress toward the mean of their group, and the low-scoring whites would regress toward the mean for their group. The same thing would have happened even if there had been no program and the children had been simply retested.

The same outcome would likely have been obtained if children had been matched on IQs instead of reading scores, since the two are probably positively correlated. So simply finding another matching variable may not be a solution. One solution would be to match very large samples of African-American and white children and then split each group, giving the reading program to one subgroup but not the other. All would be retested at the end of the one subgroup's participation in the program. (Assignment of subjects to the subgroups of African-American and white children should, of course, be random.) Regression to the mean would be expected in both subgroups, but the effect of the reading program could be evaluated against the group that had no program. Perhaps African-American children with the reading program would show much less drop (regression to the mean) than those without, indicating that the program really did have a positive effect.

Because quasi-experimental research with subject variables is conducted quite often to evaluate educational programs, its practitioners need to be aware of the many thorny problems associated with its use. One may not be able to say much with regard to the results or draw important conclusions because of confoundings. Matching helps alleviate this problem in some cases where its use is possible, but then one introduces the possibility of regression artifacts. And many researchers seem unaware of this problem. One famous blooper in such evaluational research, very similar to the hypothetical study outlined here, is discussed in Chapter 12.

When matching is a practical possibility and when regression artifacts are evaluated, we can feel somewhat more confident of conclusions from our results. But we should remember that what we have is still only a correlation, albeit a very carefully controlled one. Matching is sometimes useful, but it is not a cure-all. In our earlier example comparing schizophrenic subjects with others on mental test performance, if the schizophrenics still performed worse than the new matched control group, could we then conclude that schizophrenia *produced* inferiority in language usage? No, we could not. It could still be something else, some other difference between the two groups. We can never be absolutely sure we have matched on the relevant variables.

The study of experimental design is complex. In most chapters, we include a feature, From Problem to Experiment, that tells how to turn some issue or question into an actual experiment. We describe this feature next.

FROM PROBLEM TO EXPERIMENT
THE NUTS AND BOLTS

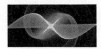

Problem *Conducting an Experiment*

Many of the decisions that go into creating an experiment are not clearly explained in journal reports of research. Although some of this brevity can be attributed to the economy imposed by journal editors who like short articles, a larger part is based on the assumption that experimental psychologists, or indeed psychologists researching any specialty, share a common background knowledge. This is true in all branches of science. For example, a physicist writing in a journal assumes that the readers already know that a dyne is a unit of force and will not bother to explain that term. Similarly, psychologists usually assume the reader knows what the terms *stimulus* and *response* mean, although these may be defined anyway. One purpose of this text is to give you some of the vocabulary necessary if you wish to read or write about psychological research.

Another problem for the new researcher is related to the "lore of the laboratory." "Everybody" knows there are certain "obvious" ways to perform certain kinds of research. These ways differ from area to area but are well known within each category. They are so well known that researchers seldom bother to explain them and indeed are quite surprised when new researchers are ignorant of these "obvious" tricks and techniques. Animal researchers often deprive animals of food for several hours before the experiment or keep their pigeons at a certain percentage of the weight the pigeons would attain if they had food continuously available. Although the reasons for this are obvious to the researcher, they may not be obvious to you. How does an experimenter know how many items to use in a memory experiment? How long should an experiment take? Why is one dependent variable selected from a set of what appear to be equally valid dependent variables? How many subjects should be used in an experiment? The From Problem to Experiment sections in the chapters of Part Two will answer such "obvious" questions as these.

From Problem to Experiment

All research aims at solving a problem. This problem can be abstract and theoretical or concrete and applied. The problem may arise from an observation made more or less casually, such as that people seem to be more aggressive during the summer. Here, the problem can be stated as "Why does summer heat cause aggression?" or even more skeptically as "Does high temperature cause aggression?" A problem may arise from an accidental discovery in a laboratory, such as the finding of mold on a piece of bread. Solving this problem—why is the mold growing here?—led to the discovery of penicillin. Finally, a problem may arise directly from a theoretical model, for instance, when we ask, "Why does reinforcement increase the probability of the occurrence of the behavior that preceded it?"

The first step the experimenter must take is to translate the problem into a testable hypothesis. The hypothesis then must be transformed into an experiment with independent, dependent, and control variables.

From Problem to Hypothesis A problem is, more or less, a vague statement that must be verified or a question that must be answered. Unless either is made specific and precise, it cannot be experimentally tested. Any hypothesis is a particular prediction, derived from a problem, often stated in this form: If A, then B. The crucial distinction between a problem and a hypothesis is that a hypothesis is directly testable, whereas a problem is not. An experimental test must be capable of disproving a hypothesis.

The purpose of any experiment is to test hypotheses about the effects of an independent variable(s) on the dependent variable. To do this, we must collect **data.** Once obtained, these data must be analyzed. Once analyzed, data must be reported. We briefly discuss these aspects in turn.

▼ DATA

Obtaining Data

Outlining an experimental design does not establish all the conditions needed for data acquisition. Although the design tells you how to assign subjects to experiments, it does not tell you how to get the subjects. Without subjects, there are no data.

Psychologists who investigate animal behavior have much more control over subject selection than those who study humans. Although animal psychologists must bear the additional expense of obtaining housing and feeding their subjects, they can select the strain they wish to purchase and always have subjects available, barring some catastrophe.

Research with humans most often uses as subjects college students enrolled in introductory psychology. Provided that this participation is used as a learning experience for the student, it is considered ethical and proper (American Psychological Association [APA], 1987). If the experiment is not used as a learning experience, the experimenter should pay subjects. Since college students are a select population, experimenters need to be careful about generalizing results to other subject populations. For example, techniques from a programmed learning system designed to teach inorganic chemistry might not prove successful in the teaching of plumbing.

Random selection means that any member of a population has an equal chance of being selected as a participant. Furthermore, each selection is independent of other selections, so choosing one person does not affect the chances of selecting anyone else. Sometimes in a typical psychology experiment it can be difficult to specify the population being sampled (Gigerenzer, 1993). Even if subjects can be drawn randomly, exactly what population does a university subject pool represent? It is not even clear if the population of students taking required psychology courses are representative of all university students. Since the student population is now so diverse, representing people with many different ages and backgrounds, researchers need be careful about extrapolating results from the test sample to other populations.

Random assignment means that each participant in the experiment is randomly assigned to experimental treatments (Holland, 1993). This is a prudent technique

because it increases our ability to make causal inferences from the experimental results. Statistical implications of sampling are discussed in Appendix B.

After your sample has been selected and your design is fixed, one major decision
remains. Should you test your participants one at a time or in a group? Both procedures have advantages and disadvantages. The biggest advantage of group testing is
economy. It takes only 1 hour to test 30 participants for an hour as a group, whereas
it takes 30 hours to test them singly. So, all other things being equal, it is faster, and
therefore better, to test participants in groups. But there are many instances where
all other things are far from equal. For example, take a listening experiment in which
separate words are presented to left and right ears. One hurried doctoral student
decided to save time and test her participants in a group. She forgot that unless participants were positioned exactly between the two loudspeakers, one message would
reach one ear before the other message reached the other ear. This invalidated the
independent variable. Of course, it would have been fine to test participants in a
group if each person wore earphones, thus avoiding this difficulty. The other problem
in group testing is the possibility that participants will influence one another, thus
influencing the data. Perhaps a participant may cheat and copy answers from another, or the sexual composition of the group may alter motivation. Sometimes these
problems can be prevented by placing participants in individual booths that prohibit
social interaction.

Analyzing Data

The immediate result of an experiment is a large series of numbers that represent behavior
under different conditions. As Sidman (1960) humorously describes it, scientists believe
that all data are tainted at birth. Data belong to Chance or to Science—but never to both.
Before the psychologist can be sure that data belong to Science, the demon Chance must
be exorcised. This is done by a ritual called *inferential statistical analysis*.

Once statistical analysis tells you which data are reliable (did not occur by chance),
you still have to decide which data are important. No mathematical calculation can
tell what hypotheses are being tested, what is predicted by the theories, and so on.
Statistics are never a substitute for thought. Statistical analysis is a theoretically neutral
procedure that serves theory and hypothesis testing. Except in the case of a what-if
experiment, the theories and hypotheses precede the statistics.

Because it is virtually impossible to grasp the meaning of the large set of numbers
an experiment produces, data are usually condensed by descriptive statistics. The most
common are the mean and the standard deviation. As part of the data analysis, means
are calculated for each level of each independent variable, as well as for combinations
of independent variables to show interactions.

Reporting Data

Data are presented in tables or figures. Figures are usually easier to understand.
Figure 3.2 is a typical example of how results of an experiment are reported. The
dependent variable is plotted on the **ordinate**—the vertical scale. The independent
variable is graphed on the **abscissa**—the horizontal scale. More than one independent

variable can be shown in the same graph by using solid and dotted lines and/or differently shaped symbols for each independent variable.

Raw (unanalyzed) data are hardly ever reported. Instead, some descriptive statistic, such as the mean, is used to summarize data. Other statistics often accompany data to tell the reader about the reliability of these data.

Many different styles and formats can be used to report data. We recommend the format given in the *Publication Manual of the American Psychological Association,* which has become the standard reference in psychology and many other fields in social science. This book will tell you more than you would like to know about every aspect of preparing the report of an experiment. If it is not in the library or bookstore, you can purchase it through the Order Department, American Psychological Association, P.O. Box 2710, Hyattsville, Maryland 20784.

▼ SUMMARY

1. An experiment is a controlled procedure for investigating the effects of one or more independent variables on one or more dependent variables. The *independent variable* is manipulated by the experimenter, whereas the *dependent variable* is observed and recorded. Experiments offer the investigator the best chance of eliminating or minimizing extraneous variation. Experiments are performed to test theories, to replicate and expand previous findings, or to show that prior research cannot be confirmed. Only rarely are experiments performed just to see what might happen.

2. Independent variables are chosen because an experimenter thinks they will control behavior. If they do not, this may mean that the manipulation was inadequate or that the experimenter was wrong. Dependent variables must be *stable*—that is, they must consistently produce the same results under the same conditions. *Ceiling* and *floor effects* result from an inadequate range for the dependent variable. *Control variables* are potential independent variables that are not manipulated during an experiment.

3. Most experiments test more than one independent variable at a time. In addition to providing economy, this allows the experimenter to gain important information about interactions. *Interactions* occur when the effects of one independent variable are not the same for different levels of another independent variable. Occasionally, experiments use more than one dependent variable.

4. Experimental design assigns subjects to different conditions in ways that are expected to minimize extraneous variation. In a *between-subjects design,* different groups of subjects experience different treatments. In a *within-subjects design,* the same subjects go through all treatments. The between-subjects design is safer, but the within-subjects design is more efficient. *Mixed designs* have some independent variables that are between-subjects and others that are within-subjects. In between-subjects designs, equivalent groups are formed by matching and by *randomization. General practice effects* and *differential carryover effects* in within-subjects designs are evaluated but not eliminated by counterbalancing. Control conditions provide a clear baseline against which the condition(s) of interest can be compared.

5. There are many pitfalls in experimental design. *Demand characteristics* result from the subject's knowledge that he or she is participating in an experiment. *Experimenter effects* are artifacts introduced accidentally, when the experimenter (through behavior or individual characteristics) provides clues regarding the purpose of the experiment or influences the subject systematically. Experimenter effects can be minimized by the use of machinery to preclude subtle differences in the experimenter's behavior.

6. Selecting participants from some population is called **sampling.** *Random sampling* means that each member of the population has an equal chance of being selected. It is more efficient to test subjects in groups, but care must be taken to avoid contaminating the experiment.

7. Quasi-experiments in psychology often employ subject variables. These variables are measures such as age, IQ, mental health, height, hair color, sex, and the myriad other characteristics that differ from one person to the next. Such variables are determined after the fact, since they are often inherited dispositions (or at least, people come to the psychological study with the variable already determined). Because it is not possible to assign people randomly to the conditions of interest, studies that use subject variables are inherently correlational in nature.

8. To attempt cause-and-effect statements from manipulation of subject variables, researchers often match subjects on other variables. Thus, if a researcher were interested in the effects of hair color on performance in some task or on the reaction from others in some situation, he or she would attempt to control as many other variables as possible to ensure that hair color was the only aspect on which people in the various conditions differed. Matching is often a useful tool for these purposes, but one must be certain that the possibility of regression artifacts does not cloud the conclusions.

9. *Regression to the mean* refers to the fact that when a subgroup with extreme scores is taken from a larger group and retested, members will tend to score nearer the mean of the whole group on the second test. If, in matching two groups on the basis of a first test, the researcher is taking high scorers from a group that generally does poorly and low scorers from a group that generally does well, then even if the groups are not treated differently in an experiment, the researcher can expect them to score differently on a second test—simply because of regression to the mean. This problem is referred to as a *regression artifact*.

▼ KEY TERMS

abscissa
baseline
between-subjects design
ceiling effect
control condition
control group
control variable
counterbalancing
critical experiment
data
demand characteristics
dependent variable
differential carryover effects
double-blind experiment
experiment
experimenter effects
floor effect
general practice effects
Hawthorne effect
independent variable

interaction
level
matching
mixed design
null results
ordinate
quasi-experiments
random assignment
random selection
randomization
regression artifact
regression to the mean
sampling
small-n design
stability
subject variable
synergism
what-if experiment
within-subjects design

▼ DISCUSSION QUESTIONS

1. Design an experiment to discover why plumbers get paid more than college professors. Take a random sample of plumbers and professors. Have half of each group perform the job of the other occupation, while the other occupation either (a) observes quietly or (b) offers advice. Name the dependent, independent, and control variables you would select for this experiment. What are some of the design problems associated with such an experiment?

2. Transform each of the following problems or statements into at least two testable hypotheses:
   (a) You can't teach an old dog new tricks.
   (b) Eating junk food lowers your grade point average.
   (c) A penny saved is a penny earned.
   (d) The best way to study is to cram the night before an exam.

3. Create a fictitious experiment with two independent variables. Draw hypothetical results that illustrate interaction and lack of interaction. Label your graphs carefully.

4. Explain the quotation by Beveridge at the beginning of this chapter.

5. Suppose you wanted to determine whether people with long noses have a better sense of humor than people with shorter noses. Nose length is, of course, a subject variable. You decide to give two groups of people with different-sized noses a series of 20 jokes (which experts have rated as excellent) to see if the people with long noses like them better than those with short noses. What steps would you take to ensure that some other variable was not confounded with nose length in your two groups of people? How would you go about selecting people for the study, assuming that you had 200 people for whom you had measures of nose length and many other characteristics?

 WEB CONNECTIONS

Explore the step-by-step presentation of **"True Experiments"** on the Wadsworth Psychology Resource Center, Statistics and Research Methods activities at:

   http://academic.cengage.com/psychology/workshops

A complete research methods course with numerous links to a variety of important topics in experimental psychology can be found at:

   http://trochim.human.cornell.edu

An award-winning set of online experiments can be found at:

   www.psychologie.unizh.ch/somi/ulf/lab/webexppsylab.html

CHAPTER 4

ETHICS IN PSYCHOLOGICAL RESEARCH

The double-edged potentiality of scientific knowledge poses ethical problems for all scientists. To the extent that psychological research deals with important problems and potent methods, psychologists must recognize and alert others to the fact that the potential for misuse of research increases its potential for constructive application. (AMERICAN PSYCHOLOGICAL ASSOCIATION, 1982, P. 16)

▼ RESEARCH WITH HUMAN PARTICIPANTS

The quotation introducing this chapter is taken from a publication of the American Psychological Association (APA). It comes from a preamble to a lengthy discussion of ethical principles covering all aspects of psychology and is presented in abbreviated form here to emphasize the ethical obligations of researchers in all areas of science. These obligations are straightforward in principle but difficult to implement. We examine both the ethical principles and the problems associated with putting them into practice in psychology. Psychologists are concerned with the ethics of research involving both human participants and animals. Although some of this concern is selfish, owing to fear of restriction of research funds and loss of access to subject populations, most psychologists are ethical persons who have no desire to inflict harm on anyone.

An experimenter cannot be completely impartial and objective in judging the ethical issues concerning his or her own research, so most universities and research institutions have peer committees that judge the ethicality of proposed research. Indeed, such a committee must approve any federally funded research before funding is granted.

Various ethical issues become obvious in the context of an actual research project. Imagine you are a psychologist interested in determining to what extent depressive feelings influence how well people remember. One very important reason why you want to study this topic is that depression is a fairly common emotional problem among college students, and you would like to determine how this problem could affect academic performance. You decide to do a tightly controlled laboratory experiment to determine the effects of depression on memory. You want to induce depression in some of your participants, and then compare their memory to that of others who were not induced to be depressed. You induce depression in your participants by a procedure devised by Velten (1968). In this procedure people read aloud 60 self-referent statements associated with the mood in question. In this case, the participant reads statements that are supposed to induce depression, beginning with relatively mild ones, such as "Today is neither better nor worse than any other day," and progressing to more extreme ones, such as "I feel so bad that I would like to go to sleep and never wake up." Velten's procedure induces a mild, temporary depression; participants report feeling depressed, and their behavior suffers on a variety of tasks.

Many details of this experiment have not been specified, but it should be obvious that the welfare of the research participants in this study could be jeopardized (for complete details of this experiment, see Elmes, Chapman, & Selig, 1984). Inducing a negative mood (such as depression) in college students could have disastrous effects on their social and intellectual functioning. How can you as an ethical researcher try to preserve and protect the fundamental human rights of your participants? What would you do to protect their welfare and at the same time conduct an internally valid experiment?

In a review of research on mood and memory, Blaney (1986) listed a number of studies in which depression was induced in college students. In some experiments, a happy mood was induced in subjects. Do the ethical considerations depend on the kind of mood—happy or sad—that is induced in a person? Also, researchers have used several different mood-induction procedures in their experiments. Besides the Velten (1968) procedure previously described, hypnosis and music have been used to induce a depressed or happy mood. Do ethical considerations depend on the mood-induction technique? These questions concerning mood-induction research illustrate how ethical issues associated with psychological research may vary from study to study.

The APA (2002) provides ethical guidelines for researchers. The association outlined the general principles governing the conduct of research and publication practices. Later in this chapter we consider ethics in animal research and scientific fraud. Now we examine the principles relating primarily to human participants. To consider how the welfare of the students was protected in the mood-induction studies, the eight principles that guide research involving human participants are outlined. Read and understand these ethical principles before you conduct a research project.

8.01 Institutional Approval

When institutional approval is required, psychologists provide accurate information about their research proposals and obtain approval prior to conducting the research. They conduct the research in accordance with the approved research protocol.

8.02 Informed Consent to Research

(a) When obtaining informed consent as required in Standard 3.10, Informed Consent, psychologists inform participants about (1) the purpose of the research, expected duration, and procedures; (2) their right to decline to participate and to withdraw from the research once participation has begun; (3) the foreseeable consequences of declining or withdrawing; (4) reasonably foreseeable factors that may be expected to influence their willingness to participate such as potential risks, discomfort, or adverse effects; (5) any prospective research benefits; (6) limits of confidentiality; (7) incentives for participation; and (8) whom to contact for questions about the research and research participants' rights. They provide opportunity for the prospective participants to ask questions and receive answers. (See also Standards 8.03, Informed Consent for Recording Voices and Images in Research; 8.05, Dispensing With Informed Consent for Research; and 8.07, Deception in Research.)

(b) Psychologists conducting intervention research involving the use of experimental treatments clarify to participants at the outset of the research (1) the experimental nature of the treatment; (2) the services that will or will not be available to the control group(s) if appropriate; (3) the means by which assignment to treatment and control groups will be made; (4) available treatment alternatives if an individual does not wish to participate in the research or wishes to withdraw once a study has begun; and (5) compensation for or monetary costs of participating including, if appropriate, whether reimbursement from the participant or a third-party payor will be sought. (See also Standard 8.02a, Informed Consent to Research.)

8.03 Informed Consent for Recording Voices and Images in Research

Psychologists obtain informed consent from research participants prior to recording their voices or images for data collection unless (1) the research consists solely of naturalistic observations in public places, and it is not anticipated that the recording will be used in a manner that could cause personal identification or harm, or (2) the research design includes deception, and consent for the use of the recording is obtained during debriefing. (See also Standard 8.07, Deception in Research.)

8.04 Client/Patient, Student, and Subordinate Research Participants

(a) When psychologists conduct research with clients/patients, students, or subordinates as participants, psychologists take steps to protect the prospective participants from adverse consequences of declining or withdrawing from participation.

(b) When research participation is a course requirement or an opportunity for extra credit, the prospective participant is given the choice of equitable alternative activities.

8.05 Dispensing With Informed Consent for Research

Psychologists may dispense with informed consent only (1) where research would not reasonably be assumed to create distress or harm and involves (a) the study of normal educational practices, curricula, or classroom management methods conducted in educational settings; (b) only anonymous questionnaires, naturalistic observations, or archival research for which disclosure of responses would not place participants at risk of criminal or civil liability or damage their financial standing, employability, or reputation, and confidentiality is protected; or (c) the study of factors related to job or organization effectiveness conducted in organizational settings for which there is no risk to participants' employability, and confidentiality is protected or (2) where otherwise permitted by law or federal or institutional regulations.

8.06 Offering Inducements for Research Participation

(a) Psychologists make reasonable efforts to avoid offering excessive or inappropriate financial or other inducements for research participation when such inducements are likely to coerce participation.

(b) When offering professional services as an inducement for research participation, psychologists clarify the nature of the services, as well as the risks, obligations, and limitations. (See also Standard 6.05, Barter With Clients/Patients.)

8.07 Deception in Research

(a) Psychologists do not conduct a study involving deception unless they have determined that the use of deceptive techniques is justified by the study's significant prospective scientific, educational, or applied value and that effective nondeceptive alternative procedures are not feasible.

(b) Psychologists do not deceive prospective participants about research that is reasonably expected to cause physical pain or severe emotional distress. APA Ethics Code 2002 Page 12

c) Psychologists explain any deception that is an integral feature of the design and conduct of an experiment to participants

as early as is feasible, preferably at the conclusion of their participation, but no later than at the conclusion of the data collection, and permit participants to withdraw their data. (See also Standard 8.08, Debriefing.)

8.08 Debriefing

(a) Psychologists provide a prompt opportunity for participants to obtain appropriate information about the nature, results, and conclusions of the research, and they take reasonable steps to correct any misconceptions that participants may have of which the psychologists are aware.

(b) If scientific or humane values justify delaying or withholding this information, psychologists take reasonable measures to reduce the risk of harm.

(c) When psychologists become aware that research procedures have harmed a participant, they take reasonable steps to minimize the harm.[1]

---

[1] Source: American Psychological Association. (2002). *Ethical practices of psychologists and code of conduct, 2002.* Copyright © 2002 by the American Psychological Association. Reprinted with permission.

Informed Consent and Deception

The ethical researcher informs participants, prior to participation, of all aspects of the research that might reasonably be expected to influence willingness to participate and explains all other aspects of the research about which participants inquire. This means that the participants must be forewarned about those aspects of the research that may have detrimental effects. In most psychological research, participants receive complete information about what they will be asked to do during the research project so that they can give **informed consent** about their understanding of the possible problems associated with participation. Participants are rarely misled as to the nature of the experiences they will have during the experiment. Furthermore, an experimenter usually states the purpose of the experimental procedure truthfully. Nonetheless, experimenters sometimes mislead participants about the true purpose of an experiment. This false description is often referred to as a "cover story." This kind of **deception** is usually done to control subject reactivity. For instance, a researcher interested in whether people behave more assertively in same-gender groups than in mixed-gender groups tells people that they will be working on problems that require group cooperation. They are also told that the purpose of the experiment is to evaluate the difficulty of these tasks.

The researcher was concerned that participants' behavior might change if they knew the real purpose of the experiment. In this case, information regarding the hypothesis under test probably will not change anyone's decision to participate, but this information might change performance on the task. Deception of this sort, although usually harmless, must be considered carefully because the participant's consent is not fully informed. A person might choose not to participate in a particular experiment because he or she does not approve of the purpose of the experiment.

Even more rare than deception concerning the purpose of an experiment is deception concerning the experiences that the participant will have during the experiment.

Such deception is, unfortunately, necessary to answer some research questions. For example, if an investigator wants to see how well people recall information that they are not actively trying to remember, he or she might not inform participants that the experiment requires a memory test. Obviously, the omission of information prevents participants from giving fully informed consent.

Thus, whenever a research question requires deception, the ethical researcher faces a dilemma. People must be warned if the procedure will place them in serious danger of physical or psychological harm. Deception in such cases is clearly unethical. When a procedure involves only minor risks, on the other hand, the decision regarding full disclosure to participants is more difficult. In all cases, the potential benefits of the research must be weighed against the actual and potential costs to the participant. However, participants should always receive as much information as possible, and they should know that they can end their participation at any time without negative consequences.

Let us reexamine the depression and memory experiment we discussed earlier, focusing on the question of informed consent. The people who signed up to participate were told that some of the things they were going to do in the experiment might make them feel unhappy, and they were given the opportunity to refuse to participate. The specific nature of the manipulation, such as the Velten technique and who was going to serve in the experimental group, was not disclosed ahead of time. People may have reacted unusually if they knew all the details. Because the effects of the mood induction were known to be temporary, the researchers believed that partial information was enough to permit informed consent. Here, although some information was omitted, participants were not misled about what to expect in the experiment.

The issues surrounding informed consent and deception often require considerable thought and deliberation to arrive at ethical solutions. Every research institution in this country should have a standing committee that must approve any experimental procedure involving human subjects. These committees try to ensure the ethical treatment of experimental participants. We discuss these committees in more detail later.

In sum, fully informed consent is the norm in most areas of psychology. Occasionally, some information is withheld or participants are misled so as to prevent subject reactivity. In such cases, experimenters, as well as members of institutional review boards, take great care in deciding whether the benefits of the procedure outweigh the risks to the participants.

Freedom to Withdraw

As mentioned briefly in the previous section, participants should be allowed to decline to participate or to withdraw at any time. Moreover, few people would deny that people who are unhappy about participating should have the **freedom to withdraw.** Where, then, is the ethical dilemma? The major problem revolves around the definition of a willing volunteer participant. Consider the subject pool for the depression and memory experiment: undergraduate students (mostly freshmen and sophomores) taking introductory psychology. They sign up to participate in experiments, and they usually receive some sort of course credit for their service. Are they volunteering when they sign up, or are they under some sort of coercion that they have inferred from the situation? If the students actually receive extra credit, they are likely to be acting on their own volition. If they must participate as part of a course requirement, then the freedom to participate or not is less obvious. When students are required to participate, they should have some optional way of fulfilling the requirement, such as writing a paper or attending a special lecture.

Generally, when the pool of potential participants is a captive audience, such as students, prisoners, military recruits, and employees of the experimenter, the ethical researcher considers the individual's freedom to withdraw or to participate. In the depression and memory experiment, volunteer students were recruited with the lure of extra credit (participation was not mandatory). When they signed up, they were forewarned about the possibility of unhappiness (they could agree to participate or not). The instructions at the beginning of the experiment informed them that they had the option of quitting at any time and would still receive full extra credit (they were free to withdraw).

Protection from Harm and Debriefing

The APA suggests an additional safeguard to provide research participants with **protection from harm.** The subjects should have a way to contact the investigator following participation in the research. Even the most scrupulously ethical project of the minimal-risk sort may have unintended aftereffects. Thus, the participant should be able to receive help or advice from the researcher if problems should arise. We have had participants cry (out of frustration and embarrassment) during what was supposed to be a standard, innocuous memory experiment. Those participants may have carried away from the experiment a negative self-image or strong feelings of resentment toward the experimenter in particular or research in general.

Because of such unintended effects, the prudent researcher provides a detailed **debriefing,** which means that the investigator explains the general purposes of the research.

Furthermore, the researcher completely describes the manipulations so that any questions or misunderstandings may be removed.

Let us apply the principles of debriefing and protection from harm to the depression and memory experiment. At the end of that project, the participants were given a list of phone numbers of people who could be contacted in the unlikely event that the subjects felt depressed following the experiment. The list of contacts included the principal investigator, a counselor, and the dean of student affairs and his assistant. Also, the day after participation, one of the experimenters, who tried to determine whether the participant was having any negative aftereffects, phoned each subject who had read the depression-inducing statements.

The participants received thorough debriefing. They were told about the mood-induction procedure and how its effects were temporary. The experimenter answered any questions asked by the participants.

Removing Harmful Consequences

Debriefing participants and giving them phone numbers may not be sufficient in a risky project. If a participant could suffer long-term consequences as a result of serving in a research project, the investigator has the responsibility for **removing harmful consequences.**

The feelings of resentful people may be difficult to reverse, because the resentment may be unintended and undetected. However, the ethical investigator must take steps to minimize known risks.

Prior to the debriefing in the depression and memory experiment, the participants read a series of self-referent statements designed to induce elation. This exercise was supposed to counteract the effects of the negative mood induced earlier. The participants were then questioned about their current feelings, and they were also asked to sign a statement that said they left the experiment feeling no worse than when they began it. All participants signed the statement, but had they not, a contingent plan was to keep them in the laboratory under the supervision of one of the experimenters until they felt better.

Confidentiality

What a person does in an experiment should be confidential unless otherwise agreed.

An ethical researcher does not run around saying things like "Bobby Freshman is stupid; he did more poorly than anyone else in my experiment." Also, personal information about particular participants, such as their attitudes toward premarital sex or their family income, should not be revealed without their permission. The principle of **confidentiality** seems straightforward, but a researcher can be faced with an ethical dilemma when trying to uphold confidentiality.

This dilemma arose in the depression and memory experiment. The experimenter was confronted with an ethical problem because he believed it was necessary to violate the principle of confidentiality in order to uphold the principle of protection from harm. How did this dilemma develop? One of the first tasks of the participants was to answer some questions concerning their mental health. They indicated whether they were currently seeking professional help for a personal problem. If they were, they provided some details about the problem and the therapeutic procedure. The participants were assured that their answers were confidential. They then completed a clinical test that assessed their current level of depression. If a participant indicated that he or she was being treated for depression and scored high on the test, the experiment was discontinued at that point. The researchers wanted to minimize harm and maximize frank, open responses by assuring the students of the confidential nature of their responses and by using the depression test to prevent a depressed person from becoming even more depressed by the mood-induction procedure. Nevertheless, an ethical dilemma arose. In the course of the experiment, two students scored very high on the depression test, and one of them was not undergoing therapy. Because the test was known to be a reliable and valid predictor of clinically serious depression, the principal investigator believed that it was necessary to warn one of the college's counselors about the two students who appeared to have very high levels of depression. Then, under the guise of a routine interview, the counselor talked to these students.

This type of dilemma occurs frequently in research. To adhere to one ethical principle may necessitate violating another. Easy choices vanish when this happens. In the case we mentioned, if the highly depressed students had suspected that the investigator had betrayed their confidence, permanent resentment and mistrust could have resulted.

On the other hand, the investigator could not ignore the fact that these students, particularly the one not undergoing therapy, were in severe distress. At the time, ensuring that the students received help seemed much more important than upholding their right to confidentiality.

As our example illustrates, ethical decisions must sometimes be made on the basis of pragmatic concerns. In other words, people involved in making decisions about a research project must focus on how best to protect the participants and at the same time conduct a meaningful, valid project. The responsibility for ethical practice rests on the researcher, review boards, and journal editors who review research for publication. In limited instances a researcher might justify deception, concealment, and breaches of confidentiality. However, such questionable ethical practices must be avoided if possible. Ethical violations are not prerequisites of good research.

▼ ETHICS IN RESEARCH WITH ANIMALS

Although the majority of research in contemporary psychology focuses on humans, an appreciable number of studies focus on animals (Miller, 1985). Animals are often used to answer questions that would be impossible or impractical to answer by using human beings. Some people believe, however, that animals should not be used in various kinds of research (Bowd, 1980). For example, Rollin (1985) has argued that if the concept of legal and moral rights can be applied to human research, it can also be applied in the same way to animal research. He suggested that the status of research with animals needs to be elevated to that of human subjects, with many of the same rules that govern human research applied to animals. Reports in the media have discussed the purported mistreatment of laboratory animals and the attempts of animal-rights advocates to limit the use of animals in research. Therefore, a consideration of why animals are used in research is important, and an understanding of the ethical safeguards for animals is necessary.

Animals are also the subjects of research because they are interesting and because they form an important part of the natural world. The numbers of bird-watchers and other amateur naturalists, as well as the numerous comparative psychologists and ethologists, readily attest to the interest. More important in terms of ethical concerns, however, is that animals serve as convenient, highly controlled models for humans *and* other animals. The APA (2003b) provides additional information regarding the use of animals in psychological research.

Arguments Against Research with Animals

Ethics prohibit experimentally induced brain damage in human beings, preclude deliberate separation of a human infant from its parents, forbid testing of unknown drugs on human beings, and generally exclude dangerous and irreversible manipulations on human beings. Animal-rights advocates believe that research on animals should have the same prohibitions. According to the animal-rights advocates, researchers need to uphold the rights of both human beings and animals because, for example, they believe that experimental destruction of a monkey's brain is as ethically reprehensible as the destruction of the brain of a human being. Three points summarize the animal-rights advocates' position: (1) Animals feel pain and their lives can be destroyed, as is true of humans (Roberts, 1971); (2) destroying or harming any living thing is dehumanizing to the human scientist (Roberts, 1971); and (3) claims about scientific progress being helped by animal research are a form of racism and, like interracial bigotry, are completely unwarranted and unethical. Neglecting the rights and interests of other species has been called **speciesism** by Singer (1995). Most psychologists have reservations about these points, which we consider next.

Arguments for Research with Animals

The first point is that animals feel pain and suffering. Certainly, this is true, but ethical standards exist in all scientific disciplines that use animals as research subjects. A major portion of these principles concerns the proscription of undue pain and inhumane treatment. No ethical psychologist would deliberately inflict undue harm on an animal. When pain and suffering are inflicted on an animal, it is only after considerable deliberation by the scientist and the appropriate ethics review boards. Such deliberations weigh the suffering of the animal against the potential benefits of the experiment. Only when the benefits far exceed the harm is the experiment approved and conducted. Finally, an important point to make about behavioral research on animals is that much of it does not involve pain or physical harm to them.

The second plank of the animals-rights platform is that the destruction of any living thing is dehumanizing to the human scientist. Presumably, plants are not meant to be included here, for as human beings, we must destroy plants, if not animals, to survive. Even if this proscription against killing living things is limited to animals, it has a number of serious implications beyond eliminating animal research. If one uses this argument against animal research, then one should not eat meat of any kind. Likewise, one should not use any products derived from the destruction of animals (e.g., leather). Finally, if the destruction of animals is dehumanizing, then is it not also dehumanizing to benefit from the destruction of animals? If so, then a true believer in animal rights should forsake most of the wonders of modern medicine because virtually all of it benefited from animal research. However, consistent adherence to a belief in animal rights is often difficult. The difficulty was illustrated in the results of a survey of activists who attended a large rally in support of animal rights (Plous, 1991). Plous reports that a substantially higher percentage of activists claim to be vegetarians or vegans (people who eat no animal products, including milk and eggs) than do people in general. Many activists say they do not use leather goods. Nevertheless, a majority of animal-rights activists (53 percent) report they buy leather goods, ingest animal flesh, or both.

Finally, there is the charge that scientific progress at the expense of animals is simply speciesism, the belief that the sacrifice of members of other species is justified if our species is benefited. As a criticism against animal research, this argument ignores the fact that a significant amount of animal research benefits the welfare of animals. For example, Miller (1985) points out that research on learned taste aversion in rats has led to new, nonlethal means of keeping coyotes away from sheep and crows away from crops. Similarly, research on the imprinting of hatchling ducks to human caretakers led to better preparation of artificially incubated condor chicks for the wild.

In any case, even if using animals for the benefit of human beings is a form of speciesism, it is doubtful that many people would give up the benefits already achieved or even give up the possible future benefits to be derived from animal research. Consider this quote from Robert J. White, an eminent neuroscientist and neurosurgeon, who conducted research on monkeys that involved removing the brain of the animal:

> As I write this article, I relive my vivid experiences yesterday when I removed at operation a large tumor from the cerebellum and brain stem of a small child. This was a surgical undertaking that would have been impossible a few decades ago, highly dangerous a few years ago, but is today, thanks to extensive experimentation on the brains of lower animals, routinely accomplished with a high degree of safety. (1971, p. 504)

In addition to the benefits of experimental neurosurgery, numerous benefits are derived from behavioral research with animals. Miller (1985) notes that psychological experiments with animals have led directly to benefits in the treatment of such diverse psychological problems as bedwetting, phobias, compulsive disorders such as anorexia nervosa, and depression. Moreover, animal experiments have given rise to behavioral technologies such as biofeedback that have been used to help individuals with neuromuscular disorders regain control over their bodies. Psychological research with animals has also demonstrated experimentally the link between psychological stress and physical health. Other studies have demonstrated that the detrimental effects of physically separating an infant from its parents—as is necessary when a newborn must be placed in an incubator to sustain its life—can be largely reversed simply by stroking the infant during three 15-minute periods during the day. Miller points to the substantial benefits of psychological research on animals, contrary to the claims made by some animal-rights activists (Plous, 1991).

Gallup and Suarez (1985) reviewed the rationale, extent, and use of animals in psychological research. They considered the possible alternatives and concluded that in many cases there is no viable alternative to the use of animals in psychological research. Professional support for the use of animals in both research and teaching has remained high even as the use of animals in research has declined over time (Rowan & Lowe, 1995). Eighty percent of respondents in a survey of APA members indicated general support for animal research (Plous, 1996a). Similar results were obtained from a sample of undergraduate psychology majors (Plous, 1996b). The psychologists did not uniformly support all animal research. Many disapproved of studies involving pain or death, and the majority supported federal protection of rats, mice, and birds equivalent to that provided for primates (Plous, 1996a).

Guidelines for Use of Animals in Research

Psychologists have focused on the humane and ethical treatment of animals used in research for a long time (Greenough, 1992). For example, one early statement of humane treatment (Young, 1928) asserted that animals used as research subjects ". . . shall be kindly treated, properly fed, and their surroundings kept in the best possible sanitary condition" (p. 487). This concern is echoed in the modern guidelines of the APA (2003a) governing research with animals, which state as a general principle the following:

> Psychology encompasses a broad range of areas of research and applied endeavors. Important parts of these endeavors are teaching and research on the behavior of non-human animals, which contribute to the understanding of basic principles underlying

behavior and to advancing the welfare of both human and nonhuman animals. Clearly, psychologists should conduct their teaching and research in a manner consonant with relevant laws and regulations. In addition, ethical concerns mandate that psychologists should consider the costs and benefits of procedures involving animals before proceeding with the research. (p. 1)

As in virtually any human enterprise, abuses of humane treatment sometimes occur in the use of animals in research. However, these abuses go against the standard practice of animal researchers. Ethical researchers treat animals humanely. When unethical treatment of animals is uncovered, the researchers in question should be punished. One should not conclude that because abuses occur, animal research should be prohibited. The typical view of animal-rights activists (Plous, 1991) is based on a philosophical position, and this position prohibits the use of animals for human benefit as a general rule, not just for research. You must decide for yourself what attitude to take toward animal research, but the importance of the issue necessitates that you critically consider each side of the debate and its implications.

The following principle outlines the primary considerations for researchers using animal subjects as specified in the APA (2002) ethics code. A more-detailed specification of these principles is in APA's (2003a) *Guidelines for Ethical Conduct in the Care and Use of Animals*.

8.09 Humane Care and Use of Animals in Research

(a) Psychologists acquire, care for, use, and dispose of animals in compliance with current federal, state, and local laws and regulations, and with professional standards.

(b) Psychologists trained in research methods and experienced in the care of laboratory animals supervise all procedures involving animals and are responsible for ensuring appropriate consideration of their comfort, health, and humane treatment.

(c) Psychologists ensure that all individuals under their supervision who are using animals have received instruction in research methods and in the care, maintenance, and handling of the species being used, to the extent appropriate to their role. (See also Standard 2.05, Delegation of Work to Others.)

(d) Psychologists make reasonable efforts to minimize the discomfort, infection, illness, and pain of animal subjects.

(e) Psychologists use a procedure subjecting animals to pain, stress, or privation only when an alternative procedure is unavailable and the goal is justified by its prospective scientific, educational, or applied value.

(f) Psychologists perform surgical procedures under appropriate anesthesia and follow techniques to avoid infection and minimize pain during and after surgery.

(g) When it is appropriate that an animal's life be terminated, psychologists proceed rapidly, with an effort to minimize pain and in accordance with accepted procedures.[1]

_____

[1] Source: American Psychological Association. (2002). *Ethical principles of psychologists and code of conduct, 2002.* Copyright © 2002 by the American Psychological Association. Reprinted with permission.

▼ SCIENTIFIC FRAUD

In Chapter 13 we discuss inadvertent researcher bias, in which the behavior of the scientist accidentally contaminates the results of a research project. Here, in the context of ethics, we consider deliberate bias by scientists—**fraud.** When scientists engage in research, they expend substantial time and effort, and their prestige and career advancement often depend on the success of their work. Under these pressures, some scientists are not completely honest in the treatment of their experiments and data. Instances of deliberate falsification can range from "fudging" or "cooking" data—in which results are manipulated so as to make them look better—to "forging" data—in which observations are reported that were never in fact made (Kohn, 1986). A survey of doctoral candidates and science faculty indicates that these kinds of fraudulent practices occur with enough frequency to merit some concern about the ethical status of science (Swazey, Anderson, & Lewis, 1993).

A frequently cited example of fudging is the case of Sir Cyril Burt. He was a well-respected psychologist who studied the role of heredity in intelligence. He published several papers reporting data collected on identical twins, some reared together, others reared apart. The data were collected in the period 1913 to 1932. In three papers, he reported a correlation in IQ scores of 0.944 for twins reared together and of 0.771 for twins reared apart. Although the correlations were identical for the three papers, each reported an appreciably different number of subjects. That the correlations remained unchanged despite the addition of new subjects is extremely improbable. This evidence, along with other suspicious facts, led some scientists and historians to conclude that Burt's data were not completely honest (Broad & Wade, 1982; Kohn, 1986).

There are a number of examples of forging data. A famous case is that of the Piltdown man discovered in England in 1912. The Piltdown man consisted of a skull of humanoid appearance and an apelike jawbone. The bones supposedly represented the "missing link" between apes and humans. The finding was widely, although not universally, accepted for 57 years until suspicious scientists used a variety of dating methods to show that the jaw was of modern origin whereas the skull was substantially older. The scientists discovered that the jaw was identical to that of an orangutan. Piltdown Man was a hoax, but who contrived the hoax is not known.

Deliberate researcher bias can be more subtle than forging or even fudging data. A researcher can choose not to report results that are incompatible with a personal theory or even with his or her political or social beliefs. Similarly, a biased scientist may design projects such that negative or ideologically bad results are unlikely.

How do we detect fraud? Science is self-correcting. The truth will win out. When an important finding is published, the scientific community takes it seriously and pursues the implications of the reported data. When other scientists try to repeat the fraudulent experiment, they will fail to get the reported results, and such failures will eventually lead scientists to conclude that the findings were not real. Thus, the repetition of experiments is important to detecting scientific fraud (Barber, 1976). Direct, specific repetitions are called **replications.** It may take many failed replications and years of effort, however, before the entire scientific community agrees that the fraudulent results should be discarded, a fact that illustrates the serious consequences of scientific fraud.

A related problem is **plagiarism,** or taking credit for someone else's ideas, data, or words. Although it may be obvious to you that you should not use someone else's data as your own, plagiarism may be much less obvious in other cases. If you are using someone else's words, you are obliged to use quotation marks with an appropriate citation. Slightly rewording someone else's writing is also inappropriate, especially without proper citation. To avoid plagiarism in this instance, you might write without looking directly at the source you are describing. The trickiest case may be that of *idea plagiarism.* If the idea came from someone else, you should give that person credit even if you are not quoting him or her directly. One potential problem is that people may accidentally lose track of who generated which ideas, especially since ideas are often generated in on-the-fly verbal discussions among colleagues. A way to avoid this problem is to agree on authorship at the beginning of a project, contingent on work progressing as allocated.

We summarize here the remainder of the ethical principles (8.10–8.15) of the APA (2002). These have to do with honesty in reporting data and in publication practices. Psychologists neither plagiarize nor fabricate data. Authorship credit is taken only for substantial contributions to work actually done. Status does not automatically confer authorship credit, and dissertation work ordinarily has the student as principal author. Researchers appropriately divulge republication of data, and they should share research data with other professionals. Finally, reviewers of papers, grants, and proposals maintain the confidentiality of the information they have reviewed.

Most ethical review boards, which are discussed in the next section, monitor the scientific practices that could lead to scientific fraud. Moreover, individuals guarantee federal granting agencies that they have not engaged in fraudulent practices. Upon discovering fraud, the granting agencies suspend the grant and may attempt to recover funds that have been expended. Researchers who are guilty of fraud will not receive additional grants. Thus, institutions and granting agencies also play a role in containing fraud.

▼ MONITORING ETHICAL PRACTICES

As you are well aware by now, the APA provides ethical guidelines for psychological research. Acceptance of membership in the association commits the member to adherence to these principles. The principles are also intended for nonmembers, including students of psychology and others working for a psychologist.

The APA established an Ethics Committee that fulfills a number of purposes. Through publications, educational meetings, and convention activities, the Ethics Committee educates psychologists and the public about ethical issues related to psychological research. The committee also investigates and adjudicates complaints concerning unethical research practices. Examples of these cases can be found in an APA (1987) publication titled *Casebook on Ethical Issues*. The Ethics Committee also publishes an annual report in *American Psychologist*. The APA Ethical Principles we describe in this chapter were approved in 2002 and went into effect in June 2003.

A substantial amount of psychological research is funded by one of the arms of the Public Health Service (PHS), which is a part of the United States Department of Health and Human Services. The PHS has a division called the Office of Research Integrity, which has as its duty protecting the integrity of PHS research programs. This is a major effort. Each year the PHS provides several billion dollars to support more than 30,000 research grants in a number of disciplines, including psychology. The Office of Research Integrity and the APA combine to consider the prevention fraud and protection of participants. Furthermore, any institution that receives money from the federal government—which means virtually every U.S. institution that engages in research—must have an **institutional review board (IRB)** that oversees the protection of human participants and an **institutional animal care and use committee (IACUC)** that oversees the protection of animal subjects. A researcher sends a detailed protocol to the IRB (or IACUC). Presumably, the protocol tries to take account of the pertinent ethical principles, and the committee members then judge the ethicality of the project. All experiments must be approved by the members of these committees. Federal regulations require that each IRB have at least five members who are qualified to review the kind of research typically conducted within the institution. Furthermore, if an IRB regularly reviews research involving vulnerable individuals (e.g., children, prisoners, the mentally disabled), the committee should include at least one member whose area of expertise deals with such individuals. There must be at least one member whose primary concern is in a scientific area and one member whose primary concern is in a nonscientific area. There must also be someone on the committee, usually an attorney, who can ascertain whether proposed research violates any laws or federal regulations. Finally, regulations require that at least one member of the committee be otherwise free from affiliation with the institution. This diversity in membership helps to ensure that the rights of individuals participating in research are protected.

How does an IRB make its decision regarding the ethicality of a particular research project? First, it assesses the level of risk involved in the procedure. Many psychological experiments are classified as involving only minimal risk. *Minimal risk* means that the experimental procedures involve no greater risk than is associated with daily activities. If the chairperson of the IRB believes that the research is of minimal risk, then the entire membership of the IRB need not review the research.

If greater than minimal risk is deemed necessary for research purposes, then this usually requires the full attention of the entire membership of the IRB. The IRB must decide if these risks are reasonable in relation to the benefits that would be gained from the research. The IRB also ensures that participants receive full information prior to the experiment, and it ensures that the research procedures provide safety and confidentiality. The deliberations of the IRB can be extensive, and their recommendations may seem onerous to some researchers, even though the intent of the IRB is clearly to ensure the ethical treatment of the participants. A recent report (Keith-Spiegel & Koocher, 2005) argues that some ethical short cuts arise from the perception of some researchers that the IRB is unfair. Keith-Spiegel and Koocher suggest that "Applied to IRBs and research scientists, striving for fairness on the part of the IRBs should enhance perceptions of fairness. The result should encourage responsible behavior by the researchers that, in turn, would serve as a preventative protection of human research participants" (p. 347).

An acquaintance with the institutional review process should help to reassure you that ethical research in psychology, and in other sciences, is the rule, not the exception. Because of safeguards built in to the structure of IRB and IACUC committees, scientists cannot simply rely solely on their own judgment to protect the humans and animals participating in their experiments. Furthermore, the boards help to emphasize honesty in research, which aids in reducing fraudulent practices.

▼ SUMMARY

1. An ethical investigator protects the welfare of research participants by following the ethical standards of the APA.

2. Informing the participant about the experiment prior to participation and minimal use of deception on the part of the investigator allow the participant to make a reasoned judgment about whether to participate.

3. The participant has the right to decline to serve in an experiment or to withdraw from an experiment at any time.

4. In an ethical investigation, the participant is protected from physical and mental harm.

5. After the data have been collected, participants should be carefully debriefed to remove any misconceptions that may have arisen.

6. Any harmful consequences resulting from an experiment should be removed by the investigator.

7. Unless the participant otherwise agrees, information relating to his or her participation is confidential.

8. Attempts to uphold ethical principles sometimes lead to a dilemma in that adherence to one principle may violate another.

9. When animal subjects are used, care should be taken to minimize their pain and discomfort.

10. Ethical scientists are honest. They do not engage in activities that misrepresent the conduct and outcome of research.

11. Scientific fraud can be detected by replications of research, and institutional boards and granting agencies (such as the Office of Research Integrity) monitor research to prevent or stop fraud.

12. IRBs and IACUCs help monitor ethical practices in research and ensure the ethical treatment of human participants and animal subjects.

▼ KEY TERMS

confidentiality
debriefing
deception
fraud
freedom to withdraw
informed consent
institutional animal care and use committee (IACUC)

institutional review board (IRB)
plagiarism
protection from harm
removing harmful consequences
replication
speciesism

▼ DISCUSSION QUESTIONS

1. Reconsider the ethical principles presented in this chapter and read the list of ethical principles presented by the APA (1987, 2002).

2. Read selections from the *Casebook on Ethical Issues* published by the APA (1987), which is probably available in your library. This book describes the background of different ethical complaints, how the complaints came to be sent to the Ethics Committee, and how the cases were adjudicated. Select two cases and consider the ethical principles involved in the case. Describe why you agree or disagree with the adjudication of the Ethics Committee.

3. Read two of the articles listed in the following Suggested Readings section. These articles describe the ethical issues associated with different types of psychological research. Consider the general ethical principles that apply in both cases. Describe how the ethical issues differ between the two types of research discussed in the articles.

▼ WEB CONNECTIONS

In addition to the treatment of ethics by the APA at **http://www.apa.org**, there is a good site containing ethical dilemmas and exercises related to those dilemmas:

http://onlineethics.org/reseth/psychindex.html

Another good site concerned with fraud, values, and other ethical issues, including responsible research, can be found at:

http://www.nap.edu/readingroom/books/obas/

▼ SUGGESTED READINGS

Bowd, A. D. (1980). Ethical reservations about psychological research with animals. *Psychological Record, 30,* 201–210.

Devenport, L. D., & Devenport, J. A. (1990). The laboratory animal dilemma: A solution in our backyards. *Psychological Science, 1,* 215–216.

Goodyear, R. K., Crego, C. A., & Johnston, M. W. (2003). Ethical issues in the supervision of student research: A study of critical incidents. In D. N. Bersoff (Ed.), *Ethical conflicts in psychology* (3rd ed., pp. 429–435). Washington, DC: American Psychological Association. (Reprinted from *Professional Psychology: Research and Practice, 23,* 203–210.)

Hoff, C. (1980). Immoral and moral uses of animals. *New England Journal of Medicine, 302,* 115–118.

Imber, S. D., Glanz, L. M., Elkin, I., Sotsky, S. M., Boyer, J. L., & Leber, W. R. (1986). Ethical issues in psychotherapy research: Problems in a collaborative clinical study. *American Psychologist, 41,* 137–146.

Melton, G., & Gray, J. (1988). Ethical dilemmas in AIDS research: Individual privacy and public health. *American Psychologist, 43,* 60–64.

Milgram, S. (1977). Ethical issues in the study of obedience. In S. Milgram (Ed.), *The individual in a social world* (pp. 188–199). Reading, MA: Addison-Wesley.

Miller, N. E. (1985). The value of behavioral research on animals. *American Psychologist, 40,* 423–440.

Scarr, S. (1988). Race and gender as psychological variables: Social and ethical issues. *American Psychologist, 43,* 56–59.

Sieber, J. E., & Stanley, B. (1988). Ethical and professional dimensions of socially sensitive research. *American Psychologist, 43,* 49–55.

Smith, C. P. (1983). Ethical issues: Research on deception, informed consent, and debriefing. In L. Wheeler & P. Shaver (Eds.), *Review of personality and social psychology* (Vol. 4, pp. 297–328). Beverly Hills, CA: Sage.

PSYCHOLOGY IN ACTION

Understanding and Remembering Consent Forms

According to the APA (2002), psychological experiments require a subject's informed consent before his or her participation. How meaningful is a subject's signature on a consent form, however, if he or she did not understand and does not remember the information from the consent form?

Mann (1994) had people read either a consent form or an information sheet about a hypothetical functional magnetic resonance imaging (fMRI) brain-scanning experiment. The information sheet was the same as the consent form, except that it did not require a signature. Subjects then answered questions about the alleged upcoming procedure. Even though they had just read the consent form/information sheet, only a minority of Mann's subjects were able to answer the following questions correctly:

▼ What type of device will we use to study your brain? (38 percent correct)
▼ How does this device work? (47 percent)
▼ Are there risks to this procedure? (48 percent)
▼ What can you do if the sound of the machine bothers you? (45 percent)
▼ What can you do if you have a complaint about the study? (39 percent)
▼ What will the researchers do for you if you get hurt? (47 percent)
▼ Name two of the four things your signature on the consent form means. (20 percent)

In addition, 62 percent of the subjects who had signed the consent form thought they had lost their right to sue the experimenter, compared with only 16 percent of those who had merely read the information sheet.

If you are planning a study of your own, you will have created a consent form that you can use in this demonstration. If not, ask your teacher for one. Design a series of questions that will test people's comprehension and memory for the consent form. Have your friends read the consent form, and then ask them to answer (from memory) your questions. How much do your friends remember about what they have just read? Do they know the risks and benefits associated with the study? If not, have they really given their informed consent even though they signed the forms? ■

CHAPTER 5

HOW TO READ AND WRITE RESEARCH REPORTS

"I couldn't afford to learn it," said the Mock Turtle with a sigh. "I only took the regular course." "What was that?" inquired Alice. "Reeling and Writhing, of course." (LEWIS CARROLL)

Trying to read a psychology journal article for the first time can be a challenging experience. Researchers write articles for other researchers, so they use jargon and a terse writing style. These features aid communication among scholars in a particular field, who can read short reports and understand them. But such writing can be difficult to comprehend for students beginning their study of a field. This chapter is designed to prepare you for your first encounter with the literature of experimental psychology. Because psychology is a science, progress is measured by the accumulation of knowledge in the various fields. Researchers spend a great deal of their time reading and writing journal articles in an effort to contribute to this body of knowledge. Even if your career in psychology extends no further than this course, you will discover that critical thinking and writing skills are invaluable for living in a world that revolves around information. To help you become fluent in the art of reading and writing research reports, in this chapter we describe the format and style most often used in journal articles. Hints are provided to help you become a critical reader, skilled at objectively evaluating an article. With some practice, you will far surpass the Mock Turtle and not have to "reel and writhe" your way through every psychology article you read. The chapter ends with some recommendations for writing a research report.

▼ HOW TO DO A LITERATURE SEARCH

Once you have come up with a research idea, the next step is usually to conduct a **literature search.** The purpose of a literature search is to find out what other researchers have previously discovered about a particular topic. This is done by tracking down published articles in which researchers have reported their scientific findings.

The easiest way to conduct a literature search is by computer. Many libraries allow you to access electronic databases that contain abstracts of articles from journals that publish psychological research. More will be said about abstracts later in this chapter, but typically they are short summaries (180 words or less) of the experiments in the article. One of the most important electronic databases is *PsycINFO,* which currently contains more than 2 million records. With an electronic database, you provide a topic and the computer scans for abstracts related to that topic. Some databases also allow you to scan for government documents and technical reports that often do not have abstracts. Another popular way to conduct a computerized literature search is to use the Internet search engine Google Scholar (http://scholar.google.com/), which scans scholarly literature in many disciplines, including psychology. (See the Psychology in Action section at the end of this chapter for an example of how to do an electronic search.)

An excellent electronic resource for learning about the latest research findings is the *Social Science Citation Index.* By entering information about a key article that you have already found, you can obtain a list of more recent articles that have cited your article and view their abstracts. Because these articles contain a discussion of your key article, it is very likely that they are directly related to your topic of interest. This is an extremely efficient way to bring yourself up to date in some specific content area.

After you have found an abstract of interest to you, you can then find the entire article in your library or send a note to the author requesting a reprint of the article or additional information. Many libraries now provide access to electronic versions of research journals, so you may be able to download the article directly from a computer.

Once you have done your literature search and obtained the articles relevant to your research interest, the next step is to read the articles.

▼ THE PARTS OF AN ARTICLE

The basic psychology article consists of seven parts: title and author(s), abstract, introduction, method, results, discussion, and references. Each part has an important function and is a necessary component of the article.

Title and Author(s)

The **title** gives you an idea of the contents of an article. Because titles must be short (10 to 12 words), the most common type of title states only the dependent and independent variables—for example, "Rate of bar pressing as a function of quality and quantity of food reward." Although this title is not particularly appealing, it conveys important information. The title and **author**(s) of each article typically occupy a prominent place in a given journal issue, such as the inside front cover, back cover, or first page.

As you continue to gain knowledge in a particular content area, you will become familiar with many researchers. You may start to pay attention to the authors first and then look at the titles. After you have read several articles published by the same author, you will grow to understand that writer's viewpoints and how they differ from those of other researchers.

So many psychology articles are published each month that no one has the time to read all of them. The table of contents is a first step to selecting those articles relevant to your own interests. But an even better decision can be made by consulting the abstract and the references of an article.

Abstract

The **abstract** is a short paragraph (not to exceed 180 words) that summarizes the key points of an article. According to the *Publication Manual of the American Psychological Association* (APA, 2001), it should be ". . . a brief, comprehensive summary of the contents of the article; it allows readers to survey the contents of an article quickly" (p. 12). The abstract is the best way to discover quickly what an article is about. A well-written journal abstract will convey the problem under investigation, the procedure used to explore the problem, the results, the conclusions, and the implications or applications of the research findings. This information provided in brief allows you to discover quickly if a particular article warrants further reading. As you gain experience and become familiar with authors in the field, you will want to consult the references as well before making this decision.

Introduction

The **introduction** specifies the problem to be studied and tells why it is important. The author also reviews the relevant research literature on the topic. A good introduction also specifies the hypotheses to be tested and gives the rationale behind the predictions.

Method

The **method** section describes in detail the operations performed by the experimenter. It is usually printed in smaller type to conserve space, but this does not mean it is an unimportant part of the article to be skimmed quickly. The method section should contain enough information that another experimenter could replicate the study.

It is customary to divide the method section into subsections that cover participants (or subjects), apparatus or materials, and procedure. The **participants** (or subjects) section tells how many subjects there were, how they were selected (randomly, haphazardly, only the investigator's relatives, etc.) and who they were (college undergraduates taking introductory psychology, paid volunteers obtained by an ad in a newspaper, a particular strain of rats purchased from a supply house). The **apparatus** section describes any equipment used to test the subjects. This section might include details such as the model number of a computer or the size of a conditioning chamber. This section is referred to as the **materials** section when questionnaires, written or videotaped sketches, and other similar means are used to test subjects. If they are long, special materials may be placed in an appendix section, usually set in smaller type. The **procedure** section explains what happened to the subjects and includes instructions (for human subjects), statistical design features, and so forth. If an uncommon statistical technique was used—that is, one that cannot be looked up directly in an advanced statistics text and cited—an extra **design** subsection is often included. Sometimes even a standard statistical technique is described in a design subsection.

Results

The **results** section tells what happened in the experiment. It is unusual to find raw data or individual scores reported in a journal article; instead, descriptive statistics are presented that summarize the data. Inferential statistics present the probability of whether the observed differences between the various experimental conditions have been produced by random, or chance, factors. This information helps both the researcher and the reader determine how confident to be that the independent variable(s) produced a change in the dependent variable. (See Appendix B for further explanation and review.) Both kinds of statistics are important and help psychologists understand the outcome of an experiment.

Either tables or graphs may be used to describe and summarize data. It is often helpful to draw a graph for yourself from the tabular data. If an article contains several figures, check that the scales are comparable, so that effects can be easily compared across different figures. The way a graph is drawn can be misleading, as the following example illustrates.

Imagine that a psychologist is interested in how people perceive written English words. Either a word or a nonword—letters that follow the pattern of written English but do not spell a real word (e.g., *nale*)—is presented visually. The participants must press one button if it is a word or press a different button if it is a nonword. This is called a *lexical decision*. In another condition, the participant must pronounce the word or nonword when it is presented. This is called *naming*. An experiment to compare naming and lexical decisions was performed by Frost, Katz, and Bentin (1987). Their results showed how long it took people to respond to high-frequency English words and to nonwords.

We have replotted their data in Figure 5.1. At first glance, the two panels look quite different. Examining panel (a), we might conclude that naming and lexical decisions are quite similar. But from panel (b) we might conclude not only that naming is faster but also that the difference between words and nonwords is greater for lexical decisions than for naming. Which figure is correct?

Actually, the same data are presented in both panels. The trick is that the vertical scales are plotted differently. One panel has reaction time (the time between the visual presentation and responding) measured in seconds, whereas the other plots reaction time in milliseconds. Since a millisecond is one one-thousandth of a second, the two graphs appear to be different. Also, the scale is "broken" in panel (b), so that measures begin at 520 milliseconds, which further dramatizes the difference. Clearly, the way a graph is drawn can emphasize or conceal results. (See Appendix B for a further example of this point.)

But which way of graphing the results is right? In a sense, both are, because both can be argued to portray matters accurately. However, if statistical tests have shown a difference to exist between the two measures, then the graph in panel (b) more accurately captures the relation between measures. This was the scale used by Frost, Katz, and Bentin (1987) to portray their results.

Inferential statistics permit the assessment of whether differences that appear in the results, as in panel (b), are real and not due to chance factors. Inferential statistics about the data appear in statements such as "$F(4, 60) = 2.03, p < .05$." All this means is that the odds for obtaining by chance an F statistic at least as large as 2.03 would be less than 5 percent if the experiment were repeated. That is, if the experiment were conducted 100 times, the results would be similar in at least 95 out of the 100 repetitions.

There is no fixed rule for setting an appropriate level of significance—.05, or 5 in 100, as opposed to .001, or 1 in 1,000, for instance. It is up to the researcher to decide if the odds are just right, too high, or too low. Depending on the import of your conclusions, you may require more (e.g., .001, or 1 in 1,000) or less certainty (e.g., .10, or 10 in 100) that what happened has not happened by chance.

Imagine the problem of a graduate student admissions officer who has been told that resources at the university are extremely limited. It has been suggested that she discriminate against women in accepting students into the program, since they are believed to be less likely to finish. She would like to put such unsubstantiated notions to rest and so commissions a statistical analysis to test this hypothesis. Here, odds of 5 in 100 to reject the null hypothesis that women are less likely than men to finish are

▼ **FIGURE 5.1**

Exaggerated Scales. Exactly the same data are presented in the two panels of Figure 5.1, but the scale in panel (a) is in seconds and that in panel (b) is in milliseconds (with a scale break indicated, too). Thus, the differences appear very small in (a) and very large in (b).

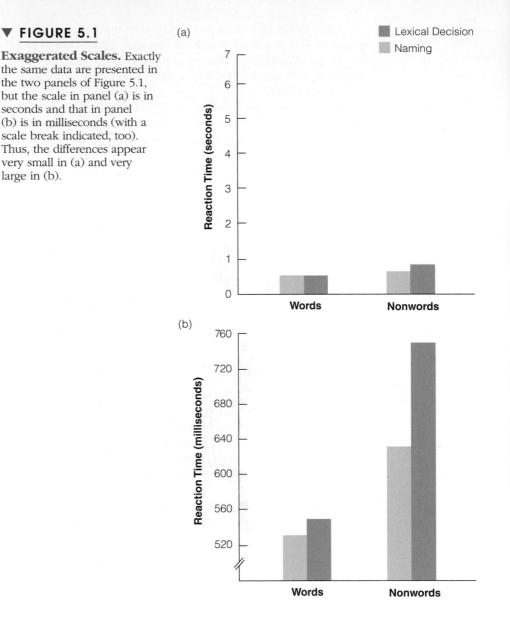

too high, because the import is so great. A level of significance of 1 in 1,000 would be more appropriate.

Or take the case of a breakfast cereal company that wishes to include a "prize" inside the box. It performs a statistical analysis to decide which of five potential prizes, all of which cost the same, is preferred by consumers. If there is any difference among prizes, the company wants to be sure to find the best one. If the firm is wrong and incorrectly selects one, when in fact all are equally attractive, no great harm is done, since each prize costs the same. Here, odds of 5 in 100 are too low. A level of significance of 50 in

100 might be more appropriate. The situation determines what the level of significance should be. Additional discussion of inferential statistics and the level of significance can be found in Appendix B.

In the results section, the author's specific choice of words is important. Beware of such statements as this: "Although the data just barely missed reaching the proposed level of significance, it appears that a trend in the predicted direction did occur." This kind of statement should be approached with caution for several reasons. First, the word trend is a technical term: Existence of a trend can be determined only by an appropriate statistical test. Second, it implies that results that are significant go beyond a trend—that is, they are true and utterly reliable—and that failure to reach a prescribed level means only that "truth" is latent rather than explicit. This implication is false: Even significant results are reliable only in a probabilistic sense—for example, 95 times in 100.

Discussion

The **discussion** is the most creative part of an article. Here, an author is permitted to restate what the data show (if he or she so desires) and to draw theoretical conclusions. Most editors have firm standards for both method and results sections, but the author is given greater latitude in the discussion. In the words of the *Publication Manual of the American Psychological Association* (APA, 2001): "You are free to examine, interpret, and qualify the results, as well as to draw inferences from them" (p. 26). Keep in mind that research results are not incontestable truths and that experimental findings are relative to the context in which they are found. Freedom for the author requires caution from the readers.

References

References are found at the end of the article. In contrast to journals in other disciplines, psychology journals list full titles of referenced articles. This practice helps to tell the reader what the article is about. Furthermore, the references are valuable as a guide for related information. They can also be used as an index of the merit of the article. Articles should refer to the most recently published works in the area, as well as to the most important previous publications. Furthermore, only articles cited in text should be included in the reference section. This is different from a bibliography, which includes as many relevant citations as is feasible.

▼ CHECKLIST FOR THE CRITICAL READER

In this section, we offer some hints that have helped us to become better consumers of the information presented in psychological journals. Our major suggestion is to avoid rushing through an article. Instead, you might deliberately stop after each section and write down the answers to the questions we shall list here. This can be difficult at first, but with practice, this process becomes automatic and requires little extra time.

Introduction

1. *What is the author's goal?* The introduction explains the reasons behind the research and reviews the previous literature on the phenomena of interest. If one or more theories are related to the research, the introduction gives the predictions the theories make. As with scientists in other areas, psychologists do not necessarily agree as to the underlying mechanisms and theoretical interpretations of behavior. The author may present a particular theory that he or she thinks provides a useful explanation of behavior. Although the author may present more than one theory in the introduction, he or she will proceed later on to demonstrate that they do not all help equally to predict and explain the obtained results. Try to figure out which of the several theories the author believes and which are slated for subsequent rejection.

2. *What hypotheses will be tested in the experiment?* The answer to this should be obvious and stated directly within the introduction section.

3. *If I had to design an experiment to test this hypothesis, what would I do?* This is the key question for the introduction. You must try to answer this *before* continuing on to the method section of the article. Many experiments are done within the context of a systematic investigation of behavior to test and support a particular theoretical framework developed by the author. If the author has any skill as a wordsmith, once you have finished the next section, you are likely to agree with the method that the author has advocated in the article. A clever author will plant the seeds to this answer in the introduction itself; this practice makes it harder for you to state a method independently. Write down the major ideas for your method of testing the hypothesis.

Method

Compare your answer to Question 3 with that of the author of the article. They probably will differ, if you have not peeked. Now answer Questions 4(a–c).

4(a). *Is my proposed method better than the author's?* Regardless of who has the better method, you or the author, this forced comparison will make you think about the method section critically, instead of passively accepting it.

4(b). *Does the author's method actually test the hypothesis?* The hypothesis is sometimes the first casualty, disappearing between the introduction and method sections. Always check that the method used is adequate and relevant to the hypothesis at hand.

4(c). *What are the independent, dependent, and control variables?* This is an obvious question and can be answered quickly. Listing the variables helps you avoid passive reading of the method section. After you have resolved differences between your proposed method and the author's, answer the next question.

5. *Using the subjects, apparatus or materials, and procedures described by the author, what results would I predict for this experiment?* You must answer this on your own before reading the results section. To help yourself, review the hypotheses and the independent and dependent variables. You may find it impossible to predict a single outcome. This is not really a problem, since the author probably also had more than one prediction originally. He or she may have done some preliminary investigations to narrow down possible outcomes; alternatively, he or she may have been surprised by the results and had to rethink the introduction once the results were in. Draw a rough sketch illustrating the most likely outcomes you have predicted.

Results

Compare the results with your predictions. If they are the same, go on to Questions 7(a), 7(b), and 7(c). If not, answer Question 6.

6. *Did the author get unexpected results?* After some thought, you will reach one of two conclusions: Either your prediction was wrong, or the results are hard to believe. Perhaps the method the author selected was inappropriate and did not adequately test the stated hypotheses or introduced sources of uncontrolled variance. Or perhaps these results would not be obtained again if the experiment were repeated. You might even try your own experiment. See if you can replicate the reported results.

7(a). *How would I interpret these results?*

7(b). *What applications and implications would I draw from my interpretation of the results?* Try to answer this question and Question 7(a) on your own, before reading the discussion.

7(c). *Can I think of another explanation for these results?* Even when the data are as predicted, there may be more than one reason why the results occurred as they did. You will often encounter multiexperiment papers in which the authors follow up their first experiment by doing additional experiments to eliminate alternate explanations. You might want to try thinking of a new experiment to test an alternate hypothesis.

Discussion

As mentioned earlier, the discussion section includes the author's interpretation of the data in the form of conclusions. A good discussion section brings the reader full circle in that it provides a narrative response to the question posed in the introduction. In addition, the author expands on his or her conclusions by offering insight regarding the applications and implications of the experimental results.

As a critical reader, you have constructed your own interpretation of the results. Compare the merits of your interpretation with the merits of the author's. Which one do you prefer? Answer Questions 8(a) and 8(b) to help you critically assess your and the author's interpretation of the results. Answer Questions 8(c) and 8(d) to help you think critically about possible future directions.

8(a). *Does my interpretation or the author's better represent the data?* Because authors are allowed more latitude in the discussion section than in other sections of a report, it is possible to find that an author has drawn conclusions that may not be warranted by the data. In other cases, authors draw conclusions that are largely appropriate and then proceed to extend these conclusions beyond what the data can support. The latter situation typically occurs when a researcher fails to recognize the limitations of the dependent variable.

8(b). *Do I or does the author offer the more cogent discussion of the applications and implications of the results?* This question is secondary to the question posed in 8(a). Nonetheless, you can gain valuable insight regarding the overall integrity of the research by considering this question. A researcher's responsibilities extend beyond that of conducting a tightly controlled experiment; he or she must also consider the rationale and theory that underlie the research. The extent to which an author demonstrates wisdom in identifying applications and implications of the results provides a good indication of the overall integrity of the research.

8(c). *What questions are left unanswered?* No study ever answers all questions. It may be that you are left with general questions about the literature, or perhaps you were puzzled by some specific data point ignored by the authors.

8(d). *What additional studies might I do?* It may be that you feel there are still alternate explanations for the results, or you want to answer one of the questions posed in 8(c). You are back to Question 3: "If I had to design an experiment to test this hypothesis, what would I do?" The research process never ends.

Checklist Summary

As you are reading your first article carefully, try to write down the answers to all eight questions. It is hard work the first several times, so do not be discouraged. In the following section, we analyze a typical psychological article according to the checklist summarized in Table 5.1.

▼ TABLE 5.1

Questions For Critical Readers

Introduction
1. What is the author's goal?
2. What hypothesis will be tested in the experiment?
3. If I had to design an experiment to test this hypothesis, what would I do?
Method
4(a). Is my proposed method better than the author's?
4(b). Does the author's method actually test the hypothesis?
4(c). What are the independent, dependent, and control variables?
5. Using the subjects, apparatus or materials, and procedures described by the author, what results would I predict for this experiment?
Results
6. Did the author get unexpected results?
7(a). How would I interpret these results?
7(b). What applications and implications would I draw from my interpretation of the results?
7(c). Is there an alternate explanation for the results?
Discussion
8(a). Does my interpretation or the author's better represent the data?
8(b). Do I or does the author offer the more cogent discussion of the applications and implications of the results?
8(c). What questions are left unanswered?
8(d). What additional studies might I do?

▼ A SAMPLE JOURNAL ARTICLE

In this section, we have reprinted a short article from *Psychological Science,* with sample answers to the checklist questions.[1] The article is about the effect of imagining oneself voting on actual subsequent voting behavior.

Most articles are written for experts in a particular area, so the authors of a report assume that their readers have some knowledge of the topic under investigation. In addition, most journals set page limits on articles, which means that some information may be missing or presented very tersely. The assumptions made by the authors and brevity of many articles pose a problem for the novice reader. The novice may have to read other articles or textbooks in order to understand a particular report. The following report was chosen to be fairly easy to understand; nevertheless, you may find parts of it confusing. Do not be discouraged. To help you, we have placed checklist items at various strategic locations throughout the article.

RESEARCH REPORT: PICTURE YOURSELF AT THE POLLS

Visual Perspective in Mental Imagery Affects Self-Perception and Behavior
Lisa K. Libby,[1] Eric M. Shaeffer,[1] Richard P. Eibach,[2]
and Jonathan A. Slemmer[1]
[1]The Ohio State University and [2]Williams College

ABSTRACT—*The present research demonstrates that the visual perspective—own first-person versus observer's third-person—people use to picture themselves engaging in a potential future action affects their self-perceptions and subsequent behavior. On the eve of the 2004 U.S. presidential election, registered voters in Ohio were instructed to use either the first-person or the third-person perspective to picture themselves voting in the election. Picturing voting from the third-person perspective caused subjects to adopt a stronger pro-voting mind-set correspondent with the imagined behavior. Further, this effect on self-perception carried over to behavior, causing subjects who were instructed to picture voting from the third-person perspective to be significantly more likely to vote in the election. These findings extend previous research in autobiographical memory and social judgment linking the observer's perspective with dispositional attributions, and demonstrate the causal role of imagery in determining future behavior.*

Imagination is the beginning of creation. You imagine what you desire, you will what you imagine and at last you create what you will. George Bernard Shaw (1921, p. 9)

Everyone faces the challenge of following through on good intentions. There are many people who intend to donate to charity, exercise more, and vote in elections, but far fewer who actually do so (e.g., Sheeran, 2002). One bit of advice sometimes given to people who are trying to achieve a goal is to picture themselves achieving it. Indeed, imagining oneself engaging in behaviors can make one more likely to actually engage in those behaviors

---

(e.g., Gregory, Cialdini, & Carpenter, 1982). Existing research has not investigated the role of visual imagery in this process; however, some researchers have suggested that imagery is a crucial component of goal representations (Conway, Meares, & Standart, 2004). The present experiment investigated whether a qualitative difference in people's mental images of themselves engaging in a desired future action—namely, voting in the 2004 U.S. presidential election—would affect their likelihood of following through with that action.

One intriguing fact about the way people picture life events is that they do not always use their own *first-person* visual perspective; sometimes they use an observer's *third-person* visual perspective so that they see themselves in the image (Nigro & Neisser, 1983). Research in autobiographical memory shows that the visual perspective people use to picture a past event affects their present emotions, self-judgments, and even behavior (Libby, Eibach, & Gilovich, 2005; McIsaac & Eich, 2002; Robinson & Swanson, 1993). Given that memory and imagination rely on many of the same cognitive processes (Bartlett, 1932; Levine et al., 1998), the visual perspective people use when picturing potential future actions should also have important effects.

Shifting visual perspective in imagery may appear to be a minor manipulation: One is still thinking about the event, regardless of the visual perspective. However, the differential effect of adopting one's own versus an outsider's perspective is crucial to understanding a wide variety of phenomena across many domains of psychology (e.g., cognitive development: Piaget, 1932; neuroscience of self-awareness and agency: Decety & Grezes, 2006; self-concept: Baldwin & Holmes, 1987; self-control: Prencipe & Zelazo, 2005; clinical disorders: Clark & Wells, 1995; attitude change: Bem, 1972; social understanding: Barresi & Moore, 1996; empathy: Batson, Early, & Salvarani, 1997). The present experiment grew out of a well-established effect from social psychology: Perspective affects perceptions of the cause of behavior. Observers tend to understand behavior as a function of the actor's disposition, whereas actors tend to understand their behavior as a function of the situation (Jones & Nisbett, 1971). One reason for this effect is the different visual perspectives that observers and actors have on the behavior. The actor is visually focal for observers, whereas the situation is visually focal for actors, and people tend to attribute cause to focal factors (Storms, 1973).

Further research in autobiographical memory has investigated the impact of this perspective difference on people's explanations for their own past behavior. People see their past behavior as more caused by their disposition when they picture that behavior from the third-person perspective, rather than from the first-person perspective (Frank & Gilovich, 1989). This effect may contribute to people's tendency to think about themselves in more dispositional terms in the distant past than in the recent past (Moore, Sherrod, Liu, & Underwood, 1979), because older memories are more likely recalled from the third-person perspective (Nigro & Neisser, 1983). Other research suggests analogous effects when thinking about the distant versus near future: People are more likely to picture their distant future selves than their near future selves from the third-person perspective (D'Argembeau & Van der Linden, 2004) and are more likely to think about their distant future selves than their near future selves in dispositional terms (Pronin & Ross, 2006).

The present experiment built on previous findings to investigate how the visual perspective people use to picture themselves engaging in a desired future behavior—voting—affects their likelihood of following through with that behavior. Given that actions are seen more as a reflection of one's own character when pictured from the third-person than from the first-person perspective, we predicted that picturing oneself voting from the third-person perspective would cause people to attribute more pro-voting sentiments to themselves and would cause people to be more likely to actually vote. To test this prediction, we recruited registered voters to participate in an on-line experiment the night before the 2004 U.S. presidential election. We manipulated the perspective they used to picture themselves voting and measured the impact of this manipulation on their self-perceptions as voters. After the election, we followed up to determine whether they voted.

1. *What are the authors' goals?* The authors seek to test whether the likelihood of voting in a presidential election depends on the visual perspective—first person or third person—from which people imagine themselves voting. Prior research has examined how visual perspective affects a variety of other psychological phenomena (e.g., how people explain their own past behavior), but the authors wanted to be the first to study whether it affects the likelihood of following through on future behavior.

2. *What hypotheses will be tested in the experiment?* The authors intend to test two related hypotheses, both of which are clearly stated in the final paragraph of the introduction. One hypothesis is that picturing oneself voting from the third-person perspective causes people to attribute more pro-voting sentiments to themselves. That is, if people "see" themselves voting in their mental imagery, they come to believe that they personally have more positive thoughts and feelings about voting. The second hypothesis is that picturing oneself voting from the third-person perspective causes people to be more likely to actually vote.

3. *If I had to design an experiment to test these hypotheses, what would I do?* Ideally, you should try to answer this question *before* reading about the authors' method of testing the hypotheses. However, in this paper, the authors have briefly summarized their method in the final three sentences of the introduction. In fact, it is not unusual for authors to provide a general overview of their method in the introduction before presenting the details in the method section itself. This practice helps the reader to get the "big picture" before getting all the details. Nevertheless, it is worth thinking about how you would design an experiment of your own to test the hypotheses before diving into the method section. In this case, it is obvious that, in any experiment you might design, you would need to assign some subjects to a condition in which they pictured themselves voting from the first-person perspective and other subjects to a condition in which they did the same from the third-person perspective. One possibility would be to bring undergraduates into a psychology laboratory in advance of a student government election and assign half of them to picture themselves voting in the election from the first-person perspective and half from the third-person perspective. You could then email students after the election and determine how many of them in the third-person condition voted versus how many in the first-person condition.

A tougher question is how to determine whether students in the third-person condition attributed more pro-voting sentiments to themselves than did students in the first-person condition. How would you measure students' thoughts and feelings about voting? One possibility would be to ask students to rate their attitude toward voting on a scale ranging from "very negative" to "very positive."

Method

Subjects   Two hundred fifty-six undergraduates (163 female) at The Ohio State University completed the preelection questionnaire online for course credit. Subjects who had already voted (n = 95), who were not registered to vote (n = 1), who did not indicate if they were registered (n = 1), or who did not indicate if they had already voted (n = 6) were excluded from analyses. Seven subjects (4 in the third-person condition) were excluded for failing the manipulation check (described later).

The final preelection sample consisted of 146 subjects (94 female), 69 in the first-person condition and 77 in the third-person condition. Their mean age was 19.3 years (SD = 3.02 years). Of this sample, 53.4% indicated that they would vote for George W. Bush, 45.2% indicated that they would vote for John Kerry, and 1.4% indicated that they were undecided. Condition assignment was independent of candidate preference, and exclusion from analysis was independent of condition and candidate preference (χ^2s < 2.90, ps > .30).

Ninety-five subjects from the preelection sample (65%) responded to the postelection follow-up questionnaire in exchange for course credit or the chance to win a $50 Amazon. com gift certificate. There were no significant differences in response rate according to condition or candidate preference (χ^2s < .74, ps > .50).

Materials and Procedure

Preelection   Subjects were recruited for an on-line study of imagination. Although it was specified that subjects must be registered voters to take part, no other connection to voting or the election was mentioned in recruitment. At 6:30 p.m. on November 1, 2004, subjects received an e-mail with a link to one of two versions of the questionnaire. Subjects were randomly assigned to these versions, which differed only in the instructions for the imagery perspective to be taken. Subjects completed the questionnaire on their own computers any time up until the polls opened on November 2, 2004, at 6:30 a.m.

After providing demographic information, subjects read that they would be asked to imagine themselves engaging in a particular action in the future and should follow instructions for how to picture the image. They received either first-person or third-person visualization instructions (third-person wording in brackets):

> You should picture doing the action from a first-person [third-person] visual perspective. With the first-person [third-person] visual perspective you see the event from the visual perspective you [an observer] would have if the event were actually taking place. That is, you are looking out at your surroundings through your own eyes [you see yourself in the image, as well as your surroundings].

Subjects were then instructed to close their eyes and use the specified perspective to picture themselves "voting in the upcoming presidential election." When they had the image in mind, they were to hold it there and respond "yes" or "no" to the following question, which varied by condition and served as the manipulation check (third-person wording in brackets):

> As you're picturing it right now, do you see [yourself in] the scene from the visual perspective you [an observer] would have if the event were actually taking place?

A response of "no" constituted failure of the manipulation check.

Next, subjects used scales ranging from *not at all* (1) to *completely* (7) to rate how well five phrases described their image: "influencing the election," "marking a ballot," "fulfilling my duty as a citizen," "making my opinions heard," and "selecting my candidate's name."

Subjects went on to complete the main preelection dependent measures, which were designed to assess their self-perceptions as voters. While continuing to use the specified perspective to picture themselves voting, subjects used a 7-point scale, ranging from *extremely good* (+3) to *extremely bad* (−3) to indicate how good or bad it was to vote in the upcoming election. Then they used 5-point scales ranging from *not at all* (1) to *extremely* or *a great deal* (5) to indicate how personally important it was to vote in the election, how likely it was that they would vote, how much their vote would make a difference, how much regret they would experience if they did not vote and their candidate lost, and how satisfied they would be if they voted and their candidate won. Next, it was explained that sometimes people plan to vote but encounter problems. Subjects considered three potential deterrents they might face on Election Day: (a) "There is a 20-min wait in line in order to vote," (b) "The candidate you support is definitely going to win in your state," and (c) "You can't find anyone to go to the polling place with you." Subjects used a 5-point scale ranging from *not at all* (1) to *extremely* (5) to indicate how likely they would be to vote if they encountered each deterrent.

Finally, subjects used 7-point scales ranging from *not at all* (1) to *extremely* (7) to indicate the extent to which they were feeling excited, scared, bored, happy, nervous, determined, inspired, sad, unmotivated, and hopeful.

The final page of the questionnaire thanked subjects for their time and presented links to information on voters' rights, voter registration, and polling locations.

Postelection   On November 22, 2004, all subjects received an e-mail inviting them to respond to an on-line survey within the following 4 days. The questionnaire began with the following item, modeled on those used to assess voting behavior in the U.S. Census Bureau's Current Population Survey and the American National Election Studies:

> In talking to people about elections, we often find that a lot of people were not able to vote because they weren't registered, they were sick, or they just didn't have time. How about you—did you vote in the most recent presidential election?

Subjects responded by choosing "No, I didn't vote" or "Yes, I voted."[1]

4a. *Is my proposed method better than the authors'?* The authors' method has three primary advantages over the one we proposed. First, by having students complete the preelection questionnaire (including the visualization task) online, the authors saved themselves the trouble of having to bring students into the laboratory as we suggested doing. We cannot say for sure, but by conducting the experiment online, the authors may have been able to collect data from more subjects than if they had run subjects in the lab, because they did not have to find the time to meet with subjects in person and because students who wished to participate could do so at their own convenience.

Second, the authors studied voting in a presidential election, as opposed to a student government election, and this naturally seems more important. If visual perspective affects voting in a presidential election, the finding will probably be more interesting to people than if it affects voting in a student government election.

Third, the authors asked a variety of questions to measure subjects' attitude about voting, instead of only one as we proposed. They asked subjects to rate generally how good or bad it was to vote in the election, which is similar to our proposed rating, but they also asked for several other ratings, such as how personally important it was to vote, how satisfied they would feel if they voted and their candidate won, and how likely they would be to vote even if they encountered problems on Election Day. As we shall see, the authors combined subjects' responses to all these questions into a single measure of pro-voting sentiments. Because this measure assesses subjects' thoughts

---

[1]Using self-administered surveys (e.g., Internet questionnaires) rather than human interviewers significantly reduces social-desirability pressures on behavioral self-reports (voting: Holbrook & Krosnick, 2006; other behaviors: Tourangeau & Smith, 1996).

and feelings about voting from a variety of angles, it should capture subjects' true attitude better than would any single question alone.

4b. *Does the authors' method actually test the hypotheses?* In this study, the authors' method is well suited to test the two main hypotheses. The method includes a manipulation of visual perspective, a measure of pro-voting sentiments, and a measure of actual voting behavior. Therefore, the authors can test whether subjects who picture themselves voting from the third-person perspective versus the first-person one attribute more pro-voting sentiments to themselves and are more likely to actually vote.

4c. *What are the independent, dependent, and control variables?* The independent variable is visual perspective (first-person or third-person). The dependent variables are pro-voting sentiments as measured by the various ratings subjects made and actual voting behavior (voted or did not vote). There are no control variables to speak of in this experiment.

5. *Using the subjects, apparatus or materials, and procedures described by the authors, what results would I predict for this experiment?* Before reading this article, you probably never considered whether visual perspective in mental imagery affects people's attitudes about the imagined activity or whether it affects people's likelihood to actually engage in the activity. You may not have ever thought about the difference between third-person and first-person perspective at all! Despite what the authors have argued, you may not believe that something as seemingly trivial as visual perspective could affect something as important as voting, so you may find it hard to predict that the third-person perspective will actually cause more people to vote than does the first-person perspective. If you continue to read articles in the field of psychology, this will probably not be the last time you encounter a prediction that is difficult to believe. Psychological research often produces results that few people would predict in advance.

Results

Building on the finding that picturing one's own actions from the third-person perspective leads to a more dispositional interpretation of the visualized behavior than does picturing one's actions from the first-person perspective, we predicted that subjects who pictured voting from the third-person perspective would adopt a stronger mind-set correspondent with voting behavior and thus would be more likely to vote in the election than would subjects who pictured voting from the first-person perspective.

Pro-Voting Mind-Set   To assess the effect of perspective on subjects' self-perceptions as voters, we created a composite pro-voting index by standardizing and averaging responses on the main preelection dependent measures (attitude, importance, likelihood, vote impact, regret, satisfaction, and responses to the three problem scenarios; $\alpha = .82$). As predicted, picturing voting from the third-person perspective caused subjects to adopt a stronger pro-voting mind-set ($M = .10$, $SD = .58$) than did picturing voting from the first-person perspective ($M = -.11$, $SD = .69$), $t(144) = 2.07$, $p < .05$, $p_{rep} = .93$, $d = 0.33$.

Voting Behavior   The next question was whether the effect of perspective on pro-voting mind-set on Election Eve would carry over to behavior on Election Day. Indeed, it did. Picturing voting from the third-person perspective caused subjects to be more likely to vote, as indicated by their responses to the postelection questionnaire. A full 90% of respondents in the third-person condition voted, compared with 72% of those in the first-person condition, $\chi^2 (1, N = 95) = 5.04$, $p < .03$, $p_{rep} = .94$. Further analysis (MacKinnon & Dwyer, 1993) suggested that pro-voting mind-set mediated the effect of perspective on voting behavior (see Fig. 1).

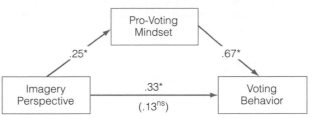

Fig. 1 Mediational analysis relating imagery perspective and pro-voting mind-set to voting behavior, Sobel $z = 1.85$, $p < .07$, $p_{rep} = .90$. Numbers on the paths are standardized regression coefficients. Imagery perspective was coded −1 for first-person and +1 for third-person. Voting behavior was coded 0 for nonvoting and 1 for voting. Asterisks indicate coefficients significantly different from zero, $*p < .05$, $P_{rep} > .93$. The number in parentheses is the standardized regression coefficient for imagery perspective when pro-voting mind-set was included in the equation.

6. *Did the authors get unexpected results?* The authors found, as they predicted, that the third-person perspective caused subjects to have a stronger pro-voting mindset and to be more likely to vote. These results were not unexpected by the authors, but they may be surprising to you.

Another important result is mentioned in only a single sentence under the heading Voting Behavior but is illustrated in Figure 1. A statistical procedure known as a mediational analysis showed that pro-voting mindset "mediated" the effect of perspective on voting behavior. What this means is that the third-person perspective did not *directly* cause subjects to be more likely to vote. Rather, the perspective caused people to have a stronger pro-voting mindset, and this mindset caused people to be more likely to vote. In other words, the analysis established a causal chain linking the third-person perspective to pro-voting mindset and pro-voting mindset to voting.

7a. *How would I interpret these results?* The results are straightforward and the interpretation is clear: Picturing oneself voting from the third-person perspective versus the first-person perspective can cause people to feel that voting is more personally important to them and this feeling can lead people to vote.

7b. *What applications and implications would I draw from my interpretation of the results?* An important implication of these results is that it may be possible to increase voter turnout by encouraging potential voters to picture themselves voting from the third-person perspective. For example, perhaps organizers at political rallies should lead the crowd in a brief third-person visualization task like that performed by subjects in this experiment.

7c. *Can I think of another explanation for these results?* Given the simplicity of the authors' method and the clarity of their results, it is difficult to think of an alternative explanation other than that the third-person perspective increased pro-voting sentiments and these sentiments led people to vote. However, if you *can* think of another explanation, you should also think about how you would design an experiment to test your explanation.

Discussion

Simply varying the visual perspective that individuals used to picture themselves engaging in a desirable future behavior affected their self-perceptions and their likelihood of following through with that behavior: Registered voters who were instructed to picture themselves voting from the third-person perspective subsequently adopted a stronger pro-voting mindset than those instructed to picture themselves voting from the first-person perspective, and were consequently more likely to vote. These results suggest an important implication of the fact that actions are perceived to be more a function of the actor's character when viewed from an observer's perspective than when viewed from the actor's perspective (Storms, 1973). Seeing oneself as the type of person who would engage in a desired behavior increases the likelihood of engaging in that behavior.

The present findings are particularly noteworthy given that the experiment was conducted in Ohio during the 2004 presidential election. That campaign focused on volatile issues of war, terrorism, and same-sex marriage and involved unprecedented efforts to mobilize voter turnout in Ohio, a crucial swing state (Dao, 2004). The fact that our manipulation affected voter turnout even in this complex field of motivational forces demonstrates the potential power of self-focused imagery. The success of this manipulation was likely due to its giving direction to a process—visual imagination—that people use naturally to plan future actions. Indeed, visual imagery of upcoming situations is quite common in everyday life (Singer & McCraven, 1961). The present findings demonstrate that with some guidance, this imagery can be harnessed to alter self-perceptions and behavior.

Specifically, we found that people are more likely to adjust their self-concepts to match a desired behavior if that behavior is imagined from a third-person, observer's perspective rather than a first-person, experiencer's perspective. Subjects who imagined voting from the third-person perspective saw themselves as more likely to vote and more motivated to overcome obstacles to voting compared with those using first-person imagery. Third-person imagery also led subjects to anticipate feelings of regret and satisfaction consistent with internalizing voting as a personal norm (Kahneman & Miller, 1986). And subjects who imagined from the third-person perspective reported beliefs about the importance and impact of voting that were consistent with stronger self-identification as voters. Cumulatively, these effects on self-perceptions compelled persons in the third-person visualization condition to turn out in greater numbers on Election Day than did persons in the first-person condition. These findings suggest that self-focused imagery can affect meaningful behaviors by altering self-perceptions. Therefore, the injunction to "picture yourself" performing a desired behavior may, in fact, be an effective strategy for translating good intentions into practical actions.

Acknowledgments

This article is dedicated to the memory of Jon Slemmer, whose expertise was integral in carrying out this research.

References

Baldwin, M.W., & Holmes, J.G. (1987). Salient private audiences and awareness of the self. *Journal of Personality and Social Psychology, 52,* 1087–1098.

Barresi, J., & Moore, C. (1996). Intentional relations and social understanding. *Behavioral and Brain Science, 19,* 107–154.

Bartlett, F.C. (1932). *Remembering: A study in experimental and social psychology.* New York: Cambridge University Press.

Batson, C.D., Early, S., & Salvarani, G. (1997). Perspective taking: Imagining how another feels versus imagining how you would feel. *Personality and Social Psychology Bulletin, 23,* 751–758.

Bem, D.J. (1972). Self-perception theory. In L. Berkowitz (Ed.), *Advances in experimental social psychology* (Vol. 6, pp. 1–62). New York: Academic Press.

Clark, D.M., & Wells, A. (1995). A cognitive model of social phobia. In R.G. Heimberg, M.R. Liebowitz, D.A. Hope, & F.R. Schneier (Eds.), *Social phobia: Diagnosis, assessment and treatment* (pp. 69–93). New York: Guilford Press.

Conway, M.A., Meares, K., & Standart, S. (2004). Images and goals. *Memory, 12,* 525–531.

Dao, J. (2004, November 1). To get Ohio voters to the polls, volunteers knock, talk, and cajole. *The New York Times,* p. 17A.

D'Argembeau, A., & Van der Linden, M. (2004). Phenomenal characteristics associated with projecting oneself back into the past and forward into the future: Influence of valence and temporal distance. *Consciousness and Cognition: An International Journal, 13,* 844–858.

Decety, J., & Grezes, J. (2006). The power of simulation: Imagining one's own and other's behavior. *Brain Research, 1079,* 4–14.

Frank, M.G., & Gilovich, T. (1989). Effect of memory perspective on retrospective causal attributions. *Journal of Personality and Social Psychology, 57,* 399–403.

Gregory, W.L., Cialdini, R.B., & Carpenter, K.M. (1982). Self-relevant scenarios as mediators of likelihood estimates and compliance: Does imagining make it so? *Journal of Personality and Social Psychology, 43,* 89–99.

Holbrook, A.L., & Krosnick. J.A. (2006). *Social desirability bias in voter turnout reports: Tests using the item count and randomized response techniques.* Manuscript submitted for publication.

Jones, E.E., & Nisbett, R.E. (1971). The actor and the observer: Divergent perceptions of the causes of behavior. In E.E. Jones, D.E. Kanouse, H.H. Kelley, R.E. Nishett, S. Valins, & B. Weiner (Eds.), *Attribution: Perceiving the causes of behavior* (pp. 79–94). New York: General Learning Press.

Kahneman, D., & Miller, D.T. (1986). Norm theory: Comparing reality to its alternatives. *Psychological Review, 93,* 136–153.

Levine, B., Black, S.E., Cabeza, R., Sinden, M., Mcintosh, A.R., Toth, J.P., Tulving, E., & Struss, D.T. (1998). Episodic memory and the self in a case of isolated retrograde amnesia. *Brain, 121,* 1951–1973.

Libby, L.K., Eibach, R.P., & Gilovich, T. (2005). Here's looking at me: The effect of memory perspective on assessments of personal change. *Journal of Personality and Social Psychology, 88,* 50–62.

MacKinnon, D.P., & Dwyer, J.H. (1993). Estimating mediated effects in prevention studies. *Evaluation Review, 17,* 144–158.

McIsaac, H.K., & Eich, E. (2002). Vantage point in episodic memory. *Psychonomic Bulletin & Review, 9,* 146–150.

Moore, B.S., Sherrod, D.R., Liu, T.J., & Underwood, B. (1979). The dispositional shift in attribution over time. *Journal of Experimental Social Psychology, 15,* 553–569.

Nigro, G., & Neisser, U. (1983). Point of view in personal memories. *Cognitive Psychology, 15,* 467–482.

Piaget, J. (1932). *The moral judgment of the child.* London: Kegan Paul, Trench, & Trubner.

Prencipe, A., & Zelazo, P.D. (2005). Development of affective decision making for self and other. *Psychological Science, 16,* 501–505.

Pronin, E., & Ross, L. (2006). Temporal differences in trait self-ascription: When the self is seen as an other. *Journal of Personality and Social Psychology, 90,* 197–209.

Robinson, J.A., & Swanson, K.L. (1993). Field and observer modes of remembering. *Memory, 1,* 169–184.

Shaw, G.B. (1921). *Back to Methuselah: A metabiological pentateuch.* New York: Brentano's.

Sheeran, P. (2002). Intention-behavior relations: A conceptual and empirical review. In W. Stroebe & M. Hewstone (Eds.), *European review of social psychology* (Vol. 12, pp, 1–36). Chichester, England: Wiley.

Singer, J.L., & McCraven, V.G. (1961). Some characteristics of adult daydreaming. *Journal of Psychology, 51,* 151–164.

Storms, M.D. (1973). Videotape and the attribution process: Reversing actors' and observers' points of view. *Journal of Personality and Social Psychology, 27,* 65–175.

Tourangeau, R., & Smith, T.W. (1996). Asking sensitive questions: The impact of data collection mode, question format, and question context. *Public Opinion Quarterly, 60,* 275–304.

**(RECEIVED 5/17/06; REVISION ACCEPTED 7/31/06;
FINAL MATERIALS RECEIVED 9/14/06)**

8a. *Does my interpretation or the authors' better represent the data?* In this case, our interpretation is the same as the authors'. That will certainly not always be the case, especially when reading longer, more complex studies.

8b. *Do I or do the authors offer the more cogent discussion of the applications and implications of the results?* The authors have a fine discussion, which includes the interesting point that the visual perspective manipulation affected voter turnout even in the context of a hotly contested presidential campaign in which there were many factors potentially affecting voting behavior. Thus, the authors conclude that visual imagery must have a relatively strong influence on behavior. They also note, as we did, that the power of visual imagery could be used purposefully to influence behavior. However, while we focused on the idea that political organizers could use visual imagery to affect the behavior of other people, the authors furthermore suggest that people could use it for themselves to increase the chances that they will carry through on their own good intentions.

8c. *What questions are left unanswered?* To better understand the power of visual perspective to influence behavior, we think it is important to compare voting given the third-person perspective to voting given no visual imagery at all. The authors found that the third-person perspective increased voting relative to the first-person perspective, but how likely would people have been to vote had they not gone through a visualization task at all but rather had simply completed an online questionnaire in which they were asked questions about their attitude toward voting? Presumably the authors would predict that third-person visualization would cause a big increase in voting relative to no visualization at all, but this study does not directly speak to that possibility because it does not include a novisualization condition.

8d. *What additional studies might I do?* It would be a straightforward matter to replicate the conditions of the current study and add a no-visualization condition in which subjects are treated exactly the same as in the conditions described here *except* that they do not receive the visualization instructions and do not answer any questions about their image. Of course, one problem is that, if you wanted to study voting in a presidential election again, you might have to wait as long as 4 years to do it!

▼ WRITING A RESEARCH REPORT

You have gotten an idea, reviewed the pertinent literature, designed a procedure, collected your data, and analyzed the results. Your course may require a written record of your research. Even if it does not, you are obligated to publicize the results of a carefully done project. We believe that to maintain the self-correcting nature of science, it is important to publish good data. However, this does not mean that journals should be cluttered with information derived from every undergraduate project. If your research is promising, you will receive encouragement from your instructor.

In this section, we will review the format of a typical report and discuss some of the stylistic considerations that make up a comprehensible paper. If you follow our suggestions for reading articles, you will have a pretty good idea about the format of a research report, and you will probably have a good feel for technical writing style. Some aspects of technical writing are not obvious, so we will discuss them here. What we present are general guidelines. If you need additional information, examine R. J. Sternberg's 1993 book, *The Psychologist's Companion*, and 1992 article, "How to Win Acceptances by Psychology Journals: 21 Tips for Better Writing"; D. J. Bem's 2004 chapter, "Writing the Empirical Journal Article," which is published in *The Compleat Academic*, a guide to a career in psychology; and H. L. Roediger's 2007 article, "Twelve Tips for Authors." The 2001 version of the *Publication Manual of the American Psychological Association* (fifth edition) will also help, because it is the official arbiter of style for almost all the journals in psychology and education.

Format

The outline of a typical report in Figure 5.2 emphasizes the sequence of pages you will have to put together in your APA-style manuscript. This version of the article is known as the *copy* manuscript and is assembled in a particular manner to facilitate the editorial and publication processes. A run through that sequence will give you an idea of what you are supposed to include.

Your cover page contains the title of your project, your name, your affiliation (your institution or place of business), and your running head. The short title that appears at the top of each page of the copy manuscript consists of the first few words of the title and is used to identify the manuscript during the editorial process only. The heading that will appear at the top of each page of the *published* article is called the **running head,** and this is typed in capital letters on the cover page of the copy manuscript. The short title and running head should not be confused. You should double space the lines on the cover page and every other page of the copy manuscript.

The next page, page two, contains the heading "Abstract" and the abstract itself. On this page, and on all subsequent ones (except the figures), the short title and the page number should be placed in the top right-hand corner of the page.

At the top of page three is the full title, followed by the introduction. Ordinarily, you will not have a heading for the introduction. After your introduction is finished, the method section begins. Generally, for a write-up of one experiment, you will type the title "Method" in the center of a line to begin the section. You should begin the method section immediately after the introduction; a page break is not used here. Note the format shown for the headings on page four in Figure 5.2. The side headings, such as "Subjects" and "Apparatus" (or "Materials") help guide the reader to pertinent information. The results section immediately follows the method. Do not include **figures** and **tables** in the body of this section; they come at the end of the report. Next comes the discussion, which ends the major textual portion of your report.

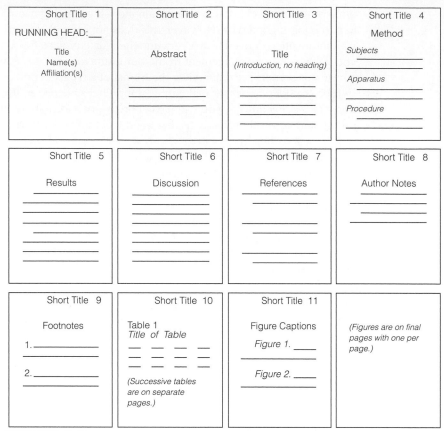

▼ **FIGURE 5.2**

Page Sequence for a Report in APA Format.

The references begin on a separate page. The format for presenting references is complex, and you should use care in preparing them. See Table 5.2 for guidelines for commonly cited sources. You should also consult the article reprinted in this chapter, which contains most of the different styles of references that you will have to document. Look them over carefully; if you have any questions, ask your instructor. You might also study the APA *Publication Manual* and recent journal articles. Any author notes and footnotes appear on separate pages after the references. For most college laboratory reports, footnotes are not necessary. When you prepare something for publication, you may acknowledge financial and intellectual support, which should appear on the author-note page. General acknowledgments are not numbered. Other, perhaps peripheral, information should appear as numbered footnotes on a separate footnote page, but such footnotes are generally discouraged.

Following the footnotes are your data tables that are mentioned in the results section. Each table should be on a separate page and numbered consecutively, according to its appearance in the results section. Make the titles of your tables short but communicative. Captions for your figures are numbered consecutively and appear on a separate page

▼ **TABLE 5.2**

General Forms for the Reference List

Type of Source	Format
Periodical *(e.g., journal)*	Author, A. A., Author, B. B., & Author, C. C. (1999). Title of article. *Title of Periodical, xx,* xxx–xxx.
Non-periodical *(e.g., book)*	Author, A. A., Author, B. B., & Author, C. C. (2004). *Title of work.* Location: Publisher.
Part of a non-periodical *(e.g., book chapter)*	Author, A. A., Author, B. B., & Author, C. C. (2001). Title of chapter. In A. Editor, B. Editor, & C. Editor (Eds.), *Title of book* (pp. xxx–xxx). Location: Publisher.
Online document	Author, A. A. (2001). *Title of work.* Retrieved month day, year, from source.

following the data tables. Finally, you insert your figures, each on a separate page. Tables and figures are separated from the text, one per page, to facilitate the typesetting process.

As mentioned before, copy manuscripts are organized in this fashion to accommodate the publisher. However, you should note that there is a special section in the APA *Publication Manual* about the accepted format for student papers submitted for a course requirement but not for publication. For example, in student papers, tables and figures may be interspersed in the text. You should check with your professor or department regarding the preferred format for class projects. However, we recommend learning the APA publication format because it provides good practice for preparing your future publications.

Sample Manuscript

A sample manuscript appears on the following pages. The research that led to this manuscript was performed by the first author (David Gallo) and the second author (Meredith Roberts) while they were undergraduates at Wesleyan University working with the third author (Dr. John Seamon). The research began as a project in a methodology course in which David Gallo was enrolled, one like the course in which most students reading this text are enrolled. These Wesleyan students, with the help of their professor, converted a student project into a publishable article contributing to the psychological literature on human memory. You should note the sequence of pages, where typing begins on a new page, and what information is provided in each section. An aspect missing from this manuscript that may appear in one of yours is a separate footnote page. Also, you may choose to include figures that depict data in a graphical form in addition to (or in place of) tables. Note carefully how the references are cited in the reference section. One aspect of this manuscript that is different from the standard APA format is the use of the term *subjects* instead of *participants*. Although the current APA format requires the use of the term *participants* for humans participating in research, some journals not affiliated with the American Psychological Association (such as the one that published the following research paper) permit the use of either *participants* or *subjects*. Hence, the term *subjects* was used in this paper at the discretion of the authors.

The full citation for the following paper is: Gallo, D. A., Roberts, M. J., & Seamon, J. G. (1997). Remembering words not presented in lists: Can we avoid creating false memories? *Psychonomic Bulletin & Review, 4,* 271–276. (Copyright 1997 by the Psychonomic Society Inc. Reprinted by permission of the authors and the publisher.)

Text continued on p. 143

Remembering Words 1

Running head: FALSE RECOGNITION

Remembering Words Not Presented in Lists: Can We Avoid Creating False Memories?

David A. Gallo, Meredith J. Roberts, and John G. Seamon

Wesleyan University

Remembering Words 2

Abstract

Can subjects avoid creating false memories in Roediger and McDermott's (1995) false recognition paradigm if they are forewarned about this memory illusion? We presented subjects with semantically related word lists, followed by a recognition test. The test was composed of studied words, semantically related nonstudied words (critical lures), and unrelated nonstudied words. One group of subjects was uninformed about the false recognition effect, a second group was urged to minimize all false alarms, and a third group was forewarned about falsely recognizing critical lures. Compared to the uninformed and cautious subjects, the forewarned subjects reduced their false alarm rate for critical lures, and they made remember and know judgments equally often for recognized studied words and critical lures. But forewarning did not eliminate the false recognition effect, as these subjects and those in the other groups made numerous false recognitions in this task.

Remembering Words Not Presented in Lists:

Can We Avoid Creating False Memories?

In a special issue of the *Journal of Memory and Language* devoted to research on memory illusions, Roediger (1996) provided an historical overview of errors in perception and memory. He defined a *memory illusion* as an instance in which a person's report of a past event seriously deviates from the actual event. One striking example offered as evidence of a memory illusion was Deese's (1959) finding of false recall in a list learning paradigm. Deese presented subjects with lists of semantic associates to nonpresented critical words. For example, for the critical word "*needle,*" the presented list consisted of *thread, pin, eye, sewing, sharp, point, pricked, thimble, haystack, pain, hurt,* and *injection.* When the subjects were given a free recall test after each list's presentation, the nonpresented critical word was often erroneously recalled more frequently than nonpresented but unrelated words. This procedure induced subjects to recall specific words that were never presented in the lists. Beginning with Roediger and McDermott (1995), there has been a revival of interest in this paradigm for studying this false memory effect (e.g., McDermott, 1996; Payne, Elie, Blackwell, & Neuschatz, 1996; Read, 1996; Schacter, Verfaille, & Pradere, 1996).

Roediger and McDermott (1995) reported two experiments that replicated and extended Deese's result. In their first experiment, the subjects were read six of Deese's lists that elicited the highest frequency of false recall. After each list was presented, the subjects were given a free recall test, followed by a recognition test after all of the lists were recalled. The recognition test was composed of studied words, nonstudied critical words (hereafter referred to as critical lures), and nonstudied unrelated words. Roediger and McDermott found that the critical lures were falsely recalled and recognized more frequently than other nonstudied words.

In their second experiment, Roediger and McDermott modified their procedure. Half of the subjects received a free recall test after each study list presentation, and half performed unrelated math problems instead. On the subsequent recognition test,

Remembering Words 4

the researchers made use of Tulving's (1985) remember vs. know judgment task. For any recognized word, the subjects had to indicate whether they specifically remembered the word's occurrence at study (a remember judgment) or they merely knew the word that had been presented in the absence of any specific recollection (a know judgment). Roediger and McDermott found that the study and recall condition led to more false recognitions of critical lures than did the study and math condition. However, the subjects in both conditions produced false alarms to the critical lures at rates that were comparable to the corresponding hit rates for studied words. Moreover, the results showed that recognized critical lures were often characterized as remembered in the remember vs. know judgment task, especially in the study and recall condition. These observations led Roediger and McDermott to describe the false recognition effect as a "powerful illusion of memory" (p. 803). An illusion that is all the more surprising, they said, because it was observed under intentional learning conditions, with short retention intervals, in a list-learning laboratory procedure that normally produces few errors, and with professional memorizers (college students) as subjects. The primary purpose of the present research was to determine whether subjects could avoid creating false memories in Roediger and McDermott's false recognition paradigm if they were forewarned about this memory illusion. To our knowledge, no one has specifically determined if this false memory effect could be diminished or eliminated by the subjects' knowledge, but prior research has asked whether different experimental conditions could influence this effect. For example, McDermott (1996, Experiment 2) gave subjects multiple study and recall tests with the same word lists presented in either a blocked or random manner. She found that random presentation produced less false recall than blocked presentation, but both forms of presentation still yielded false recalls after multiple study-test trials or a final recall test given 24 h later. Payne et al. (1996) observed a similar effect in showing that recognition of critical lures did not decrease over a 24 h retention interval. Finally, Read (1996) manipulated encoding instructions by having subjects memorize word order or engage in elaborative or maintenance rehearsal during list presentation. He found that all three encoding conditions yielded high levels of false recall for critical words, but the false recalls were lowest for the subjects who focused on word order. These studies indicate that this false memory effect persists through multiple study and test trials (McDermott, 1996), a 24 h delay between study and test (McDermott, 1966; Payne et al., 1996), and elaborative or maintenance rehearsal during encoding (Read, 1996). But false memory for critical words is diminished when the words are randomized over lists (McDermott, 1996) or the subjects attempt to memorize word order at study (Read, 1996).

Following those studies, the present research sought to determine if the false recognition of critical lures could be attenuated or eliminated by the use of forewarning instructions. Curiously, we found no published research on the effects of foreknowledge on perceptual or memory illusions. For perceptual illusions, such research may have been unnecessary as Gregory (1987) notes that these illusions occur even when people know that they are perceiving an illusion. For example, we may know that the lines in the Muller-Lyer illusion are equal in length, yet one line still appears to be longer than the other. Perceptual illusions fool us because perceptual processes work extremely rapidly and do not take everything that we know into account in the process of forming a precept (Gregory, 1987). Memory illusions also fool us, but they do so over a more extended time frame that includes study and test conditions. Memory illusions may thus provide greater opportunity than perceptual illusions to be influenced by the subject's knowledge. To the extent that foreknowledge can be used during encoding or retrieval to devise compensatory cognitive strategies, an illusion may be diminished or eliminated.

The only statements we found about the effects of foreknowledge on false memory are located in two places in Roediger and McDermott's (1995) research. One statement suggests that forewarning might be effective in minimizing the false recognition of critical lures, whereas the other statement suggests little effect of forewarning.

Remembering Words 6

For example, the authors noted that they dropped the only subject from their analysis who had no false recalls of the critical words because at the end of Experiment 2 when the subjects were asked if they "knew what the experiment was about," this subject reported that "she noticed that the lists seemed designed to make her think of a nonpresented word" (p. 808) This subject may have adopted a strategy that permitted her to overcome the memory illusion. However, Roediger and McDermott also reported that "informal demonstration experiments with groups of sophisticated subjects, such as wily graduate students who knew we were trying to induce false memories" still produced a strong false memory effect (p. 812). To the extent that these subjects were fully informed about the memory illusion before study, this observation suggests that forewarning will have a minimal effect on the false recognition of critical words.

The present research tested these foreknowledge alternatives systematically by comparing groups of subjects with different instructional sets in a modified version of the Roediger and McDermott (1996, Experiment 2) paradigm. To the extent that this false memory effect is a memory illusion that functions like a perceptual illusion, foreknowledge of the effect may have little or no effect on the recognition of critical lures. But if this memory illusion differs from perceptual illusions in that it allows greater opportunity for performance to be influenced by encoding or retrieval strategies, foreknowledge of the illusion should attenuate the effect to the extent that people can devise effective compensatory strategies. We presented subjects with blocked lists of semantically related words for study, followed by a recognition test after all lists were presented. One group of subjects was uninformed about the false recognition effect, a second group was urged to be cautious at the time of the recognition test to minimize all false alarms, and a third group was forewarned of the specific illusion by a demonstration and instructions before study. Based on Roediger and McDermott's findings, we hypothesized that the subjects in the uninformed condition would produce a strong false recognition effect. Subjects in the cautious and forewarned groups provide novel test conditions and, compared to the uninformed condition, they should produce either a comparable or diminished effect.

Method

Subjects

The subjects were 48 Wesleyan University undergraduates who served as paid volunteers. None had participated in any related memory research.

Materials

We used 16 of Roediger and McDermott's 24 word lists for study and test words (see their appendix). Each list was composed of 15 associates to a nonpresented critical word (i.e., a critical lure). Within a list, the order of the words was constant and the strongest associates to the critical lure normally occurred first. For example, the list associated with the critical lure *sleep* consisted of the following words: *bed, rest, awake, tired, dream, wake, snooze, blanket, doze, slumber, snore, nap, peace, yawn, and drowsy.* For counterbalancing purposes, the 16 lists were divided into two sets of 8 lists, labeled A and B. Half of the subjects in each condition received Set A for study and half received Set B. The set not used during study provided distracters for the recognition test.

Procedure

During study, the subjects were presented with an auditory tape containing eight lists of 15 words presented in blocked fashion. The words were spoken by a male voice at a rate of 1.5 s per word, and a tone separated each list. The subjects, who were tested in groups of up to 6, were told to remember the words for a recognition memory test that would follow.

After all 120 study words were heard, the subjects were given a visual recognition memory test consisting of 64 words. Following Roediger and McDermott's test procedure, this test contained three items from each studied list (serial positions 1, 8, and 10), the nonpresented critical lure from each studied list, three items from each

Remembering Words 8

nonstudied list (serial positions 1, 8, and 10), and the critical lure from each nonstudied list, all listed in a random order. Each word was accompanied by a plus (1) and
minus (2) sign and the letters *R* and *K* (for Remember and Know).

The subjects were instructed to examine the words in sequential order at a self-
paced rate and make a decision for each word on the list. They were told to circle
the plus sign for any word that they recognized from the study tape or the minus
sign for any word they failed to recognize. In addition, following Tulving (1985), the
subjects were instructed to make a *remember* or *know* judgment for each recognized
word by circling R or K on their answer sheets. The subjects were told to circle R if
they had a conscious recollection of the word from the study lists, such as the way
the word was presented or what they were thinking about at the time, or K if they
were sure the word was presented, but they could not recollect its actual occurrence
or any related details. These instructions for remember and know judgments were
similar to those used by Rajaram (1993) and Roediger and McDermott (1995). After
the recognition test, the subjects completed a questionnaire that assessed their awareness of the organization of the word lists at study and asked for a description of any
strategies that were used to reduce false recognitions.

The variable of primary interest in this experiment was the effect of foreknowledge
on the false memory effect. Accordingly, three groups of 16 subjects received different instructions at study or test. In the uninformed condition, the subjects were not
told about the false recognition effect. Instead, they were given standard instructions
to try to remember as many words as possible for a subsequent recognition test. This
condition is similar to the general procedure used by Roediger and McDermott (1995,
Experiment 2).

In the cautious condition, the subjects were also uninformed about the false recognition effect during study, but they were asked to be careful on the recognition
test in order to minimize their false recognitions to all words. This condition was
designed to determine if merely asking subjects to be cautious was sufficient to

minimize the false recognition effect for critical lures. Unlike the subjects in the uninformed condition who received no information about the words used in the recognition test, these subjects were told that some words on the test were similar to words heard at study but were not actually presented. No other information was provided.

In the forewarned condition, the subjects were provided with detailed information and examples of the false recognition effect prior to the presentation of the study lists. Because the subjects were specifically told that the study lists were designed to try to make them falsely recognize related but nonpresented words, this condition allowed subjects the chance to devise strategies to reduce or eliminate the false recognition effect. As part of the forewarning procedure, the subjects participated in a false recognition demonstration before instructions for the actual experiment were given. The subjects were read a sample list of words and told that they would be given a practice recognition test to familiarize themselves with the procedure. The list was obtained from Roediger and McDermott and not used elsewhere in this experiment. Following the presentation of the sample list, subjects were given an eight word recognition test, constructed in the same manner as our actual test. Three of the words were from the sample list (serial positions 1, 8, and 10), one word was the nonpresented critical lure, and four words were unrelated distracters taken from another Roediger and McDermott list not used again in this experiment. After the subjects completed the sample recognition test, the critical lure was identified, and the false recognition effect was described.

These subjects were further informed that prior research has demonstrated that presenting lists of words that were semantically associated to nonpresented words led to high levels of false recognition of the critical lures. This discussion was followed by a reading of another sample list of 15 related words, along with its critical lure from another Roediger and McDermott list that was not used again in this experiment. The subjects were told that the lists that they would hear at study were constructed in the same fashion as the sample lists. Their task was to minimize the false

Remembering Words 10

recognition of critical lures without sacrificing their recognition of words presented at study. Care was taken to ensure that the subjects understood the manner in which the study lists were constructed, the nature of the false recognition effect, and the goal of minimizing the false recognition of critical lures. Prior to the recognition test, the subjects were reminded of their task. Together, these procedures provide a strong test of any possible effect of forewarning.

Results

The primary data consisted of the responses to the recognition test for subjects in the uninformed, cautious, and forewarned conditions and the remember vs. know judgments for all of the words that were recognized. These results are shown in Table 1 for each condition and response measure.

Table 1 indicates that the hit rate for studied words varied across groups, and this observation was supported by the results of an analysis of variance, $F(2, 42) = 4.62$, $M Se = .02$, $p < .02$. The hit rate for the uninformed group (.76) was greater than that for the cautious group (.65), $t(30) = 2.33$, $SEM = .05$, $p < .05$, and the forewarned group (.63), $t(30) = 3.01$, $SEM = 04$, $p < .01$, whereas the hit rates for the cautious and forewarned groups did not vary, $t < 1$. There was also an effect of groups on the false recognition rate for critical lures, $F(2, 42) = 11.05$, $MSe = .05$, $p < .001$, as the rate for the forewarned group (.46) was less than that for the uninformed group (.81), $t(30) = 4.84$, $SEM = .07$, $p < .001$, and the cautious group (.74), $t(30) = 3.36$, $SEM = .08$, $p < .01$. The false alarm rates for critical lures for the uninformed and cautious groups did not vary, $t < 1$, and there was no overall effect of groups on the false alarm rates for nonstudied words or unrelated critical lures, both F's < 1.

In addition to producing the highest hit rate, the uninformed group also produced a strong false memory effect by falsely recognizing the nonpresented critical lures (.81) at least as frequently as the studied words (.76), $t(15) = 1.25$, $SEM < .04$, $p > .10$. On the remember vs. know judgment task, these subjects selected remember responses more frequently than know responses for recognized studied words, $t(15) = 4.43$, $SEM = .06$, $p < .001$, and falsely recognized critical lures, $t(15) = 2.40$, $SEM < .11$, $p < .05$. Their false alarm rates for nonstudied words and unrelated critical lures were the same (.15), and most of these false alarms were judged as know responses. These results closely replicate Roediger and McDermott's (Experiment 2, Table 2) results and indicate that when subjects are uninformed about this memory illusion, they cannot differentiate list items from semantically related but nonpresented items.

The finding that subjects in the cautious group had a significantly lower overall hit rate and nonsignificantly lower false alarm rates than subjects in the uninformed group suggests that the instructions to be cautious influenced recognition performance. But even though these subjects exercised caution, they still demonstrated a false memory effect by recognizing critical lures (.74) at least as often as studied words (.65), $t(15) = 1.8$, $SEM < .05$, $p > .05$. However, these subjects, who selected remember responses over know responses for recognized studied words, $t(15) = 2.67$, $SEM < .06$, $p < .05$, did not differentiate these responses for falsely recognized critical lures, $t < 1$. Their false alarm rates were the same for nonstudied words and unrelated critical lures (.12), and most of these false alarms were judged as know responses. These results indicate that instructing subjects to be cautious can lower the hit rate for studied words and reduce the likelihood that falsely recognized critical lures will be judged as remembered from the prior lists. But such instructions do not diminish the false recognition effect. Merely asking people to be cautious about their false alarms has little effect on this memory illusion.

Most important, the subjects in the forewarned group had a lower overall hit rate and a lower false alarm rate for critical lures than subjects in the uninformed group. At the same time, they had a comparable hit rate and a lower critical lure false alarm rate than subjects in the cautious group. These subjects still made more false recognitions of critical lures (.46) than unrelated critical lures (.14), $t(15) = 5.39$, $SEM = .06$, $p < .001$, demonstrating the persistence of the false memory effect.

Remembering Words 12

But their lower rate of false recognition of critical lures, relative to that rate for either the uninformed (.81) or cautious (.74) groups, and their lower rate of false recognition of critical lures relative to their hit rate, $t(15) = 3.2$, $SEM = .05$, $p < .01$, indicates that forewarning instructions diminished the false recognition effect. Moreover, unlike the uninformed subjects, these subjects did not differentiate between remember and know judgments for either recognized studied words, $t(15) = 1.0$, $SEM = .05$, $p > .10$, or critical lures, $t(15) = 1.3$, $SEM = .08$, $p > .10$. As in the previous conditions, the false alarm rates for nonstudied words and unrelated critical lures were the same (.14), with the majority of these false alarms judged as know responses. These results demonstrate that forewarning instructions can reduce the magnitude of the false recognition effect by reducing the proportion of falsely recognized critical lures and the proportion of those false recognitions judged to be remembered from study.

The Post-Experiment Questionnaire

An open-ended questionnaire was given to all subjects at the end of the experiment. It was designed to provide information about subject awareness of study list organization and the types of strategies that were used to maximize performance on the recognition test. For subjects in the cautious group, we were interested in determining how they might reduce their false alarms to all nonstudied words, whereas for subjects in the forewarned group, we wanted to know how they attempted to minimize their susceptibility to recognizing critical lures. Each subject's written statement was sorted into one of four categories based on the specific strategy that was described. Those categories consisted of the following: no strategy indicated (these subjects made no report of any strategy), maintenance rehearsal (these subjects focused on the sound of each list word or repeated them silently during study), elaborative rehearsal (these subjects focused on list themes by linking study words by semantic associations or forming visual images of the words), and determine critical lures

Remembering Words 13

(in addition to focusing on each list's theme, these subjects tried to determine and remember each list's critical lure). Table 2 shows the number of subjects in each category from each group, along with the corresponding average hit rate for studied words and false alarm rate for critical lures. False alarm rates for nonstudied words and unrelated critical lures were not included because these rates were low in each condition and did not differ across groups.

The results shown in Table 2 indicate that subjects in the uninformed and cautious groups produced a similar pattern of Results. These subjects were more apt to Report that they used elaborative Rehearsal as their primary means of remembering list words (17 of 32 or .53) than either maintenance rehearsal (3 of 32 or .09) or a strategy aimed at determining the critical lures (5 of 32 or .16). Although these subjects spontaneously used elaborative processes which are typically more effective than maintenance processes to remember the study words (e.g., Craik & Watkins, 1973), most of them were not aware of the nature of this experiment and they did not try to determine the critical lures on their own. This was true even after subjects in the cautious group were told that some nonpresented test words would be similar to study words. A far different pattern of results is seen in Table 2 for the subjects in the forewarned group. The most commonly reported strategy for these subjects was to determine the critical lures. Elaborative or maintenance rehearsal was infrequently reported, and the number of subjects who reported no strategy was comparable to the other groups.

The results in Table 2 make two important points. The first point is that the instructions given to the subjects in this task influenced the type of strategy that was used. When subjects were merely told that they would be tested on lists of words (uninformed group) or urged to be cautious for a test (cautious group), the majority of them wisely adopted elaborative rehearsal processes to maximize their memory performance. However, when they were told in advance about the memory illusion (forewarned group), many of these subjects tried to determine the specific critical lures that might appear on the recognition test. The second and more important point

Remembering Words 14

is that subjects in all conditions were susceptible to the false recognition effect, regardless of self-reported strategy. If we examine only those categories in Table 2 with the most subjects, the false recognition of critical lures was greater for subjects in the uninformed (.89) and cautious (.82) groups who used elaborative rehearsal than subjects in the forewarned (.45) group who tried to determine critical lures. But note that even those subjects in the forewarned group who tried to find critical lures falsely recognized nearly half of them. Those subjects understood the forewarning instructions and tried to minimize the false recognition effect, yet they were still influenced by the memory illusion they were actively trying to resist. Clearly, forewarning instructions diminished but did not eliminate the false recognition effect.

An In-Class Demonstration

As part of a regular meeting of the third author's class (Psychology 221, Human Memory), 25 Wesleyan University students participated in an in-class demonstration on the effect of forewarning. Prior to the demonstration, the students were given a detailed description of Roediger and McDermott's experiment, along with a sample list and critical lure. The instructor then informed them that they would be read 8 lists of words, and their job was to devise a strategy to minimize the false recognition of critical lures. The study lists and recognition test were constructed in the same fashion as the present experiment. The lists were read at a rate of approximately 1.5 s per word, and remember and know judgments were not made at test. The results closely paralleled those from the forewarned group in the present experiment for hit rate (.67), false alarms for critical lures (.49), and false alarms for nonstudied words (.19) and unrelated critical lures (.22). Even though the memory students still falsely recognized critical lures greater than unrelated critical lures, $t(24) = 7.57$, $SEM = .04$, $p < .001$, their level of false recognition for critical lures was lower than their hit rate for studied words, $t(24) = 3.40$, $SEM = .05$, $p < .01$. These findings indicate that the memory students were susceptible to this memory illusion, albeit at an attenuated level.

Thus, in both a formal laboratory setting and a less formal classroom setting, forewarning instructions served to diminish but not eliminate the effect of this memory illusion.

Discussion

The study demonstrated several important points. First, when subjects were un-informed about the memory illusion, they demonstrated a strong false recognition effect. These subjects falsely recognized critical lures at a rate that was comparable to their hit rate for studied words, and they were more likely to indicate that they specifically remembered those words from study than simply knew that they were presented. Second, when subjects were urged to be cautious about false alarms to all words, they still demonstrated a strong false recognition effect as their false alarm rate for critical lures was comparable to their hit rate for studied words. However, instructions to be cautious decreased the likelihood that falsely recognized critical lures would be remembered from study. Third, when subjects were forewarned about the memory illusion, they demonstrated a diminished false recognition effect. These subjects reduced their false alarm rate for critical lures, and they made remember and know judgments equally often for recognized studied words and critical lures. Fourth, a post-experiment questionnaire indicated that the majority of the subjects in the uninformed and cautious groups used elaborative rehearsal to try to remember the study words, whereas many subjects in the forewarned group tried to determine the critical lures. The subjects in the forewarned group who sought the critical lures were still susceptible to the memory illusion. Finally, the effects of forewarning on false recognition were shown to be reliable by the results of an in-class demonstration.

Our finding that forewarning instructions diminished but did not eliminate the false recognition effect provides an empirical link between perceptual and memory illu-sions. Earlier, Roediger and McDermott (1995) suggested that the false memory effect functions as a perceptual illusion when they stated that "Just as perceptual illusions can be compelling even when people are aware of the factors giving rise to the

Remembering Words 16

illusion, we suspect that the same is true in our case of remembering events that never happened." (p. 812). Our results do not disagree; both knowledgeable and uninformed subjects falsely recognized critical lures. The present procedures allowed forewarned subjects the opportunity to devise strategies to reduce their susceptibility to critical lures. Yet even though many subjects in this group sought to determine those critical lures, they still falsely recognized almost half of them. This memory illusion, can be influenced by a subject's knowledge because the procedures used in this task allow time for that knowledge to be used. But even when the subjects were armed with this knowledge, false recognitions still occurred. Given the extensive training procedures used in the forewarned condition, it is not obvious how we might have better informed our subjects about this illusion, nor is it clear that a better strategy exists to ward off its effect than trying to determine the critical lures. This strategy was not wholly effective, and its effectiveness would be expected to diminish as the number of study lists grows larger than the memory span. Clearly, even knowledgeable subjects make memory errors in this task.

To explain this memory illusion, some researchers have adopted Underwood's (1965) *implicit activation response hypothesis* that suggests that when subjects encode words, they think of semantic associates to those words at study (e.g., Roediger & McDermott, 1995; Schacter et al., 1996). In the present experiment, listening to lists of semantically related words may activate representations for critical lures because they are the highest semantic associates of the list items. On the subsequent recognition test, subjects may falsely recognize those words on the basis of implicit stimulus familiarity or explicit retrieval of the study context. If the representations for the critical lures are not consciously activated at study, subjects may falsely recognize those words at test, but they may be more apt to say that they know that those items were presented than to say that they specifically remember their presentation. If those representations were consciously activated at study, subjects may not only falsely recognize those items, they may also say that they remember their presentation. In both instances, subjects would be making a source monitoring error about the critical lures. Forewarned subjects in the present experiment may have reduced both their false alarm rate and their frequency of remember judgments to critical lures by rejecting any lures at test that were consciously activated at study and identified as related, but nonstudied words. However, these subjects would still be prone to false recognitions, albeit at a lower rate and with a lower frequency of remember judgments than the other conditions, because they could still be fooled by critical lures that were nonconsciously activated at study or were consciously activated, but not identified as nonstudied words.

Finally, psychologists have long known that memory errors occur in nonlaboratory settings (e.g., Bartlett, 1932; Munsterberg, 1908) and there is currently great controversy over the possibility of recovered/false memories of childhood abuse (Loftus, 1993). We do not claim that the present paradigm offers a general method for studying false memory or that the present findings can generalize to memories of child abuse (see Freyd & Gleaves, 1996, and Roediger & McDermott, 1996, for comments on these issues). Rather, we think that the present false recognition research has practical value in understanding the degree to which knowledge can be used to inoculate a person against a false memory effect. Are memory errors always likely to plague us because remembering is fundamentally constructive in nature, as Roediger and McDermott (1995) assert, or might we overcome these errors by understanding the conditions under which they are likely to occur? Our findings suggest that inoculation by knowledge may achieve only limited success as knowledgeable people could only partially control their susceptibility to remembering events that never occurred.

References

Bartlett, F. C. (1932). *Remembering: A study in experimental and social psychology.* Cambridge: Cambridge University Press.

Craik, F. I. M., & Watkins, M. J. (1973). The role of rehearsal in short-term memory. *Journal of Verbal Learning and Verbal Behavior, 12,* 599–607.

Deese, J. (1959). On the prediction of occurrence of particular verbal intrusions in immediate recall. *Journal of Experimental Psychology, 58,* 17–22.

Freyd, J. J., & Gleaves, D. H. (1996). "Remembering" words not presented in lists: Relevance to the current recovered/false memory controversy. *Journal of Experimental Psychology: Learning, Memory, and Cognition, 22,* 811–813.

Remembering Words 18

Gregory, R. L. (1987). Illusions. In R. L. Gregory (Ed.), *The Oxford companion to the mind*. New York: Oxford University Press.

Loftus, E. F. (1993). The reality of repressed memories. *American Psychologist, 48,* 518–537.

McDermott, K. B. (1996). The persistence of false memories in list recall. *Journal of Memory and Language, 35,* 212–230.

Munsterberg, H. (1908). *On the witness stand: Essays on psychology and crime*. New York: Clark, Boardman, Doubleday.

Payne, D. G., Elie, C. J., Blackwell, J. M., & Neuschatz, J. S. (1996). Memory illusions: Recalling, recognizing, and recollecting events that never occurred. *Journal of Memory and Language, 35,* 261–285.

Rajaram, S. (1993). Remembering and knowing: Two means of access to the personal past. *Memory & Cognition, 21,* 89–102.

Read, J. D. (1996). From a passing thought to a false memory in 2 minutes: Confusing real and illusory events. *Psychonomic Bulletin & Review, 3,* 105–111.

Roediger, H. L. III (1996). Memory illusions. *Journal of Memory and Language, 35,* 76–100.

Roediger, H. L. III, & McDermott, K. B. (1995). Creating false memories: Remembering words not presented in lists. *Journal of Experimental Psychology: Learning, Memory, and Cognition, 21,* 803–814.

Roediger, H. L. III, & McDermott, K. B. (1996). False perceptions of false memories. *Journal of Experimental Psychology: Learning, Memory, and Cognition, 22,* 814–816.

Schacter, D. L., Verfaellie, M., & Pradere, D. (1996). The neuropsychology of memory illusions: False recall and recognition in amnesic patients. *Journal of Memory and Language, 35,* 319–334.

Tulving, E. (1985). Memory and consciousness. *Canadian Psychologist, 26,* 1–12.

Underwood, B. J. (1965). False recognition produced by implicit verbal responses. *Journal of Experimental Psychology, 70,* 122–129.

Remembering Words 19

Authors' Note

Appreciation is expressed to Chun Luo for helpful comments on an earlier draft of this paper. This research was supported by a Wesleyan Grant in Support of Scholarship made to J. G. S. Correspondence should be addressed to him at the Department of Psychology, Wesleyan University, Middletown, CT 06459-0408 (e-mail: jseamon@wesleyan.edu).

Remembering Words 20

Table 1

Mean Recognition for Studied and Nonstudied Words and Related and Unrelated Critical Lures

Item Type	Proportion of Recognized Words		
	Overall	R	K
Uninformed Condition			
List Words			
Studied	.76	.52	.24
Nonstudied	.15	.03	.12
Critical Lures			
Related	.81	.55	.27
Unrelated	.15	.06	.10
Cautious Condition			
List Words			
Studied	.65	.41	.24
Nonstudied	.12	.03	.09
Critical Lures			
Related	.74	.37	.38
Unrelated	.12	.01	.11
Forewarned Group			
List Words			
Studied	.63	.34	.28
Nonstudied	.14	.02	.12
Critical Lures			
Related	.46	.19	.28
Unrelated	.14	.03	.11

Note: R = Remember Judgment; K = Know Judgment. Instances where remember and know proportions do not sum to the overall proportion reflect rounding to two decimal places.

Remembering Words 21

Table 2

Hits for Studied Words and False Alarms For Critical Lures According to Self-Reported Strategies

| | Self-Reported Strategy | | | |
| | None Indicated | Maintenance Rehearsal | Elaborative Rehearsal | Determine Critical Lures |
Group				
Uninformed				
N	3	2	8	3
Hits	.71	.71	.81	.74
FAs	.83	.81	.89	.58
Cautious				
N	4	1	9	2
Hits	.56	.83	.66	.71
FAs	.59	.88	.82	.63
Forewarned				
N	4	2	3	7
Hits	.49	.65	.65	.68
FAs	.28	.69	.58	.45

Note: N represents the number of subjects; hits and false alarms are proportions.

Style

Now that you have some idea of format, let us consider style. After suffering through some obscurely written article, you will no doubt recognize the advantage of clear, unambiguous writing. The APA format helps standardize the order and general content. However, making sure that the reader understands what you are saying is up to you. We have read many research reports prepared for our classes and we have found the biggest problem is transition, or flow, from one section to the next. Many students write as if they were composing a surprise-ending short story, even though their report should be as straightforward as possible. The information for each section described here is summarized in Table 5.3.

Your title should be short (10 to 12 words) and concise. Usually the title states the independent variables and dependent variables.

Your abstract should include your variables (independent, dependent, and important control variables), number and type of subjects, major results, and important conclusions. Because the abstract should not exceed 180 words, state only the most essential aspect of the paper. The body of your report should expand on the abstract. (This is why most abstracts are written last, even though the report might be clearer if the abstract were written first, as an outline for the main part of the work.)

In the introduction, you should state why you are interested in a particular issue, what other investigators have found, and what variables you will be examining. You should begin by stating a broad perspective on the issue, then quickly narrow down to the specific question that interests you. You should lead the reader through the relevant research, always keeping in mind that you are setting up your own research question. Thus, avoid discussion of tangential issues. Toward the end of the introduction, give the reader an overview of your experiment, specifying your hypotheses explicitly and outlining any predictions derived from theories you have discussed. By the end of the introduction, the reader should see your experiment as filling an important gap in our knowledge.

In the method section, state how you examined the variables you described at the end of the introduction. Here, it is important to be clear and complete. By

▼ **TABLE 5.3**

A Summary of the Information in each Section of a Research Report

Section	Information
Title	Experiments: State independent and dependent variables—"The effects of X on Y."
	Other studies: State the relationships examined—"The relation between X and Y."
Abstract	In 180 words or less, state what was done to whom and summarize the most important results.
Introduction	State what you plan to do and why (you may have to review results from related research). Predicted results may be appropriate.
Method	Present enough information to allow someone else to repeat your study exactly the way you did it. For clarity use subheadings (Participants, Apparatus, etc.) and make sure that dependent, independent, subject, and control variables are specified.
Results	Summarize important results in tables or figures. Direct the reader to data that seem most relevant to the purpose of the research.
Discussion	State how the results relate to the hypotheses or predictions stated in the introduction. Inferences and theoretical statements are appropriate.
References	In APA format, list only those references that were cited in your report.

the time you write the method section, you are quite familiar with the details and complexities of your experiment. This familiarity makes it difficult to realize that the reader of your report is learning of these details for the first time. As you write, try to tell the reader everything he or she would need to know in order to be able to repeat your experiment, but do not include any extraneous variables. Often people divide their method section into three subsections: subjects (or participants), materials (or apparatus), and procedure. The subjects section specifies the number of subjects participating in the study, the population from which they were drawn (e.g., the introductory psychology class at your university), and their incentive for participating (e.g., course credit). If any subjects were discarded for any reason, that should be mentioned in this section. The materials (or apparatus) section should describe all relevant aspects of the materials used in the experiment. The next section, the procedure section, often begins with a description of the experimental design, states the instructions given to subjects (if they are human), and generally leads the reader through the various phases of the experiment.

In the results section, state what happened when you examined the variables. Clarity is important here. Avoid simply listing your statistical analyses with minimal comment. Instead, state each finding in plain English first, then support it with statistics. Your results section should end with a summary of the purpose and results of your experiment. In your discussion, state what the effects of the variables mean for the issue at hand. The biggest danger in this section of the paper is lack of organization. Before you begin writing, you should know the points you want to make. Make them concise and easy to understand. The discussion should follow up the issues pointed out in the introduction. Also, as in the introduction, avoid straying onto tangents. When the reader has completed your report, he or she should be able to state the main conclusions in a sentence or two. Be careful, however, in the conclusions you draw; avoid grandiose statements. Science advances in small steps; your experiment need not be earthshaking to be scientifically important.

Often a research paper is not written in the order that it appears in the journal. You may consider writing the method and results sections first and the introduction and discussion sections later (the abstract last). Although it may not seem so initially, the method and results sections are less difficult to generate because they are written in a conventional manner. In other words, there are only so many ways to describe the number of participants in a study or the results of a particular statistical analysis. On the other hand, the introduction and discussion sections are often the most difficult to write and, thus, are saved for last. Usually these sections are longer and require writing skill, organization, and insight. For example, the discussion section can be difficult because an explanation of the data is required, and often the data can be interpreted in more than one way. Note that not all writers use this strategy, and you should choose an approach that suits you best.

The APA *Publication Manual* outlines writing style considerations as follows: Orderly expression of ideas, smoothness of expression, economy of expression, precision, and clarity. It also offers strategies to improve one's writing style. These guidelines warrant some discussion, so we now consider aspects of writing style.

Scientific writing demands clarity, so each word has to be chosen carefully. Consider these sentences that regularly appear in undergraduate research reports: "I ran the subjects individually." "The white albino rat was introduced to the Skinner box." Actually, none of the subjects in the study from which the first sentence was pulled did any running during the course of the project. What the author meant to say was, "I tested the subjects individually." From reading about rats introduced to Skinner boxes, you might conclude that the researcher had very clever rats. The rat did not shake hands with a box; all that happened was that the rat was put into the operant-conditioning chambers. Furthermore, "white albino" is redundant. All albino rats are white. The lesson here is that in scientific writing, you must be careful to choose the correct word or phrase and avoid ambiguity. Also, be cautious when using pronouns such as *which, this, that, these,* and *those.* Many students find it irresistible to begin a paragraph with one of these pronouns, and more often than not the referent for the pronoun is not easy to determine. You can usually avoid any ambiguity by including the referent of the pronoun each time it is used.

After you have decided on your words and phrases, put them together carefully. A common problem among some writers is to shift verb tenses abruptly. In general, use the past tense in the review of other studies in your introduction (Smith *found*) and in your method (the subjects *were*). When you are describing and discussing your data, the present tense is usually appropriate (The data *show* that . . . , which *means* that).

Make sure that collective and plural nouns agree with their verbs and pronouns. Plural words that end in *a* are troublesome, such as *data, criteria,* and *phenomena.* Each of these nouns is plural, so they require plural verbs and pronouns. "These data *are*" is correct, but "this phenomena is" is incorrect. The singular forms for these nouns are: *datum, criterion,* and *phenomenon* (this phenomenon *is*).

Many scientific writers overuse the passive voice in their reports. Consider this statement: "It is thought that forgetting is caused by interference." Although this sentence is fairly concise (and it is precise), it is also stuffy and less direct than "We think that interference causes forgetting," which is really what the writer meant. Be careful about using either the active or the passive voice too much. If you overuse the passive voice, your report sounds stuffy. If you overuse the active voice, you may take interest away from what you did and place too much emphasis on yourself (I think, I did, and so on). If you want to emphasize what was done and not who did it and why, use the passive construction. On the other hand, if you think that the agent of the activity is also important, or if the reason for the action is important, use the active voice.

The careful writer avoids language that is sexist. The APA recommends that the use of *he* (and *his* and *him*) as a generic pronoun be avoided by changing to a plural construction or by using *he and she.* Generally, the writer should strive for accurate, unbiased communication. The APA *Publication Manual* contains a section devoted to the reduction of language bias.

Scientific writing requires the use of consistent terminology; if you assign labels to things (e.g., labeling subject groups: informed and uninformed), use these labels throughout the paper. You may have been taught in English classes to try to vary descriptions of repetitive things to avoid boring the reader. However, in scientific writing, changing terminology only adds confusion. It is important for the reader to know that when you introduce a new term, it refers to a concept different from ones previously discussed.

Writing a cogent, well-organized research article is a skill that requires considerable effort and practice. More is involved than simply allocating information to the correct sections. There are many fine points of style, usage, and exposition that distinguish lucid, well-written articles from obscure and tortuous ones. While writing your report, you should make frequent use of standard references for points of style and grammar.

In addition, consult the APA *Publication Manual* regarding aspects of technical writing that are particularly relevant to psychology journal articles, including the organization and content of each section, the economy and precision in the expression of ideas, the presentation of data and statistics, and so forth. We highly recommend the aforementioned book by Sternberg (1993), the articles by Sternberg (1992) and Roediger (2007), and the chapter by Bem (2004) for excellent advice and specific examples of good and poor style, phrasing, and organization in psychology articles. Finally, and perhaps most importantly, you should allocate time for revising and rewriting your manuscript, with the aforementioned stylistic comments in mind. No one can write a publishable manuscript on the first try; revision is a crucial part of the writing process.

Publishing an Article

Assume that your article has been written, proofread, and corrected, and the last page has just emerged from your printer. Now what? Although it is unlikely that your first student effort will produce an article of professional quality, you may nevertheless find it interesting to discover what happens when a professional psychologist submits an article to a journal.

The first step is to send copies of the manuscript (the technical term for an unpublished work) to a small number of trusted associates who can check it over to make sure that it has no obvious or elementary flaws and that it is written clearly. Once the comments come back, the indicated corrections are made and, with some trepidation, the author commits the manuscript to the mail, addressed to the editor of the most appropriate journal. After this step, it is necessary to exhibit great patience for the next few months. The review process is slow. (The editor who receives the manuscript typically is extremely busy juggling many responsibilities—teaching, conducting his or her own research, supervising undergraduate and graduate students, and so on.) Two or three weeks after submitting the article, the author receives a form letter thanking him or her for interest in the journal and acknowledging receipt of the manuscript. The manuscript gets a number (such as 04-145), and if an associate editor has been assigned to handle it, the author is instructed to direct all future correspondence to that editor.

The editor sends copies of the manuscript to two or three reviewers. Some journals allow the author to have anonymous (or blind) reviewing, where the author's identity is concealed. This is for those who do not believe in the impartiality of reviewers. The reviewer, who may also review for several other journals, puts the manuscript in the pile on his or her desk. A conscientious reviewer may take a day or two to carefully read and evaluate a manuscript. The reviewer then sends a summary statement to the editor. When the reviewers are in agreement, the editor's decision is easy. If the reviewers disagree, the editor must carefully read the manuscript and sometimes may request another opinion. Finally, an editorial decision is reached and the author receives a letter stating (1) why the manuscript cannot be published, (2) what kind of revisions are needed to make the manuscript acceptable, or (3) that the journal will publish the article. Because rejection rates for manuscripts are quite high in most journals (above 70 percent), editors spend a great deal of time devising tactful letters of rejection.

Whether or not the article was accepted, the comments of the reviewers are most valuable. The best psychologists in the area have provided, free of charge, their careful opinions about the research. Of course, reviewers can also make mistakes. Any author who disagrees with a review has the privilege of writing to the editor. Although this action will usually not result in the article being accepted, it is important that rejected authors have the right to appeal or protest. Anyway, there are always other journals.

If the article was accepted for publication, the author is still not finished. Some revision of the manuscript may be required. The copyright for the article is signed over to the publisher. Some months later, the author receives galley or page proofs from the publisher. These must be carefully checked to ensure that the words and tables set in type by the printer match those in the original manuscript. After making corrections, the author returns the article to the publisher. Several months later, the article finally appears in the journal. The entire process, from submission of the manuscript until final publication, takes a year or more. Authors do not get paid for articles in journals, but on the other hand, neither do they get charged for the privilege of appearing in print.

As you might expect, it is a great thrill to see your name in print, especially the first time. An even greater thrill, however, is the knowledge that you may have added some small amount to our understanding of why people and animals think and act as they do.

▼ SUMMARY

1. When you read a research report, you should read actively and critically, so that you can derive maximum benefit from other people's research.

2. The checklist for critical readers is designed to get you into the habit of actively asking questions about the reports you read: What hypotheses are being tested? How are they being tested? Does the method test the hypotheses? Do the results apply to the hypotheses? How does the author relate the results to the purposes of the research? What interpretations and inferences are made by the author?

3. You should also consider these questions when you write your own report. The APA format provides a framework for your report, but it is up to you to write clearly. Several suggestions that help produce a clear, unambiguous style of report writing are provided.

4. The chapter concludes with a brief description of the publication process. For psychological science to progress, reports must be published, and knowledgeable consumers must read them critically.

▼ KEY TERMS

abstract
APA format
apparatus
author
design
discussion
figures
introduction
literature search
materials

method
participants
procedure
references
results
running head
subject (participant)
tables
title

WEB CONNECTIONS

The following site has links to step-by-step presentations on **"APA Style"** and **"Getting Ideas for a Study":**

http://academic.cengage.com/psychology/workshops.html

For a great guide to APA style, check out this newly updated page:

http://www.docstyles.com/apacrib.htm

How to do a literature search can be found at:

http://apa.org/science/lib.html

An interesting online journal, *Psycoloquy*, which is sponsored by the American Psychological Association, can be found at:

http://www.cogsci.ecs.soton.ac.uk/psycoloquy/

▼ LABORATORY RESOURCE

While Langston's (2002) Chapter 10 of *Research Methods Laboratory Manual for Psychology* is on a different topic (obstacle detection by the blind) than the ones covered in depth in this chapter (factors that influence voting and false memory for words), the goals are the same: (a) to develop hypotheses, (b) to test between hypotheses, (c) and to repeat the process until you've pinned down the answer.

PSYCHOLOGY IN ACTION
A Literature Search

Suppose you became interested in the effects of hypnosis on memory. Many people believe that hypnosis is a viable way to remember events that might otherwise not be retrieved, yet many courts will not let people who have been hypnotized testify as witnesses. Why is this? Are our memories susceptible to change when we are under hypnosis? Or does hypnosis help memory? These are the types of questions in which you are interested.

To obtain answers to these questions, you will do a literature search. Because you are not particularly knowledgeable in this area, you do not know the names of any researchers who have done work on the effects of hypnosis on memory. Therefore, the best place to start is probably *PsycINFO*. You do not have to be a librarian or computer expert to use electronic databases such as *PsycINFO*. Help screens are available as well as printed instructions; additionally, the reference staff at your library can answer questions and help you plan your search strategy.

To find out about the effects of hypnosis on memory, you might begin by looking up a "keyword"; to do this, you simply type in a word that captures the topic in which you are interested (for instance, *hypnosis*). However, a recent search turned up 10,261 journal articles written about the subject of hypnosis; clearly, this is too many to work with. A search of *memory* turns up even more articles: 84,630! In this situation, you will want to combine keywords to pare down the numbers. Because you are interested in the *susceptibility of memory to hypnosis,* you can combine separate searches for *susceptibility, memory,* and *hypnosis*; the result is a list of all the articles that contain information about all three concepts. You have now narrowed the field down to a more workable list of 113 references, each accompanied by a brief abstract. You skim the titles and abstracts and determine which articles look especially interesting; you will probably want to go to the journals after this step and read the articles that look most relevant to your interests. Review articles are especially helpful at this stage because they summarize and evaluate many empirical articles.

Now suppose you have found an article that contains a theory about hypnosis and memory that is particularly interesting to you; you would like to know about the implications of this theory and whether it has generally held up under experimental scrutiny. One way to do this would be to find out what more recent articles have cited this article. To do this, you would use the *Social Science Citation Index (SSCI). SSCI* allows you to enter an article's reference and find out who has cited the article. That way, you can find out the recent developments in that area.

Most libraries have printers that allow you to print out any interesting reference you might discover when using electronic searches. Additionally, you can sometimes download the references onto your own storage device. Ask your reference librarian what types of options have you at your library. ■

PART 2

PRINCIPLES AND PRACTICES OF EXPERIMENTAL PSYCHOLOGY

PSYCHOPHYSICS

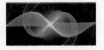

Observation is a passive science, experimentation an active science.
(CLAUDE BERNARD)

Suppose you were a dentist (or a patient at a dentist) and you wanted a way to make pain more tolerable without administering drugs. The measurement of pain is a psychophysical problem, since the degree of pain must be inferred from the behavior of the patient in the dentist's chair. This chapter discusses several sophisticated psychophysical techniques for measuring sensations such as pain.

It probably would not occur to you, as either a dentist or a patient, that odor might increase a person's tolerance of pain. But a recent psychophysical study (Prescott and Wilkie, 2007) showed that a sweet-smelling odor could make pain more tolerable. Pain was studied using the infamous **cold-pressor test,** which requires subjects to immerse their dominant hand and forearm into cold water (5° C) for up to 4 minutes. Subjects were told to leave their hand in the water for as long as they could tolerate the pain. Subjects who breathed a sweet-smelling odor kept their hand in the cold water almost three times as long as subjects in a control condition where no odor was present. Therefore, one of the authors of this text who is due for a root-canal dental procedure is bringing a copy of the research article to his dentist: yet another example of the practical benefits of psychophysical research.

▼ MEASURING SENSATIONS

This unexpected result is owing to several factors, some of which are addressed in this chapter. We will examine these issues in the context of a venerable area of investigation in scientific psychology called **psychophysics.** Psychophysics involves the determination of the psychological reaction to events that lie along a physical dimension. Edwin G. Boring (1950), the eminent historian of experimental psychology, claims that the introduction of techniques to measure the relation between internal impressions (the *psycho* of psychophysics) and the external world (the *physics*) marked the onset of scientific psychology.

Boring marked psychophysics as the beginning of scientific psychology primarily because the scientists using psychophysical techniques were able to formulate the first mathematical laws of psychological phenomena. Although the characteristics of these laws are of interest in and of themselves, their development has other important implications. First, measuring sensations is very difficult, because they are not open to public measurement as is light intensity or the weight of a stone. Second, the internal judgments are not identical to the amount of physical energy influencing the sensory apparatus. We examine each of these legacies of psychophysics now and expand on them throughout this chapter.

Gustav Fechner formalized the **psychophysical methods,** which measure attributes of the world in terms of their psychological values (1860/1966). His methods, which are detailed later in the chapter, showed that psychological judgments varied in particular ways according to the intensity of the stimulus and the particular sensory modality of

Physical Visual Intensity ——————▶ Psychological Brightness
Physical Auditory Intensity ——————▶ Psychological Loudness
Physical Measure of Weight ——————▶ Psychological Heaviness
Physical Electrical Intensity ——————▶ Psychological Pain

▼ **FIGURE 6.1**

Some Relationships Between Physical Stimuli and Psychological Judgments.

the stimulus (i.e., judgments of visual stimuli differed from judgments of auditory stimuli, which differed from judgments of taste stimuli, and so on). Since these relations held, at least approximately, for many different people, Fechner and other researchers concluded that private, internal judgments had been measured accurately. As shown in Figure 6.1, psychophysicists could measure the psychological attributes of brightness, loudness, heaviness, and pain just as physicists measured the corresponding physical attributes of light intensity, auditory intensity, and so on.

Both in the 1800s and today, a prominent use of psychophysics is to measure seemingly simple sensations such as brightness, which probably seems unnecessary. You may think it simple to decide the loudness or painfulness of stimuli. However, it turns out that there is rarely a direct one-to-one relation between physical values and psychological values. If a rock band turned up its amplifiers to produce twice as much energy as it had produced before (a doubling of the physical units), this twofold increase of energy would not result in listeners experiencing a sound twice as loud as before. For a listener to judge the sound to be twice as loud, the energy level would have to be increased roughly 10 times. Such discoveries derived from the psychophysical methods have important practical applications. For example, the amplifier or radio dial that you turn to increase volume (i.e., the perceived loudness) cannot bear a one-to-one relation between movements of the dial and increases in energy. Rather, the dial has to be calibrated so that its movements increase intensity proportional to increments in loudness. Thus, doubling the volume level on the dial has to increase physical energy about 10 times to produce a twofold increase in loudness. Telephones are also designed so that their microphones and amplifiers work in accord with this psychophysical relation between auditory intensity and perceived loudness.

The psychophysical relation between stimulus and judgment depends on the particular sensory modality that is stimulated. Pain judgments in response to increases in electrical intensity of shocks applied to the skin grow much more rapidly than do loudness judgments in response to increases in sound energy. For one shock to be judged twice as painful as another, the intensity of the shock needs to have been increased about one-third. We can see, then, that merely measuring changes in physical units does not always help us accurately determine changes in psychological units.

In this chapter, psychophysical methods are used to illustrate three scientific topics. **Operational definitions** describe the procedures used to produce a concept and allow us to communicate successfully about the concepts we are studying. What does it mean when a subject reports that he or she detects a painful stimulus? An operational definition of detection and one of pain will help to ensure that scientists use technical terms in similar ways.

A related issue has to do with **measurement scales,** the assignment of numbers or names to objects and their attributes. How do we determine whether one light intensity appears twice as bright as another? Not all psychophysical techniques permit accurate statements about the ratio of one sensation to another.

Finally, we shall discuss **small-*n* designs,** or those based on small numbers of subjects. In this context, we explain why it is often appropriate to formulate psychophysical laws that are based on large numbers of observations but that are taken from a small number of observers (the small *n*). This technique differs from that often used in psychology experiments in which large numbers of subjects are used, but few observations are taken on each person.

6.1   EXPERIMENTAL TOPICS AND RESEARCH ILLUSTRATIONS

Topic   *Operational Definition*
Illustration   *Thresholds*

No serious discussion, scientific or otherwise, can progress very far unless the participants agree to define the terms they are using. Imagine that you and your date are having a friendly argument about who is the best athlete of the year. How do you define *athlete*? You both might agree about such common sports as tennis, swimming, and gymnastics, but what about more esoteric sports, such as Frisbee throwing, hang gliding, and hopping cross-country on a pogo stick? Should practitioners of these activities be considered for your athlete-of-the-year award? Until this question of definition is answered, your discussion may just go around in circles.

Similar problems can arise in scientific discussions. One way to describe the unusual analgesia results reported by Prescott & Wilkie is that untrained observers become less sensitive to pain after inhaling a sweet-smelling odor. For ordinary conversation, this might be a perfectly adequate way to make sense of the situation. However, *common* usage and *technical* usage have different requirements: In technical discourse, precision is necessary, so that needless arguments over the meaning of scientific results do not occur. Technically, a decrease in sensitivity would imply that the body's pain receptors became less acute after smelling sweet odors. This unlikely possibility would have important implications for drug companies, doctors, and headache sufferers.

What the scientist needs to know are the operations used to produce the outcome. The scientist then can decide whether the concept so defined is a sensible way to think about the outcome. In this instance, the procedure used by Hardy (described in detail in the next section) was supposed to measure sensitivity; however, his technique did not permit the assessment of an alternative interpretation—namely, that aspirin altered the willingness of the observers to say that a stimulus was painful. We can see that it is crucial to know the procedures and operations scientists use to study the processes they say they are studying. Words and phrases such as *pain, sensitivity,* and *willingness to respond* have broad, everyday meanings that must be precisely limited when they are used in a technical, scientific context.

The most common way of providing technical meaning is by using an operational definition. An operational definition is a formula for building a construct in such a way that other scientists can duplicate it, by specifying the operations used to produce and measure it. "Take the eye of a newt, the leg of a frog, three oyster shells and shake twice" is an operational definition, although it is not entirely clear what is being defined. However,

INTRODUCING THE VARIABLES

Dependent Variables

Observers in psychophysical studies are asked to make one of two kinds of judgments about stimuli that have been presented. If only one stimulus has been presented on a particular trial, an absolute judgment is required. Absolute judgments can be simple statements about the presence or absence of a signal ("Yes, I saw it" or "No, I did not see it") or direct estimates about some property of the stimulus (answering) ("How many grams does this weigh?)." If two stimuli must be compared on a particular trial, a relative judgment is required. Again, simple statements, such as "Stimulus A is a larger than (or smaller than) stimulus B," can be made; or direct estimates, such as "Stimulus A is twice as large as stimulus B," can be given.

Independent Variables

The major independent variables manipulated in psychophysical studies are the magnitude and the quality of stimuli. Changing the intensity—the physical correlate of loudness—of a tone would be a manipulation of stimulus magnitude, as would be changing the weight of an object or the concentration of an odor. The frequency—the physical correlate of pitch—of a tone would be manipulated to produce a qualitative change in the stimulus. Other qualitative judgments could require that observers compare various foods (spinach versus turnips) or the styles of different singers (Madonna versus Tammy Wynette).

Control Variables

The main thing to be controlled in a psychophysical experiment is the observer's willingness to make a particular response. This attitude must remain constant from trial to trial. An observer who is very willing to make a positive judgment ("Yes, I saw it") should maintain this same willingness over the course of the experiment. If the criteria for making a response vary, then an inaccurate picture of sensitivities is obtained. Classical or traditional psychophysics assumed the observers could accomplish this constancy without too much difficulty. Once an observer was trained, attitude was supposedly controlled. Modern psychophysical theories, such as the theory of signal detection (to be discussed later), do not accept this assumption. They assume that the observer makes a response based on a decision that depends both on the stimulus and on the psychological factors involved, such as the relative costs and benefits of the decision. So, as will be detailed later, modern psychophysical methods incorporate special techniques to guarantee (or at least to test) the assumption that the observer maintains a constant strategy.

this recipe can be duplicated, so it meets the major criterion for an operational definition. You can tell from this example that an operational definition does not have to be entirely sensible, as long as it is clear and can be copied. For instance, we might operationally define a construct called *centigrams* as the product of your height in centimeters and your weight in grams. Since any scientist can easily determine the centigram score, this is a valid operational definition. Of course, it probably could not be used for any important scientific purpose, but the potential utility of an operational definition is an issue separate from its validity. Typically, however, operationally defined constructs are tied to a theory or body of research literature, so they do make sense and do have some validity.

In the following sections, we discuss the operational definition of a theoretical construct called a **threshold.** First, we give the common-language meaning of this term; we see then how attempts at increasing the precision of definition have led to rather sophisticated methodological techniques to improve the operational definitions of a threshold.

Thresholds: Classical Psychophysics

In common language, a threshold is the part of a doorway you step through or over to enter a room. Classical psychophysicists believed that stimuli had to cross such a (hypothetical) barrier to enter the brain or the mind. If a stimulus were strong, it could easily jump over the threshold. A crude analogy that may be helpful is to think of the stimulus as a pole-vaulter. The bar corresponds to the threshold. A good jump will put you over the bar (across the threshold), whereas a feeble jump will not. The question, then, is one of how strong a stimulus must be if a signal is to cross the threshold. Answering this question was of major concern to classical psychophysicists.

At first, the answer may seem obvious. All we have to do is slowly increase the intensity of a stimulus, such as a tone or a dim light, until the observer responds, "Yes, there it is." Unfortunately, when we try to repeat this process, the point at which an observer suddenly detects the stimulus changes from trial to trial. To deal with this variability, classical psychophysicists developed statistical methods to estimate the best value for the threshold. We will discuss only one of the methods, developed by Fechner and known as the **method of limits.**

If we performed an experiment using the method of limits to determine the threshold for a tone, results would look like those shown in Table 6.1. Each column represents data from one block of trials. The first block starts with a clearly audible tone, to which the observer responds "yes." The tone intensity is lowered in successive steps until the observer reports "no," thus ending that trial block. The next block of trials starts with an intensity so low that the observer cannot hear the tone and responds "no." On successive trials, the intensity is gradually increased, until the

▼ TABLE 6.1

Using the Method of Limits to Determine an Absolute Threshold.

Stimulus Intensity	Response				
	↓		↓		
200			Yes		
180	Yes		Yes		
160	Yes		Yes		
140	Yes	Yes	Yes		
120	Yes	No	No	Yes	
100	Yes	No		No	
80	No	No		No	
60		No		No	
40		No		↑	
20		No			
		↑			Mean
Threshold	90	130	130	110	115

Note: In the first series of trials, the experimenter starts with a strong stimulus and decreases its intensity until the observer can no longer detect it. The threshold is the mean of the stimulus intensities that yield the first "no" response and the last "yes" response. In the next series of trials, a weak stimulus is increased in intensity until it is detected. It is customary to start each series at a different stimulus intensity to make it less likely that the observer's responses will be influenced by the length of a series. Stimuli are in arbitrary units—that is, the intensities ranging from 20 to 200 could represent weight or anything else that might vary in intensity.

observer reports hearing the tone. This process of alternating trial blocks continues until Table 6.1 is complete. Each block is started at a different intensity to avoid extra cues that might mislead the observer.

If the observer were a perfect stimulus detector, the point at which responses switched from "yes" to "no" (or vice versa) would always be the same. This ideal point would be the threshold. Stimuli less intense than this value would never be detected, and stimuli greater than or equal to this ideal threshold would always be detected. Unfortunately, real data from real people do not have this ideal characteristic; instead, they look like the data in Table 6.1.

Observers are influenced by their expectations about when they think it is time to change their response from "yes" to "no" or vice versa. For example, if a series requires several "yes" responses before the threshold is reached, some observers may decide that they are giving too many "yes" responses and prematurely respond "no." Other observers may be very cautious about changing their responses and may delay too long. Indeed, the same observer at different times may commit both of these kinds of errors. So the threshold is operationally defined as the mean (average) of the points in each trial block at which the observer switches from "yes" to "no" (or "no" to "yes"). This operational definition is a statistical one. A threshold defined this way, based on an observer's ability to detect a signal, is called an **absolute threshold,** since the yes-no judgments are not based on a comparison of two stimuli but are absolute judgments about a single stimulus.

Classical psychophysics assumes that the physical stimulus produces a normal distribution of mental events (Figure 6.2). Thus, the actual mental value produced by the same physical stimulus varies from trial to trial. The threshold is a statistical concept that corresponds to the mean of this normal distribution. Since a normal distribution is symmetrical, the threshold is the stimulus value that can be detected 50 percent of the time.

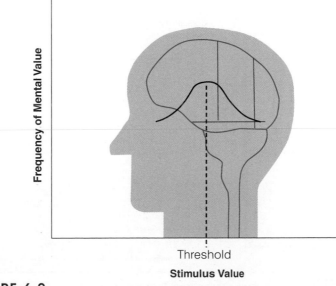

▼ **FIGURE 6.2**

The Same Physical Stimulus Produces a Range of Mental Values.

Since the absolute threshold is a statistical concept, much like the "average taxpayer," it has other statistical properties in addition to the mean. These are now illustrated by computing a **difference threshold** in Table 6.2. Difference thresholds are based on relative judgments, in which a constant unchanging comparison stimulus is judged relative to a series of changing stimuli. The question being asked by the experimenter is this: "How different must two stimuli be before they can reliably be distinguished?"

The traditional example of a difference threshold requires the observer to lift pairs of weights—one weight always remaining the same—and to judge if the new weight is heavier, lighter, or equal to the standard weight. Several series of ascending and descending trials are given. The upper threshold is the average point at which the observer changes from "heavier" responses to "equal" responses. The lower threshold is the point at which "equal" responses give way to "lighter" responses. The difference between these two values is called the **interval of uncertainty.** The difference threshold is operationally defined as half the interval of uncertainty. In Table 6.2, this equals 10 grams. The mean of the upper and lower thresholds is called the **point of subjective equality** (300 grams in Table 6.2).

Ernst Heinrich Weber, whose pioneering work in psychophysics preceded Fechner's by about 20 years, discovered some important properties of the difference threshold. One property that Weber determined was that the magnitude of the difference threshold increases with increases in the magnitude of the standard stimulus. He found that 10 grams is the difference threshold when 300 grams is the standard, and the corresponding value for a 600-gram standard stimulus is a difference threshold of 20 grams. A familiar example will illustrate this psychophysical finding. In a room lit by a single

▼ TABLE 6.2

Using the Method of Limits to Determine a Difference Threshold.

	Comparison Stimulus (grams)	Response			
		↓		↓	
	350			Heavier	
	340	Heavier		Heavier	
	330	Heavier		Heavier	
	320	Heavier	Heavier	Heavier	Heavier
	310	Equal	Equal	Heavier	Equal
Standard Stimulus	300	Equal	Equal	Heavier	Lighter
	290	Equal	Lighter	Equal	Lighter
	280	Lighter	Lighter	Equal	Lighter
	270		Lighter	Lighter	Lighter
	260		Lighter		
				↑	Mean
Upper Threshold		315	315	295	315	310
Lower Threshold		285	295	275	305	290
Interval of Uncertainty = 310 − 290 = 20 grams					

Note: For descending series, the upper threshold is the mean of the stimuli leading to the last "heavier" response and the first "equal" response. The lower threshold is the mean of the stimuli producing the last "equal" response and the first "lighter" response. The standard stimulus is always 300 grams. The difference threshold is one-half of the interval of uncertainty (10 grams, in this example).

candle, the addition of another lit candle will make the room noticeably brighter. However, in a room illuminated by several intense lamps, adding a single lit candle will not noticeably increase the brightness of the room.

Weber is famous for determining a second property of the difference threshold: *For a particular sensory modality, the size of the difference threshold relative to the standard stimulus is constant.* To return to our earlier example, the ratio of 10 grams to 300 grams is the same as the ratio of 20 grams to 600 grams, 1/30 in this case. According to Weber's discovery, this means that the difference threshold for a 900-gram standard stimulus should be 30 grams, and it should be 40 grams for a 1,200-gram standard. What should the difference threshold be for a standard stimulus of 50 grams?

Fechner called relative constancy of the difference threshold **Weber's law.** This law is usually written as $\Delta I/I = K,$ where I refers to the magnitude of the standard stimulus, ΔI is the difference threshold, and K is the symbol for constancy.

Weber's law, or the Weber fraction, as it is sometimes called, varies in size for different senses. For example, it is somewhat larger for brightness than it is for heaviness. A substantial amount of research has shown that Weber's law holds true for greater than 90 percent of the range of standard stimuli tested in a particular sensory modality. It fails to hold for very weak stimuli, such that the Weber fraction for very light standard stimuli is much larger than 1/30, which is what is found in the middle range.

You may think that the method of limits is quite inefficient, since each column contains many successive responses (in Table 6.1, either "yes" or "no") that do not change. A newer version of the method of limits, called the **staircase method** (Cornsweet, 1962), concentrates responses around the threshold. For the first trial, it is similar to the method of limits. However, once an estimate of the threshold is obtained, the staircase method never presents stimuli that are far from this estimate. This is shown in Table 6.3. As soon as the threshold estimate is crossed, the direction of stimulus intensity reverses. This improves the efficiency of the method by keeping the stimuli much closer to the threshold than is the case for the method of limits. The threshold is operationally defined as the mean value of all stimuli presented, starting with the second trial (column 2 in Table 6.3).

The staircase version of the method of limits was used to determine whether wine experts have more acute sensitivity to odors than do wine novices (Parr, Heatherbell,

▼ **TABLE 6.3**

Using the Staircase Method to Determine an Absolute Threshold.

Stimulus Intensity	Response			
	↓			
180	Yes			
160	Yes			
140	Yes	Yes	↓	Yes
120	Yes	No	No	↑
100	Yes	No		
80	No	↑		
	Threshold = 124			

& White, 2002). Novices and experts had to differentiate the smell of various concentrations of butanol, which has a fruity smell, from distilled water. Parr and associates found that wine experts and wine novices had nearly identical difference thresholds. Using other procedures, on the other hand, the researchers found that experts could recognize wine-related odors better than novices.

No Thresholds: The Theory of Signal Detection

According to the **theory of signal detection,** our perception in general is controlled by evidence and decision processes. A signal or stimulus creates (hypothetical) evidence that depends on the intensity of the signal and the acuity of the observer, which partly determine a "yes" response. There are other determiners of a decision to say "yes, there is a stimulus present," including factors that influence the willingness of the observer to say a signal is present. These response-bias influences include the payoff for being accurate, the frequency of the signal, and so on. Figure 6.3 shows the decision process is influenced by both the evidence and response biases (Pastore, Crawley, Berens, & Skelly, 2003).

Any decision you make depends on the costs and benefits associated with it. Imagine that a friend has set up a blind date for you. The costs (a wasted evening) are probably less than the possible benefits (an exciting evening now and more exciting evenings in the future); many of us would accept a blind date, even though we knew nothing about the person we would be dating. So you might be likely to respond "yes." This decision would be based mostly on costs and benefits, since you would lack information about the stimulus (the person who is your date).

Now let us imagine a situation in which costs are high: accepting or offering a proposal of marriage. Even those of us who are eager to accept a blind date would not

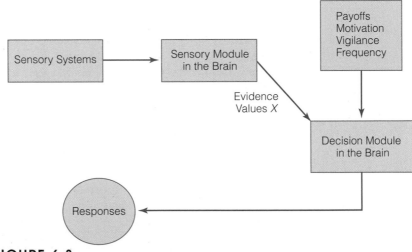

▼ **FIGURE 6.3**

A Theoretical Look at What Happens in Signal Detection. Sensory analysis sends evidence values (X) to the decision module. The values of X are a function of signal strength and the acuity of the observer. The payoffs, motivation, and attention processes send response bias information to the decision module. Together, the sensory and bias components determine the response of the observer. The X evidence values are on the abscissa of Figures 6.4 and 6.5. The payoffs and so on determine the position of the criterion.

get married if we were offered only the information that was needed to help us decide whether to go on a blind date. The costs of an unsatisfactory marriage are much greater than those of a blind date that does not pan out. In terms of decision theory, most of us are conservative decision makers when considering marriage but liberal decision makers when considering a blind date. This response bias does not depend on the stimulus—indeed, the same person could be involved in both instances—but only on the costs and benefits of the decision.

Now, we can return to the sensory end (beginning) of signal detection. The sensory process transmits a value to the decision process. If this value is high, the decision process is more likely to yield a "yes" response once costs and benefits have been considered. If this value is low, the decision process is more likely to yield a "no" response, even if costs and benefits favor a "yes" decision. What determines the value sent by the sensory process?

Signal-detection theory assumes that **noise,** a disturbance that can be confused with signals, is always present when a human attempts to detect signals. This background disturbance is owing to such things as environmental changes, equipment changes, spontaneous neural activity, and direct experimental manipulations. Just to make sure that the assumption that noise is present during attempts at detection, a typical signal-detection experiment will present white noise—a hissing sound such as that heard when you tune your television to an unoccupied channel—along with the signal. Noise can be auditory or visual or can occur in any modality; we consider only the auditory system for now.

To illustrate the detection of signals sent by the sensory process, we will examine a typical experiment on signal detection. Imagine you are sitting in a soundproof booth, wearing headphones. On each of several hundred trials, you must decide whether you hear a faint tone combined with the white noise or only the white noise by itself. A trial might begin by the presentation of a flashing light, which tells you to get ready for the test stimulus. Then you will hear a burst of white noise, which may or may not contain the faint tone signal. You say "yes" if you think a tone signal was present and "no" if you think just noise was present. Signal-detection theory assumes that any stimulus, even noise, produces distribution of evidence. The evidence on each trial is only one point, and the distributions are built up from many trials, each occurring at a different point in time (see the discussion of distributions in Appendix B). Since evidence cannot be directly observed, the distributions for stimulus trials and for noise trials are hypothetical. The evidence arising from a trial for which only noise occurred will tend to be small, so that over many trials, a (hypothetical) distribution with a small mean will be established. When a signal plus noise is presented, the evidence will be larger, so that a distribution with a greater mean will be formed over many trials.

Repeated trials generate two distributions—one for noise only and one for the signal plus noise—as shown in Figure 6.4. Since the two distributions overlap in the middle, some values of evidence are ambiguous, because they could have occurred as a result of either noise or the signal. Of course, if the two distributions were far enough apart, this problem would be minimized—but even in the laboratory, life is usually not that simple.

A criterion, shown as a vertical line in Figure 6.5, must be set to determine whether a response will be "yes" or "no." The position of this **criterion** is set by the decision process. If costs and benefits favor a liberal decision policy, the criterion will be set far to the left, so that most responses will be "yes." If a conservative policy is used, the criterion moves to the right, so that most responses will be "no." In either case,

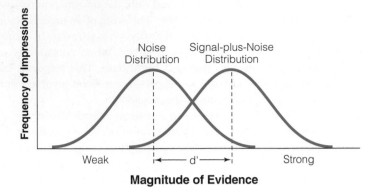

▼ **FIGURE 6.4**

Hypothetical Distributions of the Evidence Resulting from Noise and Signal Plus Noise. The frequency of the impressions is the *Y*-axis and the magnitude of evidence is the *X*-axis. The strength of the signal and the sensory acuity of the observer determine the amount of overlap of the two distributions. A stronger signal or a more sensitive observer would move the signal-plus-noise distribution to the right (toward the strong end of the *X*-axis). The dashed vertical lines are the mean (average) of each distribution, and the distance between the two means is called d'.

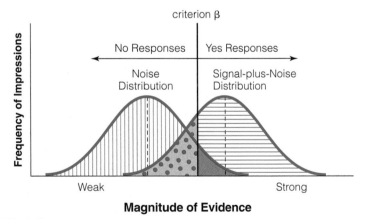

▼ **FIGURE 6.5**

Hypothetical Distributions of "Yes" or "No" Responses as a Function of the Criterion and the Magnitude of the Evidence. The decision criterion (β) determines whether a "yes" or "no" response will be made. Strong evidence to the right of the criterion will lead to "yes" responses, and weak evidence to the left will lead to "no" responses. Correct detection of the signal ("yes" responses in the horizontally striped area) are called hits. Correct "no" responses when noise occurs (the vertically striped portion) are called correct rejections. Misses occur when a "no" response occurs to weak signals to the left of the criterion (the dotted portion of the signal-plus-noise distribution). False alarms are incorrect "yes" responses to noise that is to the right of the criterion (the black portion of the noise distribution).

some errors will be made. As shown in Figure 6.5, correctly detecting a signal when it is presented is called a **hit.** Incorrectly responding "yes" when only noise is presented is called a **false alarm.** With a liberal decision strategy—criterion set to the left—the number of hits will be high; but since there are numerous "yes" responses, the number of false alarms will also be high. (If someone said "yes" on every trial, both the hit rate and the false alarm rate would be 100 percent.) With a conservative decision strategy, false alarms will be low—but so will hits. (If someone said "no" on every trial, the false alarm rate would be 0 percent, as would the hit rate.)

If we plot hits as a function of false alarms, as the criterion moves from conservative to liberal, we get the representation depicted in Figure 6.6.

This figure is called a **receiver-operating characteristic** (or ROC) function. Both hits and false alarms are infrequent (conservative criterion) at the lower left of the curve. As the criterion becomes more liberal, both hits and false alarms become more likely, and the ROC curve moves upward to the right. The slope of the ROC function tells us the criterion. Flat slopes reveal a liberal decision criterion (generally, the upper right of the curve) and steep slopes a conservative criterion (usually, the lower left of the curve).

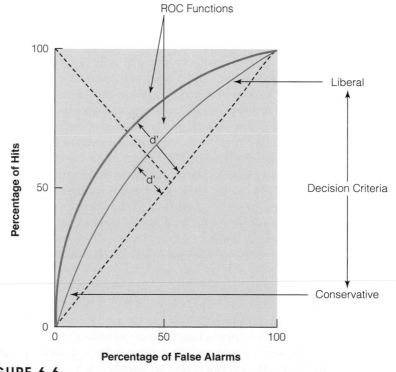

▼ FIGURE 6.6

ROC Functions. The distance from the diagonal to the center of the curve is proportional to d'. The diagonal represents chance performance, with the observer guessing about the presence or absence of a signal. Thus, the percentage of hits equals the percentage of false alarms along this "guessing" diagonal. The heavy ROC function is farther away from the diagonal than is the lighter ROC function, which means that d' is greater for the heavy curve than for the light one. A larger d' can result from a stronger signal or a more acute observer.

The slope of curves such as the ROC function is determined by the slope of a line that is drawn tangent to a particular point on the function and intersects one of the axes of the graph. There are tables, such as Table A of Appendix C, that contain values of the criterion. The distance from the diagonal to the ROC curve tells us how far apart the noise and signal-plus-noise distributions of Figure 6.4 lie. When the two distributions are far apart, indicating either a more discernible signal or a more acute observer, the ROC curve moves upward to the left, away from the diagonal, as shown by the heavy ROC function in Figure 6.6. When the signal is less detectable or when the observer is less acute and the two distributions are close together, the ROC curve moves closer to the diagonal. Thus, the ROC function tells us about both the sensory process (d', distance between signal-plus-noise and noise-only distributions) and the decision process (β, the slope). Since a single experimental condition generates only a single point on the ROC curve, many conditions are needed to alter the hit and false-alarm rates. Usually, hit and false-alarm rates are manipulated by altering the payoff associated with them (see Figure 6.10 later in this chapter). (If a hit were worth 2 dollars and a false alarm penalized you 50 cents, would you be more liberal or more conservative than if a hit were valued at 50 cents and a false alarm penalized you 2 dollars?)

Another way to manipulate the rate of hits and false alarms is to vary how often the signal occurs (see Figure 6.10 later). If, over a series of trials, a signal had occurred 90 percent of the time, you would be more likely to say "yes" on any trial than when the signal had occurred very infrequently on the previous trials.

By now, you may be wondering what all this has to do with thresholds. Nowhere does the ROC curve have a label that reads "threshold." Whether an observer will respond "yes" or "no" depends on the evidence and the decision criterion. Signal intensity may be held constant, but since there are varying payoffs for hits and false alarms, you can generate an ROC curve showing d' (sensitivity) and the slope of the curve at various points. There is no operational definition of a threshold. Instead, two quantities are operationally defined. The sensitivity of the observer is called **d'** and is defined as the distance between signal and noise distributions in Figure 6.4 or as the maximum distance between the ROC curve and the diagonal in Figure 6.6. The criterion of the decision processes is called **beta** (β) and is the slope of the ROC function at the point of interest—for example, a hit rate of 55 percent.

So, what is a threshold? As shown in Figure 6.4, signal-detection theory supposes that the evidence of a stimulus is a continuous distribution that takes on a zero value only when the stimulus intensity itself is zero. We do not have a threshold that splits the stimulus dimension into detectable and undetectable components, as classical psychophysics would lead us to believe. Rather, a stimulus must yield a sensation that exceeds the decision criterion (β) in order for a person to report having detected a weak stimulus (Figure 6.5). In a sense, then, the notion of an absolute threshold as determined by a stimulus of a particular intensity has been denied by signal-detection theory. What we have left, as D'Amato (1970) suggests, is a response or **decision threshold.** Only when a stimulus yields evidence that exceeds the decision threshold, what we have been calling β or the criterion, do we have correct detection of the signal. Of course, d' determines the detectability of the signal but not necessarily what the subject reports. This means that detecting and reporting the presence of a signal are determined by d' and β; together, these two quantities determine what a classical psychophysicist would call a threshold.

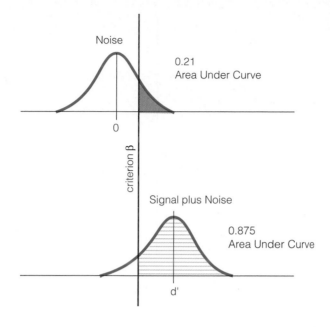

▼ FIGURE 6.7

Calculating d' on the basis of false alarms (blue area under the noise distribution curve) and hits (horizontally striped area under signal-plus-noise distribution curve).

Calculating d'.   Given a set of data, we can easily calculate d' by using tables based on the area under the normal curve (see Table A in Appendix C). Suppose you know that the hit rate is 0.875 and the false-alarm rate is 0.21. What is d'? First, draw the noise distribution, as in Figure 6.7. Since the false-alarm rate represents the area under the curve from the criterion to plus infinity on the right, it equals 0.21. Since the normal curve is symmetrical, half of its area (0.5) lies between zero and plus infinity. Therefore, the area between zero and the criterion must be 0.52 − 0.21, which equals 0.29. Now look up 0.29 in Table A of Appendix C. You will find that z = 0.8. This is the normalized distance of the criterion from zero.

Second, repeat this process for the signal distribution shown at the bottom of Figure 6.7. Since the hit rate is 0.875, this is the area under the curve from the criterion to plus infinity. Again, because of symmetry, half the area under the curve (0.5) is between d' and plus infinity. Therefore, the area between the criterion and d' is 0.875 − 0.5, which equals 0.375. Consulting Table A of Appendix C, we find that an area of 0.375 corresponds to a z of about 1.15.

We can now put these two z values together to find d' (Figure 6.8). Since the mean of the noise distribution is given the value of zero, d' is the sum of the two z values: 0.8 + 1.15 = 1.95. Our calculation of d' is now complete. Obviously, then, the larger the d', the greater the distance between the means of the two distributions. Therefore, a large d' indicates either a strong signal or an acute observer.

Advantage of signal-detection methods.   A major advantage of signal-detection methods over a classical psychophysical procedure, such as the method of limits, is the ability to measure both sensitivity and response bias. In many areas of applied psychology, the ability to distinguish between these two processes is very important. Let us return to the problem of measuring the effectiveness of analgesics.

In a large number of experiments, Hardy, Wolff, and Goodell (1952) examined people's reactions to radiant heat presented to their forearms by a piece of equipment

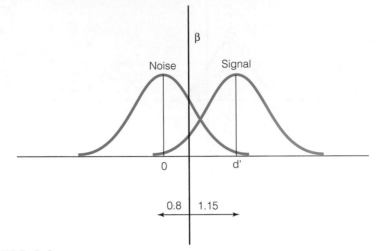

▼ FIGURE 6.8

Calculating d': the sum of the two z values yields d' . d' = 0.8 + 1.15 = 1.95.

similar to a hair dryer, called a dolorimeter. A small spot of stimulation was presented at various intensities (usually defined in terms of calories per unit area stimulated, rather than in terms of a temperature scale). The researchers' approach was to determine the intensity of heat necessary for a person to report pain—first without an analgesic such as aspirin and then when aspirin had been taken prior to the presentation of heat. An increase in the intensity needed to elicit pain after the subjects had taken aspirin would indicate that aspirin had analgesic properties. Indeed, this is what Hardy and associates found. Or, at least, that is what they observed when they used highly experienced subjects (themselves) in the experiment. Much to their surprise, when they tested naive subjects (eighty military recruits, in this case), they found that for more than half of their subjects, the heat intensity required to evoke pain actually went *down* following the ingestion of aspirin.

Hardy and associates (1952) used the method of limits to determine the absolute threshold of pain and changes in such thresholds resulting from a supposed analgesic, such as aspirin. Among other things, they found that aspirin elevated pain thresholds more consistently in trained observers than in naive ones, and they noted that various kinds of suggestion would alter pain thresholds. For example, thresholds were raised more when people believed they had taken an analgesic than when they did not believe so. Furthermore, Hardy and his associates showed that this suggestion elevated thresholds both when people took a real analgesic (say, aspirin) and when they took a **placebo** (inert) pill (see Chapter 13 for a discussion of the placebo effect). Is this result owing to a change in sensitivity (d'), or is there a change in the decision criterion (β)?

To determine how analgesics worked, Clark and coworkers (Clark, 1969; Clark & Yang, 1974) conducted a number of experiments on pain analgesia. Rather than using the method of limits, Clark used a signal-detection procedure so that both changes in sensitivity and decision processes could be assessed. In these experiments, a dolorimeter was used to evoke pain by means of thermal stimulation.

Initially, Clark found that analgesics such as aspirin reduced d', which means that the drug lowered the acuity of the sensory system with the outcome being that the aspirin reduced the ability of people to distinguish between painful and nonpainful stimuli. Clark then investigated whether placebos and acupuncture (a Chinese medical procedure of inserting needles into the skin, which is sometimes used to reduce surgically induced pain and has other medical uses) altered d' (reduced sensitivity) or whether placebos and acupuncture changed the willingness of the subjects to report pain. In both experiments, Clark found that placebos and acupuncture reduced the reports of pain and the number of times that the subjects attempted to withdraw from the painful stimuli. Did these procedures induce analgesia for pain? No; in both experiments, d' was unaffected by the manipulation. What happened was that acupuncture and placebos elevated the subjects' decision criterion, so that stronger stimuli than before were required to elicit a detection response. This does not mean that placebos and acupuncture do not work; following an acupuncture treatment or the ingestion of a placebo, people report less pain. What Clark's results do show is the way in which these procedures work to alleviate pain. They do not deaden the sensory systems; rather, they change the decision threshold for reporting that pain has been experienced.

Let us return briefly to the work by Hardy and associates (1952). Using the method of limits, they found that suggestion altered the absolute threshold. Given the signal-detection results found by Clark, it is reasonable to suppose that suggestion changed the absolute threshold determined by the method of limits by altering the decision criterion of the subjects. How are we to account for the fact that trained observers—but not naive ones—have higher pain thresholds following the ingestion of aspirin? Why do most naive observers have a lower pain threshold? We could guess that this too is a criterion shift, owing to the fact that the trained observers know all about the experiment and the supposed effects of aspirin, whereas the naive subjects are nervous after taking a drug and are more likely to report pain. In the absence of doing a signal-detection analysis, however, we can only speculate about the data. An enigma in the literature on pain relief could be cleared up with an appropriately conducted signal-detection experiment.

6.2 EXPERIMENTAL TOPICS AND RESEARCH ILLUSTRATIONS

Topic   *Measurement Scales*
Illustration   *Fechner's Law and Stevens' Law*

It is a dictum in psychophysics that anything that exists, be it the intensity of painful feelings or your attitude toward spinach, exists in some amount. Anything that exists in some amount can be measured. **Measurement** is a systematic way of assigning numbers or names to objects and their attributes. When we assign names or numbers to objects and their attributes, we need a measurement scale, which results from different measurement operations. When we measure temperature, for example, we usually use either the Fahrenheit scale or the centigrade scale. These two temperature scales are inappropriate for measuring weight, which can be measured in pounds or kilograms. As we will see, the different measurement operations yield scales that differ in the information that they provide.

Properties of Measurement Scales

Measurement scales can have four properties (McCall, 1990), and the combination of these properties determines what is measured. All measurement scales have instances that are different from each other. This fundamental property, **difference,** means that some temperatures are colder (or warmer) than others, some people are male and some female, and so on. The other scale properties are not universal. Some scales can determine the **magnitude** of attributes, which means that the scale can show that one attribute is greater than, less than, or equal to another instance of that attribute. Another property of attributes that some scales can determine is whether there are **equal intervals** between magnitudes. A 1-pound difference between two weights is the same when considering both 1 versus 2 pounds and 70 versus 71 pounds. A final property of some measurement scales is a **true zero** point on the scale, meaning that zero on the scale indicates that nothing of the attribute being measured exists. You cannot have less than zero weight—it has a true zero point of no weight—but you can have less than zero degrees centigrade.

Types of Measurement Scales

Psychologists use four measurement scales: nominal, ordinal, interval, and ratio. These scales are defined by which of the four properties of measurement scales they possess. **Nominal scales** measure just the property of difference and nothing else. **Ordinal scales** measure differences and magnitudes. **Interval scales** possess the properties of difference, magnitude, and equal intervals. **Ratio scales** have all four properties of measurement scales (difference, magnitude, equal interval, and a meaningful zero).

Nominal scales include zip codes, gender (male and female), and undergraduate major programs. Each of these scales classifies people in some way, but they do not measure magnitudes in any obvious way. Thus, useful statistics, such as the arithmetic average, cannot be used to characterize nominal measures. Even assigning arbitrary numbers to major programs (business = 1, psychology = 2, and so on) would not legitimize the "average" major at an institution. You could, however, determine the total number of people who major in each program.

Ordinal scales include a variety of ranked measures such as how nervous people are on a 10-point scale (from 1 = not at all nervous to 10 = extremely nervous), the placement in a beauty contest, or the finishing order in a horse race. Where you finish in a beauty contest tells the magnitude of beauty, but it reveals little about the intervals between the ranks. The top two finishers might be very close to each other, but the fifth and sixth could be very far apart from each other. Averaging numbers with unequal intervals is not legitimate. Nominal and ordinal numbers have special statistics (*nonparametric statistics*, described in the statistical appendix) that should be used with them.

Interval and ratio scales allow you to perform most mathematical operations on them, and ordinary inferential statistics (see appendix for *parametric statistics*) can be used on attributes measured at these levels. Most IQ measures and SAT scores are examples of interval scales, because adjacent values have equal intervals across the entire scale. The 10 units of difference between an IQ of 90 and an IQ of 100 is supposed to be the same as the 10 units of difference separating IQ scores of 110 and 120. Neither the IQ nor the SAT has a true zero point, so they are not ratio scales. Measures such as response speed and percentage correct are ratio measures, because you can exhibit zero speed or no correct responses.

You should note that the measurement scale derives from the measuring procedure, not necessarily from the nature of the attributes being measured. Temperature measured by the Kelvin scale has a true zero and is a ratio measure. The Fahrenheit and centigrade scales, however, do not have a true zero (these scales have no point for the absence of temperature), so they are interval scales. If we simply say that one thing is hotter than another, we are measuring at the ordinal level. Finally, calling one thing "hot" and another "cold" is measuring temperature at the nominal level.

Importance of Measurement Scales

Behavioral data derived from different scales tell us different things, and the kinds of conclusions we can draw depend, in part, on the scale that we use. Because a ratio scale has four measurement properties and nominal scales only one, we have more information about something, say depression, if it is measured at the ratio level than if it is measured at the nominal level. The information provided by the scale permits certain kinds of conclusions. If pain were assessed on an ordinal scale, it would be improper to say that a person with a pain score of 8 on the scale perceives twice as much pain as someone with a pain score of 4. To make such a statement, we would have to measure pain on a scale that has a meaningful zero point and equal intervals between adjacent score values (a ratio scale). The type of measurement scale can determine the amount of information you have about an attribute, and the type of scale determines, in part, the conclusions that we can draw.

We now examine two approaches toward the measurement of sensation. Both approaches have the goal of devising a ratio scale of an internal psychological dimension. The first approach is Fechner's, and it involved a reliance on the results of classical psychophysical methods to provide the data for the psychophysical scale. The second approach is a more modern one that was developed by S. S. Stevens.

Fechner's Law

Fechner relied on the psychophysical research done by Weber to try to develop a measurement scale for sensations. According to Weber's law, the difference threshold bears a constant relation to the standard stimulus: $\Delta I/I = K$. Fechner assumed that Weber's law was correct and, with two additional assumptions, developed his own law of sensation measurement. Fechner first assumed that the absolute threshold indicates the point of zero sensation. He then assumed that the **just-noticeable difference** (JND), which is the internal sensation evoked by two stimuli that differ by one difference threshold, is the unit defining the intervals of an internal psychological scale. Because Weber's law was assumed to be accurate, Fechner believed that all JNDs produce equal increments in sensation, as shown in Figure 6.9. Each JND step on the psychological scale corresponds to the physical stimulus that is one difference threshold greater than the preceding stimulus. The first unit beyond the zero point corresponds to the physical stimulus that is one JND above the absolute threshold. The next point will be one JND above that, or two JNDs above the absolute threshold.

This process can be continued to build a psychological scale. Once this is done, there is a fixed mathematical relationship between the value of the physical scale corresponding to some point on the psychological scale and the physical value corresponding to the preceding point on the internal psychological scale. To find the physical scale value that corresponds to a particular psychological value, we first take the physical value of the previous step on the external scale (e.g., X in Figure 6.9) and multiply it by the Weber fraction. We then add this product to our original value, so that $Y = X +$ the product of X times the Weber fraction in Figure 6.9 (likewise, $Z = Y +$ the product of Y times the Weber fraction). Summing in this fashion yields successive physical values that correspond to successive JNDs on the internal psychological scale. When this

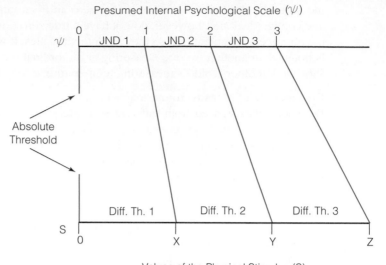

▼ FIGURE 6.9

Fechner's Law. Equal units on an internal psychological scale correspond to progressively greater units on an external physical scale (the difference thresholds): $\psi = K \log (S)$.

relationship is expanded and solved mathematically, we find that the psychological scale value **(ψ)** is proportional to the logarithm of the physical-stimulus value. This equation **($\psi = K$ log Stimulus)** is called **Fechner's law.**

According to Fechner's law, all JNDs produce equivalent increments in sensation; therefore, it appears that we have a ratio scale (D'Amato, 1970). The sensation corresponding to six JNDs should be twice the sensation of three JNDs. Two factors we have already discussed should lead you to question whether Fechner has actually devised a ratio scale of sensation. First, Fechner's zero point is arbitrary rather than absolute. The absolute threshold is defined statistically and includes many sensations that do not exceed the decision criterion (see the discussion on thresholds and signal detection). Second, we know that Weber's law is only approximately true; this could result in psychological and physical units of varying sizes. There is an additional difficulty with Fechner's formulation. Fechner assumed that each JND was psychologically equal, but if you ask people about the magnitude of the sensory effects produced by stimuli of varying JNDs above threshold, there is poor correspondence between the two (D'Amato, 1970). Thus, Fechner's work is neither a ratio scale nor an interval scale. At best, it is an ordinal scale indicating that sensations are ordered in a particular way with regard to the physical stimuli that produce them.

Stevens' Power Law

S. S. Stevens (1961) attempted to develop an internal scale of sensation more directly than did Fechner. Fechner used an **indirect scaling** method, in which the psychological scale was built up by putting successive JNDs in a row. The observers did not judge the magnitudes of the JNDs directly, so the psychological scale values are derived from measures of discrimination; therefore, they are indirect. Stevens used several **direct scaling** techniques, in which the observer responded in psychological scale units in the first place.

The primary direct scaling procedure used by Stevens was the method of **magnitude estimation,** which requires the observer to state a number that represents his or her sensation of the stimulus intensity. The first stimulus that the experimenter presents is arbitrarily assigned some convenient number, say, 100. Then other stimuli are assigned numbers, depending on how close the perceived intensity is to the first stimulus. For example, the experimenter could present a tone of moderate intensity and tell you it has a value of 100. Then a weaker tone might be presented, so you would give it a lower number, say, 87. These numbers reported by the observer represent perceived psychological values directly. When data are gathered in this way, the equation relating psychological value to physical value differs from the logarithmic relationship of Fechner's law. Instead, the equation obtained by Stevens (1961) is $\psi = K \text{ (Stimulus)}^n$, where n is an exponent. This equation is called **Stevens' law.**

The method of magnitude estimation is not limited to psychological scales that have a physical correlate. Essay exams are often graded by this method. Similarly, legal penalties, severity of crimes, works of art, and so forth, can be scaled by magnitude estimation.

If we assume that a stimulus of zero intensity always produces zero sensation (that is, there are no false alarms), then we can accept Stevens' law as a ratio psychological scale. With a true zero, and with equal stimulus ratios producing equal sensation ratios (a power relation), we have satisfied the criteria for a ratio scale. If this is the case, then it seems reasonable to accept $\psi = K S^n$ as the way in which our internal sensations are related to the external world.

Stevens' law has not escaped criticism. Is the law about sensations or about numbers? Different people use numbers differently. Some observers always produce very large exponents for Stevens' law, and Marks (1974) found that the law varies with the range of numbers used by observers. Bartoshuk (2000) showed that using a small range of numbers constricts a psychophysical scale. This constriction masks differences in judgments especially at very high stimulus values (this scale attenuation is equivalent to the ceiling effect described in Chapter 10).

To minimize idiosyncratic differences in the range of numbers used in psychophysical tasks and also prevent constriction, Bartoshuk and other sensory psychologists use a 100-point ratio scale procedure. Green, Shaffer, and Gilmore (1993) devised the **labeled magnitude scale**, which pairs numbers bounded by 0 and 100 with verbal labels. It starts at a zero value, which is labeled as *nothing*, and progresses through numbered labels of *moderate, strong, very strong,* and at the top of the scale (100 units) is the label *strongest imaginable sensation.* Thus, all observers have the same vocabulary and the same range of units to describe their sensations. Using this scale, Bartoshuk (2000) was able to identify *supertasters*, whose taste anatomy leads them to have extremely intense taste sensations. For example, supertasters feel much more heat from hot peppers and also react more to the creaminess of foods than do ordinary tasters.

Another concern with magnitude estimation relates to operational definitions. Many studies reveal that a particular sensory scale, such as brightness, has more than one scale that characterizes it. Marks (1974) notes that you can accurately describe a power function for brightness only if you specify all the variables relevant to the perception of brightness—the color and duration of the light, the sensory adaptation of the observer, and so on. Varying the latter factors changes the value of the exponent in Stevens' law. Thus, we must operationally define the psychophysical function or risk misrepresenting the relation between sensation and stimulus.

6.3   EXPERIMENTAL TOPICS AND RESEARCH ILLUSTRATIONS

Topic   *Small-n Design*
Illustration   *Psychophysical Methods*

The typical experiment in psychology measures the behavior of a large number of participants. One reason for this setup is that research participants differ substantially from one another in various complex psychological characteristics, such as personality and IQ. Furthermore, the setting in which these complex behaviors are measured may be poorly controlled. Both these problems can be handled by random assignment of large numbers of participants to the conditions. This may reduce the possibility that uncontrolled variation in people and setting will be associated with a particular treatment, which would then allow the effects of the independent variable to be observed. Since most psychophysical experiments involve somewhat less complex psychological processes that are studied in well-controlled settings, fewer subjects are often used. Psychophysical research often relies on small-*n* designs, in which a large number of tightly controlled observations are made on a small number of observers. Other areas of psychology, in particular learning, also use small-*n* designs for similar reasons (see Chapter 9).

An example of small-*n* research is shown in the two panels of Figure 6.10, where a single observer generated both ROC functions. Data in panel A were obtained by varying signal probability from low to high relative to the occurrence of noise-only trials. The observer is conservative when signal probability is low, but as signal probability increases, the observer becomes more liberal with "yes" responses. This change in decision criterion sweeps out the ROC function starting from the lower left (conservative) and moving along the curve to the upper right (liberal). In panel B, the experimenter kept the signal probability constant and varied the payoff. When the cost of false alarms is high relative

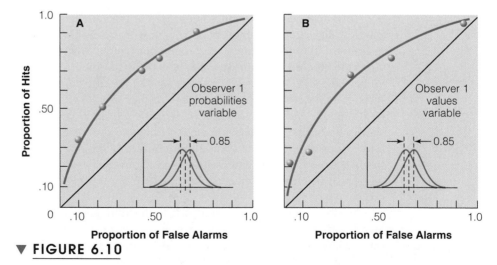

▼ **FIGURE 6.10**

ROC Graphs from the Same Observer. In panel (a) the probability that a signal occurred was varied, and in panel (b) the payoffs for hits and the costs of false alarms varied. The insert shows the hypothetical noise and sign-plus-noise distributions. The curves were fitted to the open-circle data points with $d' = 0.85$. Notice the fit to the data points and similarity in shape of the two curves. (Data from Green and Swets, 1966.)

to the payoff for hits (at the lower left), the observer is conservative. As the relative payoff for hits increases (moving toward the upper right), the observer adopts a liberal decision criterion and becomes more willing to say "yes," there is a signal.

Both ROC curves are well fitted by a d' = 0.85 (see the insert in each panel). Such a close fit to the data points (the open circles) is very impressive, because the two functions were generated by varying the decision criterion in different ways. The extreme similarity of the two curves illustrates a high degree of experimental control over the behavior of a single observer who participated in thousands of trials. As we will see, the highly reliable results of signal-detection experiments help us understand a number of important psychological phenomena.

There is another, important reason for using small-n designs. Many experiments require special participants, such as specialists in radiology (interpreting X-rays), who are scarce relative to the large numbers of undergraduates that typically are used in experiments. Thus, a psychophysical experiment on what data are used by experts to detect breast cancer might include six mammography specialists (e.g., Swets, Dawes, & Monahan, 2000). The ROC curve labeled "Standard" in Figure 6.11 (adapted from Swets et al., 2000) was produced by the behavior of five general radiologists who interpreted in their usual way 118 mammograms, half of which contained malignancies. Each X-ray was rated on a rating scale for the likelihood of containing cancer, which generated the data points (circles) in the figure. Low probability estimates of malignancy are represented on the lower left, high estimates on the upper right. With little likelihood of cancer, there were few false alarms, because the radiologist is conservative. Hits and false alarms both increase as the radiologists say "yes" more often to the increasing evidence that cancer is present. The upper ROC curve ("Enhanced") was generated on the same mammograms months later when the radiologists had available to them a checklist of features that specialists in mammography had developed. Note that the enhanced curve is farther from the diagonal, indicating greater sensitivity, and the data indicate a 13 percent increase in hits and a 12 percent decrease in false alarms. The

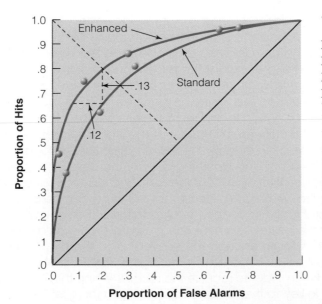

▼ **FIGURE 6.11**

ROC Graph of General Radiologists' Reading of Mammograms that Did Not Contain Malignancies. The lower ROC curve is the baseline, and the upper curve was generated when radiologists used a checklist of features developed by mammography experts. The figure is adapted from Swets, Dawes, and Monahan (2000), and used with permission of the Blackwell Publishing, Ltd.

regularity of the psychophysical data and their enhancement shows the usefulness of such methods in applied setting.

Using experts to help improve the detection of cancer by general radiologists is one example of using **statistical prediction rules** to increase the accuracy of decisions. The statistical prediction rules are based on predictor variables and diagnostic information that can be consulted during detection decisions of various kinds. Swets and associates (2000) report on studies using prediction rules to aid in detection in a variety of situations in which low hit rates might be dangerous or fatal. These include diagnosing prostate cancer, predicting violence in released prisoners, and enhancing the detection of finding cracks in airplane wings.

FROM PROBLEM TO EXPERIMENT
THE NUTS AND BOLTS

Problem   *Do pigeons have visual thresholds?*

Problem   *How can we measure a pigeon's visual threshold?*

Since this problem is based more on methodology than on content, we do not require much in the way of a formal hypothesis. Content issues would arise when the feasibility of measuring a pigeon's visual threshold was first established. Primarily for the sake of completeness, we offer the following hypothesis.

Hypothesis   *Pigeons are sensitive to different intensities of light, and their absolute thresholds will be influenced by variables that influence human thresholds, such as the wavelength (color) of the light and certain drugs.*

The first problem we must overcome is the fact that pigeons cannot talk. Therefore, we will put them into a conditioning chamber with two response keys to peck: one for "Yes, I see the light" and the other for "No, I don't see it." Our dependent variable is the absolute threshold as measured by the differential key pecks (see later discussion). Our independent variables are light intensity, light color, and the presence or absence of a drug. Control variables will include the conditioning chamber and the reward schedules used to maintain pecking. We want the pigeon to peck the Yes key when the light is visible and the No key when it is not, but we have no way of determining just from looking at the light whether it is visible to the pigeon.

Blough (1958, 1961) developed a way to get the pigeon to indicate the visibility of the light. He uses a variant of the staircase method to determine the absolute threshold. Pecks on the Yes key gradually reduce the intensity of the light, and pecks on the No key gradually increase it. Occasionally, pecks on the Yes key completely cut out the light, and subsequent pecks on the No key are rewarded with food. As Blough notes, this procedure can be described anthropomorphically as having the pigeon peck the Yes key to turn out the light and peck the No key to get the food reward. (You should note that these lights were never intense enough to be aversive to the pigeon.) What happens is that when the light is too dim for the pigeon to see, it switches from the Yes key to the No key in order to receive the reward. When the light is visible, it switches from the No key to the Yes key in order to dim the light.

Since the bird is shifting back and forth between keys in response to changes in intensity, we can determine the absolute threshold by taking the average of the intensities just prior to the switch from one key to the other. This is what is done to determine a human's absolute threshold with the staircase method. Blough reports that when the color of the light is varied, the pigeon's absolute threshold changes, just as the human absolute threshold changes. Furthermore, minute doses of LSD raise the absolute threshold of light—for both pigeons and humans.

▼ SUMMARY

1. Operational definitions that specify how concepts are produced and measured are required in science, both to make experiments more public and to increase the precision of technical terms beyond their use in ordinary conversation.

2. The method of limits, which was devised by Fechner, provides an operational definition for the concepts of absolute threshold and the difference threshold.

3. Classical psychophysics are primarily aimed at evaluating thresholds. The more modern theory of signal detection replaces the threshold concept with two other operationally defined concepts: d' and β.

4. Sensory processes are measured by d', and decision processes are measured by β. Both d' and β can be computed from ROC (receiver-operating characteristic) functions that plot hits against false alarms.

5. Measurement scales result when numbers or names are systematically assigned to objects or their attributes.

6. Measurement scales provide information to the extent that they measure differences, magnitudes, and equal intervals and have a true zero point.

7. In order of increasing informativeness, the measurement scales used in psychology are nominal, ordinal, interval, and ratio.

8. Fechner's law probably yields an ordinal scaling of psychological judgments. Stevens' law yields a ratio scale.

9. The labeled magnitude scale is a 0–100 scale with verbal labels for many numbers. The scale minimizes ceiling effects and minimizes idiosyncratic ranges of numbers used by different observers.

10. Because of the tight control and relative lack of complexity of the behavior, many psychophysical experiments use small-n designs that employ few subjects. Small-n designs are also used because of the scarcity of special types of observers, such as radiologists.

11. The ability to make accurate detection decisions can be improved by using statistical prediction rules that involve predictor variables and diagnostic information.

▼ KEY TERMS

absolute threshold
beta (β)
cold-pressor test
criterion
d'
decision threshold
difference
difference threshold

direct scaling
equal intervals
false alarm
Fechner's law ($\psi = K \log(S)$)
hit
indirect scaling
interval of uncertainty
interval scale

just-noticeable difference (JND)

psychophysical methods

labeled magnitude scale

psychophysics

magnitude

ratio scale

magnitude estimation

receiver-operating characteristic (ROC)

measurement

small-n designs

measurement scales

staircase method

method of limits

statistical prediction rules

noise

Stevens' law ($\psi = K S^n$)

nominal scale

theory of signal detection

operational definitions

threshold

ordinal scale

true zero

placebo

Weber's law ($\Delta I / I = K$)

point of subjective equality

▼ DISCUSSION QUESTIONS

1. Although the method of limits may not yield the best definition of sensory thresholds, it has many practical uses—especially for the determination of difference thresholds. The sensory effects of food flavorings are often determined this way. See if you can think of additional practical uses of the method of limits. A brief literature search in a journal such as *Ergonomics* may be of use.

2. Does either the method of limits or the staircase method offer a better operational definition of

the concept of a threshold—or are the two methods equivalent insofar as operational definition is concerned?

3. Calculate d' for the following pairs of hit and false-alarm rates: (0.90, 0.10), (0.90, 0.25), (0.90, 0.50), (0.90, 0.90).

4. What is the difference between an absolute threshold and a decision threshold?

5. Give two examples of each kind of measurement scale.

WEB CONNECTIONS

Original writings by Fechner can be found at:
        http://www.yorku.ca/dept/psych/classics/index.htm

Links to psychophysical resources are at:
        http://www.psy.ulaval.ca/~ispp/Library/links.html

PSYCHOLOGY IN ACTION
Weber's Law

This project examines Weber's law using a variant of the method of limits to calculate the difference threshold for heaviness. For this project, your apparatus and materials will be containers, some weights to put in the containers, and a scale. The containers could be drinking cups, aluminum cans, or milk cartons. You could use coins, sand, or a similar material for weight. To weigh your materials, a postal scale or a kitchen scale ought to be satisfactory. Use a moderate range of weights, say, from about 5 ounces to about 24 ounces.

A suggested procedure follows. Fill one container about one-eighth full and add slightly more to another. Ask a friend to lift them and tell you which weighs more. At first, your subject will tell you they are equal in weight. Keep adding material to the heavier container until your friend can tell which is heavier. Do not let your friend see you filling the heavier container, which should not always be lifted with the same hand.

Once the heavier container is determined, it becomes the new standard stimulus and you should make a new, slightly heavier comparison. Add material to a new container after each heaviness judgment by your friend until it is just noticeably heavier than the standard container. Keep on repeating this procedure with new comparison containers until the last container is almost completely filled. Now, weigh each of the containers, and note the differences in weight between adjacent containers.

You should find that adding a constant amount of material is not enough to produce a noticeable difference. Although x amount is sufficient to distinguish the first two containers, amounts greater than x are required to tell containers apart later in the series. You should find that a constant percentage of the weight of a container is required before the next container seems heavier. This percentage is called the Weber fraction.

Weber's law states: The difference threshold divided by the stimulus magnitude equals a constant ($\Delta I/I = K$). Weber's law usually does not hold for extreme values of stimulus magnitude. Thus, if you repeated your experiment with bricks or a small number of paper clips instead of objects weighing several ounces, you would not get results that follow Weber's law. The Weber fraction also differs for different individuals and for different tasks, such as judging line length instead of weight. You might try to verify these characteristics of Weber's law. ∎

PERCEPTION

Discovery consists of seeing what everybody has seen and thinking what nobody has thought. (ALBERT SZENT-GYÖRGY)

Imagine you are actually viewing the town of Ålesund, Norway, from the camera angle that yielded Figure 7.1 on page 182. In the standard way of conceptualizing the visual receptive process of such a scene, you first detect the presence of objects; then, this **sensation** provides the elements necessary for your **perception** of the town. According to this approach, perception is the interpretation and recognition of the objects and events that we sense. This simple and intuitively appealing theory of perception provides the background for most of the theoretical and methodological issues that confront psychologists interested in studying perception. (For additional details on the issues, see Coren, Ward, & Enns, 1994.)

▼ ISSUES IN PERCEPTION

One set of issues has to do with how the observer uses sensory information to make perceptual interpretations. Look again at Figure 7.1. If you were actually viewing Ålesund, you would perceive the mountains as farther away than the buildings in the foreground. This natural and unambiguous perception results from several cues that provide information about the distance and depth of objects in the scene. How do they enter into perception?

Direct and Indirect Perception

The **direct approach to perception** (Gibson, 1979) argues that the usually reliable cues in the optic array of a scene directly provide information about depth and distance. The direct view assumes that the perceiver picks up the information afforded by the environment naturally and without reflecting on them, which has led many to call this approach an *ecological* one (Norman, 2002). In contrast, the **indirect approach to perception** argues that our judgments of depth are made on the basis of our past experience with the depth cues (Gregory, 1970).

According to the indirect approach, we construct the scene to produce a perception of depth and distance. These perceptual processes have led some to call this the *constructivist approach* (Norman, 2002). The direct and indirect views of perception have been debated at least since the middle of the nineteenth century, when von Helmholtz (see von Helmholtz, 1962, for a modern translation) espoused an **empirical theory** of perception. He thought that all of our knowledge of visual perception resulted from our past visual experiences. When we are confronted with a new visual scene, such as that in Figure 7.1, we interpret it by inferring that the perspective cues we sense mean depth.

These **unconscious inferences,** as von Helmholtz called them, occur rapidly and without conscious thought—the inferences are a visual habit. The empirical theory is often contrasted with a version of direct perception called **nativistic theory.** According

▼ **FIGURE 7.1**

A view of the town of Ålesund, Norway.

to the nativistic view, the nature of the visual system (the eye and the brain) determines visual perception. One example of a nativistic approach to perception is Gestalt theory, which is discussed in Appendix A.

In contemporary cognitive psychology, the direct/indirect controversy is often described as a contrast between **bottom-up** and **top-down** perceptual processing. The bottom-up view emphasizes the role of sensory data in determining perception, and the top-down approach stresses the role of previously established concepts in determining perceptions. Because of these contrasts, you will also see the two aspects of perception labeled as a distinction between **data-driven processing** (the bottom-up emphasis) and **conceptually driven processing** (the top-down emphasis). With regard to the Ålesund photograph (Figure 7.1), the bottom-up analysis focuses on the gradient of texture that appears to recede into the distance toward the mountains in the background. Since this receding texture is a component of depth and distance in our three-dimensional world, we directly see the picture as containing depth. The indirect or top-down approach provides an alternative interpretation of your perception of Ålesund. The interpretation from the top-down position asserts that your perception of depth and distance in a *photograph* is an illusion.

An **illusion** is a mistaken or distorted perception. Why is your perception of these qualities in the Ålesund photograph an illusion? The small buildings near the top of the photograph could be miniature buildings, or they could be farther away than the large buildings at the bottom. However, in the photograph, both sets of buildings are equally distant from you (assuming that your eyes and the plane of the picture are parallel). On the basis of your past experience with small buildings being distant from you, you confer illusory depth cues to the two-dimensional photographic representation of Ålesund. This interpretation of depth leads to a three-dimensional percept. Since there is no real depth in the two-dimensional photograph, the depth and distance that we do perceive can be attributed to an indirect process resulting from our interpretation of the (illusory) cues in the scene.

Most perceptions involve a complex interplay between direct and indirect factors (or bottom-up and top-down processes), and many contemporary theories emphasize that interplay. For example, Norman (2002) suggests that rather than assuming they represent completely different types of perception, it may make sense to consider direct and indirect processes as working together to result in perceptual experience. We will later see a particular example of how this may work.

Awareness and Perception

If the perceiver adds meaning and interpretation to sensations, the question arises as to whether these additions result from conscious deliberation. The controversial topic in perception that we emphasize in this chapter concerns the role of conscious **aware-ness** in perception. The gist of the awareness issue is this question: Can meanings and interpretations be applied to sense data automatically, without our being verbally aware of them, or is verbal awareness a necessary part of perception? Von Helmholtz, you will remember, argued that our inferences and conclusions are unconscious.

However, perception has to do with one's experience of an event, and much research on perception has attempted to understand the nature of this phenomenal experience (Kaufman, 1974). After all, the argument goes, if perception includes an experience or a feeling of "something," then we must be consciously aware of that "something." A substantial amount of research is being undertaken to determine the relation between conscious awareness and perception. As you might expect, studying a private process such as consciousness (see Appendix A) is fraught with numerous methodological problems. We examine some of these problems in this chapter. To set the stage for our examination, we first consider a remarkable neuropsychological case study, the patient D. B.

Blindsight: Detection without Awareness   D. B. is an Englishman in his early 50s. Except for the particular neuropsychological problem that he has, D. B.'s life (medically, socially, and psychologically) can be described as ordinary or typical. What follows is a précis of a detailed case study resulting from an intensive examination of D. B. over a 13-year period (Weiskrantz, 1986). The study was restarted recently (Weiskrantz, 2002).

When D. B. was about 14, he began to experience violent headaches every 6 weeks or so, accompanied by a temporary oval of blindness in the left portion of his visual field. In his early 20s, the attacks increased in frequency, and a partial blindness remained permanently after one of the headache attacks. An angiogram, which is an X-ray picture of the head taken after an opaque substance has been injected into the bloodstream, revealed a mass of enlarged blood vessels at the tip of the visual cortex on the right side of the brain. This visual part of the brain and the distorted blood vessels were removed surgically. Immediately, his headache attacks stopped, and D. B. was able to lead a reasonably normal, productive life. However, after the operation, D. B. was blind in the left half of his visual field.

The reason that D. B. was blind in the left half of his visual field can be determined from Figure 7.2. The right visual cortex contains the information in the left visual field,

▼ **FIGURE 7.2**

A simplified top view of the eyes and brain showing how the right and left visual fields are represented in the visual cortex at the back of the brain. The left visual field is represented in the right visual cortex, and the right visual field is represented in the left visual cortex. Because the site of D. B.'s operation was in the right visual cortex, he was blind in the left visual field.

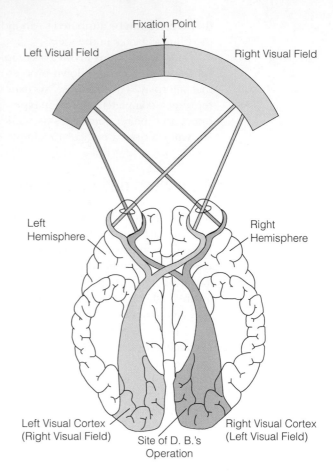

and the left visual cortex contains the information in the right visual field. Since D. B. had a large portion of his right visual cortex surgically removed to eliminate the headaches, the left visual field did not have the same representation in the brain as did the right visual field.

D. B.'s blindness was determined by a procedure called **dynamic perimetry,** which is the standard way of assessing visual field defects following accident or surgery. The procedure is a variant of ascending method of limits trials (see Chapter 6). With the patient's head kept still, a spot of light is slowly moved across the visual field of one eye, starting at the perimeter. When the light is seen by the patient, it is returned to the perimeter and brought across the field again from a different angle.

This procedure is repeated several times and results in a map of sensitive and blind areas in the visual field. Then the perimetry is repeated on the other eye. The blind part of the visual field is called a **scotoma;** D. B. had a scotoma in the left half of the visual field of each eye.

So far this blindness, though unfortunate, was as expected, given that brain tissue from the right visual cortex had been removed. However, some informal observations seemed to show that D. B. could locate objects in his blind field. For example, he could reach for a person's outstretched hand accurately, even though he could not see it.

Furthermore, he could correctly guess the orientation (horizontal or vertical) of a stick that he claimed he could not see. In fact, D. B. vehemently denied that he saw anything in a portion of his left visual field, and he attributed his success on these informal tasks to lucky guesses.

Suppose you were Weiskrantz, the psychologist who observed this odd behavior. What would you conclude? On the one hand, D. B. was blind. He did not report seeing stimuli in his left visual field. On the other hand, D. B.'s behavior indicated that he could detect and locate stimuli in the same area. Weiskrantz and his associates believed D. B.'s verbal report that he could not see objects in his left visual field, so they undertook a series of controlled experiments to determine the visual capacity of D. B.'s scotoma.

Since D. B. could not see objects in the blind field, he was asked to make forced-choice guesses about the location and the presence or absence of small patches of light. Other tests required him to guess the orientation of very small lines. All the tests were done under controlled lighting conditions, and D. B.'s head and direction of gaze were kept fixed. Sometimes, the visual stimuli were presented so briefly in the blind area that D. B. could not move his eyes quickly enough to change his focus to the good visual field. The line and dot stimuli were small and not very intense, but their size and intensity may have influenced both good and bad visual fields simultaneously. Therefore, detection of these targets in the blind visual field was compared with detection in the good field and in the blind spot.

Everyone has a blind spot in each eye. It is the part of the retina where the nerves exit the eyeball and thus is insensitive to light. If D. B. were able to detect a target in his blind spot, it would mean that the target was so intense or so big that it "leaked" out to sensitive areas of the eye. Since the blind spot was much smaller than D. B.'s field of blindness and since he could not detect targets in his blind spot, Weiskrantz had chosen target stimuli with appropriate characteristics to test in the blind field.

Weiskrantz then presented D. B. with dots and lines of either horizontal or vertical orientation. The results of the controlled tests were very interesting. Localization, detection, and guessing of orientation of targets presented to the blind field were much better than could be expected by chance. In many cases, the visual performance from the blind field was nearly as good as that from the good visual field. D. B. could not identify objects presented to his blind field, and throughout the testing he claimed not to see the targets for which he was required to make forced-choice judgments. D. B.'s reaction to his success on the forced-choice trials was one of incredulity. He attributed his success to lucky guesses, because he simply could not see the target stimuli.

Blindsight is the name that Weiskrantz used to describe visual capacity in a scotoma (the blind field) when there is no acknowledged awareness of perception. This seems a very odd phenomenon, but Weiskrantz and his associates (e.g., Weiskrantz, 1997; Weiskrantz, Cowey, & LeMare, 1998) report on another blindsight patient, G. Y., similar in etiology and behavior to D. B. Moreover, the generality of dissociation between verbal awareness and perceptual capacity is not the issue, because other neuropsychological studies have shown that different types of brain damage can result in disorders similar to blindsight. For example, Paillard and associates (1983) report the case of a brain-injured woman who was insensitive to touch on the right side of her body; yet, when she was asked to locate where she was touched on her unfeeling side, she could do so with considerable accuracy. She could also correctly guess the direction of movement on her skin, even though she could not feel the moving stimulus. Furthermore, as we will soon see, non–brain-damaged people can be induced to show a similar dissociation between awareness and perceptual behavior under controlled laboratory conditions. The issue, then, is to try to understand the relation between verbal reports of awareness and perception.

Current research on vision suggests that there are two types of visual systems in the brain: One is important for identifying objects, and the other system has to do with detection and movement. Apparently, the problem suffered by D. B. was that the system concerned with identification was destroyed during the operation performed to cure his headaches.

INTRODUCING THE VARIABLES

Dependent Variables

The simplest dependent variable is the verbal description given by an observer. Although this is the easiest measure to obtain, it often has several disadvantages. An untrained observer seldom is able to give a precise report. Although this can be corrected by proper training, there is always the possibility that the training, rather than the stimulus, is controlling the observer's report.

We shall return to properties of subjective reports in the next section. More objective measures of perception include reaction time and reports that can be verified directly by the experimenter. For example, if a string of six letters is presented in a **tachistoscope** (a device for controlling illumination and duration of stimuli) for 50 milliseconds (ms) and the observer is asked to report the letters, the experimenter can easily determine whether this report is correct. Observers are often asked to rate their confidence that their report is correct. Such rating measures, although not objective, can provide converging operations when used with other objective measures, such as reaction time.

As you can see, the major dimension for classifying dependent variables in perception is verifiability. Of course, all dependent variables must be verifiable and consistent. But some dependent variables can be verified directly, whereas others require subtle statistical methods, such as scaling, before verification can be achieved. So

we will divide dependent variables into those that can be *immediately* verified (judged as correct or incorrect) by the experimenter and those that cannot.

Independent Variables

As you might expect, the independent variables that are most common in studies of perception are those that alter the physical characteristics of stimuli. Psychologists change the size, shape, backgrounds, perspective, and angle of view of visual stimuli. Auditory stimuli can be varied according to frequency (pitch), intensity (loudness), waveform (timbre), and complexity (number of separate waveforms and their relationship to one another). The time course of perception is studied by presenting parts of a stimulus separated by short time intervals or by limiting the presentation time of the entire stimulus to tens or hundreds of milliseconds.

Another class of perceptual independent variables is more qualitative than quantitative. Animals and people have been placed in abnormal circumstances where the usual perceptual inputs are either absent or grossly distorted. Some examples of this type of manipulation would be raising animals in the dark, having people wear special goggles that distort their vision, allowing normal perception but preventing motor movements, and having a uniform visual field with no patterns or lines. Many such studies try to determine whether perception is learned like other behavior or is innate. At one time, the distinction between innate and learned perception was a major controversy in psychology. Now, as noted earlier, most psychologists admit there are both innate and learned components in perception.

Control Variables

This chapter is concerned with what might be termed the intellectual aspects of perception; however, perception has emotional and motivational aspects, which we will discuss as well. Thus, when people are asked to report taboo four-letter words, these words require greater display duration than do innocent control words. Similarly, when hungry people observe an out-of-focus image, they report seeing food-related objects more often than people who have eaten recently. Although these phenomena are interesting in their own right, when we focus on the stimulus as the most important determinant of perception, these other effects become artifacts and must be controlled. In terms of signal-detection theory (see Chapter 6), the decision aspects of perception must be held constant. Reporting a taboo word requires greater display duration not because the word is harder to perceive, but because observers are more reluctant to say a taboo word to the experimenter and hence alter their decision criterion (Zajonc, 1962).

Physical aspects of the stimulus that are not being investigated must also be controlled. The more important characteristics to hold constant when they are not independent variables include stimulus duration, intensity, illumination, contrast, and the like.

7.1   EXPERIMENTAL TOPICS AND RESEARCH ILLUSTRATIONS

Topic   *Verbal Report*
Illustration   *Perception without Awareness*

A compelling aspect of research on perception is that the dependent variables seem to provide insight into the observer's **phenomenological experience,** which is the internal awareness of the external world. This insight seems especially strong when a **verbal report** is elicited from an observer. It seems apparent that the verbal report, or what the observer says is perceived, must be correlated with his or her awareness of the experience. However, when a verbal report is elicited, the psychologist must determine whether the verbal report is a useful dependent variable that provides a reliable and valid indicator of the observer's experience.

Reconsider the discussion of psychophysics in the previous chapter. One way to view the difficulty in establishing a true threshold by the method of limits is that what the subject reports is not solely a function of what is perceived. Evidence and the subject's willingness to respond combine to determine the decision threshold; this is the reason signal-detection methods were developed.

Psychologists are likely to accept most reports from psychophysical research as valid indicators of phenomenological experience for two reasons. In the first place, d' and β can be determined under appropriate conditions. In the second place, most people report approximately the same fluctuations in experience when external stimuli are varied. The generality and regularity of the results increase our confidence in the utility of the verbal reports that are given in such experiments.

For this latter reason, the verbal reports occurring during magnitude estimation (see Chapter 6) are accepted. If a rock band increases its amplification by a factor of 10 and you report that it then sounds twice as loud, the psychologist has no direct check on your phenomenological experience. However, the fact that most observers respond in roughly similar ways to changes in stimulus energy suggests that the verbal report has some generality and thus represents a valid way of assessing the observer's perceptual experience.

Deciding on the usefulness of a verbal report is sometimes very difficult. Imagine you are confronted by a woman who claims to see little green people from Mars. Does she really see little green people? Since you and several others do not see these people, and since it is highly improbable that there is humanlike life (of any color) on Mars, you are likely to assume that the woman is demented—she is hallucinating. A **hallucination** is the report of an experience without any apparent corresponding stimulation.

Assuming that the woman is not lying, what are we to make of her verbal report that she sees little green people from Mars? Unlike the situation in a psychological experiment, in this instance there is a dramatic discrepancy between the stimulus (none or an irrelevant one) and the verbal report of the experience (green people). A psychologist interested in perception might not believe that her verbal report coincides with a perceptual experience. This is not to deny that the woman is actually experiencing the little green people. But her experience is unlikely to be a product of perception; rather, it probably results from mental pathology or the influence of drugs.

Now, reconsider the case of D. B. What are we to conclude from his verbal report, "I can't see the objects"? His verbal report did not coincide with his behavior in the presence of some kinds of stimuli. Was D. B. having a sort of negative hallucination (not seeing something that was actually there and otherwise detectable), or was his verbal report an accurate reflection of his perceptual experience? How do we decide on the utility of a report? D. B.'s verbal report was troublesome for an understanding of his perceptions, because from the standpoint of the experimenter, there was an obvious discrepancy between the presence or absence of a stimulus and D. B.'s report of his perceptual experience (Weiskrantz, 1986). This discrepancy seems to be different from the lack of direct check seen in scaling experiments, because failing to identify an object while accurately localizing it represents a paradox.

How does the psychologist know when the response of the observer qualifies as a useful dependent variable? The answer is deceptively simple: It qualifies only when a verifiable relationship between the response and a previous perceptual event can be directly inferred. Natsoulas (1967) defined a report as a presumed or confirmed relationship between some preceding or synchronous event (e_i) and the response. This relationship must be such as to make possible direct inferences from knowledge of the response to e_i (p. 250).

This definition is purposely abstract and will make more sense once we have examined another concrete example.

In the preceding chapter, we discussed how a pigeon could be trained to tell us its absolute visual threshold (Blough, 1958). You will recall that the pigeon pecked one key when it saw the stimulus and a different key when it did not. Appropriate reinforcement contingencies ensured that the pigeon's behavior was controlled by the stimulus. According to the definition just given, do the pigeon's pecking responses qualify as reports?

In this instance, the preceding event (e_i) is the stimulus, with particular reference to its intensity. A peck on one key indicates that the stimulus is below the threshold, whereas a peck on the other shows that the pigeon can see the stimulus. This relationship is the direct inference called for in the definition. Knowing the response—that is, which key is pecked—allows a direct inference as to whether the pigeon can see the stimulus. We must conclude, therefore, that the pecking responses do indeed qualify as reports.

The essential characteristic of an adequate report of a perception is the relation between it and the preceding perceptual event. To the extent that alternate relations or inferences can be proposed, the report is weakened. For example, had Blough not been careful to eliminate the possibility that the pigeon learned to switch between keys only after a long string of pecks on a single key, this alternate relation could have also explained the pecking behavior. In that case, the pecking could not have been correctly interpreted as a perceptual report.

The pecking example also illustrates the unimportance of the qualitative nature of the report. A key press is every bit as good as a verbal statement that the stimulus is or is not seen. Verbal statements can be responses to stimuli, rather than unverifiable reports. It is only the relation between the preceding event and the report that needs to be considered in order to establish whether a response is an adequate dependent variable. Just because a statement is verbal does not guarantee that it is also a report.

Now we can consider D. B.'s case in a slightly different way. His two classes of perceptual reports—the verbal one and the detection/localization one—are in conflict. The difficulty in understanding this conflict arises for two reasons. First, humans tend to place a great deal of emphasis on verbal reports as indicators of phenomenological experience. Thus, the verbal report must be the "correct" one, the cases of the demented woman and Blough's pigeons notwithstanding. Second, people make the incorrect assumption that all perceptual reports will have the same preceding synchronous event. It is logically possible (and empirically likely, as we shall soon discover) that the e_i for a verbal report is different from the e_i associated with other indicators of perceptual experience. One report can indicate a perceptual experience and another can fail to do so.

More recent work by Weiskrantz (2002) with D. B. points importantly to the e_i approach to understanding perception. An offhand comment by D. B. to Weiskrantz led to a remarkable discovery. After showing that he could not detect gratings (parallel lines) but could guess their orientation correctly, D. B. commented that he could see the gratings after he closed his eyes. Was this a hallucination? No, it was an afterimage. An **afterimage** arises after looking at a visual stimulus, usually for several seconds. After the stimulus is removed, there is initially a **positive afterimage** that is similar in brightness and color of the original stimulus (Woodworth & Schlosberg, 1954). After a brief period, the positive afterimage usually becomes a **negative afterimage,** which is opposite in brightness and complementary in color (a red stimulus appears green in the negative afterimage). What D. B. claimed was that he perceived a negative afterimage of the black lines of the gratings that he could not see. This fascinating possibility is merely a verbal report until we can verify possible e_i. Systematic testing provided the necessary information to conclude that D. B.'s afterimage was a real phenomenon.

D. B. demonstrated complementary colored afterimages, and grating afterimages with appropriate orientations. Although he could not distinguish a circle from a square visually, D. B. was perfect in distinguishing those objects in his afterimages.

The size of D. B.'s afterimages varied directly with the distance from the surface on which the images were viewed, which is true of the afterimages of normally sighted people, including D. B. in his seeing field (Weiskrantz, 2002). The proportionality of the size of the afterimage and viewing distance is called **Emmert's law.** So, what does all this mean?

D. B. had conscious aftereffects to nonconscious perceptions of external stimuli. The afterimages were reliable and behaved lawfully, so they can be considered synchronous events (Natsoulas, 1967). Weiskrantz calls D. B.'s unusual afterimages **prime sight** to distinguish it from blindsight. Both of these "sights" may strain credulity, but they are perceptions according to our analysis of synchronous events.

Are these mere curiosities of perception with little relevance to "real" perception? We do not think so, because we will now examine how one can study perception without verbal awareness in ordinary research participants. What must be done is to determine the indicators of perceptual experience in the absence of verbal reports of that experience.

Lack of Verbal Awareness

The topic of perception without awareness has had a long and controversial history (Eriksen, 1960). Marcel (1983) revived the controversy when he reported the results of a series of experiments that seemed to show the perception of meaning in the absence of verbal awareness. The normal college students who participated in Marcel's research behaved much like D. B. They claimed that they could not perceive a word, yet their behavior indicated that they were sensitive to the meaning of the unperceived word.

In one of his experiments, Marcel combined several different research techniques. His basic task was a variant of the Stroop effect—named after Stroop (1935), who first reported the phenomenon. A standard Stroop task works as follows. The participant sees a list of words and is supposed to name the ink color of each word rapidly. Compared with naming the ink color of a neutral word unrelated to color (such as *house* in red ink), color naming is slower when the word and ink color conflict (*red* printed in blue ink) and faster when the word and the ink color are congruent (*green* in green ink). The slower or faster color naming under conditions of word/color conflict or congruency define the **Stroop effect.**

Marcel modified the Stroop procedure by using a form of **priming.** Priming occurs when a word or other perceptual event biases the observer to perceive a subsequent event in a particular way. Seeing the word *red* printed in black ink could prime you to think of the color red, much like the old joke "Don't think of an elephant" makes you think of an elephant. So if you had been primed by the word *red* to think of the color red, a subsequent color, such as green, might be unexpected, and a Stroop-like conflict would be produced. In Marcel's experiment, a priming word (for example, *red*) was presented just prior to a patch of color (for example, green), and the subject was to indicate quickly the color of the color patch (the observer should say "green"). If priming works to produce a Stroop effect, then compared with a neutral word prime such as *house,* a congruent word prime *(green)* should speed up color naming of a green-colored patch, and an incongruent color-word prime *(red)* should slow down color naming of green. That is what Marcel found.

In the priming Stroop test, Marcel employed a clever technique to manipulate the observers' awareness of the priming word. He prevented the perception of the priming word on some trials by a procedure called **masking.** Masking, in this context, involves presenting a jumbled pattern of letters immediately after the onset of a priming word. The mask will prevent the detection and identification of the word when it follows the word immediately; as the interval between the word and the mask increases, detection and accurate identification of the word also increase. An effectively masked prime should not be reportable by the observer, because he or she cannot detect or identify the prime. Marcel reasoned that if perception can occur without awareness, then an effective mask should not eliminate the Stroop effect induced by the prime. Regardless of whether the subjects are aware of the prime, their color naming should be sensitive to it, if the perception of meaning does not depend on verbal awareness. Alternatively, if awareness is necessary for the perception of meaning, then masking the prime should eliminate the Stroop effect.

Marcel's procedure for part of one of his experiments is outlined in Figure 7.3. To present the stimuli, he used a tachistoscope, which is a device that allows very brief presentations. The time between prime and the patch of color was 400 ms, which is four-tenths of a second. Awareness of the prime was determined by how much later the mask followed the prime. On aware trials, the mask was presented at the same time as the color patch (400 ms after the prime). This interval is long enough for the prime to be detected and identified.

On unaware trials, the interval between the onset of the mask and the onset of the prime was very short. Prior to the start of the Stroop test, the exact interval

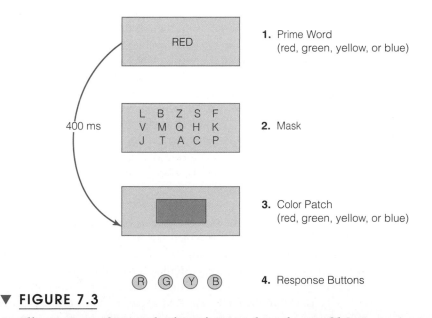

▼ **FIGURE 7.3**

An Illustration of Marcel's (1983) Procedure (part of his experiment 3). A color patch (red, green, yellow, or blue) appeared 400 ms after a prime word (no word, *red, green, yellow, blue,* or a noncolor word). The mask on aware trials occurred with the color patch. On unaware trials, the mask was presented just after the prime. The time between prime onset and mask onset on unaware trials was determined separately for each subject, such that the subject could determine the presence of the prime no more than 60 percent of the time (chance detection would have been 50 percent—"yes" or "no" the prime was present). When the color patch appeared, the subject indicated the color by pressing a button corresponding to red, green, yellow, or blue.

between prime and mask was determined individually for each subject. The color words were followed by a mask, and the observer was to detect the presence of the prime. The detection threshold was determined by the method of limits and was defined as the prime-mask interval that yielded detection less than 60 percent of the time, with 50 percent being chance performance for detecting the presence of the prime. During the Stroop test, an interval 5 ms shorter than the detection interval was used on unaware trials.

On some Stroop trials, a prime was not presented. The remaining trials were defined by the relation between the prime and the color patch: neutral, congruent, or incongruent. The materials included four colors (red, green, yellow, and blue), four color words (*red, green, yellow,* and *blue*), and three neutral words (*cough, kind,* and *water*). After the color patch appeared, the observers pressed one of four buttons to indicate the color of the color patch. The reaction time to press the correct button was the primary dependent variable.

The results were straightforward. On both aware and unaware trials, a typical Stroop effect was obtained. Compared with neutral primes and no prime at all, color identification (for example, yellow) was slower following incongruent primes (for example, the word *blue*) and faster following congruent primes (*yellow*)—regardless of whether the subjects were aware of the primes. Based on these results and the results of other experiments that he did, Marcel concluded that people can perceive meaning without awareness.

In Marcel's experiment, the observers' behavior on the Stroop test showed that meaning had been registered, even though their verbal reports indicated that the priming stimuli had not been perceived. Cheesman and Merikle (1984) questioned the awareness interpretation of the results. They noted that Marcel's detection threshold of 60 percent allowed for the possibility of true detection on some trials (see Chapter 6 on the distribution of responding in signal detection). Furthermore, Cheesman and Merikle reasoned that verbal reports of awareness may have a higher threshold than does differential responding to the meaning of words. If this is the case, then perhaps Marcel may have inadvertently determined the wrong threshold when he adjusted the prime-mask interval to obtain less than 60 percent detection. Marcel's procedure may have resulted in a threshold that was below the observers' threshold for making a verbal report but above their detection threshold.

Cheesman and Merikle tested the idea that the inappropriate threshold had been determined by replicating Marcel's Stroop experiment with a few important changes. First, they altered the way in which the detection threshold for the prime was determined. Instead of having the observer judge the presence or absence of the prime, as in Marcel's work, Cheesman and Merikle forced the subjects to report which color word had been presented. This was done to minimize response bias in reporting the presence of a prime. In the forced-choice procedure, each prime is presented equally often, followed by a mask. Over an extensive series of trials, the observers responded equally often with each of the choices available (the same four color words Marcel used—*red, green, yellow,* and *blue*). Thus, the observers' criterion for saying a particular color was the same for all the primes.

The second important change that Cheesman and Merikle introduced was the calculation of several prime-detection thresholds for each subject. Using the method of limits, they varied the interval between the prime and mask so that forced-choice detection of the prime was 25 percent, 55 percent, or 90 percent. Chance level of detecting the prime in choosing among four alternatives is 25 percent. Thus, the lowest threshold they calculated was chance detection. The 55 percent level of responding was approximately equal to the threshold used by Marcel. The 90 percent threshold yields near-perfect performance. At all levels of detection, the mask was usually effective in eliminating verbal awareness of the prime. That is, even though the subjects could differentially detect the color words, depending on the prime-mask interval, they claimed not to be aware of what the words were—they claimed to be guessing.

In the Stroop portion of the experiment, Cheesman and Merikle followed Marcel's procedure (see Figure 7.3), except that they had four conditions instead of two. The four conditions were the three prime-mask intervals, which yielded 25 percent, 55 percent, and 90 percent detection, as well as a no-mask condition. As in Marcel's experiment, the prime bore a neutral, congruent, or incongruent relation to the color patch.

The results of the Cheesman and Merikle experiment are shown in Figure 7.4. The standard Stroop effect was obtained in each condition, except when the prime was detected at a chance level. Even though the observers claimed to be unaware of the

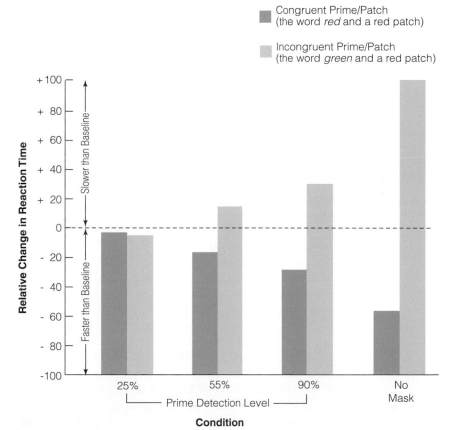

▼ **FIGURE 7.4**

Results of Cheesman and Merikle (1984), showing reaction times to congruent and incongruent primes relative to the neutral primes in each of the four conditions. The Stroop effect is seen in all conditions except the 25 percent prime-detection condition.

primes in the 55 percent and 90 percent conditions, their behavior showed that they were sensitive to the meanings of the primes. At a very short prime-mask interval that leads to chance detection (the 25 percent condition), the subjects were not sensitive to the meaning of the primes.

If we take the chance-detection threshold as the one indicating no awareness of the prime, then we can interpret the results of Cheesman and Merikle as providing no evidence for perception of meaning without awareness. On the other hand, behavior at the 55 percent and 90 percent prime-detection levels (where subjects say they are unaware of the prime) shows that there is perception of meaning. Cheesman and Merikle (1984, 1986) theorized that their data are congruent with the idea that there are two thresholds. One is an **objective threshold,** where the level of discriminative responding is at a chance level of performance. The other is a **subjective threshold,** where the level of discriminative responding is above the chance level, but the observers *claim* that they cannot detect or recognize the perceptual information. Thus, they are hypothesizing that discriminative response thresholds require a weaker synchronous event (e_i) than do verbal response thresholds.

To test this theory directly, Cheesman and Merikle (1984) conducted a second experiment in which they varied the intensity (energy level) of the prime to determine the two thresholds. At the objective threshold, observers detected at a chance level and were verbally unaware of the words. At the subjective threshold, observers detected the words 66 percent of the time but claimed to be unable to identify them. The Stroop test was then repeated, and the Stroop effect was found for primes presented at the subjective threshold—but not for primes presented at the objective threshold.

The two-threshold theory is illustrated in Figure 7.5. Between the two thresholds, people make verbal reports that they are unaware of the primes, but their responses to stimuli indicate that they are sensitive to meaning. Below the objective threshold, awareness cannot be determined, because the subjects both respond at a chance level and are verbally unaware. According to this way of viewing the masked-prime Stroop effect, Marcel had determined in his experiments the subjective threshold, not an objective one.

The theory derived from the work by Cheesman and Merikle has some important implications for understanding the role of verbal reports in perceptual research. In the first place, a coherent way of thinking about the difference between verbal reports believed to indicate awareness and other perceptual responses has been provided. For normal subjects, we now have ways of determining when such discrepancies should occur, and for patients such as D. B., we now have a sensible way of thinking about seemingly bizarre behavior. Weiskrantz reports that very strong stimuli presented to D. B.'s blind field produced some feelings of awareness—but not ordinary seeing. We can conclude that one consequence of damage to the visual part of the brain is a marked elevation of the subjective threshold (as noted later, there are additional factors, as well).

A second implication of the two-threshold theory is that there is not necessarily anything special about a verbal report. At each threshold level in the research by Cheesman and Merikle, the verbal report provided little information beyond that given by forced-choice discriminative responses. This suggests that such indexes of perception are perfectly adequate, and the premium that people place on the veracity of and necessity for verbal reports of awareness may be misplaced. In many instances, all that

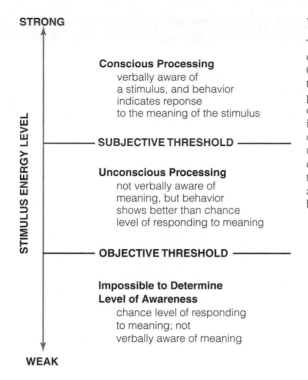

STRONG

STIMULUS ENERGY LEVEL

Conscious Processing
verbally aware of
a stimulus, and behavior
indicates reponse
to the meaning of the stimulus

—— **SUBJECTIVE THRESHOLD** ——

Unconscious Processing
not verbally aware of
meaning, but behavior
shows better than chance
level of responding to meaning

—— **OBJECTIVE THRESHOLD** ——

**Impossible to Determine
Level of Awareness**
chance level of responding
to meaning; not
verbally aware of meaning

WEAK

▼ FIGURE 7.5

The two-threshold theory developed by Cheesman and Merikle (1984, 1986). Between the subjective and objective thresholds, people claim they are unaware of the stimulus, but their behavior shows otherwise. Below the objective threshold, people are unaware and their behavior is at a chance level. Above the subjective threshold, people are verbally aware of the stimulus and their behavior is sensitive to meaning.

is needed to understand a perception is an indicator response; statements of awareness are not essential.

Nevertheless, the strong phenomenological component of perception remains, and people are aware of some things and not of others. The threshold of awareness cannot be the objective threshold. So Cheesman and Merikle (1986) conclude:

> Given that perceptual awareness or consciousness is a subjective state, we propose that the subjective threshold, or the threshold for *claimed* awareness, better captures the phenomenological distinction between conscious and unconscious perceptual experiences and that the subjective threshold, therefore, provides a better definition of the boundary between conscious and unconscious processes than is provided by the objective threshold. (p. 344, emphasis in the original)

Cheesman and Merikle have offered an operational definition of awareness (see the discussions of operational definitions in Chapters 6 and 12). Simply defining awareness does not allow us to distinguish conscious from unconscious processes and to determine the validity of a verbal report. At face value, Cheesman and Merikle simply allow each subject to use his or her own subjective confidence to establish the awareness threshold. They point out that this is a serious problem, because subjective confidence cannot be distinguished from response bias. If we have only the subjective threshold as a measure of the awareness threshold, then we are nearly back where we started: We have an unverifiable report. To solve this problem adequately, we need to use converging operations, a topic to which we now turn.

Topic   *Converging Operations*
Illustrations   *Perception without Awareness and Perception*
with Explicit Awareness

The distinction between the experience of perceiving and responding to stimuli, discussed in the preceding section, was a major impetus for the idea that a set of two or more operational definitions is needed to define the psychological concept of perception. In a classic article titled "Operationism and the Concept of Perception," Garner, Hake, and Eriksen (1956) showed that perception was more than just a response. This may seem obvious to you after reading the preceding section, so we must take a step backward in time.

Fifty or so years ago, experimental psychology was barely starting to recover from the throes of a rigidly applied framework of Watsonian behaviorism. Observers made responses that discriminated one stimulus pattern from another; for many psychologists, such responses were equivalent to perception. We now realize, largely owing to Garner, Hake, and Eriksen, that such a limited concept of perception arises from a very literal and incomplete interpretation of operationism. According to **operationism,** concepts are defined by the operations used to measure and produce them. If weight were defined as the movement of a meter located in a small rectangular box on your bathroom floor, then the response indicated on the scale dial when you stepped on the scale would define weight. If perception were defined as an observer saying one stimulus looks different from another, then that response would be perception.

Garner and associates pointed out that this was only part of operationism. Equally important was the need for a *set* of operations to define each concept. They cited the physicist Bridgman (1945) to emphasize this neglected aspect:

> Operational definitions, in spite of their precision, are in application without significance unless the situations to which they are applied are sufficiently developed so that *at least two* methods are known of getting to the terminus. Definition of a phenomenon by the operations which produced it, taken naked and without further qualification, has an entirely specious precision, because it is a description of a single isolated event. (p. 248, emphasis added)

Operationally defining perception as a discrimination response—that is, a response of A or B—is not enough. At least two operations are required.

When only a single operation is used, it is impossible to distinguish between limitations of the perceptual system and those of the response system. Since perceptual and response systems are to some extent independent, two or more operations are required to separate the limitations of each system.

Converging operations are a set of two or more operations that eliminate alternate concepts that might explain a set of experimental results. This abstract definition is best understood through several examples. We start with a discussion of further work undertaken by Cheesman and Merikle.

Perception without Awareness

In the experiments by Cheesman and Merikle (1984), the phenomenological claims of unawareness to stimuli occurring below the subjective threshold cannot be distinguished from a response bias to withhold a verbal report of awareness. To bolster our confidence in the distinction between perception with awareness and perception without awareness, a converging operation is needed to show that perceptual processing under the two levels of awareness is qualitatively different. Otherwise, all we can say about the results is that the Stroop effect is sometimes accompanied by reports of awareness of the prime and sometimes not accompanied by awareness. Later experiments by Cheesman and Merikle (1986) provided the converging operations by showing that an independent variable (the frequency with which congruent prime-color patch trials occurred) had a qualitatively different effect on unconscious perceptual processing than it did on conscious perceptual processing. In addition to the subjective threshold, another variable distinguished between aware and unaware perception.

Cheesman and Merikle (1986) decided to vary the frequency with which congruent prime-color patch combinations occurred. Earlier research using different forms of the Stroop test had shown that the facilitation and inhibition of reaction time on congruent and incongruent trials (see the no-mask condition of Figure 7.4) increased with increases in the frequency of congruent trials (Glaser & Glaser, 1982). The congruent trials (the word *red* and red ink) occurred twice as often as mismatches between the word and ink color. Observers had a strong tendency to say the color named by the word, and this anticipation speeded up the response time on congruent trials. Since this anticipation would lead to an incorrect response on incongruent trials, reaction time was very slow on trials having a mismatch between word and color (for example, the word *yellow* and a blue ink color). Frequency effects such as this one represent a voluntary strategy on the part of the observers (Lowe & Mitterer, 1982). When congruent trials occur with high frequency, the subjects become biased toward making the most frequent response, based on their identification of the relative frequency of various types of trials. This results in a facilitation of reaction time on the majority of trials (the congruent ones) and a disruption of reaction time on only a small subset of trials (the incongruent ones).

Since the congruent, incongruent, and neutral primes each occurred on one-third of the trials in their earlier work, Cheesman and Merikle reasoned that the effects of increasing the frequency of congruent-prime trials (to two-thirds of the trials) would depend on whether the primes were above or below the subjective threshold. They argued that if the frequency effect resulted from the observers' identification of the most frequent type of trial, then when the primes were presented below the subjective threshold and could not be consciously identified, the frequency effect would not occur. If the primes were above the subjective threshold and could be consciously identified, then the frequency effect would be observed.

After showing that congruent primes presented on two-thirds of the no-mask trials enhanced the Stroop effect, Cheesman and Merikle then varied the frequency of congruent-prime trials: They occurred on one-third or two-thirds of the trials. They also had primes either below the subjective threshold or well above it.

The results of this experiment are shown in Figure 7.6. As in their earlier work (see Figure 7.4), the Stroop effect did not depend on whether the primes were above or below the subjective threshold. However, the frequency of congruent trials had an effect only when the primes were above the subjective threshold and were consciously identified. Observers can use strategies only when they are consciously aware of the stimuli as defined by the subjective threshold. Thus, converging operations indicate that conscious and unconscious perceptual processing methods are qualitatively different, and the phenomenological distinction between different levels of awareness in perception is on firm experimental ground. These conclusions required two sets

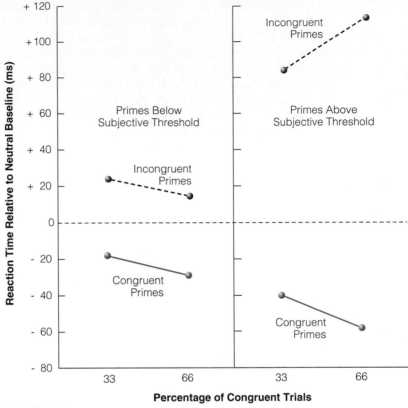

▼ FIGURE 7.6

Results of Cheesman and Merikle (1986), showing an enhancement of the Stroop effect for primes above subjective threshold when the frequency of congruent trials is increased. The magnitude of the Stroop effect for unaware primes is not influenced by the frequency of congruent trials.

of observations: the determination of different awareness thresholds and demonstration of the differential effect of congruent trial frequency across levels of awareness. Both sets of observations converge on the adequacy of the distinction between perception with awareness and perception without it (Merikle & Cheesman, 1987, report supporting results).

Most experimental psychologists agree that the phenomenon of perception without awareness rests on solid ground (Kihlstrom, Barnhardt, & Tataryn, 1992). The confidence results partly from the qualitative differences that independent variables have when people claim perceptual awareness than when they do not (Merikle & Reingold, 1992; Merikle, Smilek, & Eastwood, 2001). The converging evidence just described provides one major example. Confidence in the generality of the idea of perception without awareness also derives from the wide variety of experimental circumstances in which unaware effects have been obtained (Greenwald, 1992; Loftus & Klinger, 1992; Sergent & Dehaene, 2004). Converging operations provide precision in definition, and the replications of results across tasks point to a general phenomenon.

Blindsight Reviewed

Our analysis of D. B.'s perception is incomplete. Converging operations are needed to verify the claim that he could not see objects in his blind field, despite his ability to detect and localize them accurately. To provide converging operations to show that D. B.'s perception of objects in his blind field was qualitatively different from that in his good field, Weiskrantz used a tactic similar to the one used by Cheesman and Merikle.

The procedure used by Weiskrantz to provide converging operations is called **double dissociation of function** (Weiskrantz, 1997). In this procedure, opposite behaviors are elicited by two different tasks from different areas of functioning. Specifically, Weiskrantz wanted to find a set of conditions under which detection and localization were *poorer* in the good field than in the blind one, while at the same time demonstrating that recognition and identification still were absent in the blind field and present in the good one. If there were opposite perceptual deficits in the two fields under these conditions, then Weiskrantz could be sure that the kind of vision in the blind field was qualitatively different from that in the good field and that the blindness was not just a poorer version of normal vision.

Weiskrantz presented an *x* or a triangle to the periphery of the good field; for brief and dim presentations, detection there was poorer than detection in the center portion of the blind field. Despite the poor detection in the good field, D. B. could still say whether an *x* or a triangle had been presented on these trials. As was the case in other experiments, accurate detection in the blind field was accompanied by blindness for the identification of the stimuli. That is, D. B. could tell when the targets were presented to the blind field, but he could not tell whether they had been an *x* or a triangle. From his experiments on D. B., Weiskrantz concluded that the dissociation is consistent with the idea that there are two visual systems. As mentioned earlier, one is a "what" system that concerns identification and recognition. The other is a "where" system that deals with detection and localization. In the absence of brain damage, these systems work together, so that detection is accompanied by recognition and, in adult humans, verbal awareness.

Other kinds of research indicate a double dissociation between the what and where visual systems. Physiological research (Cowey, 1995) has demonstrated dissociations in monkeys when parts of their visual systems have been surgically altered. Lesions in one part of the visual system lead to disordered recognition of what is there, but localization is intact; lesions elsewhere in the visual system result in an absence of spatial capacity, but object recognition is intact. Similar sorts of results have been reported in the neuropsychological literature. Farah (1990) discusses two different kinds of brain-damaged people. With damage to one part of their visual system, people cannot see or imagine objects, but they can figure out and imagine where objects are located. Conversely, people with damage to other areas of the brain can locate objects and imagine their locations, but these people cannot recognize or imagine the objects themselves. So, two additional combinations of results provide further converging evidence for a visual system composed of two functional systems. The behavioral, physiological, and neuropsychological data result in an impressive pattern of converging evidence, which strongly supports Norman's (2002) theory that both direct and indirect processes are involved in normal vision.

Perception with Explicit Awareness

Thus far we have divided perception in several ways: direct/indirect, top-down/bottom-up, what/where, and unaware/aware. Recall that in the original blindsight work, D. B.'s reports of object blindness did not correspond with his ability to locate an object. The focus then and in Merikle's work was on improving our understanding of lack of awareness on perception. We have yet to analyze the role of converging operations in supporting the effect of explicit awareness on perception, which we do here. Research clearly reveals the value of converging operations in bolstering our understanding.

Most of the work on explicit awareness is by Proffitt and associates, and Proffitt (2006) provides a review of most of that research. Proffitt's review outlines his agenda by noting that the visual processes involved in perceiving the immediate environment—say, those in observing the degree of slant of a hill—are immutable except for the conditions of the spatial layout. Explicit awareness, on the other hand, varies with both the optical array and the emotional and physical costs of intending to do things in that environment. As we will discuss, wearing a heavy backpack while viewing a hill, as opposed to a light pack, seems to make the hill appear steeper. Thus, Proffitt (2006) argues that "perceiving spatial layout combines the geometry of the world with behavioral goals and the costs with achieving those goals" (p. 110). Let us examine some of the research that leads to that conclusion.

The first series of studies we consider examined the perception of the steepness of hills (Proffitt, Bhalla, Gossweiller, & Midgett, 1995). Observers made three judgments of hill slant in a counterbalanced order: a verbal judgment of explicit awareness in degrees, a visual estimate of explicit awareness done by moving a semicircle to reveal a schematic cross section of the hill, and a haptic (touch) judgment done by moving a board with the palm of the hand, trying to match the feeling of the board with the incline of the hill while looking at the hill. Proffitt and associates assumed that the haptic condition was an implicit, visually guided oculomotor task. Observers drastically overestimated hill slant when making the explicit awareness estimates, but they were more conservative and more accurate with the haptic task. Next they had experienced runners make the three types of judgments of hill slant two times: just before a 1-hour run and just after the run. The runners estimated the slants of two different hills, and the researchers counterbalanced these hills across the pre-and postrun conditions (see Chapters 2 and 9) for two groups of runners. The visually guided haptic judgments were reasonably accurate and not influenced by running for an hour. In general, the runners exaggerated slant in their explicit awareness judgments, and they made much steeper explicit judgments after the run than before it. Thus, the effort of running increased the explicitly estimated grade of hills.

In a second series of studies, Bhalla and Proffitt (1999) examined the physical cost of observers in three different ways while they made the explicit awareness and visually guided estimates. First, they found that wearing a heavy backpack increased the explicit estimates of slant but did not influence the haptic judgments. Second, they assessed the fitness of varsity athletes and general undergraduates by a stress test and then had them judge the slant of four hills. Explicit awareness judgments of slant were negatively correlated (see Chapter 2 on correlation) with fitness; that is, they found that the less fit the participant, the greater the visual and verbal steepness estimates. Visually guided estimates did not vary with fitness. Third, elderly people made estimates of the slant of hills. The explicit but not the visually guided judgments varied positively with age. Older people made higher slant estimates. Bhalla and Proffitt also found that self-reported poor health influenced the age effect—the poorer the health, the greater the explicit judgments of slant. Healthiness had no influence on the visually guided judgments.

The methodology employed in these studies by Proffitt and collaborators includes experiments (heavy backpack or not, before and after a run) and quasi-experiments with subject variables (age and fitness). The experiments alone allow for causal statements, but they are not as interesting as the effects associated with subject variables.

The latter, of course, do not permit a causal analysis (see Chapters 2, 3, and 12). The package of research is compelling in demonstrating the conclusion that nonvisual processes can influence the visual perception of our world.

Proffitt's work has led to additional interesting studies related to athletic performance, showing that batting average in softball players is positively correlated with the estimated size of the ball (Witt & Proffitt, 2005), and the size of a dart-board target is positively correlated with dart-throwing proficiency (Wesp, Cichello, Gracia, & Davis, 2004). Apparently, the ability to succeed in an endeavor has an influence on perception. We conclude this section by revisiting the point made by Proffitt (2006) at the beginning of the section: Perceiving the world combines visual analysis with explicit awareness of the goals and the costs afforded by them.

FROM PROBLEM TO EXPERIMENT
THE NUTS AND BOLTS

Problem   *The Color–Distance Illusion*

It is well known in the visual arts that warm colors (yellow, orange, red, and transitions between these colors) give the appearance of moving toward the viewer, whereas cool colors (blue, green) seem to recede from the viewer. A two-dimensional picture can be made to look three-dimensional by such artistic devices as having blue backgrounds and warm-colored foregrounds. This illusion can be quite convincing. One of us remembers viewing an exhibition of stained glass in which one work of art had several deep blue panes of glass surrounding a red circle. The illusion of three dimensions was so strong that the circle looked as if it floated about 10 centimeters in front of the blue background. The author had to go up and touch the glass to convince himself that the red and blue pieces of glass were in the same plane. Imagine that an experimental psychologist wishes to investigate this warm–cool color illusion. We can state the problem as follows:

Problem   *Why do warm colors appear to come forward and cool colors appear to recede?*

Before trying to answer this question in any detail, a careful experimental psychologist would first attempt to demonstrate the phenomenon in controlled laboratory circumstances. He or she would want to rule out the possibility that the illusion occurs because of other artistic devices, such as perspective or variations in brightness, both of which can create an appearance of distance.

So a general hypothesis that color serves as a cue to depth would first be advanced. As is always true, we can formulate several more specific testable versions of this general hypothesis.

Hypothesis   *When pairs of color patches are presented in the same plane, the warmer color will be judged closer by a person viewing these stimuli with one eye (monocularly).*

The major independent variable is, of course, the color (or, more technically, the hue) of the visual test patches. Another independent variable that would probably be manipulated at the same time is the distance between the eye and the stimuli. This variable would be included because the experimenter would have no prior reason to select some particular viewing distance. Since there is nothing special about the viewing distance, you might think that this independent variable is unnecessary. Any distance selected at random would do.

Although this reasoning is correct if the assumption that distance does not matter is true, this is only the experimenter's best guess. Since it is easy and inexpensive to use three or four viewing distances instead of only one, most experimenters would go ahead and manipulate distance. Data showing that viewing distance has no effect on the depth cue of color, although a null finding, is still of interest, since it would allow certain explanations of the illusion to be ruled out. Finally, the experimenter's guess might be wrong, and the two independent variables (hue and viewing distance) might interact.

How many hues should be tested in this experiment? If all possible pairs of hues are to be presented to the observer, we find that the number of stimuli (a stimulus is one pair of color patches) increases dramatically with the number of hues to be tested. The minimum experiment would have three hues: one warm, one cool, and one neutral gray. This would require a total of three stimuli to present all possible pairs. Although this total is most reasonable in terms of demanding experimental effort, three stimuli (and only two real colors) are too few to establish the generality of the effect. We could use five hues: two warm colors, two cool colors, and one gray. This would require 10 stimuli. Seven colors would require 21 stimuli and nine colors 36 stimuli. To keep the experimental session from being too long, we might select five colors and four viewing distances.

The dependent variable is a forced-choice judgment, with the observer being required to state which of the two color patches appears closer. (Actually, they are both the same distance from the observer.) This would be scored by creating a matrix, with all the hues listed down the columns and also across the rows. Each cell in the matrix specifies a combination of two colors. The main diagonal would not have any entries, since the same color would not be presented twice within a stimulus. Cell entries would be the number of times (or the percentages) that color X was judged to be closer than color Y.

As with any perceptual experiment, many control variables need to be considered. What the person in the street calls color is actually composed of three independent attributes: hue, saturation, and brightness. *Hue* is the frequency of the light and corresponds to shade of color—red, green, and so on.

Saturation corresponds to the strength of color—that is, whether it is pale and washed-out or deep and strong. *Brightness* refers to the amount of light reflected from a surface. Since our experiment has hue as its major independent variable, both saturation and brightness must be controlled. Brightness especially is an important cue to depth, with brighter objects being perceived as closer to the viewer, all other things being equal. So we must be extremely sure that all our stimuli are of equal brightness. Another control variable has already been given in the hypothesis, which specified monocular (one-eye) viewing conditions.

Because each eye sees external objects from a slightly different location, binocular vision (both eyes) is an important cue for depth perception. Since we are primarily interested in color as a possible depth cue, all other cues to distance must be eliminated from the experiment.

We do not know what the results of this experiment would be. However, for purposes of further discussion, let us pretend that warm colors were judged as closer. We would then formulate another hypothesis, trying to provide a converging operation to bolster the results and interpretation of this first experiment.

Hypothesis   *When an observer is asked to move an adjustable colored stimulus so that it appears in the same plane as a fixed colored stimulus, the observer will set the adjustable stimulus closer if it is a cool color and the fixed stimulus is a warm color, and vice versa.*

This hypothesis is more complicated than the first, so we explain it in more detail. Imagine two colored circles in front of you, with one of them sitting on a pulley so that it can move forward and backward. The other circle cannot be moved. Your task is to adjust this pulley until both stimuli appear equally distant from you. The hypothesis predicts that, since warm colors will appear closer to you, a cool color (which appears farther away) placed on the pulley must be moved closer in order to appear even with the fixed warm color. Similarly, if the fixed color is cool, it will appear farther away, so that a warm color (which will appear closer) on the pulley must be moved farther away from you than the fixed color.

The independent and control variables are as before. The dependent variable is now the distance between the observer and the adjustable stimulus.

However, in scoring this distance, we probably would take the position of the fixed stimulus as zero and record a negative number if the adjustable stimulus is closer to the viewer and a positive number if it is farther away.

Whereas the first experiment yielded a qualitative assessment of the warm–cool illusion, this experiment gives a number based on perceived distance.

Therefore, it provides an indication of how strong or weak the illusion might be for different combinations of colors. If we were bold enough, this hypothesis could be made even more specific by predicting that the size of the illusion would depend on the difference in frequency between the hues of each pair of stimuli. As stimuli were farther apart in the visual spectrum, greater distance settings would result.

So far, our two experiments have been aimed more at establishing the replicability and reliability of the (hypothetical) finding that warm colors move forward and cool colors recede than at explaining why this happens. The converging operations provided by the two experiments are weak, since they are quite similar and differ only in the precision with which the dependent variable is measured. In particular, the judgments made by the viewer are relative judgments concerning two colors viewed simultaneously. One next step toward explaining our (hypothetical) result would be to provide a stronger converging operation by requiring an absolute judgment about a single stimulus.

Hypothesis   *When an observer, using both eyes, is required to estimate the distance of a single colored stimulus chip, warm colors will be judged to be closer than cool colors.*

Our independent variable is unchanged, as are the control variables. The dependent variable is a direct estimate of distance. There are several scaling techniques that could be used, but for the sake of simplicity, we shall let our observer make a judgment in distance units that are familiar to him or her, such as inches or centimeters. Of course, it is unlikely that, even for a neutral gray stimulus, such estimates will be highly accurate, but that is not the issue we wish to investigate. All we care about in this experiment are the relative values of the distance estimates for warm versus cool colors. If results agree with those hypothesized for the first two experiments, we have learned that there is some absolute property of color that serves as a cue for distance. If no differences are found—that is, if distance estimates are the same for all colors—there remain two possibilities. You have probably noticed that the hypothesis states that normal binocular vision (both eyes) was to be tested. This is another converging operation.

If results were negative, a careful experimenter would replicate this third experiment, using monocular vision as before. If results still were negative with monocular vision, then we would be forced to conclude that the warm–cool distance illusion was a property of relative judgments and that a contrast between two stimuli was necessary to produce it. This would be a major step in explaining the effect, but still only a beginning. The remaining steps are left as exercises for future experimenters. (If you want to find out more about this, look up *chromatic aberration* in a perception text, such as Coren et al., 1994.)

▼ SUMMARY

1. Perception is often described as the interpretation of sensation. Issues in the study of perception include the role of direct and indirect approaches to perception (often referred to as bottom-up and top-down processes), the ways native and experiential factors influence perception, and the part played by awareness.

2. Verbal reports allow the psychologist to study another person's perceptual and phenomenological experiences. However, care is needed to make sure that the verbal reports are adequate dependent variables. Examples of perceptual issues that have been studied by verbal reports are blindsight and perception without awareness.

3. In the Stroop effect, work by Cheesman and Merikle indicates that there is a difference in verbal awareness for items presented above a subjective threshold and for those presented below the subjective threshold and above the objective threshold.

4. Converging operations allow inferences about perceptual operations that are stronger than inferences from a single experiment or experimental condition. Converging operations have allowed psychologists to have a better understanding of blindsight, perception without awareness, and perception with explicit awareness.

▼ KEY TERMS

afterimage

awareness

blindsight

bottom-up processing

conceptually driven processing

converging operations

data-driven processing

direct approach to perception

double dissociation of function

dynamic perimetry

Emmert's law

empirical theory

hallucination

illusion

indirect approach to perception

masking

nativistic theory

negative afterimage

objective threshold

operationism

perception

phenomenological experience

positive afterimage

priming

prime sight

scotoma

sensation

Stroop effect

subjective threshold

tachistoscope

top-down processing

unconscious inference

verbal report

▼ DISCUSSION QUESTIONS

1. If you have ever taken prescription drugs to alleviate surgical or dental pain, you may have experienced a dissociation between the feeling or pain (the hurt) and your ability to localize the source of pain. Relate this to blindsight and perception without awareness.

2. Consult Garner (1974), and discuss how converging operations are used to bolster the concepts of dimensional integrality and separability.

3. Design your own experiment to investigate further the warm–cool color–distance illusion.

4. Consult a perception text (such as Coren et al., 1994), and discuss additional examples of illusions and phenomenological reports.

▼ WEB CONNECTIONS

An analysis of the perception of odors and tastes can be found at:

http://www.hhmi.org/senses/

A fascinating treatment of visual and auditory illusions can be found at:

http://www.illusionworks.com/

▼ LABORATORY RESOURCE

An interesting experiment on perception is considered in Chapter 6 of Langston's (2002) manual. This experiment examines how room color influences a person's mood.

°PSYCHOLOGY IN ACTION

The Stroop Effect

You can easily try the Stroop test for yourself. All you need are some index cards, colored markers, and a watch with a second hand or, even better, a stopwatch.

Take sixteen index cards, and using your markers, write the name of the color in its color—that is, with a green marker, write *GREEN,* and so on. If you have eight markers, each color will be repeated twice. If you have only four markers, repeat each color four times. Take another sixteen index cards and write color names that do not correspond to the ink—that is, with a green marker, write *RED,* and so on. Your stimuli are now completed.

Pick one of the two decks; for each card, name the color of the ink. Time how long it takes you to go through all sixteen cards. Do the same for the other deck. Were you faster for the deck that had compatible color names and inks? It would be better to test several people to obtain more reliable results than just testing yourself.

Another way that you can study the Stroop effect is to use number stimuli. Determine how quickly your participants can read through a long column of single digits in which the numbers 1 through 4 are repeated several times. Then determine how long it takes them to count the numbers of arbitrary symbols in a column. The column should be as long as the first one, and you should use a symbol such as a dollar sign in such a way that there are one, two, three, or four of them on a line. Now, you are ready to try the Stroop conflict condition. Work up a column as long as the previous two in which you have stimuli such as *2 2 2 2, 1 1, 3,* and *4 4 4.* The participants' task is to name the number of digits; that is, they are to say "four" when they see *2 2 2 2,* and so on. An interesting addition to either of the above experiments would be to have a separate group of participants read all the stimuli when lists are presented upside down.

This will make reading and counting more difficult and slow down the rate of responding.

What happens to the magnitude of the Stroop effect? Why? ■

CHAPTER 8

ATTENTION AND REACTION TIME

The great tragedy of Science—the slaying of a beautiful hypothesis by an ugly fact. (T. H. HUXLEY)

In this chapter, we examine two basic cognitive processes: attention and the time taken to respond to stimuli. We focus on the aspects of attention concerning how people switch their cognitive resources from one task to another. With regard to the second topic, we consider both overt behavior—the reaction time to respond—and the nature and timing of the brain waves that occur during cognitive activity. The methodological issues examined are confounding, selection of the dependent variable, and interactions.

▼ THE ABC OF REACTION TIME

Interest in reaction time began in the eighteenth century, when an assistant at the Royal Observatory in England was fired because his reaction times did not agree with his employer's reaction times. Astronomers in those days recorded the time and position of astral events by observing when a celestial body crossed a line in the eyepiece of their telescope. A nearby clock ticked every second, and the observer was expected to note the crossing time to the nearest tenth of a second. When the crossing times of Kinnebrook, the unfortunate assistant, were checked by his boss, they were always too great. Kinnebrook was warned but could not shorten his observation times, so he was fired.

A German astronomer, Bessel, heard of Kinnebrook's firing and wondered whether the difference between the crossing times of Kinnebrook and his boss was caused by something other than incompetence. Bessel suspected that people might observe the crossing with slightly different reaction times. When Bessel and other astronomers compared their crossing times, they consistently found systematic differences. Some astronomers always made faster estimates than others. This difference among astronomers in reacting to the crossing times of celestial bodies was called the **personal equation,** a name that highlights the fact that people differ in their reaction times and, thus, have their own equation for estimating crossing times.

The personal equation remained only a problem for astronomers until Donders, a Dutch physiologist, realized that he could use people's reaction times to calibrate the time required for various mental operations. Donders developed three kinds of reaction-time tasks that are still known as **Donders A, B,** and **C reactions** (illustrated in Figure 8.1).

In the A reaction, which is often called the **simple reaction,** a single stimulus, say, a light, comes on, and the observer responds by quickly pressing a key or button. There is only one stimulus and one response. When you turn off your alarm clock in response to its loud signal, the time between the onset of the sound and your depression of the alarm button is your simple reaction time. Donders believed that the A, or simple, reaction provided a baseline of the cognitive operations involved in more complicated reactions. A more complex reaction is going to require what goes on in a simple reaction, which includes sensory processes, nerve conduction time, motor movement time, and so forth, but it also will have additional cognitive operations.

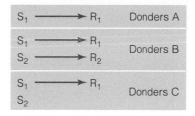

▼ FIGURE 8.1

At the top is the Donders A reaction task. In this simple reaction-time procedure, one stimulus is linked to one response. In the middle is the Donders B reaction task. In this reaction-time procedure, two stimuli are linked to two responses. At the bottom is the Donders C reaction task, in which there are two stimuli but only one is linked to a response.

The more complicated reactions, B and C, are also illustrated in Figure 8.1. In a B reaction, which is also known as **choice reaction time,** there is more than one stimulus and more than one response. Each stimulus has its own unique response. As shown in Figure 8.1, the observer is supposed to make R_1 when S_1 occurs and R_2 when S_2 occurs. When your car is at a traffic light, you are faced with a B (or choice) reaction. If the light is green, you step on the accelerator; if it is red, you step on the brake pedal. What cognitive operations in addition to the baseline ones are necessary for a choice reaction? First, you must identify the light as red or green. Then you must select the pedal you should press. Therefore, a choice reaction includes the baseline operations occurring in a simple reaction as well as the cognitive operations of stimulus identification and response selection.

To estimate the time required for identification and selection, we need to determine a third kind of reaction: the Donders C reaction, which is the bottom one in Figure 8.1. Here, as in the B reaction, there is more than one stimulus, but only one stimulus is linked with a response. If S_1 occurs, the observer is supposed to make R_1; if any other stimulus occurs (S_2), the correct behavior is to withhold responding and do nothing. Waiting in line at a takeout restaurant would be an example of a C reaction—until your number is called, you should not respond. What cognitive operations are needed to perform a C reaction? As in the B reaction, you must identify your number when it is called. However, once this is accomplished, there is no need to select a response, since only one response is appropriate. So the C reaction adds stimulus selection to the baseline operations but does not include response selection.

We can now estimate the time required for the cognitive operations of identification and selection by subtracting appropriate pairs of reaction times. The C reaction measures identification plus assorted baseline times. Therefore, subtracting the A reaction time (RT) from the C RT tells us how long identification takes. Similarly, subtracting the C RT from the B one estimates stimulus selection time, since the B reaction includes identification, selection, and baseline times, but the C reaction includes only identification and baseline times. This procedure of estimating the time it takes to perform various cognitive operations is called the **subtractive method.** The subtractive method using the Donders A, B, and C reactions is illustrated in Figure 8.2.

Early in the history of psychology, Wundt (see Appendix A) and his students devoted much effort to studying reaction time using the subtraction method. However, the method soon came under attack from psychologists who relied on introspection as

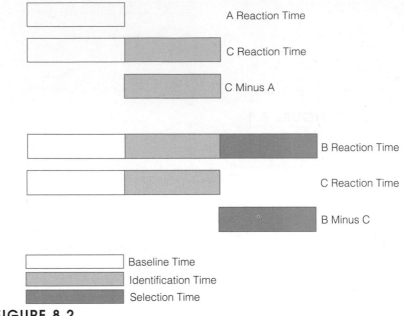

▼ **FIGURE 8.2**

Illustration of Donders's Subtractive Method.

a method of gathering data. As noted in Appendix A, **introspection** was a systematic way of examining one's own consciousness, which was heavily used by Titchener, the American structural psychologist, and his students. When trained introspectionists performed the Donders reactions, they noted that a C reaction did not feel like an A reaction plus something else, nor did a B reaction feel like a C reaction plus something else. Instead, the three reactions all felt completely different. Because many psychologists at that time thought that introspection was a powerful tool for understanding cognitive processes, Donders's subtractive method was discredited. Today, experimental psychologists rely less heavily on introspective data, and Donders's methods provide the basis for substantial amounts of important research and theorizing, some of which is examined later in this chapter.

8.1   EXPERIMENTAL TOPICS AND RESEARCH ILLUSTRATIONS

Topic   *Confounding*
Illustration   *Pure Insertion*

The contemporary study of complex mental processes, such as attention, tries to divide a complex process into a set of component parts or modules. How can we identify these component modules? An important criterion is **separate modifiability** (Sternberg, 2001). This is a form of independence that occurs when one component module can be changed without changing the other. If module A, for example, response execution, can be changed without altering the mental functioning of module B, for example, perception, and module B can be changed without altering module A, then the two mental processes are separately modifiable.

INTRODUCING THE VARIABLES

Dependent Variables

In studies of attention, the range of dependent variables is considerably more restricted than that of independent variables. Reaction time is by far the preferred variable and is extensively used. Percentage of correct responses is also used, especially in studies of attention in which memory plays a role. When an experiment is framed within the context of a particular model, such as the theory of signal detection (see Chapter 6), derived statistics such as d' and β are also used as dependent variables. Another common statistic is amount of information in bits, where one bit is the information present in the toss of a fair coin that can come up either heads or tails. These derived statistics may be combined with reaction time to yield measures of the rate of performance, such as bits/sec or d'/sec.

Dependent variables in electroencephalography (EEG) and event-related potential (ERP) studies focus on the location of the voltage change, its pattern over time, and the direction and timing of change after stimulus onset. Recent technological advances have allowed researchers to examine changes in the patterns of electrical activity of the whole brain across time. The resulting pictures of brain activity yield information similar to that seen in various kinds of brain scans, such as computed tomography (CT) scans.

Independent Variables

Although studies of attention and reaction time have used an impressive variety of independent variables, these variables center around the need for the human to make decisions and the rate at which such decisions can be made. Thus, varying the number of alternatives in a choice reaction task increases the number of decisions that must be made to identify the correct stimulus and select its associated response. Varying the presentation rate of a series of stimuli limits the amount of attention that can be devoted to processing each stimulus and is a common technique used to study the upper bounds of attention. Another way of increasing the attention demanded by some task is to increase its complexity; thus, a simple version of a task may require naming a visually presented digit, whereas a more complex decision may require subtracting the digit from nine.

The key point in manipulating attention is to gradually increase task demands until the person is hard pressed to keep up with them. The use of overload as a diagnostic device has been borrowed from engineering, where it is quite common. For example, the strength of materials is tested by placing them in a hydraulic press and gradually increasing the pressure until the material fails. This gives the metallurgical engineer information about the material that could not be easily gained from the intact structure. Although a far gentler method of imposing overload is required for the study of human attention, the underlying goals and techniques are similar to those of the engineer. By discovering how the human system reacts to overloads of information, the psychologist gains insight into human performance and information processing with more reasonable attentive loads.

Control Variables

Research in attention and reaction time is usually quite carefully controlled. Perceptual factors, such as the intensity and duration of stimuli, are often under the control of a computer or other automated equipment that conducts the experiment. Even speech sounds can be presented in exactly the same way trial after trial by using a "talking computer." This precise control is necessary if psychologists are to interpret small changes in reaction time on the order of tens of milliseconds (1 millisecond being equal to one one-thousandth of a second).

Likewise, to record electrical changes in microvolts, precise control is needed in research using EEGs and ERPs as dependent variables. Sophisticated recording equipment that can filter out extraneous electrical activity is used along with amplifiers and computers that allow precise specification of the electrical changes that are of interest.

Thus, the three components of a Donders B reaction (Figure 8.2) are distinct and separate modules (or stages) of information processing. This is a theoretical statement and needs to be confirmed by appropriate experiments. If Donders was correct, then we would expect the three stages to be separately modifiable. In order to test this theoretical model of information processing, we must find some measure (dependent variable) that is influenced by all the processing stages or modules. As Figure 8.2 shows, reaction time is such a measure. But we cannot yet test separate modifiability until we first specify how each processing stage contributes to the measure. One simple combination rule is that total reaction time is the sum of the individual stage reaction times. Because this rule states that we should add up the individual stage times, this method of analysis is called the additive-factor method (Sternberg, 2001).

When mental processes are separately modifiable, the addition (or deletion) of one process does not affect the other processes. The method of additive factors includes the assumption that the duration of a stage (stage-processing time) does not depend upon the duration of other stages. Thus, when some other mental process is added or deleted, nothing happens to the duration of the original stage. This is called the assumption of **pure insertion:** A mental module can be added or deleted without altering the duration of other modules.

It is important to realize that while Donders stage model predicts an ordering of A, B, and C reaction times, it does not directly test the assumption of pure insertion. In mathematical terms, there are three equations and three unknowns that are estimated by these equations. Since the number of equations and unknowns is equal, it is not mathematically possible to test the validity of the assumption of pure insertion. (In other words, the assumption was used to generate the results and there are no remaining degrees of freedom to validate the assumption.) While early researchers rejected the assumption of pure insertion based upon introspective reports (Kulpe, 1893), contemporary researchers prefer more objective tests of behavior.

Thus, it might prove helpful to add another measure in addition to reaction time. Response force, the amount of pressure exerted on a response key, has been shown to be a useful additional measure in studies of human information processing. For example, response force increases as stimulus intensity is increased (Miller, Franz, & Ulrich, 1999) and can even be observed and related to independent variables when no overt response is demanded and reaction time cannot be measured (Kantowitz, 1972).

A series of five experiments that measured both reaction time (RT) and force-dependent variables for A, B, and C reactions was conducted by Ulrich, Mattes, and Miller (1999). Their first experiment presented a visual stimulus (green LED) either to the left or right of a central fixation point. For the A reaction, participants responded to either light with the same hand. For the B reaction, they responded to the left light with their left hand or to the right light with their right hand. Figure 8.3 shows their results. B RT was significantly higher than A RT, as we would expect. However, integrated force (the area under a curve showing force as a function of time) did not differ for the two reactions. This outcome is consistent with the hypothesis of pure insertion, because response force is the same regardless of type of reaction.

However, there are some potential problems with this experiment. **Confounding** occurs when more than one independent variable is simultaneously varied so that we cannot be entirely sure which variable is responsible for the outcome. In a standard Donders A-reaction experiment, usually only one stimulus is mapped to the response. In this experiment, two stimuli (left and right LEDs) were mapped to the response.

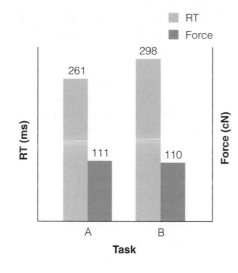

▼ FIGURE 8.3

RT and Integrated Force for A and B Reactions. (Data from Ulrich et al., 1999, experiment 1.)

Thus, the possibility exists that having to divide attention between two lights, instead of having to focus only on a single light, might change the way this modified Donders A reaction is performed. Furthermore, RT is also proportional to the intensity of a visual stimulus (Ulrich & Mattes, 1996) so that brighter stimuli yield faster RT. This becomes especially important for C reactions where the participant only needs to look at the light that is mapped to the response. The authors were concerned that apparent brightness was confounded in the C reaction and did a special experiment (experiment 5) to check for possible confounding. We will get to that experiment shortly, but first we must discuss their experiments that compared B and C reactions.

Figure 8.4 shows the results of an experiment that measured force and RT for B and C reactions. In the C reaction, participants were required to respond only to the LED on one side of the fixation point; no response was required for the other LED. Again, there was no difference in integrated force. However, there was also no difference between B and C RTs! This is not at all what we should expect: The B reaction should

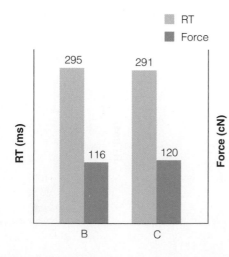

▼ FIGURE 8.4

RT and Integrated Force for B and C Reactions. (Data from Ulrich et al., 1999, experiment 3.)

take longer than the C reaction. While the authors attempt to explain this result, they are not convincing. Strictly speaking, equal RTs argue against the model presented in Figure 8.2. Thus, the authors of your textbook (especially the one writing this chapter) are skeptical about the results and interpretation of this experiment in the series.

Figure 8.5 shows the results of an experiment that measured force and RT for A and C reactions. In this experiment both RT and force were significantly different for A and C reactions. The RT difference is what we would expect from Figure 8.2. However, the greater force for the C reaction is not consistent with the hypothesis of pure insertion.

The authors performed another experiment because of the possible confounding of apparent stimulus intensity in the C reaction where participants could focus their vision entirely on one of the two stimuli. In this experiment the LEDs were replaced by the letters *X* and *S* on a computer screen. Since the letters were always presented in the center of the screen, participants could not focus on just one side for the C reaction. Figure 8.6 shows the results. These results are very satisfying. First, the B reaction takes longer than the C reaction, as expected. Second, force is the same for both reactions, which is consistent with pure insertion.

▼ **FIGURE 8.5**

RT and Integrated Force for A and C Reactions. (Data from Ulrich et al., 1999, experiment 4.)

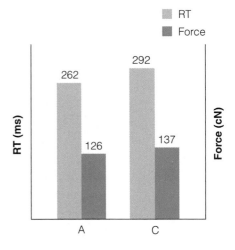

▼ **FIGURE 8.6**

RT and Integrated Force for B and C Reactions. (Data from Ulrich et al., 1999, experiment 5.)

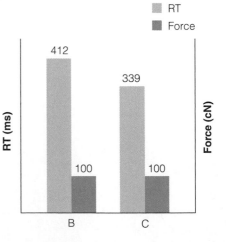

How might we summarize the results and conclusions of these experiments? The results are more difficult to compare because each experiment tested only two kinds of Donders reactions. The experimenters did this intentionally to minimize negative transfer across reactions. In within-subject designs, there is the possibility that exposure to one condition changes performance in a subsequent condition. However, the best way to avoid negative transfer is to use a between-subjects design where each participant is exposed to only one kind of Donders reaction. If negative transfer is not anticipated, within-subject designs where each participant experiences all three Donders reactions are more efficient. The experimenters chose a weak compromise by including only two Donders reactions. If they were truly concerned about negative transfer, a between-subjects design would have been preferable. If they were not very concerned about negative transfer, it would make more sense to test all three Donders reactions in the same experiment.

Results from the experiment shown in Figure 8.4 are problematic. It would be a good idea to replicate this experiment including all three Donders reactions in the same experiment. However, based on the other experiments in the series, it seems reasonable to conclude that the model proposed by Donders (Figure 8.2) is correct and that the assumption of pure insertion is valid. However, the experimenters accept this conclusion only for Donders A and B reactions and argue that the force data reject pure insertion for the C reaction. Their argument depends, in part, on discussions of the best way to score response force that are too detailed for this textbook. It is clear that even five experiments are not sufficient to evaluate pure insertion, and although it has been more than a century since Donders (1868) introduced the method of subtractive logic, modern researchers will continue to study and ponder his ideas.

8.2   EXPERIMENTAL TOPICS AND RESEARCH ILLUSTRATIONS

Topic   *Selection of the Dependent Variable*
Illustration   *Speed–Accuracy Trade-Off*

As discussed in Chapter 3, the experimenter selects one or more dependent variables from the large number that are possible. In that chapter, we suggested that it is often very important to have more than one dependent variable in an experiment. We will illustrate just how important it is to have more than one dependent variable in this section.

An extremely popular dependent variable used in research on attention and information processing is RT. Indeed, this variable is so popular that the study of reaction time has become virtually a content area in itself. When experimental psychologists get together, it is quite common for some of them to identify their research interests by stating, "I'm in reaction time." This may sound odd to you, since a psychologist studying memory would not say, "I'm in percent correct," but it does indicate that a dependent variable may become so important that it is not only a means of investigating specific content areas but also an object of study in its own right.

At first, one might think that RT would be a poor topic to illustrate selection of a dependent variable, since by naming reaction time we have already made the selection. It is true that some psychologists routinely measure RT with little thought about the implications of this selection decision. Right now, RT is "in." The speed with which a task can be performed is often taken as an indication of the attentional requirements of the task. Things that can be done quickly are interpreted as having small attentional requirements. This logic is not always correct, since attention can be operationally defined in ways that need not involve reaction time.

There is an inverse relationship between the speed and accuracy of performance. When you try to do something very fast, you make more mistakes than if you do it slowly. Conversely, if you try to do something, such as type a term paper, very accurately, you must go more slowly to achieve the desired accuracy. Psychologists call this relationship the **speed–accuracy trade-off.** It has important implications for studies that measure RT as the dependent variable.

This can be illustrated by an experiment conducted by Theios (1973), in which the task of the participant was quite simple. A digit was presented visually; the participant needed only to name the digit. The independent variable was the probability (relative frequency) of the digits, which varied from 0.2 (a particular digit was presented 20 percent of the time) to 0.8. RT data from this experiment are shown in Figure 8.7. Theios concluded that stimulus probability had no effect on reaction time.

This conclusion appears quite reasonable when errors are ignored. But when the error data also shown in Figure 8.7 are considered, another interpretation emerges (Pachella, 1974). The average error rate of 3 percent may not seem very high to you, but stop and think about how simple the task was. All that was required was to name a digit—hardly a devastating task for college students. Even worse, the error rate varied

▼ **FIGURE 8.7**

RT and Error Rate as a Function of Stimulus Probability. Although reaction time is fairly constant, error rate declines as stimulus probability increases. (Data from Theios, 1973, and Pachella, 1974.)

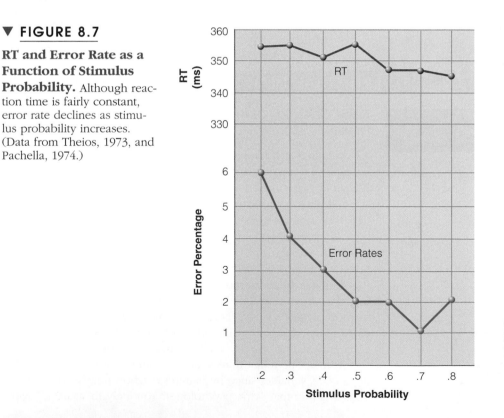

systematically according to stimulus probability, the independent variable. The highest error rate (6 percent) occurred with the lowest stimulus probability; as the probability increased, error rate decreased. What would the RTs have been if the error rates were equal for all levels of stimulus probability? According to the speed–accuracy trade-off, reaction times in the low stimulus–probability conditions would have to increase in order to decrease the error rate. Pachella (1974) has suggested that to lower error rates to 2 percent, RT in the 0.2 stimulus–probability condition might have to be increased as much as 100 milliseconds. So the conclusion that stimulus probability does not affect RT must be questioned once error rates are considered.

The basic problem here lies with the selection of RT as the *only* important dependent variable. Since reaction time depends, in part, on the error rate, we must consider both speed and accuracy as dependent variables. In short, RT is not a univariate dependent variable but a multivariate variable. It may reduce to a single dependent variable in some cases where error rate is constant across all levels of the independent variables; but in general, two dependent variables—RT and error rate—must be jointly considered.

This point will be emphasized by reference to divided attention experiments conducted by Pashler (1989). These experiments also illustrate that examining more than one dependent variable can be crucial to understanding the psychological processes involved in the experimental task. In a series of six experiments, Pashler used a modification of the Donders B (choice reaction time) task (see Figure 8.1). The important modification was that S_1 and S_2 were not presented simultaneously. Rather, there was a brief delay between the two stimuli. An interval between S_1 and S_2 is called **stimulus onset asynchrony (SOA),** and the procedure is shown in Figure 8.8.

Pashler was interested in looking at the effects of varying SOA between S_1 and S_2 because it had long been known that as the SOA became shorter, the reaction time to S_2 became longer (e.g., Herman & Kantowitz, 1970). Thus, there is an inverse relation between the length of SOA and the speed of making R_2. This phenomenon has been dubbed the **psychological refractory period,** a period in which additional cognitive activities are difficult to manage. Apparently, there must be a fairly long delay between stimuli so the activities necessary to make R_2 do not intrude on the refractory period. If you reexamine Figure 8.2, you will see that there are several possible reasons why a shorter period between stimuli would lead to a slowing of the second response. There could be problems in identifying S_2, selecting R_2, or executing R_2. Pashler hoped to determine which of these was responsible for the refractory period.

An example of the psychological refractory period is illustrated in Figure 8.9. The reaction time of R_2 is shown by the solid line. As the length of the SOA is shortened (the interval between the two stimuli), the time to make R_2 gets longer. Notice, too, that

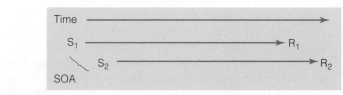

▼ FIGURE 8.8

The Two-Stimulus Paradigm for Studying the Psychological Refractory Period. The interval between S_1 and S_2 is the stimulus onset asynchrony (SOA).

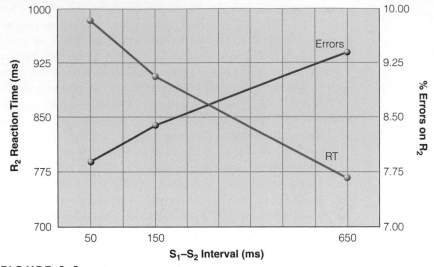

▼ **FIGURE 8.9**

RT and Errors for R_2 as a Function of SOA Between S_1 and S_2. The increase in errors with decreases in RT is an example of the speed–accuracy trade-off. The slow RT associated with the shortest SOA is an example of the psychological refractory period. (Adapted from data presented by Pashler, 1989, experiment 4.)

errors increased as reaction time decreased. This is a clear example of a speed–accuracy trade-off. Although the increase in errors across SOAs is small (about 1.5 percent), it is a statistically significant increase.

The results shown in Figure 8.9 come from an experiment (Pashler, 1989, experiment 4) in which S_1–R_1 were tones leading to key presses with the left hand and S_2–R_2 were a display of digits and a vocal response—the observer called out the name of the highest digit in a display of eight digits. This task is not very demanding, especially since R_1 and R_2 are markedly different, but note that lengthening the SOA by 100 ms (a tenth of a second) led to a speedup in reaction time of about 75 ms. Lengthening the SOA from 150 milliseconds to 650 milliseconds further reduced the time to make R_2 by about 140 ms. Thus, even with rather elementary behaviors, the psychological refractory period puts severe limitations on our ability to respond quickly to a second stimulus. The speed–accuracy trade-off in this experiment is interesting, because in an otherwise identical experiment Pashler showed that R_2 accuracy was unrelated to SOA when the subjects were not required to respond quickly to S_2. Thus, the accuracy of R_2 suffers only when it must be made quickly. Had Pashler just examined the accuracy of R_2, he would have observed the converse of a psychological refractory period. This illustrates the importance of having multiple measures of behavior.

What are the causes of the refractory period effect seen in Figure 8.9? One possibility holds that the closer in time the two stimuli are, the more difficult it is to execute two responses. This seems unlikely, given that the two responses were very different— one manual, the other vocal. Indeed, making vocal and manual responses in everyday tasks, such as driving, seems trivially easy. Is it a stimulus selection difficulty? This too seems unlikely, because the stimuli are very different from each other. In experiments in which S_1 and S_2 are highly similar, Pashler found that the error rate on R_2 is highest for very short SOAs. This is the opposite of what is seen in Figure 8.9. The selection effect at short SOAs probably arises because of the overlap of similar perceptual processes when the two stimuli are highly similar. Stimulus selection problems cannot account for the psychological refractory period when the stimuli are dissimilar.

Pashler argued that the effect of short SOAs on the slowing down of R_2 is the result of response-selection difficulties, and to clarify that position he looked at another dependent variable. He examined the time to make R_2 after fast and not-so-fast R_1 times. He expected that R_2 should occur more quickly after fast R_1 responses than after slow ones, because if R_1 were out of the way quickly, it would allow more rapid selection of R_2. In several experiments, he found that the faster that R_1 is executed, the faster is R_2, especially when SOA is very short. This seems to indicate that the observer must postpone selecting the second response until the first response is selected. The fact that the refractory period effect is about the same regardless of the similarity between R_1 and R_2 is also consistent with the idea that shortened SOAs lead to a postponement in selecting the second response and not to stimulus identification difficulties.

The work by Pashler is especially clear in illustrating the utility of carefully selecting the dependent variables in an experiment. He was able to increase our understanding of the psychological refractory period by a judicious selection of several dependent variables.

Theoretical Explanations of the Psychological Refractory Period
As was explained in Chapter 1, science requires both data and theory. The psychological refractory period paradigm has been quite productive in generating models to explain how people process overlapping tasks. The first model (Telford, 1931) was based upon an analogy to the refractory period of a single neuron: When a neuron is excited, it is unable to fire again within a short period after the original excitation. This explanation of overlapping tasks maintained that the entire brain was refractory and that processing the first stimulus prevented, for a brief time, any subsequent processing of stimuli. While this model has been rejected for many reasons (Herman & Kantowitz, 1970), the incorrect descriptive title "psychological refractory period" remains as sort of an historical vermiform appendix.

Current theoretical models fall into two classes: **central bottleneck** and **central capacity sharing.** Central bottleneck models (Navon & Miller, 2002; Pashler, 1994) state that some common internal-processing stage is required by both tasks so that processing of the second task must be deferred until the stage that is busy processing the first task becomes available. Central capacity sharing models (Broadbent, 1971; Kantowitz & Knight, 1976; Tombu & Joliceur, 2003) postulate a theoretical resource called capacity, in many ways similar to the information-processing throughput capacity of a computer system that must be shared across tasks. While two tasks may be processed simultaneously, this will be accomplished with lesser efficiency than if the system had only one task to process.

Figure 8.10 shows how bottleneck models explain longer RT to the second stimulus as SOA decreases. The processing bottleneck is the shaded bar. At short SOAs processing for task 2 must wait until the task 1 bottleneck is cleared. At long SOAs there is no overlap in bottleneck processing, so that RT to the second stimulus is not delayed. At intermediate SOAs there is partial overlap so that RT to the second stimulus is partially delayed.

Central capacity models make the same prediction but for a different reason. At short SOAs each stage is operating at less than full efficiency since capacity must be

▼ **FIGURE 8.10**

Bottleneck Explanation of Psychological Refractory Period Effect.

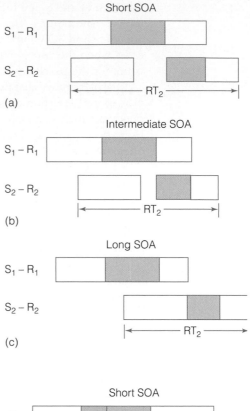

(a) Short SOA

(b) Intermediate SOA

(c) Long SOA

▼ **FIGURE 8.11**

Capacity Sharing Explanation of Psychological Refractory Period Effect.

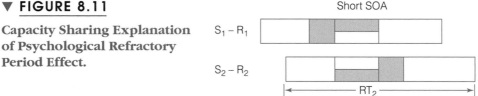

Short SOA

shared during task overlap, as indicated by the center shaded portion of Figure 8.11. Hence RT is increased.

Since both classes of models predict the psychological refractory period effect, how can we determine which is correct? One way is to examine RT to the first stimulus. At short SOAs, this is also delayed (Herman & Kantowitz, 1970). Bottleneck models predict no delay in RT because the processing for task 2 does not start until task 1 processing is completed. Capacity-sharing models predict a delay because capacity for task 1 processing decreases as soon as task 2 processing begins.

Tombu and Joliceur (2003) carefully reviewed both kinds of models and have concluded that capacity-sharing models are preferable, in large part because of delayed RT to the first stimulus. Their conclusions are based on data and theory published more than 30 years ago as well as recent experiments. In science, good data and models are eternal. Unlike fashion, the latest publication is not automatically the best. The worth of earlier ideas and results does not necessarily fade over time. This is one reason that scientists place a high value on publication of results: It is possible that our work will remain useful long after we are no longer active researchers.

8.3   EXPERIMENTAL TOPICS AND RESEARCH ILLUSTRATIONS

Topic   *Interaction Effects*
Illustration   *Cognitive Control*

An **interaction** occurs when the effects of one independent variable are not identical across different levels of other independent variables. As we mentioned in Chapter 3, the search for interactions is a major reason for including more than one independent variable in an experiment. You can spot interactions in graphed results by looking for lines that are not parallel. Understanding interaction effects often poses some difficulty for the new researcher, so we discuss them here and again in Chapter 10.

The ability to dynamically shift your focus of attention from one aspect of a stimulus to a different aspect is termed **cognitive control** and is a mainstream topic in the study of attention that has been of interest to psychologists for many years. Imagine an experiment where you must respond as fast as possible to one of four stimuli: a red square, a red circle, a blue square, and a blue circle. If you have no advance information before the stimuli are presented, this is a four-choice Donders B reaction-time task. But if you had partial advance information that limited the set of possible alternatives to only two stimuli—for example, if you knew in advance that a square would be presented—your reaction time will be faster than a four-choice RT. If the time between the cue that presents partial advance information and the stimulus is sufficiently long, RT to the cued stimulus will equal two-choice RT (e.g., Kantowitz & Sanders, 1972). The time between the cue and the stimulus is called the cue-stimulus interval; it is often in the range of 100 to 1000 ms.

Stress and Cognitive Control

It is interesting to wonder how stress might affect cognitive control. There are two major possibilities. First, handling stress could require capacity or attention, thereby decreasing performance because resources devoted to stress are no longer available for processing stimuli (Broadbent, 1971). Second, people might adapt to depleted resources by selecting a more efficient processing strategy for dealing with perceptual stimuli so that increased selectivity improves performance (Steinhauser, Maier, & Hubner, 2007). (There are, of course, even more possibilities, such as stress creating new additional capacity, that we will not consider here.)

To answer this question, does stress improve cognitive control, Steinhauser and associates (2007), performed a straightforward experiment. They created two levels of stress, High and Low, by presenting multiple-choice questions that were easy or difficult: Indeed, some of the high-stress questions were insoluble. After this IQ test was completed, they presented stimuli consisting of a digit and a letter (e.g., 6M). Cues specified that subjects should respond to the digit or to the letter. For the letter task, subjects had to decide if the letter was a consonant or a vowel. For the digit task, subjects had to decide if the digit was odd or even. Subjects responded by pressing one of two buttons and RT was recorded. The cue-stimulus interval was either Short (200 msec) or Long (1000 msec). Blocks of Short and Long cue-stimulus intervals alternated, and the starting block was counterbalanced across subjects (see Chapters 3 and 9 for discussions of counterbalancing). On successive trials within a 48-trial block, tasks could either be Repeated (e.g., digit followed by digit) or Shifted (e.g., digit followed by letter).

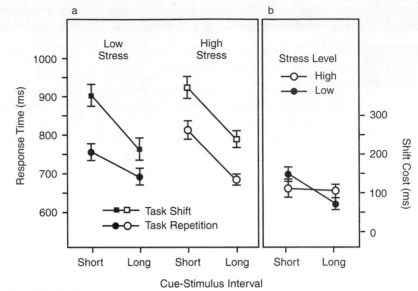

▼ **FIGURE 8.12**

Mean response times as a function of cue-stimulus interval for Low- and High-stress conditions. Shift costs in panel b are difference scores from panel a. Error bars represent standard errors of the means. (From Steinhauser et al., 2007, with permission.)

Results of this experiment are shown in Figure 8.12. For the Low-stress condition, there was an interaction between Cue-stimulus Interval and Task Shift-Repetition. This interaction disappeared for the High-Stress condition. Although mean RT was similar for both groups, the patterns of cognitive control were different. Under Low stress there was a relatively greater cost for shifting tasks at the Short cue-stimulus interval. In other words, the difference between the two RTs for the Short interval was greater than the difference for the Long interval when stress was Low. But under High stress the cost of shifting tasks was the same for Short and Long cue-stimulus intervals. This outcome is consistent with the second prediction given at the start of this section: Introducing stress causes a change in cognitive strategy.

FROM PROBLEM TO EXPERIMENT

THE NUTS AND BOLTS

Problem   *Measuring Attention*

Some of the things we do seem to proceed fairly automatically, and others seem to require great concentration. Motor skills such as walking do not require much mental effort, whereas doing mental arithmetic can be quite taxing. To study the attention requirements of various tasks, we must have some way to measure it.

Problem   *How can we determine the amount of attention or mental effort that any arbitrary task might require?*

As is usually the case, this problem must be refined further; some hypotheses must be formulated before any meaningful solution can be attempted.

Hypothesis   *Increased attentional demands will be accompanied by increased stress, which will show up as a change in some physiological measure of body function.*

This hypothesis is a little vague, because it fails to specify the dependent variable precisely. There are many physiological correlates of behavior, and it is not clear from the hypothesis whether the experimenter should record heart rate, galvanic skin response, or brain waves or perform a chemical analysis of breathing exhalations. This difficulty could be bypassed by deciding to record every physiological measure that could be conveniently instrumented. Use of several dependent measures is indeed quite common in studies that investigate physiological correlates of attention, and this approach, although not terribly efficient, would strike some psychologists as reasonable. Although some of the dependent variables might prove to be useless, presumably they could be thrown out and only the "good" physiological measures retained.

Let us arbitrarily select three dependent variables: heart rate, brain waves, and pupil (a part of the eye, not a student) diameter. We hope that one or more of these will be correlated with attention. Now we must choose an independent variable. To do this, we need first to select a task for which we are fairly certain that (1) attention is required and (2) the amount of attention required can be varied by changing task difficulty. This is not as easy as it first appears; to do this properly, we must search the available literature to find converging operations (see Chapter 7 or 14), where the same task has been used in different situations. Without going into details of how this can be accomplished (see Miller & Ulrich, 1998), let us assume that one task that meets this requirement is the psychological refractory period discussed earlier in the chapter. We will further assume that attentional requirements can be controlled by varying SOA. So our independent variable will be SOA. How many different SOAs should be used? Clearly, at least two, since we cannot manipulate attention required with only a single SOA. The actual number selected would be a compromise between having as many different SOAs as possible and the limitations of time, money, and so forth. Let us say that four SOAs will be used: 50, 100, 200, and 400 milliseconds.

Control variables include modality and intensity of stimuli. The most important factor to be controlled is the presence of the second task. Thus, it is essential to include a single-task control condition (not a control variable) that is only S_1–R_1. We will also need to control for variables that are likely to influence heart rate, brain waves, and pupil diameter. This list of variables is quite extensive, and our present discussion will illustrate control on only two dependent variables. Heart rate is known to change with respiration (breathing) rate. It is difficult to control someone's breathing rate without resorting to unpleasant chemical and mechanical treatments. Most experimenters would not take this kind of risk and would simply monitor breathing rates. Technically, this kind of control adds another dependent variable. The control achieved is statistical rather than experimental—in this case, the correlation of heart and breathing rates. Pupil diameter is very sensitive to amount of illumination, with bright light causing the pupil to contract, so the experimenter would take care to keep the level of illumination constant throughout the study. Control would then be experimental rather than statistical, unlike the control of heart rate.

If we actually did this kind of experiment, we might expect only ERP to be related to attention. However, there are data (see Kahneman, 1973) suggesting that all three of our dependent variables are related to attention and amount of mental effort. It is often important to have more than one dependent variable because some dependent variables may be more sensitive to manipulation than others.

Hypothesis   *The amount of attention required by driving can be measured by reaction time for a simultaneous Donders B reaction task.*

Here, the dependent variable is specified precisely. It is choice reaction time. The logic behind this hypothesis is that the choice reaction task requires attention, so that attention devoted to the other task (usually called the primary task) must be diverted away from the reaction task, leading to increased reaction time. A further assumption is that both the primary task and the choice reaction task draw on a common source of attention or capacity.

The primary task would be driving a vehicle. For safety reasons, this kind of research is often carried out in a driving simulator. Our independent variables could be type of road environment defined by traffic density (high or low) and roadway curvature (straight, sharp curve, shallow curve). Some specific hypotheses might be that high traffic density requires greater attention and also that negotiating sharp curves requires greater attention. Performance on the driving task could be measured by deviations in lane position from the center of the lane.

The secondary task would be a Donders B reaction presented during driving. For example, the driver could hear a high- or low-frequency tone and could respond by pressing one of two buttons on the steering wheel.

Control variables would be the intensity of the tones and the vehicle handling characteristics. We would also use single-task control conditions (these are not control variables) of driving with no secondary task and the Donders B reaction with no driving. Unless driving performance was the same in control and experimental conditions, we could not reach any conclusions about the attention demands of driving. For example, if drivers did much better when no reaction task was required, this could indicate a shift of attention from driving to the Donders B reaction when they were performed together. The logic behind using secondary tasks to evaluate attention demands that the same amount of attention always be devoted to the primary task.

▼ SUMMARY

1. Interest in reaction time began with the personal equation, a systematic difference in RTs found among eighteenth-century astronomers. This phenomenon led Donders to formulate his subtractive method.
2. If the Donders A RT is subtracted from the C RT, an estimate of stimulus identification time is obtained. Donders B RT minus C RT yields an estimate of selection time.
3. Confounding occurs when a factor that is covariant with an independent variable may account for observed changes in behavior.
4. Dependent variables must be carefully selected, and the prudent researcher obtains as many measures of behavior as feasible. Studies that measure RT should also record error rate, because errors tend to be higher when a task is completed quickly. This leads to a trade-off between speed and accuracy.
5. When the time to respond between two signals is very short, the response to the second stimulus slows down. This psychological refractory period is better understood now that researchers have measured several dependent variables in the same experiment.
6. Interactions occur when the effect of one independent variable differs across levels of other independent variables manipulated in the same experiment. An interaction between stress level and cue-stimulus interval showed that stress alters cognitive strategy.

▼ KEY TERMS

central bottleneck
central capacity sharing
choice-reaction time
cognitive control
confounding
cue-stimulus interval
Donders A reaction
Donders B reaction
Donders C reaction
interaction

introspection
personal equation
psychological refractory period
pure insertion
separate modifiability
simple reaction
speed–accuracy trade-off
stimulus onset asynchrony (SOA)
stress level
subtractive method

▼ DISCUSSION QUESTIONS

1. What arguments could Kinnebrook have used to keep his job at the Royal Observatory?
2. Discuss the confoundings that can limit the usefulness of the assumption of pure insertion.
3. List five examples of the speed–accuracy trade-off that occur in everyday life outside the laboratory. Select one of your examples and design a laboratory experiment that will measure the trade-off. See if you can determine whether an additional dependent variable would be useful in understanding your example.
4. What is the importance of the interaction between stress level and cue-stimulus interval? Can you think of some examples?
5. Discuss possible interaction between traffic density and road curvature when using a secondary task to measure attention demands of driving.

WEB CONNECTIONS

Explore the step-by-step presentation of **"Confounds: Threats to Validity"** at:

http://psychology.wadsworth.com/workshops/workshops.html

You can test yourself in several experiments concerned with attention and reaction time at:

http://coglab.psych.purdue.edu/coglab/

An informative discussion of attention deficit hyperactivity disorder can be found at:

http://faculty.washington.edu/chudler/adhd.html

PSYCHOLOGY IN ACTION
Speed–Accuracy Trade-Off

The following demonstration requires a pencil, a newspaper, and a watch with a second hand. It helps if you have a friend to time you, but a timer with a buzzer can be used instead. Set your timer (or your friend) to 30 seconds. Now, going at a comfortable speed, work your way through a newspaper article, crossing out every letter *e* that occurs. Stop after 30 seconds and count the number of lines that you have completed. This is your baseline figure. (Enter it in Table 8.1.) Next, keep the time constant at 30 seconds, but try to increase the number of lines that have crossed-out letter *e*'s by 10 percent. Third, repeat this process with 10 percent fewer lines than your baseline—that is, go slower this time.

Repeat with 15 percent more lines (go faster); finally, with 15 percent fewer. Now take a well-deserved rest. When you have recovered, go back over each of the five passages you have crossed out and count the number of letter *e*'s you should have crossed out and the number you actually crossed out. Dividing the number crossed out by the total number gives you your error rate or percentage. Did you systematically make more errors as you tried to go faster and include more lines, thus revealing a trade-off between speed and accuracy? ■

▼ TABLE 8.1

Empirical Determination of Speed–Accuracy Trade-Off.

	Number of Lines	Number *e*'s Crossed Out Correctly (1)	Number *e*'s Missed (2)	Total *e*'s (1) + (2)	Percent (2) ÷ [(1) + (2)]
Baseline (*B*)	____	____	____	____	____
B + 10%	____	____	____	____	____
B − 10%	____	____	____	____	____
B + 15%	____	____	____	____	____
B − 15%	____	____	____	____	____

CONDITIONING AND LEARNING

We should be careful to get out of an experience only the wisdom that is in it—and stop there; lest we be like the cat that sits down on a hot stove-lid. She will never sit down on a hot stove-lid again—and that is well; but also she will never sit down on a cold one anymore. (MARK TWAIN)

The above quote by Mark Twain describes a learning experience that shares many characteristics with a kind of conditioning called **classical conditioning.** In classical conditioning, the experience, as Twain indicates, is usually not under control of the organism.

The cat does not seek out a hot stove lid to sit on; rather, the stove just happens to be hot when she sits on it; there is nothing she can do about it. Twain also notes that the effects of conditioning can be far reaching—the cat will not choose to sit on any stove lid again, regardless of whether the lid is hot. This sort of conditioning is a prominent part of our lives. Some of the more important examples of classical conditioning have been studied by Ader and his associates.

Following work by Herrnstein (1962), Ader and Cohen (1982) wanted to see if a conditioned placebo (see Chapter 6) could influence the body's immune response. Herrnstein showed that when a saline solution was paired with a drug that can slow down behavior (scopolamine), the saline solution alone resulted in a slowing down of behavior. Just as Twain's cat associated heat with stove lids—even cold stove lids—associating the salty solution with scopolamine led to its producing behavior similar to the behavior produced by scopolamine. Ader and Cohen paired the taste of a novel liquid with a drug that suppresses the immune system. After several pairings, the novel stimulus became a placebo, because it could also suppress the immune system. In turn, the immune suppression by the placebo prevented the development of lethal kidney problems in mice that were susceptible to kidney disease. Such findings helped lead to the development of **psychoneuroimmunology,** which is an interdisciplinary study of the interrelationships among behavior, neural, endocrine, and immune processes (Irwin & Miller, 2007). A major focus of this new field is to understand how conditioning can modulate immune responses.

Not all conditioning involves events that simply happen to the organism. In **instrumental conditioning,** the behavior of the organism is instrumental in producing consequences, often called rewards and punishments, which alter the rate of the behaviors that have produced the consequences. Let us examine an example of instrumental conditioning in an infant.

The behavior of infants between 2 and 6 months old is not very complicated, but they do show excited body movements to interesting stimuli. Rovee-Collier (1993) took advantage of this excitement to look at learning and retention in infants. She taught infants an instrumental kick response, by following a kick with the movement of a mobile that was suspended over the infant in his or her crib. A ribbon attached to the infant's leg and the mobile permits the infant's kick to activate the mobile. The rate of kicking when attached to the mobile is compared with the rate of kicking in a baseline phase (see Chapter 3) when the ribbon does not connect the infant and the mobile. Kicking is the instrumental response, and Rovee-Collier observed increases in kicking above the baseline in 2-, 3-, and 6-month-old infants. The infants learned an instrumental response—kicking—to activate the mobile.

Classical conditioning allows an organism to represent its world by learning relations among events (Rescorla, 1988)—a novel taste predicts an immune response. Instrumental conditioning, on the other hand, leads primarily to an organism learning relations between behavior and the outcomes it produces—a kick activates a mobile. These two fundamental types of learning will provide the background to illustrate several methodological issues. Before discussing these issues, we describe the basic features of these two types of conditioning.

▼ TYPES OF CONDITIONING

Classical Conditioning: Does the Name Pavlov Ring a Bell?

Early in this century, some fundamental psychological discoveries were made by Ivan P. Pavlov (1849–1936). The basic discovery that he made, which is now called Pavlovian, respondent, or classical conditioning, is well-known today, even by those outside psychology—but the fascinating story of how it came about is not. Pavlov was not trained as a psychologist (there were no psychologists in Russia, or elsewhere, when he received his education), but as a physiologist. He made great contributions in physiology concerning the measurement and analysis of stomach secretions accompanying the digestive process. He carefully measured the fluids produced by different sorts of food, and he regarded the secretion of these stomach juices as a physiological reflex. For this important work on the gastric juices involved in digestion, Pavlov received the Nobel Prize for medicine in 1904.

After he won the Nobel Prize, Pavlov turned to some more or less incidental discoveries that he had made in the course of his work. His fame in experimental psychology today arises from the systematic work that he did on these incidental discoveries, especially those concerning salivation. In one type of physiological experiment, Pavlov cut a dog's esophagus so that it would no longer carry food to the stomach (Figure 9.1). But he discovered that when he placed food in the dog's mouth, the stomach secreted almost as much gastric juice as it did when the food went to the stomach. Of course, food in the mouth produced reflexive salivation, but the reflexive action of the stomach seemed to depend on stimuli located in other places besides those in direct contact with the stomach lining. However, then Pavlov made an even more remarkable discovery. He found that it was not even necessary to place food in contact with the mouth to obtain salivary and gastric secretions. The mere sight of food would produce the secretions, or even the sight of the food dish without the food—or even the sight of the person who usually fed the animal! Obviously, then, secretion of the gastric juices and saliva must be caused by more than an automatic physiological reflex produced when a substance comes into direct contact with the animal. A physiological reflex is one that is shown by all physically normal animals of a certain species; it is "wired" into the nervous system. Pavlov had discovered a new type of reflex, one that he sometimes called a psychic reflex and sometimes a conditioned reflex. An outline of the standard paradigm for studying Pavlovian conditioning in the laboratory appears in Figure 9.2.

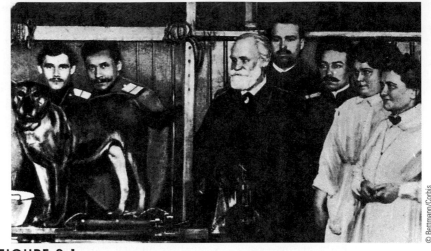

▼ **FIGURE 9.1**

Ivan Pavlov and his staff are shown here with one of the dogs used in his experiments. The dog was harnessed to the wooden frame shown in the picture. Saliva was conducted by a tube to a measuring device that could record the rate and quantity of salivation.

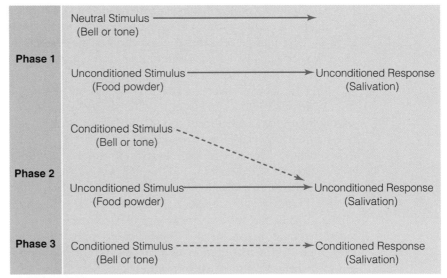

▼ **FIGURE 9.2**

An Outline of the Stages in Classical Conditioning. A neutral stimulus, such as a bell, that elicits no salivation when presented by itself is delivered to the organism slightly before an unconditioned stimulus, such as food powder, that produces an unconditioned response, salivation. If the neutral stimulus predicts the unconditioned stimulus, then after a number of pairings (as in phase 1), the neutral stimulus becomes associated with the unconditioned response, indicated by the broken line in phase 2. The neutral stimulus is now called the conditioned stimulus. Eventually (phase 3), the conditioned stimulus will elicit salivation in the absence of the unconditioned stimulus, and this salivation is called the **conditioned response (CR).** If the conditioned stimulus is repeatedly presented without the unconditioned stimulus, the CR will grow weaker and eventually extinguish.

Pavlov's very important discovery demonstrates that nearly any stimulus that does not normally elicit a particular response can come to control that response by being paired with another stimulus that reliably produces a reaction. For example, if a person is subjected to a stressful event in a particular situation (say, his or her office or room), then the body will respond with defensive reactions: The heart may race, blood pressure increases, adrenaline flows, and so on. These responses might become conditioned to the situation, so that even without a stressful event a person may show all these physiological changes in the situation. Some researchers in the field of behavioral medicine have argued that many disorders so prevalent today—hypertension, gastric ulcers, headaches—are in part caused by conditioned reactions that occur when people are in situations where they have repeatedly experienced stress. As indicated by the case in which a novel taste produced immune suppression, Pavlovian conditioning also seems to play a role in the development of other important human behaviors, including phobias (irrational fears) and other aversions.

Pavlovian conditioning does not, however, indicate that you are entirely at the mercy of arbitrarily paired events. Research has shown that although contiguous pairing of events (say, an office and stress) may be necessary for classical conditioning to occur, such pairing may not be sufficient. Several years ago, Kamin (1969) showed that it is important for the **conditioned stimulus (CS)** to *predict* the **unconditioned stimulus (US)** and not just coincide with it. Kamin first demonstrated that rats could easily learn to associate CSs that were a light, a noise, or a combination of light and noise with a mild electric shock (the US). He then showed that if a rat first learned that one CS was associated with shock (say, the noise), the rat would not learn much at all about the light–US relation when the light was subsequently presented with the noise CS in combination with the shock. Kamin reasoned that the rat first learned that noise predicted shock. Then when the noise and light appeared together, the light was redundant to the noise and the animal did not learn to associate it with the shock. Such **blocking** of learning to redundant stimuli compounded with the original CS also appears in experiments with humans (Mitchell & Lovibond, 2002). According to these results, a person who showed a stress reaction to his or her office would not learn to associate stress with a new piece of office furniture because the office itself would be a good predictor of stress. When one event predicts another, a *contingent* relation (or a **contingency**) is said to exist between the two events.

Instrumental (Operant) Conditioning

The earliest examples of the second type of conditioning were experiments by E. L. Thorndike at Columbia University, who put cats in puzzle boxes from which they were supposed to escape. These experiments were performed at about the same time as Pavlov's. They are described in detail in Chapter 11; briefly, the experiment concerned learning from the consequences of some action. Thorndike's cats performed some response that allowed them to escape from the puzzle box; then, when they were placed in the box again, they tended to perform the same response. The consequences of a behavior affected how it was learned. Since the behavior was instrumental in producing the consequence (the reward), this form of learning was called instrumental conditioning. It was seen as obeying different principles from those of Pavlovian conditioning and was also viewed as a more general type of learning.

Over the years, a great number of psychologists have devoted much effort to understanding instrumental conditioning. The most famous investigator and popularizer of the study of this type of conditioning is B. F. Skinner. He called this type of conditioning **operant conditioning,** because the response operates on the environment. This is distinguished from what Skinner called **respondent conditioning,** the classical conditioning studied by Pavlovians, in which the organism simply responds to environmental stimulation. The primary datum of interest in the study of operant conditioning is the rate at which some response occurs. The primary responses that have been studied are lever pressing by rats and key pecking by pigeons in operant-conditioning apparatuses (or, more colloquially, in Skinner boxes). A Skinner box is simply a small, well-lit box with a lever or key that can be depressed and a place for dispensing food (Figure 9.3).

In operant conditioning, the experimenter waits until the animal makes the desired response; he or she then rewards it, say, with food. If the entire response is not performed, the experimenter must reinforce successive approximations to it until the desired response occurs. For example, if you want to teach a pigeon to walk around in figure eights, you must first reward quarter-circle turns, then half-turns, and so on. This procedure of reinforcing greater and greater approximations to the desired behavior is called **shaping** the behavior; in principle, it is similar to the "getting warmer" game played by children. Operant conditioning works on the law of effect (see Chapter 11 for additional details): If an operant response is made and followed by a reinforcing stimulus, the probability that the response will occur again is increased. What will serve as a reinforcing stimulus is not specified ahead of time but must be discovered for each situation. Using this straightforward principle, Skinner and many others have undertaken the experimental analysis of numerous behaviors.

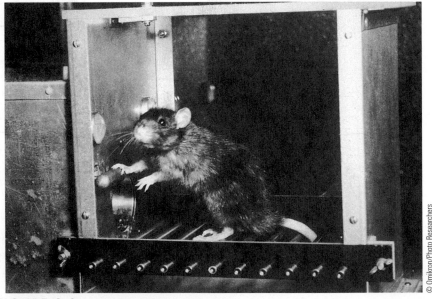

© Omikron/Photo Researchers

▼ FIGURE 9.3

A typical Skinner box equipped with a response lever and a food cup below it. A lever press by the animal makes a pellet of food drop into the cup. All of this machinery is controlled by programming equipment that allows the experimenter to set different tasks for the animal.

A reinforcing stimulus is one that strengthens the response that it follows. Generally, two different classes of reinforcing stimuli are identified: **positive reinforcing stimulus** and **negative reinforcing stimulus.** Positive reinforcers are the familiar rewards that are given following a particular response: food pellets in the Skinner box, a gold star on a good spelling test, a moving mobile in a crib, and so on. Behaviors that produce positive reinforcers increase in likelihood. Negative reinforcers are aversive events, and responses that remove or avoid them are strengthened. For example, a rat can learn to press a bar in a Skinner box to terminate a shock or to postpone it. In a similar fashion, you receive reinforcement on a bitterly cold day by putting on a warm coat to avoid getting uncomfortably chilly.

Do not confuse negative reinforcement with **punishment.** Behaviors that produce aversive events are said to be punished. Punished behaviors decrease in frequency. If a rat has been positively reinforced with food for pressing a lever and is now punished for each lever press with a mild electric shock, the rate of pressing the lever will decrease.

The role of stimuli other than the reinforcing stimulus is also important in the study of operant conditioning. A **discriminative stimulus (SD)** signals when a behavior will be followed by a reward. For example, a pigeon might be trained to peck a button for food only in the presence of a red light. If any other light is on, pecking will not be followed by food. Animals learn such contingencies between stimuli and responses quite readily. A discriminative stimulus may be said to "set the stage" or "provide the occasion" for some response. One of the primary tasks of operant conditioning is to bring some response "under stimulus control." An organism is said to be under stimulus control when it responds correctly and consistently in the presence of a discriminative stimulus and not in its absence. Rovee-Collier's infants were under stimulus control when they responded to the mobile that resulted in reinforcement.

Recall that effective CSs in classical conditioning are those that are contingently related to the US (the CS predicts the US). Operant conditioning also has important contingent relations: namely, the relation between the response and the reinforcing stimulus. In operant conditioning, organisms can learn that there is a positive contingency between behavior and reinforcement, which is the standard Skinner box arrangement. Organisms can also learn that there is a negative contingency between behavior and reinforcement, such that if they respond, reinforcement will not occur. One way of examining this contingency is to use a procedure called **experimental extinction,** in which reinforcement is withheld after an organism has learned to make a particular response. After several times of having reinforcement fail to follow the response, the organism ceases to make the response. (See the "From Problem to Experiment" section at the end of this chapter for an additional discussion of extinction.)

Finally, organisms can learn that there is a null contingency between their behavior and reinforcement. A **null contingency** is one in which the reinforcer is independent of behavior—sometimes a behavior leads to reinforcement, and sometimes the reinforcement occurs in the absence of a particular behavior. When organisms learn that no matter what they do, aversive events will happen, they learn to be helpless and show various signs of depression (LoLordo, 2001). Likewise, some research shows that when positive events occur independently of behavior, organisms tend to become lazy (Welker, 1976). It is tempting to generalize the latter effect to "spoiled brats" who receive substantial numbers of noncontingent positive reinforcers and then fail to work hard to get them when it becomes necessary to do so.

INTRODUCING THE VARIABLES

Dependent Variables

One important dependent variable in animal learning research is the rate of responding, often plotted over time. Another important dependent variable commonly used in classical conditioning is the amplitude of the response. Rather than just noting whether or not a dog salivates to a conditioned stimulus, we can measure the amplitude of the response by seeing how much saliva is produced. Another commonly measured characteristic of responses is their latency, or the time it takes the animal to accomplish the response. This measure is widely used in maze-learning experiments, where the time it takes an animal to complete the maze is recorded. Often results are plotted in terms of speed rather than latency, speed being the reciprocal of latency (1/latency).

A derived measure of learning is resistance to extinction. After a response has been learned, if the experimenter no longer applies reinforcement when the animal executes the response, the response gradually grows weaker or extinguishes. Resistance to extinction, then, can be used as an index of how well the response was learned in the first place. It is considered a derived, rather than basic, measure because what is still being measured is frequency, amplitude, or speed of response. These all decline during extinction, but they may decline at different rates after different manipulations of the independent variable. Thus, resistance to extinction is a derived measure of the effectiveness of some independent variable on learning.

Independent Variables

A great many independent variables may be manipulated in studies of animal learning and conditioning. Many have to do with the nature of reinforcement. Experimenters can vary the magnitude of reinforcement in Pavlovian and instrumental conditioning.

Experimenters can also vary the schedule by which reinforcement is administered, as well as the delay after the response, before they present the reinforcing stimulus to the subject. (Typically, longer delays produce less learning.) Another popular variable is the motivation of the animal. This can be manipulated by varying the amount of time the organism has been deprived of the reinforcing stimulus (e.g., food or water) before the experiment. These are, of course, just a few of the possible independent variables.

Control Variables

Control of extraneous variation is typically quite sophisticated in basic animal learning research, but even here, there are subtle problems. One of these is the problem of **pseudoconditioning** in classical conditioning experiments. Pseudoconditioning refers to a temporary elevation in the amplitude of the conditioned response (CR) that is not caused by the association between the CS and US. Thus, it is not true conditioning but only mimics conditioning. It is recognized by being relatively short lived and variable and is usually caused by the general excitement of the experimental situation for the animal, including the presentation of the CS and US. The appropriate control for pseudoconditioning is to have one group of animals in the experiment exposed to the same number of CS and US presentations as the animals in the conditioning group but to have the presentations unpaired and presented randomly. Both the experimental and the pseudoconditioning control groups should be affected by the general excitement induced by the experimental situation; any difference between the two groups should be due to the learning produced by the CS–US pairings in the case of the experimental group (Rescorla, 1967).

9.1   EXPERIMENTAL TOPICS AND RESEARCH ILLUSTRATIONS

Topic *Within- and Between-Subjects Designs*

Illustration *Stimulus Intensity*

One fundamental question about classical conditioning is how the intensity of a neutral stimulus affects the conditioning process. For example, if a tone is paired with food given to dogs, will the intensity of the tone affect how quickly the dog becomes conditioned, so that the tone alone (now called the conditioned stimulus) produces salivation? A reasonable hypothesis is that the stronger the stimulus, the more quickly conditioning will occur. Animals should be very sensitive to more-salient stimuli and thus more likely to associate them with unconditioned stimuli. We might predict that the stronger the conditioned stimulus, the faster and stronger the conditioning will occur.

Many researchers have investigated this question over the years; the surprising finding from most of the early research was that stimulus intensity did not seem to have much effect on Pavlovian conditioning. Relatively weak stimuli seemed to produce just as good conditioning as did strong stimuli (Carter, 1941; Grant and Schneider, 1948). Since most theories of the time predicted that conditioning should be affected by the intensity of the stimulus (Hull, 1943), the failure to find the effect constituted something of a puzzle. The researchers who did these experiments on stimulus-intensity effects in conditioning typically used between-subjects designs, so that different groups of subjects received different stimulus intensities. Before discussing the reason for their doing this, let us consider some of the general advantages and disadvantages of between-subjects and within-subjects experimental designs.

Between-Subjects Versus Within-Subjects Designs

Consider the simplest sort of experimental design in which there are two conditions, experimental and control, with different groups of participants assigned to each. In a **between-subjects design,** a different group of participants usually receives just one level of each independent variable. One potential problem that can arise from using a between-subjects design is that a difference obtained on the dependent variable might be caused by the fact that different groups of participants are used in the two conditions. This means that in the standard between-subjects design *participants are confounded with the levels of independent variable.* Experimenters try to overcome this problem by randomly assigning subjects to the levels of the independent variable in between-subjects designs. Thus, *on the average,* the groups should have similar characteristics in all conditions. In all between-subjects designs, then, participants should be randomly assigned to the different conditions to ensure that the groups are equivalent prior to the manipulation of the independent variable. We must try to have equivalent groups, because otherwise any difference observed between the groups on the dependent variable might be merely because participants in the different groups differed in ability. If we have a large number of subjects and randomly assign them to groups, then we can minimize the possibility of this sort of confounding and be more confident that any difference we find on the dependent variable actually results from the independent-variable manipulation. When subjects are randomly assigned to conditions in a between-subjects design, this is referred to as a **random-groups design.**

There are two primary drawbacks to between-subjects or random-groups designs. One is the fact that they are wasteful in terms of the number of subjects required.

When a different group of subjects is assigned to each condition, the total number of participants required for an experiment can quickly become quite large—especially if the experimental design is at all complex. Thus, between-subjects designs are impractical when, as is often the case, there is a shortage of participants available for an experiment.

The second problem is more serious; it has to do with the variability introduced by using different groups of participants. One basic fact of all psychological research is that subjects differ greatly in their abilities to perform almost any task (on almost any dependent variable). When numerous participants are used in between-subjects designs, some of the differences in behavior in the experimental conditions will result from differences among the participants. This can have the unfortunate effect of making it difficult to determine whether subject differences or the independent variable determined the results. In summary, participants are confounded with groups, and in between-subjects designs this variability caused by their subject differences cannot be estimated statistically and taken into account.

Both of the problems with between-subjects designs can be reduced by using **within-subjects designs,** in which all participants receive every level of the variable. Within-subjects designs usually require fewer subjects than between-subjects designs, because each participant serves in all conditions. Also, statistical techniques can take into account the variance produced by the differences between subjects. This is possible because each one serves as his or her own control—another way of saying that participants are *not* confounded with groups, as in a between-subjects experiment. A within-subjects design is usually more effective than a between-subjects design in detecting differences between conditions on the dependent variable, because this variance owing to participant differences can be estimated statistically and taken into account. The exact statistical techniques for analyzing within-subjects experiments are not discussed here. In general, the within-subjects design is more powerful—more likely to allow detection of a difference between conditions if there really is one—than the between-subjects design. This advantage makes the within-subjects design preferred by many investigators whenever it is possible to use it.

Although there are advantages to using within-subjects designs, new problems are introduced by them. Unfortunately, within-subjects designs simply cannot be used in investigating some types of experimental problems, and even when they can be used, they have requirements that between-subjects designs do not. Within-subjects designs cannot be used in cases where performing in one condition is likely to completely change performance in another condition. This problem is usually called **asymmetrical transfer,** or a **carryover effect.** If we want to know how rats differ in learning a maze with and without their hippocampuses (a part of the brain related to learning and memory), we cannot use a within-subjects design, since we cannot replace a hippocampus once it is removed. The same problem occurs any time the independent variable may provide a change in behavior that will carry over until the subject is tested under the other condition.

If we want to test people on a task either with or without some specific training, we cannot test them first with training and then with no training. And we cannot always test them in the reverse order (no training and then training), because then we have confounded conditions with practice on the task. For example, if we want to see if a specific memory-training program is effective, we cannot teach people the program (the training phase), test them, and then test them again with no training. Once a person has had the training, we cannot take it away; it will carry over to the next part of the experiment. We cannot test people in the other direction, either, with a memory test, a training phase, and then a second memory test. The reason is that if people improved on the second test, we would not know whether the improvement was a result of training or merely practice at taking memory tests. In other words, training and practice would be confounded. A between-subjects design is appropriate in this case. One group of people would have their memories tested with no training; the other group would be tested after receiving the memory training program.

Within-subjects designs are also inappropriate when participants may figure out what is expected of them in the experiment and then try to cooperate with the experimenter to produce the desired results. This is more likely to happen with within-subjects than between-subjects designs, because in the former case, the people participate in each condition. This problem makes within-subjects designs all but nonexistent in certain types of social psychological research.

Even when these problems do not eliminate the possibility of using a within-subjects design in some situations, there are additional problems to be considered. In within-subjects designs, the subjects are always tested at two or more points in time; thus, the experimenter must be on guard for factors related to time that would affect the experimental results. The two primary factors that must be considered are **practice effects** and **fatigue effects,** which tend to offset one another. Practice effects refer to improved performance in the experimental task simply because of practice, and not the manipulation of the independent variable (as in the memory experiment just discussed). Fatigue effects refer to decreases in performance over the course of the experiment, especially if the experimental task is long, difficult, or boring. The effects of practice and fatigue may be taken into account and minimized by systematically arranging the order in which the experimental conditions are presented to subjects. This technique is referred to as **counterbalancing** of conditions and is discussed later in the chapter.

As we have said, when appropriate, within-subjects designs are generally preferred to between-subjects designs, despite the fact that they involve a number of additional considerations. The primary advantage, once again, is the fact that within-subjects designs are typically more powerful or more sensitive, because the possibility of error resulting from subject variability is reduced relative to that in between-subjects designs.

A third design, the **matched-groups design,** tries to introduce some of the advantages of a within-subjects design to a between-subjects comparison. The matched-groups design attempts to reduce participant variability among groups by matching them in the different groups on other variables. Thus, in a human memory experiment, people might be matched on the basis of IQ before they were randomly assigned to conditions. (Each subgroup of people matched for IQ is randomly assigned to a particular group.) Matching on relevant variables can help reduce the variability caused by the simple random assignment of participants to each group (the random-groups design). Also, it is very important that assignment to conditions still be random within matched sets of people; otherwise, there is the possibility of confounding and other problems, especially regression artifacts (see Chapters 2 and 12). In many situations, matching tends to involve much work, since participants must be measured separately on the matching variable.

One matching technique used in animal research is the **split-litter technique.** This involves taking animals from the same litter and then randomly assigning them to

238   PART 2   PRINCIPLES AND PRACTICES OF EXPERIMENTAL PSYCHOLOGY

groups. Since the animals in the different groups are genetically similar, this helps reduce variability resulting from subject differences that occurs in random-groups designs.

Stimulus Intensity in Classical Conditioning

Let us now return to the problem we considered earlier. How does the intensity of the conditioned stimulus affect acquisition of a conditioned response? Common sense, as well as some theories, led to the prediction that more intense stimuli should lead to faster conditioning than should less intense stimuli. However, as mentioned earlier, the first research on this topic failed to find such effects. For example, Grant and Schneider (1948) varied the intensity of a light as a conditioned stimulus in an eyelid-conditioning experiment. In such experiments, people are attached to an apparatus that delivers puffs of air to the eye and records responses (eye blinks). The unconditioned stimulus is the air puff, the **unconditioned response (UR)** is the blinking, and the conditioned stimulus is a light that precedes the air puff. Originally, the light does not cause a person to blink; but after it is repeatedly paired with the air puff, eventually the light by itself causes the blinking, which then is the conditioned response. Grant and Schneider asked simply whether more intense lights would cause faster conditioning. Would a bright light cause people to develop a conditioned response faster than a dim light? They tested different groups in the two cases, one with each intensity of light, and discovered that, contrary to expectations, conditioning was just as fast in the condition with the dim light as it was in the condition with the bright light. Other researchers obtained similar results when they examined the effects of stimulus intensity on conditioning in between-subjects designs, even when they used different stimuli (such as tones instead of lights).

The choice of a between- or within-subjects design is usually determined by the nature of the problem studied, the independent variables manipulated, the number of participants available to the researcher, and other considerations described in the preceding section. Rarely do researchers consider the possibility that the very outcome of their research could depend on the type of design they choose. However, this is exactly the case in the issue of the effects of stimulus intensity on conditioning, as was discovered after Grant and Schneider's (1948) research.

Years later, Beck (1963) again asked the question of whether the intensity of the stimulus affected eyelid conditioning. She was also interested in other variables, including the intensity of the unconditioned stimulus (the air puff) and the anxiety level of her participants. For our purposes, we will consider only the effect of the intensity level of the conditioned stimulus, which was varied within subjects as one factor in a complex experimental design. Beck used two intensity levels and presented them in an irregular order across 100 conditioning trials in her experiment. She found a large and statistically significant effect of stimulus intensity on development of the conditioned response, contrary to what other researchers had found.

Grice and Hunter (1964) noticed Beck's effect and wondered if she had found an effect where others had found none because she had used a within-subjects design, whereas most others had used between-subjects designs. To discover this, they tested three groups of people: In two groups, the variable of intensity of the conditioned stimulus was varied between subjects, and for the remaining group, it was varied within subjects. They used a soft tone (50 decibels) or a loud tone (100 decibels) as the conditioned stimuli in an eyelid-conditioning experiment. People in each group participated in 100 trials. On each trial, participants heard a buzzer that alerted them that a trial was beginning. Two seconds later, they heard a tone (soft or loud) that lasted half a second, and then after another half-second, they received a puff of air to the eye. The tone was the conditioned stimulus, the air puff the unconditioned stimulus. The loud group received the 100-decibel tone on all 100 trials, whereas the soft group received the 50-decibel tone on all 100 trials. These two groups represent a between-subjects comparison of stimulus-intensity level in eyelid conditioning. People in the third group (the loud/soft group) received 50 trials with the loud tone (L) and 50 trials with the soft tone (S). The trials occurred in one of two irregular orders, such that one order was the mirror image of the other. In other words, if the order of the first 10 trials was L, S, S, L, S, L, L, L, S, L, the other order would be S, L, L, S, L, S, S, S, L, S. In the loud/soft group, half the people received each order.[1]

The results are shown in Figure 9.4, where you can see the percentage of the last 60 trials on which participants showed a conditioned response—that is, blinking—to the

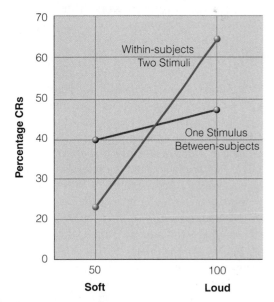

▼ FIGURE 9.4

Results of Grice and Hunter's (1964) Experiment. When stimulus intensity was varied between subjects so that every subject had experience only with the loud or soft stimulus, no reliable effect of stimulus intensity was found. However, when there was a within-subjects manipulation of stimulus intensity so that every subject experienced both intensities, a large effect was obtained. (The measure was the percentage of the last 60 trials on which a conditioned response occurred.) The results show that the type of experimental design can affect the results obtained in an experiment. *Source:* From "Stimulus Intensity Effects Depend upon the Type of Experimental Design," by G. R. Grice and J. J. Hunter in *Psychological Review,* 71, 247–256. © 1964 by the American Psychological Association. Adapted with permission.

---

[1] You may have noticed that there is a confounding in the design of the experiment by Grice and Hunter. People received 100 trials with either a soft or a loud CS in the between-subjects case, but subjects received half as many of each CS in the within-subjects case. More trials should yield better conditioning to each CS for the between-subjects case, but as shown in Figure 9.4, it did not—loud led to better learning in the within-subjects case, and soft led to better learning in the between-subjects case.

tone before the air puff came. One line represents the between-subjects comparison, in which each subject had experience with only the loud stimulus or the soft stimulus. Notice that the percentage of trials on which participants responded did not vary as a function of stimulus intensity in the one-stimulus, between-subjects case. (The slight difference seen is not statistically reliable.) On the other hand, when stimulus intensity was varied within subjects in the loud/soft group, a large effect of stimulus intensity was found. People responded just slightly more than 20 percent of the time to the soft stimulus but almost 70 percent of the time to the loud stimulus, a significant difference.

The results of Grice and Hunter's experiment show that the choice of a between-subjects or within-subjects design can have far-reaching effects. In this case, the actual outcome of experiments designed to examine the effects of stimulus intensity was determined by the choice of design. When people experienced both stimuli, they reacted to them differently; but when they experienced only one stimulus or the other, they showed no difference in responding. Grice (1966) reports other situations in which a similar pattern of results occurs. In many experimental situations, researchers cannot tell whether their findings would be changed by switching from a between-subjects to a within-subjects design (or vice versa), because it is impossible to ask the experimental question with the other design, for reasons discussed earlier. However, Grice and Hunter's (1964) research reminds us that the choice of an experimental design can have ramifications beyond mundane considerations of the number of subjects used and the like. The actual outcome of the research may be affected.

Consider an alternative way of interpreting these results. Perhaps the between- and within-subjects designs result in different effects because the within-subjects design automatically produces a carryover effect by allowing the participants in the experiment to experience all values of the relevant stimuli. Compared with people in the between-subjects version, people in the within-subjects design may have been able to perceive the loud stimulus as louder and the soft stimulus as softer because they had the opportunity to experience both intensities on successive trials and could therefore compare one stimulus with another. People who perceived only one value of the stimulus could not make such a comparison. Likewise, Kawai and Imada (1996) have found that the greater aversiveness of a longer electrical shock than a shorter one is more likely to be noticed in a within-subjects design than in a between-subjects one. Later, in the "From Problem to Experiment" section on page 253, you will see that the choice of design can determine the course of extinction in instrumental conditioning for humans (Svartdal, 2000) and nonhuman animals (Papini, Thomas, & McVicar, 2002). In the next section we examine another sort of contrast that can occur in conditioning, and it also suggests that being able to compare events by virtue of the experimental design results in different kinds of behavior.

9.2   EXPERIMENTAL TOPICS AND RESEARCH ILLUSTRATIONS

Topic   *Counterbalancing*

Illustration   *Simultaneous Contrast*

Whenever a within-subjects design is used, one needs to decide with care the order in which the conditions should be presented to the subjects. The arrangement must be such that, on the average, the conditions are presented at the same stage of practice, so that there can be no confounding between the experimental conditions and stage of practice. Counterbalancing is also necessary to minimize the effect of other variables besides time that might affect the experiment. Often, the experimenter must counterbalance across variables in which he or she has little interest, even in between-subjects designs, so that these extraneous variables do not affect the conditions of interest. An example of this problem should make it clearer.

In learning an instrumental response, the particular magnitude of the reward greatly influences performance. Typically, performance improves as the magnitude of reward increases. However, the particular magnitude of reward used does not have an invariable effect on performance but depends instead on the experience that the organism has had with other reinforcement conditions. One example of this effect is provided by an experiment done by Bower (1961) on **simultaneous contrast,** in which some subjects experienced two contrasting magnitudes of reward.

Bower's experiment consisted of three groups of 10 rats, each of which received four trials a day in a straight-alley maze for 32 days, for a total of 128 trials. The independent variable was the magnitude of reward used. One group of rats received eight food pellets in the goal box on their four trials. Since they received a constant eight pellets on each trial, this condition is referred to as Constant 8. Another group received only one pellet after each trial (Constant 1). These two groups can be considered as controls for the third (Contrast) group. Subjects in this group received two trials each day, in two different straight alleys. The two alleys were quite discriminable, one being black and one being white. In one alley, the rats always received a one-pellet reward; in the other alley, they always received eight pellets. Bower wanted to see how the exposure to both levels of reinforcement would affect running speed, as compared with exposure to only one level all the time. Would rats run at a different speed for a one-pellet (or eight-pellet) reward if they had experienced another level of reward, rather than having had constant training at one particular level?

Before examining the results, consider some design features that Bower had to face for the contrast rats. Since magnitude of reward varied within subjects in this condition, there were two problems to consider. First, he had to make sure that not all subjects received the greater or lesser reinforcement in either the black or white alley, because alley color then would be confounded with reward magnitude, and rats may simply have run faster in black alleys than white (or vice versa). This was easily accomplished by having half the animals receive eight pellets in the black alley and one pellet in the white alley and having the other half of the animals receive the reverse arrangement. For the control animals that received only one reward magnitude, half received the reward in a white alley and half in a black alley. All this may sound rather complicated, so we outlined the design scheme in Figure 9.5.

The second problem concerns the order in which the rats in the contrast group should be given the two conditions on the four trials each day. Obviously, they should not first be given the two large-reward trials followed by the two small-reward trials (or vice versa), since time of testing would be confounded with reward magnitude. Perhaps a random order could be used for the 128 trials. But random orders are not preferred in such cases, since there can be, even in random orders, long runs in which the same occurrence appears. So it would not be surprising to find cases where there were two trials in a row of the same type (large or small magnitude of reward), although across all subjects there would be no confounding with practice. A preferable way to handle this problem involves counterbalancing the conditions rather than

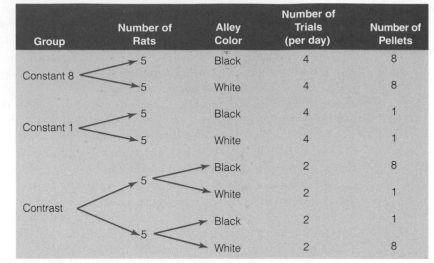

Group	Number of Rats	Alley Color	Number of Trials (per day)	Number of Pellets
Constant 8	5	Black	4	8
	5	White	4	8
Constant 1	5	Black	4	1
	5	White	4	1
Contrast	5	Black	2	8
		White	2	1
	5	Black	2	1
		White	2	8

▼ **FIGURE 9.5**

An outline of the design of Bower's experiment showing some of the features used to minimize confounding. Alley color is not confounded with group or magnitude of reward (number of pellets). For the contrast group, additional counterbalancing is needed to balance the order of one- versus eight-pellet trials within the daily session (see text).

varying them randomly. *Counterbalancing,* you will remember, refers to any technique used to systematically vary the order of conditions in an experiment to distribute the effects of time of testing (such as practice and fatigue), so that they are not confounded with conditions.

When two conditions are tested in blocks of four trials, there are six possible orders in which the conditions can occur within trials. In the present case, if *S* stands for a small (one-pellet) reward and *L* for a large (eight-pellet) one, then the six orders are SSLL, SLSL, SLLS, LLSS, LSLS, LSSL. Bower solved the counterbalancing problem by using each of these orders equally often. On a particular day of testing, he would pick an order for the trials for half the rats (e.g., LSSL) and then simply test the other half using the opposite order (SLLS). The next day he would pick another order for half the rats, while the others received the reverse order, and so on. This led to no confounding between order and conditions, and all the orders were used equally often, so that the experiment did not depend on just one order. We shall return to this point in a moment.

Bower's results are presented in Figure 9.6, where the mean running speed for each of the four conditions is plotted across blocks of 2 days (eight trials). For the rats that received constant reward, those rewarded with eight pellets performed better after the first few days than those rewarded with one. It was not exactly big news, of course, that rats ran faster for more, rather than less, food. The real interest was in how fast rats in the contrast conditions ran for large and small rewards. Although there was no statistically reliable effect between speeds of the Constant 8 and Contrast 8 conditions in Figure 9.6, the Contrast 1 rats ran reliably more slowly for the reward than did the Constant 1 rats, at least toward the end of training. This is referred to as a **negative contrast effect,** since the contrast subjects ran more slowly for the small reward than did the rats that always received the small reward.

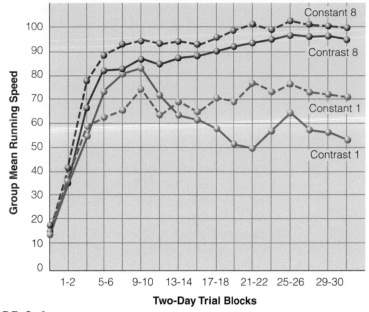

▼ FIGURE 9.6

These are the group mean running speeds for the conditions of Bower's experiment, averaged over blocks of eight trials (2 days). The rats that received both one-pellet and eight-pellet trials ran more slowly for the one-pellet reward than rats that always received one pellet. This is called a negative contrast effect. *Source:* Bower, G. (1961). "A contrast effect in differential learning," *Journal of Expermental Psychology, 62,* Figure 1.

One interpretation of this phenomenon considers emotional states induced in the contrast rats owing to their experience in the situation. Since the contrast rats were familiar with both levels of reward, when placed in the distinctive alley that told them that they would receive a small reward, they were annoyed or frustrated at having to run down the alley for only one crummy pellet. These results prompt an interesting question as to why Bower did not find a **positive contrast effect,** or faster running for the Contrast 8 subjects relative to the Constant 8 subjects. Should not the Contrast 8 rats be happy or elated to learn, when placed in the distinctive alley signaling a large reward, that they would get eight pellets rather than only one? One possibility is that they *were* more elated but that a ceiling effect prevented this from being reflected in their running speeds. Perhaps performance was already very good in the Constant 8 condition. Because of the large reward, there was no room for improvement in the Contrast 8 condition. The rats in the control (Constant 8) condition were already running as fast as their little legs would carry them, so no matter how much more elated the contrast rats might be, this could not be reflected in their performance. Although this ceiling-effect interpretation of the present data is bolstered somewhat by other reports of positive contrast effects (Padilla, 1971), negative contrast effects seem more easily obtained than positive ones. We discuss the problem of ceiling effects in data analysis more fully in Chapter 10.

The results of Bower's experiment should remind you of the lesson in the previous section contrasting between- and within-subjects designs. As in Grice and Hunter's experiments on stimulus-intensity effects, Bower found that the effect of a reward of a particular magnitude depended on the type of design used. In a within-subjects design, in which the animals had experience with both reward magnitudes, the effect on behavior was greater than in the between-subjects comparison, in which a different group of animals received constant rewards over the series of trials. Once again, the nature of the design can affect the experimenter's conclusion about how strong an effect is produced by the independent variable.

Further Considerations in Counterbalancing

A great variety of counterbalancing schemes can be used in various situations. Some of these become very complex. Here, we discuss only some of the simpler counterbalancing designs to provide you with a few tricks of the trade.

The case represented by Bower's (1961) contrast group is in many ways typical of the counterbalancing problem as it usually arises. Two conditions were to be tested within subjects; thus, they had to be counterbalanced so as not to be confounded with stage of practice. One solution to this problem, and the one most psychologists would pick, would be to use an ***ABBA* design,** where *A* stands for one condition and *B* stands for the other. This would remove the confounding of particular conditions with time of testing, since each condition would be tested at the same time on average ($1 + 4 = 5$ for *A*, and $2 + 3 = 5$ for *B*, where the numbers refer to the order of test). But perhaps the specific order of testing might also matter. For example, let us assume that there is a very large practice effect on the dependent variable but that it occurs very early in training, on the first trial. Then it would contribute to the *A* condition but not to the *B* condition, so that the *ABBA* design would not eliminate the confounding of conditions with practice.

Two solutions to this problem of large effects of practice early in training can be suggested. One is to give a number of practice trials in the experimental situation before the experiment proper begins. Thus, the subjects are given practice, and performance on the dependent variable is allowed to stabilize before the experimental conditions of interest are introduced. Another solution is to employ more than one counterbalancing scheme. For example, half the subjects might get the reverse of the scheme that the other half receives. So half the subjects would get *ABBA* and the other half would get *BAAB*. Bower's solution to the counterbalancing problem was the ideal extension of this logic, since he used every possible counterbalancing scheme equally often. But when more than two conditions are involved, this becomes unwieldy. In most situations, an adequate solution to the problem of practice effects at the beginning of a testing session would be to give subjects practice and then use two counterbalancing schemes, one of which is the reverse of the other. Grice and Hunter (1964), in the experiment on stimulus intensity described earlier, did just this.

For situations in which there are more than two conditions, we would recommend one particular scheme for counterbalancing as generally desirable. This is the **balanced Latin square design.** Suppose there were six conditions in a counterbalanced order so that practice effects would not confound the results. For example, in a simultaneous contrast experiment such as Bower's, six different reward magnitudes could be used rather than only two. A balanced Latin square design would ensure

▼ **TABLE 9.1**

Balanced Latin Square for Six Experimental Conditions (1–6) Presented to Each Subject. Rows Indicate the Order in Which Subjects *a* through *f* Receive the Experimental Conditions.

Subjects	Order of Testing Conditions					
	1st	2nd	3rd	4th	5th	6th
a	1	2	6	3	5	4
b	2	3	1	4	6	5
c	3	4	2	5	1	6
d	4	5	3	6	2	1
e	5	6	4	1	3	2
f	6	1	5	2	4	3

that when each condition was tested, it would be preceded and followed equally often by every other condition. This last feature is very useful in minimizing carryover effects among conditions and makes the balanced Latin square preferred to other counterbalancing schemes. Constructing a balanced Latin square is easy, especially if the experiment has an even number of conditions. Let us number the six conditions in an experiment from one to six. A balanced Latin square can be thought of as a two-dimensional matrix in which the columns (extending vertically) represent conditions tested, and the rows represent the subjects. A balanced Latin square for six conditions is presented in Table 9.1. The subjects are labeled *a* through *f*, and the order in which they receive the conditions is indicated by reading across the row. So subject *a* receives the conditions in the order 1, 2, 6, 3, 5, 4. The general formula for constructing the first row of a balanced Latin square is 1, 2, n, 3, $n - 1$, 4, $n - 2$, and so on, where n stands for the total number of conditions. After the first row is in place, just number down the columns with higher numbers, starting over when you get to n (as in Table 9.1). When a balanced Latin square is used, subjects must be tested in multiples of n, in this case six, in order to counterbalance conditions appropriately against practice.

When an experimental design has an odd number of conditions, it becomes a bit more complicated to use a balanced Latin square. In fact, two squares must be used, the second of which is the reverse of the first, as seen in Table 9.2, where once again letters indicate subjects and numbers stand for conditions in the experiment. When a balanced Latin square is used with an unequal number of conditions, each subject must be tested in each condition twice. The case represented in Table 9.2 is for five conditions. In general, the first square is constructed in exactly the same manner as when there is an even number of conditions, and then the second square is an exact reversal of the first.

The balanced Latin square is an optimal counterbalancing system for many purposes, since each condition occurs, on the average, at the same stage of practice and each condition precedes and follows every other equally often. This latter feature is not true of other counterbalancing schemes, and thus there is more concern that testing in one condition may affect testing in another condition.

▼ **TABLE 9.2**

Balanced Latin Square for the Five Experimental Conditions (1–5) Presented to Each Subject. Rows Indicate the Order in Which Subjects *a* through *e* Receive the Experimental Conditions. When the Number of Conditions Is Odd, Each Condition Must Be Given to Each Subject Twice for a Balanced Latin Square.

	Square 1					Square 2				
	Order of Testing									
Subjects	1st	2nd	3rd	4th	5th	1st	2nd	3rd	4th	5th
a	1	2	5	3	4	4	3	5	2	1
b	2	3	1	4	5	5	4	1	3	2
c	3	4	2	5	1	1	5	2	4	3
d	4	5	3	1	2	2	1	3	5	4
e	5	1	4	2	3	3	2	4	1	5

9.3   EXPERIMENTAL TOPICS AND RESEARCH APPLICATIONS

Topic   *Small-*n *Designs*
Illustration   *Behavior Problems in Children*

In the simplest case, an experiment involves a comparison between control and experimental conditions. Both between- and within-subjects designs usually include a large number of subjects, although the number is often less in the within-subjects case. Large numbers of subjects are required so that an unusual participant does not skew the results. Such designs are called **large-*n* designs** and have become the norm in psychological research; powerful statistical techniques (see Appendix B) allow the researcher to determine whether differences between the conditions are worth worrying about. An alternative approach to such designs is the **small-*n* design,** in which a very few subjects are intensely analyzed. Two areas within experimental psychology often use small-*n* designs. You may recall from Chapter 6 that psychophysics often uses small-*n* designs. Experimental control is the hallmark of the second research area that uses small-*n* designs—the experimental analysis of behavior in terms of operant conditioning. Skinner (1959) urged the use of small-*n* designs in operant research, because he wanted to emphasize the importance of experimental control over behavior and deemphasize the importance of statistical analysis. Skinner believed that statistical analysis often becomes an end in itself, rather than a tool to help the researcher make decisions about the experimental results. The experimental control usually achieved in traditional research with large numbers of subjects and statistical inference is strived for in small-*n* research by very carefully controlling the experimental setting and by taking numerous and continuous measures of the dependent variable. Small-*n* methodology is especially appropriate to the clinical application of operant techniques to modify behavior. Typically, a therapist deals with a single client at a time, which is the limiting case of a small-*n* design. Although a therapist may treat more than one patient at a time with similar methods, the numbers are very small relative to those seen in most large-n research. We examine small-n design in the context of behavior problems in children.

Consider the following scenario: Concerned parents seek psychological help for their child because she has temper tantrums several times a day. These tantrums are noisy, with a lot of yelling and crying, and they are violent—she often kicks things and bangs her head on the floor. When the therapist, who specializes in behavior modification using operant-conditioning techniques, first sees the child, what conclusions might he or she draw? What causes this behavior? What can the therapist do to remove it and return the child to a more normal existence? A behavior therapist seeks to discover what in the learning history of the child has produced such troublesome behavior, focusing on the contingencies of reinforcement that produce and maintain the child's crying, kicking, and head banging. Perhaps the parents only paid close attention to the child when she threw a tantrum—inadvertently rewarding her tantrum behavior. The proposed therapy tries to change the contingencies of reinforcement, so that the child receives rewards for appropriate and not maladaptive behavior.

The AB Design

Before examining valid small-n designs, we look at a common but invalid way to evaluate the effectiveness of a therapy. Research concerning the effectiveness of a therapy should be incorporated into the treatment whenever possible. This seems like a fairly simple matter: Measure the frequency of the behavior that needs to be changed, then institute the therapy and see if the behavior changes. We can call this an ***AB* design,** where A represents the baseline condition before therapy, and B represents the condition after therapy (the independent variable) that is introduced. This design is used frequently in medical, educational, and other applied research, where a therapy or training procedure is instituted to determine its effects on the problem of interest. However, the AB design (Campbell & Stanley, 1966) fails completely as a valid experimental design and should be avoided. It fails because changes occurring during treatment in the B phase may be caused by other factors that are confounded with the factor of interest. The treatment might produce the change in behavior, but so could other sources that the researcher is not aware of or has failed to control. We cannot conclusively establish that change resulted from the therapy because of a lack of control comparisons. A confounding variable might have produced the change in the absence of an independent variable. Remember, confounding occurs when other variables are inadvertently varied with the primary factor of interest—in the case of the little girl, the therapy. It is crucial to control carefully the potential confounding variables, so that the primary one is producing the effect. This is impossible in the AB design, since the therapist-researcher may not even be aware of the other variables.

A standard solution to the problem involves a large-n design. We have two groups to which subjects have been randomly assigned. One, the experimental, receives the treatment; the other, the control, does not. If the experimental condition improves with the therapy and the control does not, we may conclude that the treatment and not some extraneous factor produced the result. In the case of therapy on an individual, such as the case of the tantrum-throwing girl, there usually is no potential control group and only one subject in the experimental "group." Since a large-n design depends on having a substantial number of subjects in the experimental and control conditions, it is inappropriate for use in evaluating many therapeutic situations.

The ABA or Reversal Design

As an alternative to the flawed *AB* design, the experimenter may reverse the conditions after the phase to yield an ***ABA* design,** which is also called a **reversal design.** The second *A* phase in the *ABA* design serves to rule out the possibility that some confounding factor influenced the behavior observed in the *B* phase. Returning the conditions of the experiment to their original baseline level, with the independent variable no longer applied, allows the experimenter to determine if behavior returns to baseline level during the second phase. If it does, then the researcher can conclude that the independent variable effected change during the *B* phase. This generalization would not apply if a confounding variable happened to be perfectly correlated with the independent variable. Such a situation is unlikely. Here we consider an example of a reversal design.

Hart, Allen, Buell, Harris, and Wolf (1964) investigated the excessive crying of a 4-year-old nursery school pupil, Bill, who otherwise seemed quite healthy and normal. The crying often came in response to mild frustrations that other children dealt with in more effective ways. Rather than attribute his crying to internal variables, such as fear, lack of confidence, or regression to behavior of an earlier age, the investigators looked to the social learning environment to see what reinforcement contingencies might produce such behavior. They decided, with reasoning similar to that already discussed in the case of our hypothetical little girl, that adult attention reinforced Bill's crying behavior. The researchers set about testing this supposition with an *ABA* (actually ***ABAB***) design.

First, they needed a good measure of the dependent variable, crying. The teacher carried a pocket counter and depressed the lever every time there was a crying episode. "A crying episode was defined as a cry (a) loud enough to be heard at least 50 feet away and (b) of 5 seconds or more duration." At the end of each nursery school day, the teacher totaled the number of crying episodes. We could, perhaps, quibble some with this operational definition of a crying episode (did the teacher go 50 feet away each time to listen?), but let us assume it is valid and reliable.

In the initial baseline of phase *A*, Bill received normal attention by the teacher to his crying. During the 10 days of the first baseline period, the number of crying episodes was between 5 and 10 per day, as shown in the leftmost panel of Figure 9.7, where the frequency of crying episodes on the ordinate is plotted against days on the abscissa. For the next 10 days (the first *B* phase), the teacher attempted to extinguish the crying episodes by ignoring them, while rewarding Bill with attention every time he responded to minor calamities (such as falls or pushes) in a more appropriate way. As shown in Figure 9.7, the number of crying episodes dropped precipitously, so that there were between zero and two during the last 6 days of the first *B* phase. This completes the *AB* phase of the design; once again, we cannot be certain that the reinforcement contingencies were responsible for Bill's improved behavior. Perhaps he was getting along better with his classmates, or his parents were treating him better at home. Either of these things (or others) could have improved his disposition.

To gain better evidence that the reinforcement contingencies changed Bill's behavior, the investigators returned to the baseline: Bill was again reinforced for crying. At first, he was rewarded with attention for approximations to crying (whimpering and sulking); after crying had been established again, it was maintained with attention to each crying episode. As the third panel in Figure 9.7 shows, it took only 4 days to reestablish crying. This led to the conclusion that the reinforcement contingencies, and not

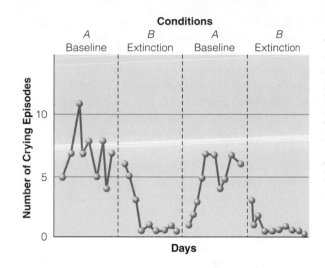

Conditions

▼ FIGURE 9.7

The number of crying episodes exhibited by Bill, a nursery school student, during the four phases of an *ABAB* design initiated to control his problem crying. Wolf, M. M., & Risley, T. R. (1971). Reinforcement: Applied research. In R. Glaser (Ed.), *The Nature of Reinforcement* (p. 316). New York: Academic Press.

any number of other factors, were responsible for the termination of crying in the first *B* phase. Finally, since this was a therapeutic situation, the investigators instituted a second *B* phase similar to the first, in which Bill's crying was once again extinguished.

In this investigation, no inferential statistics were employed to justify the conclusions drawn. Rather, with good control of the independent variable and repeated measures on the dependent variable, the differences between conditions in this experiment were striking enough to decrease the need for inferential statistics. Use of *ABA* small-*n* designs can allow powerful experimental inferences.

Alternating-Treatments Design

As in the standard within-subjects experiments, small-*n* experiments often include carryover effects that prohibit use of the reversal design. If the treatment introduced in the *B* phase has long-term effects on the dependent variable, then reversal is impractical. Furthermore, the experimenter may want to obtain several samples of the subjects' behavior under the same independent variable or under several independent variables. There are a number of ways to solve these problems, but we consider just two.

Rose (1978) used what could be called an *ACABCBCB* design, where *A* phases refer to baseline conditions, and *B* and *C* phases represent different levels of the independent variable(s). When presentation of different levels of the independent variable alternate, we have an **alternating-treatments design.** Rose wanted to determine the effects of artificial food coloring on hyperactivity in children. Two hyperactive 8-year-old girls were subjects. They had been on a strict diet, the Kaiser-Permanente (K-P) diet (Feingold, 1975), which does not allow foods containing artificial flavors and colors and foods containing natural salicylates (many fruits and meats). On the basis of uncontrolled case studies (*AB* designs), Feingold reported that the K-P diet reduced hyperactivity.

Rose's *A* phase counted the behavior of the two girls under the ordinary K-P diet. The *B* phase examined another kind of baseline. It involved the introduction of an oatmeal cookie that contained no artificial coloring. The *C* phase included the level of interest of the independent variable: oatmeal cookies containing an artificial yellow dye. Rose chose this artificial color because it is commonly used in the manufacture of foods, and it had the additional benefit that it did not change the taste or appearance of the cookies. (When asked to sort the cookies on the basis of color, judges were unable to do so systematically with regard to the presence of the dye.) The subjects, their parents, and the observers were blind to when the children ate the dye-laced cookie. Various aspects of the two girls' behavior were recorded during school by several different observers. One dependent variable that Rose measured was the percentage of time that the girls were out of their seats during school. Rose found that the girls were most active during the C phases, when they had ingested a cookie with artificial coloring in it. Rose also noticed that there was no placebo effect. That is, the percentage of time out of their seats was essentially the same during the A phases (no cookie) and the B phases, in which the girls ate cookies without artificial coloring. So, Rose concluded that artificial colors can lead to hyperactivity in some children.

Multiple-Baseline Design

Rose's extension of the reversal design allows an experimenter to examine the effects of more than two levels of the independent variable. However, the extension does not permit experiments involving independent variables that are likely to have strong carryover effects. The **multiple-baseline design,** illustrated in Figure 9.8, is suitable for situations in which the behavior of interest may not reverse to baseline levels (i.e., when there are permanent carryover effects).

Two features of the multiple-baseline design are noteworthy. First, notice that different behaviors (or different subjects) have baseline periods of different lengths prior to the introduction of the independent variable. The baseline periods are to the left of the vertical lines, and the treatment periods, in which the independent variable has been introduced, are to the right of the vertical lines. Using such a design in the case of Bill (described earlier) might involve a continual baseline monitoring of some other unwanted behavior (say, picking fights) when the extinction period for crying was introduced. Then after several days, perhaps, the extinction procedure could be applied to the fighting behavior. Behavior A in Figure 9.8 could be crying, and

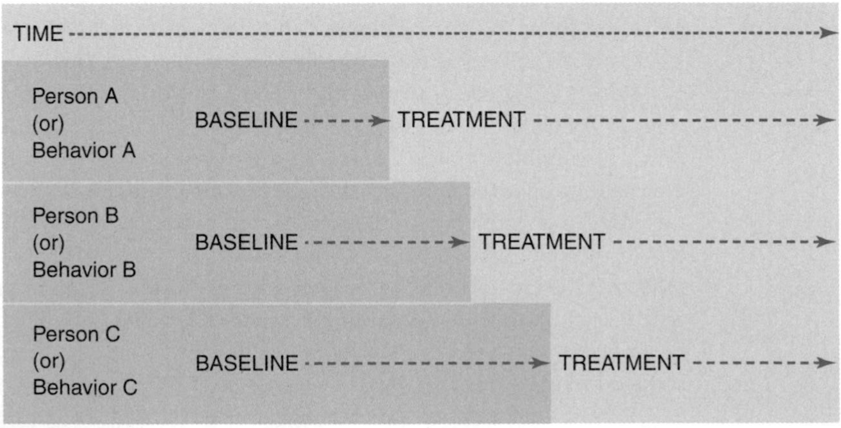

▼ **FIGURE 9.8**

An Outline of the Multiple-Baseline Design. Different people (between subjects) or different behaviors (within subjects) have baseline periods of different lengths. The vertical lines indicate when the independent variable (the treatment) was introduced.

Behavior B could be fighting. Fighting behavior occurs under baseline conditions while the crying behavior is treated. If the untreated behavior holds steady prior to the introduction of the independent variable and then changes afterward, we can assume that the independent variable alters the behavior and not something else that also happens to change during the observation period. Suppose, however, that crying and fighting typically go together. So, the treatment of one behavior could influence the occurrence of the other. If Bill's fighting decreased as crying extinguished, then we could not attribute the changes in one of the behaviors to the independent variable.

This problem leads us to the second important feature of the multiple-baseline design. The multiple-baseline design can be used as a small-n equivalent of the between-subjects design. As shown in Figure 9.8, instead of several behaviors being monitored as in a within-subjects design, different people can be monitored for different periods prior to the introduction of the independent variable. This type of multiple-baseline design, as is true of the ordinary between-subjects design, should be appropriate for situations in which the independent variable will have strong carryover effects. The between-subjects multiple-baseline procedure is also appropriate for cases where target behaviors are likely to be influenced by each other, such as could have occurred in our hypothetical experiment concerning Hart and coworkers' subject, Bill.

An experiment by Schreibman, O'Neill, and Koegel (1983) nicely illustrates the between-subjects form of the multiple-baseline design. Schreibman and her co-workers wanted to teach behavior-modification procedures to the normal siblings of autistic children so that they could become effective teachers of their autistic siblings. Autism is a behavior disorder of unknown origin. It is characterized by impoverished social behavior, minimal language use, and self-stimulation of various kinds. For each of three pairs of siblings—one normal (mean age was 10 years) and one autistic (mean age was 7 years)—several target behaviors, such as counting, identification of letters, and learning about money, were chosen for the normal sibling to teach the autistic sibling. Since the normal siblings had to learn correct behavior-modification techniques, such as reinforcement for appropriate responding, the experimenters first recorded baseline measures of the normal siblings' use of correct behavior-modification techniques and the correct performance of the target behaviors by the autistic children. The baseline data for each pair of children appear left of the vertical lines in Figure 9.9. Since learning behavior-modification techniques is likely to influence a wide variety of behaviors of the teacher and the pupil (the normal and autistic child, respectively), a multiple-baseline design across pairs of children was used. Changes in the behavior of normal and autistic children after the normal siblings were trained to use behavior-modification procedures appear right of the vertical lines in Figure 9.9. Correct performance by both children in each pair increased after the beginning of training. Schreibman and associates concluded that the training, and not some other confounding factor (such as changes resulting from being observed), altered the behavior.

Note the data points represented by plus signs and bull's-eyes. These symbols show the children's behavior in a setting that was entirely different from the training room, one in which the children did not know they were being monitored by the experimenters. Behavior in this generalization setting was very similar to the behavior in the training room, so the treatment program was effective in making general changes in the children's behavior.

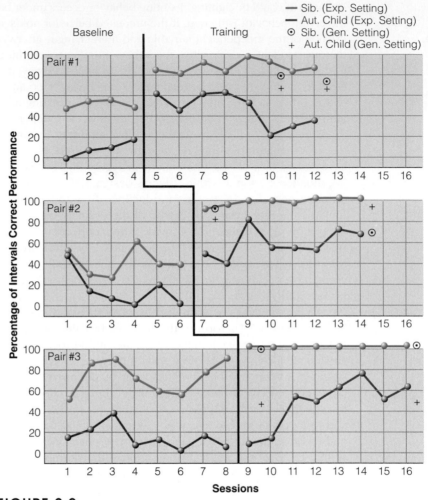

▼ FIGURE 9.9

The normal siblings' use of correct behavior-modification procedures, and the autistic children's appropriate responses. The baseline period is to the left of the vertical line for each pair of children. The pluses and bull's-eyes show behavior in a generalization setting (Schreibman et al., 1983, in *Journal of Applied Behavior Analysis, 16,* p. 135. Copyright 1983 by the Society for the Experimental Analysis of Behavior, Inc.) Reprinted with permission of Blackwell Publishing, Ltd.

The operant-conditioning research designs described are representative of the powerful research techniques developed by Skinner and his followers. Careful control has provided an enormously valuable database for psychology. As we have seen, the procedures have been used in clinical settings with substantial success. The interested reader will see how broadly the techniques have been applied in Kazdin (2001). The small-*n* procedures of operant analysis are important tools for psychologists who wish to understand thought and behavior.

Changing-Criterion Design

The **changing-criterion design** involves changing the behavior necessary to obtain reinforcement. For example, a rat may have to press a lever for food reinforcement five times for several minutes, and then the criterion behavior could change to seven lever presses to get the reinforcement. This procedure could then repeat with several other criteria. Here the independent variable is the criterion behavior necessary to obtain the outcome, and the underlying logic is similar to that of other small-n designs. If behavior changes systematically with the changing criteria, then we assume that the criteria are producing the change.

Therapists use a changing-criterion design in a variety of behavioral therapy situations. Kahng, Boscoe, and Byrne (2003) used such a design to increase food acceptance in Clara, a 4-year-old girl. She would drink out of a bottle, but she would not eat food. The therapist used a clever procedure of having escape from the meal contingent on a certain number of bites of food. Further, if Clara accepted a bite of food, she received praise and then later in therapy a Blues Clues token that she could play after the meal. The therapist increased the criterion number of bites to escape the meal setting for her favorite food (applesauce). She gradually accepted applesauce more readily with increases in the criterion. Acceptance of other foods gradually increased as well. At the end of therapy she met a 15-bite criterion of all foods in about 16 minutes. At a follow up meal 6 months after therapy, she ate more than 90 percent of 50 bites in 10 minutes.

McDougall and his associates (McDougall, Hawkins, Brady, & Jenkins, 2006; McDougall & Smith, 2006) have developed interesting variations of the changing-criterion design. The **range-bound changing criterion** involves criteria that specify upper and lower bounds of the target behavior. Thus, a child who needed more aerobic exercise might have criteria that specify the minimum and maximum amount of running for each exercise period. The **distributed-criterion design** shares features of the multiple-baseline design and the alternating-treatments design. In this design, a child who did not play well with others might have criteria for the amount of time spent in solitary and in social play during recess. These percentages and criteria are distributed across two or more behaviors and could be changed across time to increase the desired behavior (social play in this case). A lesson to take away from McDougall's work is that the various designs are powerful ways of changing behavior and that combining these designs can enhance the therapeutic situation.

FROM PROBLEM TO EXPERIMENT
THE NUTS AND BOLTS

Problem   *The Partial Reinforcement Extinction Effect*

To produce instrumental learning (operant conditioning), we follow with a reinforcement stimulus the behavior that we are interested in having the animal learn. The animal soon learns that the reward is forthcoming in the situation if the appropriate response is emitted. For example, suppose we want to teach an animal to learn a maze. The simplest sort of maze is the straight alley, which is composed of a start box where the animal is placed, an alley through which the animal runs when the start box door is opened, and the goal box where the animal is reinforced. The reinforcement is typically food, and usually the animal has been deprived of food prior to the experiment. The dependent variable is running speed or time to run the straight-alley maze. Often the animal's speed in each section of the runway is measured so that the experimenter finds speeds for its leaving the start box, traversing the alley, and approaching the goal. Learning is indicated by the fact that after a number of trials the rat's speed increases (the latency decreases). At first, the rat dawdles along, but on later trials, it really hustles.

Problem   *How is learning affected by the amount of reinforcement?*

Suppose we now wanted to ask a straightforward question about learning in this situation: How is learning affected by the amount of reinforcement? Intuitively, you might expect that learning would increase as the amount of reinforcement increases. But if you read the first part of this chapter carefully, you should realize that this depends on how "amount of reinforcement" and "learning" are defined. We could vary the amount of reinforcement by varying the percentage of trials on which subjects receive reward or by varying the magnitude of reward after each trial. We could also measure learning in several ways: one might be running speed, another might be judgments of persistence (by humans, of course, Svartdal, 2003), or we could measure resistance to extinction. The latter measure, discussed in the "Introducing the Variables" section, is found by seeing how long after training an animal will continue running a maze when it no longer receives reinforcement.

Problem   *What is the effect of percentage of reward on resistance to extinction?*

Let us confine our interest to the case in which we vary the percentage of rewarded trials. Our experiment has now become more manageable.

We vary the percentage of trials on which the animals receive rewards for running the maze (the independent variable), and we measure the time it takes the animals to run the maze and their resistance to extinction (or running speeds during extinction training).

In many experiments such as these, researchers have found that resistance to extinction is generally greater the *smaller* the percentage of trials during which the animal receives reinforcement during training. If an animal receives **continuous reinforcement** (i.e., is reinforced after every trial), its running behavior will extinguish much more rapidly when reinforcement is withdrawn than will animals that receive reinforcement on only some percentage of the acquisition trials. In general, the smaller the percentage of reinforced trials, the greater will be the resistance to extinction (i.e., the faster the animal will run when reinforcement is withdrawn). The fact that infrequent reinforcement will lead to greater persistence in responding than continuous reinforcement is called the **partial reinforcement extinction effect (PREE).** Several explanations of it have been proposed (Amsel, 1994; Capaldi, 1994).

A number of variables may contribute to the typical PREE. When rats are rewarded on only some proportion of trials, a number of factors may vary simultaneously. One factor is the number of nonrewarded trials (or *N*-trials) that precede a rewarded (or *R*) trial. Another factor is the number of transitions from nonrewarded to rewarded trials (or *N–R* transitions) during the course of partial-reinforcement training. A third factor is the number of different *N*-lengths (or number of different sequences of nonrewarded trials preceding a rewarded trial) during partial reinforcement. All these variables could be (and have been) examined; let us consider the first by way of an experiment in animal-learning research.

Hypothesis   *Resistance to extinction will increase with increases in the number of nonrewarded trials that precede a rewarded trial (the N-length).*

Basically, we want to design an experiment in which the number of nonrewarded trials would be varied before a rewarded trial. There could be three *N*-lengths of one, two, and three nonrewarded trials before a rewarded trial, with the hypothesis being that resistance to extinction should increase with *N*-length. The greater the number of nonrewarded trials, the faster the rats should run during extinction.

A simple straight alley is used as the training apparatus, and the time for the rat to run the maze is the dependent variable. Do we want to use a within-subjects or between-subjects design? If we use a within-subjects design, we have to counterbalance the three schedules of reinforcement. But even if we do this, there is a serious problem of a carryover effect, or the effect that training rats under one schedule has on training them on the next.

When just one response is examined, such as running in a straight alley, a between-subjects design is used. However, it is possible to avoid a carryover problem by having the subjects learn different responses under different schedules of nonrewarded trials. Animals could receive one *N*-length in a straight alley painted black and a different *N*-length in a white alley. This kind of within-subjects experiment on the PREE has often yielded the surprising result of a *reversed* PREE, in which the animal shows greater resistance to extinction for the response that has the larger percentage of reinforced trials (for a discussion of some of the issues involved in a within-subjects PREE, see Rescorla, 1999). In a single experiment with human participants, Svartdal (2000) observed the usual PREE in a between-subjects comparison and a reversed PREE in a within-subjects comparison. If you are interested in tying together an understanding of design effects, contrast effects, and partial reinforcement, we suggest you examine the work by Rescorla (1999) and Svartdal (2000) and design your own experiment.

Stable results in a between-subjects partial-reinforcement situation could probably be achieved with only 15 subjects in each of three groups. Before the experiment is begun, it is usual to pretrain the animals to get them used to the experimental situation. This reduces the amount of within-subjects variability caused by extraneous factors, such as fear of being handled by the experimenter. Thus, for several days, the animals are handled for an hour or so each day by the experimenter. The rats should also be placed in the goal box with food pellets in the food dish to ensure that they will eat the pellets. Otherwise, as you might readily suppose, the pellets are unlikely to serve as a reinforcer. Finally, the rats should be placed in the straight alley and allowed to explore it for a few minutes on each of several days before actual testing. This is to ensure that they will not be frightened when they are placed in it for testing. On each trial of the experiment proper, the experimenter takes the rat from its home cage and places it in the start box. The start box door is opened, which starts a timer, and the rat moves down the alley to the goal box. Near the goal box, the rat passes through a photoelectric beam, which stops the timer. When the rat enters the goal box, the goal box door is closed, so that the rat cannot return to the alley. Typically, the rat is confined to the goal box for a constant period of time in all conditions—say, 30 seconds. Then the rat is placed in a separate cage to await the next trial. In this experiment, the independent variable is the number of nonrewarded or N-trials (one, two, or three) preceding a rewarded or R-trial. This is straightforward, since it is easy either to provide or not to provide food when the rat runs the maze. The only tricky aspect is that the experimental procedure confounds the number of nonrewarded trials with the amount of rewarded trials that the rats receive during a series of tests. The rats with greater N-lengths receive less reward. One way to correct this confounding is to provide subjects in conditions with N-lengths of two and three with intertrial reinforcements. These are simply periods when rats are given rewards between trials in the neutral cage. The rewards are not dependent on the instrumental response.

The rats should be given a number of days of training, perhaps 10, to ensure that they learn their particular schedule of reinforcement. Twelve trials per day would be an appropriate number. After 10 days of learning, extinction training is introduced. This consists of simply running the rats at 12 trials per day for perhaps 4 days with no reward at all and measuring the time the rats take to run the maze. This phase of the experiment is critical, since we want to ascertain the effect of the training schedules on resistance to extinction. But a problem enters here. It is common during extinction for at least some rats to simply stop running. Either they refuse to leave the start box, or they stop halfway down the alley. What happens to our dependent measure in cases such as this? The convention adopted to avoid this problem is to allow the rats a fixed amount of time to traverse the alley and to remove them and begin the next trial if they fail to beat the cutoff. A limit of 90 seconds is often used; if a rat has not made it a few feet down the maze in 90 seconds, it is unlikely that it will make it at all. Thus, the experimenter simply removes the animal, records its time as 90 seconds, and places it in the neutral cage in preparation for the next trial. Since different schedules of training sometimes produce lopsided or skewed distributions of running times, it is often necessary to use the median time for each animal rather than the mean to eliminate the effect of a few extremely long times. (See Appendix B for a discussion of medians.)

The basic purpose of the experiment is to see whether the number of nonrewarded trials produces greater resistance to extinction. In other words, if subjects receive greater N-lengths, will they run faster when given no reward during extinction? In an experiment similar to the one described here, Capaldi (1964) found that greater N-lengths were associated with greater resistance to extinction.

▼ SUMMARY

1. The study of animal learning and behavior has identified two basic types of conditioning. In classical (or Pavlovian or respondent) conditioning, a neutral stimulus, such as a light or tone, precedes an unconditioned stimulus that produces an automatic or unconditioned response.

    After a number of such pairings, the originally neutral stimulus produces the response if there is a contingent (predictive) relation between the neutral stimulus and the unconditioned stimulus.

2. In instrumental (operant) conditioning, a particular behavior that is followed by a reinforcing stimulus will increase in frequency. A positive reinforcing stimulus (the familiar rewards) increases the frequency of the response that produces it. A negative reinforcing stimulus increases the frequency of the response that removes it. A response that is followed by a punishing stimulus decreases in frequency.

3. In all experimental research, whether with humans or other organisms, a fundamental question is whether to use the same organisms in each condition of the experiment (a within-subjects design) or to use different organisms in the different conditions (a between-subjects design).

4. Within-subjects designs are preferred when they can be used, because they minimize the amount of variability caused by differences among subjects. Also, within-subjects designs employ fewer subjects than between-subjects designs, though, of course, it is necessary to test each individual for longer periods.

5. The primary danger in within-subjects designs is that of carryover effects, the relatively permanent effects that testing subjects in one condition might have on their later behavior in another condition. In such cases, it is necessary to use between-subjects designs, even though more subjects will be needed and subject variability is less controllable.

6. The choice of an experimental design may in some instances strongly affect the outcome of an experiment. For example, stimulus intensity appears to play little role in classical conditioning when manipulated between subjects but a great role when manipulated within subjects. Thus, the type of experimental design chosen can sometimes be critical.

7. In within-subjects designs, it is necessary to counterbalance conditions or to vary the conditions in a systematic way so that they are not confounded with time of testing. If conditions are not counterbalanced, then time-related effects, such as fatigue or practice, rather than manipulation of the independent variable may account for the results. It is also necessary to counterbalance in between-subjects designs across variables that are not of central interest. One quite useful counterbalancing scheme is the balanced Latin square design, in which each condition precedes and follows every other one equally often.

8. The traditional large-n research methodology is often inappropriate in applied settings, where there is only one subject. Often an *AB* design is used as a small-n design. A baseline of behavior is established (the *A* phase), and then some treatment is imposed (the *B* phase).

    The conclusion that changes in behavior during the *B* phase resulted from the treatment is faulty because other variables may be confounded with the treatment (such as practice or fatigue effects).

9. The *ABA* design is a powerful alternative to the *AB* design. The second *A* phase, introduced after the *B* (treatment) phase, removes the treatment to determine whether any changes observed during the *B* phase were caused by the independent variable or by confounding factors. The alternating-treatments design permits an examination of several independent variables or of independent variables with more than two levels.

10. The multiple-baseline design is another small-n design in which different behaviors or different people receive baseline periods of varying lengths prior to the introduction of the independent variable. For use within subjects, this design is preferable to the *ABA* design if the independent variable has strong carryover effects.

▼ KEY TERMS

AB design
ABA (reversal) design
ABAB design
ABBA design
alternating-treatments design
asymmetrical transfer
balanced Latin square design
between-subjects design
blocking
carryover effect
changing-criterion design
classical conditioning
conditioned response (CR)
conditioned stimulus (CS)
contingency
continuous reinforcement
counterbalancing
discriminative stimulus (SD)
distributed-criterion design
experimental extinction
fatigue effect
instrumental conditioning
large-*n* designs
matched-groups design

multiple-baseline design
negative contrast effect
negative reinforcing stimulus
null contingency
operant conditioning
partial reinforcement extinction effect (PREE)
positive contrast effect
positive reinforcing stimulus
practice effect
psychoneuroimmunology
pseudoconditioning
punishment
random-groups design
range-bound changing criterion
respondent conditioning
reversal (*ABA*) design
shaping
simultaneous contrast
small-*n* designs
split-litter technique
unconditioned response (UR)
unconditioned stimulus (US)
within-subjects design

▼ DISCUSSION QUESTIONS

1. Discuss the advantages of within-subjects designs. What complications and problems are entailed by using a within-subjects design?
2. Discuss the advantages and disadvantages of using a between-subjects design.
3. In each of the following cases, tell whether it would be best to examine the independent variable in a within-subjects or a between-subjects design. Justify your answer in each case.
   a. A social psychological study of helping, in which the researchers are interested in how group size affects whether or not an individual will help someone else in the group.
   b. A study of the effect of varying loudness of a tone in measuring how quickly people can respond to the tone.
   c. An experiment designed to answer the question of whether the color of a woman's hair affects the likelihood that she will be asked out for dates.
   d. A study in which three different training techniques are compared as to their effectiveness in teaching animals tricks.
4. Tell what a balanced Latin square is and explain why it is a preferred counterbalancing scheme in many situations. Draw two balanced Latin squares similar to those in Tables 9.1 and 9.2 for cases in which there are (a) three conditions and (b) four conditions.
5. The results of some experiments described in this chapter showed different effects of an independent variable when it was manipulated between

and within subjects. Make a list of three variables for which you think between- and within-subjects designs would show the same effects, and provide two further instances in which you think the two types of designs would produce different results. Justify your reasoning in each case.

6. Discuss the sorts of confounding that may arise from the use of an *AB* design.

WEB CONNECTIONS

Explore the step-by-step presentation of "**Between vs. within Designs**" at:
> **http:// academic.cengage.com/psychology/workshops/student_resources/ workshops/between1.html**

A helpful overview of learning is available at:
> **http://www.funderstanding.com/theories.cfm**

A good discussion of research design can be found at:
> **http://trochim.human.cornell.edu/kb/expfact.htm**

PSYCHOLOGY IN ACTION.
Knowledge of Results as Reinforcement

People receive many reinforcements in the form of knowledge of results rather than as biological rewards, such as food pellets given to hungry rats in Skinner boxes. "That's good" or "You've almost got it correct" are frequently given as feedback. So, in addition to being rewarded for approximations to a correct response, we also are told how close we are to a target response.

The following is based on a famous experiment done by Thorndike (1932). We provide a variant of his procedure that was suggested by Snellgrove (1981). Thorndike blindfolded subjects and asked them to draw lines that were 3 inches long. Little or no improvements in accuracy occurred when the subjects did not receive knowledge of results, but Thorndike found rapid shaping of behavior when knowledge of results was given: People were told "right" when they were within one-eighth inch and "wrong" when they were off by more than one-eighth inch. You will vary the type of feedback: Some participants will be told nothing, others will be told "good" when they are within one-eighth inch of 3 inches, and a third group will be told exactly how long a line they drew (to a sixteenth of an inch). You will need paper, pencils, a ruler, and a blindfold. Each person will receive 10 trials, with a single kind of knowledge of results. Record the accuracy (to a sixteenth of an inch) on each trial for each person, so you can compare the rate of progress across the 10 trials for each form of feedback.

You could use a within-subjects design, in which a person tries drawing different lengths of line (e.g., 2 inches, 3 inches, and 5 inches) under one of each of the feedback conditions. With a within-subjects design, you will need to counterbalance the type of feedback across line length, as well as the ordering of conditions throughout the experiment. This experiment is probably best done with a between-subjects design, because of relatively permanent carryover effects resulting from the different kinds of feedback.

If you use a between-subjects design, you should combine your efforts with classmates, so that you can have a large sample of participants in each feedback group.

Be sure to agree on a protocol, because all experimenters must treat the participants identically (except for the levels of independent variable) during testing. The timing for giving feedback must be the same for each feedback condition. Delayed knowledge of results usually yields better learning than immediate knowledge (e.g., Swinnen, Schmidt, Nicholson, & Shapiro, 1990), so do not confound how quickly feedback is supplied with the nature of the feedback. On each trial, measure and record performance, then give the appropriate knowledge of results before going on to the next trial. ∎

REMEMBERING AND FORGETTING

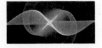

The whole of science is nothing more than refinement of everyday thinking. (ALBERT EINSTEIN)

What experiences can you recall from your year in the eighth grade? Think of them for a moment. You learned many facts there; lots of things happened to you. Probably you will never recall even a small fraction of the facts you learned or experiences you had then. What has happened to these memories? Are they lost forever? Or are the memories still stored somewhere but never actively recalled because you have not had an appropriate situation to bring them to mind? There are some things you will never forget, even if you want to, but others you cannot recall, no matter how urgent the need. If a budding romance had a catastrophic ending, this memory from your days in the eighth grade may stick with you long after other events have been relegated to the dim recesses of the past. Why?

The humorist Robert Benchley, in an essay called "What College Did to Me," attempted to recall the things he had learned in college years before and to classify these by the year in which they were learned. There were 39 items in the list. He remembered 12 things from his freshman year; this decreased to only 8 things recalled from his senior year. A selective sampling from Benchley's list appears in Table 10.1. It is selective only with regard to the number of pieces of information included, so that it does give a fair representation of the depth and range of the lasting knowledge acquired in college. You should, of course, be happy and proud to know that you too may soon have a college degree, a certificate that proclaims your knowledge of certain basic facts such as these.

Is this all Benchley really remembers from his college days? If you made a list from your days in the eighth grade, it would probably be similarly brief. This leads to an interesting question: How can we study memories that cannot be recalled? If a person cannot recall an experience, can we assume that the memory trace representing that experience has vanished?

▼ EBBINGHAUS'S CONTRIBUTION—WHEN MEMORY WAS YOUNG

The experimental investigation of human memory was begun by a German psychologist, Hermann Ebbinghaus (Figure 10.1; see Boneau, 1998, for a biographical sketch). Ebbinghaus was a true scientific pioneer. He believed, unlike his famous contemporary, Wilhelm Wundt (see Appendix A), that experimental psychology could be developed to study the higher mental processes and not just sensory processes. His main achievement was demonstrating how empirical research could answer interesting questions about memory. This research was published in 1885 in a remarkable book, *Memory: A Contribution to Experimental Psychology*. One of the first questions Ebbinghaus faced was the one we have been considering: how to measure memory. Ebbinghaus served as the only subject in all his experiments; the materials he invented to be memorized are

▼ **TABLE 10.1**

Selected Items Robert Benchley Recalled from His Years in College

Things I Learned—Freshman Year
1. Charlemagne either died or was born or did something with the Holy Roman Empire in 800.
2. By placing a paper bag inside another paper bag you can carry home a milkshake in it.
3. There is a double l in the middle of "parallel."
4. French nouns ending in "aison" are feminine.
5. Almost everything you need to know about a subject is in the encyclopedia.
6. A tasty sandwich can be made by spreading peanut butter on raisin bread.
7. The chances are against filling an inside straight.
8. There is a law in economics called The Law of Diminishing Returns, which means after a certain margin is reached returns begin to diminish. This may not be correctly stated, but there is a law by that name.

Sophomore Year
1. A good imitation of measles rash can be effected by stabbing the forearm with a stiff whiskbroom.
2. Queen Elizabeth was not above suspicion.
3. You can sleep undetected in a lecture course by resting the head on the hand as if shading the eyes.
4. The ancient Phoenicians were really Jews, and got as far north as England where they operated tin mines.
5. You can get dressed much quicker in the morning if the night before when you are going to bed you take off your trousers and underdrawers at once, leaving the latter inside the former.

Junior Year
1. Emerson left his pastorate because he had some argument about communion.
2. Pushing your arms back as far as they will go fifty times each day increases your chest measurement.
3. Marcus Aurelius had a son who turned out to be a bad boy.
4. Eight hours of sleep are not necessary.
5. Heraclitus believed fire was the basis of all life.
6. The chances are you will never fill an inside straight.

Senior Year
1. There is as yet no law determining what constitutes trespass in an airplane.
2. Six hours of sleep are not necessary.
3. Bicarbonate of soda taken before retiring makes you feel better the next day.
4. May is the shortest month of the year.

Source: Adapted from "What College Did to Me" in *Inside Benchley* by Robert Benchley. © 1921, 1922, 1925, 1927, 1928, 1942 by Harper & Brothers. Copyright renewed 1970 by Gertrude D. Benchley. Reprinted by permission of HarperCollins Publishers, Inc.

called **nonsense syllables.** He typically used meaningless syllables that contained a vowel sandwiched between two consonants (therefore called CVC syllables), such as ZOK, VAP, and so on. By using these syllables, he hoped to minimize the influence of linguistic associations that would have been present had he used words, sentences, or (as he sometimes did) passages of poetry as materials to be remembered. (Later research has shown that "nonsense" syllables is a misnomer, because a few items he used were words. Also, in learning even nonsense words, people imbue them with meaning.)

Ebbinghaus selected these syllables at random from a master set of 2,300 and placed them into lists that varied in length. If the list contained, say, 30 nonsense syllables, Ebbinghaus would read the syllables aloud to himself at a uniform rate. Immediately afterward, he would cover up the list and then try to repeat it back to himself

▼ **FIGURE 10.1**

Hermann Ebbinghaus began the experimental study of verbal learning and memory.

© Bettmann/Corbis

or write it down. Obviously, on the first trial, this feat was impossible, but he could measure the number of syllables he was able to recall correctly. He would then read the list aloud a second time, attempt recall, and so on. One measure of the difficulty of recalling a list that Ebbinghaus used is the number of such study/test trials (or the amount of time) needed for one perfect recitation of the list. This is called a **trials to criterion** measure of memory; it was widely used in memory research for years, though it is rare now.

Suppose Ebbinghaus wanted to test his memory of a list a month after learning it. He might, as an initial cue, provide himself with the first nonsense syllable in the list. But suppose this did not help him recall the list and that, try as he might, he could recall nothing further. Would this mean that the series he had memorized a month earlier had left no lasting impression? How could we ever know? Ebbinghaus invented an ingenious method of answering this question. In measuring memory for a series of nonsense syllables, Ebbinghaus attempted to relearn the series, just as he had learned it in the first place, by repeatedly reading it aloud and then attempting to recite it or write it. Once again, he could measure the number of trials or the amount of time necessary to learn the list. The memory for the list at the time of relearning could be measured by the savings in terms of fewer trials or less time needed to relearn the list; this measure of memory would be obtainable even when a person could recall nothing of the material before relearning it. Ebbinghaus found that even when he could recall none of the nonsense syllables in a list, he often still exhibited a considerable savings in the number of trials or amount of time it took him to relearn the list, indicating that memory for the list could exist without active recall.

The **savings score** that Ebbinghaus used was the percentage of trials saved in relearning a list relative to the original number of trials it took to learn the list in the first place. For example, if Ebbinghaus took 10 trials to learn a list of nonsense syllables in order, and then a week later, he took only 5 trials to relearn the list, this would represent 50 percent savings ($\frac{10-5}{10} \times 100\%$). To put it more generally, percentage savings is defined as the difference between the number of trials in original learning (OL) of a list and its relearning (RL) divided by the number of trials in original learning (OL), with this ratio multiplied by 100. (The equation is $\frac{OL - RL}{OL} \times 100\%$.) To show you that it makes sense, consider that immediately after learning a list perfectly, it will take no additional trials to relearn it, so the savings would be 100 percent ($\frac{10 - 0}{10} \times 100\% = 100\%$). However, if a person waited 10 years to relearn the list, it would probably be like starting over, so the savings would be 0 percent (if it took the same number of trials to relearn the list as it did to learn it originally: $\frac{10 - 10}{10} \times 100\% = 0\%$).

The examples we just used were hypothetical, but what is the relation between savings and time since original learning? Ebbinghaus asked this question and in answering it provided one of his best-known findings, which is shown in Figure 10.2.

The graph shows the relation between the amount of savings and the time since original learning, or how forgetting is related to time. As you can see, Ebbinghaus found that forgetting is rapid soon after learning but then slows. The **savings method** is still used today to ask important questions about memory (e.g., MacLeod, 1988; Keisler & Willingham, 2007).

Although Robert Benchley may have exhibited poor recall for information he learned in college, if he had been required to retake his courses, he probably would, like Ebbinghaus, have exhibited considerable savings. (He tells us that these courses included such gems as Early Renaissance Etchers, the Social Life of Minor Sixteenth-Century Poets, and the History of Lace Making.) Perhaps you may recall little of your geometry course in high school (or Chapter 2 of this book, for that matter), but presumably you would find the course much easier if you were to take it again.

You may wonder whether Ebbinghaus's findings are representative of human memory in general, since he studied only one subject (himself) repeatedly, a method that is rarely acceptable in modern research.

However, his findings have been replicated many times with larger groups of subjects and are still considered valid. (The importance of "replicability," or repeatability of experimental results, is discussed in Chapter 11.)

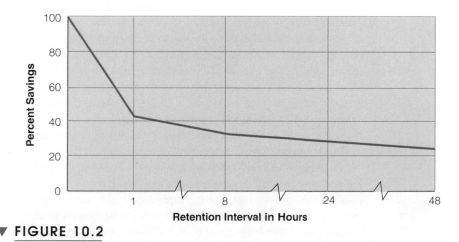

Retention Interval in Hours

▼ FIGURE 10.2

The Forgetting Curve. Ebbinghaus measured the savings in relearning a list of nonsense syllables after various periods of time had elapsed since original learning. Notice that forgetting is rapid at first and then levels off.

Ebbinghaus's work in memory was truly original. But besides his seminal memory research, his other achievements include an interesting discussion of the problem of experimenter bias, production of one of psychology's earliest mathematical models, one of the earliest examples of explicit hypothesis testing, and an advanced (for the time) discussion of statistical problems in research. He also wrote an interesting psychology text and designed an early intelligence test (Tulving, 1992).

Mary Calkins also provided an important contribution in the area of memory research. Calkins, a former student of William James, was interested in how associations were formed (see Furumoto, 1991). The method she invented is known as paired-associate learning. In this technique, subjects learn a list of arbitrary associations such as *spoon-airplane* and *chair-trust*. Later, memory of the associations is tested by presenting the first word in each pair (e.g., spoon) as a retrieval cue for the second word (airplane). Throughout the years, researchers interested in memory have used this method, and it continues to be popular today.

▼ VARIETIES OF MEMORY

The term *memory* is quite broad and covers many different kinds of skills and abilities. All have in common the properties that something is learned, retained over time, and then used in some particular situation, but beyond that, types of memory may differ considerably (see Roediger, Marsh, & Lee, 2002, for a summary). You have probably had an experience like this: You are introduced to three people and utterly forget the first person's name by the time you shake the third person's hand. This spectacularly fast forgetting seems quite different from the slower forgetting studied by Ebbinghaus. Remembering information such as a telephone number over a brief interval reflects **short-term** or working memory, and some psychologists believe that it has different properties from **long-term memory** (the kind Ebbinghaus studied) and that it should properly be considered a distinct memory system or store. One way of defining short-term memory is the recovery of information shortly after it has been perceived, before it has even left conscious awareness (James, 1890). Long-term memory, then, refers to retrieval of memories that have disappeared from consciousness after their initial perception.

This general definition of long-term memory today seems too broad to most psychologists, who make further distinctions among types of memory. These are discussed more fully later in the chapter, when we illustrate how memory is studied in different ways. One basic distinction that guides much research today is explicit memory versus implicit memory (Graf & Schacter, 1985; Schacter, 1987). **Explicit memory** (sometimes called **episodic memory**) refers to the conscious recollection of events (or episodes) in one's life. People may be asked to recall what they learned in a particular time or place or to distinguish things that happened to them from plausible distractors. Examples would be answering the question of what you did last Saturday night, what you learned in your introductory psychology course, or what you have done thus far today. Tasks typically used to measure both short-term and long-term memory would be classified as explicit memory tests, because people are explicitly told to retrieve information from their past.

Implicit memory, on the other hand, refers to the expression of past learning in which a person need not make any conscious effort to retrieve information from the past (Roediger & McDermott, 1993; Schacter, 1990). It just happens, more or less automatically. For example, when you bend over to tie your shoelaces, you need not say to

INTRODUCING THE VARIABLES

Dependent Variables

Remembering may be measured in numerous ways; these often involve either **recall** or **recognition.** In recall tests, reproduction of material is required, whereas in recognition tests, material is presented to people and they are required to judge whether or not they have seen it previously. Three popular recall tests are **serial recall, free recall,** and **paired-associate recall.** In serial recall, people are required to recall information in the serial order in which it was presented, whereas in free recall, the order of recall is irrelevant. In paired-associate recall, people are presented with pairs of items, such as *igloo-saloon;* at recall, they are given one member of the pair (*igloo*, referred to as the stimulus) and are asked to produce the other member (*saloon*, the response).

Recognition tests are generally of two types. In **yes/no recognition** tests, people are given the original material they studied, such as words, mixed in with a number of new but generally similar items (words). Subjects respond yes or no to each word, depending on whether they believe it was in the original list. **Forced-choice recognition tests** are multiple-choice tests. Several alternatives are presented, only one of which is correct, and the subject in the experiment is forced to choose the correct alternative. Forced-choice tests are preferred to yes/no tests because correcting for guessing is less of a problem.

Recall and recognition tests are not dichotomous; rather, they may be viewed as lying on a continuum, with the dimension being the amount of information given about the material, or the power of the retrieval cues presented. If *GRA* is presented as a cue for the word *GRAPH*, which appeared in the list, is this a test of recall or recognition?

In each case, the dependent measure in tests of recall and recognition is the number or proportion of items correctly recalled or recognized in different conditions or the number of errors, which amounts to the same thing. Sometimes a derivative measure is used, such as d' from the theory of signal detection (see Chapter 7). Recently, investigators concerned with recognition have used reaction time as a dependent measure, as discussed in Chapter 8.

The study of implicit memory tests has intrigued cognitive psychologists lately (Roediger, 1990). Although these tests do not require people to consciously remember the material they have studied, performance on these tasks is influenced or "primed" by previous exposure to the material. That is, implicit memory tests are tasks that can be performed without specific reference to the previous experiences in the laboratory, such as filling in a fragmented word such as "s_r_w_e_r_." On these types of tasks, "memory" is reflected by the fact that performance on the test is primed or biased by the previous study episode. For example, your ability to complete the preceding word fragment as *strawberry* would be greatly enhanced if you had read the word *strawberry* earlier, even though you were not explicitly asked to remember having done so. These tests are especially interesting because they behave very differently from traditional explicit memory tests, such as recall and recognition. In some sense, the "laws of memory" are different when examined with these implicit tests than with standard explicit memory tests. Later in the chapter, we examine these implicit tests more closely.

Independent Variables

Many types of variables are manipulated in experiments on human memory. One of the most popular variables historically has been the nature of the material presented for memory. It can be letters, digits, nonsense syllables, words, phrases, sentences, paragraphs, or long passages of prose; the characteristics of each of these types of material can also be varied. For example, words that refer to concrete objects (*cigar, rhinoceros*) are better recalled than abstract words (*beauty, dread*), when other relevant factors such as word length are held constant (Paivio, 1969). Several other important independent variables will be considered in the experiments

Continued

discussed in this chapter. One is quite obvious: the retention interval between presentation of material and test, which Ebbinghaus first studied (see Figure 10.2). How fast does forgetting occur? What are its mechanisms? Another variable attracting much attention is modality of presentation. Is information better remembered if it comes in through the ears or the eyes, or is there no difference? Study strategy is also important, such as how a person tries to learn (or encode) the material. A final variable under consideration is the nature of the memory test given to people. For example, do recall tests show results different from recognition tests? How are implicit memory tests different from explicit tests? This is just a sample of the variables that are investigated in memory studies.

Control Variables

Memory experiments are typically quite well controlled. Important variables that are usually held constant across conditions are the amount of material presented and the rate of presentation, though these can be interesting variables in their own right. The modality of presentation is another factor that must not vary, unless it is a variable of major interest. If some characteristic of the material is being varied, then it is necessary to hold constant other factors. If a researcher is interested in varying the concreteness or abstractness of words, then other characteristics, such as word length and frequency of occurrence in everyday use, must be held constant across the different conditions.

yourself, "How do I do this? When did I learn to do this? Can I remember how?" Instead, the behavior occurs relatively effortlessly, and if you stop to reflect on exactly how you are doing it, you may actually do worse. Of course, information expressed implicitly was learned, but the crux of the distinction is that, unlike explicit remembering, implicit expressions of memory do not require people consciously to retrieve information from their past. In fact, as we shall see later in the chapter, patterns of performance on explicit and implicit tests of memory are often quite different (Roediger, 1990).

10.1   EXPERIMENTAL TOPICS AND RESEARCH ILLUSTRATIONS

Topic   *Scale Attenuation*
Illustration   *Modality Differences*

The first topic we are considering here is important but often overlooked in psychological research. The general problem is how to interpret performance on some dependent variable in an experiment when performance is either very nearly perfect (near the "ceiling" of the scale) or very nearly lacking altogether (near the "floor"). These effects are called **scale-attenuation effects** (or, more commonly, **ceiling** and **floor effects**). As usual, we shall embed our discussion in the context of an actual research problem.

One subject in memory research that has attracted a great deal of attention is that of modality differences. Do we remember information better if it comes through our eyes or through our ears? Or is there no difference? Is information better remembered if it is presented to both the ears and the eyes simultaneously relative to a condition in which it is presented to only one or the other? These questions are of not only theoretical but also practical importance. When you look up a phone number and need to remember it while you cross the room to the telephone, is it sufficient to simply read the number silently to yourself as you usually do, or would you be better off to also read the number aloud so that information entered both your ears and your eyes?

The Eyes Have It: Scarborough's Experiment

One attempt to answer these questions was reported by Scarborough (1972). He used a short-term memory task called the **Brown-Peterson technique** after its inventors (Brown, 1958; Peterson & Peterson, 1959). Here, people are presented with information to remember for a short period and then are distracted from rehearsing (repeating it to themselves) by being required to perform some other task until they are later asked to recall the information. Typically, subjects are given a single *CCC* trigram (three consonants, for example, *NRF*). They are then required to count backward by threes from a three-digit number (464, 461, 458, etc.) for varying periods (the retention interval) up to about 30 seconds before attempting recall. (Again, the counting is to prevent people from rehearsing the letters or repeating them silently.) Try it yourself. Three letters and a three-digit number will appear after the next sentence. Read the letters and the number out loud, look away, and then count backward by threes from the number for about 30 seconds before you try to recall the letters.

XGR 679

How did you do? Chances are you recalled the trigram perfectly. People almost always do on the first trial in experiments using this task. However, recall drops off when multiple trials are used with a different trigram on each trial, so that after four or five trials, subjects are typically recalling trigrams correctly only 50 percent of the time, with an 18-second retention interval (Figure 10.3). This phenomenon is named **proactive interference,** since the early trials in this task interfere with recall on later trials.

In Scarborough's (1972) experiment, all subjects received 36 consonant trigrams presented for 0.7 seconds in the Brown-Peterson technique. There were three groups of six subjects; the method in which the trigrams were presented differed for each

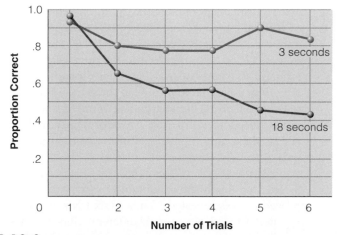

▼ **FIGURE 10.3**

Retention of a Stimulus Trigram as a Function of the Number of Trials (1–6) and the Retention Interval on Each Trial (3 or 18 seconds). On the first trial, there is very little forgetting of the trigram, even with an 18-second retention interval. However, after a number of trials, recall becomes poorer due to the prior tests, especially with the 18-second retention interval (Keppel & Underwood, 1962). This phenomenon is known as proactive interference.

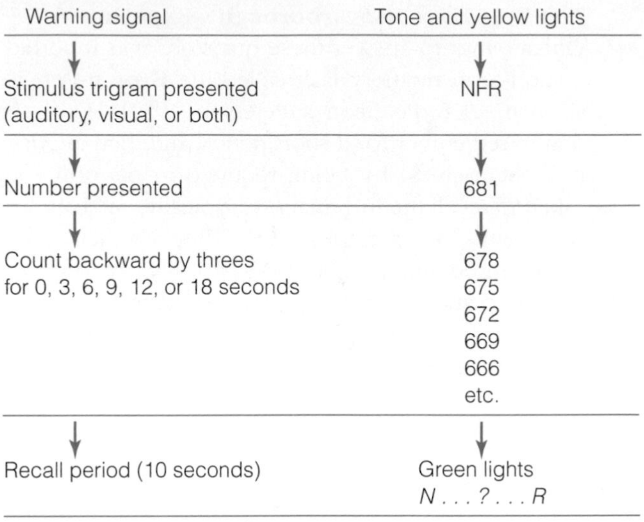

Warning signal	Tone and yellow lights
↓	↓
Stimulus trigram presented (auditory, visual, or both)	NFR
↓	↓
Number presented	681
↓	↓
Count backward by threes for 0, 3, 6, 9, 12, or 18 seconds	678 675 672 669 666 etc.
↓	↓
Recall period (10 seconds)	Green lights N . . . ? . . . R

▼ FIGURE 10.4

Schematic overview of a typical trial in the Brown-Peterson short-term memory procedure, as used in Scarborough's experiment.

group. One group of subjects *saw* the trigrams (visual only condition), one group *heard* the trigrams (auditory only), and a third group both saw and heard the trigrams (visual + auditory). Presentation time was carefully controlled by having the trigrams presented over a tape recorder or a tachistoscope, a device for quickly exposing and removing visual information. One second after presentation of the trigram, subjects heard a three-digit number, except in one condition in which subjects were requested to recall the trigram immediately (the 0-second retention-interval condition). Subjects in each condition were required to retain the letters during retention intervals of 0, 3, 6, 9, 12, or 18 seconds. Once the three-digit number was presented, subjects were required to count backward by threes aloud at the rate of one count per second (in time with a metronome) to keep them from rehearsing the trigram. At the end of the retention interval, the metronome stopped and two green lights came on, signaling the 10-second recall period. Therefore, each trial consisted of a warning signal (two yellow lights and a tone) indicating that the trigram was about to be displayed; presentation of the trigram; presentation of the three-digit number (with the one exception just noted); the retention interval during which the subjects counted backward by threes; and finally the recall period. A typical trial is exemplified in Figure 10.4. This procedure was repeated 36 times (six trials at each of the six retention intervals, in a counterbalanced order) with different trigrams. In summary, three between-subjects conditions (visual only, auditory only, visual and auditory) were combined with six within-subjects conditions (retention intervals of 0, 1, 3, 6, 9, 12, or 18 seconds) in the experiment.

The results of Scarborough's experiment are reproduced in Figure 10.5, where the percentage of times a trigram was correctly reported is plotted as a function of retention interval. This figure (and the statistics that Scarborough reports back this up) shows that subjects who received only visual presentation of the trigrams generally recalled them

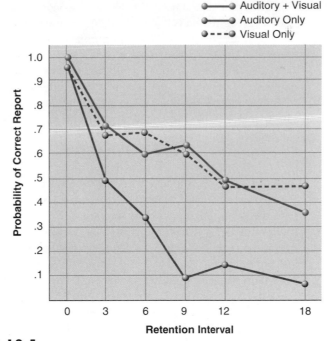

▼ FIGURE 10.5

The probability of correctly recalling a stimulus trigram as a function of the three presentation conditions and the duration of the counting task. Notice that (1) visual presentation is generally superior to auditory presentation, and (2) simultaneous auditory and visual presentation is no better than only visual presentation (Scarborough, 1972).

a greater percentage of the time than subjects who received only auditory presentation. Furthermore, receiving information in both modalities simultaneously did not produce any better recall than presenting the information only visually; the percentage correct at each retention interval is roughly the same for visual only and visual plus auditory subjects. So far so good. But what else can we conclude from Figure 10.5? Specifically, can we conclude anything about the rates of forgetting for information that is presented auditorily and visually? Is the rate of forgetting the same or different in the two cases?

Scarborough (1972) was quite careful on this score. Although the auditory only and visual only functions appear to diverge increasingly as the retention interval becomes longer, he did not draw the conclusion that the rate of forgetting is greater for information presented through the ears than through the eyes. However, consider what another writer said about this experiment in his textbook:

> The figure shows that the curves intercept the *Y* ordinate at roughly the same point and diverge significantly. The intercept value at zero sec. provides a measure of the original perception and storage of the stimuli, since it measures how much information the subject has immediately after the presentation of the stimuli, when no forgetting has taken place. The rate of forgetting can be determined from the slopes of the forgetting functions. According to this analysis, Figure 10.5 shows that the items presented auditorily are forgotten much faster than the items presented visually (Massaro, 1975, pp. 530–531).

Unfortunately, although it seems reasonable, this conclusion must be called into question. The reason is that performance at the 0-second retention interval is very nearly perfect in all conditions. When performance is perfect, it is impossible to tell whether there are any "real" differences among conditions because of scale attenuation—in this case, a ceiling effect. If the scale of the dependent measure were really "long" enough, it might show differences between auditory and visual presentation, even at the 0-second retention interval. So Massaro's conclusion that the rate of forgetting is greater for auditory than for visual presentation cannot be accepted on the basis of the argument we just quoted, because the assumption of equivalent performance at the 0-second retention interval may not be correct.

All this may be a bit confusing at first, so let us take a clearer case and demonstrate the same principle. Suppose two obese men decided to make a bet as to who could lose the greatest amount of weight in a certain amount of time. One man looked much heavier than the other, but neither was sure what he actually weighed, since they both made a point of avoiding scales. The scale they decided to use for the bet was a common bathroom scale that runs from 0 to 300 pounds. On the day they were to begin their weight-loss programs, each man weighed himself while the other watched. To their great surprise, both men weighed in at exactly the same value, 300 pounds. So despite their different sizes, the two men decided that they were beginning their bet at equal weights.

The problem again is one of ceiling effects in the scale of measurement. The weight range of the bathroom scale simply did not go high enough to record the actual weight of these men. Let us imagine that one would be found to actually weigh 300 pounds and the other 350 pounds, if their weights had been taken by a scale with a greater range. After 6 months of their weight-loss program, let us further suppose, both men had actually lost 100 pounds. They would both reweigh themselves at this point and discover that one now weighed 200 pounds and the other 250. Since they believed that they both had started from the same weight (300), they would reach the erroneous conclusion that the person who presently weighed 200 had won the bet. See Figure 10.6(a).

The problem here is really the same as that in interpreting the results of Scarborough's experiment as evidence that information presented auditorily is forgotten at a greater rate than information presented visually. There is no better way for us to know the rate of forgetting in the two conditions of interest in that experiment than there is for the two men to know the rate of weight loss in judging who won their bet. In neither case can we assume equivalent initial scores before the measurement of loss begins.

One way to avoid this problem in Scarborough's experiment would be to ignore the data points at the 0-second retention interval and ask whether the rate of forgetting is greater between 3 and 18 seconds for auditory than for visual presentation. This could be done by computing an interaction between presentation and retention interval over the range of 3 to 18 seconds; but by simply inspecting Figure 10.5, you can get some idea as to whether the auditory only and visual only points are increasingly divergent. They are between 3 and 9 seconds, but after that, the difference between them remains constant. However, this lack of an increasingly larger difference over the last three points may be caused by a floor effect in the auditory only condition, since performance is so poor, especially on the last point (only 7 or 8 percent correct). One must be very careful in interpreting data when there are ceiling or floor effects. A prudent investigator would hesitate to draw any conclusion from the data in Figure 10.5 about rates of forgetting—Scarborough's

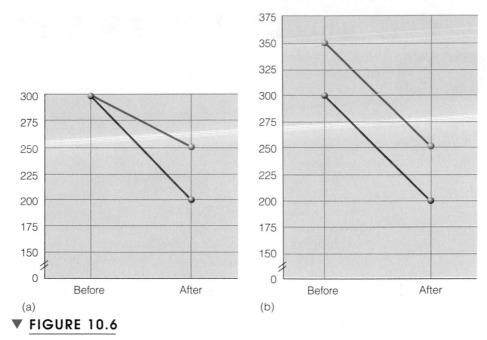

(a)   (b)

▼ **FIGURE 10.6**

Panel (a) illustrates the situation as the overweight men believed it to be: They started at the same weight, and one lost twice as much as the other. Panel (b) reveals the actual case, with the ceiling effect in the scale of measurement removed. In fact, both men lost 100 pounds. Scale attenuation (ceiling and floor effects) can hide actual differences that may exist between conditions in an experiment.

approach exactly. But we should also note that over the retention intervals where there are neither ceiling nor floor effects (3, 6, and 9 seconds), there seems to be greater forgetting with auditory than with visual presentation, in agreement with Massaro's conclusion quoted earlier.

How can problems of ceiling and floor effects be avoided in psychological research? Unfortunately, no hard-and-fast rule can be given. Researchers usually try to design their experiments so that they avoid extremes in performance; then, they often test their intuitions about performance on the task by testing small groups of pilot subjects. If these subjects perform near the ceiling or floor of the scale, it will often be necessary to revise the experimental task. For example, if performance in a memory experiment is too good, the amount of material being given can be increased so as to lower performance. Similarly, if the task is so hard that people hardly remember anything, the task can be made easier by reducing the amount of material, presenting it more slowly, and so on. The idea is to design tasks and performance scales so that people typically score in the middle ranges. Then, as the independent variables are manipulated, improvements or decrements in people's performance can be observed. The prudent investigator will usually make the effort to test pilot subjects before launching into an experiment that may turn out later to have been flawed by ceiling or floor effects. The testing of pilot subjects also permits the researcher to learn about other problems in the design or procedure of the experiment.

10.2   EXPERIMENTAL TOPICS AND RESEARCH ILLUSTRATIONS

Topic   *Generality of Results*
Illustration   *Levels of Processing*

We mentioned in Chapter 3 that there are many ways to test a hypothesis and that single experiments that test a hypothesis, although informative to a certain extent, need to be viewed against a background of other experiments designed to test the same hypothesis in other ways. Ideally, researchers would like experiments that test a particular hypothesis in a variety of situations to converge on one conclusion, but in reality, this is often not the case. The issue is one of **generality of results:** Often the conclusion drawn from one experimental situation does not generalize to other situations. This is frustrating but inevitable. It is also important. We should always ask these questions after some experiment has shown an effect of some independent variable on some dependent variable: To what subject populations does this effect generalize? (Just because an effect holds for rats does not necessarily mean that it will hold for people; see Chapter 15.) Under what settings, either experimental or extraexperimental, does this conclusion hold? Will the conclusion hold when the independent and dependent variables are operationalized or defined in a slightly different way than they are in the original experiment? The question of generality crops up in all types of research. If huge doses of some drug produce cancer in laboratory mice, should this drug be banned from human consumption, even when the dosage level is much smaller and the organism entirely different? Of course, testing with animals is a critical first step in discovering if a substance is harmful (or helpful) before it is tried on humans, but effects in one species do not necessarily mean that the same effects will be found in another species.

To illustrate the issues surrounding the problem of generality of results, we consider experiments bearing on the **levels of processing** approach to memory. Craik and Lockhart (1972) proposed that memory could be viewed as a by-product of perception and, further, that perception could be conceived as progressing through various stages or levels. For example, consider your perception and comprehension of the word *YACHT*. Craik and Lockhart (1972) noted that a person pays attention to features at different cognitive "levels" when reading such a word. A first level is that of surface features of appearances: the word has five letters, includes one vowel, is in uppercase type, and so on. Perception of the word's letters is a first step in reading it; a **graphemic** (letter) level of analysis is required. Second, the reading of many words is accompanied by translating the written form into some common (phonemic) code that is shared with words that are heard. The code is called **phonemic** (or **phonological**) because it is assumed to be based on phonemes, the basic sound patterns of a language. We would rely on a phonemic code when we decide that *yacht* rhymes with *hot*, even though the words do not look alike. A third stage, or level, of processing is the determination of a word's meaning. The purpose of reading is to derive the meaning of the words, to know what a yacht is. This is referred to as a **semantic** level of analysis.

Craik and Lockhart (1972) proposed that perceiving words (or anything else) involved progress through the stages from appearance (shallow levels in the cognitive system) to meaning (deep levels in the cognitive system). Furthermore they argued that later memory for experiences was directly tied to their depth of processing during initial perception: The deeper the level of processing during initial perception, the better should be memory for the experience.

An experiment reported by Craik and Tulving (1975) illustrates the type of evidence supporting the levels of processing approach to memory. The researchers presented undergraduate subjects with 60 words and had them answer questions about each word. The questions were designed to manipulate the level of processing of the words. For example, the subjects might see the word *BEAR* on a screen and be asked one of the following three questions: Is it in uppercase letters? Does it rhyme with *chair?* Is it an animal? In each case the subject should answer yes but in doing so should process the word to different levels. In the first case, only superficial (graphemic) characteristics of the word must be checked to answer the question about typeface. In the second case, the sound of the word (or its phonemic code) must be consulted. Finally, in the third case, the subject must access the word's meaning, or process it semantically. The researchers predicted, in line with the levels of processing theory, that words processed to deeper levels should be better remembered than those processed to shallower levels (semantic > phonemic > graphemic).

Craik and Tulving's (1975) results confirmed those predictions impressively. They tested memory by a recognition test on which their subjects were given the 60 old words (those about which they had answered questions) along with 120 new words. The subjects were told to try to pick out and circle exactly 60 words that they had seen in the earlier phase of the experiment. Because subjects had to pick out 60 words, chance performance (i.e., the level expected for people who had never seen the words) would have been 33 percent (60 of 180). The results are shown in Figure 10.7 for those words receiving a yes response during the study phase. Recognition increased from just above chance with superficial, graphemic processing of the word's appearance to nearly perfect with a deep, semantic level of processing. The only difference among the three conditions during the study phase was the very brief mental process that occurred when the person answered the question, so this experiment shows the power of even very rapid encoding processes on memory. The results conformed nicely to the predictions from levels of processing theory.

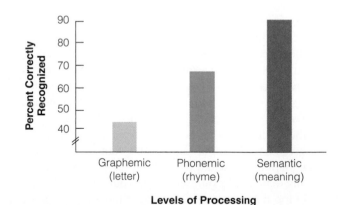

Levels of Processing

▼ **FIGURE 10.7**

Results of Craik and Tulving (1975). Subjects answered questions about words that were designed to effect different levels of processing: graphemic (Is it in uppercase letters?), phonemic (Does it rhyme with ____?), and semantic (Is it in the ____ category?). In line with the levels of processing approach, the deeper the level of original processing, the more accurate was recognition on the later test. (After Craik and Tulving, 1975.)

The levels of processing approach and the experiments designed to test it have greatly excited experimental psychologists and have produced a large amount of research (see Gardiner, Java, & Richardson-Klavehn, 1996; Lockhart & Craik, 1990). In fact, the journal *Memory* published an entire special issue on the topic (2002, vol. 10, issue 5–6). Our concern here is with the generality of the basic experimental results, as seen in Figure 10.7, rather than with the theory itself. The theory has been criticized as being circular and untestable, because there is no independent way of assessing depth or level of processing except for performance on a memory test (Nelson, 1977). Without converging operations (see Chapters 7 and 14) on the construct of levels of processing, the theory does run the risk of being circular: Processing that produces good retention is deep processing, and vice versa. Despite this difficulty, the levels of processing framework has generated a massive amount of research, in part because the basic experimental effects are so strong. Few variables in the study of memory take performance from almost chance levels to almost perfect, with all other variables held constant.

The Craik and Tulving (1975) results are powerful, but how general are they? The subjects in the experiment were highly selected college students; the materials were single words about which questions were asked; the test was recognition, with subjects forced to respond with a fixed number of words (so they had to guess); and level of processing was operationalized (manipulated) in a particular way. Were any or all of these features critical in producing Craik and Tulving's (1975) results? As we discussed in Chapter 3, every experiment involves many choices in deciding how a particular theory or hypothesis is tested. Further research is necessary to determine the generality of the findings.

Jenkins (1979) has proposed an interesting way to think about the issue of generalizability of results, as represented in his **tetrahedral model of memory experiments** shown in Figure 10.8. (A tetrahedron has four faces; hence, the name.) Jenkins (1979) noted that any researcher exploring memory must make choices along four dimensions, whether or not that particular dimension is of interest in the experiment (i.e., even if it is a control variable). These are (1) the subjects being tested, (2) the material used for learning and testing, (3) the orienting tasks (or the features of the setting in which subjects are tested), and (4) the type of test used. Roediger (2008) recently observed that there are even more dimensions that need to be considered, but we will focus on Jenkins's original four here. In the Craik and Tulving (1975) experiment, the researchers were interested in how the orienting task (the questions orienting the subjects to process the words in particular ways) affected retention. The other three were not of interest, and so these potential variables were controlled: All subjects were college students, the memory test was recognition, and the materials used were words. Jenkins's (1979) framework points out that any experimental result should be viewed in the context of other potential variables that could have been manipulated. The issue of generality of results can then be framed as follows: If the other control variables were manipulated, would the same results hold? If the independent variable was operationally defined in a different way, would the result replicate? We turn now to research that helps answer this question about the levels of processing effect. (The following coverage is not complete but illustrates the points by selective use of examples.)

Subjects

Do people other than college students show the levels of processing effect (better memory for material processed meaningfully)? In general, the answer here to date is yes. For example, Cermak and Reale (1978) tested patients with Korsakoff's syndrome,

▼ FIGURE 10.8

Jenkins's (1979) Tetrahedral Model of Memory Experiments. Each corner represents a cluster of factors in which memory researchers may be interested. Even if only one factor (say, type of material) is of interest in an experiment, the outcome of the experiment may still be influenced by the values selected on the other dimensions as control variables.

a brain disorder suffered by some chronic alcoholics due to a vitamin deficiency. One hallmark of Korsakoff's syndrome is a severe memory deficit on explicit memory tests, such as recall or recognition. Nonetheless, Cermak and Reale (1978) discovered that Korsakoff patients did show a level of processing effect when tested in a manner similar to Craik and Tulving's (1975). Although performance was much lower overall for

Korsakoff patients than for normal control subjects, the patients still showed somewhat better retention following meaningful encoding than following shallow encoding.

Other experiments have been directed at the variable of age. Murphy and Brown (1975) tested preschool children (under age 5) by giving them 16 pictures and having different groups judge them on three different dimensions. One group was asked if the pictures belonged to a particular category. A second group was asked if the pictures represented something nasty or nice. The children in a third group were asked to name the dominant color in the pictures. This last task was judged to involve shallow encoding, whereas the first two were thought to be deep. The results came out just this way: Children who had named pictures' colors during the study phase recalled 18 percent of the pictures later, but those who had performed the more meaningful encoding tasks recalled about 40 percent. It has been argued that even 3-month-old infants show levels of processing effects; manipulations that selectively directed their attention during encoding affected their later recognition of mobile stimuli (Adler, Gerhardstein, & Rovee-Collier, 1998). At the other end of the life span, older adults also show strong levels of processing effects (Craik, 1977). In short, the levels of processing effect is relatively robust across those subject variables studied thus far.

Materials

Can level of processing effects be found with materials other than lists of words? Obviously, the effect would be of little interest if it does not generalize beyond this restriction. Smith and Winograd (1978) showed people faces at the rate of one every 8 seconds. One group was told to decide whether or not each person had a big nose (a superficial judgment). Another group was told to judge whether each person was friendly (a deep judgment). On a later recognition test, subjects who judged the faces on friendliness recognized them better than those who judged them on nose size, confirming the basic levels of processing effect with faces.

As mentioned in the preceding section, Murphy and Brown (1975) tested preschool children with pictures in a level of processing paradigm and replicated the basic effect, too. Lane and Robertson (1979) also found a level of processing effect in chess players' memories for positions on chessboards. Levels of processing effects have also been found with such diverse materials as Chinese characters (Lee, 2002) and simple actions (Zimmer & Engelkamp, 1999).

In general, evidence exists that the level of processing ideas can be extended to nonverbal material, although it is certainly true that the great bulk of levels of processing research has used verbal material. However, Intraub and Nicklos (1985) have reported an exception to this pattern. They had people look at pictures and answer either physical questions (Is this horizontal or vertical?) or questions requiring access to meaning (Is this edible or inedible?). Later they asked subjects to recall the pictures by writing a one- or two-sentence descriptive phrase. Surprisingly, they found that physical questions led to better retention than did meaningful questions, a reverse of the usual pattern. The outcome cannot be dismissed as a fluke, because they replicated the finding in six experiments under various conditions. The unusual finding by Intraub and Nicklos (1985) represents something of a mystery; as yet no one has satisfactorily explained why they found a reverse level of processing effect (physical judgments superior to meaningful judgments) in retention of pictures. But exceptions to a general pattern can lead to opportunities for theoretical advancement, as we shall see in the next section.

Orienting Tasks and Settings

This category of variables refers to the many aspects of the particular experimental context, including the instructions subjects are given, the particular version of the experimental task, the strategies subjects use, and so on.

The basic level of processing effect (deep encoding producing greater retention than shallow encoding) has been shown to hold over a wide variety of changes in experimental setting. For example, one dimension often considered in memory experiments is whether subjects know before they are exposed to the study material that their memories will be tested. When subjects are told that their memories will be tested, it is referred to as intentional learning; when they are given material with no such warning (but think they are performing some other task), it is called incidental learning (because learning the material is perceived, by the subject, to be incidental to the purpose of the experiment). Craik and Tulving (1975) tested subjects under both incidental and intentional learning conditions and showed that the level of processing effect occurred in both cases.

Another dimension of interest in the level of processing experiment is the particular questions (or the orienting tasks) used to induce shallow and deep processing. Craik and Tulving (1975) had subjects judge the typeface of words (uppercase or lowercase) for the shallow, physical dimension and judge whether or not the word belonged to a particular category (animal?) for the deep level. But many other types of questions could be used to direct subjects' attention to superficial or meaningful aspects of the words. For example, Hyde and Jenkins (1969) asked subjects whether words contained particular letters (an *e*?) as the shallow task and to rate the words' pleasantness as the deep task. This manipulation also produced a robust level of processing effect. In general, numerous manipulations with verbal materials converge on the same conclusion: Retention is poorer after physical (shallow) orienting tasks than after meaningful (deep) orienting tasks. Thus, the level of processing effect is generally robust over many variations on the basic experimental paradigm with verbal materials and with recall or recognition as the memory tests.

Type of Test

The fourth dimension in Jenkins's (1979) model of memory experiments is the type of test used to assess memory. The standard measures of memory have been variations on recall and recognition tests. Level of processing effects have been found repeatedly with both types of test. However, researchers have found other kinds of tests on which level of processing has no effect (Fisher & Craik, 1977; Jacoby & Dallas, 1981; McDaniel, Friedman, & Bourne, 1978) or even a reverse effect (Morris, Bransford, & Franks, 1977). This discovery has helped refine ideas about levels of processing and led to a new approach, transfer-appropriate processing. The basic idea guiding this research is that the form of a test—what kind of knowledge it taps—may determine what encoding activities are useful for the test.

Morris and associates (1977) conducted an experiment similar in many ways to the original Craik and Tulving (1975) experiment. They used college students as subjects and asked them to make judgments about words. The questions about the words (e.g., *EAGLE*) were designed to induce a phonemic level of processing ("— rhymes with *legal*?") or a semantic level ("— is a large bird?"). Subjects answered phonemic questions for half the words and semantic questions for the other half, with the correct answer "yes" half the time and "no" half the time. According to the levels of processing view, the meaningful questions should produce deeper encoding and better retention. This prediction was upheld in a standard recognition test (such as that used by Craik and Tulving) in which studied words were mixed with nonstudied words and the subjects' task was to pick out the studied words. As shown in the left panel of Figure 10.9, subjects recognized words 84 percent of the time following semantic encoding but only 63 percent of the time following phonemic encoding.

But Morris and associates (1977) gave a second group of subjects a different test called a rhyme recognition test. The subjects' job in this test was to examine a list of words and to pick out words that rhymed with words they had studied earlier. So if *beagle* were on the test list, they should pick it because it rhymes with the studied word *eagle*. (None of the words on the test list had appeared on the study list, just words that rhymed with them.) Subjects performed better on the rhyme recognition test if they had studied words in the phonemic condition (49 percent correct) than in the semantic condition (33 percent correct), a reversal of the usual finding. Thus Morris and associates (1977) argued that one type of processing is not inherently superior or inferior to another type but that effects of encoding manipulations depend on how the information will be used or tested. Instead of fixed levels of processing, they argued for **transfer-appropriate processing:** Performance on a test will benefit to the extent that the knowledge acquired (or the operations performed) during study match the knowledge or operations required by the test. On a recognition test that required use of phonemic (rhyme) knowledge, prior phonemic encoding led to better performance than did semantic encoding.

Although levels of processing effects are robust across many variables, they do not generalize to all types of tests. For tests that require access of meaningful information,

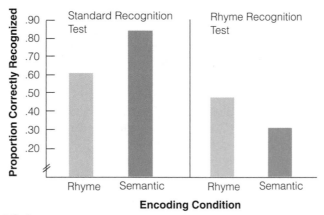

▼ FIGURE 10.9

Results of Morris, Bransford, and Franks (1977). After answering questions about words designed to make them think about the word's sound (phonemic coding) or meaning (semantic coding), subjects took either a standard recognition test (left panel) or a rhyme recognition test in which they had to select words that rhymed with the original studied words (right panel). The usual levels of processing effects were found with the standard recognition test, but phonemic coding produced better performance than semantic coding on the rhyme recognition test. Thus, types of processing are not inherently shallow or deep but depend on the way the information must be used. Poor processing for one type of test may be good processing for another test.

standard level of processing effects are found. However, this is not so for other types of tests (see Jacoby & Dallas, 1981; Roediger, Weldon, Stadler, & Riegler, 1992).

This section has been oriented around Jenkins's (1979) model of memory experiments shown in Figure 10.8, but his model also can be broadened to apply to all psychology experiments. That is, in any line of inquiry one should ask if the results will generalize across types of subjects, across research settings, across different dependent measures, and across different ways of manipulating the independent variables.

Whenever an experimental result does not generalize across some variable, noting this fact is only the first step. The real problem is to find out why. Scientists often tend to disbelieve or ignore exceptions to firmly held beliefs, at least until the exception has been replicated enough times to be made salient. Changing one's mind about strongly held beliefs is always uncomfortable, but one way science sometimes progresses by leaps is when an empirical exception to a widely accepted theory becomes understood. Often, understanding the exception causes us to discard or greatly modify our theory. Thus, failures of generalization are not necessarily to be lamented; they can be great opportunities. The finding that levels of processing effects do not hold on all tests has thus led to a new theoretical approach named transfer-appropriate processing, which has been applied in other domains, too (see Blaxton, 1989; Roediger, 1990).

10.3   EXPERIMENTAL TOPICS AND RESEARCH ILLUSTRATIONS

Topic   *Interaction Effects*
Illustration   *Implicit and Explicit Memory Tests*

Interaction effect is a statistical term that arises from the use of analysis of variance in evaluating multifactor experiments, or those having more than one independent variable. Interaction effects are more commonly referred to as **interactions** and were discussed previously in Chapters 3 and 8. (The analysis of variance is described in Appendix B.) However, because the concept of interactions is so important, we consider it again in somewhat more detail. Also, we have discovered that it is a concept that is somewhat bothersome to students, so repeated treatments should provide a better grasp of the topic.

Multifactor experiments, you will recall, are those in which two or more independent variables are manipulated at the same time. An interaction effect occurs when the effect of one independent variable differs depending on the level of the other independent variable. You have already been exposed to interaction effects several times in this chapter, although we did not refer to them as such. For example, Scarborough's (1972) results seen in Figure 10.5 show that the superiority of visual to auditory presentation in his short-term memory paradigm depended on the retention interval used. Similarly, the results of Morris and associates (1977) shown in Figure 10.9 show an interaction between the level of processing during study and the type of test taken. The examples used in this section are similar to those of Morris and associates (1977).

Implicit and Explicit Tests

We will use differences between implicit and explicit memory tests to illustrate various types of interactions. The distinction between these types of tests was described briefly at the beginning of the chapter and are amplified here.

Explicit memory measures are those that require a person to consciously recollect the material that he or she studied during an earlier part of the experiment. Examples of such tests are free recall, cued recall, and recognition; in each case, people are told to recollect previous experiences. Thus, these tests are explicitly presented as tests of memory.

In contrast, implicit memory tests are tasks that can be performed without specific reference to the previous experiences in the laboratory. One example of an implicit test is the **word fragment completion task.** In this task, subjects see words that have letters missing from them and are required to fill in the blanks to form complete words (e.g., __l__p__a__t for elephant). People are typically told just to produce whatever word fits the frame as quickly as possible; they are not told that some of the fragments are made from previously studied items. The fragments are quite difficult, and a person can typically complete only 20 to 35 percent of them if he or she has not seen them recently. The proportion of fragments that can be completed without a subject's ever having studied the items is the control condition, often called the "nonstudied baseline." However, if the person has read the words that complete the fragments at some time prior to performing the fragment completion test, he or she can complete many more of the fragments: typically, about 25 percent more of them. This occurs even when people are not told that the fragments come from the words studied earlier. Memory is said to be tested implicitly, because even though the subjects do not have to try to remember the studied words in order to perform the task, their performance is spontaneously improved by the prior exposures.

This improvement in performance is called **priming.** To measure priming, researchers test subjects on a random mixture of fragments for both words they studied and words they did not study. Each person's priming score can then be computed by subtracting the proportion of nonstudied items that were solved (the nonstudied baseline) from the proportion of studied items completed. For example, suppose you have studied 10 words. Later, you receive a fragment test with fragments for the 10 words you have studied, plus 10 other fragments for words you have not studied, randomly mixed together. If you solve fragments for 5 out of the 10 studied words (50 percent), but only 2 out of the 10 nonstudied words (nonstudied baseline of 20 percent), then your priming score would be $0.50 - 0.20 = 0.30$. (To make sure that the difference between studied and nonstudied words is not simply due to the studied items being easier, the items are counterbalanced across subjects. That is, half the subjects study one half of the items, whereas the other subjects study the other half of the items. Thus, during the course of the experiment, each item appears as a studied and as a nonstudied item equally often. See Chapter 9.)

Another example of an implicit memory test is the word stem completion test. On this test, people see word stems that are the first three letters of a word, such as ele___, and are told to complete the stem with the first word that comes to mind. What word did you think of to complete this stem? Most likely, you thought of "elephant" instead of "element" or "elegant," or so on, because you were primed with that word in a previous paragraph. The same priming occurs when people study a list of words before taking the word stem completion test.

Several other types of implicit memory tests have also been used, but we will not describe them here (see Roediger & McDermott, 1993). The critical feature of these tests is that they can all be performed without people necessarily being aware that they are remembering the prior study episode, even though their answers are influenced or "primed" by the material they have seen earlier. These tests are sometimes said to reflect "memory without awareness" (Jacoby & Witherspoon, 1982) because improved performance does not require that people be aware of the relation between the test and study materials.

Amnesia

Interest in the distinction between implicit and explicit memory measures originally arose out of research with amnesics (e.g., Warrington & Weiskrantz, 1970). Patients with **amnesia** have brain damage from any one of a number of sources, such as chronic alcoholism (Korsakoff's syndrome), anoxia (loss of oxygen to the brain), surgery, or head injury; they show severe memory deficits on explicit retention measures. Typically, they can recall or recognize very little about recently presented information, even though their other cognitive functions are intact. Some cases are so profound that the patient's doctors must reintroduce themselves each time they meet with the patient! The following excerpt is taken from a book by Wayne Wickelgren (1977), who worked with amnesic patients.

> Once in the course of testing one of these people, I had a rather eerie experience. The patient was a young man in his twenties who had recently suffered brain damage because of an unusual fencing accident. Suzanne Corkin introduced me to the patient saying something like, "This is Wayne Wickelgren." The young man replied "Wickelgren, that's a German name isn't it?" I said, "no." Then he said "Irish?" Again I said "no." Then he said "Scandinavian?" and I answered "yes." I talked with him for perhaps five minutes, and then I had to leave to make a telephone call. When I returned, everyone was standing in approximately the same locations as before. Sue, realizing that the patient would have no knowledge of ever having met me before, reintroduced me to him. After she said, "This is Wayne Wickelgren," he proceeded to say, "That's a German name, isn't it?" I replied, "no." Then he said, "Irish?" I said, "no," and he said "Scandinavian?"—exactly the same series of questions he had asked the first time he met me (p. 326).

For more examples of the difficulties faced by amnesics in daily life, the interested reader should acquire Philip Hilts' (1995) book about H. M., who is probably the most famous amnesic. Hilts, a reporter, recounts how H. M. was unable to remember witnessing an accident (even though H. M. was in a car that had to swerve to avoid hitting the overturned car) and how H. M. continued to be unsure of his father's status 4 years after his father's death. Thus, amnesics' explicit recollection is severely impaired, as compared with that of normal subjects. It was often hypothesized in the past that amnesics lacked the ability to learn and to store new verbal information.

In 1970, Elizabeth Warrington and Lawrence Weiskrantz decided to test amnesics' memory in a different way and made a discovery that has greatly changed the way scientists think about amnesia, in particular, and memory functioning in general. Warrington and Weiskrantz asked amnesics and control subjects (patients without neurological disease) to study lists of 24 words and then tested their memories in several different ways. (They studied different lists for each memory test.) We discuss two of the tests here.

The first test was a traditional explicit free recall test, in which the subjects were simply instructed to recall as many of the words as possible. As expected, the amnesics recalled many fewer items (33 percent) than did the controls (54 percent). The second test was an implicit test, in which subjects saw perceptually degraded words (pieces of each letter were obliterated, so that none of the words could be identified by the subjects before the test); they were simply instructed to try to figure out and name the word. (All the words had been presented previously during the study phase.) The interesting question was whether amnesics would show their typical poor performance on this implicit memory task or whether something different would happen.

To introduce the concept of interactions, in the following section we examine several possible outcomes that might have been obtained in this experiment.

Interactions

In general, two independent variables are said to interact when the effect of one variable (on the dependent variable) changes at different levels of the other variable. We have chosen to illustrate this concept with our discussion of implicit and explicit memory tests because they exhibit many interesting interactions. That is, implicit and explicit memory tests respond differently to manipulations of certain independent variables. Variables that have a large effect on an implicit test may have no effect—or even the opposite effect—on explicit tests. We will now illustrate interactions involving implicit and explicit memory tests by examining some different patterns of results that might have been obtained in the Warrington and Weiskrantz experiment, described in the preceding section.

Figure 10.10 contains four sets of hypothetical data illustrating different patterns of results that Warrington and Weiskrantz might have observed in their experiment comparing implicit and explicit memory in amnesic and control subjects. The data in the tables on the left are illustrated in corresponding bar graphs (in the middle panels) and line graphs (on the right). Note that, technically, the variables represented here should not be plotted on line graphs; they are plotted this way here only to facilitate the comparisons of the different formats for presenting the data. We will discuss each display in turn. As we discuss each example, examine the pattern of data in the table and then look at how the data appear when plotted on the graphs.

Example A is included as the starting point to demonstrate how data might look when there is no interaction between the variables. Here, the control subjects perform better than the amnesics on both the explicit and the implicit tests, showing a **main effect** of the subject group. That is, subjects whose memories are intact (controls) have better memories than amnesics, regardless of how memory is tested. Thus, there is no interaction between memory group and test type in this example. Main effects are generalizations; they tell us that at each level of one variable (here, test type), the same effect was observed on the other variable (here, controls performed better than amnesics).

Example B illustrates one possible type of interaction that might be obtained. In this case, controls perform better than amnesics on the explicit free recall test, but amnesics perform as well as controls on the word identification task. In other words, the traditional difference between the amnesic and control groups disappears when memory is measured implicitly. Thus, the effect of one independent variable (the presence or absence of a memory deficit) changes, depending on the level of the other independent variable (test type). This is one example of what is meant by an interaction between two variables.

Example C illustrates a type of interaction that researchers typically find most interesting, known as a **crossover interaction.** The reason for this name is best illustrated in line graph C. In our example, the control subjects show better memory than amnesics on the explicit test, but the amnesics show better memory than the controls

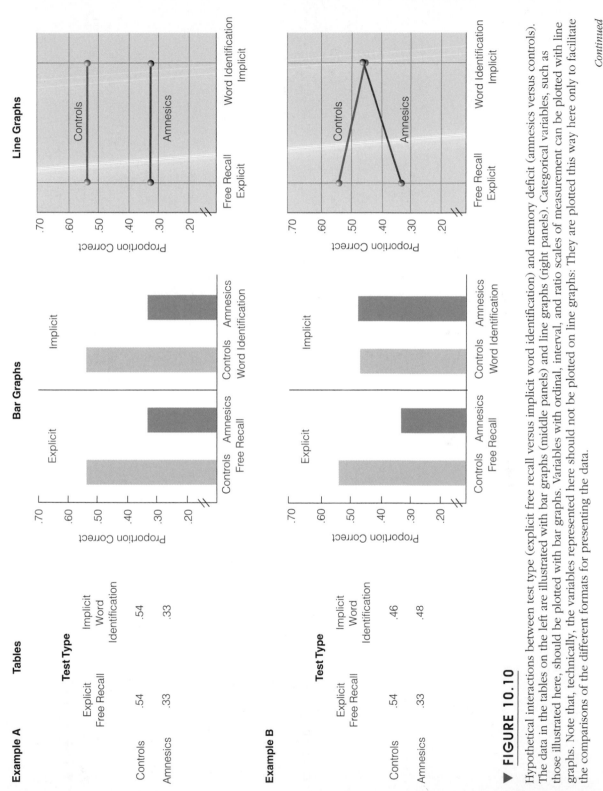

▶ **FIGURE 10.10**

Hypothetical interactions between test type (explicit free recall versus implicit word identification) and memory deficit (amnesics versus controls). The data in the tables on the left are illustrated with bar graphs (middle panels) and line graphs (right panels). Categorical variables, such as those illustrated here, should be plotted with bar graphs. Variables with ordinal, interval, and ratio scales of measurement can be plotted with line graphs. Note that, technically, the variables represented here should not be plotted on line graphs: They are plotted this way here only to facilitate the comparisons of the different formats for presenting the data.

Continued

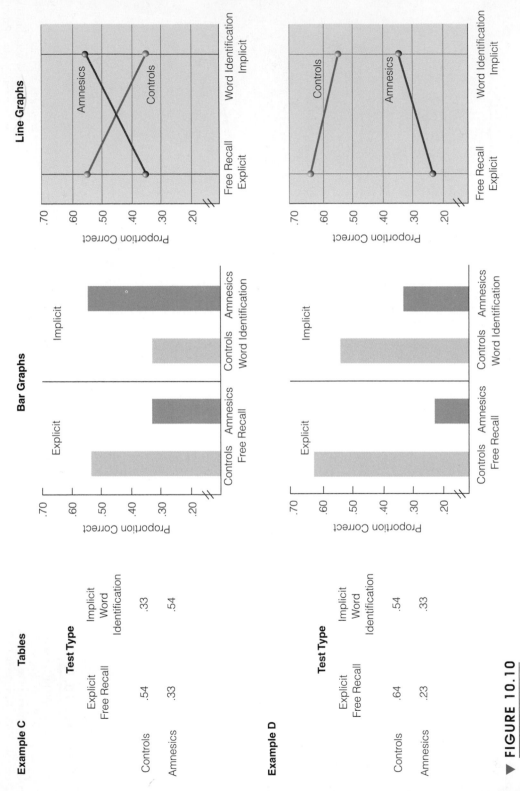

▶ **FIGURE 10.10**
cont'd.

on the implicit test. Thus, in a crossover interaction, the first independent variable has one effect at one level of the second independent variable, but it has the opposite effect at the other level of the second independent variable. If we obtained the data in Example C in our experiment, we would conclude that amnesics have better memory than the control subjects if memory is measured implicitly (at least on this test) but that the reverse occurs on the explicit test.

Although many other types of interactions exist, we will end our illustrations with the interaction depicted in Example D. If these data were obtained in our experiment, we would conclude that the amnesic deficit is more pronounced on the explicit test than on the implicit test. That is, although control subjects perform substantially better than amnesics on the implicit test, the superiority of controls' memory to amnesics' memory is even greater on the explicit test. These data would suggest that the implicit test is a less-sensitive measure of amnesic deficits than is the explicit test.

We will not keep you in suspense any longer. It turns out that Warrington and Weiskrantz obtained the results depicted in Example B. They found that although amnesics performed very poorly on the explicit recall test, the amount of priming they showed on the word fragment identification task was identical to performance of normal control subjects! (Recall that no subjects could identify any of the fragmented words before they started the experiment, so the proportions of items identified are priming scores.) That is, the amnesic deficit disappears when memory is tapped implicitly, with tests that can be performed without referring to the prior learning episode.

Since Warrington and Weiskrantz's important discovery, many other experimenters have obtained similar results with a variety of implicit tasks (Dunn, 1998; Gabrieli, Keane, Zarella, & Poldrack, 1997; Shimamura, 1986). That is, although amnesics perform poorly on explicit tests, they show preserved priming on implicit tests. The reasons for these interactions are not entirely understood, but they certainly dispel the notion that amnesics preserve no memorial record of recent experiences. At least part of the amnesics' problem seems to lie in gaining conscious access to these stored experiences.

One interesting outgrowth of the work comparing performance on explicit and implicit tests is the examination of normal people's memories. Can interactions between these measures be found in normal people? If so, this would argue that the explicit/implicit contrast generalizes to other subjects. In this case (unlike the previous levels of processing instance), we ask whether findings obtained with an unusual population (amnesic patients) generalize to more typical groups. Many experiments have indeed shown interactions between independent variables and the type of test in normal subjects (Roediger, 1990); we consider here one reported by Weldon and Roediger (1987).

Weldon and Roediger (1987) were interested in the picture superiority effect, the finding that pictures are remembered better than words. However, this effect has typically only been studied with explicit memory tests (recall and recognition), and Weldon and Roediger (1987) wanted to extend the study of picture/word differences to implicit tests. (They suspected, for various reasons, that the picture superiority effect would not be found on implicit tests, such as those used by Warrington & Weiskrantz [1970]). In their experiment, college student subjects studied a long series of pictures and of words in anticipation of a later memory test, the nature of which was unspecified. There were three sets of items; subjects studied one set as pictures and one set as words and did not study the third set. The item sets were counterbalanced across subjects, so that if subjects in one group saw a picture of an elephant, those in another group saw the word *elephant,* and those in a third group did not see the item in either form.

After studying the words and pictures, subjects took either an explicit free recall test or an implicit word fragment completion test. In the free recall test, subjects were given a blank sheet of paper and asked to recall the names of the pictures and words as well as possible (i.e., they recalled pictures by writing down their names, not by try-ing to draw them). Despite the fact that the response mode was always verbal, pictures were better remembered than were words, as shown in the left side of Figure 10.11. The picture superiority effect was not large in this experiment, but it was statistically significant and replicates many other reports (Madigan, 1983).

In the word fragment completion test, subjects were given a long series of frag-mented words (e.g., __l__p__a__t) and told simply to complete each one with a word, if possible. In this case, the measure of interest was priming—the advantage in completing a fragment when its prior presentation was either a picture or a word, relative to the case when neither form has been studied. When subjects did not study the concept, they completed 37 percent of the fragments. The data in the right side of Figure 10.11 show the priming from prior study of pictures and words over this level. Unlike the results on the left and the entire previous literature, words produced more priming than pictures on the implicit word fragment completion test. The pattern in Figure 10.11 shows an interaction between *explicit* and *implicit retention* in normal subjects. In some ways, this

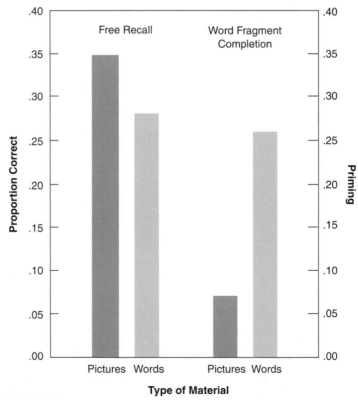

▼ FIGURE 10.11

Results of Weldon and Roediger (1987). Pictures were better remembered than words in the explicit free recall tests, but words produced more priming than pictures on the implicit word fragment completion test. The overall pattern reveals a crossover interaction.

interaction is even more striking than the interaction between tests shown in amnesics, because it represents a crossover interaction.

The topic of interactions is also related to the first problem considered in the chapter, that of scale attenuation. Often, ceiling and floor effects make the interpretation of interactions hazardous. Look back at the results of Scarborough's experiment, shown in Figure 10.5. An interaction is pictured there between modality of presentation and retention interval. Modality of presentation has an effect, but only at the longer retention intervals. However, we decided that this interaction could not be meaningfully interpreted, since it might have been produced by a ceiling effect at the 0-second retention interval. Now we can state a general rule: Extreme caution should be used in interpreting interactions where performance on the dependent variable is at either the floor or the ceiling at some level of one of the independent variables.

Multifactor experiments are extremely useful and much preferable to single-factor experiments for the very reason that they help us answer the question of generality. As we discussed in the preceding section of this chapter, one thing we very much want to know about the effect of some independent variable on a dependent variable is the conditions under which it holds. By independently varying a second (or even a third) variable in the same experiment, we can gain at least a partial answer to this question.

We have considered cases in which two factors are manipulated simultaneously. However, this logic can be extended to design experiments that involve simultaneous manipulation of three, four, or even more variables. (In practice, researchers hardly ever design experiments with more than four independent variables of interest.) When the nature of an interaction effect between two variables changes depending on the level of some third variable, the interaction is referred to as a **higher-order interaction,** since it involves several variables.

For example, suppose an investigator designs an experiment in which test type and memory deficit are manipulated, as in the Warrington and Weiskrantz experiment; in this experiment, level of processing is also manipulated. People in one condition are told to count the number of vowels in each word, whereas people in the other condition are told to form a sentence using each word. When people count vowels, they are encoding the words at a shallow level, because they are focusing their attention on the surface, or graphemic, features of the words. On the other hand, when people form sentences, they are focusing on the meaning, or semantic aspects, of the words and are thus processing words at a deeper level. So, the three factors in the experiment would be (1) encoding condition (counting vowels versus forming sentences), (2) subject group (amnesic versus control), and (3) word fragment completion and free recall. If the researcher were to find the pattern of results represented in Figure 10.12, then a higher-order interaction would exist. Here, the results show that when the control subjects study the words by forming sentences, they recall many more words on the explicit recall test than when they simply count the vowels. However, the amnesics do not show this improvement in performance on the explicit test. On the implicit test, there is no change in performance for either the controls or the amnesics when they study the words by forming sentences. Therefore, manipulation of a third variable (level of processing) changes the nature of the interaction between the other two variables. (Note that the data in Figure 10.12 are hypothetical.)

Many other intriguing interactions involving implicit versus explicit memory tests have been obtained; they are opening a whole new area of research (Roediger & McDermott, 1993). To date, this research has generated many new insights and theories about human memory. Thus, interactions between implicit and explicit tests not only

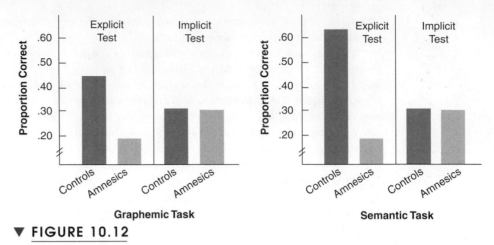

▼ FIGURE 10.12

A hypothetical higher-order interaction involving test type, memory deficit, and level of processing (graphemic versus semantic).

have revealed interesting things about memory disorders, such as amnesia, but also are providing a wealth of new information about normal memory.

Graphing the Data

During the preceding discussion, you probably figured out that the easiest way to detect interactions is to graph the data and then examine the patterns in the graphs. When the patterns of the effect of one variable are consistent across the levels of the other variable (e.g., Example A in Figure 10.10), then the two variables do not interact. When the patterns change at different levels of the independent variables (i.e., the means converge, cross over, or diverge), then interactions between the variables probably exist. Of course, appropriate statistical tests must be performed to determine the degree to which the interactions are real effects and are not simply due to chance variation.

Different types of graphs are appropriate for plotting different types of variables. Bar graphs should be used when the independent variable is categorical or qualitative—that is, when the levels of the independent variable bear no quantitative relation to one another. Examples of categorical variables are one's major in school; modality of stimulus presentation; type of study material (e.g., pictures versus words); and the two variables used in Warrington and Weiskrantz's experiment, test type and memory impairment. Categorical variables should not be plotted with line graphs because a continuous line implies that the underlying variable is continuous, or at least ordered in a meaningful way. How would you order study materials, for example? Are pictures "more" or "less" than words? Obviously, they are simply different types of items. Strictly speaking, we know the line graphs in the right-hand panels of Figure 10.10 are inappropriate for graphing the data in the example, because categorical dimensions are plotted on the abscissa (*X*-axis). The proper modes for presenting these variables are bar graphs or tables.

To use line graphs, give the variable plotted along the abscissa (*X*-axis) at least an ordinal scale and preferably an interval or ratio scale (see Chapter 6). An example of an ordinally scaled variable is the rank order of items according to some attribute (e.g., unpleasant, neutral, pleasant). Different levels of ordinal variables imply "more" or "less" of some attribute, but the magnitude of the difference is not known. Because the distances between points on an ordinal scale are not meaningful, ordinal variables are often more appropriately plotted with bar graphs than with line graphs.

Interval scales have meaningful distances between points, such as temperature (Celsius or Fahrenheit) or IQ, but have arbitrary zero points.

Ratio scales also have meaningful distances between points; in addition, they have true zero points, so that the ratios between measures are meaningful. Examples are distance, weight, retention interval (the elapsed time between study and test), and drug dosage. Both interval and ratio scales are continuous; independent variables that have these properties can be plotted on line graphs. Tables can always be used to present such data, too.

FROM PROBLEM TO EXPERIMENT
THE NUTS AND BOLTS

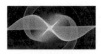

Problem   *Which Is More Effective, Reading or Listening?*

We have discussed the problem of modality differences in memory tasks that involve a short string of stimuli, such as three letters. A question of more general interest is whether there are differences in the comprehension and memory of information that is read as opposed to heard. If the same information were presented by a lecturer or read in a book, which would be more effective? Reading might allow us to go quickly over material we understand well and to tarry over difficult ideas. But while reading, we may be more apt to just glide our eyes over the page and daydream; a lecturer moving about and talking might better capture our attention.

Problem   *Is reading better than listening?*

Numerous hypotheses can be formed and operationally defined in different ways to answer this question. One such hypothesis will be considered here.

Hypothesis   *Subjects who read a long passage of material will be better able to answer multiple-choice questions about the material than will subjects who listen to another person reading the material.*

Even though this hypothesis is fairly specific, there are still a great many matters open to interpretation in actually performing the experiment. The variables need to be given operational definitions. How long is a "long passage"? What should be the subject matter of the passage? Should we use more than one passage? How should the passage to be read be presented? How long should the presentation take? Who should read the passage—or should we vary that? What kinds of questions should we ask on the multiple-choice (forced-choice recognition) test? Should we use a between-subjects or within-subjects design? These are only some of the questions that must be answered in translating the hypothesis into an actual experiment. How we decide these matters may affect the outcome of the experiment.

Let us consider the last question first and work through these questions in reverse order. Should we use each subject in both the reading and listening conditions, or should we use different groups of subjects in the two conditions? In general, it is best to use the same subjects in each condition, since in that case we do not have to worry about differences between conditions being caused by differences between subjects in the two conditions. As long as we counterbalance the conditions for practice effects by testing half the subjects in the Read condition before the Listen condition and the other half in the reverse order, there is nothing to prevent us from using the advantageous within-subjects design.

This decision helps determine the answer to another question. Since we are using each subject in two different conditions, we should obviously use at least two passages of test material, one for one condition and one for the other. We might even use more passages, since we would like to have some confidence that our results generalize to other reading material besides the particular passages used in the experiment. This issue of the generality of results over materials is an important one, especially since it is widely overlooked in certain types of research, with the result that statistical tests are often misapplied (Clark, 1973).

What kinds of passages should be used? Presumably, material that is relatively unfamiliar to the subjects would be the best choice, since we want to test knowledge they gain during the reading of the passage and not that which they acquired before the experiment. If subjects could answer almost all the questions on the multiple-choice test before coming into the experiment, there would be no chance for our independent variable (reading versus listening to the passage) to exert any influence over our dependent variable (recognition), since we would have a ceiling effect in the recognition test (close to 100 percent performance). In attempting to avoid familiar materials, researchers investigating memory for "naturalistic" prose passages have often chosen passages that contain so many words and concepts foreign to the subjects that we might wonder how "natural" these bizarre stories are. We would probably be better off using passages with mostly familiar words but new information. Passages might be taken from parts of articles from *Scientific American* or other magazines at a similar level of difficulty.

How long should the passage be? This is closely tied in with how long the presentation should take. Suppose we decide that the recognition tests should take about 7 minutes in each case. We might then want to limit time of presentation of each passage to 15 minutes in order to make the experiment last only an hour. (There should be about 15 minutes allotted for instructions, handing out and picking up tests, and explaining the experiment when it is finished.)

Perhaps the trickiest aspect of designing this experiment is deciding exactly how the passages are to be presented during the minutes in each presentation condition. Suppose we pick passages that take 15 minutes to be read out loud in the Listen condition. In the condition in which subjects read the passage, should we also simply allow them 15 minutes to read it? Then they could quite likely have more actual presentation time, since most people can read silently faster than they can read aloud. Thus, subjects who read the passage could spend more time on the difficult material. Do we want to try to eliminate this in some way—for example, by instructing subjects to read the passage once straight through? Or do we want to leave it in as one of the natural differences between reading and listening that we are trying to investigate? If we somehow remove or minimize regression (reading back over the material) in the Read condition and then find listening to be better than reading, we may be open to the criticism that our conclusion holds only in artificial laboratory situations and not in the "real world." So, to maximize the possibility for generalizable results, let us allow subjects in the Read condition 15 minutes to read the material—the same amount of time as is allowed for oral presentation—and then see what differences occur. If reading is superior to listening (or vice versa), we will have to do further research to see exactly what aspects of the process are important.

The same problem arises with oral presentation of the passage. Should we vary who reads it? The sex of the person? His or her attractiveness? Should it be read in a monotone or with zest and enthusiasm, such as a lecturer might try to convey? Let us decide to have one woman read it with normal intonation as much as possible and not in a monotone.

Designing the multiple-choice test is also important, especially with regard to making it neither too hard nor too easy, to avoid ceiling and floor effects. Should the test tap only surface-level questions (was it discussed in the third paragraph?) or more meaningful questions about the text? Or should we vary this? We could probably agree to use meaningful questions. Or why not use a recall test in the first place? (Because it is more difficult to derive quantitative measures of recall of prose, though it is possible.)

There are even more choices and difficulties than we have discussed here, even though we have only a 2×2 within-subjects within-subjects design with two types of presentation (read versus listen) and two passages (passage is a variable we are not primarily interested in). Since it is obvious that we could have operationalized the basic conditions differently and used a different dependent variable, it would be important to consider results of the present experiment against a background of other experiments in which the variables are operationalized differently. A series of such converging experiments is necessary if we are to gain some idea as to the generality or limitation of any particular experimental result.

This area of research examining modality differences in long-term retention of prose materials has received surprisingly little attention. However, two relevant references are King (1968) and Kintsch and Kozminsky (1977). More recently, researchers have been interested in the implications of this question for journalism (Eveland, Seo, & Marton, 2002; Furnham, 2001). That is, do people remember more of the news if they read a news story or if they hear a report on the TV or radio? You might think about how you could modify the study described in this section to be more applicable to the applied journalism question.

▼ SUMMARY

1. Ebbinghaus was the first psychologist to study learning and memory systematically. He solved the problem of how to study unrecallable memories by relearning material and measuring the savings in the number of relearning trials compared with those needed for original learning. Although savings methods are still used today, most researchers measure memory in other ways: typically, with some variation of recall (production) and recognition (discrimination of studied from nonstudied material) tests.

2. Scale attenuation in psychological research refers to situations in which a measurement scale is too restricted to measure differences that may exist between conditions. When performance is nearly perfect, the problem is referred to as a ceiling effect, since performance is bumping into the top, or roof, of the scale. When performance is nearly absent altogether, the problem is referred to as a floor effect.

3. It is an error to assume that performance in two conditions is equivalent when it is at the ceiling or floor of a measurement scale. Although subjects in two conditions may score equivalently on the dependent variable (near either 0 percent or 100 percent), there may be a true difference between conditions, but the measurement scale of the variable may be too restricted (too "short") to show the real difference. Recall the case of the two men weighing themselves on a bathroom scale that only registers up to 300 pounds. The examples in this chapter illustrate ceiling effects, but floor effects are as common and as important. If the mean recall in a memory experiment involving 2- and 3-year-old children is 2 percent for each age group, are we justified in concluding that memory capacity is the same for both groups of children? Similarly, there can be errors in interpreting interactions when performance in some conditions is constrained by ceiling and floor effects.

4. A critical issue about any experimental result is its generalizability beyond the conditions under which it was discovered. Jenkins's tetrahedral model of memory experiments provides four dimensions across which such generality can be assessed: (1) Would the finding hold with different subject populations? (2) Would the finding be obtained with different experimental materials? (3) Would the finding occur with different types of memory tests? (4) Would the same results occur with a different experimental setting and different ways of operationalizing the independent variables?

5. Researchers are interested in whether a particular result will generalize across several dimensions: subject populations, materials, situations, dependent measures, and so on. Multifactor experiments, or those in which more than one variable is manipulated simultaneously, are extremely important in determining generality of results. Such experiments tell us whether the effect of an independent variable on a dependent variable is the same or different when other variables are manipulated at the same time.

6. When an independent variable has an effect that is the same at all levels of the second independent variable, this is referred to as a main effect. Two independent variables are said to interact when the effect of an independent variable on the dependent variable is different at different levels of a second independent variable. Main effects can be thought of as allowing generalizations to be made across other conditions, because the independent variable has the same effect at all levels of the other independent variable. Interactions indicate that simple generalizations about an independent variable are not safe; the effect of this independent variable depends on the level of the second independent variable in the multifactor experiment.

7. Implicit and explicit memory tests interact with a variety of independent variables. For example, even though amnesics perform poorly on explicit tests, such as free recall, they show just as much priming as control subjects on implicit tests, such as priming in word identification. Pictures produce better retention than do words on explicit memory tests, but words produce more priming than do pictures on verbal implicit memory tests. By studying the way these types of tests interact with other variables, scientists are gaining a new understanding of both normal and abnormal memory function.

 KEY TERMS

amnesia
autobiographical memory
Brown-Peterson technique
ceiling effect
crossover interaction

episodic memory
explicit memory
flashbulb memory
floor effect
forced-choice recognition test

free recall	recall
generality of results	recognition
graphemic code	savings method
higher-order interaction	savings score
implicit memory	scale-attenuation effects
interactions	semantic
levels of processing	serial recall
long-term memory	short-term memory
main effect	tetrahedral model of memory experiments
nonsense syllables	transfer-appropriate processing
paired-associate recall	trials to criterion
phonemic (phonological) code	word fragment completion task
priming	yes/no recognition test
proactive interference	

▼ DISCUSSION QUESTIONS

1. Identify two situations, besides those presented in the chapter, in which ceiling and floor effects would probably make interpreting experimental observations difficult. How could problems caused by these effects be overcome in the experiments?

2. Researchers often lament the discovery that some result does not generalize to a new setting. Discuss why failures of generalization can often lead to progress in understanding a phenomenon. Can you think of discoveries in science sparked by an anomalous result when past knowledge failed to generalize to a new situation?

3. What are the advantages of multifactor experiments that make them so popular among researchers, despite their complexity? Discuss the relation of multifactor experiments to the problem of generality of results.

 ## WEB CONNECTIONS

An excellent site that covers basic information about memory and how to develop a better memory can be found at:

http://www.muskingum.edu/~cal/database/general/memory.html

The Web site of the Practical Memory Institute includes a list of frequently asked questions (and answers) about memory. It can be found at:

http://www.memoryzine.com/index.html

▼ LABORATORY RESOURCES

Langston's (2002) Chapter 5 describes a semantic memory task: Subjects retrieved words to definitions like "an arch or hoop in croquet that balls have to be hit through" (the answer is *wicket*). Of interest was ability to do this task either with or without gestures (some subjects were forced to hold a rod in their hands while others were free to gesture if they wished to do so). The hypothesis was that gesturing helps people to retrieve words. Read these experiments, and use Jenkins's model of memory to generate experimental variations.

PSYCHOLOGY IN ACTION

Remembering the 9/11 Terrorist Attacks

Can you answer the following questions?

1. What time of day did you first hear the news of the 9/11 attacks?
2. Where were you?
3. What were you doing?
4. Who told you?
5. Who else was there?
6. How did you feel about it?
7. Can you describe at least three vivid details of the experience?
8. What did you do immediately after hearing the news?

Ask a few of your friends these questions as well. The chances are good that both you and your friends will be able to confidently answer at least five of the questions, and that your memories for hearing the news of 9/11 fit into the category of **flashbulb memories.** What is striking about flashbulb memories is their vividness; people report remembering such peripheral details as what they were wearing when they heard the news. The term was coined by Brown and Kulik (1977) to describe people's vivid memories for hearing shocking news. They chose the term *flashbulb* because "it suggests surprise, an indiscriminate illumination, and brevity."

So-called flashbulb memories are really vivid **autobiographical memories,** and as such, they are just as prone to error as are other personal memories. For example, Neisser and Harsch (1992) found changes in people's memories for hearing the news of the *Challenger* explosion when they compared initial reports to those collected 32 to 34 months later. Of the 36 subjects, only 3 correctly remembered all the major attributes. Twenty-two subjects were wrong on two out of three major memory attributes (location, activity, and source of news); the remaining subjects erred on all three. Such memory distortions appear to develop over time. Schmolck, Buffalo, and Squire (2000) examined memories for hearing the verdict in the O.J. Simpson trial; 15 months after the verdict, 50 percent of the reports were considered highly accurate (as compared with initial accounts), whereas after 32 months only 29 percent were labeled highly accurate.

There are many reasons why these memories may become distorted over time. People continue to talk and think about events long after they have occurred. Depending on their audience or goals, they may tell their stories differently, with consequences for memory (e.g., Tversky & Marsh, 2000). People also listen to other people's accounts, and listeners may later incorporate details from others' stories into their own memories (e.g., Niedzwienska, 2003). People also have beliefs about how things should have been and may reconstruct their memories to match those beliefs (e.g., Ross, 1989).

Many psychologists collected 9/11 memories immediately after the attacks. Follow-up studies are ongoing, and numerous reports have now been published (e.g., Luminet et al., 2004; Talarico & Rubin, 2003; Wolters & Goudsmit, 2005). You might think about what questions about memory would be interesting to ask if you had access to the same sample of people repeatedly over a period of years. ■

CHAPTER 11

THINKING AND PROBLEM SOLVING

Life does not consist mainly—or even largely—of facts and happenings. It consists mainly of the storm of thoughts that is forever blowing through one's head. (MARK TWAIN)

In case you do not have any problems at the moment, let us give you one. Read the following problem carefully and examine its representation in Figure 11.1. Give the problem some careful thought before you continue reading the text.

Two train stations are 100 miles apart. At 2 P.M. one Saturday afternoon, the two trains start toward each other, one from each station. One train travels at 60 miles per hour, the other at 40 miles per hour. Just as the trains pull out of their stations, a bird springs into the air in front of the first train and flies ahead to the front of the second train. When the bird reaches the second train, it turns back without losing any speed and flies directly toward the first train. The bird continues to fly back and forth between the trains at a rate of 80 miles per hour. How many miles will the bird have flown before the trains meet?

Were you able to solve the problem? Most people have a great deal of difficulty with it, but some people solve it almost immediately. They must be very good mathematicians, you might be thinking. Not at all.

Let us consider how most people try to solve this problem. Because of the way it is stated and the way the picture in Figure 11.1 is drawn, most people begin worrying immediately about how long it will take the bird to go from the first to the second train, how far the second train will have moved by the time the bird arrives, then how long it will take the bird to trek back to the first train and how far that train will have moved, and so on. The general strategy is to try to figure out how long it will take the bird to make each trip between the trains, then add these times together to find out how many miles the bird will have flown before the trains meet. This is a quite reasonable strategy, and it will give you the answer, provided you have plenty of time, a good calculator, and knowledge of calculus.

Since it is quite likely that you do not have one or more of these three resources, you might need to find a simpler solution. **Thought** can be defined as "the achievement of a new representation through the performance of mental operations" (Posner, 1973, p. 147). We can say that thought is necessary to find a simpler solution to the bird-and-train problem. To solve the problem, you must reconceptualize it. In fact, after you make an appropriate reconceptualization, the solution to the problem is simple. What you need to focus on is how long the trains will be traveling before they meet. Since one is traveling at 60 miles per hour and the other at 40 miles per hour and they are 100 miles apart, they will meet in an hour. Once you think of recasting the problem in this way and using one other piece of information, the solution is obvious. Since the trains will meet in an hour and the bird is flying at 80 miles per hour, the bird will have flown 80 miles before the trains meet. Not much time is needed; nor is a calculator; nor is higher mathematics. Just thought.

Just thought? That is simple enough to say, but the process is very complicated. What happens mentally while a person is trying to discover a solution to a problem?

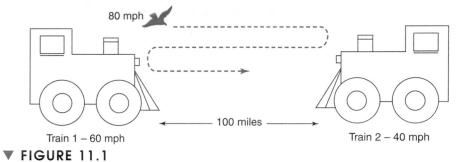

80 mph

100 miles

Train 1 – 60 mph   Train 2 – 40 mph

▼ **FIGURE 11.1**

An illustration of the bird-and-train problem.

How does a person go about discovering a simpler solution to the problem (thinking)? Can we find general psychological laws of thought? How can we even study this hidden process? These are among the difficult questions that we will be considering in this chapter.

The experimental topics covered in this chapter include the issue of **reliability of results** (or replicability), the problem of **extraneous variables** and **experimental control,** and the use of **verbal reports** in psychological research. The first concern is the reliability of results: If we were to perform an experiment a second time, how likely would we be to obtain data that would allow us to reach the same conclusion as in the first experiment? This problem exists in all research but, for reasons to be discussed later, may be heightened in research on thinking and other complex processes. Second, the topic of problem solving and thought is so complicated that great ingenuity is needed to perform interesting and useful experiments in this area. How can we gain control over some independent variable while controlling the extraneous variables, since there are so many that might influence the thought process? The final issue is one of **subjective (verbal) report** and its value in psychological research. In an area such as problem solving and thinking, people are quite willing, usually, to tell how they think they set about solving a problem. Are we to accept their reports as useful evidence on the nature of the processes involved?

Historically, there have been two primary approaches to the study of problem solving that have different emphases. Both have been very influential on the study of thinking and the study of learning. The two approaches represent a bottom-up (data-driven) analysis and top-down (conceptually driven) analysis analogous to the ways of examining perception that were discussed in Chapter 7.

▼ TWO APPROACHES TO THINKING

Thorndike's Trial-and-Error Learning

In some interesting early experiments, Thorndike (1898) studied problem solving in cats. He placed them in specially constructed puzzle boxes with food placed outside. The cats' problem was how to escape from the box and obtain the food. In some cases, the appropriate solution was simply clawing down a rope, but sometimes there were as many as three different solutions the cat could use. Thorndike observed the cats' performance on successive trials in the puzzle box and measured the amount of time it took them to escape on each trial. On the first trial, the cat would try a variety of strategies in attempting to escape the box and would strike out in an undirected manner at nearby objects. Eventually, the cat would claw at the rope that released it from the cage. It apparently learned by trial and error. Its success in escaping from the box seemed completely accidental, at least at first. On successive occasions, though, the cats began to escape from the box more quickly and systematically each time. Nonetheless, the guiding principle that seemed to govern the cats' solution attempts was one of trial-and-error learning.

In his analysis of trial-and-error learning, Thorndike was particularly concerned with success. It seemed obvious that the success of a correct movement caused it to be impressed or learned. The effect of the movement was to lead to success, which "stamps-in" the movement, as Thorndike put it. These early experiments led to the **law of effect** and the concept of reinforcement (see Chapter 9). The historical impact of this bottom-up research has been much greater in the field of animal learning, where its importance is overwhelming, than in research concerned with thinking and problem solving. The emphasis in research on human thinking and problem solving has been much more on higher-level conceptually driven processes, in the tradition to be discussed next. Nonetheless, there have been attempts to analyze human thought processes in terms of trial-and-error learning, or operant conditioning (see Skinner, 1957, Chap. 19).

Insight in Köhler's Chimpanzees

Wolfgang Köhler, a German psychologist, was posted by his country to the island of Tenerife (a part of the Canary Islands) during 1913 to study anthropoid apes. Soon after, World War I broke out, and Köhler remained on Tenerife. While there, he conducted research on the problem-solving capacities of chimpanzees. Many of the problems he used could not be solved in a simple, direct way, as could Thorndike's puzzle-box problem, in which the cat merely had to claw at a rope. Instead, solutions required a more roundabout approach. Köhler discussed his research in a book published in German in 1921 and translated into English as *The Mentality of Apes* (1927).

In one problem, Köhler dangled a banana out of reach of the chimpanzees. It was too far above them for them to reach it, even with the aid of a stick placed within their enclosure. A more indirect solution to the problem was required. Köhler describes in detail attempts of the chimps to obtain the banana. Usually, they would first try out various direct strategies of obtaining it, like reaching and poking at it with the stick. Failing with these methods, they would then seem to engage in various random acts or often apparently give up on the problem altogether. Somewhat later, however, a chimp would suddenly implement the appropriate solution to the problem. The solution in this case was to stack some crates that were in the enclosure on top of one another and then climb up them to reach the banana (Figure 11.2).

Köhler emphasized the importance of insight in solving the problem. Insight refers to the ability to conceptualize a problem in a unique way that allows it to be solved. As in the case of the chimps, insight often seems to occur in an instant.

After a period of random activity or no activity at all, the chimp (presumably) suddenly conceived of the boxes as related to the problem. Once this insight was achieved, implementing the solution was quite simple.

▼ FIGURE 11.2

One of Köhler's chimpanzees stacking boxes on top of one another to reach the bananas. From *The Mentality of Apes* (Plate V), by W. Köhler, 1927, London: Routledge and Kegan Paul.

Köhler's top-down approach to problem solving emphasized its structured, planned, and conceptual nature, rather than its trial-and-error aspect. Köhler was a member of the Gestalt school of psychology (see Appendix A), which in general was opposed to the more elementary type of analysis of behaviorism that grew, in part, from work such as Thorndike's. However, both behaviorist and Gestalt approaches have been tremendously influential in the psychology of thinking and problem solving (Holyoak, 1990).

11.1   EXPERIMENTAL TOPICS AND RESEARCH ILLUSTRATIONS

Topic   *Reliability and Replication*
Illustration   *Analogical Reasoning*

The basic issue of reliability of experimental results is simply this: If an experiment were repeated, would the results be the same as those found the first time? This is a crucial topic in psychological research, for an experimental outcome is worthless if we cannot have reasonable certainty that the results from it are reliable.

The key to ensuring the reliability of our observations is the number of observations we make. The greater the number of observations, the more confident we can be that our sample statistics approximate the true population parameter values. If we take a random sample of persons in the United States and ask them survey questions (e.g., about their preference in an upcoming presidential election), we can be more confident that the results accurately represent the population if the sample consists of 100,000 people than if it consists of only 100.

This is similar to the way that Las Vegas casinos ensure profitability. On games such as blackjack, craps, and roulette, the population parameters (the true odds) are known. The more individual observations (bets) that are made, the more likely the results will reflect the population parameters. Because the odds favor the casinos, the casinos come out on top.

The thing to keep in mind, then, is that our confidence in the reliability of a particular result increases with the number of observations on which the result is based. So, in general, we should attempt to maximize the number of observations in the conditions of our experiments. This increases not only our confidence in the reliability of the result but also the **power** of the statistical tests we employ, or the ability of the tests to allow rejection of the **null hypothesis** if it is in fact false. The null hypothesis is the prediction that the independent variable will have no effect on the dependent variable.

Reliability involves not only sample size and statistics but also different types of experimental replicability. The key to experimental replicability is the identification of the relevant variables, because they must be systematically manipulated or controlled to produce consistent results. In general, in the study of more complex processes, there should probably be greater concern with reliability of results than in the study of simpler processes. One reason is that in research concerned with complex processes, it is often necessary to use between-subjects designs, or designs in which a different group of subjects serves in each experimental condition, because of the carryover effects that would occur from within-subjects designs (see Chapter 9). The use of between-subjects designs rather than within-subjects designs tends to increase variability of observations, since differences among individual subjects are not as well controlled.

But there is another reason that experimental reliability can be a problem in researching complex cognition. Typically, for practical reasons, it is difficult to obtain many observations per condition in the study of complex processes with between-subjects designs. This is true because it is often necessary to test subjects individually, which takes a great amount of time. In experiments on complex processes such as problem solving, it might take an hour to test an individual subject. Thus, even if there were only four conditions in the experiment and we wanted only 25 observations in each condition, that would still amount to up to 100 hours of testing of subjects. Because of these practical considerations, then, we often find very few observations per experimental condition in the study of complex processes, even though this means we will have less confidence in the reliability of the results and our statistical tests will have less power.

Analogical Reasoning

We will illustrate some further points about reliability of research by discussing problem solving by **analogy.** When people comprehend some point by analogy, they understand one thing in terms of another. If you were told in high school physics that the structure of the atom was similar in some ways to the organization of the solar system, or in chemistry that molecules of gas bumped off one another like billiard balls on a pool table, or in psychology that human memory could be compared with a giant library or dictionary, your teacher was employing analogical reasoning. She or he was trying to get you to understand something unfamiliar in terms of something you already understood. Psychologists interested in thinking have long recognized the importance of analogies in thinking and making discoveries. The art of discovery often lies in perceiving a resemblance between two items in different domains of knowledge

INTRODUCING THE VARIABLES

Dependent Variables

There are three primary ways to measure the process of problem solving. Let us assume that we either do or do not present an illustration along with the train-and-bird problem. One group of subjects attempts to solve it with Figure 11.1 present, and one group attempts to solve it without the illustration. What do we measure? The first and most obvious thing to measure is the number or proportion of subjects in the two conditions that are able to solve the problem within a time limit (say, 45 minutes). But most problems chosen for study are likely to be fairly easy or at least solvable within the time limit. What if everyone in both groups solves the problem? Then it is impossible to tell whether the independent variable had any effect, because of a ceiling effect in performance (see Chapter 10). It is, of course, improper to conclude that the variable had no effect just because the percentage of people solving the problem is equivalent, since the problem was too easy to reveal any possible differences. What we can do is look at a second measure of performance in solving the problem: latency, or the time taken to solve the problem. Even though all subjects in both groups solved the problem, they might have taken different amounts of time to do this in the different conditions. So although there may be no differences in percentages of people solving the problem, measurement of the time taken to solve the problem may prove a more sensitive index of problem difficulty in the two conditions (picture versus no picture). In fact, even if there were no ceiling effect, but the percentages of people solving the problem were still equivalent at, say, 60 percent, differences in performance might still be revealed by latencies. Therefore, we can say that latencies are likely to be a more sensitive dependent variable than that of percentage correct, since this measure is more likely to indicate an effect of the independent variable in most situations. (It would be very unusual to find the reverse: an effect on percentage correct but not on latency.) Of course, we would normally expect a high negative correlation between percentage correct and latency,

such that in conditions where fewer subjects are able to solve a problem, they also take longer to do so.

A third measure that can be used in some problem-solving situations where more than one solution is possible is the quality of the solution. It must be possible to rank the solutions on an ordinal scale; in other words, it must be possible to order them from best to worst. Then, even if percentage correct and latency measures indicate no difference between subjects solving problems under two conditions, subjects in one condition may still achieve more satisfactory solutions than subjects in another condition.

One might want to use all three measures of problem solution as converging operations of some problem-solving construct, but there may well be no straightforward relationship among them. For example, subjects in one condition may take much longer to solve a particular problem than subjects in another condition, and perhaps a smaller percentage of subjects will solve the problem in the first condition, but the solutions the subjects achieve in this condition might be superior to those in the other. In other words, variation in the independent variable might allow subjects in one condition to frequently produce a poor solution in a relatively short period, as opposed to subjects in another condition who may less frequently produce a better solution and take a longer time doing so. So there may be no simple relation among measures. This problem is a variant of the speed–accuracy tradeoff problem discussed under reaction-time measures in Chapter 8.

Independent Variables

The primary independent variable in the study of problem solving is the manner in which the problem is presented. This can be varied in several different ways. Let us consider the problem concerning how long it takes the bird to fly between the two trains before the trains meet, which was presented at the beginning of the chapter. One thing we could vary is the order and prominence of the information needed to solve the problem. The critical fact that the bird was flying at 80 miles per hour is buried in the description of the problem. If it were made more prominent, subjects might get the idea of using this fact earlier in their attempts to restructure the problem. A second factor that might be varied is the amount of irrelevant information presented. For example, the information that the trains began at 2 P.M. on a Saturday is completely irrelevant to solving the problem and should be ignored. It may well be that the more irrelevant information presented along with the few relevant facts, the longer it will take to solve the problem. Whether or not an illustration is presented and the nature of the illustration could also be varied. Presenting or not presenting an illustration with the problem may aid or hinder its solution, depending on the nature of the problem. Other sorts of psycholinguistic variables could be studied too, such as whether active or passive sentences are used in describing the problem. Besides those dealing with how the problem is presented, other variables of interest might be whether there is time pressure (or some other sort of stress) that people are working under when attempting to solve the problem; whether the magnitude of a reward offered affects the solution; and whether there are individual differences among classes of people (e.g., high versus low IQ) solving the problem.

Control Variables

Experiments concerned with problem solving and thinking are often more complicated than others in human experimental psychology; thus, this area (along with others, such as social and environmental psychology, that deal with complex processes) requires a great deal of care to produce experimental control. Since it is typical in this field to use between-subjects designs (independent groups of subjects are assigned to different conditions), care must be taken to ensure that subjects in the different conditions are statistically equivalent, either by randomly assigning them to conditions or by matching them on some dimension such as IQ. Similarly, one must control as tightly as feasible all extraneous variables (such as the way the problem is stated or how it is presented).

(Hadamard, 1945). For example, in the seventeenth century, William Harvey developed a hydraulic model of blood circulation after he conceived of the heart as a pump.

The study of reasoning by analogy is quite difficult. Problem solving, thinking, and discovery are topics that have long resisted understanding by psychologists. However, in the last 20 years or so, some real gains have been made in this area on numerous fronts (Mayer, 1983). Here we consider examples from experiments by Gick and Holyoak (1980, 1983) to illustrate how interesting research can be done on these topics and to show the importance of determining the reliability of experimental phenomena.

Gick and Holyoak were interested in the effects of analogical reasoning on problem solving. Before discussing this research, we will give you the problem they used, to let you mull it over before you continue. It is called the radiation problem and was first used by Duncker in 1945. It can be stated as follows:

Suppose you are a doctor faced with a patient who has a malignant tumor in his stomach. It is impossible to operate on the tumor, but unless the tumor is destroyed the patient will die. There is a kind of ray that can be used to destroy the tumor. If the rays reach the tumor all at once at a sufficiently high intensity, the tumor will be destroyed. Unfortunately, at this intensity the healthy tissue that the rays pass through on the way to the tumor will also be destroyed. At lower intensities, the rays are harmless to healthy tissue, but they will not affect the tumor either. What type of procedure might be used to destroy the tumor with the rays, and at the same time avoid destroying the healthy tissue? (Gick & Holyoak, 1980, pp. 307–308).

Shut your book and think about how to solve this problem before you read on. Do not read ahead until you have thought of at least one solution to the problem.

How did you do? Many students have difficulty solving the problem, given all the constraints placed on them. Many "solutions" depend on advanced technology, such as immunizing the healthy tissue with some drug and then passing the ray through it to the cancerous tumor. A more practical solution is to operate on the patient and insert a tube into the affected area or otherwise expose the tumor, so that the radiation can be directly applied to the diseased organ. However, perhaps the most creative and effective solution to the problem would be to aim several weak rays at the tumor from different directions, so that they converged on it. Each of the rays would be weak enough not to hurt the tissue through which it passed, but the strength of all the rays when they converged would be sufficient to destroy the tumor. This solution is generated by very few students; in the original studies of this problem by Duncker (1945), only 2 out of 45 subjects (4 percent) came up with this solution.

Gick and Holyoak (1980, 1983) were interested in seeing whether they could get more people to solve this problem by giving them an analogous problem and solution before the radiation problem. The idea is that people will abstract the guiding principle from the first problem and then be able to apply it to the second. With this in mind, Gick and Holyoak developed other "analog stories" that embodied the same principle as that which applied to the most effective solution to the radiation problem.

In one story, called "The Commander," the leader of a tank corps needed to mount an attack on an enemy headquarters. By attacking with many tanks, he had a good chance of winning, but he had to attack across narrow, rickety bridges that would permit only a few tanks to pass. An assault with such a small force across one bridge would be easily repulsed. To achieve victory, the tank commander hit on the plan of sending a few tanks to each of the small bridges that circled the headquarters. All the tanks were then able to attack across the bridges at once and overtake the enemy headquarters.

The similarity between the tank-attack problem and the radiation problem should be apparent. In both cases, it is necessary for the problem solver to forgo a direct attack on the headquarters (or cancerous tumor) and disperse forces (or radiation) for a simultaneous converging attack from different directions. But would subjects in an experiment use the principles derived from reading a story such as "The Commander" to solve the radiation problem? Gick and Holyoak (1980) performed a series of experiments in which subjects attempted to solve the radiation problem either after reading a story similar to "The Commander" or after reading no story (or an irrelevant story). They found in several experiments that subjects who were given no story or an irrelevant story before the radiation problem solved the problem with the most effective solution only about 10 percent of the time. However, when subjects were given an analog story before the radiation problem, about 75 percent solved it within the time limit. Since this result was obtained in several experiments, the basic phenomenon was replicated several times. Obviously, people can profit from analogy in solving problems.

The results of one of their experiments led Gick and Holyoak (1980) to consider more closely the processes involved in reasoning by analogy. In experiment 4 of their series, they gave all subjects the analog story to read and then the radiation problem to solve. However, in the "hint" condition of experiment 4, subjects were told, after they had read the story but before they got the radiation problem, to use the story as a hint on how to solve the problem. (This instruction had also been included in all of Gick and Holyoak's prior experiments in the series.) For subjects in the "no-hint" condition, no mention was made about the relation between the story they had just read and the problem-solving task ahead. The results revealed that the hint was indeed a critical component to solving the problem by analogy. When the hint was given, 92 percent of the subjects solved the problem; when the hint was not given, only 20 percent of them solved it. The results seem to show that it is not enough to have been exposed to the analogy; one must be led to make active use of it during the attempt to solve the later problem. (The higher percentage of students solving the problem in experiment 4 relative to earlier experiments—92 percent to about 75 percent—was likely due to somewhat different stories being used across experiments.)

This fact may not seem surprising: Telling people to use a source of knowledge does indeed lead them to do so. But what is surprising is how few subjects (20 percent) came upon the solution spontaneously, without the hint. The first question we ask ourselves about a surprising discovery in any experimental field is this: Is it real? This brings us back to the question of reliability: If the experiment were repeated, would the same result be obtained?

One way to answer this question is to compute inferential statistics, the logic of which is described in Appendix B. Briefly, inferential statistics are used to determine whether a difference obtained between conditions is due to operation of the independent variable or to chance factors. If the difference between the conditions is great enough so that it would occur by chance in fewer than 5 cases in 100, then the researcher rejects the possibility that chance factors produced the result and instead accepts the result as evidence for a real effect of the independent variable—in this case, the presence or absence of the hint. In fact, Gick and Holyoak (1980) performed the appropriate inferential statistics and concluded that the difference in the percentage of solutions between the two groups was not a result of chance factors but was caused by the presence or absence of the hint. Thus, we can conclude on the basis of such a test that the difference has **statistical reliability.**

Statistical reliability is a necessary condition for taking seriously an experimental result, but many researchers prefer to see an experimenter also establish **experimental reliability.** If the experiment is repeated under essentially the same conditions, will the results be the same as they were before? An adage among researchers is that "one replication is worth a thousand *t* tests." (The *t* test is a well-known statistical test used to evaluate the statistical reliability between two conditions.) The gist of the adage is that many researchers are more convinced by repetitions of the experiment than by inferential statistics applied to the original outcome. Although an outcome may be deemed statistically reliable, the possibility remains that it could have occurred by chance (statistical reliability still allows a 5 percent error rate) or because of some unintentional confounding or error on the part of the experimenter. For example, perhaps smarter subjects happened to be assigned to one condition rather than another. Although these possibilities might seem unlikely, they do sometimes occur. In some experiments, subjects are randomly assigned to conditions, and then, prior to the main experiment, the various groups are given a pretest to determine whether the groups are actually equivalent (on the average) in ability. Occasionally, pretests of this sort turn up differences, before the independent variable has been introduced (see, e.g., Tulving & Pearlstone, 1966). Since such problems can occur even in well-controlled research, researchers encourage replication of experiments, even when inferential statistics indicate that some effect is reliable.

There are three types of experimental replication: **direct replication, systematic replication,** and **conceptual replication.** Direct replication, as the name implies, is the attempt to repeat the experiment as closely as is practical, with as few changes as possible in the original method. If Gick and Holyoak (1980) had attempted to repeat their fourth experiment as precisely as possible with the exception of testing new groups of subjects randomly assigned to conditions, this would have constituted a direct replication of their experiment.

A more interesting type of replication is systematic replication. In systematic replications, the experimenter attempts to vary factors believed to be irrelevant to the experimental outcome. If the phenomenon is not illusory, it will survive these changes. If the effect disappears, then the researcher has discovered important boundary conditions on the phenomenon being studied. Actually, experiment 4 of the Gick and Holyoak series might itself be considered a systematic replication that led to important new information. In their first three experiments, Gick and Holyoak had compared conditions in which subjects solved the radiation problem either after studying a story that embodied an analogous solution (the experimental condition) or after studying one that did not (the control condition). As previously discussed, they found that a greater percentage of subjects solved the radiation problem with the "convergence solution" (aiming the rays from various sides) when tested in the experimental condition than when tested in the control condition. They replicated this observation several times. However, in each of the first three experiments, subjects in the experimental condition were told that they should use the story in attempting to solve the problem. In experiment 4, Gick and Holyoak attempted to repeat the experiment but varied this one (seemingly small) feature; this small variation allowed the experiment to be considered a systematic replication. They discovered that this hint was actually a critical part of the experimental manipulation; simply having subjects study the story and then try to solve the radiation problem without the specific hint produced a much lower percentage of subjects solving the problem than instructing them to use the hint.

In a conceptual replication, one attempts to replicate a phenomenon, but in a way radically different from the original experiment. In experiments that followed up the ones already described, Gick and Holyoak (1983) attempted to determine conditions that would promote positive transfer of analog stories to problem solutions. In three experiments with the radiation problem and another problem, Gick and Holyoak had subjects process the analog story in different ways (the experimental conditions) to see whether the amount of positive transfer could be increased, as compared with the case in which the analogy was simply presented by itself with no special instructions (the control condition). They found that the amount of positive transfer (indexed by a greater percentage of subjects solving the problem in the experimental conditions) did not improve when (1) subjects were told to summarize stories rather than study them for a test of recall (experiment 1); (2) subjects were given or not given a verbal principle along with the story that captured the essence of the strategy (experiment 2); or (3) subjects were given diagrams along with the story (experiment 3).

Gick and Holyoak (1983) did manage to uncover conditions that produced positive transfer of the story analogs to solving the radiation problem. When subjects studied two analogs and then described their similarities (before being given the problem), greater positive transfer occurred than when subjects studied only one analog. Gick and Holyoak argued that subjects who processed two analogs and thought about their similarities could generate a better underlying idea (or schema, in their terms), which could then be spontaneously applied to solving new problems.

Although the experiments reported by Gick and Holyoak (1983) were not direct or systematic replications of their earlier experiment indicating that subjects had difficulty spontaneously using analogies to solve problems, they converged on the same conclusion that it is difficult to improve reasoning from analogies. Thus, these later experiments may be considered conceptual replications, in the sense that they reproduced the essence of the phenomenon of the difficulty of reasoning from analogies without overt direction to do so, even though the experimental techniques were not exact replicas of those used in the original experiment.

The problem of replicability is interwoven with the topic of **generality of results.** In the case of systematic and conceptual replications, a researcher is not repeating an experiment exactly but really asking whether the phenomenon of interest generalizes in one way or another. In systematic replications, the variables manipulated (and across which generality is sought) are typically not dramatically different from those of the original experiment, whereas in conceptual replications, the differences in procedure are usually much greater. In a certain sense, it is best if the researcher eventually finds conditions under which the phenomenon *cannot* be replicated.

For example, Spencer and Weisberg (1986) replicated Gick and Holyoak's (1983) condition in which subjects were given two analog stories before solving the radiation problem. They added an interesting twist, however, by changing the pretext under which the two initial training stories and the radiation problem were administered. In the "same-context" condition, subjects were led to believe that all three stories were part of a pilot experiment and were tested on all three by an experimenter who came into their classrooms. In the "different-context" condition, the subjects were told that only the first two stories were part of an experiment. After they performed the training stories, the experimenter left the classroom, and then their instructor gave them the radiation problem to solve as part of a "class demonstration." In addition, the radiation problem was given either immediately or 45 minutes after the training problems. Different classrooms of subjects participated in the four different combinations of conditions, and no subjects received hints that the radiation problem was related to the first two problems.

The results are presented in Figure 11.3. When there was no delay between the first two problems and the radiation problem, there were equal amounts of transfer in the same- and different-context groups. However, when there was a 45-minute interval between the training and radiation problems, only subjects who tried to solve the radiation problem in the same context showed transfer. Subjects in the different-context condition showed no transfer after the 45-minute interval. Subjects did not see that the radiation problem was like the first two problems when the apparent relation among them was destroyed by changing the pretext for performing the radiation task. These results represent an interaction of context and time of test and support the notion that analogical reasoning is not readily generalized to new problems and situations. They also help define the conditions under which analogical transfer will and will not be obtained.

Much research has focused on the use of analogy in educational situations (e.g., Bulgren, Deshler, Schumaker, & Lenz, 2000; Kolodner, 1997). But many other situations are also of interest to researchers, including (but not limited to) how people use analogies during negotiations (Gentner, Loewenstein, & Thompson, 2003), and how people

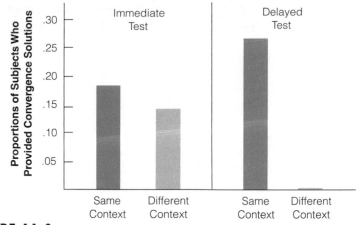

▼ FIGURE 11.3

Proportion of subjects in Spencer and Weisberg's (1986) experiment who showed transfer when solving similar types of problems. When the test problem was given 45 minutes after the two training problems, subjects in the different-context condition, who were told that the training problems were part of an experiment but that the test problem was part of a class demonstration, showed no transfer from having previously solved the training problems. Subjects in the same-context condition, who were told that all three problems were part of an experiment, showed transfer on both the immediate test and after the long delay.

make analogies between political events and leaders (Holyoak & Thagard, 1997). One creative new line of research is investigating how concrete analogies help people to understand abstract concepts (Boroditsky, 2000). For example, consider how you talk about time: You borrow such spatial terms as "ahead," "forward," and "behind." That is, you use your personal experience with physical space as an analogy for talking and thinking about time (which you can't actually see or touch). In a series of clever experiments, Boroditsky and Ramscar (2002) demonstrated how people's physical positions affected their answers to questions about time. They asked people the ambiguous question "Suppose you are told that next Wednesday's meeting has been moved forward 2 days. What day is the meeting, now that it has been rescheduled?" Depending on your perspective, you might reasonably answer either "Monday" or "Friday" (most people are very confident in their answer, but ask a few of your friends—you will find people do answer this question differently!). Your answer depends on how you think about time. If you view time as moving toward you (the time-moving perspective), then you will think of time advancing (coming forward) 2 days closer, and answer "Monday." If you view yourself as moving through time (the ego-moving perspective), "forward" implies your movement into the future—and you will answer "Friday." Boroditsky and Ramscar (2002) asked this question of people at the airport. As expected due to the ambiguous nature of the question, half of people waiting to pick up passengers answered "Friday" and half answered "Monday." But more than half of airline passengers (people who were either waiting to get on a plane or who had just got off a plane) chose "Friday"—because air travelers were in the mode of thinking of themselves as moving, as traveling through physical space, and thus used the ego-moving spatial perspective to answer the temporal question. Boroditsky and Ramscar found converging evidence for the use of spatial metaphors to answer temporal questions from such diverse sources as a laboratory experiment, passengers on a train, and people waiting in a lunch line. For example, the closer people were to the front of a long lunch line, the more likely they were to answer the ambiguous question with "Friday"—they had just experienced themselves moving through space and so used that perspective to answer the question.

Given the research we have just described, we might reasonably ask, "What conditions allow a person to use analogies to solve problems in an efficient way?" Holyoak (1990; Holyoak & Thagard, 1989) has developed a theory that describes the conditions under which successful analogical transfer will occur. According to Holyoak, having experience with the tank-attack problem will help a person solve the tumor problem only if the person finds the best set of correspondences between the original problem and the transfer problem. Holyoak calls the ways in which a person relates the elements of one problem to another **mapping.** In the tank/tumor case, for example, the person trying to solve the problem needs to recognize that the goals of capturing the fortress and destroying the tumor correspond. Furthermore, the person needs to realize that the rays' capacity to destroy corresponds to the army's ability to capture.

According to the theory, the correspondences that are noticed must be considered in a unified fashion. That is, the mapping or correspondence between the original problem and the target problem must have **structural consistency,** which means that the elements that correspond in the two problems need to be related to each other in a way that is consistent with other mappings.

Consider the structural mappings illustrated in Figure 11.4. Holyoak assumes that if the perceived relationship of one pair of elements in the two problems is consistent, then the relationships among other elements also have to be consistent. If the problem solver notices the analogy between the fortress and the tumor, then capturing would have to correspond to destroying, and the destroyer (rays) would have to map onto the capturer, which would be the army in this instance. The pattern of such analogical mappings would be structurally consistent.

The correspondences among the components of the two problems shown in Figure 11.4 form a coherent set and thus support each other. For example, if a person first recognizes one point of correspondence—say, army is the same as rays—then the person is more likely to notice another correspondence, such as between general and doctor. Holyoak believes that his theory of structural consistency helps to specify conditions under which analogous solutions are easy or difficult. If a person is able to recognize one or two mappings, then the other consistencies will fall into place, and the problem should be solved.

Experiments by Novick (1990) show that the amount of generalization depends on how problems are represented or conceptualized. If general problem-solving strategies, such as thinking about using a two-dimensional matrix as an aid to solution, are valuable in solving one type of problem, then people will use the technique again on other problems that do not have analogous solutions.

If a researcher cannot find variables that control the presence or absence of the phenomenon, then an understanding of the topic will be hampered. Performing systematic and conceptual replications should permit a researcher to delineate the **boundary conditions** of a phenomenon: the conditions outside of which the phenomenon does not hold. When the variables that control a phenomenon can be discovered, the researcher can construct a better theory about it, because the relevant factors are known.

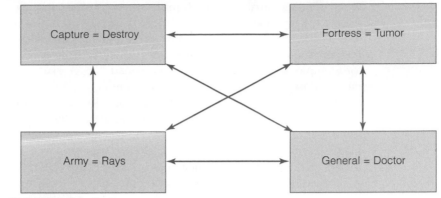

▼ **FIGURE 11.4**

An Outline of Holyoak's Model of Analogical Correspondences Between the Tumor Problem and the Fortress Problem.

11.2   EXPERIMENTAL TOPICS AND RESEARCH ILLUSTRATIONS

Topic   *Experimental Control*
Illustration   *Functional Fixedness*

The topic of experimental control runs throughout this book, as it should, since it is crucial to all types of experimental research. The purpose of any experiment is to observe the effect of manipulation of certain variables—the independent variables—on the measurement of dependent variables. For a conclusion about the effect of an independent variable on a dependent variable to be sound, it is necessary that we gain a sufficient amount of experimental control over the situation to ensure that no other factor varies with the independent variable. In this book, these other variables are usually called control variables, although they are also referred to as extraneous variables, or even nuisance variables. If an extraneous variable is allowed to vary at the same time as the independent variable of interest, we cannot know whether the effect on the dependent variable is caused by variation in the independent variable, the extraneous variable, or both operating together. In such cases, we say that the two variables are confounded.

In the study of complex processes, there are often greater problems of experimental control than in other types of research. In the study of such topics as problem solving, there is frequently a great deal of variation in the measures taken on the dependent variable. We have already discussed some of the reasons for this. Because it is necessary to use between-subjects designs in much of this research, individual differences among subjects contribute greatly to the uncontrolled variation, or "error variance." Also, it may not be possible to tightly control all the nuisance variables that may affect a situation. Instead, they may be left to vary in an unsystematic way, since unsystematic variation will not affect one experimental condition more than another. Still, these randomly varying factors may serve to increase the variability of measurements.

Because of the effect of these variations on the dependent variable, detecting a reliable effect of the independent variable may be more difficult. One other reason for experimental control, then, is to reduce these extraneous sources of variation on the dependent variables. But given that they do occur and may be more prevalent in the study of problem solving and other complex processes, it becomes necessary to increase the number of observations in experimental conditions to get reliable results. For practical reasons that we have already discussed, this is not always possible. Therefore, employing as much experimental control over extraneous variables as can be mustered in these situations becomes even more important and desirable.

Our intent in discussing all these considerations is not to imply that solid research on interesting, complex processes is practically impossible. However, it is necessary to keep firmly in mind the difficulties one encounters in such research. Some experimental psychologists view research in these complex areas as relatively "sloppy," since it often lacks tight experimental control and employs relatively few observations in experimental conditions (leading to the possibility of unreliable results). It is as though some researchers in this area believe that the greater difficulty in studying complex psychological processes somehow justifies lesser, rather than greater, experimental control. But it is quite obvious that the problems inherent in studying complex processes can be overcome: We have instances of exemplary research in this area.

A good example is the research on **functional fixedness** in problem solving. This work began with an important series of studies by Karl Duncker (1945, pp. 85–101). The general idea behind the concept is that if an object has recently been used in one particular way in a given situation, its use in a second, different way to solve a new problem is likely to be overlooked. Duncker invented a number of problems that he used to test this general idea, but we focus on only one, the well-known "box" problem. This problem is a classic, and is still under investigation today (e.g., Carnevale & Probst, 1998; German & Defeyter, 2000).

Duncker's Box Problem

In the box problem, subjects were told that their task was to affix three small candles onto a door at eye level. The materials they were to use were placed on a table. Among the objects were several crucial ones: some tacks, matches, three small pasteboard boxes about the size of a matchbox, and the candles. The appropriate solution to the problem was to tack the boxes to the wall and use them as platforms on which the candles could be attached with some melted wax. In the control condition, the boxes were empty; but in the functional-fixedness condition, the boxes were filled with the needed material. There were several candles in one, tacks in a second, and matches in a third. Thus, in the latter condition, the function of the box as a container was to be "fixed" in the subjects' minds. This should have been less the case in the control condition, since the boxes were not used as containers. Duncker also employed a third condition, which we will refer to as the neutral-use condition. Here, the boxes were also used as containers, but they contained neutral objects (such as buttons) not needed as parts of the solution.

A between-subjects design was necessary in this experiment, since once subjects had been exposed to the problem, they could not, for obvious reasons, be tested again in a different condition. In this particular experiment, Duncker employed only seven subjects in each condition. The results for the three conditions are reported in Table 11.1 as the number of subjects who solved the problem in each condition. All seven subjects in the control condition solved the problem, but only 43 percent of the subjects in the functional-fixedness condition (three out of seven) were able to do so. In the neutral-use condition, only one subject (14 percent) was able to solve the

▼ **TABLE 11.1**

Number of Subjects Who Solved Duncker's Box Problem in Three Different Experimental Conditions. When Subjects Were Given the Boxes That Contained Material (The Functional-Fixedness and Neutral-Use Conditions), a Smaller Number Were Able to Solve the Problem than When the Boxes Were Given to Them Empty (Control). Presumably, in the Former Cases, the Function of the Box Was "Fixed" as a Container, and Thus Subjects Did Not as Readily Think of the Boxes as Potential Platforms for the Candles.

Condition	Boxes	Solved Problem ($n = 21$)
Control	Empty	7 (100%)
Functional fixedness	Filled with candles, matches, and tacks	3 (43%)
Neutral	Filled with irrelevant materials (buttons, etc.)	1 (14%)

problem. Of course, these differences among conditions were not evaluated statistically, but the difference between the control and functional-fixedness conditions was replicated with four other problems. The difference between the functional-fixedness and neutral-use conditions was replicated with two independent groups solving one other problem. The functional-fixedness effect has since been replicated a number of times, so we can be assured it is reliable, despite the small number of subjects used in the original studies.

Duncker's findings can be interpreted within the framework of Gestalt principles of problem solving, discussed earlier in this chapter. Recall that Gestaltists believed that many problems are solved through insight, or a sudden restructuring of the problem in a way that leads to the correct solution. In Duncker's experiment, subjects in the functional-fixedness condition seemed unable to overcome the bias induced by seeing all the objects serving their ordinary functions and could not restructure their perceptions to see different uses for the objects.

Adamson's Replication

A study by Adamson (1952) is interesting in this regard. He sought to replicate Duncker's original experiment by comparing subjects in the functional-fixedness and control conditions on the solution to three problems. These included the box problem we have already discussed, as well as two others, referred to as the paper clip problem and the gimlet problem. (The exact nature of these problems need not concern us.) In each situation, the comparison was between subjects who had previous experience with an object (and who thus should have been thinking of the function of the object as fixed) and control subjects for whom this was not the case. Adamson was primarily concerned about how few subjects were used in Duncker's original experiment, so he used between 26 and 29 subjects in each of his six separate conditions (3 problems × 2 experimental conditions). The dependent measures he used were the percentage of subjects who were able to solve the problem in the 20-minute period and the amount of time it took successful subjects to solve the problem.

The results are quite instructive. When Adamson used Duncker's dependent measure of the percentage of subjects who were able to solve the problem, he was able to replicate the functional-fixedness effect in only the box problem. A full 86 percent of the control subjects but only 41 percent of the subjects in the functional-fixedness condition were able to solve the box problem. However, performance on the other two problems was impossible to interpret with this measure, because of **ceiling effects** in both conditions. That is, almost all subjects in both conditions solved the problem, so performance did not differ; for both problems, it approached 100 percent in each condition. This problem is discussed in the "Introducing the Variables" section in this chapter (see also Chapter 10); once again, we are not justified in concluding that there was no difference between the two conditions under these circumstances. The conclusion, rather, is that the dependent variable was not sufficiently sensitive to allow detection of any possible differences between conditions.

Fortunately, Adamson also used a second dependent measure. He also measured how long it took to solve the problems, what is usually called **latency.** The results, in terms of mean time to solution for subjects in the two conditions, are presented in Figure 11.5 for both the gimlet and the paper clip problems. Only data concerning subjects who actually solved the problems are included. Although almost all subjects were able to solve the problems, the amount of time it took to do so varied greatly in the two conditions, as is apparent from Figure 11.5. In each case, subjects in the control condition solved the problem much faster than subjects in the experimental (functional-fixedness) condition. Thus, having the function of the objects fixed by the way the problem was presented slowed but did not prevent solution to the problem. The important point is that functional fixedness was demonstrated in all three of Adamson's problems, but in two of them, it was necessary to use a latency measure that was more sensitive than simply the percentage of subjects solving the problem.

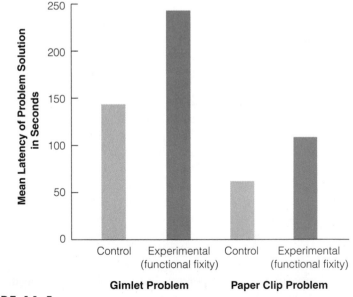

▼ FIGURE 11.5

Time taken to solve the gimlet and paper clip problems in the control and experimental (functional-fixedness) conditions of Adamson's (1952) experiment. It took subjects in the functional-fixedness condition longer to solve the problems than the controls.

Latency measures can also be difficult to interpret because of **floor effects.** For example, in Adamson's experiments, if the time to solve a problem was very fast (at the bottom end of the measurement scale) in both the experimental and control conditions and no significant difference was observed, it would have been difficult to conclude that the manipulation had no effect. Although this was not the case, clearly it can be seen in Figure 11.5 that when the overall latency was faster (the paper clip problem), the difference between the experimental condition and the control condition was less than when the overall latency was slower (the gimlet problem).

Why was Adamson unable to replicate Duncker's results with the gimlet and paper clip problems, when the percentage of subjects solving the problem was the dependent measure? Adamson suggests that he simply may have had more able subjects, which is certainly a possibility. But another real possibility is that Adamson allowed 20 minutes for his subjects to solve the problem, whereas Duncker seems to have allowed much less time, though it varied somewhat from individual to individual, depending on the progress of each toward a solution.

The Adamson study is an excellent example of a systematic, well-controlled replication that served to clean up an original demonstration of an interesting phenomenon. Such replications are quite valuable, especially since they often lead to new knowledge on the generality of the phenomenon in question. However, after a novel phenomenon has been replicated once or twice in independent laboratories, further research effort directed at simple replications is to be discouraged. (The chances are excellent that journal editors would not see fit to publish further studies of direct or even systematic replications at this point.) The research effort must turn to developing an understanding of the factors that influence the phenomenon and developing a theory or model of the psychological processes involved.

In the area of functional fixedness, Glucksberg and his associates have provided systematic research on the effect of verbalization and labeling on functional fixedness (Glucksberg & Weisberg, 1966; Glucksberg & Danks, 1967, 1968). For example, it has been found that when objects in the candle problem are given verbal labels (candle, tacks, box, matches) when they are shown to the subjects, the problem is solved by more subjects than when no labels are given. The trick is to have the subjects think of the box not merely as a container of tacks, but as a separate object capable of being used to solve the problem. Labeling the objects aids this process. As Glucksberg has pointed out, "It is not the way the world *is* that influences what we do as much as it is how we *represent* that world symbolically" (1966, p. 26; italics are Glucksberg's).

11.3 ° EXPERIMENTAL TOPICS AND RESEARCH ILLUSTRATIONS

Topic   *Verbal Reports*
Illustration   *Overconfidence in Judgments*

Early in the history of experimental psychology, there was an emphasis on the use of introspective reports as a method for discovering the structure of the mind. As is discussed in Appendix A, introspection was not a casual, moody reflection on the contents of the mind during some experience or other, but a rigorous, methodical technique of describing experience. Its basic problem was one of reliability: Investigators who used introspection in different psychology laboratories often arrived at different conclusions about the structure of the mind. The method would probably have fallen into disuse for this reason alone, but its departure from psychology was hastened by Watson's (1913) attack on the entire enterprise of structural psychology and by the subsequent rise of behaviorism. Since introspection has a technical meaning in the vocabulary of structural psychology, we will use the term *verbal report* to refer to the use of subjects' reports in psychological experiments (see Chapter 7 also). These are sometimes called *subjective reports,* as well.

Despite the success of behaviorism in sweeping away the structural approach, the use of the subjective report has kept its place in psychology. In fact, the use of verbal report is quite in accord with the scientific rules of behaviorists, since verbal reports are, of course, overt behavior. In fact, Watson, the founder of behaviorism, states this quite clearly in a section called "The Behaviorist's Platform" in *Behaviorism:*

> The behaviorist asks: Why don't we make what we can *observe* the real field of psychology? Let us limit ourselves to things that can be observed, and formulate laws concerning only those things. Now what can we observe? We can observe *behavior—what the organism does or says*. And let us point out at once: that *saying* is doing—that is, *behaving*. Speaking overtly or to ourselves (thinking) is just as objective a type of behavior as baseball. (1925, p. 6; italics are Watson's)

The use of verbal report, then, was endorsed by the founder of behaviorism. But as Spence (1948) pointed out, the use of verbal report is very different for structuralist and behaviorist psychologists. For the former, introspective reports are facts or data about internal mental events that are thought to directly mirror these events. For behaviorists, on the other hand, verbal reports are simply one type of behavior that may be worth studying as a dependent variable. They are to be considered no more nor less worthwhile or "real" *a priori* than any other type of response or dependent variable (see Chapter 7). If one wants to use verbal reports as evidence for some particular mental construct, they are to be considered as only one of several needed converging operations. Verbal reports are, of course, more likely to be useful in certain areas of psychology than others. Research on thinking is one area in which extensive use is made of verbal reports.

One critical component in thinking is the ability to evaluate one's knowledge. A number of experiments have explored the **feeling-of-knowing** phenomenon, first studied systematically by Hart (1965). A representative experiment is one by Freedman and Landauer (1966). Subjects were given a long series of general-knowledge questions (What is the capital of Ecuador? Who was the fifth president of the United States?) and asked to provide answers. For each question for which subjects could not provide an answer, they were asked to rate on a four-point scale how confident they were that they could recognize the answer if it were presented with similar alternatives. The four judgments were "definitely know" the answer, "probably know" it, "probably don't know" it, and "definitely don't know" it. After making these feeling-of-knowing judgments, subjects were given the questions again and asked to pick the correct answer from among six alternatives.

The subjects recognized 73 percent of the items that they had judged they would definitely know, 61 percent they had said they would probably know, and 51 percent and 35 percent of the answers to questions they had thought they either probably or definitely did not know. The fact that the ratings are generally correlated with later recognition performance may be taken as an indication that people's subjective feelings of what they know (following a failure of recall) are fairly accurate. Other experiments have revealed a similar feeling-of-knowing effect (e.g., Koriat & Levy-Sadot, 2001; Schacter, 1983; but see Perfect & Hollins, 1999, for an exception), and recent research has illuminated the specific brain activity associated with the feeling (Maril, Simons, Mitchell, Schwartz, & Schacter, 2003). However, one other interesting feature of the data is that even when people were convinced they knew the answer to a question, they were able to respond correctly only 73 percent of the time. Obviously, the ability to monitor the state of one's knowledge is rather imperfect. Often we seem overly confident that we know something when in fact we do not or at least cannot remember it at the time we are tested.

Other studies using slightly different techniques have shown that people have this tendency to be overly confident of their knowledge. One technique is to ask people to answer questions with two alternative answers, and then ask them to rate the probability of their having answered them correctly. Suppose you were given the following item: "Bile pigments accumulate as a result of a condition known as (a) jaundice or (b) gangrene." After choosing the answer you believed to be correct, you would then be asked to estimate the probability from 0.50 to 1.00 that you are in fact correct. (Since there are two alternatives, 0.50 is chance.) Lichtenstein and Fischhoff (1977) reported that although there was a general correlation between judgments of confidence and accuracy, subjects were generally much more confident than warranted by their knowledge. For example, for items that subjects estimated they would answer correctly 80 percent of the time, the actual accuracy was only 70 percent. This overconfidence does not seem to result from subjects' not taking the task very seriously, for other studies have reported the same tendency even when subjects are given elaborate instructions emphasizing accuracy and when they are given the opportunity to bet on their answers with the possibility of losing money as a result (Fischhoff, Slovic, & Lichtenstein, 1977).

These studies show that although verbal reports of our factual knowledge are generally correlated with that knowledge, they are by no means perfect reflections of what we know. This points out a shortcoming of retrospective verbal reports of cognitive processes. The vagaries of memory may produce an inaccurate or biased judgment of what we thought while performing some act. Many factors—motivational, emotional, social—may lessen the accuracy of verbal reports. Indeed, researchers in some areas have long been leery of accepting verbal reports at face value.

Nisbett and Wilson (1977) reviewed many experiments that related individuals' verbal reports to their behavior in experimental situations and reached the rather startling conclusion that "there may be little or no direct introspective awareness to higher order cognitive processes" (p. 231). They used many lines of evidence to draw this conclusion; one general type involves experiments comparing performance of people in between-subjects designs. Some experimental variable is manipulated and shown to have a strong influence on behavior; later, subjects in the different groups are asked why they responded the way they did. If subjects are consciously aware of the forces guiding their behavior, they should report the influence of the independent variable as a critical determinant of their performance. In many cases reviewed by Nisbett and Wilson, subjects could not do this and, in addition, often denied that the independent variable could have affected them, even when the experimenter suggested it as a possibility.

Nisbett and Wilson (1977) used such reports as the basis for their claim that people have no direct introspective access to the cognitive processes that mediate behavior. A corollary of this position would seem to be that subjective reports are generally inaccurate as descriptions of cognitive events. (Nisbett and Wilson argue that even when such reports are accurate, they may be based on general knowledge and not on some special self-knowledge.) Others argue that Nisbett and Wilson's position is too extreme (see Ericsson & Simon, 1979; Smith & Miller, 1978). They maintain that under many conditions, people can be shown to have generally accurate access to their mental states. After all, the feeling-of-knowing studies discussed earlier showed that subjects are generally accurate in judging whether they know information, even when they cannot recall it. Many of the studies described by Nisbett and Wilson had features such as between-subjects designs and reports from subjects after the task was completed. Subjects likely would show better awareness if they participated in experiments that used within-subjects designs, since they would be exposed to the full range of the independent variable. Similarly, if subjects were asked to make reports during the actual performance of a task (e.g., by reporting out loud to the experimenter), reports might be more accurate. Using retrospective reports rather than ones taken "on line" makes subjects rely on fallible memory; perhaps they knew what they were doing at the time they were doing it, but then forgot (or distorted) their reasons later.

Janet Metcalfe (1986) conducted an experiment in which she obtained such on-line reports. Metcalfe wondered whether people who are trying to solve certain types of problems experience premonitions that they are approaching the solution or whether the solution comes to them suddenly. Notice that this question relates to the issue of trial-and-error versus insight learning, discussed at the beginning of this chapter. Metcalfe asked subjects to solve a variety of problems, such as anagrams (unscrambling the letters in scrambled words, such as *valert* for *travel*) and other brainteasers. As they worked on the problems, a click sounded every 10 seconds; at each click, subjects rated how close they thought they were to solving the problem by writing a number from 0 to 10. A 0 meant they were very "cold" and had no idea what the solution was; intermediate values meant they felt they were getting "warm"; and a 10 meant they had solved the problem, at which point they wrote the solution.

Metcalfe reasoned that if problem solving proceeds in a gradual trial-and-error fashion, people will achieve the solutions step by step, and their "feeling-of-warmth" ratings will get increasingly high as they approach the solution. On the other hand, if people solve problems through a sudden insight, then their feelings of warmth should stay relatively low and constant during the intervals preceding the solution and then jump to a 10 when they solve the problem. Finally, if people can accurately assess whether they are reaching a correct solution, then the "feeling-of-warmth" judgments should be higher preceding correct than preceding incorrect answers.

To summarize, the experiment addressed two interesting questions. First, do people have the subjective feeling that they solve problems gradually, or do they discover the answers in a flash of insight? Second, do people have accurate subjective premonitions that they are successfully reaching a problem solution? That is, do they know when their line of reasoning is leading to a correct solution?

The results of Metcalfe's experiment were quite interesting. First of all, the "feelings-of-warmth" ratings that subjects gave tended to follow an insight pattern. That is, while trying to solve the problems, subjects felt relatively "cold" and did not indicate that they were getting warmer or closer to the solution until the interval in which they solved the problem. Therefore, for the type of problems she used, people tended to achieve the solutions with rather sudden insights. The most surprising result, however, was that the subjects' feeling-of-warmth judgments were very inaccurate. That is, when subjects indicated that they thought they were very close to a solution (i.e., their warmth ratings were relatively high), they actually were more likely to give an incorrect than a correct solution! Thus, Metcalfe's experiment shows that people's subjective intuitions about whether they will solve a problem may not be reliable. Again, subjective reports must be interpreted cautiously (see Chapter 7, as well).

Where do all these considerations leave us in evaluating the use of subjective verbal reports as a research tool? Although the issue is complex, we can venture a few summary statements. First, it is probably unwise in many instances to place too much emphasis on verbal reports by using them, for example, as the sole dependent measure in an experiment. Some psychologists have suggested that for experiments that might be impractical or unethical to conduct, researchers should describe the procedure and various conditions to subjects and have subjects say how they would react (e.g., Brown, 1962; Kelman, 1966). However, the assumption that one's predictions while role-playing always (or even usually) accurately reflect how one will behave when placed in an actual situation seems risky. Second, verbal reports may very well be useful in some situations, but a researcher will have to analyze each situation carefully to determine the potential for error in using verbal reports. Most researchers consider subjective reports as useful extra sources of information in experiments but not as the primary dependent variable of interest. However, Ericsson and Simon (1979) detail conditions under which they believe verbal reports can serve as primary data. Finally, we believe that verbal reports can serve as interesting dependent measures, whether or not such reports accurately reflect cognitive states of the individual. Even if Nisbett and Wilson are correct in asserting that people have little or no accurate introspective awareness of the causes of their behavior, studying people's beliefs and reports about those causes would be of interest in itself.

FROM PROBLEM TO EXPERIMENT
THE NUTS AND BOLTS

Problem   *Incubation in Problem Solving*

Many writers on the subject of thinking and problem solving have described a rather mysterious process that seems to aid in solving problems. Consider the following account of the French mathematician, Henri Poincaré. (The mathematical terms in the quotation should not dismay you; just examine the passage for the psychological principle involved.)

> Just at this time I left Caen, where I was then living, to go on a geologic excursion under the auspices of the school of mines. The changes of travel made me forget my mathematical work. Having reached Coutances, we entered an omnibus to go some place or other. At the moment when I put my foot on the step the idea came to me, without anything in my former thoughts seeming to have paved the way for it, that the transformations I had used to define the Fuchsian functions were identical with those of non-Euclidean geometry. I did not verify the idea; I should not have the time, as, upon taking my seat in the omnibus, I went on with a conversation already commenced, but I felt a perfect certainty. On my return to Caen, for conscience's sake I verified the result at my leisure.

Then I turned my attention to the study of some arithmetical questions apparently without much success and without a suspicion of my connection with my preceding researches. Disgusted with my failure, I went to spend a few days at the seaside, and thought of something else. One morning, walking on the bluff, the idea came to me, with just the same characteristics of brevity, suddenness, and immediate certainty, that the arithmetic transformations of indeterminate ternary quadratic forms were identical with those of non-Euclidean geometry. . . .

I shall limit myself to this single example; it is useless to multiply them. In regard to my other researches I would have to say analogous things. . . .

Most striking at first is this appearance of sudden illumination, a manifest sign of long, unconscious prior work. The role of this unconscious work in mathematical invention appears to me incontestable. (Poincaré, 1929, p. 388)

There are many reports of similar experiences from writers, mathematicians, and scientists. Koestler (1964) cited several examples of a problem being solved in a sudden flash of illumination after all apparent progress on it had ceased and in fact the solver had turned to other matters. (Recall the similar appearance in Köhler's chimps.) But what are we to make of these reports? How are they to be evaluated? Can we accept them as useful evidence on the nature of thought? If so, then apparently the search for problem solutions can proceed without conscious attention; the mind may inexorably grind away at solving a problem without any conscious direction on the part of its owner.

Experimental psychologists are unlikely to be convinced by these reports that such a process is central to thought, rather than representing a more or less rare and curious accident. Instead, they are likely to consider such reports as hypotheses in need of experimental tests. On the basis of his own intuitions, Pioncaré outlined four stages in the thought process. First is **preparation,** during which a person becomes immersed in trying to solve a problem and learns the numerous relevant facts and considerations. Second is **incubation,** during which a person turns to other matters after failing to solve the problem. The problem is said to incubate, much as eggs do while a hen sits on them. (The same idea is expressed when you say "Let me sleep on it.") Next comes the stage of **illumination** (which Köhler calls **insight**), when the idea is hatched. Finally comes the stage of **verification,** when the solution to the problem must be carefully checked. These stages were identified on the basis of intuition and have thus been given only loose verbal definitions.

Although Poincaré collected many instances that seemed to confirm his theory of problem solving—and in particular the incubation process—as we all know, an example or two can be found to support almost any idea or theory, no matter how silly. And surely we can find many counterexamples in which problems are solved without incubation and sudden illumination. Instead of providing anecdotes, we must subject the concept of incubation to experimental test.

Problem *Can we find evidence for the concept of incubation?*

At present, this concept is rather fuzzy. We need to provide it with a more precise operational definition, so we will know exactly what we are looking for. Let us examine a definition by Posner (1973): "Incubation refers to an increase in the likelihood of successfully solving a problem that results from placing a delay between the period of intense work which initiates the problem solution and another period of conscious effort which finalizes the solution" (p. 171). This is somewhat precise, but a number of points still must be specified. In fact, it is a rather curious operational definition, since we do not even know if the defined phenomenon exists at this point! What we have done, really, is to suggest a hypothetical operational definition that can serve as the hypothesis of an experiment in search of the concept.

Hypothesis *Subjects who are allowed a break between two periods of work on solving a problem will be more likely to eventually find a solution (or to find one faster) than subjects not provided a break.*

Further, the longer the break, the more likely that the subjects will find the solution (and find it faster), at least up to some limit.

There remain, as always, a host of considerations to which we must turn our attention. How long should we allow subjects to solve the problem? Two 15-minute periods, or a total of 30 minutes, might be appropriate. The primary independent variable is the delay that is to be introduced between the two periods of work on the problem. At a minimum, we would want three independent conditions, so appropriate delays might be 0, 15, or 30 minutes between the two work periods. (More conditions with a wider range of delay intervals might be appropriate, too.) The experiment should probably employ a between-subjects design, since the amount of time required for subjects to serve in all three conditions would be prohibitive. The number of subjects to serve in each condition would depend on the available resources but should be as great as possible. A minimum of 20 may be sufficient, but the power of statistical tests based on this small a sample would not be great. It would be much better to have 75 or 100 subjects per condition. Since groups of subjects could be tested rather than individuals, the amount of effort in testing 300 subjects would not be prohibitive, if this many people were available. The length of the entire procedure would vary from perhaps 45 minutes in the zero-delay condition to 75 minutes in the 30-minute-delay condition.

Another important consideration is the type of problem to be used. It would probably be best to test subjects in the three conditions on more than one problem to ensure that the phenomenon, if found at all, is not specific to only one problem. If 75 subjects were used in each condition, 25 could be tested on each of three problems. It would be necessary to pretest the problems on subjects similar to those to be used in the experiment to ensure that (1) very few subjects could solve the problems in 15 minutes, or before the independent variable is introduced; and (2) around half (at least) could solve the problem in 30 minutes with no delay. The latter requirement is to guard against floor effects, or performance too poor to allow manipulation of the independent variable to reveal any effect. A sample problem might be the following:

> A man had four chains, each three links long. He wanted to join the four chains into a single closed chain. Having a link opened cost 2 cents, and having a link closed cost 3 cents. The man had his chains joined into a closed chain for 15 cents. How did he do it?

Another consideration is what subjects should be doing during the delay intervals. They should not simply be allowed to sit there and mull over the problem, since then they are essentially not given a delay at all. Subjects should be occupied with mental arithmetic problems or the like; it might even be wise to lead them to believe, at the beginning of the break, that they are going on to a new phase of the experiment and will not be returning to the problem they have failed to solve. This would ensure that subjects would not be trying to devote some attention to the problem while working on the filler activity.

The primary dependent measures would be the percentage of subjects in each condition who solved the problem and the amount of time it took them to do so. If the problems were selected carefully enough so that there were several solutions, the quality of solutions might also be evaluated. Even if the problems did not have this feature, subjects could be asked at the end of the second 15-minute period to write down how they were attempting to solve the problem, and the quality of these attempts could be evaluated to see whether the different conditions affected the quality of the terminal-solution attempts. The evaluations, of course, should be made by someone who does not know the conditions of the subjects (i.e., someone who is blind with respect to conditions).

These are the essentials, then, for an experiment on incubation. The predictions are that subjects who experience a delay between the two 15-minute periods of working on the problem will solve the problem more often (and will do so faster) than subjects who work on the problem continually for 30 minutes. Also, subjects who have a 30-minute break should achieve a solution more often (and do so faster) than those who have the shorter, 15-minute break.

Experiments such as this can make real contributions to the understanding of incubation. Perhaps the best evidence for incubation comes from a doctoral dissertation by Silveira (1971), which is a somewhat more complicated version of the type of experiment we have just outlined here. It is discussed briefly in Posner's book (1973, pp. 169–175). Published experiments yield mixed results. Olton and Johnson (1976) failed to find any evidence for incubation, whereas Steve Smith's data support incubation effects (e.g., see Smith & Blankenship, 1989; Smith & Blankenship, 1991; Smith, 1995).

If the phenomenon of incubation has been established experimentally, this is only the beginning of our attempts to understand it. What factors influence incubation? What kind of psychological theory could explain it? Saying that it is caused by "unconscious thought processes" is as bad as saying nothing at all. Actually, it might even be worse, since it gives the illusion of providing an explanation when, in fact, it does nothing of the kind. Can you think of explicit, testable hypotheses that could account for incubation? This is the path we must take to even begin to understand the phenomenon.

(By the way, the solution to the chain problem is that the man opened all the links in one of the chains—three opened at 2 cents each, for 6 cents—and then used the three open loops to join the remaining three chains together—three closed at 3 cents each, for 9 cents.)

▼ SUMMARY

1. Studies of complex psychological processes, such as thinking and problem solving, have special problems in terms of reliability of results and experimental control. One main problem concerns the relatively great variability that is likely to occur in observations under different experimental conditions. The individual differences that people exhibit in performing a complex task, such as solving a problem, are apt to be much greater than in performing simpler tasks.

2. In complex experiments, it is often necessary to use between-subjects designs, in which an independent group of subjects serves in each experimental condition. Unfortunately, less control over variance introduced by differences between subjects is possible than in within-subjects designs. A partial solution to these problems is to obtain as many observations per condition as possible to produce stable results and to control as tightly as feasible all extraneous variables, so they will not increase the variability within conditions.

3. Reliability of results from a single experiment can be assessed through the logic of statistical inference by employing appropriate statistical tests. Such tests allow us to assess how likely it is that the effect of some experimental variable is actually caused by the operation of that variable and not random (chance) factors.

4. Experimental reliability, which is preferred to statistical reliability by many psychologists, refers to actual replicability of experiments. Three types are identified. In direct replications, the attempt is to repeat the experiment as exactly as possible to see whether the same results will be obtained a second time. Systematic replications involve changing variables not thought to be critical to the phenomenon under consideration to make sure it survives such changes. Conceptual replications attempt to demonstrate the phenomenon with a wholly new paradigm or set of experimental conditions.

5. Systematic and conceptual replications also address the generality of results. Do results of an experiment generalize across the rather slight changes in procedure in systematic replications and the greater changes in procedure in conceptual replications? Often, advances in understanding a phenomenon are enhanced when researchers are able to find conditions under which the phenomenon does not replicate. When such boundary conditions are established and the researcher understands what factors control the presence or absence of the phenomenon, better theories can be constructed.

6. Subjective reports are verbal reports about people's awareness of their cognitive processes. They are sometimes used in the study of thinking, but caution must be exercised. In some instances, people are overly confident in judgments of their knowledge. In experiments on various complex judgments, people provided erroneous subjective impressions regarding the influence of particular variables that were shown to actually control their behavior. Verbal reports are sometimes useful in psychological research, but their trustworthiness will likely vary with the topic being studied.

▼ KEY TERMS

analogy
boundary conditions
ceiling effect
conceptual replication

confirmation bias
direct replication
experimental control
experimental reliability

extraneous variables
feeling of knowing
floor effects
functional fixedness
generality of results
illumination
incubation
insight
latency
law of effect
mapping
null hypothesis

power
preparation
reliability of results
statistical reliability
structural consistency
subjective report
systematic replication
thought
verbal report
verification
Wason Card Selection Task

▼ DISCUSSION QUESTIONS

1. A researcher in the biology department of your university has just demonstrated extrasensory perception (ESP) in rats. The rats were placed in a maze, where they had to choose between two possible runways, one of which led to food. The rats could not see or smell the food at the place in the maze where they had to make their decision, and the runway in which the experimenter put the food varied randomly from trial to trial. Over a series of 50 trials, the researcher found that there were 2 rats out of 100 tested that seemed to perform better than would be expected on the basis of chance. One picked the correct runway 64 percent of the time; the other picked it 66 percent of the time (with chance being 50 percent). Which of the two following tests would be more convincing to you as confirmation of these rats having ESP?

   a. The researcher performs statistical tests showing that the two rats had indeed performed better than chance in making their choices; or

   b. a different researcher tests the two rats on several hundred more trials and does succeed in replicating the first researcher's findings.

   Defend your choice. If you were the second researcher, what safeguards would you introduce into the experiment to ensure that the rats were not using sensory cues to solve the problem (assuming the rats again performed above chance)?

2. After seeing the results of the first experiment (namely, 2 out of 100 rats apparently scored better than chance on the test of extrasensory percep-

tion), we ask the experimenter how many of the rats scored below chance by 10 percent or more. The researcher reports that three did and says he is fascinated by this discovery, which seems to indicate that some rats have "negative extrasensory perception." What do you, as a dispassionate observer, conclude about these claims?

3. Distinguish among direct replications, systematic replications, and conceptual replications. Should the three types be considered qualitatively different, or do they lie on a continuum? If they lie on a continuum, what dimension underlies it?

4. The reward system in science discourages replications of other people's work. Researchers are rewarded much more for novel contributions than for "merely repeating" the work of others. Some have argued that this reward system tends to create fragmentation and disarray in many areas of psychology, because people are rewarded for going their own way and (sometimes) ignoring progress in other closely related areas. Thus, basic phenomena will often be unreplicated. Do you think replication should be more strongly encouraged? If so, how?

5. Many psychological journals encourage researchers to report a series of experiments about some phenomenon rather than a single experiment. Do you think this is a good idea? If so, why? What dangers might be inherent in requiring that research reports contain numerous experiments?

6. Verbal reports are likely to be more useful in some areas of psychology than in others. For each of the following topics, discuss the pros and cons of using verbal reports. For those cases in which you think verbal reports cannot be used, suggest better methods:

a. Studying strategies by which people remember their childhood experiences when asked to do so

b. Studying sexual behavior of college students

c. Studying people's mental processes that occur when they decide to buy one product rather than another

d. Studying the reasons why one person likes another

e. Studying what factors affect visual illusions

 WEB CONNECTIONS

The following website has links to many classic problem-solving puzzles, including the prisoner's dilemma:

http://www.psychnet-uk.com/games/games.htm

The following website has links to different problem-solving demonstrations and studies:

http://psych.hanover.edu/research/exponnet.html#Cognition

PSYCHOLOGY IN ACTION
Confirmation Bias

Consider the following problem: Each of the cards below is two-sided; on one side is a letter and on the other is a number. Your task is to figure out which cards need to be turned over to test the following rule: "If a card has a vowel on one side, it has an even number on the other."

| A | G | 4 | 7 |

Which card(s) did you choose? Most people pick either just the A card, or the A and 4 cards. But in reality, you need to select the A and 7 cards, as both these cards will allow you to disconfirm the hypothesis (if the 7 has a vowel on the other side, or the A card turns over to an odd number, then the rule must be false. Checking the 4 card will only allow you to confirm the hypothesis). This task is the classic **Wason Card Selection Task** (e.g., Wason, 1968), and the **confirmation bias** is the name for people's tendency to search for evidence that supports their hypothesis.

People do better on this task when the task is conceptualized within a more familiar domain; for example, they know which cards to turn over to test the rule: "to drink alcohol, one must be at least 21 years old" (a card has an age on one side and a drink on the other).

Now, people don't bother checking the drinks of 21 year olds (because it doesn't matter for the rule); they know they need to see how old the beer-drinkers are and what the 16-year-olds are drinking (e.g., Ahn & Graham, 1999; Cox & Griggs, 1982).

Try these problems out on your friends. You might consider doing a variation on the Gick and Holyoak studies described earlier: If your friends do the easier beer version first, are they more likely to solve the traditional version? If not, does a hint help them to transfer their knowledge? ∎

CHAPTER 12

INDIVIDUAL DIFFERENCES AND DEVELOPMENT

Theoretically, we can distinguish between learning and growth, but practically they are inseparable: there is no behavior that is independent of the animal's heredity, or its growth to maturity, or the supporting environment; and no higher behavior that is uninfluenced by learning. (DONALD HEBB)

When Balamural Krishna Ambati was an undergraduate premedical student, he enjoyed chess, basketball, and various kinds of biological research. What distinguished him from other undergraduates? Well, for one thing, he was 13 when he completed his undergraduate program. For another, he hoped to become the youngest graduate of a medical school. Bala, as he is called, is a child prodigy who mastered calculus at age 4. His grade point average and his test scores indicated that he should graduate from medical school before his eighteenth birthday (Stanley, 1990), and he did at age 17 in 1995 (Baker, 2006). When he started his medical career at age 24, he was too young to rent an automobile (Baker, 2006).

Clearly, Bala is different from most physicians, who might begin medical school at age 22 and finally finish in their mid-20s. Why was Bala so far ahead of the typical person entering the medical profession? How and why did he develop so quickly that he went to school with students much older than he? These sorts of questions are addressed by psychologists interested in individual differences and development. In this chapter, we examine some methodological issues relevant to undertaking research on how people differ and develop.

The study of individual differences began because of important practical decisions that had to be made about people, but it is a topic that has been mostly ignored by experimental psychologists, who are primarily interested in finding general laws and explanations for behavior. Investigation of individual differences is really just getting under way by psychologists who employ experimental methods, although it has long been a topic of concern for psychologists with more practical and applied interests.

The experimental investigation of individual differences illustrates the need for **reliability** of measures of individual characteristics. If individuals' decisions concerning future action are to be based on their particular mental abilities, interests, and ways of responding to events, then measures of these factors must yield similar results on different test occasions. In addition, the characteristics in which a psychologist is interested need to be defined in a way that can be communicated to others. It would be unreasonable to expect consistent measures of intelligence if everyone who measured it used a different definition of intelligence. The most useful kind of definition, because it is the most easily communicated, describes a procedure for producing and measuring the characteristic of interest. Such procedures are called **operational definitions** and are a necessary component of all research. One use of operational definitions is to separate people into classes or categories on the basis of the definitions, so researchers can study these classes of people in experimental settings. When people are classified this way, the variables are referred to as **subject variables.** Examples of subject variables are age, intelligence, sex, degree of neuroticism, or any characteristic of people that can be precisely specified. Age is a subject variable of particular interest to developmental psychologists, who study changes in behavior across the life span. Later in the chapter, we consider problems associated with studying age-related changes.

Once an investigator has operationally defined an individual characteristic and found the measure to be reliable, she or he may then wish to change that characteristic through some type of learning experience. One of the hazards in interpreting such a change is known as **regression to the mean,** which may lead an investigator to believe a change has been produced when, in fact, it has not, or vice versa. In this chapter, we discuss reliability, operational definitions, subject variables, and regression in the context of research on individual differences and development.

▼ APPROACHES TO INDIVIDUAL DIFFERENCES

A general issue in science, and particularly in the psychology of individual differences, concerns which methods and theories best allow predictions of future events. Historically, the study of individual differences has been characterized by debate about the appropriate ways to understand how people differ and, therefore, how their future behavior can be predicted.

Methodological Approaches to Individual Differences

One set of issues involves the methods used to derive predictions. Two methods of approaching the problem are the empirical and analytical, which are equivalent to the inductive and deductive approaches discussed in Chapter 1. The **empirical approach** aims to achieve the greatest degree of predictive precision possible by any means available. This often involves a search for a combination of measures that will predict the events in question. The traditional intelligence test given to schoolchildren is an example of this approach to prediction. Early in the last century, the French government commissioned Alfred Binet and Theodore Simon to devise tests that would determine which children could and which could not profit from an education. Thus, the original purpose of intelligence tests (and the main one today) was to predict school performance. Binet and Simon reasoned that as normal children develop, they should be able to handle more difficult problems. Younger children who do well on questions devised for older ones are thought to be intelligent, and those who do not perform up to their age level are considered less intelligent than average. Binet and Simon employed tests of memory, comprehension, attention, and the like. They operationally defined (see Chapter 6) intelligence as the ability to succeed in school, and one predictor of this success was the child's score on the tests that they constructed.

Intelligence tests became highly popular because they accomplish the important goal of determining which children will profit from what types of education. Correlations between intelligence and measures of academic success generally run in the neighborhood of +0.60. When a test predicts a criterion behavior well, it is said to have **predictive validity** (sometimes called **criterion validity**). In addition to predictive validity, tests may have considerable **face validity,** which means that they seem to measure something most people would be willing to call intelligence. This occurs when success in school is better predicted by test items that appear to measure mental ability than by tests that measure some ability that is unrelated to academics, such as prowess in shooting billiards. Knowing *what* works in science often leads to a better understanding of *how* and *why* something works. For this reason empirical solutions to specific problems often precede theoretical and analytical understandings of those problems.

An **analytical approach** toward measuring intelligence involves a theoretical analysis of what produces the effects we attribute to intelligence. Once we have analyzed the components of the concept, we can measure them. In the nineteenth century, Sir Francis Galton believed that the ability to form mental images and the ability to respond quickly to a stimulus were components of high intelligence. When he compared these abilities in scientists and statesmen with those of common workers, he was surprised to find no differences. He concluded that these abilities do not contribute heavily to intelligence, contrary to his own and others' views.

Contemporary researchers have had better success in breaking down intelligence into its components (Gardner, 1983; Hunt & Lansman, 1975; Sternberg, 1988). However, we are still some distance from being able to predict scholastic performance as well as the empiricist's intelligence tests. The analytical and theoretical approaches are best viewed as complementary rather than antagonistic, which is the way in which Jean Piaget, the eminent developmental psychologist, attempted to understand intellectual development. Piaget (1932) spent many years observing children (primarily his own). From the empirical regularities that he observed in cognitive and social development, Piaget developed a comprehensive theory of development (Piaget & Inhelder, 1969). The theory, in turn, became the guiding force behind a substantial portion of research in developmental psychology. As we noted in Chapter 1, individual scientists may focus on a particular approach toward understanding; however, a combination of empirical and analytic work will best lead to scientific progress.

Variables Leading to Individual Differences

A second set of issues underlying the study of individual differences concerns the basic variables that lead to them. Just as in the study of perception (see Chapter 7), some researchers have argued for a nativistic (nature) basis for individual differences, whereas others have proposed an empirical (nurture) basis. This nature–nurture contrast is an old one in psychology (Schultz & Schultz, 1987), and it is still alive with much controversy.

According to **nature theory,** genetic differences underlie individual differences. A recent study by Herrnstein and Murray (1994), *The Bell Curve,* illustrates a heritability theory of intelligence. In particular, Herrnstein and Murray argue that there is a "genetic factor in cognitive ethnic differences" (p. 270), which accounts for differences in intelligence between blacks and whites, as well as other ethnic group differences. Several scientists (Fraser, 1995; Sternberg, 1995) have vigorously undermined their proposal and some of its implications, and Nisbett (1995) noted that much evidence opposes Herrnstein and Murray's view that black–white differences in intelligence test scores have a genetic basis.

A **nurture view** of individual differences focuses on experiential factors that influence how organisms develop. An example of this kind of proposal was developed by Ericsson, Krampe, and Tesch-Romer (1993) to account for differences in the abilities of violinists and pianists. Contrary to Galton's (1869/1979) widely held view that genius is hereditary, Ericsson and associates present a variety of evidence to show that quality of musicianship is a function of the amount and quality of practice. They argue that extensive practice for at least 10 years is the major contributor to musical ability.

As is true of other dichotomous views that we have examined, neither pole by itself is likely to reveal the correct state of affairs. Hebb has long advocated a more sophisticated analysis of the effects of nature and nurture on behavior (e.g., Hebb & Donderi, 1987). He notes that the effects of heredity must take place in an environment of some kind, which means that genetics never acts alone. On the other hand, he notes that experience (nurture) always requires an organism that has a genetic background, which means that experience cannot act alone. So, he has proposed that we should consider six interacting factors when we examine the development of an organism. The first factor is genetics. The second is the prenatal nutritive environment, which has long been known to have important effects on development. A pregnant mother who has measles can have a child with retarded cognitive development, and the ingestion of large amounts of alcohol during pregnancy can produce birth defects. For example, work has shown that spatial–visual reasoning is compromised in 14-year-old children whose mothers had ingested some, but less than excessive, amounts of alcohol during pregnancy (Hunt, Streissguth, Kerr, & Olson, 1995). Hunt and associates found that the more a mother reported drinking during pregnancy, the faster but less accurately did the children respond to how triangles and squares could be combined to form a figure. The third factor that Hebb identified was postnatal nutrition, and cognitive development after birth is critically related to the adequacy of the diet. These three factors can be considered as the physical or constitutional variables associated with how people grow. In the case of intelligence, we know that the three variables relate to the development of the brain. In turn, Duncan and associates (2000, 2003) have shown the relation between general intelligence and parts of the brain, in particular the prefrontal lobes.

The fourth and fifth factors that Hebb identifies are those usually associated with experience, namely, cultural and individual learning. Hebb notes that we need to consider the environment shared by all members of a particular group or species—the cultural learning in the case of humans. People growing up in the cold of Mongolia share experiences that are markedly different from those who develop in a tropical climate, as in parts of Brazil. The second kind of learning (the one discussed in Chapter 9) concerns the unique experiences of an individual. Even identical twins living in the same culture do not have identical learning experiences. Hebb's sixth and final factor is physical trauma, which might involve such things as a brain tumor or the loss of sight resulting from an accident.

We can consider Hebb's factors as an outline of development rather than a theory. However, these interacting factors certainly complicate the analysis of development, and they point to the futility of opting for a purely genetic or experiential explanation of a behavior. Zuckerman (1995) has explored the hormones and neurotransmitters that are associated with certain personality traits. His survey convincingly implicates certain classes of hormones and neurotransmitters to such behaviors as extraversion and impulsivity. However, Zuckerman carefully notes that "we do not inherit personality traits or even behavior mechanisms as such" (p. 331). He indicates that our inherited chemical templates interact in as-yet-unknown ways with the kinds of factors proposed by Hebb. "Only cross disciplinary, developmental, and comparative psychobiological research can provide the answers" (p. 332) to how the factors interact.

INTRODUCING THE VARIABLES

We consider here just one type of individual difference, intelligence, but the general principles also hold for other individual differences.

Dependent Variables

The dependent variables in the study of intelligence are the *measures* of intelligence used by each experimenter. Since notions of what intelligence really is differ widely among experimenters, it is difficult to devise a single measure that would be acceptable to all. Empirical approaches are generally based on the observation that as children grow older, they are able to perform more complicated and more difficult tasks. For individuals of any given age, an average level of performance on certain tasks can be determined by testing a large and representative sample. The particular tasks or test items will be selected on the basis of their correlations with objective criteria of success in school, such as grades and reading level, and possibly also with subjective criteria, such as teacher ratings.

At any particular age level, there will be some average number of items that children can pass.

If a 7-year-old child can pass the same number of items as the average 9-year-old child, we would say that this child has a **mental age** of 9. The intelligence quotient, or IQ, is defined as mental age divided by **chronological age** $\times$ 100, or (in this case) 9/7 $\times$ 100 = 129. By definition, a score of 100 means that an individual scored the average for his or her age, and every 15-point variation from this average represents one standard deviation (see Appendix B) from this mean. Variants of the IQ are used as an index of intelligence.

A purely analytic intelligence test (none is currently in general use) would contain many subtests designed to measure specific properties of a person's information-processing system. Examples of these properties might be short-term memory capacity and scanning rate, long-term memory organization and access time, maximum information transmission rates in various types of tasks, and the ability to allocate attention. Performance on these tasks could be compared with normative performance, as with empirical tests. A combined score computed from all the separate task results may possibly be used as a predictor of scholastic performance.

Independent Variables

All individual differences, including intelligence, are subject variables and not true independent variables. Studies of human intelligence are often aimed at determining the relative importance of genetic, as opposed to environmental, factors in producing intelligence. One of the techniques employed in this research has been to examine monozygotic (identical) twins, dizygotic (fraternal) twins, other siblings, and unrelated children who are reared in the same household or in different households. Genetic similarity varies in these studies as follows: Identical twins (of course) have the same genetic inheritance, fraternal twins and other siblings are genetically similar to a lesser degree than identical twins, and unrelated children have the least degree of genetic similarity. Environmental similarity varies in that children reared in the same household have more similar experiences than children reared in separate households.

A number of objections to the definition of environmental similarity can be raised. In the first place, it seems unreasonable to assume that all pairs of children in the same household have continued equally similar experiences. Twins, and particularly identical twins, are often treated more alike than other pairs of children, if for no other reason than that they are at the same age when various family events occur. Also, foster children and biological children may be treated somewhat differently even when they are of the same age. A second objection is based on the fact that foster children enter the family at later ages than biological children, even if by only a few weeks or months. Although this difference may appear trivial when intelligence is measured at ages of 10 to 15 or more, many studies have shown that early experiences are quite important in the development of intelligence. A third objection is based on the potential influence of experiences that occur even earlier than those of the first few weeks in the home, namely, those that occur in the prenatal environment. As with genetic inheritance, these prenatal experiences will generally be most similar for twins, less similar for siblings, and least similar for unrelated children. Similarity of prenatal and early postnatal experience may thus be correlated with genetic similarity, making it risky to interpret correlations of one or the other with measured intelligence.

Control Variables

In studies of intelligence, it is difficult to define an exhaustive set of control variables. The single most important factor to control, however, is generally thought to be specific learning that could affect test performance. If certain individuals have learned answers to a number of the test questions, rather than having to "reason out" the answers, they will appear more intelligent than other individuals who have not previously learned these particular facts, words, or relations.

Although many items have been deleted from modern intelligence tests in order to make them more "culture-fair," or less influenced by particular learning experiences, it is impossible to eliminate all the effects of learning, language usage, motivation, cultural knowledge, testing experience, and other factors that are known to affect intelligence measures. This is not a problem if intelligence is interpreted simply as probability of success in school, since these other factors no doubt influence school performance. But if intelligence is interpreted as "mental capacity" or some such construct, the effects of these extraneous variables must be minimized.

12.1   EXPERIMENTAL TOPICS AND RESEARCH ILLUSTRATIONS

Topic   *Reliability of Measures*
Illustration   *Intelligence and Developmental Research Designs*

When psychologists speak of reliability, they are referring to the consistency of their measures of some quantity. You might suppose that several attempts to measure the same thing would all yield the same numbers, unless of course someone had made an error. In fact, there is nearly always some variability in a group of measures; the amount of variability determines the reliability of the measuring instrument and procedure. The "error" to which psychologists refer is meant to imply not that someone goofed, but merely that certain unavoidable factors caused unpredictable variability in the data. These sources of error are usually beyond the control of the researcher and result from people's behaving differently on successive occasions. Psychologists try to reduce this variability—hence, increasing the reliability of their measures—by taking their measures under the same conditions on successive occasions.

If identical conditions could be ensured, then variability in measurement would have to be caused by a real change in the measured quantity. If your height is measured on two occasions, with the results 5'8" and 5'10", is this variability owing to error or to a real change in your height? The answer could be either or both. But the more similar the conditions—shoes worn, posture—the less likely you would be to attribute the difference to error. Also the closer the two measures were in time, the less likely you would be to attribute the difference to a real change in stature. You have some notion of how quickly stature can change, or of the stability of a person's true stature.

Intelligence is more difficult to measure than stature, however, and sources of error are likely to be hard to detect. A person's performance on an intelligence test may be momentarily altered by extraneous factors, such as the amount of sleep the person has had, whether he or she ate a good meal before the test, and so on. It is also more difficult to develop a notion of its stability. Does intelligence vary at all, or does it remain fixed throughout life? If it changes markedly, can it do so within a week, a month, a year, or 10 years? If it changes, can we determine those factors that produce the change? These are questions that psychologists would like to answer; the answers require measurement of intelligence. But the alert reader will realize that we have now reasoned ourselves into a logical circle. Let us go around again and try to get out.

Several measures of the same quantity will not, in general, exactly agree. This variability may be a result of error or of real change in the measured quantity. We cannot tell, without some additional assumptions, how much error there is in our measurement. Thus, how can we ask if intelligence changes? A useful assumption—one that allows the logical circle to be broken—holds that the measured quantity is stable over relatively short periods. (If a researcher measures your intelligence in the morning and then again in the afternoon, any change can be assumed to be caused by measurement error rather than a real change in intelligence.) With this assumption, a psychologist can estimate measurement error and attempt to improve and specify the reliability of the measuring instrument. Questions concerning the stability of the underlying quantity, in this case intelligence, can then be answered. We first review some of the techniques that test developers use to assess the reliability of their measures, and then we review a study that attempted to determine the stability of intelligence over many years.

Test Reliability

We noted previously that the concept of intelligence is not well defined theoretically. Some theorists postulate a number of separate mental abilities, perhaps more than 100 (Guilford, 1967). Others believe that there is one primary mental ability and that although other, more specific abilities may be isolated, they are less important (Herrnstein & Murray, 1994). This primary ability has been described as "a capacity for abstract reasoning and problem solving" (Jensen, 1969, p. 19). To test for this ability, we assemble collections of problems or tasks and present them to individuals to solve, generally within a specified period. The score that an individual achieves is then compared with scores obtained by others. Before placing much confidence in an individual's score, however, we need to know how reliable it is. Would the individual achieve about the same score if we were to test him or her again the next day or a week later? Because we believe that the underlying ability does not change appreciably during so short a time, we attribute a large change in scores to measurement error, indicating unreliability in our test. This procedure of giving the same test twice in succession over a short time interval is used to determine what is called the **test–retest reliability** of a measure. It is generally expressed as a correlation between first and second scores obtained from a large sample of subjects.

A slightly different procedure can be employed to avoid such problems as specific practice effects. This technique involves giving alternate or **parallel forms** of the test on the two testing occasions. Again, if correlations between first and second scores are high, they indicate reliability of the tests. Also, the equivalence of the two forms of the test can be determined in this way.

A third procedure can be used to evaluate reliability with a single test presentation. This technique provides **split-half reliability;** it involves dividing the test items into two arbitrary groups (such as odd and even items) and correlating the scores obtained in the two halves of the test. If these correlations are high, the test reliability is confirmed. In addition, the equivalence of the test items is established.

Stability of Intelligence Measures

Modern intelligence tests are usually found to yield quite high test–retest reliabilities (correlations of about 0.95). If we accept these tests as reliable, we can then proceed to ask how stable measured intelligence remains over an individual's lifetime. A number of longitudinal studies have been initiated to examine this question, and reports are published every 10 years or so to bring the results up to date. One report (Kangas & Bradway, 1971) includes data on a group of subjects who were tested with the Stanford-Binet test in 1931, at a mean age of a little more than 4 years, and then tested again in 1941, 1956, and 1969. The original sample consisted of San Francisco Bay Area children who were part of a nationwide standardization population for a revision of the Stanford-Binet scale. Scores were obtained on two alternate forms of the test. In 1941, 138 of these subjects were retested with the same form of the test, and in 1956, 111 received the Wechsler Adult Intelligence Scale and the Stanford-Binet test. In 1969, 48 individuals agreed to be retested yet again.

Before examining the results of this study, we should recall that these results will be descriptive of the population of subjects from which the data were gathered. They will also, one hopes, be representative of data from similar subjects. They may or may not be representative of subjects who differ in important respects from the subjects in this study.

Kangas and Bradway provided data to show that the 48 subjects tested in 1969 did not differ from the larger group of 111 subjects tested in 1956. They provided means and standard deviations for both chronological age and IQ as assessed by the Stanford-Binet test at each age and found no differences between the two samples.

The authors reported correlations between scores obtained at each pair of test administrations, with scores from the parallel forms administered in 1931 averaged. The tests used at each age were the Stanford-Binet (S-B) intelligence tests and, for the 1956 and 1969 tests only, the Wechsler Adult Intelligence Scale (WAIS). The results are presented in Table 12.1. Notice that the WAIS has a verbal component and a performance component, which together give the full score. As you look from left to right across the table, you see that correlations between successive testings decrease with the amount of time between testings. The drop is especially pronounced when preschool intelligence, taken when the children's mean age was 4.1, is correlated with the other scores (the top row of the table). The correlations are much higher when adult scores are correlated. However, all the correlations in Table 12.1 are statistically significant; scores obtained when children are about 4 years old can be said to predict to some extent (a correlation of 0.41) how well they will do much later, at age 41.6. (We should also note that intelligence tests given to 4 year olds are quite different in types of questions from those given to older children; this may help account for the low correlations.)

You can view the increase in correlation between the 1969 measures and previous ones as the subjects' ages increase as you look from the top of the table to the bottom. The correlations are higher when S-B scores are correlated with each other rather than with WAIS scores, and vice versa. Since the S-B test is verbal, it does not correlate too highly with the performance part of the WAIS. The results presented in Table 12.1 indicate that intelligence is fairly stable across 37 years for this sample.

Another interesting finding of the Kangas and Bradway study is that the test scores increased at each testing age from 4.1 to 41.6. This increase was examined separately for males and for females (24 of each), and these groups were further separated into high-, medium-, and low-scoring groups by taking the top eight, middle eight, and bottom eight subjects of each sex. The results are presented in Figure 12.1, where gains in S-B IQ are plotted for the high- and low-scoring men and women. As already mentioned,

▼ **TABLE 12.1**

Correlations Between IQ Test Scores at Four Administrations from 1931 to 1969.

Test	1941 (N =138) S-B (Form L)	1956 (N =109 − 111*) S-B (Form L)	WAIS Full	WAIS Verbal	WAIS Performance	1969 (N = 48) S-B (Form L-M)	WAIS Full	WAIS Verbal	WAIS Performance
1931 S-B (Forms L & M)	.65	.59	.64	.60	.54	.41	.39	.28	.29
1941 S-B (Form L)		.85	.80	.81	.51	.68	.53	.57	.18
1956 S-B (Form L)			.83	.89	.46	.77	.58	.68	.14
1956 WAIS Full				.87	.84	.72	.73	.69	.41
Verbal					.59	.73	.63	.70	.20
Performance						.36	.67	.47	.57
1969 S-B (Form L-M)							.77	.86	.36
1969 WAIS Full								.87	.74
Verbal									.38

Note: S-B is the Stanford-Binet test, given at all ages, and WAIS is the Wechsler Adult Intelligence Scale, given in 1956 and 1969. All correlations are significant beyond the .01 level. From "Intelligence at Middle Age: A Thirty-Eight Year Follow-Up," by J. Kangas and K. Bradway, 1971, *Developmental Psychology, 5,* pp. 333–337, Table 2. The 1931–1956 portion of the table is reprinted from an article by Katherine P. Bradway and Clare C. Thompson, 1962, *Journal of Educational Psychology.* Copyright 1962 by the American Psychological Association. Reprinted by permission. *Because of incomplete data for two of the subjects, the number of total subjects on which any one correlation is based varies from 109 to 111.

continual gains were recorded for all groups, including the medium groups, which are not shown. But one group seemed to gain much less than the others: the high-scoring group of women. This result may or may not be caused by a ceiling effect (see Chapters 10 and 11), because the men with high scores show a substantial increase. Since we do not know whether the men and women scoring highly were equivalent initially, and since the low-scoring women improved dramatically, a ceiling effect is a possibility.

Although this study cannot be considered conclusive in itself, it is in general agreement with others in showing that measured intelligence does remain *relatively* stable over a large portion of one's life, from early childhood to middle age. This also means that early measures of mental development can predict later intelligence, which Bornstein and Sigman (1986) confirmed in an important longitudinal study.

Age as a Variable

In the Kangas and Bradway study, the primary variable of interest was age. As discussed previously, age is a subject variable. Subject variables, by definition, cannot be experimentally manipulated. Instead, a researcher can only select instances that satisfy different categories and study those instances. Thus, research with subject variables is largely correlational in nature; researchers can identify dependent variables that change with variations in a subject variable, but it is difficult to pin causation on the subject variable and not on some possibly confounded factor that varies with the subject variable. Studies with age as a subject variable clearly illustrate the difficulty of showing age as a causative variable.

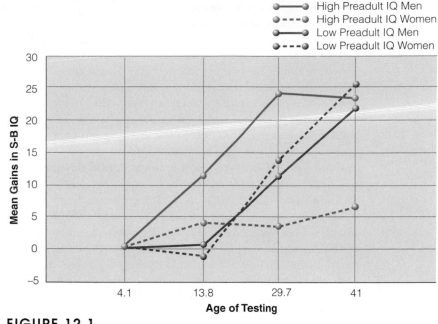

▼ FIGURE 12.1

Mean Gains in S-B IQ at Successive Mean Ages for Men and Women of Differing Preadult IQ Levels. From "Intelligence at Middle Age: A Thirty-Eight Year Follow-up," by J. Kangas & K. Bradway, 1971, *Developmental Psychology, 5,* pp. 333–337, Figure 1. Copyright 1971 by the American Psychological Association. Reprinted by permission.

The most typical experimental design in which age is varied is called a **cross-sectional design.** In this design, a researcher takes a cross section of the population and tests the subjects in the experiment or procedure of interest. If a researcher were interested in how intelligence varied with age, she or he might test people who were 5, 10, 15, 20, 25, 30, 35, 40, 45, 50, 55, 60, 65, 70, and 75 years old. If 25 people were tested at each age, then 375 people would need to be tested. In fact, this is a quite common research design, although the large number of ages sampled is atypical. This design for developmental research has been faulted on important grounds. It has been argued that many other factors are likely to be confounded with age in this sort of design. For example, people who are 25 in 1997 are likely to differ from people who are 65 or 75 on a number of important dimensions: The older subjects will have been raised differently and educated differently, are more likely to have immigrated to the United States, are more likely to have served in the armed forces, and so on. These confoundings have been called **cohort effects,** which refer to effects of the different sorts of people (the **cohorts**) who grow up with people of differing ages.

Your cohorts, such as your classmates, are necessarily different from the cohorts of your grandparents. Another crucial difference in many studies of intellectual performance is that older people are likely to have had fewer years of formal education than younger people. Thus, if in using a cross-sectional research design, researchers discover differences among people of different ages, they will have difficulty showing that age is responsible for the difference rather than any number of confounded factors.

Many cross-sectional studies of intelligence that have been conducted show a common pattern of performance: Intelligence (as measured on a standard test) increases steadily into the early 20s, then drops gradually until about age 60, and then declines more quickly thereafter. The conclusion, then, is rather gloomy, since many researchers inferred that intelligence leveled off or even dropped after people turned 20. However, in retrospect and with evidence from other studies, it seems a more likely conclusion that cross-sectional studies of intelligence are flawed by all the factors just mentioned, particularly differences in education over the decades. In fact, as we have just seen, when Kangas and Bradway used a different research design to ask the question of how age affects intelligence, they concluded that intelligence continually *increased* across the ages in the study.

Kangas and Bradway used a **longitudinal design.** In these designs, the same group of subjects is tested repeatedly over time, all the confoundings inherent in the cross-sectional design are avoided. Thus, a researcher may be more confident in some cases that age rather than confounded subject variables is responsible for whatever changes observed in performance. However, the longitudinal design is not without problems, either. Imagine that a researcher in 1950 was interested in how age affected people's attitudes toward war and whether the United States should have a strong military capability. If people were measured in 1950, their attitudes might generally have been quite favorable, since the United States had recently experienced the success of World War II. However, if these people were tested 20 years later, at the height of the unpopular Vietnam War, their attitudes might have been much less favorable.

This example illustrates the problem of **history effects,** the confounding of test date with age. That is, societal events (e.g., World War II and the Vietnam War) unique to the time of test may have a significant effect on the behavior of interest (e.g., expressed attitudes about the war). Obviously, a researcher would be rash to conclude that people's attitudes toward war and defense grow less favorable as they age.

Another problem with the longitudinal design involves repeated testing. Subjects in longitudinal studies are, by definition, measured multiple times. Therefore, the careful researcher must try to ensure that performance does not reflect previous experience with the test. A final problem with longitudinal studies is subject attrition. Across time, people may drop out of the experiment (from death or moving away), and this dropout rate increases across time. In fact, dropout rates can be as high as 50 percent in some longitudinal studies (Pedhazur & Pedhazur Schmelkin, 1991). Unfortunately, subjects do not drop out of studies randomly. In other words, there may be important differences between subjects who stay in a study and those who do not. In general, longitudinal designs will not lead to sound conclusions about how age alters behavior when experiential changes during the period between tests may have produced the change.

Given these problems of cross-sectional and longitudinal designs, how can psychologists perform sound research on developmental differences? In fact, many of the developmental studies on which psychologists depend have employed cross-sectional and longitudinal studies (with the former predominating).

However, Schaie (1977) advocated other research designs that allow more unambiguous assessments of age changes in performance. One of these, the **cross-sequential design,** is illustrated in Figure 12.2, which shows how people born in 4 successive years (1987–1990) might be tested later in 4 successive years (2006–2009). Each column of the figure represents a cross-sectional design, since people of different ages are being tested in one year. Similarly, each row represents a longitudinal design, since people of the same age are tested repeatedly as they age.

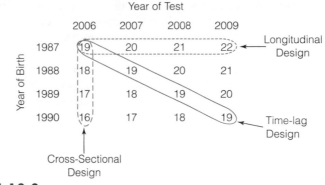

▼ **FIGURE 12.2**

The Cross-Sequential Research Design for Investigating Developmental Differences. People born in 1987–1990 are tested repeatedly in 2006–2009. The number in each cell is the age of the person when tested.

In addition, Figure 12.2 illustrates a third type of design in the diagonal. This is the **time-lag design,** which aims at determining the effects of time of testing while holding age constant. Age at testing is held constant at 19 in the time-lag design, so that any changes observed may be attributed to the changing eras in which people are tested. However, age in this design is confounded with both the year of birth and the year of test. In the entire cross-sequential design, if both the longitudinal and cross-sectional components show some dependent variable changing with age and the time-lag component shows no change with time of testing while holding age constant, then a researcher may safely attribute the observed changes to age itself and not some confounded factor.

12.2   EXPERIMENTAL TOPICS AND RESEARCH ILLUSTRATIONS

Topic   *Operational Definitions*
Illustration   *Intelligence*

Consider the following game, which is called the **imitation game.** The imitation game is a hypothetical experiment devised by Turing (1950) in an article titled "Computing Machinery and Intelligence." Turing's purpose was to devise a situation that would allow one to assess whether a machine could think.

It is played with three people, a man (A), a woman (B), and an interrogator (C) who may be of either sex. The interrogator stays in a room apart from the other two. The object of the game for the interrogator is to determine which of the other two is the man and which is the woman. He (the interrogator) knows them by labels X and Y, and at the end of the game he says either "X is A and Y is B" or "X is B and Y is A." The interrogator is allowed to put questions to A and B thus: C: "Will X please tell me the length of his or her hair?" Now suppose that X is actually A; then A must answer. It is A's object in the game to try to cause C to make the wrong identification. His answer might therefore be, "My hair is shingled, and the longest strands are about nine inches long." To ensure that tone of voice does not help the interrogator, the answers should be written or, better still, typewritten. The ideal arrangement is to have a teleprinter communicating between the two rooms. Alternatively, the question and answers can be repeated by an intermediary. The object of the game for the third player (B) is to help the interrogator. The best strategy for her is probably to give truthful answers. She can add such things as "I am the woman, don't listen to him!" to her answers, but it will avail nothing as the man can make similar remarks.

We now ask the question, "What will happen when a machine takes the part of A in this game?" Will the interrogator decide incorrectly as often when the game is played like this as he does when the game is played between a man and a woman? These questions replace our original question, "Can machines think?" (Turing, 1950, pp. 433–434).

The imitation game is usually called the **Turing test.** Presumably, the test could determine whether any machine, computer or otherwise, had intelligence. The criterion for intelligence in machines is specified in Turing's test: A machine would be called intelligent if an interrogator physically separated from a machine and a person could not distinguish between their typewritten answers to questions. More bluntly, a machine whose output is capable of imitating a human has intelligence.

Turing argued that, in principle at least, a machine would be taken for a human in the imitation game. To many psychologists and computer scientists, the Turing test is a valid one for determining intelligence. On the basis of the arguments supporting the Turing test, the belief in the possibility of **artificial intelligence (AI)** has become widespread. There are two general views about AI (Searle, 1980). The first, called **strong AI,** is the belief, following Turing, that machines can have intelligence. Put another way, the strong AI position states that it is possible for machines to possess a cognitive state that would be called intelligence if a person possessed that cognitive state. The cognitive state is realized in the program that runs the machine. Intelligence in this view is simply the manipulation of the formal symbols in the program. The second type of AI, called **weak AI,** involves using computer programs to model human intelligence; it tests theories of cognition by means of computer programs. The weak AI approach has not generated much disagreement, and we will not consider it here. Instead, we will focus on the strong AI position, because it has generated substantial controversy.

Operational Definitions

Many consider the Turing test valid because it has two important features. The first is the fact that evaluation of machine intelligence using the imitation game involves an experiment: whether an interrogator believes a machine is equivalent to a person. The second feature is more important for our purposes. The experiment described by Turing yields an operational definition.

Operational definitions were discussed in Chapter 6, using the concept of threshold as an example. Recall that an operational definition is a formula for building a construct, such as intelligence, in a way that other scientists can duplicate, by specifying the operations used to produce and measure it. An operational definition of hunger might specify withholding food from a dog for a time and then measuring how much the dog eats. Likewise, according to Turing's operational definition of intelligence, we specify the production of intelligence, a machine program that answers questions, and we measure intelligence by the amount of deception that the answers produce. This seems to be a perfectly acceptable operational definition, so why has it generated so much debate?

The primary reason that the Turing test is controversial is the fact that operational definitions are reliable in principle but not necessarily valid. The major value of an operational definition is to facilitate communication. In this case, if someone claims that machines are intelligent, it refers to the fact that the machine passed the Turing test and, presumably, nothing more.

In terms of clarity of expression, the Turing test appears to be adequate. The conditions necessary for consistently (i.e., reliably) producing what Turing calls intelligence are precisely given. However, the debate about strong AI centers on the issue of whether the Turing test adequately captures what we would call intelligence in humans. Thus, there are disagreements about the validity of the Turing test as a definition of intelligence. Validity in the current context refers to the truth or soundness of the definition. The term **construct validity** refers to the extent to which the test (e.g., the Turing test) measures the construct (e.g., intelligence) that it is supposed to measure. Is the Turing test defining intelligence, or is it defining something else? Does the amount of deception produced by the computer reflect intelligence?

Operational definitions nearly always are limited in their applicability, which means that their validity will suffer. Reconsider the operational definition of hunger that was presented earlier: withhold food for a time and observe the amount eaten. Does this adequately specify what we mean by hunger? Probably not. Humans eat for a variety of reasons, only one of which has to do with food privation. Sometimes we eat to be sociable, sometimes we eat because we desire a particular type of food, and sometimes we eat because we have not eaten for several hours. Furthermore, the preceding operational definition is not symmetrical, because not eating does not mean that our stomachs are full. Sometimes we do not eat because we have an upset stomach, sometimes we do not eat because we are trying to lose weight, and sometimes we do not eat because we have just eaten. To characterize the concept of hunger in a way that accounts for these kinds of observations, we need to have multiple operational definitions that fit together in a coherent theory. We have to use converging operations (see Chapters 7 and 14).

Much of the criticism against strong AI is of the sort that could be leveled against our definition of hunger. "Machines are not human. But can a computer talk? Can it write sonnets?" Turing anticipated some of these criticisms and believes that they can be answered in time—yes, a computer program can do those things in such a fashion that an observer (interrogator) would not know that a machine produced them. As Turing (1950) said,

> The question and answer method seems to be suitable for introducing almost any one of the fields of human endeavor that we wish to include. We do not wish to penalize the machine for its inability to shine in beauty competitions, nor to penalize a man for losing in a race against an airplane. The conditions of our game make these disabilities irrelevant. The "witnesses" can brag, if they consider it advisable, as much as they please about their charms, strength or heroism, but the interrogator cannot demand practical demonstrations. (p. 435)

Some of the critiques and Turing's rebuttal may be empirical questions that could be resolved by observation and experiment, but even if machines were developed that could do these things, there are additional criticisms. We now address a criticism of the validity of the Turing test.

The Chinese Room

A major argument against the possibility of strong AI was developed by the philosopher Searle (1980, 1990), and his objections relate to the fundamental validity of the Turing test. Searle also uses a hypothetical experiment to bolster his argument. He asks us to imagine a person who does not know the Chinese language. For purposes of our discussion, let us suppose that the person is you. You are isolated in a room, and in it is a complete instruction book written in your native language that specifies what you are to do when a piece of paper comes into the room with certain squiggles on it. The instructions tell you to match those squiggles to certain cards that are in the room with you. These cards have different patterns of lines on them as well. When you have found the card or cards you were instructed to find, you then put them in a slot that drops the card(s) outside the room.

Unbeknownst to you, the cards have Chinese characters on them, and also unbeknownst to you, you are actually answering questions in Chinese that were asked in Chinese. The thought experiment assumes that your instructions are detailed enough to allow you to answer the questions adequately even though you do not understand any Chinese—you do not even know that you are manipulating Chinese symbols. Thus, you are taking part in a version of the Turing test, because people are asking "the room" questions in Chinese (hence the name **Chinese room**), and the interrogators should not be able to distinguish your answers from those given by a person who speaks Chinese. You are adequately manipulating a set of formal symbols, but these symbols have no meaning for you.

Searle believes that you would pass the Turing test in a real Chinese room competition. Does that mean you are intelligent in Chinese? Searle's answer is no. You do not understand any Chinese, yet you pass the Turing test. You are functioning just the same as a computer that fools an interrogator into believing that a human rather than a machine is answering questions. The computer program, like you in the Chinese room, manipulates symbols, and, like you, the computer does not attach meaning or understanding to the symbols. According to Searle, this must mean that the Turing test is an invalid way to show that machines have intelligence.

Searle adds to his argument by suggesting that true understanding apparently requires a brain that has causal powers in the situation under examination. You do not understand Chinese in the same way that you understand your native language, because you cannot produce it. All you can do with Chinese, and presumably all a computer can do in any "intelligent" activity, is follow the instructions on how to manipulate symbols. To produce intelligent behavior, the symbols that are manipulated must have content or meaning. Since human minds have meaningful contents and computer programs do not, programs cannot be intelligent. Searle (1990) contends that biologically based machines such as our brains may not be the only things that can think, but he regards the possibility of creating artificial thinking devices as, at best, a project for the distant future.

Searle's Chinese room argument and his position about brains have not gone unchallenged (see Churchland & Churchland, 1990; Hauser, 1997). The basic issues seem to be these: What counts as an adequate test for intelligence? Is the behavior of a device that simply manipulates symbols enough to count as intelligence? The strong AI answer is yes. Searle's reply is no—a program that simulates a speaker of Chinese does not understand Chinese, just as a program that simulates digestion does not digest food.

Defining Intelligence

A question you might now ask is, "Aren't there other operational definitions of intelligence that are generally accepted?" The short answer is no. Intelligence has been associated with all kinds of measures. For example, recently, fluid intelligence has been associated with working memory ability (Engle, 2002; Engle, Tuholski, Laughlin, & Conway, 1999) and certain brain locales (e.g., Duncan, 2003). Here we examine some other definitions of intelligence and some additional problems associated with operationally defining concepts.

You may have noticed that we did not define intelligence when we discussed reliability in the first section of this chapter. We omitted it because test developers usually have a pragmatic problem at hand. Binet merely wanted to determine the appropriate grade level for students in French schools. In these pragmatic circumstances, the validity of the test is determined by some criterion, such as success in school. In fact, the Stanford-Binet and Wechsler tests do a good job of predicting academic performance. So, you might be tempted to say that intelligence is what tests measure if they have good criterion validity (the tests predict academic performance). The problem here is twofold. On the one hand, most intelligence tests focus on mathematical and verbal abilities, which means that they ignore other kinds of important intellectual activities, including musical ability and the ability to understand other people. On the other hand, intellectual ability in an academic sense is often viewed as a limited and culturally biased way of defining intelligence. The typical IQ test does not measure one's ability to succeed in life or adapt to the environment. So, the argument goes, the IQ scores of people may have nothing to do with common sense or leading a productive life. Furthermore, even if people were productive and had common sense, their IQ scores would not predict their success in another context, such as surviving on a desert island or faring well in the jungle. In addition, the IQ tests are, according to some critics, a reflection of white upper-middle class values and do not reflect what intelligence means for society as a whole. The finding that cultural stereotypes affect performance on other tests supports this alleged bias (Steele & Aronson, 1995). For example, women do worse on a difficult math test after they have been exposed to the stereotype that "women can't do math" (Spencer, Steele, & Quinn, 1999).

Thus, accepting the definition of intelligence as what intelligence tests measure does not solve many problems. It is limited in its range of expertise, and the definition is likely to be contested by the general public's conception of what intelligence is all about (Sternberg, 1995).

Let us briefly consider a contemporary attempt to define intelligence operationally. It is a theory of **multiple intelligences** and was developed by Gardner (1983, 2000a). His goal was to broaden the standard academic definition of intelligence to include intelligences (to use his terms) that are less tied to Western cultural values than those associated with the standard intelligence test. Gardner presents cross-cultural, psychological, psychometric, developmental, and neurological evidence for the existence of seven facets of intelligence. These multiple intelligences are bodily-kinesthetic, linguistic, logical-mathematical, musical, self-understanding (intrapersonal), social success (interpersonal), and spatial. Of these, only linguistic, logical-mathematical, and spatial are tested on standard IQ tests. For each of the seven intelligences, Gardner tries to show that there are separate neural structures associated with them, that each has a separate developmental history, that a person can be very good in one area and poor or mediocre in others, and that cross-culturally each of the areas can be shown to play prominent roles, though in different ways. Gardner (2000a) suggested that there may be more than seven different intelligences. In the 2000a book, he explores the possibility of a naturalist intelligence to add to the original list of intelligences. The naturalist intelligence concerns how people glean information about the natural world. Gardner has also explored the possibility of a spiritual intelligence and an existential intelligence (for a sampling of the various positions, see Edwards, 2003; Emmons, 2000; Gardner, 1998a; Gardner, 2000a; Gardner, 2000b; Kwilecki, 2000).

Rather than examine each of the intelligences, let us consider how Gardner analyzes one: music. First, Gardner shows that the underlying neural structures for music are different from those associated with other intelligences. Musical ability is associated with the right hemisphere of the brain, unlike linguistic ability, which is associated with the left hemisphere. People with damage to the left hemisphere are often **aphasic,** which means they have a disorder of language. Interestingly, although aphasics often have trouble speaking, they can usually sing, and, even in the rare case that they cannot sing words, their musical abilities are otherwise undisturbed. Contrarily, people with damage to the right hemisphere often suffer from **tonal agnosia.** Tonal agnosics are unable to sing, and their ordinary vocal inflections are diminished. Otherwise, the language facility of people suffering from tonal agnosia is intact.

The next thing that Gardner notes is the tremendous individual differences in musical intelligence. This can be assessed by special tests (i.e., psychometrically), but it is also obvious in everyday observation. Mozart was obviously a musical genius. At an early age, this prodigy was composing elegant symphonic music, and he was performing before the royal courts of Europe before adolescence (see Gardner, 1998b, Chap. 4, for a discussion of Mozart).

Gardner presents further evidence for a separate musical intelligence, which we need not consider here. The point is, for each of the intelligences he proposes, he tries to define them operationally along several dimensions. This means that he is using converging operations to refine his concept of intelligence. Is he successful in defining intelligence? Is Gardner's theory of multiple intelligences *the* definition of intelligence? As you might expect, the answer to those questions is no, or at least the answer is no for some psychologists.

One naysayer of Gardner's theory is the psychologist Robert Sternberg, who has taken the information-processing approach to defining intelligence (an accessible treatment of Sternberg's work is *The Triarchic Mind,* 1988). Sternberg's major criticism of Gardner's approach argues that the processes underlying the seven intelligences are not specified. Sternberg suggests that Gardner simply names the intelligences without specifying exactly what they are and what they are not. A second criticism that Sternberg makes is to say that intelligence is general, but Gardner's intelligences are specific. According to Sternberg, Gardner has identified talents rather than intelligences. Lacking musical talent should not be too damaging to a person and may go unrecognized. However, a person who could not plan or reason, which are important components of intelligence for Sternberg, could not function in the world.

Sternberg's criticisms are taken into account in his own theory of intelligence (e.g., Sternberg, 1997), which emphasizes the ability to process information, synthesize information in novel ways, and adapt to new situations. Sternberg's operational definition of intelligence suggests that intelligent behavior reflects the ability to solve problems established in a social context (see Sternberg & Salter, 1982). This view is prominent and is accepted by many psychologists interested in the information-processing approach (see Kantowitz, 1989a).

Partially in response to Sternberg's approach, Gardner (2007) argues that there are several ways in which to view minds and intelligence. One way is to consider the adaptation to the needs of the world (sound familiar?). In his book *Five Minds for the Future*, he describes the cognitive abilities that people should develop "if we are to thrive in the world during the eras to come" (p. 1). The five features of future minds are: the disciplinary mind—one that has mastered a school of thought (science, history, law, etc.); the synthesizing mind—one that can integrate ideas from several disciplines; the creating mind—one that can pose and solve new problems; the respectful mind—one that is sensitive to human differences; and the ethical mind—one that satisfies a person's responsibilities as a citizen.

But is the adaptive problem-solving ability of Sternberg and now Gardner a kind of intelligence? In these views, would writing a poem or composing a symphony be a manifestation of intelligence or simply a talent? Likewise, are we to consider the ability to solve everyday problems associated, say, with plumbing or automobile mechanics an intellectual ability? Answers to these questions require a cogent theory bolstered by confirming data based on converging operations derived from many operational definitions. Although operational definitions clearly play an important role in the development of scientific theories, the use of operational definitions has both advantages and disadvantages. On the plus side, operational definitions can facilitate scientific communication and, hence, the reliability of scientific research. Such reliable work sets the stage for elaboration and refinement of concepts. On the negative side, operational definitions can be controversial definitions of the concepts in question. Although they can be valid, their meaning is often subject to debate. The definitions need to fit into a network of other concepts that lead to the description and prediction of behavior. Certainly, progress in understanding both natural and artificial intelligence depends on a satisfactory definition of what the concept of intelligence entails.

12.3   EXPERIMENTAL TOPICS AND RESEARCH ILLUSTRATIONS

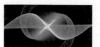

Topic   *Regression Artifacts*
Illustration   *Educational Assessment*

An issue related to the study of intelligence and individual differences revolves around attempts by psychologists and educators to improve the performance of individuals and the importance of evaluating such attempts. As you might suspect, accurate measurement lies at the heart of assessing change. Whenever measurement error occurs, the possibility exists that we will wrongly conclude that some sort of change has occurred or failed to occur. Although this statement may appear less than profound to you, a number of psychological studies have been faulted for failing to take adequate account of its truth.

Certain designs or procedures for gathering data are particularly susceptible to bias caused by measurement error. Those designs, remember, are termed **quasi-experimental designs,** because subjects are not randomly assigned to treatment and control groups (Campbell & Stanley, 1966). Subjects in these groups may be matched on a number of factors by a researcher, but it is difficult to ensure that important differences between the groups did not exist prior to the start of the treatment. This problem is amplified when the experimental (treatment) group and control (no treatment) group are not matched prior to the study on the variable they will be tested on at the end of the study. For example, a group of children from one neighborhood might be selected as an experimental group to test a new training course for teaching running. A second group of children might be chosen from the same neighborhood to serve as a control group. After 6 weeks of training of the experimental group, both groups might be tested for running speed. This would be a quasi-experimental design, because the children were not assigned randomly to one of the two groups. Even if the experimenter reported that the two groups had been of the same average height, weight, and age, we would not know for certain that the average running speed of the two groups had been the same prior to the treatment. In fact, even if control subjects had been picked to match the running speeds of the experimental group, we could not be sure that group differences following training were owing to the effects of training. The possibility would remain that the two groups had been sampled from populations that differed prior to the study. When population differences exist, there is the possibility of being misled by what are known as **regression artifacts,** or experimental effects produced by "statistical regression," rather than by experimental manipulations. We discussed regression artifacts in Chapter 2.

Perhaps an example will help here. Suppose that you are an A student and that your neighbor is a C student, although you both have similar backgrounds. On one particular assignment, you both receive a B. In an effort to improve, your neighbor decides to attend a series of help sessions. Your instructor decides to evaluate the effectiveness of the help sessions by comparing the future grades of help-session students with future grades of non–help-session students who are similar in background and received the same grades on the previous assignment. You are selected as the matched student to be compared with your friend.

On the next assignment, you receive an A-, and your friend receives a C+. The course of events in this evaluation program is illustrated in Table 12.2. Note the changes in the criterion grade as a function of the person's mean grade. Should the instructor conclude that help sessions are harmful because your friend went from a B to a C+, whereas you went from a B to an A-? Probably not, since both of you merely regressed toward your mean grades. The effect seen in this little study is probably not a true treatment effect but rather a regression artifact caused by the fact that you and your friend were not truly equivalent students. The help session may even have

▼ **TABLE 12.2**

Illustration of How Regression to the Mean Can Confuse the Interpretation of the Outcome of a Quasi-Experiment. Although Both People Were Matched as B Students, Their Performance, with or without the Help Session, Regressed Toward Their Actual Average Grade. Did the Help Session Help?

Person	Mean Grade	Matching Grade	Help Session	Criterion Grade
You	A	B	No	A−
Neighbor	C	B	Yes	C+

benefited your friend, since her or his grade was higher than the usual grade of C. If B students on the first assignment had been randomly assigned to help-session or non–help-session groups and then compared on the basis of grades on the second assignment, accurate assessment of the effect of help sessions on students' grades could have been obtained.

The phenomenon of regression to the mean occurs because all psychological measures are subject to a certain amount of variability. With any measure that is not perfectly reliable, the group of subjects obtaining the highest scores contains not only those who really belong in the highest category but also others who were placed in this category by chance errors of measurement. On a retest, these chance measurement errors will not necessarily occur in the same direction. Thus, the scores of the highest group will tend to average lower on a retest. Similarly, a group selected for poor performance on an original test will tend to average higher on a retest. The Psychology in Action section at the end of this chapter is intended to give you a better understanding of this point through a simple demonstration of regression to the mean. The importance of regression artifacts such as this in quasi-experimental studies of compensatory education has been the subject of much debate. One influential study of the effects of the Head Start program of the 1960s (Cicirelli & Granger, 1969) received particular attention. In this study, called the Westinghouse–Ohio study, children completing their Head Start experience were randomly selected for evaluation. Then they defined a control population of children from the same area who had been eligible for the program but had not attended. Control children were selected at random to be matched with experimental children on the basis of sex, racial-ethnic group membership, and kindergarten attendance. Note that the children were selected from two different groups: one that did attend Head Start and one that did not. After researchers made the final selection of experimental and control subjects, they compiled and compared additional measures of socioeconomic status, demographic status, and attitude for the two groups. Differences were slight. Measures of experimental (Head Start) and control (no Head Start) children's academic achievement and potential were then computed and compared. The general conclusion from this large study was that Head Start was not effective in removing the effects of poverty and social disadvantage.

Other psychologists (Campbell & Erlebacher, 1970a) were quick to criticize this study on several grounds. First, they pointed out that the results of the study were undoubtedly caused partially by regression artifacts. Worse, the magnitude of the artifacts could not be estimated, casting doubt over the entire set of findings.

The basic problem is one of matching (see Chapter 2 for a similar example). Cicirelli and coworkers laudably tried to match a sample of disadvantaged children who had been in the Head Start program with others from the same area who had not been in the program. Later differences between the two groups should have been due to the program, right? Not necessarily. It is right only if the two samples came from the same underlying population distributions, which is unlikely. What is likely is that the two populations differed, with the disadvantaged "treatment" children coming from a population that was poorer in ability than the "control" children. The "treatment" children who attended Head Start were usually preselected to be from a disadvantaged background (which is why they were included in the program), whereas the "controls" who were not in the program may have come from a different population that was greater in ability. The basic problem is that subjects were not randomly assigned to conditions, so the researchers had to try to match control subjects with experimental subjects. To match two samples from these different populations, the experimenters would have had to select children *above* the population mean for the disadvantaged treatment group and *below* the mean for the control group. But when this is done, the dreaded regression artifact will always be introduced. When each group is retested, the performance of individuals will tend to regress to the mean of the group; in other words, the disadvantaged group will tend to perform worse in this example, and the control group will tend to perform better.

This regression to the mean will happen in the absence of any treatment being given to either group and despite matching. The effect is the same as that in the previous example of the grades of the superior student increasing to A- from B and the other's decreasing from B to C-, when the two students were erroneously "matched" as B students. Since we already expect a difference between the groups (favoring the control) in this situation because of regression to the mean, how do we evaluate the outcome of our study? Cicirelli and coworkers found no difference between the groups. Since we might expect the treatment (Head Start) group to actually be worse owing to regression artifacts, does this mean the group actually improved owing to Head Start? It is impossible to answer this question, because in the Westinghouse–Ohio evaluation of Head Start, the direction or magnitude of regression artifacts could not be assessed.

In the preceding paragraph, we made reasonable suppositions concerning regression artifacts in this type of study. But the conclusion that Head Start had no effect cannot be drawn from the Westinghouse–Ohio study. More properly, no conclusion can be drawn on the basis of that study, since it is not known how regression artifacts affected the results.

In general, then, regression artifacts of a difficult-to-estimate magnitude are highly probable in this type of study, and this fact is acknowledged by all. Why, then, would such studies be conducted, particularly when very important political, economic, and social decisions might be based on their results? This question was raised by Campbell and Erlebacher (1970a, 1970b) and by Cicirelli and his supporters (Cicirelli, 1970; Evans & Schiller, 1970). Their answers were quite different, and they represent the type of issue that frequently confronts scientists but that science can never resolve. Campbell and Erlebacher proposed that bad information was worse than no information at all: If properly controlled experiments could not be performed, then no data should be gathered. On the other side of the issue, Evans and Schiller replied, "This position fails to understand that every program *will* be evaluated by the most arbitrary, anecdotal, partisan and subjective means" (p. 220). Campbell and Erlebacher concurred but stated, "We judge it fundamentally misleading to lend the prestige of science to any report in a situation where no scientific evaluation is possible" (1970b, p. 224). As an ultimate solution, they proposed that a commission "composed of experts who are not yet partisans in this controversy" be convened to decide the matter.

It may be impossible to decide this issue on strictly rational grounds, but we can all agree that a research study should be conducted according to the best scientific procedures available. How could the Westinghouse–Ohio study have been done appropriately?

One solution would be to randomly assign all the children to different groups and put them in different programs, to pit the effectiveness of the programs against one another. One difficulty here would be that the training programs might turn out to be equally effective. Then one could not know if any of them were better than no program at all.

The best way to design the Westinghouse–Ohio study would have been to randomly assign participants to either the no-treatment or the treatment (Head Start) condition in the beginning. There is no substitute for random assignment in eliminating confounding factors. But it seems unfair to give half the children who seek the help of a remedial program no training whatsoever. Of course, there is no guarantee at the outset that the program will do them any good; that is what the study is intended to discover. The same issue occurs in medical research when a control group with a disease is given a placebo rather than a treatment drug. It is possible in both cases that in the end, more people benefit from careful research into the effectiveness of treatments than may be harmed because treatment is withheld.

What happens when children are randomly assigned to treatment and no-treatment conditions? Consider a 4½-year longitudinal experiment conducted by Breitmayer and Ramey (1986). The subjects in their work were 80 children from disadvantaged families in a large U.S. city. At birth, half the children were randomly assigned to be in the no-treatment control group. The control children attended a day care center until the end of the experiment, but they did not receive any special educational treatment. The other half of the children were randomly assigned to the treatment group. Their day care center included a Head Start–type program that was designed to prevent mental retardation. All subjects in the experiment had a normal birth and weighed at least 5 pounds. In the first minute after birth, the neonates were assessed for their biological responsiveness on a scale similar to the one devised by Brazelton that was described in Chapter 3. The results of this testing indicated that slightly more than one-half of the babies in the control and experimental groups were not biologically optimal immediately after birth. So, we wind up with four groups in this experiment: experimental (educationally enriched day care)/optimal; control (ordinary day care)/optimal; experimental/nonoptimal; and control/nonoptimal.

Measures of intelligence at age 4½ indicated three important findings. First, the children who were biologically optimal in the first minute after birth scored higher on the intelligence tests than did the children who were biologically nonoptimal.

Second, the educationally treated children fared somewhat better than control subjects on the verbal portion of the test, and the experimental subjects far exceeded the control subjects on the performance component. Finally, most of the effect of education was owing to an interaction: the nonoptimal control subjects did especially poorly on all aspects of the intelligence test. Illustrative results are shown in Figure 12.3. This interaction is similar to the example of synergism mentioned in Chapter 2. Since after-the-fact examination revealed highly similar home situations for the two groups, Breitmayer and Ramey were able to safely conclude that early education has some important benefits— especially for children who are not biologically optimal at birth. For the reader who is intrigued by this finding, we recommend Ellsworth and Ames' (1998) book on Head Start, which provides a broad picture of the program and its aims (see also Arnold, Fisher, Doctoroff, & Dobbs, 2002; Mantzicopoulos, 2003; Slaughter-Defoe & Rubin, 2001).

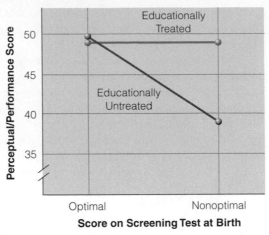

▼ **FIGURE 12.3**

The results of Breitmayer and Ramey (1986), showing an interaction of educational treatment and health at birth on the perceptual/performance score obtained at age fifty-four months. Similar, though not as pronounced, interactions were seen for scores on the verbal and quantitative portions of the intelligence tests.

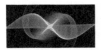

FROM PROBLEM TO EXPERIMENT

THE NUTS AND BOLTS

Problem   *What Roles Do Motivation and Emotion Play in Intellectual Performance?*

Many of you may be math phobic; others of you may hate multiple-choice exams. If you fall into either of those groups, or if you have particular intellectual likes or dislikes that can influence your performance on exams, then you are showing the effects of motivation and emotion on intellectual performance. Such likes and dislikes should be particularly important for elementary school teachers to identify, because once a student starts to dislike something, a snowball effect could arise. For example, suppose a young student begins to dislike math for some reason. That student not only will find math tests aversive but also will find learning about math aversive. Not learning newer math concepts will lead to poor test performance, which will increase the aversion, and so on.

The emotional views toward cognitive pursuits need not be specific. Dweck and her associates have identified two general goals that children seem to have when undertaking intellectual activities, and these goals are manifest in the primitive theories that children have about intelligence (Dweck, 1999; Dweck & Bempechat, 1983; Dweck & Elliott, 1983; Levy, Plaks, Hong, Chiu, & Dweck, 2001). Some children adopt what are called *performance goals*. These children seem to be motivated by not looking foolish; they want to look smart and not receive negative evaluations from their peers or their teachers. Children who adopt performance goals have what Dweck calls an *entity theory* of intelligence. These children believe that the fixed intelligence that they have is best assessed by how well others evaluate them and how well they do on intellectual tasks. Other children tend to be motivated by *learning goals*, in which they try to become smarter by learning new skills and knowledge. Children who are motivated by learning goals believe in what Dweck calls an *instrumental incremental theory,* which refers to their belief that intelligence is a set of skills and knowledge that can be increased through hard work and effort. How do these goals affect youngsters' performance? Are the goals beneficial under some circumstances? These are the issues addressed here.

Problem   *How do the motivational goals of children influence their intellectual performance?*

We might expect that how the children's goals influence their performance would interact with the task demands (Hetherington & Parke, 1986). If the situation demands quick, accurate, and correct performance, then we might expect the entity theorists to perform better than if the situation requires new learning and substantial effort. For the instrumental incremental theorists, on the other hand, better performance should occur in the latter situation, which requires effort and new learning.

Hypothesis   *The nature of the task and the children's motivational goals will interact such that intellectual performance will be best in those situations that place emphasis on goals congruent with the children's, and intellectual performance will suffer in those situations in which the task demands and motivational goals are in conflict.*

One experimental design to test this hypothesis calls for two groups of children: *entity* and *instrumental incremental.* Each of these groups should be tested under two conditions: *performance goals* and *learning goals.* Thus, the design would be a mixed one with subject group as a between-subjects variable and test condition a within-subjects variable.

The primary reason for including these two variables is to look for the interaction between them. This is very important when one of the variables is a quasi-independent variable, as subject variables are. Since the subject variable must be selected and not manipulated, it is important to look for the differential effect of a real independent variable on the different levels of the subject variable.

The first thing that must be done in this research is to select subjects in the two groups. Unfortunately, there are no published tests that serve this purpose. However, Dweck has provided a rather straightforward way of distinguishing between entity theorists and instrumental incremental ones. Children are asked to choose one of two statements about intelligence, where one statement reflects performance goals and the other reflects learning goals. So, you would have to make up a number of such pairs of statements (say, 16). A child's score on this test would be the number of times a particular type of statement was selected. An entity score could range from 0 to 16 in this example. Some examples of the types of statements you might generate are:

1. **(a)** You can learn new things, but how smart you are stays pretty much the same.
   (b) Smartness is something you can increase as much as you want to.

2. (a) I feel smart when I don't make mistakes.
   (b) I feel smart when I figure out how to do something.
3. (a) I like school work when I can hand in my papers first.
   (b) I like school work when I learn something new.
4. (a) I feel smart when I get easy work.
   (b) I feel smart when I'm reading a hard book.

The easiest way to determine to which group a child belongs is to calculate the median entity score (i.e., the middle one) for all the children who took the test. Then you assign children to the entity group who scored about the group median, and you assign the rest of the children, those who scored below the median, to the instrumental incremental group. Devising a reliable and valid test could be extremely difficult and time consuming. You may also find it difficult to get a wide spread in scores on your test. To ensure that you obtain many children who score very high and many who score very low, you may need to revise your set of test questions until you find a set that yields a good spread of scores.

After determining the group membership of a number of children (about 15 in each group would be a good minimum number), you will need to devise test situations. Here, the previous work of Dweck and her associates may be of some help. Dweck and Bempechat (1983) describe several kinds of tasks that they asked children in the entity and instrumental incremental groups to choose between and to make estimates as to how well they would do. These tasks differed in their difficulty and in the performance goals (learning or looking smart). After making their choices, all children were given the same task, which was of moderate difficulty. Thus, they manipulated the children's perception of the task by prior instructions. The same sort of procedure could be done in the present experiment. You could use instructions similar to those used by Dweck and have the children then engage in some task. For purposes of testing most children, it is often useful to suggest to them that the test procedure is a game of some sort. This is done to maintain their motivation and interest. For the learning-oriented task, children could be told the following: "In this game you'll probably learn some new things, but you'll also make some mistakes. You might get confused and feel dumb, but you should learn some neat stuff." For the performance-oriented task, the instructions might be: "This game is a lot of fun because it is easier than some. Although you won't learn a lot, it will really show me just how much kids can do." You will then need two tasks, one for each set of instructions. To maintain the children's interest, the two tasks should not be too similar. But with two different tasks you will have to counterbalance the tasks across instructions for the two groups of children. Selecting tasks could be difficult, but the most straightforward way to find them would be to elicit help from a teacher of children who are the same age as your test subjects. The teacher should be able to help you select two intellectual tasks that the typical third-grader, for example, would find to be of moderate difficulty. Let us call the two tasks you select A and B. Adequate counterbalancing and an overview of the design are illustrated in Table 12.3.

It is predicted that the entity group subjects will do more poorly on the task preceded by learning instructions than on the task preceded by performance

▼ **TABLE 12.3**

Design and Counterbalancing for the Combinations of Two Tasks (A and B) and Two Types of Instructions (Performance and Learning). The Numbers in the Table Indicate the Number of Subjects in Each Condition. The Total Number of Subjects in Each Group Is Assumed to Be Sixteen.

Group	First Test	Second Test
	(4) Task A/Performance	Task B/Learning
	(4) Task B/Performance	Task A/Learning
Entity	(4) Task A/Learning	Task B/Performance
	(4) Task B/Learning	Task A/Performance
	(4) Task A/Performance	Task B/Learning
Instrumental	(4) Task B/Performance	Task A/Learning
Incremental	(4) Task A/Learning	Task B/Performance
	(4) Task B/Learning	Task A/Performance

instructions. On the other hand, we expect the instrumental incremental subjects to do better on the task preceded by the learning instructions and more poorly on the task preceded by the performance instructions.

This research project seems to be manageable, with the possible exception of developing the entity theory test. However, research on subject variables, especially with children, poses many difficulties for the researcher. One problem has to do with ethics. Since it is unlikely that a child can give true informed consent to participate in an experiment, the children's parents must be allowed to indicate whether they want their child to participate. This means that you would have to approach an elementary school teacher, elicit his or her consent to test the students, and then have the parents sign a consent form. Your professor will be able to help you devise a consent form that would be acceptable for these purposes.

Another issue that must be resolved is the age of the children. Most earlier work has used children in the primary and middle school grades, and that would be a safe bet here. If the children are too young—say, of preschool age—they may not have a well-developed idea of what it means to be smart. On the other hand, high school students may be too sophisticated in their beliefs about intelligence to allow you to generate different groups of subjects. However, Dweck, Mangels, and Good (2004) report on experiments that successfully enhanced intellectual motivation in college students.

Still another issue has to do with gender. Do you want to test just boys, just girls, or a mixture? Dweck and colleagues (2004) report that boys and girls respond differently to learning and performance situations, so at the very least you would like to make sure that you had the same proportion of each sex in each of your test groups, such as 45 percent boys in each group. On the other hand, if you are interested in the ways in which boys and girls might differ in your situation, you might consider including gender as an additional subject variable.

Research on subject variables is often particularly interesting, and it frequently concerns questions that have practical importance. However, do not lose sight of the fact that subject variables are selected and not manipulated. The conclusions you draw must recognize that you are not working with a true independent variable.

▼ SUMMARY

1. The empirical approach to individual differences is based on finding correlates of the difference in question, such as intelligence tests designed to predict school scores. Analytical theories of individual differences attempt to provide explanations by pointing to differences in the underlying psychological processes. Nature theories of individual differences hold that genetics underlies them, whereas the nurture view focuses on the experiential factors that influence how an organism develops. A more comprehensive view, by Hebb, proposes to account for individual differences by considering six interacting factors.

2. Reliability of measuring instruments and devices is crucial to all scientific investigation, including the study of individual differences. Devising reliable measures of complicated mental abilities such as intelligence is difficult, but if reliable measures are derived, they can be used to investigate such interesting questions as the stability of the quantity, measured over long periods.

3. The most common design used in developmental research is the cross-sectional design, in which people of different ages (a cross section of the population) are tested. Unfortunately, any differences found may be owing to factors confounded with age, such as differences in education or other particular life experiences. In the longitudinal design, the same group of people is tested repeatedly as they age, thus eliminating much of the confounding that occurs in the cross-sectional approach. Unfortunately, in some cases the longitudinal design can also be misleading, when the observed changes are not owing to age per se but to life experiences that just happen to be correlated with age. The cross-sequential design embeds multiple

cross-sectional and longitudinal designs within it and permits evaluation of variation caused by changing times or eras (rather than age) through examination of the time-lag design built into it. In the time-lag design, people of the same age are examined over different eras, thus revealing the effect of era rather than age. The cross-sequential design allows stronger inferences to be made about the effects of age, unconfounded with other factors, but unfortunately such designs are difficult to implement in practice. Most developmental research still relies on the cross-sectional approach, with attempts made to match people on other factors, such as socioeconomic status.

4. Operational definitions of psychological constructs involve specifying the construct in terms of the experimental operations used to study it. The Turing test defines intelligence in such a way that machines could possess intelligence. The controversy raised by this test points to the problem of the validity of operational definitions.

5. When individual differences such as intelligence, weight, or age are examined in experiments, they are referred to as subject variables. By their nature, subject variables preclude random assignment of subjects to conditions; one must avoid concluding that experimental effects are produced by subject variables, because some confounded factor may have produced the effect.

6. In studies in which subjects in two groups (a treatment and a control) are matched on some criterion rather than being randomly assigned to the two groups, there is a great likelihood that statistical regression will affect the results and conclusions drawn. When extreme groups of subjects are selected (extreme on one dimension), their scores

upon retesting will tend toward the mean of the group. This occurs despite matching on other criteria. This can materially affect the outcome of a study, because we expect the scores of the groups to change even without any intervening treatment.

Therefore, it becomes difficult or impossible to evaluate the effect of the treatment in studies employing such *ex post facto* quasi-experimental designs. The only sure way to avoid the problem is to assign subjects randomly to conditions in the first place.

▼ KEY TERMS

analytical approach
aphasic
artificial intelligence (AI)
Chinese room
chronological age
cohort effects
cohorts
construct validity
cross-sectional design
cross-sequential design
empirical approach
face validity
history effects
imitation game
intelligence
longitudinal design
mental age
multiple intelligences

nature theory
nurture view
operational definitions
parallel forms
predictive (criterion) validity
quasi-experimental designs
regression artifacts
regression to the mean
reliability
split-half reliability
strong AI
subject variables
test–retest reliability
time-lag design
tonal agnosia
Turing test
weak AI

▼ DISCUSSION QUESTIONS

1. Often, psychological tests are constructed to measure some psychological construct, such as intelligence, depression, or dietary restraint. One prime requirement is that such tests be reliable. What is reliability? Discuss three different ways of assessing reliability in a psychological test.

2. Discuss reasons that operational definitions are necessary in psychology. Provide two operational definitions for each of the following constructs:
   a. Thirst
   b. Intelligence
   c. Memory capacity
   d. Sexual satisfaction
   e. Fear of snakes
   Does it worry you that there can be more than one definition of the "same" construct?

3. Discuss the advantages and disadvantages of each of the following research designs for developmental research:
   a. Cross-sectional
   b. Longitudinal
   c. Cross-sequential

4. Discuss the strong AI approach to intelligence. Are computers intelligent?

5. A psychotherapist is interested in evaluating the effectiveness of the new therapy she has invented. It is called pet therapy and involves convincing depressed people to keep a dog as a pet, with the hope that caring for a dog will cheer them up. To evaluate the therapy, the therapist gives each of her patients a dog from the Humane Society to care for. She measures depression using a written test

(which has been shown to be reliable) a week before they get the pets and then again 2 months later. She discovers that patients are much less depressed when assessed the second time and thus concludes that pet therapy is a success. Discuss several things wrong with this piece of research and the conclusion drawn from it. How are regression artifacts likely to have played a part? How could the research have been done better?

6. Discuss the following statement: "All experiments involving subject variables are quasi-experiments; the results obtained are always correlational in nature and possibly contaminated by confoundings." Is this statement true? Can you think of exceptions to it? In trying to do so, make a list of all the subject variables you can think of that might be of interest to psychologists.

WEB CONNECTIONS

You can find the home page for Dr. Bala Ambati at:

http://www.mcg.edu/eyes/Ambati_Page.html

The following sites have papers you can download about Howard Gardner's work on multiple intelligences:

http://pzweb.harvard.edu/PIs/HG.htm

http://www.howardgardner.com/Papers/papers.html

The following site details the history of intelligence testing and theories, and it has links to descriptions of major researchers:

http://www.indiana.edu/~intell/

PSYCHOLOGY IN ACTION
A Demonstration of Regression Artifacts

A serious problem in many research domains is known as statistical regression to the mean, or a regression artifact. You can better appreciate this phenomenon by allowing yourself to become a victim of it. Try the following experiment, proceeding through the steps as given:

1. Roll six dice on a table in front of you.
2. Place the three dice showing the lowest numbers on the left and the three dice showing the highest numbers on the right. In case of ties, randomly assign the dice to the two groups.
3. Compute and record the mean number per die for each group of three dice.
4. Raise both hands over your head and loudly proclaim, "Improve, in the name of science."
5. Roll the three low-scoring dice and compute a new mean number per die for the low group.
6. Roll the three high-scoring dice and compute a new mean number per die for the high group.
7. Compare the pretreatment and post-treatment scores for both groups. Combine your data with those of your classmates, if possible.

On the average, this procedure will produce an increase in the performance of the low group and a decrease in the performance of the high group. You might be tempted to conclude that invoking the name of science has a beneficial effect on underachieving dice and that overachieving dice require more individualized attention to maintain their outstanding performance. Such conclusions, however, fail to consider the effects of regression, which reflect the tendency for many types of measures to yield values close to their mean. You know that the roll of a fair die can yield values from 1 to 6 but that the average value from many rolls will be about 3.5. The likelihood of the average of three dice being close to 3.5 is higher than the likelihood of this average being close to 1 or 6. Thus, when you select three dice that give you a low average and roll them again, they will tend to yield a higher average value (a value closer to the mean of 3.5). In the same way, the three dice in the high group should yield a lower value when rolled again. In both cases, what you are observing is regression to the mean. ■

CHAPTER **13**

SOCIAL PSYCHOLOGY

We know more about the atom than ourselves, and the consequences are everywhere to be seen. (CARL KAYSEN)

The behavior of every human is potentially determined by a web of complex social and cultural influences. Many of the acts we perform every day are determined by the culture and society into which we are born and raised. Our experience is limited by our culture, so that we are exposed to only a very small set of the potential actions humans might perform. Most people in our society will never speak Hottentot, sail outrigger canoes, or hunt wildebeest, for the very good reason that these activities are not part of our culture. In each society, the individual's behavior conforms to a large extent to that of his or her "significant others," that is, family, peers, teachers, and so on.

The psychological study of how society affects the individual is part of the field of **social psychology.** This is a large field: A tremendous variety of research topics falls under the general rubric of social psychology. Among other things, it is concerned with how people are influenced to change their attitudes, beliefs, and behavior; how they form impressions of other people; why they like one another; the roots of aggression and violence; and the conditions determining altruism and helping. The list could easily be doubled. But with few exceptions, the topics studied by social psychologists have to do with the impact of society (other people) on the behavior of the individual. Many experiments are motivated by real events of societal importance. For example, later in the chapter we will describe work stimulated by the killing of Amidou Diallo, a black man shot 41 times by white police officers. Diallo was reaching for his wallet; officers believed he was reaching for a weapon. The officers' acquittals provoked protests, legislation, and litigation—all aimed at possible race biases in policing. Could the police officers have been biased by Diallo's race? That is, did his being black play a key role in their misidentification of the wallet as a gun? We return to these questions later in the chapter.

▼ THE ORIGINS OF SOCIAL PSYCHOLOGY

The enterprise of scientific psychology is only about 100 years old, and the application of the scientific method to the study of the interesting and complex phenomena of social psychology is even younger. The first two texts on social psychology appeared in 1908; one was written by William McDougall, a psychologist, and the other was written by E. A. Ross, a sociologist. In both books, the treatment of social psychology is very different from the approach used today. However, McDougall's book had a great impact in the field of psychology as a whole.

He argued strongly that social behavior is largely determined by a variety of instincts that are inborn and relatively unaffected by either the history of a particular person or her or his present social situation.

No one today believes that instinct can explain complex human social behavior in the way that McDougall tried to apply it. More sophisticated notions of how biology and culture interact (recall the discussion of Hebb's views in Chapter 12) in social behavior can be seen in contemporary accounts of a phenomenon such as mate selection. Evolutionary processes (e.g., Buss & Schmitt, 1993) and cultural influences (e.g., Shweder & Sullivan, 1993) must interact to produce mate-selection behavior. Nevertheless, recent analyses point to a crucial role for social and cultural norms in determining how people choose a mate (Eagly & Wood, 1999).

Social psychology became established as an independent field of empirical study during the 1920s and 1930s. Significant work by Sherif (1935) is a highlight of this era. Sherif studied **social norms,** which are the generalized rules of conduct that tell us how we ought to behave. He researched the surprisingly powerful impact of social norms and their development using a perceptual illusion, the **autokinetic phenomenon.** When a person is placed in a room that is completely dark and a single spot of light is shown on one of the walls, the light appears to move. This apparent movement occurs despite the fact that the light is actually stationary. The light seems to "move itself," thus giving rise to the name of the phenomenon.

Sherif was interested in how other people's judgments would affect those of a person perceiving the light. What Sherif discovered from a number of experiments was that a person's judgments of how the spot of light moved were greatly influenced by reports of other participants. If the experimenter (or another subject) led a subject to expect the light to move in a wide arc, then the subject would usually report that, in fact, it did seem to move in a wide arc. These experiments indicated that a person's perceptual reports could be manipulated by social influence in a dramatic way and that this process could be studied experimentally.

In Sherif's experiments, subjects were in quite an ambiguous situation. Perhaps they were easily influenced by others because they were so unsure of their own perceptions. Could we still find evidence for such great effects of social influence on perception and behavior if we made the situation less ambiguous? Solomon Asch (1951, 1956, 1958) asked this interesting question in his landmark experiments on conformity. Asch (1956) remarked on the importance of the problem as follows: "Granting the great power of groups, may we simply conclude that they can induce persons to shift their decisions and convictions in almost any desired direction, that they can prompt us to call true what we yesterday deemed false, that they can make us invest the identical action with the aura of rightness or the stigma of grotesqueness and malice?" (p. 2). The answer to this question provided by his experiments was a qualified yes, and **conformity,** which is how groups influence individual behavior so that the behavior agrees with social norms, became a popular topic in social psychology following Asch's work.

The basic procedure Asch used was as follows. A group of students gathered in a room to take part in what was described as a study of visual discrimination. They were shown a single line and then three comparison lines. Their task was to say which of the three comparison lines matched the standard. An example appears in Figure 13.1. There were seven people in the group in one experiment, but there was only one real subject. The other six were confederates of the experimenter, or assistants. The situation was arranged so that the real subject always responded with his or her answer next to last, after five other "subjects" had already given their judgments. Everyone responded aloud, so that the rest of the group knew each person's response.

There were 18 trials; in each case, one comparison line was equal to the standard. The confederates were instructed to give the correct answer on 6 of the trials but a consistently wrong answer on 12 trials. The question of interest was whether the real subject in the procedure would conform to the group judgment and go against his or

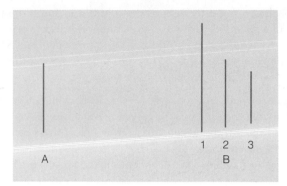

▼ FIGURE 13.1

Subjects in the perceptual discrimination task used by Asch were asked to decide which of the comparison lines (B) was the same length as that of the standard (A). How do you think you would respond if five people before you had all said that comparison line 3 was the correct answer?

her own perception. Most did conform to the erroneous judgments of the group on one or more of the 12 trials. A control group was also used, in which the confederates did not make any errors; under these conditions, only 5 percent of the real subjects made an error. Ironically, Asch's classic study was intended to demonstrate that people resist group influence when they have the objective evidence of their senses on which to rely. Indeed, 63 percent of responses in Asch's study were correct, despite group pressure to the contrary. Social psychologists, however, have tended to emphasize how much subjects conformed, probably because conformity is more surprising or controversial than is independence in American society (Friend, Rafferty, & Bramel, 1990). More recently, Asch's results have been extended into the memory domain. Subjects viewed slides of common household scenes; pairs of subjects then took turns recalling the items in the slides. Unbeknownst to the subject, the other participant was actually a confederate who deliberately suggested household items that had *not* been in the slides. Of interest was the "social contagion of memory"; subjects later claimed to have seen objects in the slides that had only been suggested by the confederate (Meade & Roediger, 2002; Roediger, Meade, & Bergman, 2001). Research suggests that social contagion may also distort eyewitnesses' memories of criminal events (Gabbert, Memon, & Allen, 2003).

In sum, Sherif's and Asch's experiments indicate that group judgments can have much power over the individual. However, later research has uncovered many factors that can lessen the influence of the group. For example, if just one confederate, responding before the subject, does not go along with the group but answers correctly, then the subject will usually fail to follow the lead of the majority, too, and will respond with the correct answer.

At about the same time Sherif was writing about social norms, Kurt Lewin was also writing extensively about social psychology. Lewin provided a theoretical account of social behavior, known as field theory, as well as some interesting experiments. He was also quite concerned with applying the knowledge social psychologists were gathering to the solution of social problems. He helped found the Research Center for Group Dynamics (now at the University of Michigan) for the study of such topics as leadership and group productivity. He also played a major role in establishing "sensitivity training" as a method of coping with complex human relationships.

Today, social psychology is one of the largest subdisciplines within scientific psychology. Social psychologists employ experimental methods in attempting to understand many issues that are of interest to most individuals, such as aggression, attraction, and altruism and helping. But because most people are interested in social psychology and have probably given some thought to the topics it includes, they sometimes tend to regard its phenomena and theories as mere common sense. Worse yet, some people even believe this area is one that should not be approached in a scientific way with the logic of experimental method. Lewin (1948) argued against this sort of reasoning some years ago:

> For thousands of years man's everyday experience with falling objects did not suffice to bring him to a correct theory of gravity. A sequence of very unusual, man-made experiences, so-called experiments, which grew out of the systematic search for the truth were necessary to bring about a change from less adequate to more adequate concepts. To assume that first-hand experience in the social world would automatically lead to the formation of correct concepts or to the creation of adequate stereotypes seems therefore unjustifiable. (pp. 60–61)

13.1   EXPERIMENTAL TOPICS AND RESEARCH ILLUSTRATIONS

Topic   *Experimental Control*
Illustration   *Obedience to Authority*

Psychologists perform experiments to discover the causes of behavior. First, the investigator selects a problem of interest: Why does some behavior occur? Second, a hypothesis is suggested that provides a tentative understanding of the behavior. Usually the hypothesis will specify factors that cause or determine the behavior. The researcher will then try to create experimental conditions to test the hypothesis. If one factor has been pinpointed by the hypothesis as the alleged cause of the behavior, will the behavior in fact be affected when the factor is manipulated in a systematic way? In the experiment, the factor that is manipulated is called the independent variable, and the behavior measured is called the dependent variable. **Experimental control** has to do with the researcher's gaining control over other factors in the situation so that he or she can be certain that the change in behavior is caused by the independent variable and not some other factor. The more complex the behavior of interest, the harder it is to gain control over all other relevant aspects of the situation.

Experimental error occurs when a change in the dependent variable—the behavior of interest—is produced by some factor other than the independent variable. Experimental control attempts to minimize or eliminate experimental error. One main source of experimental error is **confounding,** which occurs when a second variable is unintentionally varied along with the independent variable of interest. When this happens, the researcher cannot be certain whether the independent variable or the second, confounded, variable has produced the change in the dependent variable.

Several ways are available to reduce experimental error caused by confounding. The most direct approach is to control all other variables of interest so that only the independent variable is manipulated. The other factors that are kept constant are referred to as **control variables,** as we have discussed previously (see Chapter 3).

Sometimes it is not possible to rigidly control a variable across all conditions of an experiment; at such times, other techniques must be used. This problem occurs, for example, when a between-subjects experimental design is used. If there are two conditions, an experimental and a control condition, that differ in the manipulation of the independent variable, a researcher does not want to have any second variable on which the two groups

INTRODUCING THE VARIABLES

Dependent Variables

The dependent variable in social psychological research is often a measure of preference (or liking, or belief, and so on) obtained by having subjects fill out a questionnaire after experiencing some experimental treatment. For example, people might be asked to judge on a seven-point scale how much they liked or disliked the other people in the experiment or how much they agree with the position that abortion is murder. These measures would usually be taken only after an experimental treatment was designed to influence the judgments in some way. Although much useful information has been gained through the questionnaire technique, social psychologists are increasingly turning to techniques that do not depend on self-report. For example, the experimenters may also include behavioral measurement. Instead of asking a person how much animosity he or she feels toward another subject in an aggression experiment, the experimenter might set up the situation so that the subject had an opportunity to deliver mild electric shocks to the other subject in the guise of a learning experiment. Thus, aggression could be measured in terms of how many shocks were delivered. (Actually, the other person, a confederate of the experimenter, would receive no shocks.) Most recently, social psychologists have been using many of the same techniques as cognitive psychologists, relying on dependent measures such as reaction time and memory. For example, subjects might selectively remember only those actions of the other participants that fit with how much they liked them. Generally, the more converging measures we can obtain of the same hypothetical entity (e.g., aggression) that agree, the more

faith we can place in the relation discovered in the experiment.

Independent Variables

Independent variables in social psychology experiments usually are characteristics of a social situation or of the people in a situation that can be manipulated. In an experiment on attitude change, the persuasiveness of a message might be varied by manipulating the number of arguments used in support of the position being argued (e.g., that abortion is murder). In an experiment testing the hypothesis that aggression increases as the temperature rises, the experimenter might vary the temperature of the room in which an aggressive activity might occur between a person and a confederate. In an experiment on conformity, an investigator might vary the number of people who disagree with some judgment that a person has made to see whether the subject will be more likely to change his or her mind. Variables concerning the characteristics of the people in the experiment, such as sex and race, also can be examined. Are people more likely to help (or show aggression against, or like, or agree with) people of their own sex or race?

Control Variables

The introduction of experimental control in social psychological research is quite tricky, since the situations dealt with are usually complex. It is often very difficult to vary one or several factors while keeping all others constant, the prerequisite for providing firm inferences about the relation between independent and dependent variables in experiments. The next section deals with this issue.

also differ. However, in a between-subjects design, there is at least one other difference in conditions, which is built in: Different groups of people are tested in the two conditions.

When it is not possible to control a variable, as with people in a between-subjects design, the experimenter randomizes the variable to discount its influence. Thus, if a between-subjects design is used, the researcher randomly assigns participants to conditions. (The assignment is based on some scheme that guarantees true randomization, such as the random-numbers table, described in Table H in Appendix C at the end of the book.) As participants arrive for the experiment, the researcher could use the numbers in the table's rows to assign people to the conditions. If there are two conditions, odd numbers would indicate people in one condition and even numbers would represent those in the other condition.

Randomization minimizes the likelihood that there will be systematic differences between groups of participants in an experiment. Without randomization, an experimenter runs the risk that between-group differences will be confounded with the independent variable, thereby influencing the outcome of the experiment. Although different people are assigned to the two conditions, the researcher can rest assured that, on average, participants in the two conditions are similar in all important respects. Thus, if there is a statistically reliable difference in behavior between the two conditions, it could be safely attributed to the operation of the independent variable and not to the fact that there were different people in the two conditions.

In social psychological research, investigators are interested in situations that are generally more complex than those considered thus far in the book. In social situations, many factors may influence people's behavior, such as the number of other people present, the behavior and attitudes of these other people, interpersonal dynamics, and other events or social interactions that may occur in an uncontrolled or unpredictable manner. That is, in social situations, many variables besides the independent variable must be controlled or randomized before the researcher can be certain that any change in a dependent variable is caused by the independent variable.

How do we go about studying a complex social phenomenon in a controlled setting? Consider, for example, the problem of **obedience** to authority. How might one person or group of people in authority induce others to follow commands, especially when those commands may be to perform social or immoral acts? The most ghastly case of this in the twentieth century occurred in Nazi Germany, where a small cadre of Nazi fanatics instituted a program for the systematic murder of a large portion of the populace of Germany and of the countries it had conquered. Implementation of the plan involved both tacit acceptance by the bulk of the German population and the actions of otherwise normal people.

To study obedience in the laboratory, a great number of factors need to be considered, such as the perceived power of the authority figure, the behavior the participant is expected to perform, the perceived consequences of disobedience, the effects of peer pressure, the political or ideological issues involved, and so on. And how do we measure obedience? How can we bring such a complex phenomenon into a controlled setting to study the critical factors underlying it, while holding the others constant?

Milgram answered this question in a fascinating series of experiments that culminated in a book on the topic (Milgram, 1974). We will consider these experiments as a case history of bringing a complicated social psychological topic into the lab for close scrutiny. The original experiments (Milgram, 1963, 1964a, 1965) all used a common methodology to establish obedience to authority in a controlled experimental setting. In the first study, Milgram (1963) used male participants who responded to advertisements to participate, for pay, in a study of memory and learning at Yale University. When a participant appeared at the laboratory, he met another participant (actually a confederate of the experimenter) who was a 47-year-old accountant specially trained for his role. The confederate appeared rather mild-mannered and likable (Figure 13.2). Participants were told that very little was known about the effects of punishment on memory and

▼ **FIGURE 13.2**

The learner (or victim) in Milgram's original study on obedience to authority. Would you risk seriously harming this man in an experiment if someone told you to? Milgram's findings suggest that you would. From THE OBEDIENCE distributed by The Pennsylvania State University Media Sales.

© 1965 by Stanley Milgram.

that one of them was to be the teacher and one the learner in a scientific study of this topic. The men drew slips of paper from a hat to determine who was to appear in which role, but in actuality, the drawing was rigged so that the naïve participant was always the teacher and the confederate was always the learner. The experimenter was played by a rather severe 31-year-old biology teacher who wore a white lab coat. The learner was strapped into an electric chair to prevent excessive movement, and electrodes were placed on his wrists with paste "to avoid blisters and burns." In response to a question by the learner, the experimenter said, "Although the shocks can be extremely painful, they cause no permanent tissue damage" (Milgram, 1963, p. 373).

The teacher-participants were required to read a paired-associate list to the learner (see Chapter 10) and then later to test him on the list by presenting a stimulus and four alternatives, one of which was correct.

The learner-confederate was required to pick the correct response from among the four alternatives and say it aloud. If he made an error, the teacher-participant was instructed to give him an electric shock by pressing a switch on an imposing shock generator. Although the confederate actually received no shocks, the real participant had been given a mild sample shock at the beginning of the experiment to convince him that the generator was real. During the course of the experiment, teachers were required to increase the amount of shock every time the learner made an error. The primary dependent measure was the amount of electric shock the naïve participant was willing to give. The shock generator consisted of 30 lever switches, clearly labeled as proceeding from 15 to 450 volts. There were seven switches (in each of four groups), and participants were given the following verbal descriptions of the switch labels (from left to right): slight shock, moderate shock, strong shock, very strong shock, intense shock, extreme-intensity shock, and danger: severe shock. Two other switches at the far right were marked XXX.

From the beginning, the learner-confederate made errors; thus, the teacher-participant was supposed to administer ever-increasing electric shocks. In the original study, the confederate was out of sight of the teacher, but he could be heard. His responses were standardized on tape. "Starting with 75 volts the learner begins to grunt and moan. At 150 volts he demands to be let out of the experiment. At 180 volts he cries out that he can no longer stand the pain. At 300 volts he refuses to provide any more answers. . . . The experimenter (then) instructs the naïve person to treat the absence of an answer as equivalent to a wrong answer, and to follow the usual shock procedure" (Milgram, 1965, p. 61).

All people who participated in this procedure appeared very nervous and upset and frequently asked the experimenter what they should do next. Whenever people seemed unwilling to continue, the experimenter had a series of statements (which accelerated to commands) that the person was to obey. The first was rather gentle: "Please go on." Next was "The experiment requires that you continue," which progressed to "It is absolutely essential that you continue." Finally, the experimenter said, "You have no other choice. You must go on."

Milgram's (1963) results are truly remarkable. Of the 40 people originally tested in this situation, 26 (65 percent) "went all the way" and gave the confederate the full series of shocks, whereas the other 14 broke off the experiment by refusing to continue at or after the 300-volt level. The results are portrayed in Figure 13.3. The participants here were not impassive, cruel torturers. They were (just like you and me) normal people who felt

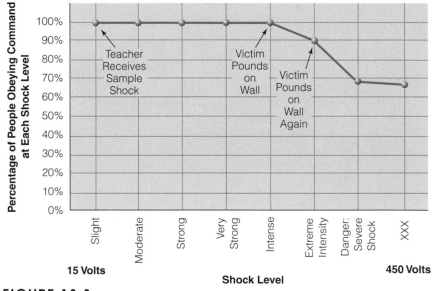

▼ FIGURE 13.3

Percentage of People Who Obeyed Commands to Continue Shocking the Victim at Various Levels of Shock Intensity. Even when the victim reacted as if in pain and stopped responding to the memory task, almost two-thirds obeyed the experimenter and administered shocks at the level of "danger" and beyond. (From *Social Psychology: Understanding Human Interaction* [p. 292], by R. A. Baron and D. Byrne, 1977, Boston: Allyn and Bacon.)

a great deal of conflict in this situation. One chapter of Milgram's (1974) book contains transcripts that show that many subjects felt anguish but nonetheless continued under the directions of the experimenter. Most were sweating profusely and many were trembling. Another symptom of their discomfort was the occurrence of nervous laughter, which became uncontrollable in several subjects. One viewer of the experiment commented:

> I observed a mature and initially poised businessman enter the laboratory smiling and confident. Within 20 minutes he was reduced to a nervous, stuttering wreck, who was rapidly approaching a point of nervous collapse. He constantly pulled on his earlobe and twisted his hands. At one point he pushed his fist into his forehead and muttered: "Oh God, let's stop it." And yet he continued to respond to every word of the experimenter, and obeyed to the end. (Milgram, 1963, p. 377)

It is interesting to note that Milgram's demonstration may actually underestimate people's willingness to obey. Because Milgram wanted to study obedience in a controlled laboratory setting, one source of obedience was lacking: genuine power over the person's behavior. That is, the men could have simply walked out of the experiment and never have suffered any negative repercussions for disobedience. However, in most real-world situations, an authority figure has the power to inflict harm if his or her orders are not followed. Parents, teachers, and law enforcement officials can punish those who disobey. Therefore, Milgram's study did not capture all the essential components of obedience as it naturally occurs. This difference between real-world settings and Milgram's laboratory setting does not devalue his contribution, however. Rather, it makes his demonstration all the more astonishing when one realizes that he obtained such high levels of obedience without the threat of punishment for disobedience. We might predict that people would have been even more obedient if the experimenter had possessed any real power over them.

Conditions Encouraging Obedience

You might have noticed something lacking in the description of Milgram's study, something crucial to an experiment. There was no variation of an independent variable in the research. Thus, no information was gained about the conditions that enhance or diminish obedience to authority in this situation. Although Milgram employed a controlled setting to produce laboratory obedience, his first study is better referred to as a demonstration rather than an experiment, since there was no manipulation of an independent variable. Milgram, of course, realized this and made no claims to the contrary. In the original report, he outlined areas in which systematic variations in the procedure might lead to useful new information about conditions necessary for obedience; he also provided some of these variations in later experiments.

One factor that could have encouraged obedience in the original study was the setting; it was conducted at Yale University, an institution presumably held in high regard by the participants (at least before the experiment). Perhaps the general Yale aura helped foster obedience, since presumably this well-known institution would not allow its premises to be used for shady purposes. Milgram (1965) reported a later study similar to the original in most details, except that it was done in an old office building in a rather sleazy part of Bridgeport, Connecticut, under the auspices of Research Associates of Bridgeport, a fictitious company. Although compliance was reduced in the Bridgeport study (48 percent delivered the maximum shock versus 65 percent in the original Yale sample), the difference was apparently not statistically significant; Milgram concluded that Yale's reputation was not responsible for the original high level of compliance. Because this conclusion is based on a failure to reject the null hypothesis, it is suspect (see Chapter 3), especially since there was a rather large absolute difference between the two studies (17 percent).

It is of interest to ask what conclusions Milgram could have reached from this study if there had been a significant reduction in obedience in Bridgeport relative to the original Yale study. Could he have concluded that it was the nature of the setting (Yale versus a dilapidated office building) that produced the results? The answer is *no,* or at least *not strictly,* since many other conditions varied between the two situations besides the setting (e.g., the city and the time of year). Thus, at least several variables were potentially confounded. It may have been that the different settings produced the result, since the experimenter and the confederates were the same in the two studies. But, in general, drawing conclusions from a comparison of conditions across different experiments is hazardous, since one can never be certain that all other conditions were held constant and that no confounding occurred. What could Milgram have concluded if the Bridgeport volunteers responding to his advertisement had turned out to differ in occupation or socioeconomic status from the Yale sample? (In fact, the two samples did not differ in any obvious way.) To determine the reasons for the differences in obedience, he would have had to conduct additional experiments. First, he could have formulated reasonable hypotheses regarding which factors were causing the differences (e.g., socioeconomic status, age, occupation). Then, he could have conducted a series of experiments in which he manipulated each factor until he had identified the ones that affected obedience. In other words, when various uncontrolled factors change across experiments (i.e., are confounded) and different results are found in those experiments, then the confounded factors must be isolated and varied independently to determine which ones produce the differences in behavior.

In subsequent real experiments, other variables have been found to have a great effect on obedience. When other people serve in the experiment as teachers who are supposed to provide shocks (though they are actually confederates), their behavior markedly affects that of the naïve participant. In one case, Milgram (1965) had the two confederates refuse to continue at predetermined levels of shock. The results are portrayed in Figure 13.4, which indicates that the naïve people were much better able to refuse to continue when others did. On the other hand, in another experiment when two conforming peers encouraged the naïve subjects to increase the shock level, they administered much greater shock than when they determined the shock level themselves (Milgram, 1964a).

Another interesting manipulation Milgram (1965) tried was to vary the closeness of the victim, so that in one condition the teacher could only hear the victim moan and complain; in another condition, he was in the same room so he could also see the victim; and in yet another condition, the participant was actually instructed to force the learner's arm down onto the metal shock plate on each trial (Figure 13.5). Although obedience decreased with closeness of the victim, from 74 percent to 40 percent to 30 percent obeying the experimenter's instructions to the end in the different conditions, it is still remarkable that almost one-third continued to give the shocks even when they had to hold down the person's hand.

Milgram's research on obedience allows us to see how an interesting and complicated problem concerning social influence can be investigated in the relatively controlled

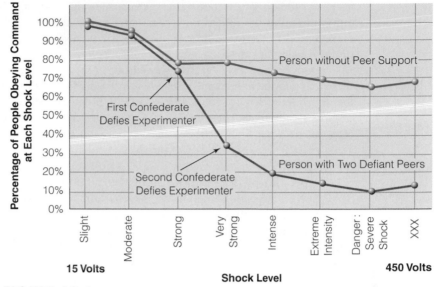

The y-axis is labeled "Percentage of People Obeying Command at Each Shock Level" with values 0%, 10%, 20%, 30%, 40%, 50%, 60%, 70%, 80%, 90%, 100%.

Labels on chart: "Person without Peer Support", "First Confederate Defies Experimenter", "Second Confederate Defies Experimenter", "Person with Two Defiant Peers".

X-axis ("Shock Level"): Slight, Moderate, Strong, Very Strong, Intense, Extreme Intensity, Danger: Severe Shock, XXX. "15 Volts" on the left, "450 Volts" on the right.

▼ **FIGURE 13.4**

Group Pressure as an Influence in Defying Authority. When people do not have peer support, 65 percent continue to obey the experimenter's commands to give stronger and stronger shocks throughout the experiment. When people are with peers who defy the experimenter, only 10 percent continue to obey the experimenter's commands. (From *Social Psychology: Understanding Human Interaction* [p. 297], by R. A. Baron and D. Byrne, 1977, Boston: Allyn and Bacon.)

© 1965 Stanley Milgram.

▼ **FIGURE 13.5**

An obedient participant shocking a confederate while forcing his arm onto the metal plate. From THE OBEDIENCE distributed by the Pennsylvania State University Media Sales.

setting of the social psychology laboratory. Although not all aspects of obedience are transported into the lab (e.g., as mentioned earlier, the person issuing commands had no real power over the naïve participants), the situation was still compelling enough to produce a dramatically high level of compliance.

Before leaving this topic, we should briefly mention three more issues. Many people who encounter Milgram's research say, "I wouldn't do that." The point is that, given the appropriate setting, you probably would. Yale college students were tested in the original situation; their results were no different from those of the "real people" in the New Haven community. Perhaps after reading this you would not participate in a situation exactly like Milgram's, but you would probably do similar things without giving them much thought. (See Geher, Bauman, Hubbard, & Legare, 2002, for more recent data on people's predictions of what they would do.)

A second aspect of Milgram's studies that often provokes comment is whether or not it was (and is) ethical to put people through this procedure, since their cooperation is obtained under false pretenses and the procedure is quite stressful. These issues have been debated by Baumrind (1964) and Milgram (1964b) at some length, so we will simply refer the interested reader to these articles and Appendix I of Milgram's (1974) book for comment on the ethical issues involved in this research. (We considered the problem of ethics in Chapter 4.)

Finally, as Milgram points out repeatedly in his writing, obedience in itself is not necessarily bad. In fact, if almost all of us did not obey the numerous laws and persons in authority in our society, life would be all but unbearable. It is only when one is asked to obey commands that produce harm that obedience is undesirable.

Obedience and the legacy of Milgram's work still receive high interest in social psychology (see Blass, 1999, 2002; Miller, Collins, & Brief, 1995; Zimbardo, 2007). Alternative theoretical explanations of the obedience seen by Milgram have been offered (Nissani, 1990). In addition, an entire issue of the *Journal of Social Issues* (*51*:3) is devoted to obedience to authority. In light of recent war-related atrocities in central Europe and the Middle East, additional understanding of blind obedience seems warranted.

13.2   EXPERIMENTAL TOPICS AND RESEARCH ILLUSTRATIONS

Topic   *Demand Characteristics and Experimenter Bias*
Illustration   *Hypnosis*

Psychological experiments typically employ as much experimental control as can be mustered by the prudent investigator. This section is concerned with two sources of bias that even the most conscientious researcher may well overlook: bias introduced by the experimenters and by the subjects themselves. The problem of **experimenter bias** is potentially prevalent in all sciences. The most blatant form of bias is the deliberate faking of data. The social pressures that exist to be productive, to publish many articles, and to find spectacular results so as to receive more money from granting agencies have led some investigators to fake results. Broad and Wade (1982) consider a number of documented cases of such fraud and discuss the problem at length. Unfortunately, nothing much can be done to reduce this sort of fraud, except to be vigilant and to punish offenders whenever they are caught. Such frauds may be uncovered when other researchers try to replicate and confirm the work. Additional considerations of fraud in research are discussed in Chapter 4.

Experimenter bias refers not only to the conscious cases of fraud but also to the much more subtle influences that experimenters may unknowingly exert on the outcome of their research. That such effects do occur has been established by much research, as well as by anecdotal observations. This more covert form of bias may be inadvertently introduced in a number of ways. The experimenter may interact with the participants in the different conditions in slightly different ways; the tone of voice and emphasis may change when the instructions are read; and, similarly, facial cues, gestures, and so forth may differ. The experimenter may not even be aware of such effects, but expectations of the way the participants should behave in the different conditions may change her or his behavior very slightly to help produce the expected effect.

Rosenthal (1966, 1969, 2002) reviewed work (much of it his own) on the influence of experimenter expectancies and discussed various solutions to the problem. One of the most effective solutions is for the experimenter to keep himself or herself insulated in some way from knowing either the hypotheses being considered or the particular conditions of the subject being tested. In such a case, the experimenter is said to be **blind** with respect to conditions. Unfortunately, it is difficult or impractical to satisfy this condition in much research, because the experimenter must administer the conditions.

The problem of experimenter bias, although potentially dangerous, may not be as serious as is sometimes assumed. Barber and Silver (1968) exhaustively analyzed the research on experimenter expectancy effects and argue that there is still not enough evidence to conclude that such effects are proven phenomena. Regardless of the validity of this claim, other factors make us believe that the importance of experimenter effects is often exaggerated. We have emphasized repeatedly throughout this book that the results of any individual experiment need to be viewed in the context of other, similar experiments before one can make a generalization. If a particular experimental result is considered important, one can rest assured that much future research will be directed toward discovering the conditions under which it holds, explicating the mechanisms involved, and so on. In the course of such research, there will be many occasions for the basic phenomenon to be replicated by experimenters with many different views on the subject, some hoping to find it, some hoping not to. If the phenomenon is replicated by all, then we can assume that it is not produced by experimenter bias; if not, we can suspect experimenter bias of being responsible for part of the difficulty. The important point is that experimenter bias, or even the blatant dishonesty of an isolated investigator, will be discovered in the normal course of scientific inquiry. Such effects should still be guarded against with all possible caution, of course. In the long run, however, effects of experimenter bias will likely be winnowed out in the scientific process.

A potentially more powerful source of bias, which is unique to the social sciences, has to do with the participant and what she or he expects to encounter in a psychological experiment. Martin Orne (1962, 1969) was a pioneer in making psychologists aware of this problem. He pointed out that people entering an experiment have some general notions of what to expect and are probably trying to figure out the specific purpose of the experiment. They are likely to believe that reasonable care will be taken for their well-being and that whatever the experimenter asks them to do will serve a useful purpose. They will also want to know this purpose and seek clues in the experimental situation. Because many psychological experiments, especially ones in social psychology such as Milgram's obedience studies, would provide uninteresting results if the true purpose of the study were known (everyone would soon refuse to obey the experimenter), elaborate deceptions are often involved to mask the true purposes of the experiment. However, as Orne points out, these might sometimes be rather transparent. At any rate, the general problem exists as to how the person's expectations affect or determine her or his behavior in an experiment. As Orne (1969) notes:

> Insofar as the subject cares about the outcome, his perception of his role and of the hypothesis being tested will become a significant determinant of his behavior. The cues which govern his behavior—which communicate what is expected of him and what the experimenter hopes to find—can therefore be crucial variables. Some time ago I proposed that these cues be called "demand characteristics of an experiment." . . . They include the scuttlebutt about the experiment, its setting, implicit and explicit instructions, the person of the experimenter, subtle cues provided by him, and, of particular importance, the experimental procedure. (p. 146)

If results of an experiment are produced by **demand characteristics** of the experimental situation, they will not generalize to other situations. It is well known that someone's awareness that he or she is part of an experiment will greatly affect their behavior. In "Psychology in Action" at the end of the chapter, we suggest an exercise you can carry out to demonstrate this point.

In all laboratory experiments, people realize that they are being observed and that their behavior is being carefully monitored. Their expectations of how they are supposed to behave may greatly determine their performance in the experiment. Another phenomenon of this sort is well known to medical researchers; it is called the **placebo effect.** This refers to the fact that when patients in medical research are given a chemically inert substance and told that it is medicine that should help them, they often show an improvement in the illness or find relief from their pain. Thus, when a drug is evaluated in medical research, it is not enough to compare a group of patients that receives the drug with a group that does not because the patients who receive the drug may improve simply due to the placebo effect (see Chapter 6). Instead, the drug group is also compared with a placebo group so that the effect of the drug can be measured in relation to the placebo effect. The term **single-blind experiment** is often applied to this type of research because the people, in this example, do not know whether they are receiving medication or a placebo. Experimental safeguards usually are extended in medical research so that the doctors who administer the drugs are also blind to the patients' treatment. The advantage of this type of **double-blind experiment** is that neither the patients' nor the doctors' expectations of improvement can affect the results.

In one line of laboratory research, Orne (1962) sought to find a task that was so meaningless and boring that normal participants would refuse to perform it. He was interested in finding such a task because he then wanted to see whether or not participants under the influence of hypnosis would perform the task when instructed to do so. One experiment involved giving subjects 2000 sheets of paper filled with rows of random digits. The people were instructed to add together the many pairs of digits in each row on all the sheets. Clearly, it was an impossible task; Orne assumed that the control people would quickly realize this and refuse to go on. But instead, the people, who were deprived of their watches, kept at the task for hours on end, with little decrement in performance. People in a later study (that aimed at making the task even more onerous and meaningless) were told that after each sheet was completed, they were to pick up a card and follow the direction written on it. Each card instructed them to tear up the sheet of paper into a minimum of 32 pieces and continue on to the next sheet. Still they persisted for hours. When questioned, they explained their behavior by saying that since they were in an experiment, they figured there must be a good reason for the request (an endurance test or the like).

Investigators have asked participants under hypnosis to do all sorts of things, often with notable success. One apparently well-established finding is that participants under hypnosis can be led to perform various antisocial and destructive acts, such as throwing acid in someone's face and handling venomous snakes (Rowland, 1939; Young, 1952). Orne and Evans (1965) suspected that this behavior might have been attributable more to the demand characteristics of the situation than to the effects of hypnosis. They asked people to perform a series of seemingly dangerous acts, such as grasping a venomous snake, taking a coin from fuming acid, and throwing nitric acid in the experimenter's face. (The procedures were designed to appear threatening, but the acts were really safe.) There were several treatment conditions: (1) people who were under deep hypnosis; (2) people who were told to simulate or pretend that they were under hypnosis; (3) awake controls who were not asked to simulate hypnosis but who were pressed by the experimenter to comply with the requests; (4) awake controls who were not pressed to comply; and (5) people who were asked to perform the tasks without being made part of an experiment. The experimenter in this study was blind to the conditions of the subjects, so as not to affect their behavior. The results are summarized in Table 13.1. As would be expected, people not in the experimental setting refused to carry out the antisocial tasks, but as other investigators had reported, a high percentage of hypnotized people did carry out the tasks as instructed. However, all simulating control participants also performed the tasks; even the nonsimulating controls performed them to a large extent if they were pressed to comply, which demonstrates the power of the experimental situation.

The conclusion to be drawn is that hypnosis is not necessarily responsible for performance of the antisocial acts. Rather, demand characteristics of the experimental situation, including the setting, the instructions, and the way people think they are supposed to behave while under hypnosis, are sufficient to produce the antisocial acts. Perhaps people can be induced to perform antisocial acts under deep hypnosis, but studies currently available do not offer reliable evidence to support the idea that hypnosis is responsible for the behavior.

▼ TABLE 13.1

Percentage of Participants Who Performed Dangerous Tasks in Response to Requests by the Experimenter. (Adapted from Orne & Evans, 1965.)

Participant Group	Grasp Venomous Snake	Take Coin from Acid	Throw Acid at Experimenter
Real hypnosis	83	83	83
Simulating hypnosis	100	100	100
Waking control—pressed to comply	50	83	83
Waking control—without being pressed to comply	50	17	17
Nonexperimental	0	0	0

The use of **simulating control participants,** as in the Orne and Evans experiment, is one way of attacking the problem of demand characteristics. The logic is essentially the same as that of using a placebo condition in medical research. The demand characteristics of the situation are assumed to be the same for participants in both the experimental condition and the simulating control condition. If the experimental manipulation (say, hypnosis) is truly effective, then the behavior of the experimental participants should differ reliably from that of the simulating controls. One problem with this logic, of course, is the implication that because no difference was found, no difference exists. This is an example of the logical error of accepting the null hypothesis (see Appendix B). However, the failure to find a difference between the hypnotized and simulating control participants does not prove that hypnosis has no effect on behavior. Rather, Orne and Evans's experiment simply makes the point that there is an alternative explanation of hypnotized peoples' compliance with requests to perform dangerous acts: They may be responding to the demand characteristics of the situation, rather than demonstrating a unique effect of hypnosis. For additional examples of the use of simulating control participants, see work by Bryant and Barnier (1999) and Reed and colleagues (Reed, Kirsch, Wickless, Moffitt, & Taren, 1996).

The problem of demand characteristics is a thorny one, especially in social psychological research. As Orne (1969, p. 156) points out, these concerns are less important in those experimental studies that do not involve deception and that encourage people to respond as accurately as possible. But in studies where optimal performance may not be encouraged for various reasons and where deception is often involved, results may be contaminated by demand characteristics. In the hypnosis study, people in all experimental conditions said they performed the acts because they were in an experiment and felt assured, despite rather convincing pretenses to the contrary, that the experimenter had taken precautions against harming them and himself. (They were correct.)

13.3   EXPERIMENTAL TOPICS AND RESEARCH ILLUSTRATIONS

Topic   *Field Research*
Illustration   *Bystander Intervention*

The problems of demand characteristics in laboratory settings, along with other factors, have caused many social psychologists to turn to **field research.** Rather than attempting to bring some phenomenon into the laboratory for study in a controlled setting, the researcher instead attempts to introduce enough control into a setting (in "the field") to allow inferences to be made about how variations in an independent variable affect a dependent variable. In such cases, there is no problem of generalizing to the real world—the experiment is conducted in the real world to begin with. However, in some ways, field research in social psychology is even more difficult to conceive and carry out than laboratory research. We shall discuss some of these problems before examining a field study.

The crux of experimental method in laboratory research is to abstract relevant variables from complex situations in nature and then reproduce parts of these situations, so that by varying different factors we may determine their contribution to the behavior of interest. By bringing the phenomenon into the laboratory, we gain control over the situation. The main problems in field research have to do with this issue of control. How can we gain control over and manipulate the independent variable in a field setting?

Presuming we can do this, how do we then simultaneously go about controlling or randomizing all the other factors that are likely to be varying willy-nilly in complex situations? And what do we measure, anyway, in a naturally occurring setting? What should our dependent variable be? There are all sorts of things we could measure, but how directly related are they to the phenomenon of interest? These are very difficult questions; the answers will depend to a great extent on the problem investigated and the ingenuity of the individual researchers in providing control in a complex situation.

The issue of specifying dependent variables is treated systematically by Webb and associates in a book called *Unobtrusive Measures: Nonreactive Research in the Social Sciences* (1966). The authors are concerned with the problem of people's changes in behavior when they know they are being observed or studied. They discuss a number of "unobtrusive" measures that can be taken on behavior without the subject's knowledge and that are thus suitable for use in field research in psychology and other social sciences (see Chapter 2). Although their book contains many clever and ingenious suggestions, most of the unobtrusive measures they describe have little bearing on many psychological problems under active investigation by psychologists. The primary problem in obtaining a good dependent measure, or providing a good operational definition of whatever underlying construct one is trying to measure, is ensuring that a plausible link exists between the construct and what is measured. This is a problem in all research, as is that of finding converging operations on a construct, but in field research, these problems are magnified. The dependent measure seems often only tangentially related to the underlying construct, as when, say, a standard mortality ratio is used as an index of social pathology (see Chapters 2 and 14).

Another problem in field research is the question of ethics. Can we justify involving people in research in the name of science when they do not volunteer and are in fact unsuspecting? Should we allow ourselves to manipulate our fellow citizens (via the independent variable) and then record their reactions (the dependent variables)? This is especially a problem when the manipulation involves inducing stress or embarrassment or some other undesirable state. In the lab, psychologists can (and are required to) debrief participants after the experiment and tell them why they were placed in this uncomfortable situation, but in the field, this is usually not done, since the participants are not even aware that they are being manipulated and observed by psychologists. Psychologists have decided, not without a certain amount of self-interest, that field research conducted in a public setting is allowable as long as no great stress or harm is occasioned on the "participants." Whether citizens themselves will agree with this judgment when (if) the legitimacy of field research ever becomes an issue is another matter. Certainly we do not tolerate manipulation and eavesdropping by government agencies, and it seems unlikely that the public at large will find psychologists' scientific motives any more acceptable. The issue has not yet arisen to a great extent, but when it does, it may spell the death knell for field research.

Before discussing a field study concerned with bystander intervention, let us examine how social psychologists became interested in this topic. Consider the following actual incidents:

> Kitty Genovese is set upon by a maniac as she returns home from work at 3 A.M. Thirty-eight of her neighbors in Kew Gardens come to their windows when she cries out in terror; none come to her assistance even though her stalker takes over half an hour to murder her. No one even so much as calls the police. She dies.

Andrew Mormille is stabbed in the stomach as he rides the A train home in Manhattan. Eleven other riders watch the seventeen-year-old boy as he bleeds to death; none come to his assistance even though his attackers have left the car. He dies.

An eighteen-year-old switchboard operator, alone in her office in the Bronx, is raped and beaten. Escaping momentarily, she runs naked and bleeding to the street, screaming for help. A crowd of forty passersby gathers and watches as, in broad daylight, the rapist tries to drag her back upstairs; no one interferes. Finally, two policemen happen by and arrest her assailant.

These vignettes are taken verbatim from a fascinating book by Bibb Latané and John Darley called *The Unresponsive Bystander: Why Doesn't He Help?* (1970, pp. 1–2), in which they describe their research aimed at answering this question. Although there are potentially many reasons the bystander may not help in such crisis situations, one that cropped up early in this research had to do with the number of bystanders. The more people who observe a crisis and who are potential helpers, the less likely any one bystander is to help the victim. Social psychologists call this the **bystander effect.** In one laboratory experiment (Darley & Latané, 1968), participants were led to believe that they were participating (via an intercom system) in a discussion on personal problems in college life, with either one, two, or five other students. The experimenter left the scene after the person had been given instructions. The discussion began with the students introducing themselves, but suddenly one of the students started to act, in a very convincing way, as though he were undergoing an epileptic seizure. (Actually, only one true participant participated at a time; the other voices heard were recorded.) The interest was in seeing how they would behave when they thought there were zero, one, or four other bystanders. The results are shown in Table 13.2, where it can be seen that the percentage of people trying to help the stranger decreased as the number of other bystanders increased. Even when people did respond to the emergency, they were slower when they thought others were also present in the situation. There is apparently a "**diffusion of responsibility,**" so that the more people present (and the more people there are to potentially witness one's making a fool of oneself), the less any individual feels compelled to intervene. A student in a class with 100 other students feels less responsible for answering an instructor's question than a student in a class with five others.

▼ **TABLE 13.2**

Both the Percentage of People Who Help a Person Having an Epileptic Seizure and the Speed with which They Respond Are Affected by the Number of Others in the Situation. As the Number Increases, Fewer Individuals Try to Help and More Time Passes before Help Is Given. (From Darley and Latané, 1968.)

Number of Perceived Bystanders	Percentage of Participants Trying to Help Stranger	Number of Seconds Elapsing before Person Tries to Help
1	85	52
2	62	93
5	31	166

An interesting field study on bystander intervention was conducted on a New York City subway by Piliavin, Rodin, and Piliavin (1969). They picked an express run between two stations that lasted 7.5 minutes and produced an emergency in order to observe who responded and how fast. Four teams of students conducted the experiment, which involved the collapse of one person (the victim) on the train about 70 seconds after it left the station. The independent variables were the race of the victim and whether the victim appeared to be ill (he carried a cane) or drunk (he carried a liquor bottle wrapped in a brown paper bag and also smelled of liquor). Two other experimenters served as observers and recorded the dependent measures, which were whether help was offered and the time that elapsed before help was offered. In addition, they recorded the race of the helper, the number of helpers, and the number and racial composition of the group of bystanders or observers.

Some of the predictions were that people would be more likely to help a person of their own race than of another race, that help would more likely be given when the victim was perceived as ill rather than drunk, and that the tendency to help would decrease with the number of observers. Interestingly, these predictions (which seem to accord with common sense) were only partially verified. There was a clear tendency for help to be offered more readily to ill than drunk victims (on 95 percent of the trials for the ill victim versus 50 percent for the drunk victim). But in both these conditions, the number of observers did not in any way affect the likelihood that help would be offered or the speed with which it was offered. Also, the race of the ill victim did not affect whether one or the other race helped. However, when the victim was drunk, people of the same race helped the victim more than did people of a different race.

Let us consider again the diffusion-of-responsibility theory. This hypothesis was developed by Darley and Latané when they analyzed factors that might have influenced bystanders who failed to respond to crises in natural settings. They tested this idea in a laboratory situation by systematically varying the number of bystanders and found support for it. But when the idea was tested in the natural circumstances of the field (where the phenomenon was first noticed), no evidence was found for it! Presumably, the results differed not because of any greater difference between field and laboratory research but because of other subtle factors that influence helping in such complex situations.

How can we determine what these factors are? First, the researcher would have to formulate hypotheses to answer this question: When does an increased number of bystanders reduce other people's willingness to intervene? After deciding which variables may be important, the experimenter must systematically vary them to see which influence bystander intervention when different numbers of bystanders are present. In this case, the experimenter would be searching for an **interaction** between the number of bystanders and some other factor that he or she is trying to discover.

One other lesson to be drawn from bystander intervention studies is that the responses of others greatly determine what we perceive as the social reality of a situation. If 40 other people stand around watching a murder, you and I will, too. Such behavior is seen as appropriate, since everyone else is doing it. Why risk our necks, when all these others could help? Where are the police when you need them? Research has shown that if people are made to feel responsible for a crisis or see someone else intervene, they are more likely to intervene (Moriarity, 1975). Type of event also matters. In one study, a bystander effect was more likely when people witnessed a confederate painting graffiti in an elevator than when people saw him littering in a public park (Chekroun & Brauer, 2002). Presumably people felt more responsibility for the shared, public park than for the corporate elevator.

The field experiments on bystander intervention are good examples of well-conducted field research. Although it is not possible to control variables as tightly as could be done in a laboratory setting, the independent variables can be manipulated without being confounded with other variables. This is achieved by randomizing over the other variables. For example, on each train run in the Piliavin and associates (1969) study, the condition of the experiment was randomly determined. Thus, other variables—such as differences among the particular people riding on the trains—were randomized across the conditions, which greatly reduced the probability that they affected the conclusions drawn from the study. However, we can ask if there was an ethical problem in conducting this research, since the "participants" did not know they were in the experiment. Suppose one of the bystanders had fainted (or had had a heart attack) while observing the crisis that was staged repeatedly in the course of the experiment. Would the knowledge gained from the experiment be worth the ordeal of the participants? This issue confronts anyone who chooses to investigate problems through field research.

13.4   EXPERIMENTAL TOPICS AND RESEARCH ILLUSTRATIONS

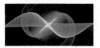

Topic   *Choosing the Dependent Variable*
Illustration   *Measuring Stereotypes and Prejudice*

Suppose you wanted to study whether students at your university are prejudiced against black people. What would you do? You could survey your fellow students, but would you believe what people told you? When studying socially sensitive topics such as racism, social psychologists are often unwilling to accept people's verbal self-reports. People may be unaware of their own prejudices (because they are motivated to believe otherwise), or they may misreport their attitudes to be more consistent with social norms against racism (a form of demand characteristic). Thus, although social psychologists still use questionnaires about racism (e.g., the Modern Racism scale; McConahey, Hardee, & Batts, 1981), they also have developed other ways of measuring prejudice. That is, social psychologists have worked to create dependent variables that are not sensitive to problems of self-report and social desirability.

In Chapter 10 ("Remembering and Forgetting"), you read about **implicit memory tests** that allow psychologists to measure memory without explicitly asking people to remember back to the study episode. Social psychologists have taken a similar approach, creating **implicit attitude measures** that allow them to observe hypothesized correlates of prejudice without explicitly asking subjects to report their attitudes.

One recent implicit attitude measure was spurred by a real event, the killing of a black immigrant by white police officers. As described earlier in the chapter, in February 1999, four New York City Police officers shot Amidou Diallo 41 times as he reached for his wallet. Diallo was unarmed, but police shot because they believed he was reaching for a weapon. Might the police officers have been biased by Diallo's race? That is, could his being black have affected their misidentification of the wallet as a gun?

To study this experimentally, Payne (2001) created a **priming** experiment with the following structure: On each trial, a face was briefly flashed on the screen for 200 ms, followed by an object presented for 200 ms. **Visual masks** began and ended each trial. The face **prime** was either black or white, and the **target** object was either a weapon or a tool. The (white) subjects' task was to ignore the faces and press one key if the object was a gun and another if it was a tool. This procedure is depicted in Figure 13.6. In one

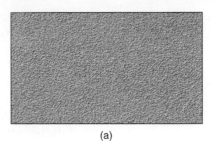

(a)

(b)

OR

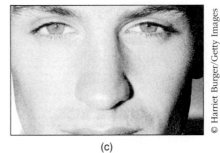

(c)

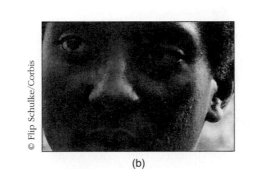

(d)

OR

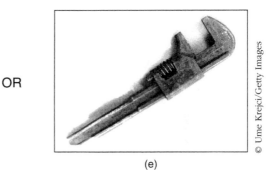

(e)

(a)

▼ FIGURE 13.6

On each trial, a black or white face was briefly flashed, followed by a gun or tool. Visual masks began and ended each trial. The task was to press a key indicating "gun" or "tool." Adapted from Payne (2001).

experiment, Payne gave subjects as long as they needed to make their object identifications; in the second experiment, a deadline was imposed. That is, in experiment 2, subjects had to respond within 500 ms of the target object's onset. Feedback given during a training phase ensured that subjects learned to respond quickly in the second experiment.

In experiment 1, because subjects could take as long as they wanted to make an object decision, there were few errors. It is a good thing that Payne included a second dependent variable, namely, the speed with which people made their gun–tool decisions. As shown in the left side of Figure 13.7, a stereotypic pattern emerged in reaction time. Overall, subjects were faster to identify guns. However, given that a gun had been presented, subjects were much faster to press the "gun" key if the picture had been preceded by a black face rather than a white face. An opposite pattern was observed for tools. There was an interaction between the race of the face prime and the identity of the target object. Viewing a black face primed identification of guns.

In experiment 2, because subjects had to respond quickly (in less than 500 ms), they made more errors than in the first experiment. Now you can see evidence of racial bias in the error data. The data are shown in the right side of Figure 13.7. Overall, subjects were more likely to make errors for tools than guns, mistakenly calling tools "guns." However, critically, subjects misidentified more tools as guns after a black face than after a white face.

Returning to the case of Amidou Diallo, you can envision that the police officers were reacting quickly and under stress. Payne's data suggest that when people are responding quickly, seeing a black person will increase their likelihood of misperceiving a harmless object as a gun. When in a hurry, people are forced to rely on stereotypes (which can act as a heuristic or shortcut); unfortunately, Americans have a stereotype of black people as dangerous (Devine & Elliot, 1995). The gun–tool paradigm is becoming

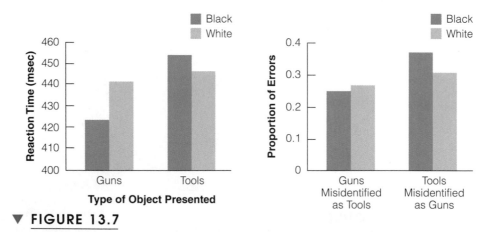

▼ FIGURE 13.7

The left panel shows the results from Payne's first experiment, in which subjects were given as much time as needed to make their gun–tool decisions. Racial bias was present in the reaction time data; subjects were particularly fast to respond to guns when they had been preceded by a black face. The right panel shows the results of the second experiment, in which subjects had to respond quickly. Now they made errors: Critically, they were more likely to misidentify a tool as a gun after having seen a black face. Adapted from Payne (2001).

popular for studying a variety of questions about racial bias (e.g., Amodio, Harmon-Jones, & Devine, 2003; Payne, Lambert, & Jacoby, 2002), and similar results have been obtained when the task is a shoot/don't shoot decision in a video game (Correll, Park, Judd, & Wittenbrink, 2002). The news is not all bad, however. Advances have also been made in understanding how to eliminate bias in the video game paradigm (Plant, Peruche, & Butz, 2005).

FROM PROBLEM TO EXPERIMENT
THE NUTS AND BOLTS

Problem   *How Does the Presence of Other People Affect an Individual's Performance on a Task?*

The presence of other people can affect our behavior in many ways. Certainly, when we know someone is watching us, we behave differently than when we believe we are unobserved. One example of this effect is known as **social facilitation,** which is the phenomenon that the presence of others can facilitate an individual's performance on a task. You may have noticed this effect yourself when you are exercising at a gym or playing a sport, for example. When spectators are present, you probably exert just a bit more effort and perform a little better. From this observation, we might predict that when people work together on a task, they will actually do better than when they work alone.

Problem   *Do people perform better when they work on a task with other people?*

This is an important consideration in industry, for example. Should jobs be designed so that people work alone or in groups? Are there conditions under which individual performance may be helped or hindered by others? What are those conditions?

Hypothesis   *When a person shares responsibility for a task with others, she or he will perform better on the task than if she or he performs it alone.*

To test this hypothesis, we must first find an appropriate task for people to perform in the laboratory. We must select something that can be performed both alone and with a group of people. Furthermore, the task must have an outcome that is measurable and comparable in both the individual and group situations. For example, suppose the task were to design a better telephone for the handicapped. Naturally, we would expect most group designs to be better than most individuals' designs (with the exception of an occasional genius, perhaps). But how would we compare the performance of each individual working in the group to his or her performance working alone? When working alone, the individual is solely responsible for the product. When working in a group, the individual is a member of a team and contributes only partially to the final product. It would be difficult to determine how much the individual contributes to the group product relative to his or her individual product. What we need is a task that is essentially the same whether performed alone or in a group and that also reflects the effects of group effort, while still allowing us to assess the individual's relative contribution.

A potential candidate for this task is one involving physical exertion, such as the force with which one can pull on a rope, a task discussed in research described in Chapter 1. Let us see if this task meets the criteria outlined earlier. First, the performance measure is easily quantified. The rope can be attached to a mechanism that measures the amount of force exerted when a person pulls on it. Second, the measure is meaningful whether one or several people pull the rope, since the metric of performance—that is, force—is the same in both situations. Finally, individual performance can be easily compared with group performance. We can ask each person to pull on the rope alone as hard as possible, then add up all the force scores. This sum would represent the potential contribution of each individual to the group effort and would serve as a baseline for comparing the effect of group performance. Next, we could have all the participants pull on the rope together and compare the force exerted by the group to the sum of the individuals' forces. If the group's total is greater than the sum of the individuals' scores, we would conclude that people's individual performance improves when they perform this task with others. We would know that in general the participants exerted more effort in the group than when alone.

One interesting question that arises in connection with this experiment is whether the size of the group affects individual performance. For example, if we believe that other people's presence will facilitate performance, then maybe the more people present, the more performance will be facilitated.

Hypothesis   *The larger the group working together, the greater will be the improvement in the individuals' performance.*

We can easily test this hypothesis with our rope-pull task. We can simply vary the size of the groups that we test: groups of two, three, five, and eight subjects.

Now, let us summarize the experimental variables so far. We have two independent variables, group size (two, three, five, or eight) and social environment (alone versus with the group). Group size will be a between-subjects factor; we cannot manipulate this within subjects because the groups are of different sizes, so by definition, we must have different people in each group. Social environment will be compared within subjects: Each person will perform the rope-pull task alone and also with a group.

Our dependent variable will be the total force exerted by the group members. In the alone condition, the individuals' scores will be summed to obtain the total score. There is one difficulty with this measure, now that we have decided to compare groups of different sizes. The total forces will be much greater in the larger than in the smaller groups, since more scores contribute to the total in the large groups. To make the groups comparable, we can convert the group scores to ratios. That is, we can measure the total force exerted by the group, then divide this by the sum of the individual forces of the members of this group. For example, if a group exerted 500 pounds of tension on the rope when they pulled together and a summed total of only 400 pounds when they pulled alone, the ratio would be 5:4. If we predict that the group will facilitate individual performance, these ratios should be larger than 1.00: The group force (the numerator) should be larger than the sum of the individual forces (the denominator). Furthermore, if we predict that larger groups produce more facilitation, the ratio should increase as group size increases (e.g., 5:4 for a group of three versus 6:4 for a group of eight).

What other factors must we consider? First, we must test more than one group in each condition. Even though a few people will participate in each group, each group will provide only two data points: the sum of the force exerted by the members alone and the total force exerted by the group pulling together. Obviously, we cannot make meaningful comparisons if we have only one observation in each group-size condition. Ideally, we should test 20 to 30 groups in each condition. Second, we should counterbalance the order of the pulling conditions. For each group-size condition, the individuals in half the groups should perform the individual pull first; the other half should perform the group pull first. Third, people should have an adequate rest between their individual and group pulls, so that their muscles are not more fatigued in one condition than in the other.

Now let us think back over our experiment. First, do you think that we will find evidence for social facilitation? That is, do you think that people will exert more effort when they pull with the group than when they pull alone? Second, do you think that people in the larger groups will exert more effort than people in the smaller groups? Can you think of any reason that we might actually predict that the opposite will happen—that is, that the group situation will actually produce poorer performance? Recall that in the last section (and in Chapter 1) we introduced the idea of diffusion of responsibility to explain bystander apathy. That is, in many settings it has been observed that the more people who witness an emergency, the less likely it is that any one person will intervene, perhaps because individuals feel personally less responsible when others are around to help. Interestingly, we can invoke this theory to predict that sharing the work with other people will actually reduce individual performance: The opposite prediction to that made by our social-facilitation hypothesis. Therefore, our proposed experiment provides a test of two competing theories, a desirable situation from a scientist's point of view.

As you will recall from Chapter 1, experiments very similar to the one we have proposed have been conducted: The research indicates that, in fact, people work less hard in a group than when alone. The earliest such study (by Ringelmann, reported in Kravitz & Martin, 1986) suggested that groups of two work at only 93 percent of their total individual capabilities and groups of four and eight dropped to 77 and 49 percent, respectively. Thus, contrary to our original predictions (social facilitation), individuals' performance is lower in groups and becomes lower still as the group size increases. This phenomenon has been called **social loafing** (Latané et al., 1979) and seems consistent with the notion that responsibility diffuses among the members of a group.

Does our experiment disprove the hypothesis of social facilitation? Not at all. As further research has shown, the critical variable determining whether the presence of other people facilitates or impairs an individual's performance is the issue of whether the individual's behavior can be uniquely observed in the situation. Social loafing occurs when an individual is an anonymous member of a group. However, when the individual knows that his or her performance can be identified, the effect can be eliminated. For example, relay racers swim faster when their individual lap times are announced than when only the overall team time is announced (Williams, Nida, Baca, & Latané, 1989). Therefore, when people know that their personal performance can be assessed, they are likely to work harder when others are present. However, if a person can "fade into the crowd," then he or she is likely to expend less effort. ("After all, why should I knock myself out when nobody notices, anyway?")

The advice to the business manager would seem to be that work groups should be designed so that a person's output can be observed by others (to produce social facilitation) and also so that each individual's efforts can be assessed independently of those of the group (to prevent social loafing).

▼ SUMMARY

1. Social psychological research is in many ways more difficult to perform than other types of research discussed in this book because the situations examined are often quite complex, with many variables affecting behavior. Thus, introducing experimental control into the situation so that sound inferences can be made about the effects of different experimental treatments on the dependent variable often requires great effort.

2. Experimental control combats the problem of experimental error, or any variation in the dependent variable that is not caused by the independent variable. Such extraneous factors should be controlled as much as possible by equating them across conditions. If control is not possible, then these factors should be randomly distributed over conditions.

3. The expectations of both the experimenter and the participants can create problems in social psychological (and other) research. The experimenter may subtly bias results in several ways—for example, by treating people slightly differently in the different conditions. A solution to this problem is for the experimenter to be blind with respect to the condition at the time of testing—but this is not often feasible, since the experimenter must provide the experimental manipulation in some way. Experimenter-bias effects are likely to be discovered in the normal course of scientific research.

4. The problem of participants' behavior being shaped by the demand characteristics of the experimental setting is potentially more dangerous than that of experimenter bias because demand characteristics are likely to be common across experiments in different laboratories. Demand characteristics include participants' expectations of how they should perform in the experiment. Orne developed some ingenious techniques for evaluating the effect of demand characteristics. He used quasicontrol groups such as simulating participants, which often enable investigators to assess whether demand characteristics affect a particular experiment but not what the outcome of the experiment would be were the demand characteristics removed.

5. One way to avoid the problem of demand characteristics is to conduct an experiment "in the field," or in a natural setting. Demand characteristics are then excluded, since the people are not even aware that they are in an experiment. Many social psychologists are turning to field research, since generality of results is no longer a problem as it is in laboratory research. However, severe problems can occur with field research, too. It is often difficult to manipulate effectively an independent variable while controlling extraneous "nuisance" variables, and it is also difficult to know what to measure, since participants do not even know they are in an experiment and cannot be asked to perform some task, rate how they feel, or so on. Even if these problems are overcome, we are left with an important ethical problem—even harder to solve—as to whether psychologists are justified in experimenting on unsuspecting members of society.

6. Recently, social psychologists have adapted the techniques of cognitive psychologists to study such topics as attitudes. We can make inferences about people's attitudes and preferences based on how long they take to respond to situations or what they remember.

▼ KEY TERMS

autokinetic phenomenon
blind
bystander intervention (bystander effect)
conformity
confounding
control variables
demand characteristics
diffusion of responsibility
double-blind experiment
experimental control
experimental error
experimenter bias
field research
implicit attitude measures
implicit memory tests

interaction
obedience
placebo effect
prime
priming
randomization
simulating control participants
single-blind experiment
social facilitation
social loafing
social norms
social psychology
target
visual masks

▼ DISCUSSION QUESTIONS

1. Why is experimental control often more difficult to achieve in social psychology experiments than in other sorts of research? To illustrate, make a list of variables that would have to be controlled (or randomized) in a typical bystander intervention study that is done
   a. in a laboratory situation, and
   b. in a field experiment.
2. Evaluate the following statement: "If an extraneous variable is in danger of being confounded with the independent variable of interest in an experiment, it is better to randomize the influence of the variable across conditions than to control it so that it cannot vary between conditions." Explain why you think this statement is true or false.
3. Discuss the problems of unintentional experimenter bias and demand characteristics of the experimental situation. How can the influence of these

problems be minimized in experimental situations? Are these problems equally likely to occur in all types of research?
4. Discuss the advantages and disadvantages of field research. Would you mind being the unwitting participant in an experiment on bystander intervention if you later found out that your reactions in the situation had been recorded?
5. Make a list of topics that you think could best be studied
   a. in laboratory experiments, and
   b. in field experiments.
   Explain why you choose the topics you do in each case.
6. Milgram's (1963) research on obedience to authority was harshly criticized by a number of psychologists. One of the most vocal critics, Baumrind (1964), argued that the long-term, psychological

risk to participants outweighed any potential contribution to psychological science. Milgram conducted follow-up sessions (immediate and 1 year later) to determine whether participants had suffered any long-term, negative effects from their participation in his obedience experiments. This follow-up included self-report questionnaires and verbal reports to a psychiatrist. Given the dubious validity of verbal and self-reports, what would you do to determine whether a person has incurred long-term, negative effects from participating in an obedience study such as Milgram's?

7. Assess the validity of Payne's weapon identification task. That is, how do you feel about studying racial bias in a priming paradigm? What are the strengths and weaknesses of this approach?

WEB CONNECTIONS

A good overview of social psychology can be found at:
http://www.spsp.org/what.htm

This site covers nearly all aspects of social psychology:
http://www.socialpsychology.org/

This site will let you measure your own implicit attitudes toward blacks and whites, men and women, the young and the elderly, and an ever-expanding variety of other groups.
https://implicit.harvard.edu/implicit/

▼ LABORATORY RESOURCES

In this chapter, you read about racial stereotypes. There are other types of biases you could study, such as sexism, age discrimination, and homophobia. Langston (2002) Chapter 8 describes experiments on sex stereotypes. For example, truck drivers and doctors are often assumed to be male, whereas secretaries and nurses are assumed to be females. Evidence for these gender biases can be found in an examination of people's reading times. That is, people are slower to read sentences in which a stereotypically male occupation is associated with a female pronoun than a male pronoun. For example, subjects read the sentence *"A lawyer must frequently argue his case out of court"* faster than the sentence *"A lawyer must frequently argue her case out of court."* In addition to replicating this basic effect, it would be interesting to think about how the size of the effect might differ across types of people. For example, do you think gender stereotypes would be more or less prevalent in older or younger adults? Conservatives or liberals? Men or women? You might also think about how this task could be modified to study other stereotyping domains (e.g., ageism).

PSYCHOLOGY IN ACTION
The Power of Being in an Experiment

People's knowledge that they are participating in an experiment often strongly affects their behavior. People do things when they are in an experiment that they would not do under other circumstances. You can demonstrate this by performing a simple experiment with your friends. Make a list of 10 friends and randomly assign them to one of two conditions, either the experimental condition or the control condition. The independent variable for the two groups is the statement you make at the beginning of the experiment. Say to the experimental participants, "I would like you to do some things for me as part of a psychology experiment for one of my courses." Say to the control group, "I would like you to do me a favor." Then tell each friend that you have a request: You would like the person to do five jumping jacks, six sit-ups, four push-ups, and make a paper airplane as fast as possible.

Of course, the small number of participants in the experiment makes it difficult for you to draw any strong conclusions. But you will probably discover that the friends who are asked to help you out with a psychology experiment are likely to be much more cooperative. They probably will do more of the activities, do them faster, and ask fewer questions. People in the control group will probably think you have been studying too hard.

The point of this demonstration is to show that psychology experiments do not just provide neutral surveys of behavior; they also can create the behaviors that are studied. When people know they are being observed in an experiment, they may react differently. Thus, the psychologist is in danger of studying behavior produced in the laboratory that may bear little relation to behavior occurring in the outside world. The cues in the experiment that guide people's behavior in this way are called demand characteristics. ■

CHAPTER **14**

ENVIRONMENTAL PSYCHOLOGY

Science is built up with facts, as a house is with stones. But a collection of facts is no more a science than a heap of stones is a house. (J. H. POINCARÉ)

In their two-volume handbook on environmental psychology, which has more than 1,500 pages, Stokols and Altman (1987) describe environmental psychology as an interdisciplinary study of "human behavior and well-being in relation to the sociophysical environment" (p. 1). In addition to psychologists studying environmental psychology, an amazingly broad group of researchers and practitioners has focused on person–environment interactions. These people come from such fields as architecture, geography, public health, sociology, and urban planning. This diversity of disciplinary interest has led to the growth of a broad-based field that includes the study of spatial behavior, crowding, stress, and territoriality in a variety of environments, including schools, residences, workplaces, the natural environment, and extreme and unusual locales (such as deserts or the Arctic). Furthermore, many researchers have studied various applications of environmental psychology in such areas as conserving resources and encouraging recycling. From this broad array of topics, we have selected a few to illustrate three methodological problems.

The problem discussed in greatest depth in this chapter is **generality of results.** One study of noise (Cohen, Glass, & Singer, 1973) showed that children who lived on the lower floors of an apartment building that was built directly over a busy freeway were poorer readers than those children living higher up, where the noise of passing traffic was less intense. As a result of this study, the building occupants demanded that a roof be built over the freeway (Figure 14.1). Did the problem justify this demand? Investigators must be able to show—as did Cohen and his colleagues—that the conclusions drawn from their data can be meaningfully generalized.

A second problem that environmental psychologists share with experimental psychologists is the effects of noise on behavior. Experimental psychologists are most likely to approach this problem with laboratory experiments. However, environmental psychologists generally prefer field studies, so that quasi-experiments replace true experiments. Thus, we will discuss effects of airplane and construction noise upon students who have not been randomly assigned to experimental conditions.

A third problem, one that is perhaps more troublesome for environmental psychologists than for other researchers, involves **ethical issues** in research. The scientist has a responsibility to ensure that individuals are not harmed in the search for knowledge. Often, however, some degree of risk is involved. How, then, can the psychologist ensure that research complies with established ethical principles?

▼ IS SCIENCE THE ONLY PATH TO TRUTH?

Our society places a high value on science and technology. The landing of astronauts on the moon symbolizes the power and prestige of American science. Many citizens believe that our high standard of living, directly attributable to such technological devices as automobiles, televisions, and computers, will continue to increase as science

▼ **FIGURE 14.1**

These apartments are built over the approach to the George Washington Bridge in New York City. Highway noise is a severe problem for the residents.

Courtesy of Dr. Shelden Cohen

advances. Hence, the quest for scientific knowledge is widely justified on the practical grounds that science creates better lives for people, as well as on the philosophical grounds that science, rather than art, religion, literature, and so on, offers the best chance for finding truth.

Psychology has yet to achieve as many stunning successes as other sciences, such as physics and chemistry. Therefore, it is more difficult to justify the scientific benefits of psychology on purely practical grounds. However, some people claim that our understanding of physical processes such as those related to nuclear energy has so far outstripped our understanding of human processes that we have become captives of our science, rather than beneficiaries. As pollution, crowding, and related environmental problems decrease the quality of life, the importance of social science becomes more and more obvious. Environmental psychology deals with issues that directly affect our everyday lives.

Since physical scientists have built up impressive accomplishments, both theoretically and practically, it seems reasonable for social scientists to emulate their more established colleagues. Virtually all social scientists believe that powerful truths can and will be discovered by applying the scientific methods used by physical scientists. Science will grant us a better theoretical understanding of the nature of human activity, and this will eventually lead to a technology capable of improving the quality of life.

Not all scientists are aware of the limitations of science, despite brief exposure to these points as part of their education. The practicing scientist may eventually discard assorted philosophical points as being of only limited value in his or her daily work (Medawar, 1969, Chapter 1).

Nevertheless, it is appropriate to present the other side of the coin and to discuss these limitations. Science focuses on only certain questions and ignores other issues. It would be extremely difficult to answer the question "Does God exist?" scientifically, so most scientists are content to pursue other matters. Similarly, psychologists tend to concentrate on the study of behavior rather than on other kinds of human experience. Aldous Huxley (1946) comments on this aspect of science:

> Pragmatically [scientists] are justified in acting in this odd and extremely arbitrary way; for by concentrating exclusively on the measurable aspects of such elements of experience as can be explained in terms of a causal system they have been able to achieve a great and increasing control over the energies of nature. But power is not the same thing as insight and, as a representation of reality, the scientific picture of the world is inadequate for the simple reason that science does not even profess to deal with experience as a whole but only with certain aspects of it in certain contexts. All this is quite clearly understood by the more philosophically minded men of science. But some scientists . . . tend to accept the world picture implicit in the theories of science as a complete and exhaustive account of reality; then tend to regard those aspects of experience which scientists leave out of account, *because they are incompetent to deal with them,* as being somehow less real than the aspects which science has arbitrarily chosen to abstract from out of the infinitely rich totality of given facts. (pp. 35–36, emphasis added)

Weizenbaum (1976) makes this same point using an anecdote about a drunkard looking for lost keys. The drunkard, kneeling under a streetlight, is approached by a police officer. The drunkard explains he is looking for his keys, which he lost somewhere over there in the darkness. When the police officer asks why he isn't looking over there, the drunkard replies that the light is better here under the lamppost. Science is somewhat like the drunkard, since it looks where its tools provide the best illumination.

Environmental psychology is particularly hard pressed when this criticism of science is applied. The real world, as distinct from the somewhat artificial world of the carefully controlled laboratory studies of the experimental psychologist, is chock-full of problems outside the circle of light given off by a streetlight. Psychologists know that scientific progress comes about, slowly but surely, if they stay within the rays of the streetlight until a new breakthrough yields a more powerful light. But this traditional approach offers small hope for the rapid solution of pressing environmental problems. If environmental psychologists move slowly and traditionally, they are open to the criticism that their research is irrelevant to the needs of society. This is a serious charge, since ultimately society pays the price for this research through federal research grants and such. On the other hand, the unwary psychologist who immediately rushes in to solve the ills of society runs a high risk of obtaining results that may later prove to be inadequate. And if public policy is formulated on the basis of such incomplete research (or no research at all), the price to society may be quite high (Figure 14.2).

Discovering the Truth about City Life

All of us, whether we dwell in large metropolitan areas or in rural communities, have opinions about the quality of urban life. For some, the city represents the height of culture and achievement. For others, the city is a cesspool of violence, pollution, and noise. How can we discover the truth about city life?

One of the most insightful views of city life can be found in a fascinating book, *Death and Life of Great American Cities,* by Jane Jacobs (1961). As one example of her insight, we will briefly discuss Jacobs's views on the functions of the sidewalk.

© Corbis/Bettmann

▼ **FIGURE 14.2**

Demolition of Part of the Pruitt-Igoe Housing Project in St. Louis. These buildings, although physically sound, were rendered unfit for occupation because of vandalism. Since then, research conducted by environmental social scientists has revealed how to prevent such tragedies.

For most of us, the sidewalk exists to get us from one place to another. Most of us, including psychologists, have not given much thought to the psychological functions of the common sidewalk. Jacobs shows that the sidewalk makes a great contribution to social interaction within the city. She notes that owners of small shops that line local streets—tailors, drugstores, candy stores—provide a multitude of social services for the neighborhood street users. These services go beyond the nature of each individual business. Thus, a tailor might keep an eye out for children running into the street and warn their parents; the candy store owner might let children use his toilet facilities so they won't have to run upstairs; the delicatessen owner might receive mail for a customer who is out of town for a few days. Each such service by itself is small. But when added together, Jacobs argues, they form the basis for positive feelings about a neighborhood as a good place to live.

Anyone who has lived on such an old-fashioned city street intuitively accepts the truth of Jacobs's statements. Yet, her conclusions are based only on naturalistic observation. Although observation is an important origin for science (see Chapter 2), a better method would add credibility to her statements. There is nothing experimental about the way Jacobs collected her data. No systematic attempts were made to manipulate independent variables and record dependent variables; no replications were conducted; no control variables enter her descriptions of behavior. Although no scientist would reject her conclusions outright, few would accept them. Most scientists would claim that an adequate test of her suggestions, which are not clear hypotheses that can be tested easily, has yet to be accomplished. Until the formal procedures required by science are duly performed, Jacobs's conclusions cannot be sanctified as scientific truth but only regarded as interesting possibilities.

The problem takes us back to our example of the streetlight. Jacobs is operating outside of the light. This makes scientists reluctant to accept her truths. Yet to many people, her conclusions seem obviously correct. Why is the scientific method any better than astute observation? The answer to this important question is given in Chapter 1, where we discuss the fixation of belief. You will recall that the great advantage of the scientific method is that it is self-correcting. If a different observer reached different conclusions about the functions and value of sidewalks, how could you decide which view was correct? So far we do not have a better way than science to decide such issues. Science as a method of fixing beliefs is much like democracy as described by Winston Churchill: "Democracy is the worst system of government except for all the others." Accepting the scientific method does not imply that any other method of arriving at truth—such as Jacobs's observations of city life—is necessarily invalid. Indeed, psychological research has confirmed many of Jacobs's suggestions. There most certainly is more than one path to truth. But when we must agree on some particular truth over which there is some dispute, then the scientific method, with all its limitations, offers the best long-term solution.

14.1   EXPERIMENTAL TOPICS AND RESEARCH ILLUSTRATIONS

Topic   *Generalization of Results*
Illustration   *Crowding*

No experiment is an end in itself. Experiments are steps along the way to the psychologist's ultimate goal of predicting and explaining behavior. Unless results of past experiments can be applied to new situations, the experiments are of little value. Thus, models explaining the flow of electricity are designed to deal not only with the small number of electrons that have been studied in the laboratory but also with the electrons in the wall sockets of your house.

An important criterion for judging the utility of an experiment is its **representativeness.** Experiments that are representative allow us to extend their findings to more general situations. When researchers discovered that cigarette tars caused cancer in laboratory beagles, many cigarette smokers felt that such research demonstrated only that dogs should not smoke. In short, they doubted the representativeness of the findings and did not believe that the results could be generalized to humans. However, later studies confirmed these earlier findings; now, the surgeon general is so convinced of the dangers of cigarette smoking that all cigarette packages must be labeled with a warning to the user.

The cigarette–beagle experiment is one example of the problem of generalizing results from one sample to a different sample or to a different population. We shall term this **sample generalization.** It occurs in many forms. The most studied human organism is the college student taking an introductory psychology class who, as part of the educational process, is often required to participate in several experiments. Let us pretend that we have just completed a study about different methods of improving reading speed and comprehension using a small sample of Rice University students enrolled in Introductory Psychology. If such a study yields appropriate results, it could have important implications for education. But first, before these implications can be made, several questions about sample generalization need to be answered. First, are these results typical or representative of all Rice students taking introductory

INTRODUCING THE VARIABLES

Dependent Variables

Environmental psychologists often record feelings and emotion in addition to observable behavior. Such internal states are inferred from rating scales. Thus, a study on crowding might ask persons to rate such things as their opinion of the other people involved in the study, the pleasantness of the experience, and the perceived size of the room. Merely labeling a scale with some descriptive title, however, does not guarantee that the scale measures that, and only that, particular facet of human experience. Consider a rating question such as the following, for which the reader must circle a number from 1 to 5:

In terms of physical attractiveness, my partner was:

Extremely good looking				A real dog
1	2	3	4	5

The subject's response could well be influenced by nonphysical behavioral characteristics. A partner who was helpful and cooperative might be judged more physically attractive than the same partner (in a different experimental condition) who was insulting and rude.

Independent Variables

Studies of crowding, spatial behavior, and territoriality manipulate **density,** which is most often defined as the number of people per unit area—for example, six people in 10 square meters (or feet). Since we can count the number of people and can measure area, density so defined satisfies our requirements for a clear operational definition. Because density has two components, we can manipulate it in two ways. First, we can hold the number of people constant and vary the size of the room that contains them. Second, we can hold room size constant and vary the number of people in the room. Although these two kinds of density manipulation may at first appear equivalent, it turns out that they have different

psychology? Again, if our sample consists only of Rice freshman, we cannot be sure that Rice seniors would yield the same results. And even if our results generalized to all Rice undergraduates, it would probably not be worthwhile to institute a drastic change in reading methodology, unless it could be demonstrated that college students across the country could benefit. Even then, we might ask if high school and grade school students could use this new reading method. Clearly, a single experiment will seldom generalize to every population of interest.

Similar problems about generalization of independent and dependent variables also exist. Environmental stress can be induced by such diverse means as increasing temperature, increasing noise level, and depriving a person of sleep the night before an experiment. To the extent that our concern is with environmental stress in general, rather than specific effects of noise, temperature, and sleep deprivation, we must ensure that these different manipulations of related independent variables allow us to make representative statements about stress. We shall call this **variable representativeness.** Let us say we are concerned with the effects of temperature on urban riots: Does the long, hot summer lead to aggression? When this is studied in the laboratory (Baron & Bell, 1976), we find that high temperatures do not necessarily lead to increased aggression. But before we can reject this explanation of summertime urban problems and advance to other hypotheses (e.g., more young people are idling in the streets during the summer months), we must ensure that independent and dependent measures generalize from the laboratory to the urban scene. Most of us would be willing to accept the assertion effects on behavior and feelings (e.g., see Marshall & Heslin, 1975). So the usual operational definition, although precise and clear, is inadequate, because it confounds two separate variables: number of people and amount of space. For example, if density is manipulated by increasing the number of people and holding room size constant, we do not know if observable differences are best attributed to density effects or to the effects of numbers of people. The issue is further complicated by the fact that psychological density often is not the same as physical density. The feeling of being crowded depends not only on physical density but also on social context (Rapoport, 1975). A crowded discotheque has far more pleasant associations than an equally crowded subway car.

Another set of independent variables studied by environmental psychologists falls into the category of stressors: those agents that produce stressful situations. Loud noise, high temperatures,

and air pollution are examples of this kind of independent variable.

Control Variables

Studies in environmental psychology often lack the careful control variables found in laboratory work done in psychology. Although gross physical features of the environment, such as room temperature, are controlled, more finely grained variables—for example, the relative position of participants (side by side or face to face)—are often neglected. This defect is particularly evident in field studies that by their very nature do not offer the experimenter much control over the situation. Environmental psychologists who conduct field studies are aware of this problem but think that the greater reality of the field situation as opposed to the more artificial laboratory setting is ample recompense.

that a temperature of 95°F in the laboratory is equivalent to the same temperature in the city street. But this equivalence is less clear when we consider common laboratory measures of aggression. The most widely used technique calls for the subject to administer an electric shock to a confederate, as used in Milgram's work that was outlined in Chapter 13 (see also Figure 14.3). (In reality, no shock is delivered, but the experimenter hopes that the subject thinks he or she is controlling an electric shock.) Higher shock

Estate of Bunji Tagawa

▼ FIGURE 14.3

A Typical Shock Machine Used in Laboratory Studies of Aggression. The buttons control the (hypothetical) shock intensity.

© Lionel Delevingne/Stock Boston

▼ **FIGURE 14.4**

Aggression in a Nonlaboratory Situation. Do you think this is the same kind of aggression tested in Figure 14.3?

intensities and longer shock durations are interpreted as evidence for greater aggression. Is the aggression involved in pushing a button the same aggression involved in hurling a brick through a storefront window or sniping at police and firefighters with a rifle (Figure 14.4)? Although the ultimate effect—harming someone else—appears to be the same in aggression inside and outside the laboratory, civil disorder may add another dimension to aggression. Establishing a physical analogy in the laboratory—as when rats are trained to "hoard" money—does not necessarily imply a psychological identity. Indeed, it is this considerable difficulty in establishing variable representativeness that has turned many environmental psychologists away from laboratory studies and toward field studies, despite the fact that considerably less experimental control results.

In this chapter, we discuss four studies on crowding and carefully examine how their results might be generalized. The first study uses animal subjects; the rest use humans. The three human studies differ in that one is based on demographic data correlated by sociologists, one uses field study techniques with experimental control instead of post hoc statistical control, and one is a laboratory experiment.

Crowding in Animals: A Laboratory Study

A long series of studies conducted by John Calhoun (1962, 1966, 1971) at the National Institute of Mental Health produced some astonishing findings about the long-term effects of crowding in rats. Calhoun placed his rats in a "rat universe" (Figure 14.5) with four compartments. Since compartments 1 and 4 were not connected (Figure 14.5), they became dead ends, and the rats congregated in compartments 2 and 3. This overcrowding caused several pathological types of behavior to develop. The mortality rate for infant rats was as high as 96 percent in pens 2 and 3. Female rats were unable to build proper nests and often dropped infant rats. These infants died where they were dropped

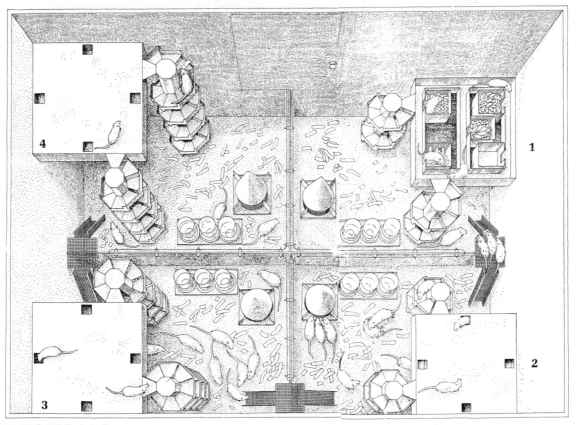

▼ FIGURE 14.5

The Rat Universe Studied by Calhoun. Note that the pens are not all joined together by ramps, so that two of them become dead ends. (Reprinted by permission of the Executor of the Estate of Bunji Tagawa.)

and often were eaten by adult rats. The high mortality rates had the greatest implications for the rat universe. Odd sexual behavior was also exhibited by male rats. The strangest rats were called "probers" by Calhoun. Instead of engaging in normal rat courtship, these probers would pursue female rats into their burrows, where they would eat dead infant rats. Thus, the independent variable (high density) caused strange maternal and sexual behaviors (dependent variables) to evolve.

These results are frightening, to say the least; if generalized to human crowding, they strongly imply that overcrowding will eventually destroy society as we know it today. But before we forsake our high-rise apartments for the wide-open spaces, let us first examine a newer study conducted with nonhuman primates.

The classic work of Calhoun just described established a model that links crowding and aggression. But more recent work with primates suggests a coping model is more accurate. Nonhuman primates cope with crowding by developing compensatory behavior that reduces aggressive encounters. For example, van Wolkenten, Davis, Gong, and de Waal (2006) observed brown capuchins under uncrowded and short-term (30 minutes) crowded conditions. They found no differences in aggressive behaviors, which supports the coping model and rejects Calhoun's density/aggression model. However, in the crowded condition the capuchins exhibited greater grooming behaviors; the authors interpreted this result to mean that grooming reduces aggression, which is consistent with the coping model. However, as the authors duly noted, the relatively short exposure to crowding does not rule out the possibility of aggression with much longer crowding durations.

In summary, the classic finding from research with rats is that crowding produces aggressive behaviors, but crowded primates may avoid aggression by developing coping behaviors. Let us turn to studies of crowding with humans to discover if crowded humans cope with high density (like capuchins) or become aggressive (like rats).

Crowding in Humans: A Correlational Demographic Study

Calhoun's studies with rats imply that high density causes pathological behavior. Since it would be highly unethical for an investigator to crowd people for long periods in the way Calhoun crowded rats, a direct experimental test analogous to Calhoun's experiments is impossible.

However, there are parts of our big cities where society has created high densities, and it is certainly ethical to observe the effects of these densities in the real world. The advantage of studying such real-life situations is that we have less difficulty generalizing results, for example, from one city to another, than from a laboratory to a city. The disadvantage is that there is virtually no experimental control over the independent variable and possible extraneous variables. One solution often used when experimental control is not feasible is after-the-fact statistical control.

This is the approach taken by Evans, Palsane, Lepore, and Martin (1989), who studied crowding and social withdrawal in Pune, India. These researchers hypothesized that people would cope with crowding by withdrawing from social interactions. This, in turn, would decrease social ties, resulting in poorer psychological health. Social support was measured by a questionnaire with 40 items designed to indicate relationships with family and friends. Psychological symptoms were measured by additional interview items that asked if a particular symptom had been experienced in the last 2 months. Subjects were 175 male heads of household living in Pune, India.

The statistical technique used to evaluate results was correlation. It is important when using correlation to examine a wide range of the independent variable to avoid restriction of range (see Chapter 2), which can produce a low correlation. Because the study was conducted in India, residential density ranged from 11 persons per room to 2 persons per room, a greater range than is typically available in the United States (Galle, Grove, & McPherson, 1972).

Figure 14.6 shows the correlation between density and psychological symptoms and between density and social support. Both correlation coefficients are statistically reliable at the 0.05 level of significance. The positive correlation shows that increasing density is associated with more psychological symptoms, whereas the negative correlation shows that increasing density is associated with less social support.

Because this is a correlational study, we cannot automatically conclude that density causes psychological symptoms and decreased social support. It is logically possible that people with these characteristics have chosen to live in higher-density housing. Demographic studies like this are not able to assign people randomly to different density conditions, as is usually the case in laboratory studies. However,

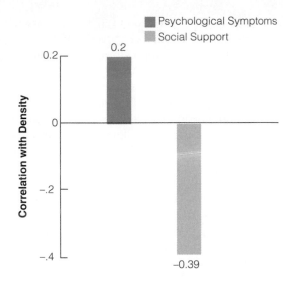

■ Psychological Symptoms
▢ Social Support

Correlations Between Density and Psychological Symptoms and Social Support. (Adapted from Evans et al., 1989.)

after considering the self-selection explanation, the researchers cautiously concluded that density was more likely to be a causal factor despite the limitations of the correlational method. Thus, these results are similar to conclusions drawn by Calhoun in his studies of animal crowding.

Crowding in Humans: Field Studies in Railroad Environments

Only a study that manipulates independent variables permits statements about causation. Saegert, Mackintosh, and West (1975) took their subjects to Manhattan's Pennsylvania Railroad Station to test the effects of crowding on performance and affect (feelings). Density, the most important independent variable, was manipulated by choosing the time at which the station was visited: either 10 A.M. to 11:30 A.M. (not a busy time) or 5 P.M. to 6 P.M. (at the height of rush hour). This manipulation confounds time of day with density, but the experimenters felt that time of day would not have any significant effects on the tasks. However, this assumption was not tested empirically. The experimenters were careful to make some population counts to ensure that the number of persons actually present was within the desired ranges.

The subjects were given a list of 42 tasks that they were to perform inside the station: such things as looking up a telephone number, finding the ticket counter, buying something at the newsstand, and so forth. They were given 30 minutes to complete as many tasks as they could; this was one dependent variable. Then subjects filled out a Mood Adjective Checklist. This is a rating scheme that permits people to describe their feelings.

The main finding was that "crowding did seem to interfere somewhat with tasks requiring knowledge and manipulation of the environment," since in the high-density condition, subjects completed about 25 tasks, versus about 29 for the low-density condition. Statistically, however, this effect was significant only at the 0.10 level, which means it could have occurred by chance in 1 experiment out of 10. The conclusions drawn by Saegert and coworkers are not very representative. The tasks required subjects to walk back and forth through the crowds in the railroad station. Even if no cognitive demands had been made—that is, if subjects had merely been asked to walk back and forth as many times as possible—we would expect crowds to have slowed them down. It is harder to move around in a dense crowd than in an empty station. Hence, it does not seem reasonable to generalize these results, as do the authors, to mean that cognitive functioning is impaired in crowded situations. However, the rating scales confirmed that subjects felt more anxious and more skeptical in the crowded condition. Since the checklist had 11 scales, it is not surprising that some of them showed an effect of density. This shotgun approach, where large numbers of rating scales are routinely administered in the hopes that some of them will yield significant results, can lead to a self-fulfilling hypothesis that can be misleading. Although it is quite reasonable that subjects felt more anxious in the crowded condition where they were bumped and shoved, the authors do not interpret the finding of greater feelings of skepticism.

When this study is compared with the Evans demographic study, one conclusion is obvious. Although studies that manipulate independent variables should generally be preferred to studies that only correlate variables, this does not necessarily mean that any experimental study is automatically superior to any correlational study. Good research, even of the correlational variety, is always preferable to poor research, even of the experimental variety.

Environmental psychologists often hang around railroad stations to observe crowding, and a more recent study shows that trains can be used for careful research. Evans and Wener (2007) studied train commuters traveling between New Jersey and Manhattan during rush hour and recorded two measures of density (car density: people/number of seats in car; seat density: people/number of seats in row) and three measures of stress (salivary cortisol, proofreading performance, and a self-rating of mood).

Using multiple-regression analysis, their results showed no significant correlations of car density and stress, but for seat density all three stress indices were significant. Commuters cope with car density by arranging themselves so as to avoid close physical proximity to other passengers when possible; for example, a commuter could choose to stand instead of taking an empty seat between two other passengers. So the proximity of other people nearby is a much more important stressor than the number of passengers in a train car.

Crowding in Humans: A Laboratory Study

In this laboratory study, Bateson and Hui (1992) used photographic slides and videotapes to simulate behavior at a London, England, railway ticket office. The slides and videos were all taken from the same spot. Density was manipulated by dividing the slides and videos into three categories based on the number of people present in the ticket office. In the low-density condition, only one or two people were in line at each ticket window. More people were present in the medium-density condition, and the high-density condition was quite crowded.

Subjects then completed a questionnaire, which was the dependent variable. It contained scales related to perceived crowding, perceived control, pleasure, and approach-avoidance. A structural model was built to explain the relationships between these dependent variables and independent variables such as density. This model predicted that density influences crowding through perceived control and that perceived control and crowding together determine people's emotional and behavioral responses as measured by the questionnaire. A complex statistical procedure (LISREL) was used to determine that the results fit the model.

Of special interest in this study was an additional field quasi-experiment that interviewed actual passengers buying railway tickets in the same ticket office where the laboratory stimuli were photographed. Three different correlation matrices (slides, videotapes, and field) were computed. Statistical analyses could not reject the hypothesis that all three matrices were equal. Thus, the laboratory methodology was validated. The authors concluded that slides and videotapes are quite appropriate ("ecologically valid") for studies of density and crowding.

Comparison of Crowding Studies

We have examined the effects of crowding in four studies: an animal study, a correlational demographic study, a field study, and a laboratory experiment. The kinds of generalizations we can draw from each study differ substantially. You are probably wondering which study is the best. There is no straightforward answer to this question: Psychologists do not agree on which is best, although experimental psychologists tend to prefer laboratory studies.

The purpose of this section is to acquaint you with the difficulties involved with generalizing the results of any study, regardless of type. By now, you may feel that these difficulties are so great that it hardly seems worthwhile to do research at all. But this conclusion is unduly pessimistic. Although it is difficult to generalize from any single study, a set of studies may indeed lead us to representative conclusions.

14.2   EXPERIMENTAL TOPICS AND RESEARCH ILLUSTRATIONS

Topic   *Quasi-Experiments*
Illustration   *Noise and Cognitive Performance*

True experiments require random assignment of participants to experimental conditions. This can be difficult to achieve in the area of environmental psychology, and so **quasi-experiments** (see Chapter 3) are often substituted for true experiments. This section discusses two recent quasi-experiments that investigated the effects of noise on elementary school and college students.

A European study (Hygge, Evans, & Bullinger, 2002) took advantage of the simultaneous opening and closing of the Munich airport to create a quasi-experiment. Two experimental groups consisted of children who either were exposed to aircraft noise at the old airport or would be exposed at the new airport. Two control groups, matched on sociodemographic variables, were not exposed to aircraft noise. Data were collected in three waves: Wave 1 was 6 months prior to the opening of the new airport, Wave 2 was 1 year later, and Wave 3 was 2 years later. Testing was conducted in a sound-isolated mobile van so that there was no confounding with immediate noise effects.

Figure 14.7 shows results for a long-term memory test where children recalled information a day after reading it. At the old airport, memory with aircraft noise was worse before the airport closed (Wave 1). Once the airport closed, however, the effects of noise disappeared. We would expect the opposite findings at the new airport. At Wave 1 there was no statistically significant effect of noise. However, at Wave 3 performance was better without noise. These results show that noise influences memory but that this effect is reversible when the noise source is removed.

▼ **FIGURE 14.7**

Mean Score on the Long-Term Memory Task as a Function of Airport, Noise Group, and Measurement Wave. Error bars show standard errors of the mean. (From Hygge et al., 2002, with permission.)

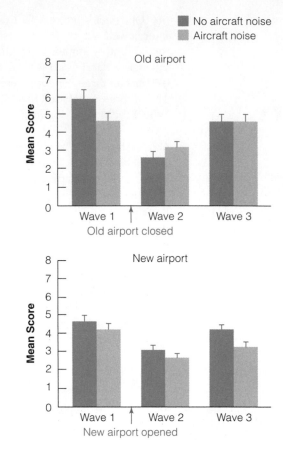

It is interesting to compare this quasi-experiment with an **ex post facto** (see Chapter 2) study of aircraft noise around Heathrow Airport in London. Haines, Stansfeld, Head, and Job (2002) correlated standardized tests in mathematics, science, and English with aircraft noise exposure; exposure varied according to distance from the airport. Exposure was statistically related to poorer reading and mathematics test scores. However, when other socioeconomic variables were statistically controlled, this correlational association disappeared. In general, results from quasi-experiments are more robust than results from ex post facto studies because scientists prefer statements about causation to statements about correlation.

Another quasi-experiment studied effects of construction noise on residents of college dorms (Ng, 2000). The noise level from outside building construction varied in three dorm wings (near, central, far). Four kinds of measures were taken: a questionnaire survey, self-completed activity logs, resident-turnover record, and external observation of windows open or closed. Higher percentages of residents in the noisier wings reported interference with activities such as telephone conversations. The near-wing residents reported keeping their windows closed more often than residents of quieter wings. However, while the objective external observation of windows found more open windows in the quieter wings, there was no reliable effect or interaction of whether construction was going on. The most important correlate of number of open windows was outside temperature.

All quasi-experiments are not automatically equally useful just because they are quasi-experiments. Comparing the two quasi-experiments discussed in this section reveals that the European study was more sophisticated and elegantly designed. Many of the measures taken in the college dorm study did not discriminate between construction noise being present or absent. This is a weakness shared with ex post facto studies of noise. In contrast, the Munich study controlled several variables, such as the presence of noise during data collection.

14.3 EXPERIMENTAL TOPICS AND RESEARCH ILLUSTRATIONS

Topic *Ethical Issues*
Illustration *Deception and Concealment*

Psychologists are extremely concerned with the ethics of research when human participants are involved. Although some of this concern is pragmatic, caused by fear of restriction of research funds and loss of access to subject populations, most psychologists are ethical persons who have no desire to inflict harm on anyone. The mad researcher who will do anything to obtain data is largely a myth.

Since it is difficult for an experimenter to be completely impartial and objective in judging the ethical issues concerning his or her own research, most universities and research institutions have institutional review boards (see Chapter 4) that judge whether the proposed research is ethical. Indeed, all federally funded research must be approved by such a board before any funding is granted. As noted in Chapter 4, these boards are guided by several principles advocated by the American Psychological Association (2002). One important principle is the right of **informed consent.** This means that every potential participant in an experiment is given both an explanation of all salient features of the research before the experiment is conducted and the opportunity to decline to participate in the research. Thus, the experimenter has a clear ethical obligation to inform participants of any possible harmful effects of the experiment. For example, if an environmental psychology experiment calls for loud noises as stressors, participants must be told this in advance, so that anyone with a history of sensitivity to sound, resulting perhaps from a childhood illness, can decline to participate. (Even with informed consent, no ethical researcher would use extremely loud sounds that might cause permanent hearing loss.)

It is extremely difficult for many proposed studies in environmental psychology to comply with the principle of informed consent. There are many situations in which, if people knew they were being observed, they might not behave normally. In such cases, the researcher would like to conceal the fact that an experiment is under way, only informing or debriefing participants after the study has ended. Clearly, this procedure violates the principle of informed consent, since the person has neither been informed nor given consent: Such research could be banned outright. However, many psychologists think that such a severe restriction would seriously impair their ability to design studies aimed at understanding human behavior in real-life environments—that is, it would greatly reduce the ability to generalize research. They argue that the potential worth of the research must be balanced against the potential harm to participants.

Imagine that you are serving on an ethics review board. Decide whether you would allow the following examples of proposed research:

1. An environmental psychologist sits in a crowded library and keeps detailed records of seating patterns.

2. An environmental psychologist makes videotapes of seating patterns in a library. These tapes are maintained indefinitely; library patrons do not know they have been filmed.

3. An experimental psychologist tells students that she is interested in their reading comprehension when in reality she is recording the speed of their responses rather than their comprehension.

4. A social psychologist is studying bystander intervention in a liquor store. Permission has been obtained from the store manager. In clear view of a patron, an experimenter "steals" a bottle of liquor. A second experimenter approaches the patron and asks, "Did you see him steal that bottle?"

5. A social psychologist connects surface electrodes to male participants with their prior approval. These participants are told that the electrodes are connected to a meter in front of them that measures sexual arousal. In reality, the meter is controlled by the experimenter. Participants are then shown slides of nude males and females. The meter gives high readings for pictures of males, leading the participants to believe they have latent homosexual tendencies.

There are no absolutes in ethics, and we cannot state that some of these examples are clearly ethical and others are clearly not. However, informal discussions with our colleagues revealed that only number 1 was unequivocally considered ethical. Since the psychologist is merely observing and does not know the people (they are represented only by symbols on the data sheet), informed consent is not deemed necessary. Any individual, psychologist or not, could easily observe these same people in the library. The potential harm to participants is negligible.

You may be astonished that objections were raised to every other example. Number 2 was thought to invade personal privacy, since the tapes were not erased after data had been abstracted. Number 3 would be acceptable only if the experimenter carefully debriefed participants by explaining the nature and reasons for this minor deception. Number 4 was actually performed; a patron denied seeing the theft and then called the police as soon as she left the store. The investigator had to go down to the police station to bail out the experimenters. Number 5 was considered unethical, even with debriefing. It is not clear that the potential psychological harm of the participants' thinking they had hidden homosexual tendencies could be removed by even immediate debriefing, especially if they did indeed have latent homosexual tendencies that until the experiment had been successfully suppressed.

An experiment that generated some ethical controversy was done by Middlemist, Knowles, and Matter (1976). They were interested in the effects of crowding in a men's room. Men appear to prefer to stand apart at urinals whenever possible, so the experimenters controlled the spacing of males at a row of three urinals adjacent to a toilet by placing a mop bucket and a "Don't Use" sign in one of the urinals. A confederate of the experimenter was stationed at one of the end urinals. The distance was varied between the participant and the confederate by putting the bucket and sign either adjacent to the confederate or one urinal away. This forced the participants to select a urinal immediately adjacent to the toilet stall, so the confederate was either next to the participant or one urinal away from the participant. Middlemist and associates reasoned that crowding would result in stress, which would, in turn, delay the onset and shorten the duration of urination by the participant. To determine whether this was the case, one of the experimenters was seated in the toilet stall with a hidden periscope through which he could secretly view and measure the onset and duration of urination.

Although the participants could not be identified by the person peering through the periscope, this seems to be a particularly unethical invasion of privacy, especially since the urinal users were unknowing participants. In a criticism of the ethics of the urinal experiment, Koocher (1977) noted that ethical principles require that psychologists must maintain the dignity of their participants and that when dignity and privacy are threatened, the experimenter must carefully weigh the benefits of the research against its costs. Koocher pointed out that although this was a public lavatory, people using it expect some degree of privacy. Middlemist and associates (1977) defended their project by noting that since the participants did not know they were being observed, they could not be embarrassed or otherwise hurt.

These examples, especially the urinal study, should show that there often is no clear answer as to what is ethical. The responsibility rests with the experimenter and the review boards. Although deception and concealment may be justified in limited instances, great caution is demanded in such experiments, and informed consent should be obtained whenever possible.

FROM PROBLEM TO EXPERIMENT
THE NUTS AND BOLTS

Problem   *Is Exposure to Noise Bad for You?*

An issue that concerns nearly everyone is the psychological effect of noise on humans. Airports, factories, and city streets expose citizens to long-term noisy environments. How might we evaluate possible effects of such exposure to noise?

Problem   *Does noise cause psychological harm?*

As always, several hypotheses can be derived from this vague problem. First, we will try a laboratory approach by formulating a hypothesis that can be tested under highly controlled circumstances.

Hypothesis   *Exposure to loud (110-decibel sound pressure level) and continuous white noise will cause decreases in the number and accuracy of arithmetic problems that can be performed in 25 minutes.*

How did we arrive at some of the variables specified in the hypothesis? The independent variable, noise intensity (set at 110 decibels, roughly as loud as a riveter), is close to the limit for safe exposure to 25 minutes of noise. Any louder noise might be harmful, and any softer noise might not yield experimental effects; that is, if no effects of noise on performance were obtained with noise much less than 110 decibels, we might be tempted to conclude that our noise just was not loud enough. White noise (which is roughly similar to the sound you hear when your radio is tuned between stations) contains all frequencies of sound and is a convenient noise source often used in the laboratory.

Why 25 minutes of exposure to the noise? Since we expect to use college students as participants, we know that they find it most convenient if an experiment takes roughly 1 hour—that is, about the same time as a class. Since our hypothesis implies a no-noise control condition, we have divided our hour experiment into two 25-minute segments, one with noise and one without. This leaves 10 minutes for instructions and debriefing.

Our dependent variable is performance on an arithmetic task. This task was chosen because it is a simple task that college students are familiar with, so no training is needed during the experiment. Performance—number of correct and number of incorrect problems—is easy to measure. Because practice or fatigue effects might be present, we should be careful to counterbalance our experiment by having half the participants start in the quiet condition and half start in the noise condition. Since all participants complete all conditions, this is a within-subjects experimental design, offering greater experimental precision than a between-subjects design. In a within-subjects design, each person is compared with herself or himself, so that differences among people do not increase the error in an experiment. However, if we are concerned that performance following noise might be different from performance following quiet—that is, that noise effects might linger on even after the noise is no longer physically present, a better experimental design would be to use separate groups of participants for each 25-minute segment, giving us a between-subjects design.

Although our experiment is well controlled, we have several problems when we attempt to generalize results. If no effects of noise were obtained (if arithmetic performance was the same for noise and quiet segments), it could be argued that a 25-minute sample of life is far too short to tell us about a worker who has been exposed to 110-decibel noise for 8 hours a day for many years. On the other hand, if effects of noise were obtained (if arithmetic performance was worse in noise segments), it could still be argued that eventually a worker adapts to noisy environments, so that if we had tested participants for several days or weeks, our initial effect might have disappeared. We will now formulate another hypothesis, so that results can be more easily generalized.

Hypothesis   *Residents of a noisy city street will (a) move more frequently and (b) score lower on a rating scale for residential satisfaction than residents of a quiet street.*

Since this hypothesis deals with the long-term effects of permanent residence, it avoids the problems of generalization seen in the preceding experiment. However, this hypothesis is not nearly as precise as the other hypothesis. Sound levels for noisy and quiet streets are not specified in advance but have to be measured during the experiment. The experimenter has to decide whether to measure sound levels only at certain times—for example, during rush hours—or to take a 24-hour average. This quasi-independent variable is not completely under the experimenter's control. Furthermore, it may be confounded with such things as income and status, since persons with lower socioeconomic status are more likely to reside on noisier streets.

The dependent variables are not entirely satisfactory, either. Even if residents desire to move more often from noisy streets, economic factors may prohibit them from doing so. On the other hand, the turnover in an area is an objective number that can be reliably measured. The second dependent variable depends to a great extent on the validity of the rating scale used to assess residential satisfaction. The experimenter will attempt to find a scale that has already been used in several studies and previously validated. If the experimenter is forced to construct a scale, then the scale must first be validated—a time-consuming and difficult process. Thus, the price of the greater ease of generalization in this study is a considerable loss of experimenter control.

When we compare both studies as solutions to the problem posed at the start of this section, it is clear that neither is perfect. This is always true with research. No single experiment can answer a question. The scientist is forced to focus on a more specific hypothesis, thus answering only a small part of the problem. This is a major source of frustration for all psychologists, since no general answers are possible until many tiny pieces, each corresponding to a specific hypothesis, are put together. An environmental psychologist could easily spend an entire career trying to understand the problem of noise and its psychological effects. For more information about the psychology of noise, see Kantowitz and Sorkin (1983), Chapter 16.

The evidence that noise pollution is a health hazard has spread beyond experimental and environmental psychology. For example, architects now realize that their designs must muffle sounds (Bronzaft, 1993). When citations to psychological research are found in journals of architecture, we can be sure that the message of environmental psychology—that human behavior and health are profoundly affected by characteristics of the environment—is getting through.

▼ SUMMARY

1. Science is not the only path to truth, and only certain portions of human experience are presently open to scientific analysis. However, the scientific method is self-correcting, whereas other methods of fixing belief are not. Therefore, science is preferable wherever its tools are appropriate.

2. Experiments are steps along the way to the psychologist's ultimate goal of predicting and explaining behavior. This goal can be most rapidly achieved by conducting experiments that are representative and that can be generalized to related situations. Two types of representativeness are sample generalization and variable representativeness. Four types of crowding studies are discussed; the kinds of generalizations we could draw from each differ substantially.

3. Since most environmental psychologists prefer field research to laboratory research, it is seldom possible to assign participants randomly to experimental condition and to manipulate all independent variables. Thus, quasi-experiments and ex post facto studies are more likely.

4. Aircraft noise influences memory, but this effect can be reversed when the noise is removed.

5. Psychologists are extremely concerned with the ethical aspects of participation in research. The right of informed consent cannot always be granted in research. In such cases, the potential harm to participants must be balanced against the potential worth of the research. Experiments involving deception and concealment must be conducted only with great caution, if at all.

▼ KEY TERMS

density
ethical issues
ex post facto
generality of results
informed consent

quasi-experiment
representativeness
sample generalization
variable representativeness

▼ DISCUSSION QUESTIONS

1. A priest, a rabbi, and a scientist were walking along the beach, discussing whether it was possible to walk on water. As an empirical test, the priest and the rabbi waded into the ocean while the scientist watched in amazement from the beach. Soon the priest was up to his chin, while the rabbi was dry from his knees up. "How are you managing to stay dry?" asked the priest. "Easy," replied the rabbi, "I walk on the rocks." What did the two clerics say about empiricism to the scientist when they returned to the beach, and what was his reply?

2. Select two areas in which science is not the appropriate path to truth. Discuss why the tools of science are irrelevant or inapplicable in these two fields. Will it be possible for science to handle these areas in the distant future?

3. Rush to the library and read the latest issues of *Environment and Behavior* and *Human Factors*. These two journals specialize in applied research. Discuss whether the articles you read can be more readily generalized than articles published in the *Journal of Experimental Psychology*.

4. Make up a short list of unethical experiments you would like to do. Visit faculty members who specialize in the research areas of your experiments and ask them if they would be willing to supervise the experiments. How many faculty members tell you that they refuse because your experiment is unethical? Is this assignment ethical?

▼ WEB CONNECTIONS

General information about environmental psychology is available at:

http://www.edra.org

http://psy.gu.se/iaap/envpsych.htm

Several links related to environmental psychology can be found at:

http://www.apa34.org/

▼ LABORATORY RESOURCES

Langston (2002) Chapter 6 describes a laboratory experiment to explore the effects of room color and mood on people. The theory to be tested claims that red is an "expansive" color that causes people to pay more attention to the external environment while green is a "contractive" color that induces introspective states. While the independent variable is clear, there are several possibilities for dependent variables and tasks to be performed in the colored environment. If enough different tasks are tested, there is a statistical possibility that false significant results could be obtained. If you wish to improve on the methodology suggested by Langston, find out how to perform a MANOVA (see Chapter 3 on more than one dependent variable) from your instructor.

PSYCHOLOGY IN ACTION
Noise and Memory

This exercise gives you several options for investigating the effects of noise on two kinds of memory: item recall and probe recall. Make up a set of seven index cards and write a day of the week on each: Monday, Tuesday . . . Sunday. These cards will be the stimuli presented to your participants, and you will shuffle the deck to rearrange the order each time you present them. In the item recall task you present only six cards. The participant must name the missing day. Recall of the missing item does not depend upon the order in which the days were presented. In the probe recall task the participant has to recall the day that followed the probe stimulus in the list. For example, if your six-item list had been Monday, Friday, Wednesday, Sunday, Saturday, and Tuesday and the probe was Saturday, the correct response would be Tuesday. In this task, knowledge of the order in which the days were presented is crucial.

Our research question is how noise affects these two types of memory recall. Do you anticipate that noise will affect both tasks the same way? Does the kind of noise matter? What about the intensity of the noise?

The simplest experiment we could devise would have only two levels of the noise independent variable: quiet (a no-noise control condition) and noise. Most experimenters would design a more complex experiment. For example, you could vary the type of noise and also its intensity. Possible noise types include instrumental music, vocal music, speech, tones, and white noise, a special noise that contains all frequencies. (You can create a sound very similar to white noise by tuning a radio to the hissing sound that occurs when the dial is between radio stations.) Sound intensity is measured in decibels, often using the A scale of the meter. (If your instructor does not have access to a sound-level meter, they can be purchased inexpensively at Radio Shack stores.) If you want to vary intensity, sound levels of 55 decibels (A scale) to 90 decibels (A) would be appropriate.

We intentionally are not specifying the hypotheses for this experiment. More information on recall and noise can be found in Banbury, Banbury, Macken, Trembley, and Jones (2001, p. 22) and Jones (1999). Effects of type of noise upon verbal memory can be found in Iwanaga and Ito (2002). You can formulate hypotheses either on the basis of your experience with noise, such as trying to study when listening to the radio, or by looking up these articles. Resist the temptation to design an experiment that combines many noise types and intensities—it will be too difficult to acquire and analyze so much data. Instead, select a subset of these independent variables that you find interesting.

Formulate your hypotheses, get your experiment approved to ensure protection of human participants, and collect your data. Your dependent variable will be either percent correct or errors on the memory tasks. For the authors of this book, the most exciting part of experimental psychology is discovering if data support or reject hypotheses. Have fun and may at least some of your hypotheses be confirmed. ■

HUMAN FACTORS

When our sciences of human nature and human relations are anything like as developed as are our sciences of physical nature, their chief concern will be with the problem of how human nature is more effectively modified. The question will not be whether it is capable of change, but how it is to be changed under what conditions. (JOHN DEWEY)

The major justification for laboratory research is its ability to provide precise statements about causality. Once some effect or phenomenon is understood from laboratory research, the applied psychologist can then use this information to improve some aspect of the world outside the laboratory. This applied enterprise serves a scientific function, in addition to solving some practical difficulty. If an important effect has been correctly identified inside the laboratory, then the behavioral laws and relationships that describe or explain this effect should also operate outside the lab. Indeed, if they do not, serious doubts about the validity of the original laboratory research can be raised. To be useful, knowledge must be applied; laboratory research is thus a beginning, not an end (see Chapter 1). In this chapter we show how some findings originally discovered and refined in the experimental psychology laboratory can be applied usefully and meaningfully to practical human factors problems. Solving practical problems sometimes means additional laboratory work. At other times, the researcher must go outside the laboratory to seek solutions. We do not intend these few human factors examples to be interpreted as the ultimate justification for experimental psychology, since it is far too early to determine how basic research findings will shape our lives in the future. The lesson to be learned in this chapter is the generalization of basic experimental psychology principles; the specific applications discussed are intended to illustrate this point.

▼ HUMAN FACTORS AND HUMAN BEHAVIOR

Definition

Human factors is defined as "the discipline that tries to optimize the relationship between technology and the human" (Kantowitz & Sorkin, 1983, p. 4). Technology can refer to something small and commonplace, such as a can opener, or something large and esoteric, such as a space station. The common denominator of technology is people; all systems large and small must be used by people. If we had sufficient understanding of how the human operates, we could in principle design all technology to better interface with people.

The central role of the person in human factors explains why experimental psychology has had such a strong influence on human factors research. More than half the members of the Human Factors and Ergonomics Society were trained as psychologists. A substantial portion of the articles published in the journal *Human Factors* can be considered applied experimental psychology. Understanding how humans function in applied settings is a crucial aspect of human factors research.

Honor Thy User

The first commandment of human factors is "Honor thy user." If there is one thing you should remember 25 years from now about human factors, it is "Honor thy user." Everything else merely embellishes this dominant theme.

Before you can honor the user, you must first know who the user will be. Different user populations have different human factors requirements. When Japan first started manufacturing automobiles, it designed cars for Japanese citizens. This created a problem when the cars were exported to the United States. American men were unable to depress the brake pedal without simultaneously depressing either the clutch or accelerator pedals. In hindsight, the reason for this design error was clear. Americans are, on average, physically larger than Japanese and have bigger feet. Although pedal spacing was satisfactory for the smaller Japanese foot, the pedals were too close together for the larger, American foot. Since American feet had not been specified in the original design characteristics, the first commandment of human factors had been violated.

This same error can occur in more sophisticated ways. A large American telecommunications company, highly regarded for its human factors efforts, was designing a system for presenting recorded messages by telephone at times specified by the user. Since the hardware for this effort was specified, the human factors designers had to come up with the equivalent of a miniature computer language with which the user could enter appropriate commands. So computer scientists were selected to create this new mini-language. After several months of effort, they came up with a powerful language that could efficiently control recorded messages. Furthermore, being prudent designers, they tested their new system by using secretaries as test subjects. Since this device was intended for use by secretaries, this was the ideal test population. Alas, none of the secretaries was able to master the new language. After some thought, the designers decided they needed a greatly improved instruction manual and so spent several more months perfecting a tutorial manual with many examples and illustrations. A second test found a few secretaries able to use the device, but most were still baffled. The designers were very unhappy and questioned the few successful secretaries carefully. It turned out that all the secretaries who were able to use the device had prior experience with computer programming. Now the problem was clear. The designers, being computer programmers themselves, had created a system that was optimal for anyone who could think like a computer programmer. But the typical user lacked computer skills. Therefore, the designers created a new inefficient language that required many more instructions to complete any given recording schedule. But this new language was easy to learn and easy to use. A final test showed that the great majority of secretaries could now accomplish the task. The designer's training, which had stressed efficiency in minimizing the length of a program, had tricked them into violating the first commandment. They had designed for themselves rather than for the user. But disaster was prevented because the designers were wise enough to test their product before sending it out the door. So an important aspect of honoring the user is to test using the same population that will eventually operate the system.

The last example of a violation to be discussed is the design of a lathe (Figure 15.1). Here, the user population is known. But, as Figure 15.1 shows, the controls on the lathe were designed for a human with a very short trunk and extremely long arms. No humans have these body dimensions. This example demonstrates that it is easier to change the machine than to change the person who must operate it.

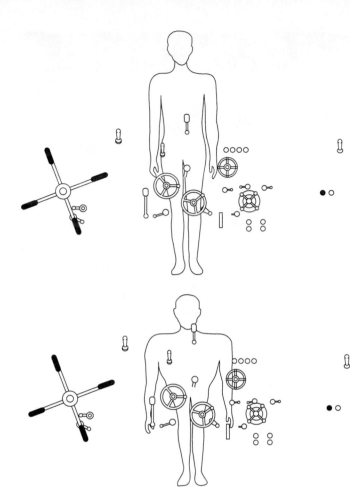

▼ **FIGURE 15.1**

The controls of a lathe in current use are not within easy reach of the average person. They are placed so that the ideal operator should be 1,372 mm (4½ ft) tall, 640 mm (2 ft) across the shoulder, and have a 2,348 mm (8 ft) arm span. (Courtesy Butterworth Heinemann, Ltd.)

The Value of Life

One important, but often neglected, topic in human factors is the value of life. It may seem crass to place an economic value on death, but this is done all the time when manufacturers decide how much safety equipment should be built into systems and what kinds of safety warnings are needed. No product is ever perfectly safe. Even a small button could prove fatal if swallowed by an infant.

A presidential address to the Human Factors Society (Parsons, 1970) discussed life and death. The value of a human life has been assessed in many ways, ranging from a few cents corresponding to the value of chemicals that comprise the human body to million-dollar insurance policies on the lives of corporate executives. Parsons estimated that choosing to return the Apollo astronauts to Earth, instead of allowing them to expire in space, cost the U.S. taxpayer about half a billion dollars per astronaut. Although Parsons was not advocating a kamikaze Apollo mission, it is clear that not all lives are valued equally.

How could one evaluate the utility of a decision by an American automobile manufacturer to include air bags in its 2004 model cars? One statistical procedure to answer

INTRODUCING THE VARIABLES

Dependent Variables

The most common dependent variable in human factors research is error rate. This is an obvious choice since decreasing human error is a major goal of human factors as a discipline. Time is also an important dependent variable. Total time to complete a task is often measured as well as component times, such as reaction time and movement time. In practical situations, excessive response time can be equivalent to an error. For example, if you correctly decide to step on the brake pedal of your car but delay your response until just before your vehicle goes over a cliff, the outcome would be the same as not stepping on the brake pedal.

Independent Variables

Human factors psychologists study a broad range of issues. As a result, a wide variety of independent variables is studied. A researcher interested in the role of visual illusions in aircraft crashes would study the same independent variables as an experimental psychologist interested in perception. Similarly, a researcher interested in training would manipulate some of the same independent variables—for example, practice, distribution of practice, and presentation modality—as a memory researcher. A human factors scientist studying mental workload would use some of the same independent variables as an experimental psychologist involved in attention research.

However, a human factors specialist interested in such complex systems as nuclear power plants or military command, control, and communication systems might manipulate communication pathways in small groups in ways similar to those that social and organizational psychologists or sociologists might use. Environmental independent variables, such as noise, temperature, and vibration, are of interest in applied settings. Subject variables, such as people with different leadership styles, might be selected. Schedules for shift work and time of day are also manipulated in human factors research.

Control Variables

Although not altogether absent, control variables are minimal in much of applied research. The field settings in which most of this research is conducted prevent the kind of experimental control we would demand inside the laboratory. For this reason, researchers must be vigilant in identifying potential confounding variables that could provide competing explanations of the experimental results. Alternatively, when relevant extraneous variables are allowed to vary, they may obscure real treatment effects.

this question is called the **quality-adjusted life year (QALY).** It is calculated in three steps (Thompson, Graham, & Zellner, 2001). To illustrate this, assume some new vehicle safety device that will prevent 1,000 deaths and 50,000 long-term injuries per year:

1. Compute the numbers of years of life preserved by the device. If the average death decreases life span by 40 years and the average injury reduces life expectancy by 0.5 years the total gain is 65,000 life years (1,000 × 40 plus 50,000 × 0.5).
2. Adjust for the quality of life-years saved. If the new device does not permit people to function at full quality (1.0) but instead allows only a quality of 0.9, then instead of 40,000 QALYs there are only 36,000 QALYs (1,000 × 40 × 0.9).
3. Account for the quality of life of survivors with injuries. Suppose the device improves the average quality of life from 0.6 (accident with no device) to 0.9. Then 50,000 survivors will gain 0.3 QALYs per year for the rest of their lives. Assuming on average this is 40 years, this produces an additional 600,000 QALYs.

QALYs saved for common vehicle-safety improvements in a cohort of 10 million vehicles are 219,629 for seat belts, 312,735 for driver air bags, and 334,531 for dual air bags (Thompson, Segui-Gomez, & Graham, 2002). The incremental cost effectiveness of adding safety equipment beyond seat belts is $24,000 per QALY for driver air bags and $61,000 per QALY for dual air bags. By comparison, the cost effectiveness of annual mammograms for women age 40 to 50 is $227,000 per QALY; screening of health-care workers to prevent HIV transmission to patients has a cost effectiveness of $465,000. Society must decide how much it is willing to spend for a life-year saved.

15.1   EXPERIMENTAL TOPICS AND RESEARCH ILLUSTRATIONS

Topic   *Small-n Design*
Illustration   *Dynamic Visual Acuity*

Many practical situations require the detection and recognition of a moving target. A center fielder running to catch a long fly ball must find the target (baseball) in his visual field before he can predict where the ball will land. An airplane pilot operating in a crowded terminal area under visual flight rules must detect and avoid oncoming aircraft. An astronaut attempting to dock a space shuttle must judge relative motion between her craft and the docking gate. An automobile driver passing another car on a highway must detect oncoming traffic to decide if it is safe to pass. All these situations are examples of dynamic visual acuity at work.

Dynamic visual acuity is defined as the ability to perceive detail in moving objects. It is usually compared with static visual acuity, the ability to perceive detail in a fixed object. Visual acuity is often measured by presenting a letter C (called a **Landolt-C**) with a small gap (Figure 15.2). If the gap is large, it is easy to notice. If the gap is very small, the letter C may be perceived as the letter O. The size of the gap that will allow you to discriminate reliably between the letter C and an apparently closed letter O is an index of your visual acuity. If the Landolt C does not move, we are measuring static acuity. If the Landolt C has a trajectory, we are measuring dynamic acuity. When you try to read a Snellen eye chart at the optometrist's office, your static visual acuity is being determined.

Although static and dynamic visual acuity are related (Scialfa et al., 1988), using static acuity to predict dynamic acuity can result in technical problems. Thus, for determining a person's ability to perform successfully in occupations that demand good dynamic acuity, the prudent researcher measures dynamic visual acuity directly. Furthermore, dynamic visual acuity has important design implications for complex systems. The designer would like to choose values that make it easier for a human to detect and recognize moving targets.

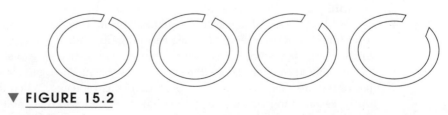

▼ **FIGURE 15.2**

Landolt C's.

Ophthalmologists are interested in the relationship between dynamic visual acuity and pupil size (Ueda, Nawa, Yukawa, Taketani, & Hara, 2006). As part of standard testing procedures, eye drops are used to dilate the pupil (a part of the eye, not a student). Some research has suggested that pupil dilation may limit a driver's ability to recognize and avoid road hazards (Wood, Garth, Grounds, McKay, & Mulvahil, 2003), so that driving should not be permitted immediately after an eye exam in which the pupil was dilated. Since dynamic visual acuity is needed when driving, Ueda and colleagues (2006) wondered if dilating the pupil decreased dynamic visual acuity. They found that pupil dilation increased dynamic visual acuity, despite their prediction that acuity would decrease. While this unexpected result does not imply that we could improve driving by taking eye drops to dilate our pupils, it does suggest that the driving decrements observed previously may not be attributed to dynamic visual acuity deficits. Of course, a single experiment never proves an explanation (see Chapter 1), so that more research will be needed to explain this result by examining other independent variables such as target size and illumination.

Effects of Target Wavelength on Dynamic Visual Acuity

As with all interesting human factors problems, the effect of color on the resolution of a moving target has both practical and theoretical import. Design decisions involving such disparate items as computer display screens and street signs are influenced by the knowledge that some particular color is easier to perceive. From a theoretical viewpoint, the blue cone color receptors are known to differ from the other color receptors, having lower static acuity and being more sluggish (Long & Garvey, 1988). Thus, Long and Garvey (1988) had both practical and theoretical reasons for studying the effect of wavelength (color) on dynamic visual acuity.

In their study, only two male observers were used in all experimental conditions. Both observers had static acuity of 20/20 when wearing eyeglasses, which, of course, were worn during the experiment. Although this is a small number of subjects, each observer participated in more than forty 40- to 60-minute sessions over a 12-month period. Small-n designs are not used to minimize experimental effort. Instead, they are appropriate in highly controlled experimental situations where data can be easily replicated.

The Experiment

Landolt C targets were projected onto a white screen. Wavelength or color was one independent variable, with individual targets presented in one of four wavelengths: white, blue, yellow, or red. The gap in the targets had four possible locations: upper left, upper right, lower left, lower right. The position of the gap varied randomly from trial to trial. The observer, in order to be correct, had to report the position of the gap. Figure 15.2 depicts a sample of the gap sizes used in the experiment. The **method of limits**—a psychophysical technique (see Chapter 6)—was used to determine the threshold or gap size that was too small to allow subjects to correctly identify the position of the gap. Gap size, then, was a second independent variable. A trial run always started with a large target gap. Following a correct response, gap size was decreased. This continued until an incorrect response was given. Then gap size was increased to that of the preceding trial, and the procedure was repeated. When the observer erred for the second time with a given gap size, testing under those conditions was stopped. The threshold was recorded as the next larger size gap.

Another important independent variable was adaptation level of the observer's eye. In night-viewing conditions, vision is controlled by the rods; this is called **scotopic vision.** In brighter day-viewing conditions, vision is controlled by the cones; this is called **photopic vision.** Rods and cones have different sensitivities to wavelength (color). Even though the rods cannot recognize color, they still respond with different sensitivity to various wavelengths. So it was prudent to study effects of wavelength under scotopic conditions, where rods dominate, versus photopic conditions, where cones dominate vision. In this study, a night-viewing condition was used to produce scotopic vision, and a day-viewing condition was used to produce photopic vision.

Finally, the last independent variable we discuss is target velocity. Three values of angular velocity were chosen based on values used in earlier studies and because a deleterious effect of target motion on acuity was expected for the chosen range of velocities.

Long and Garvey (1988) examined the two observers' data separately, because small-n research does not generally average data from different observers. They discovered that as target velocity increased, the threshold (gap size) also increased. Faster-moving targets were harder to perceive. Blue targets were easier to perceive (had a lower threshold) than targets presented in white, yellow, or red in the night-viewing condition (scotopic vision) but not in the day-viewing condition (photopic vision).

These results have some interesting practical implications. For example, red illumination is customarily used to maintain human dark adaptation (i.e., to keep a person's eyes adjusted to seeing in the dark). Long and Garvey's research suggests that blue (rather than red) illumination would allow people to more easily detect and recognize moving targets in night-viewing conditions.

15.2   EXPERIMENTAL TOPICS AND RESEARCH ILLUSTRATIONS

Topic   *Selection of Dependent Variable*
Illustration   *Mental Workload*

Eastern Airlines Flight 401 was approaching Miami International Airport when the pilot realized that the indicator light for the nose wheel was not illuminated. He therefore diverted and flew over the Everglades at a low altitude while the crew tried to determine if the problem was the signal light itself or if the nosegear was not down and locked in its landing position. Although landing a plane with a failed nose wheel is not a very dangerous procedure, the crew naturally wanted to lower the wheel manually if the signal light correctly showed a nosegear failure.

The plane was flying on autopilot while the entire three-man crew tried to determine if the light bulb was defective and if the gear was down. However, unknown to the crew, the autopilot had been accidentally disengaged, and the plane had begun a gradual descent. The crew's attention was focused on the signal light; quite a while passed before a copilot noticed the altimeter reading. In the 8 seconds remaining before Flight 401 crashed into the ground, the crew made no attempt to increase altitude. The mechanical cause of this accident that killed 99 people was a burned-out light bulb. The psychological cause was the mental process of attention. The crew was so mentally locked into solving the problem of the signal light that no one paid attention to the more important problem of flying the airplane and monitoring altitude.

Basic research on divided and focused attention provides models and data that bear directly on this kind of practical problem (see Chapter 8). But the practical utility of the research cannot be evaluated in the laboratory. **Field research** is needed to determine if laboratory research performed in universities works in the real world. In aviation, it is expensive and possibly dangerous to conduct field studies in airplanes in actual flight. Thus, most field research is performed in flight simulators. These simulators so closely duplicate the reality of flight that they are approved by the Federal Aviation Agency for training and recertification of professional pilots. In aviation, the flight simulator provides a "halfway house" between the carefully controlled laboratory and the airways. We review here a series of studies conducted in flight simulators at the National Aeronautics and Space Administration (NASA) Ames Research Center in California and then conclude with a field study from the flying observatory stationed at Ames. Our goal is to explain how to measure and evaluate the attentional requirements of flight: the effects of **workload** on the pilots' ability to control the simulators.

The NASA GAT Experiments: Measuring Workload in a Simulator

Starting in 1983, a series of experiments was carried out in the General Aviation Trainer (GAT) at NASA. This is a relatively inexpensive flight simulator that trains pilots to fly a generic single-engine airplane. It is mounted on a base that allows the entire cockpit to move according to the pilot's actions. It is most often used with the cockpit window covered over, so that the pilot must depend on instrument readings to guide flight.

The goal of this research effort, expressed in a general way, was to provide objective workload measurement methods, especially using secondary-task methodology, that would work in a flight simulator. A **secondary task** is an extra task inserted with the important task (called the **primary task**) under investigation. Often, performance on the secondary task can be interpreted as an index of attention required by the primary task. If secondary-task performance is poor, this might indicate high attention demands or mental workload for the primary task. The problem was how to use the large body of attention research to help solve a practical predicament in a field setting.

Many studies completed in the laboratories of experimental psychologists studying attention suggested that secondary tasks were useful indicators of attentional load (Kantowitz, 1985). The challenge was to use this basic research knowledge, most of which was not aimed at solving any practical problems in the near future, in a more realistic setting. The GAT environment was a reasonable compromise between the rigor and control of the experimental psychology laboratory and the high validity of a real aircraft.

Field research in pilot workload uses both objective and subjective dependent variables. **Objective measures** include variables, such as reaction time and percent correct, that can be easily verified by the experimenter. **Subjective measures** are verbal reports given on rating scales; for example, a pilot could be asked to judge workload on a scale of 1 to 10. Subjective ratings cannot be directly verified by the experimenter. In the early 1980s, investigators studying workload in flight simulators were having trouble finding satisfactory objective measures. The typical study would investigate many objective and subjective measures. It was common to find subjective measures that yielded statistical significance, but useful objective measures were rare. A study that found one objective measure out of perhaps a dozen to yield reliable statistical results was state of the art. Therefore, investigators began to prefer subjective measures to objective measures. This preference is quite understandable, since no one wants to waste resources studying effects that do not meet appropriate statistical criteria.

Theoretical Assumptions

A major problem in the human factors of aviation is the absence of meaningful theoretical frameworks to help guide research and practice. Much of the psychological literature seems irrelevant to the practitioner; therefore, most of the previous workload studies did not rely on any theoretical viewpoints. A kind of loose engineering approach was taken, based on the notion that if enough objective measures were studied, the researchers would discover one that was affected by pilot mental workload. Although some consideration was given to copying the methods used in laboratory studies of attention, little effort was devoted to understanding the theoretical implications of these methods.

Fortunately, this situation is starting to improve as investigators accept the idea that a good theory is the best practical tool (Kantowitz, 1989b). For example, recent research on the mental workload of air traffic controllers (Loft, Sanderson, Neal, & Mooij, 2007) starts with a qualitative model that emphasizes the importance of controller cognitive strategies in managing workload. Indeed, as the use of theory in transportation human factors increases, we can expect greater use of quantitative or computational models (Kantowitz, 1998), such as a recent computational model that detects driver lane changes (Salvucci, Mandalia, Kuge, & Yamamura, 2007).

One common secondary task is a **choice-reaction task.** In choice-reaction tasks, several stimuli are possible (e.g., tones of different frequencies); each one has its own unique response. Since choice reaction requires attentional capacity, there is always the danger that it will interfere with the primary task. If this happens, performance on the primary task will suffer and we will not be able to draw any conclusions about the attentional demands of the primary task. Fortunately, pilots are extremely well trained. They have learned that no matter what else happens, their first responsibility is to fly the plane. Recall that it was the failure to follow this rule that doomed Flight 401.

The Experiment

A choice-reaction task was used to test pilots in simulated flight scenarios. The main goals of the experiment were (1) to discover if a choice-reaction secondary task could meet the assumption of noninterference with the primary flying task; and, if it could, (2) to see if it was an appropriate dependent variable for measuring pilot mental workload. Not all the results are discussed here; the interested reader should see the published report by Kantowitz, Hart, and Bortolussi (1983).

The secondary task consisted of either two or four auditory tones. (Reasons for using both two- and four-choice tasks are related to theoretical issues beyond the scope of this chapter; see Kantowitz & Knight, 1976.) Pilots responded to the tones by pushing a switch, mounted under the pilot's left thumb, in the appropriate direction, depending on the pitch of the tone. Tones occurred every 22 seconds during simulated flight.

Each pilot flew one hard and one easy flight scenario, lasting 22 minutes each. Scenarios were constructed based on earlier rating data (Childress, Hart, & Bortolussi, 1982). Each scenario was flown three times: once alone as a control condition, once with a two-choice secondary task, and once with a four-choice secondary task.

Figure 15.3 shows error on the flying task as a function of level of the secondary task. The hard flight scenario showed greater error, as expected; this confirmed predictions based on the rating data used to construct the flight scenarios. Of greater importance is the effect of the secondary task. Appropriate statistical analysis shows that the two curves in Figure 15.3 are flat. There is no statistical difference between no secondary task (labeled "none" in the figure) and either two- or four-choice secondary

▼ FIGURE 15.3

Primary-Task (Flying) Error as a Function of Levels of Secondary Task.

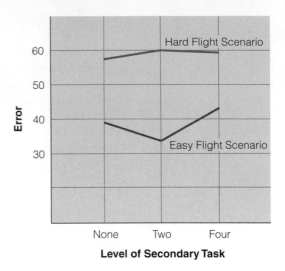

tasks. Thus, the key assumption that pilots first fly the plane and do not let secondary tasks interfere with the primary flying task was validated.

Figure 15.4 shows performance on the secondary tone task as a function of flight segment. The vertical axis shows transmitted information in bits per second. This is a measure that takes both speed and accuracy of the response into account. Higher scores indicate better performance. There are reliable statistical differences among these points. In particular, the last flight segments showed the lowest scores. This means that attention and workload were greatest during this segment. Relatively less attention was available for the secondary task during this segment, and so the bits-per-second score is low. This result makes intuitive sense to pilots, who believe that workload is highest during landing. However, their opinion is subjective. The objective results of Figure 15.4 are not based on opinion.

▼ FIGURE 15.4

Transmitted Information on the Secondary Task as a Function of Flight Segment.

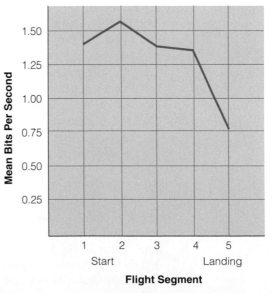

The experiment briefly described has shown that theory is indeed a practical tool. In the GAT simulator, an environment that is less controlled than the laboratory settings that created the theory, we were still able to find an objective measure of pilot workload by using choice reactions. We also found that pilots' subjective reports or opinions about their mental workload converged with the objective choice-reaction measure. The convergence of the subjective and objective measures increases our faith in the result that landing causes high mental workload.

Measuring Pilot Workload in the Air

The NASA Kuiper Airborne Observatory (Figure 15.5) is a "flying telescope" that permits astronomers to get above much of the atmosphere by flying at high altitudes—more than 40,000 feet, with 85 percent of the earth's atmosphere below it—thereby getting better images of astral events. In conjunction with the observatory's regular mission, workload researchers were able to go along to monitor four measures of pilot workload: communications analysis, subjective ratings of workload, subjective ratings of additional factors related to workload, and heart rate (Hart, Hauser, & Lester, 1984).

Because the workload research could not interfere with normal flight procedures, the researchers had to accept several limitations on the research design. For example, no measures (except for heart rate) were taken during takeoffs and landings, for safety reasons. It was also not practical to obtain objective measures by introducing a secondary task. Nevertheless, some useful information was still obtained. The most interesting result was a difference in mean heart rate between pilots and copilots. The pilots, who were responsible for flying the plane, had higher mean heart rates than the copilots, who were responsible for navigation and communication. This difference could not be attributed to differences in training, because all the pilots were fully qualified; indeed, it was often the case that someone who had functioned as a copilot on one flight would be the pilot for another flight. However, practical scheduling difficulties prevented a complete experimental design by which all pilots could be tested in both pilot and copilot jobs.

▼ **FIGURE 15.5**

The NASA Kuiper Airborne Observatory.

Similarly, it was not possible to obtain nonflying baseline heart-rate data. There was a large difference in heart rate (72 to 87 beats per minute) for the pilot; no such increase was obtained for the copilot. However, subjective workload estimates, although differing significantly across flight segments, did not differ between pilots and copilots.

As with most in-flight studies of workload, these results are not as easy to interpret as laboratory or simulator studies. Heart rate is very sensitive to amount of physical effort: The higher heart rate for pilots could reflect physical activity more than mental activity. Heart-rate variance is a measure of mental workload that is less affected by physical effort, but the researchers did not report variance results. The best approach seems to be a combination of objective, subjective, and physiological measures conducted in laboratories and simulators. The objective measures can be used to calibrate the other kinds of measures that are more appropriate for in-flight tests. Future progress in measuring pilot mental workload depends on linking present results to theories of attention. This is not an easy task and will require better cooperation between basic and applied researchers (Kantowitz, 1982).

Heavy-Vehicle Driver Workload

The methods used for measuring pilot mental workload have been applied successfully to measuring workload of professional truck drivers. Recall that the major assumption for measuring workload is that insertion of the secondary task does not alter operator performance on the primary task (Figure 15.6). Although this assumption is usually true for professional pilots who require a great deal of specialized training before they can obtain and keep a pilot's license (Kantowitz & Casper, 1988), there is no guarantee that this assumption holds for truck drivers.

Kantowitz (1995) tested this assumption in a driving simulator using drivers who had commercial driver's licenses. Primary-task measures of lane position and vehicle speed

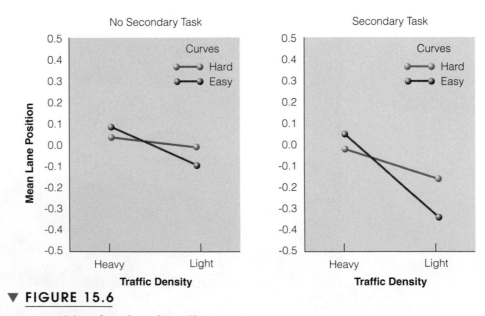

▼ FIGURE 15.6

Lane Position (Feet) and Traffic Density.

were not affected when secondary tasks were added; thus, the major assumption was met for professional truck drivers. Two secondary tasks were used. In the tachometer task, drivers were instructed to read the vehicle tachometer, which had been rigged to show only values 1,000, 2,000, 3,000, or 4,000 rpms. Drivers responded by pressing a four-position switch mounted on the steering wheel. In the immediate memory task, drivers had to repeat a seven-digit phone number that was presented auditorily. Figure 15.7 shows that reaction time to the tachometer task depended on traffic density and road geometry. The statistically significant interaction in this figure shows that driver workload was highest for heavy traffic on tight curves. Figure 15.8 shows that immediate recall was better in light traffic. This implies that driver workload is higher in heavy traffic.

These results show that the concept of operator workload is not limited to airplane pilots. The same tools and techniques that have been successful in measuring pilot workload can be used in driving simulators. However, truck driver workload must be tested on the road before we can conclude that the concept of workload can be completely generalized to ground vehicles. Vehicle manufacturers are currently using simulators and virtual prototyping to evaluate new in-vehicle devices (Bullinger & Dangelmeier, 2003).

Driving and Cellular Phones

Is it safe to use a cell phone while you are driving? Common sense and research results (Reed & Green, 1999) agree that dialing a phone is unsafe, in part because this requires taking your eyes off the road. Indeed, New York State has banned the use of handheld cell phones, and similar legislation is being considered in many other states and localities. One disadvantage of such legislation is that it implies that using a hands-free cell phone is safe. This is an important research question currently being studied in several laboratories.

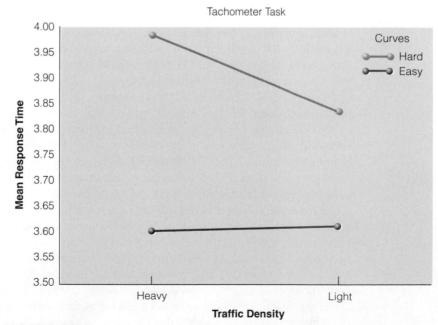

▼ **FIGURE 15.7**

Response time (seconds) and traffic density for the tachometer secondary task.

▼ **FIGURE 15.8**

Immediate Digit Memory and Traffic Density.

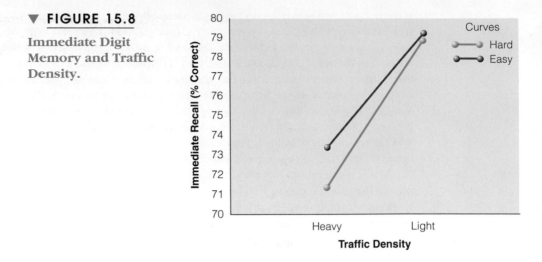

Dual-task methodology is ideal for evaluating hands-free cell phone use, although it is necessary to include the appropriate single-task control conditions (Kantowitz & Simsek, 2000). Does the cognitive load imposed by conversation on a cell phone (secondary task) interfere with performance of the primary (driving) task?

A recent study (Strayer & Johnston, 2001) used a primitive simulated driving task to answer this question. This task, called pursuit tracking, requires people to use a joystick to control a cursor on a computer display that must follow (or track) a moving target. Occasionally the target would flash red or green and participants had to press a button on the joystick to respond to the red flash; thus, a Donders C reaction was used as the secondary task. The authors then added what they called a dual-task condition where participants either listened to the radio or entered into conversations on either a handheld or hands-free phone. Actually, this was really a triple-task condition since participants had to perform (1) pursuit tracking, and (2) a Donders C reaction, and (3) either converse or listen to the radio.

The Donders C reaction time was elevated in the phone conditions (triple task) relative to the dual-task no-phone pursuit-tracking condition. Results were the same for handheld or hands-free phone conditions. Reaction time was not elevated for the radio condition. While these results are consistent with the hypothesis that any kind of cell phone should not be used while driving, there are several limitations in the study.

First, the authors did not demonstrate that the pursuit-tracking task, although widely used for decades in experimental psychology (Jagacinski & Flach, 2003), is a valid substitute for actual driving and did not cite any research directed at this point. Second, the authors were negligent in not reporting performance on the pursuit-tracking task. It is possible that differences between using handheld and hands-free phones would have been reflected in tracking performance. Third, the authors failed to recognize that they had created a triple task and that their baseline condition itself was a dual-task condition. Therefore, appropriate single-task conditions of tracking without a C reaction, and C reaction without tracking, were not included in their experiment.

This experiment was widely cited in the media as proof that hands-free cell phones should also be banned. While the authors of this text agree with that conclusion, the Strayer and Johnston (2001) study by itself is not sufficient to justify legislation. Other studies in validated driving simulators and on the road using instrumented vehicles are needed to provide a sound scientific basis for banning all cell phones in moving vehicles. Indeed, a more recent study by the same investigators (Strayer, Drews, & Johnston, 2003) used a driving simulator and found increased braking reaction time when drivers were conversing on a hands-free cell phone.

We advise you not to talk on any kind of phone while driving since studies of accident data show this to be a dangerous practice (Goodman, Tijerina, Bents, & Wierwille, 1999) somewhat akin to driving under the influence of alcohol. If you need to use your cell phone in your vehicle, pull over to a safe place (a rest area, not the side of an interstate highway) and stop your car before calling. Answering a cell phone while driving is even more risky (Reed & Green, 1999).

15.3   EXPERIMENTAL TOPICS AND RESEARCH ILLUSTRATIONS

Topic   *Field Research*
Illustration   *The Centered High-Mounted Brake Light*

As mentioned in the previous research illustration, traffic safety is a major concern of human factors psychologists. America's love affair with the automobile shows no signs of abating despite rising operating costs, air pollution, and the increasing frequency and severity of traffic jams in many of our major cities. Traffic accidents pose a serious threat to the young in our society; motor vehicle crashes represent the single leading cause of death among Americans aged 1 to 34 (National Safety Council, 1999). If your car was manufactured in 1986 or more recently, you are a direct beneficiary of one of human factors psychology's success stories—the centered high-mounted brake light. The impetus for the development of this light was the finding that 25 percent of all multivehicle accidents and 7.4 percent of fatal accidents involve rear-end collisions. In early 1977, Malone and Kirkpatrick conducted a large-scale field study involving taxicabs in the Washington, D.C., area to test different brake light configurations in an attempt to reduce the incidence of rear-end collisions. Malone (1986) outlined the details of this study in the bulletin of the Human Factors Society.

Brake Light Configurations and the Incidence of Rear-End Collisions

Malone and Kirkpatrick divided a total of 2,100 taxicab drivers into four equally sized groups: three experimental groups and one control group. The taxicab drivers had been matched for age, gender, and prior accident history. The independent variable was how brake lights were mounted on the back of the car. Four different configurations were used. The control condition was the (then) existing arrangement of two brake lights on each side of the car at a low level. The three experimental configurations tested included (1) a high-mounted brake light in the center of the car, (2) dual separated high-mounted brake lights, and (3) a separated function condition that separated the present (taillight) function from the stop and turn functions.

The dependent variables, rear-end collisions and miles driven, were collected over a 1-year period. During the course of the study, the taxicab drivers accumulated more than 60 million miles under a variety of road and weather conditions.

Malone and Kirkpatrick found that the drivers using a centered high-mounted brake light experienced significantly fewer rear-end collisions than did drivers in any other configuration condition. Figure 15.9 shows the number of accidents across the four

▼ **FIGURE 15.9**

Number of Accidents for Different Brake-Light Configurations.

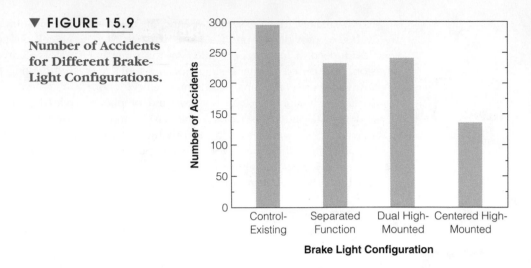

experimental conditions. As you can see, drivers in the centered high-mounted brake light condition had 54 percent fewer accidents than did drivers in the control condition (the existing configuration). When accidents did occur, the centered high-mounted brake light reduced the extent of damage by 38 percent. Malone and Kirkpatrick speculated that this brake light configuration resulted in faster brake application in the following vehicle, resulting in slower speeds at impact and less damage to both vehicles. What allowed the following vehicle to brake more quickly when the taxicab was equipped with the centered high-mounted brake light? Malone and Kirkpatrick concluded that it was closer to individuals' **normal line of regard**—that is, where individuals normally look when driving. This study helped change the brake light configuration on all cars sold in the United States. Now all new cars are required to have the centered, high-mounted brake light.

Unfortunately, later research has shown that the high-mounted brake light has not resulted in anywhere near a 50 percent reduction in accidents (Mortimer, 1993). The actual benefit ranges from 22 to 3.5 percent. A recent study based on crash data from insurance claims found only a 5 percent benefit (Farmer, 1995). We don't know why the benefit was so much less than anticipated. Part of the reason for this decreased benefit may be novelty: as more vehicles were equipped with high-mounted brake lights, drivers became more accustomed to them and so the lights become less effective. Nevertheless, human factors research on these brake lights continues to document the benefits of a center high-mounted stop lamp (Theeuwes & Alferdinck, 1995).

Human factors is an exciting and challenging area of psychology. Many researchers are drawn to this area because of the opportunity to apply principles of experimental psychology to the problems of everyday life. The research discussed in this chapter reflects this general approach. For example, Long and Garvey (1988) applied the method of limits developed in psychophysics to study the effects of target wavelength on dynamic visual acuity. Malone and Kirkpatrick used basic principles of perception to test the centered high-mounted brake light. Ultimately, the success of the experimental psychologist, as evaluated by the society that supports psychological research, is related to how well his or her research addresses problems that concern society. As you have seen in this chapter, human factors psychologists have been successful in addressing a number of these problems.

FROM PROBLEM TO EXPERIMENT
THE NUTS AND BOLTS

Problem   *Measure Pilot Mental Workload in Flight.*

Field research almost always has limitations that prevent the straightforward application of laboratory methods and solutions. Although we can measure mental workload in the laboratory and in flight simulators with some degree of success (see Kantowitz & Campbell, 1996, for a review), at present there is no universally accepted in-flight technique for continuous monitoring of pilot mental workload. This is the problem discussed here.

Problem   *Find an unobtrusive way to measure pilot mental workload in flight.*

The key word here is *unobtrusive*. This means that our method cannot interfere with normal flight procedures. So the best laboratory technique, using an objective secondary task, must be ruled out. Under high workload, the extra attention that might be diverted to a secondary task could present a safety hazard. The same argument could be made against having pilots continuously report subjective workload ratings.

This suggests that a physiological measure might be most suitable as a dependent variable. Pilots would not be bothered if painless electrodes could be attached to record heart rate or brain waves, to name two possible physiological measures. Independent variables could be the phase of the flight and pilot versus copilot.

Hypothesis   *Brain waves index pilot mental workload in flight.*

This hypothesis is far more complex than it appears to be at first. The major experimental problem is how to score brain waves. The technology for recording brain waves (called evoked potentials) from surface electrodes attached painlessly to the scalp is well established, but the interpretation of these signals is quite another matter. There are many components inside the evoked potential; sophisticated computer programs are needed to distinguish true components from electrical noise. Even after components have been correctly identified and scored, they must still be related to pilot workload.

For the sake of discussion, let us assume we have been able to locate some specific evoked potential component and have a small but powerful computer system in the airplane that can continuously process the brain waves of the pilot and the copilot. We would like to demonstrate that the magnitude of the evoked-potential component increases with increasing pilot workload. We might also predict that the pilot would exhibit a larger magnitude than the copilot.

The details of our experimental design would probably depend on the flight requirements of the mission. Field researchers usually do not have the luxury of designing missions to fit their research needs. Instead, the research problem must be piggybacked onto some existing mission. This greatly limits experimental design. We hope we would be able to identify different phases of flight (landing, cruising, and so on) that provided different levels of pilot workload. Of course, we would have to use published results from prior experiments to relate workload and phase of flight.

If our experiment worked, the greatest brain wave components would occur during the most difficult phases of flight. If, however, this was not the case, there could be many sources of potential error in this field of study that could prevent the desired outcome—even if our hypothesis were correct. Perhaps the phases of flight did not differ sufficiently in pilot workload. Perhaps the wrong brain wave component was selected. Perhaps we could not obtain sufficient data to create a powerful statistical test of our results. Perhaps our sample of pilots was much too small. Perhaps the skill level of our pilots was so high relative to a mission that was at the low end of the workload continuum that no overload occurred. Many other problems could be listed here.

▼ SUMMARY

1. Human factors is the discipline that tries to optimize the relationship between people and technology. Many human factors researchers and practitioners were originally trained in experimental psychology. However, the scope of human factors includes more than experimental psychology.

2. The main principle of human factors is "Honor thy user." Since people are the common element in various technological systems, we cannot improve system performance and quality without understanding how the human functions as part of the system.

3. In many human factors settings, the traditional large-*n* research methodology of psychological research cannot be employed. Dynamic visual acuity is one research topic in human factors where psychophysical research techniques are most appropriate. Color and movement velocity affect dynamic visual acuity.

4. Experiments in human factors can be conducted in the laboratory, in simulators, or in the field on working systems. For reasons of safety and economy, simulator research is used in areas such as aviation and nuclear power.

5. Both objective and subjective measures are used to study mental workload. Subjective measures are easier to obtain, whereas objective measures are easier to verify by researchers.

6. Theories are as important in guiding human factors research as they are in guiding basic research. Models of color vision have been applied to studying dynamic visual acuity. Models of attention are useful in directing simulator studies of mental workload.

7. Human factors psychologists are increasingly concerned with traffic safety. This is studied in driving simulators, on test tracks, and on the road in traffic. Simulator studies are safest and offer high experimental control. On-road studies are riskier and offer less control but are more realistic.

▼ KEY TERMS

choice-reaction task
dynamic visual acuity
field research
human factors
Landolt C
method of limits
normal line of regard
objective measures

photopic vision
primary task
quality-adjusted life year (QALY)
scotopic vision
secondary task
subjective measures
workload

▼ DISCUSSION QUESTIONS

1. What ethical factors must a human factors researcher consider when undertaking an investigation that has the potential to alter people's work environments?

2. How might a system designer take into account safety features that add cost to the system but can protect human lives?

3. List some practical situations in which object color might be an important aspect of dynamic visual acuity.

4. Discuss some of the difficulties inherent in field research. Can you think of methods to combat these problems?

5. Compare the advantages and disadvantages of studying pilot mental workload in a flight simulator rather than in an airplane during flight.

6. The study reviewed in the chapter showed that brake lights, which had been kept in one arrangement on cars for years, could be configured differently to produce safer cars. Is there a way to do the same for headlights, so they will help the driver to see better and be less likely to blind oncoming drivers? Suggest some ideas that might be tested.

WEB CONNECTIONS

An interesting site that catalogues bad designs of objects and the environment can be found at:

http://www.baddesigns.com

An excellent overview of human factors along with numerous links is available at:

http://www.ergonomics.org.uk

The website of the Human Factors and Ergonomics Society is also interesting:

http://www.hfes.org

PSYCHOLOGY IN ACTION
Understanding Traffic Sign Symbols

Many drivers, especially older drivers, do not understand all the symbolic traffic signs on U.S. highways (Dewar, Kline, & Swanson, 1994; Hanowski, Kantowitz, & Kantowitz, 1996). Once human factors experts can determine which signs are difficult to comprehend, these signs can be redesigned and improved. Take the following short quiz and discover how many traffic signs you understand. Then show the quiz to an elderly driver, perhaps a grandparent, and see how they do. Compare your results to the answers given at the end of this section. ■

1.

2.

3.

4.

5.

6.

7.

8.

9.

10.

11.

12.

13.

14.

15.

16.

17.

18.

19.

20.

Icon	Percent Correct	
	Younger Drivers	**Older Drivers**
1. No right turn	99	93.5
2. No U-turn	99	94.5
3. Hiking trail	86	76
4. Emergency medical services	80	64.5
5. Divided highway ends	73	62.5
6. Slippery when wet	41	43.5
7. Bicycle crossing	47	41
8. Amphitheater	32	28
9. Added lane	37	11.5
10. Library	62	43
11. Speed bumps ahead	100	100
12. Ambulance approaching	100	100
13. Trunk open	100	95
14. Ferry	100	100
15. Propane next exit	90	93
16. Fog lights on	95	60
17. Low tire pressure	95	62
18. Train station	100	78
19. School crossing	32	45
20. Water recreation	100	88

Items 1 to 10 are from Dewar et al. (1994). Younger drivers were aged 18 to 39; older drivers were 60+. Items 11 to 20 are from Hanowski et al. (1996). Younger drivers were aged 18 to 22; older drivers were 65+.

EXPERIMENTAL PSYCHOLOGY: A HISTORICAL SKETCH

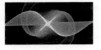

Psychology has a long past, but only a short history.

(HERMANN EBBINGHAUS)

Curiosity and wonder are the prime motivations for science, and there are few topics that people have found more interesting than the workings of their own minds. Many of the writings of the great philosophers, from Aristotle's time to the present, have been concerned with what can be called psychological problems. How do we perceive and know the external world? How do we learn about it and remember what we learn? How do we use this information to build concepts of the world and solve the problems that the world presents to us? What are the roots of abnormal behavior? Are there laws that govern social and political behavior? Is there meaning to dreams?

Although such topics have been discussed for centuries, the methods of science were not applied to the study of the human mind and behavior until three or four hundred years after they found a solid place in physics (thus Ebbinghaus's quote). In fact, psychology today is to be compared, perhaps, with sixteenth-century physics. As many students of psychology realize (to their dismay), we still have much to learn about many important areas of human behavior. This appendix provides a brief and very rough sketch of the intellectual history of experimental psychology. Full histories can be found in Boring (1950), the classic in the field, and in a more recent and readable work by Schultz and Schultz (1987) (see also Pickren & Dewsbury, 2002; Rieber & Salzinger, 1998).

▼ ORIGINS OF EXPERIMENTAL PSYCHOLOGY: PHILOSOPHY AND PHYSIOLOGY

An important issue in the history of philosophy is the mind–body problem. Are the mind and body essentially the same or different in nature? A once-popular position on this issue, which probably greatly retarded the development of a scientific psychology, held that the mind and body are separate entities and operate according to different principles. According to this theory, often called **dualism,** the body is governed by physical laws, as are inanimate objects, but the mind is not governed by such laws because it possesses free will. It makes no sense to apply scientific methods in an attempt to discover laws of mental life if one is a dualist and believes that such laws do not exist. Early dualists argued that although the mind could control the body, there was little influence in the opposite direction.

The influential philosophical writings of René Descartes (1596–1650) helped weaken the belief that the body and mind do not interact. Descartes advanced the idea of mutual interaction: the body could affect the mind, and the mind could affect the body. Although the dualist position remained and the mind was still regarded as immortal and as possessing free will and a soul, the body could be studied as a mechanical system by rational, scientific means. Because animals were regarded as not possessing souls, they too could be studied by the methods applied to the inanimate objects of physical science. Thus, the application of the scientific method began to expand beyond the study of purely physical systems to the study of organic systems.

Over the years, the idea became more prevalent that even the human mind could be treated as something that could be profitably studied to discover mental laws. The British empiricist philosophers (Locke, Berkeley, Hume, Hartley) were impressed by the power of mechanistic models for explaining physical systems (for example, astronomy and physics). They believed that the mind could be modeled in a similar fashion—that is, in terms of elements (ideas) and forces (associations) that act on those elements in lawful ways. The empiricists emphasized the mechanical nature of mental phenomena; they discussed the "laws" of association in thought and the physical basis of the perception of the external world. The idea was beginning to take hold that for scientific study, the mind could be treated like a machine.

The British philosophers also emphasized the importance of learning in our understanding of the world. Descartes had argued that some ideas are innate, or develop without having information from the external world impinge on the senses. Kant expanded on this position, and aspects of it were later incorporated into the Gestalt school of psychology. The British empiricists received their name by rejecting this idea (*empiric* comes from the Greek *empeiria,* meaning experience). John Locke wrote thus in *An Essay Concerning Human Understanding:*

> Let us suppose the mind to be, as we say, white paper, void of all characters, without any ideas:—How comes it to be furnished? Whence comes it by that vast store which the busy and boundless fancy of man has painted on it with an almost endless variety? Whence has it all the *materials* of reason and knowledge? To this I answer, in one word, from EXPERIENCE. In that all our knowledge is founded. (1690/1959, Book II, Chap. 1)

Philosophers were preparing the way for a scientific psychology by treating the mind as subject to natural laws, but their method of study was simply anecdote and reflection. No matter how brilliant the ideas, these methods were likely to advance our knowledge little past the careful reflections of Plato and Aristotle centuries before. What was needed was application of the experimental methods and logic of science to the study of the mind and behavior. As Boring observed, "The application of the experimental method to the problem of mind is the great outstanding event to which no other is comparable." This method came to psychology by way of physiology.

German physiologists in the middle of the nineteenth century were interested in what is today considered sensory physiology: the physiology of the sense organs (the eyes, ears, and so on) and the transmission of information from these organs to the brain via the nervous system. Many of the German physiologists hoped that physiology could be reduced ultimately to physics, and, as they became interested in the physiology of the human nervous system, they came increasingly close to treating the mind as a physical machine. The Berlin Physical Society was formed in the 1840s with an overriding commitment to the belief that ultimately all phenomena could be explained in terms of physics. Four of the radical young scientists in the society, all in their twenties, signed in blood (so the story goes) an oath stating their belief that all forces in the human organism were chemical and physical ones.

The Contribution of Helmholtz

One of these young scientists was Hermann von Helmholtz (1821–1894). He was primarily a physicist and physiologist and was not concerned with establishing psychology as an independent discipline, but his research is given much credit in having had this effect. His work in vision and audition was overwhelmingly important, but what we should emphasize here is his role in conducting what may be considered transition experiments between physiology and experimental psychology.

One famous case was his use of what is now known as a **reaction-time experiment** to study the speed of neural impulses. Johannes Müller, a famous German physiologist, had argued that transmission of nervous impulses was instantaneous, or perhaps approached the speed of light. If you pinch your hand, do you notice any time elapse between the time you see yourself do the pinching and the time you feel the pinch? Probably not. At any rate, Müller also stated that we could probably never calculate the speed of nervous impulses. Only a few years later (in 1851), Helmholtz measured the speed experimentally. The basic idea was ingeniously simple: Stimulate a nerve at two different distances from the brain and measure the difference in time it takes for the organism to respond to the stimulation. If one knows the distance between the two points of stimulation and the difference in time taken to respond, then one can calculate the rate of the nervous impulse, since rate equals distance divided by time. Helmholtz stimulated blindfolded people on either the shoulder or the ankle and measured how fast they could react with their hand (by pushing a lever) in each case. Since he could measure approximately how much farther the impulse would have to travel to the brain from the ankle than from the shoulder, he was able to estimate the speed of nervous impulses at the relatively slow rate of 50 meters per second—not even the speed of sound, much less that of light! Helmholtz's most careful experimental work on this issue was with frogs (where of course the technique, but not the logic, was different), and the estimates were not too different. In fact, the estimates have more or less withstood the test of time, although we know today that the speed of the nervous impulse depends on the diameter of the nerves involved.

An interesting footnote is that Helmholtz so despaired of the great variability (or differences) in the reaction times that he found among subjects, and even within the same subject on different trials, that he gave up altogether on this line of research (Schultz & Schultz, 1987). Many psychologists since Helmholtz have also lamented the variability one finds in psychological research, although most have not given it up for this reason. Much of this book is concerned with the problem of variability in measures of animal or human behavior and how to overcome this problem.

▼ EARLY SCIENTIFIC PSYCHOLOGY

Scientific psychology had its birth and early life in Germany. In this section, we mention the contributions of four early pioneers: Weber, Fechner, Wundt, and Ebbinghaus. Table A.1 summarizes their contributions and Helmholtz's.

▼ **TABLE A.1**

Five Historic Scientists

Hermann von Helmholtz	1821–1894	Measured speed of neural impulses
Ernst Weber	1795–1878	Discovered Weber's law, which relates the size of an increase in physical stimulation to the just-noticeable difference
Gustav Fechner	1801–1887	Extended Weber's law (Fechner's law) and founded psychophysics
Wilhelm Wundt	1832–1920	Established first laboratory of experimental psychology in 1879
Hermann Ebbinghaus	1850–1909	Wrote *Memory* in 1885, showing complex mental phenomena could be studied

Ernst Weber

Ernst Weber (1795–1878) was an anatomist and physiologist in Leipzig whose research centered on cutaneous sensation, or the sense of touch. His most important contribution to psychology grew out of some experiments he conducted to investigate whether active engagement of one's muscles affected one's judgment of the weights of objects (see Chapter 6). He had people compare two weights, one of which was called a standard. In one case, blindfolded subjects picked up first a standard weight and then a comparison weight and indicated to the experimenter whether the two weighed the same amount. In another case, the subjects were passive; they simply had the weights placed in their hands successively, and then made their decisions.

Weber discovered that judgments were more accurate when subjects actively engaged their muscles; but more important, he noted something interesting in subjects' abilities to detect a difference between the standard and comparison weights. The greater the weight of the standard, the greater the difference between the standard and comparison weight had to be before the subjects could notice the difference. When the standard weight was small, only a small difference between the standard and comparison was necessary for subjects to detect a difference. But when the weight was large, the difference necessary for detection (called the **just-noticeable difference,** or **jnd**) was correspondingly larger. Weber further discovered that for any of the senses, the ratio of the amount of difference necessary to produce a jnd to the standard was a constant. Thus, not only does the amount of difference necessary to produce a jnd increase with the size of the standard, but it does so in a quite systematic way. This fact has come to be known as **Weber's law** (see Chapter 6).

Gustav Fechner

Weber thought that his finding was an interesting and useful generalization, but he was by no means staggered by its importance. Gustav Fechner (1801–1887) was. Fechner was eccentric in many ways, but his importance to psychology was great. He was trained as a physicist but also contributed to philosophy, religion, aesthetics, and psychology. Among numerous other academic ventures, he wrote one book on life after death and another (antedating a recent revival of interest in this topic) that argues that plants have a "mental life." In the 1830s his interests turned to the psychological topics of color vision and afterimages.

He badly injured his eyes while staring at the sun through colored lenses; this, combined with severe depression and strain from overwork, forced him into retirement in 1839. Fechner recovered, however, to the lasting benefit of psychology. In 1850, he was worrying about the fundamental problem of whether there were laws that governed the translation of physical energy into its psychological or mental representation. He began searching for laws that would relate the intensity of physical stimuli to the subjective impression of these stimuli. While grappling with this problem, he came upon Weber's work and greatly celebrated the principle Weber discovered, naming it Weber's law. Fechner elaborated on it somewhat; as we discuss in Chapter 6, this extension is called **Fechner's law.** To Fechner, this was the fulfillment of his hope that exact quantitative relationships exist between the physical and mental worlds. Thus, we say that Fechner founded the important discipline of **psychophysics,** which we consider in Chapter 6.

Wilhelm Wundt

Perhaps the first person to consider himself primarily a psychologist, although late in his career, was Wilhelm Wundt (1832–1920). Trained in physiology and medicine (by Helmholtz, among others), he gradually became interested in psychology. In 1874 his *Principles of Physiological Psychology* was published; the eminent historian Boring called it the most important book in the history of experimental psychology. In it, Wundt systematically reviewed everything known about psychology at the time and also presented his system of psychology. The book went through six editions and helped lay the groundwork for a systematic psychology. Wundt's contributions were primarily in organizing psychology and helping to establish it as an independent discipline, more than in making important scientific discoveries. Wundt trained many people who were later to make important contributions in their own right. He also is given credit for establishing the first laboratory of experimental psychology in 1879 in Leipzig and for establishing the first psychology journal.

Although Wundt was instrumental in establishing experimental psychology as a separate discipline, he did not believe that the higher mental processes such as memory, thought, and creativity could ever be studied experimentally. Experimental method, he claimed, could be applied only to the study of sensation and perception. He thought that the higher mental processes should be studied through the examination of the works of civilization over the centuries in various cultures or through cultural history or cultural anthropology. Wundt contributed ten volumes of research to this latter pursuit.

Hermann Ebbinghaus

In the same year (1879) that Wundt was establishing his laboratory, work was being done to discredit his belief about the extreme limits of experimental method in psychology. In this year, Hermann Ebbinghaus (1850–1909) initiated his pioneering experiments on human learning and memory, which culminated in his important book,

Memory, in 1885. This text showed that interesting experimental work could be done on more complex psychological topics, such as memory. His investigations spawned the critical area of inquiry concerning human learning and memory and are discussed more fully in Chapter 10.

▼ SCHOOLS OF PSYCHOLOGY

It is customary to divide psychology into a number of schools when considering the years 1890–1940 or so, although this damages certain trends in psychology that resist being neatly fit into these pigeonholes. Nonetheless, we shall briefly describe here some of the main features of the schools of structuralism, functionalism, behaviorism, and Gestalt psychology.

Structuralism: The Structure of Mental Life

Many psychology textbooks connect Wundt to the structural school of psychology, but the ideas attributed to structural psychology are more closely tied to Edward Bradford Titchener (1867–1927). Titchener, one of Wundt's students, brought this view to the United States and advanced it from his lab at Cornell University. Although these men differed on some particulars, we can treat their views together.

As its name implies, structural psychology, or **structuralism,** was primarily concerned with uncovering the structure of the mind. According to the structuralists, the three primary questions for psychology were these: (1) What are the elements of experience? (2) How are they combined? and (3) Why? What is the cause? The basic elements of experience were considered to be **sensations:** sights, sounds, tastes, smells, and so forth. The other two elements of experience were **images,** or **ideas,** which represented experiences not actually present, and **affections,** which were emotional reactions, such as hatred, joy, and love. Each element of experience could also be evaluated by its attributes of duration, intensity, quality, and clearness.

The work of structural psychology was to break down complex mental experiences into their components in the belief that by understanding the fundamental elements of conscious experience, one could understand how they combine into complex mental phenomena. Thus, it was elementaristic, since it sought the basic elements of mental experience. Elementary sensations and images were thought to be compounded through principles of association to become complex mental events. The method of decomposing these mental events was **introspection.** For structural psychologists, introspection did not refer to casual reflection, or even to critical reflection, but rather to a specific, technical method of viewing experience. To naïve observers (that is, all of us), consciousness seems to be all of one piece, or a stream, as William-James described it. Trained introspectionists were weaned from this view. They were to report the conscious contents of an experience, instead of the focal object under consideration. A trained introspectionist would not report seeing a table in the environment but rather would report seeing a particular spatial pattern, color, brightness, and so on. In other words, introspectionists were trained to see the elements of the experience of seeing a table. If one naïvely reported seeing a table, this was considered to be a case of committing the **stimulus error.**

Introspection was a rigorous and difficult method that people outside the structural camp felt to be sterile. It was also unreliable; introspectionists in different laboratories were not able to agree on the contents of the same experience. Titchener believed that the structural program set the pattern for the way psychology should develop, and all that remained was simply to fill in the details. He railed against the newer trends in psychology, trends that eventually pushed the structural school from the scene after 1920. Nonetheless, Titchener trained many psychologists who were later to become prominent, and structuralism served an important function, since the other schools were, in part, a reaction against it.

Although Wundt has been associated with structuralism, there are important differences between his brand of psychology and that attributed to the structural school. For example, Wundt strongly criticized the method of introspection, claiming that it was not a valid scientific technique (Benjamin, 1997). Also, like the Gestalt psychologists, Wundt argued that perception could not be explained in terms of a synthesis of sensory elements. Instead, he stated that perception was unique because it included both the elements of sensation and the attentional processes of the mind.

Functionalism: The Uses of Mind

Just as the structuralists were concerned with the structure of mental life, the functionalists were concerned with the functions of mental processes and structures. During the late 1800s, Darwin's theory of evolution swept through intellectual circles in England and the United States. Thus, it was quite natural that people began asking about the adaptive significance of psychological processes. What is the function of psychological processes? What differences do they make?

John Dewey (1859–1952) initiated **functionalism** at the University of Chicago after his arrival in 1894. Arriving at about the same time were George Herbert Mead, James Rowland Angell, and A. W. Moore. Dewey was greatly influenced by Darwin's concept of natural selection. In 1896 he published a paper called "The Reflex Arc Concept in Psychology," in which he criticized the trend toward elementarism in psychology, which is the breaking down of psychological processes into their supposed elementary parts. Interestingly, he did not attack Titchener in the paper but was more concerned with other issues. He argued that psychological processes were continuous, ongoing events and that psychologists should be careful to remember that distinctions they introduced to study the process were to some extent artificial and not part of the act itself. Dewey emphasized studying behavior in its natural context to determine its functions.

The functionalist school was more vague and amorphous than Titchener's tight little band of structuralists. The functionalists had little use for introspection, thought it was impossible to study mental processes devoid of their context and function, and were much more prone to endorse practical or applied programs in psychology. Yet the functionalists had no specific program for psychology, as did Titchener, and the closest they ever came to providing a manifesto was Angell's presidential address to the American Psychological Association (1907). Besides emphasizing applied activities, such as mental tests and education (the field to which Dewey migrated), functionalism helped introduce the study of lower organisms into psychology. This naturally followed from its emphasis on evolution and the developmental function of psychological processes.

Functionalism spread from Chicago in numerous directions, especially to Columbia University. Its position, never too systematic or dogmatic, was simply absorbed by psychology at large. And while functionalism was enjoying its heyday at the University of Chicago, a young psychologist named John Watson received his degree there in 1903.

Behaviorism: Rejecting Mental Explanations

In 1913 John Watson published a paper called "Psychology as the Behaviorist Views It." Thus began the behaviorist revolution in psychology. Watson's ideas about what was later to be called **behaviorism** had begun to take shape during his days at the University of Chicago but were not fully developed until some years later, when he was teaching at Johns Hopkins University. In his 1913 paper, Watson sharply attacked structural psychology and introspection, with its emphasis on consciousness and mental contents. Watson argued that we should sweep away all this nonsense, which could not even be reproduced from one lab to another, and study something that all reasonable people could agree on: behavior. He endorsed a statement by Pillsbury that "psychology is the science of behavior" and continued:

> I believe we can write a psychology, define it as Pillsbury, and never go back upon our definition: never use the terms consciousness, mental states, mind, content, introspectively, verifiable, imagery, and the like. It can be done in terms of stimulus and response, in terms of habit formation, habit integration, and the like. Furthermore, I believe it is really worthwhile to make this attempt now. (1913, pp. 166–167)

Watson's clear, concise statement of the position of behaviorism was quite influential. For many psychologists, it justified throwing out a lot of the murky nonsense that had occupied the field for so long. Watson's flair for straightforward, interesting writing was evident also in his other works, among which is his notable book *Psychology from the Standpoint of a Behaviorist* (1919).

The behaviorists were intent on establishing psychology as a natural science, a status they thought it lacked in 1913. Its subject matter was to be behavior. There was no need to become engaged in complicated arguments about such terms as consciousness, imageless thought, and apperception, whose meanings were unclear. Watson and the other behaviorists attacked both structuralism and functionalism on the grounds of vagueness. The behaviorists did not say that consciousness, imagery, and so forth did not exist; they just maintained that such terms were not useful scientific constructs.

Behaviorists believed that most important behaviors were learned, so the study of learning became the central focus of interest. The pioneering studies of Pavlov and Thorndike, reviewed in Chapters 9 and 11, indicated the possibility of an objective psychology of learning, and the focus of behavioral psychology has been on learning ever since.

The issues of behaviorism brought on a revolution within psychology, a revolution that is still with us. Much of the behaviorist point of view has by now been absorbed into the mainstream of psychology, though debates remain over many particulars. There is, indeed, no one position that today can be called behaviorism, except the general one that endorses the study of behavior as the appropriate subject matter of psychology. (Presumably, all experimental psychologists subscribe to this view today, since all are observing behavior.) Rather, there are a number of different behaviorist positions identified with a number of different people. Some of Watson's most prominent successors in the behaviorist line are E. B. Holt, Karl Lashley, E. C. Tolman, E. R. Guthrie, Clark Hull, Kenneth Spence, and B. F. Skinner. These psychologists all have considered themselves behaviorists, though they have differed widely on a number of issues regarding how psychology should be approached. For example, Lashley and Hull were quite concerned with the physiological bases of behavior, whereas Skinner shunned such inquiries. Critics these days who argue against behaviorism usually are arguing against the position of B. F. Skinner, who has attracted much attention for the extremity of some of his views as a radical behaviorist. But, of course, Skinner's position is not to be identified as the only form of behaviorism in psychology, since there are numerous other behaviorist positions.

It is popular to say these days that behaviorism is on the decline. Mental constructs (such as attention) have been reintroduced in psychology, even in the study of animal behavior. But these mental constructs are closely tied to observable responses. (We discuss in Chapters 7 and 14 how to find evidence for unobservable psychological constructs.) Behaviorism has had a wide impact on all areas of experimental psychology and thrives today in many forms.

Gestalt Psychology: Perception of the Whole

Functionalism and behaviorism developed in the United States partly as a reaction to structuralism. Another revolt against structuralism developed on its home ground, in Germany. The structural view of perception can be characterized as a brick-and-mortar view: Sensations (the bricks) are held together by associations (the mortar). Gestalt psychologists argued against this elementaristic position and claimed that perception of objects was of wholes, not complicated sums of parts. In the terms of **Gestalt psychology,** people perceive the world in unitary wholes.

Max Wertheimer (1880–1943) and the other Gestalt psychologists produced many demonstrations of the unity of the perceptual process that seemed incompatible with the structuralist position. One of these was the phenomenon of **shape constancy.** If you stand in front of a table with a book on it, a rectangular image may be produced on your retina, but if you move sideways several feet in one direction or the other, the retinal image may become trapezoidal. Despite this change in the retinal sensations, you perceive the book as being the same and having the same shape in both cases. The shape remains constant in your perception. Similar constancies of size and brightness, as well as numerous other perceptual phenomena, demonstrate the same point. Perception appears to have qualities of wholeness independent of the changing sensations projected on the receptors.

Gestalt psychology began, as did behaviorism, as a successful protest against structural psychology but soon found itself competing with behaviorism. The Gestaltists found the same unsatisfactory elementarism in the behaviorists' descriptions of behavior as they had in the structuralists', but now the elements were stimuli and responses. The behaviorists in turn found the Gestaltists' constructs every bit as fuzzy and ill defined as they had the structuralists' and functionalists'. In addition, the Gestaltists were often content to make some point or other through simple demonstrations, without devising clear theories and testing them experimentally. To some extent, Gestaltists and behaviorists were investigating different areas, with the Gestaltists concerned primarily with perception and the behaviorists with learning. But the later Gestalt psychologists, most notably Kurt Koffka and Wolfgang Köhler, began applying Gestalt constructs to other areas of psychology, such as the study of learning, memory, and problem solving. Thus, behaviorists and Gestaltists often have come into conflict, with the experimental battles usually ending in draws. It may well be that Gestalt theorists were describing behavior at a more general level than behaviorists and that their seemingly disparate accounts of the same psychological phenomena might not be as incompatible as they seemed at the time.

Gestalt psychology has not been as integrated into the mainstream of psychology as have functionalism and behaviorism, but its influence in certain areas of psychology has been overwhelming. This is certainly true of modern **cognitive psychology,** especially in the areas of perception, problem solving, and thought.

▼ SOME MODERN TRENDS

The era of these schools of psychology declined around 1940 or so, and this way of strictly dividing the field of psychology is no longer profitable. The influence of the schools lives on in contemporary research, but the organization of the field lies along different lines. Very little has been written about the history of psychology since 1940 because there are few unifying themes yet apparent. We sketch here, however, some modern trends.

World War II and the Extension of Psychology

During World War II, psychologists were employed in such diverse occupations as studying public opinion and propaganda, aiding race relations in the armed services, training animals to aid in combat situations, designing cockpits of complicated aircraft, constructing tests for personnel selection, and dealing with clinical problems of battle fatigue, depression, and so forth. Psychologists were forced from their scholastic retreats and encouraged to apply their knowledge to the numerous problems at hand. In many cases, this contact with real-world problems allowed them to see the inadequacy of their concepts and provided them the opportunity to develop new and better ideas. Thus, the war had a healthy influence on many areas of psychology. During this period human factors, then called human engineering, came into its own as a discipline.

Another trend occurring at about the same time was the extension of experimental method to problem areas to which it had not previously been applied. Experimental social psychology and experimental child psychology received considerable attention during the 1930s and 1940s.

Cognitive Psychology: The Return of Mind

Behaviorism dominated American psychology through the 1930s and 1940s, and because the study of unobservable events was eschewed, the study of mental processes was virtually abandoned during this time. However, several developments in the 1950s reinstated the scientific study of higher mental processes as a legitimate and feasible (albeit difficult) endeavor.

First, psychologists showed that many mental operations are difficult to explain in terms of conditioned associations between environmental stimuli and responses (e.g., Chomsky, 1959). Humans are actively involved in controlling mental activity, and the variety and complexity of many interesting human behaviors (for example, language, problem solving, creativity) cannot be entirely and satisfactorily explained by simple behavioristic mechanisms. Richer theories of mental mechanisms provide more powerful means of explaining the complexities of mental life. The current challenge is to study these unobservable mental events with objective, scientific methods that tie mental constructs to observable responses. Many clever inferential techniques have been developed to do so (see Chapters 7 and 14).

Cognitive psychology also has benefited from modern technology. The principles of **information theory,** which were borrowed from engineering in the late 1940s, allowed the quantification of concepts previously measured poorly, if at all (for example, the amount of "information" in a stimulus). Although the approach did not solve many of the traditional problems in psychology, it was influential in the development of information processing models, which represent human cognitive processes in terms of information flow through the system. These models have stimulated much research.

Another major influence from outside psychology has been computer science. Because computers are capable of performing complex computational tasks, many scientists have suggested that the computer may provide a model for the way the human mind encodes, stores, processes, and retrieves information. The field of artificial intelligence is aimed at exploring the relation between human and machine intelligence. Computer science has also paved the way for **parallel distributed processing (PDP)** approaches to cognition (e.g., Seidenberg & McClelland, 1989). A PDP model consists of a network of simple processing units that fall in distinct layers, with all of the processing units within a layer connected to all of the processing units in adjacent layers. Realization of particular models is accomplished via computer simulation, and PDP models have been used to simulate a wide variety of cognitive processes (Balota & Cortese, 2000). More recently, the use of cognitive and computational approaches has spilled over into other experimental areas of psychology, such as social psychology (e.g., Queller & Smith, 2002).

Cognitive Neuroscience: The Decade of the Brain

The U.S. Congress declared the 1990s the decade of the brain. Cognitive psychologists eagerly seized on neuroscience to expand our understanding of cognitive functioning (Posner, 1993; Posner & Raichle, 1994). **Psychophysiology** is the intersection of psychology and physiology. Two important goals of psychophysiology are to (1) discover if psychological phenomena have measurable physiological correlates and (2) develop plausible psychological models derived from knowledge of physiological states (Kantowitz, 1987).

Using such measures as heart rate, pupil (a part of the eye, not a student) dilation, and brain waves can help the cognitive psychologist investigate fundamental properties (Jennings & Coles, 1991a). Brain-imaging techniques such as **functional magnetic resonance imaging (fMRI)** are becoming increasingly popular among cognitive neuroscientists; fMRI works by measuring a correlate of brain activity, namely blood flow and oxygenation, in response to a targeted cognitive activity (e.g., see McDermott &

Buckner, 2002). For example, an important issue in cognitive psychology is whether mental capacity is limited and, if so, where the mental bottleneck occurs: in perception, translation, or motor control? The cognitive psychologist, who can measure only input–output relations, is limited to inferences from global measures of performance such as reaction time. But the neuroscientist has the potential to peer inside the "black box" to obtain intermediate measures that bear on hypothetical mental events.

Of course, the interpretation of psychophysiological measures is not without risk. Such dangers have been illustrated by relating the study of brain waves to earlier studies of phrenology (Kantowitz, 1987). Phrenologists assumed that the mind consisted of a set of separate mental functions. Each function was mediated by a specific physical location and was related to the size of the bumps on the head. Modern "bumpologists" study electrical bumps recorded from heads and attempt to map these bumps to psychological processes. It is easy to be too literal and interpret these electrical signals as direct manifestations of psychological processes, just as the phrenologists mapped physical bumps to processes, an enterprise that has been discredited in modern psychology.

As long as one avoids literal interpretation of psychophysiological data as directly reflecting psychological processes, neuroscience has much to offer the cognitive psychologist. Many useful physiological correlates of behavior have already been discovered, and neuroscientists are working hard to develop better theoretical integration of behavior and physiology (Buckner & Tulving, 1995; Jennings & Coles, 1991b).

Specialization

Perhaps the most notable recent trend in psychology is specialization. The schools of psychology tended to be all-encompassing; they had something to say about every phase of what they considered psychology. For example, behaviorists did not concern themselves with just learning, although this was their primary interest; they also applied their concepts to the areas of thought, language, and child development. Now psychologists no longer identify themselves by schools but by areas of interest. Most psychology departments are organized along these lines, as are Chapters 6 through 15 of this book.

Psychologists may be social psychologists, or animal-learning psychologists, or developmental psychologists, or cognitive psychologists (sensation, perception, memory, language, thinking, information processing, and so on), or personality psychologists, and so forth. Or psychologists may specialize in psychobiology, clinical psychology, or organizational or industrial psychology. And all these areas have subareas, such as those just listed for cognitive psychology. Workers within these fields are often quite likely to know little about the other areas. This trend toward specialization is often decried as unfortunate, but there seems little alternative. Such specialization is simply the mark of a maturing science, because the possibility is slight that a psychologist could be knowledgeable in all the areas of psychology today.

Experimental psychology is only one of the fifty-three divisions of the American Psychological Association. However, many psychologists belonging to other areas employ experimental method in their work. (On the other hand, members of some fields oppose the use of experimental method in psychology.) The list in Table A.2 gives you some idea of the great diversity and specialization found among present-day

The Divisions of the American Psychological Association

APA Division Number	APA Division Name
1.	Division of General Psychology
2.	Division on the Teaching of Psychology
3.	Division of Experimental Psychology
5.	Division on Evaluation, Measurement and Statistics
6.	Division of Behavioral Neuroscience and Comparative Psychology
7.	Division on Developmental Psychology
8.	The Society of Personality and Social Psychology—A Division of the APA
9.	The Society for the Psychological Study of Social Issues—A Division of the APA
10.	Division of Psychology and the Arts
12.	Division of Clinical Psychology
13.	Division of Consulting Psychology
14.	The Society for Industrial and Organizational Psychology, Inc.—A Division of the APA
15.	Division of Educational Psychology
16.	Division of School Psychology
17.	Division of Counseling Psychology
18.	Division of Psychologists in Public Service
19.	Division of Military Psychology
20.	Division of Adult Development and Aging
21.	Division of Applied Experimental and Engineering Psychologists
22.	Division of Rehabilitation Psychology
23.	Division of Consumer Psychology
24.	Division of Theoretical and Philosophical Psychology
25.	Division for the Experimental Analysis of Behavior
26.	Division of the History of Psychology
27.	Division of Community Psychology
28.	Division of Psychopharmacology
29.	Division of Psychotherapy
30.	Division of Psychological Hypnosis
31.	Division of State Psychological Association Affairs
32.	Division of Humanistic Psychology
33.	Division on Mental Retardation and Developmental Disabilities
34.	Division of Population and Environmental Psychology
35.	Division of Psychology of Women
36.	Division on Psychology of Religion
37.	Division of Child, Youth, and Family Services
38.	Division on Health Psychology
39.	Division on Psychoanalysis
40.	Division of Clinical Neuropsychology
41.	Division of American Psychology—Law Society
42.	Division of Psychologists in Independent Practice
43.	Division of Family Psychology
44.	The Society for the Psychological Study of Lesbian and Gay Issues
45.	Society for the Study of Ethnic Minority Issues
46.	Division of Media Psychology
47.	Division of Exercise and Sport Psychology
48.	Division of Peace Psychology
49.	Division of Group Psychology and Group Psychotherapy
50.	Division of Addictions
51.	The Society for the Psychological Study of Men and Masculinity
52.	International Psychology
53.	Society of Clinical Child and Adolescent Psychology
54.	Society of Pediatric Psychology
55.	American Society for the Advancement of Pharmacotherapy

Note: There are no division numbers 4 or 11.

psychologists. In addition to the American Psychological Association, several other societies hold great importance to experimental psychologists. The Psychonomic Society was founded in 1958. Full membership is restricted to scientists who have already made scholarly contributions by publishing articles in scientific journals. The Psychonomic Society publishes several influential journals of experimental psychology and sponsors an important annual meeting where scientists can exchange information. The American Psychological Society, founded in 1988, is the newest society. Its goals are to advance the discipline of psychology, to preserve the scientific base of psychology, to promote public understanding of psychological science and its applications, to enhance the quality of graduate education, and to encourage the "giving away" of psychology in the public interest. Finally, reflecting the recent upsurge of interest in cognitive neuroscience, many experimental psychologists now belong to either the Society for Neuroscience (founded in 1970) or the Cognitive Neuroscience Society (founded in 1994).

▼ SUMMARY

1. Scientific psychology is about one hundred years old, give or take a decade. The roots of psychology lie in the questions asked by philosophers for thousands of years. The original techniques for studying psychology experimentally were devised by physicists and physiologists who became interested in psychological topics, particularly those concerned with reception of stimuli by the senses.

2. Four early pioneers of psychology were Helmholtz, Weber, Fechner, and Ebbinghaus. In an early reaction-time experiment, Helmholtz measured the speed of the nervous impulse, thus showing how experimental techniques could provide information about psychological topics.

3. Weber examined how much a stimulus had to change for an observer to notice the difference. He discovered that the amount of change needed for a just-noticeable difference (jnd) was a constant proportion of the magnitude of the standard stimulus, a fact that became known as Weber's law. Fechner continued Weber's work and coined the term *psychophysics*, which was concerned with how changes in the physical world are related to a person's perception of the changes.

▼ TABLE A.3

Summary of Four Primary Schools of Psychology

School	Subject Matter	Research Goals	Research Methods
Structuralism	Conscious experience	To break down conscious experience into its basic components: sensations, images, affections	Analytic introspection
Functionalism	The function of mental processes and how they help people adapt	To study mental processes in their natural contexts; to discover what effects they have	Objective measures; informal observation and introspection
Behaviorism	Behavior: how it is changed under different conditions, with emphasis on learning	Description, explanation, prediction, and control of behavior	Objective measures of behavior; formal experiments
Gestalt psychology	Subjective experience, with emphasis on perception, memory, and thinking	To understand the phenomena of conscious experience in terms of the whole experience (not to break down experience into arbitrary categories)	Subjective reports; some behavioral measures; demonstrations

4. Ebbinghaus performed the first systematic experiments on memory. His research methods and findings had tremendous impact on the field because they showed that even higher mental processes could be studied experimentally.

5. A number of different schools of psychology came into being between 1890 and 1940. Four primary ones were structuralism, functionalism, behaviorism, and Gestalt. A summary of their primary characteristics is presented in Table A.3 on page 446. The influence of the schools lives on today, but contemporary psychology is divided along lines of various subject matters of interest to researchers. As psychology has matured, the focus of most psychologists has become increasingly specialized.

▼ KEY TERMS

affections
behaviorism
cognitive psychology
dualism
Fechner's law
functional magnetic resonance imaging (fMRI)
functionalism
Gestalt psychology
ideas
images
information theory

introspection
just-noticeable difference (jnd)
parallel distributed processing (PDP)
psychophysics
psychophysiology
reaction-time experiment
sensation
shape constancy
stimulus error
structuralism
Weber's law

 ## WEB CONNECTIONS

A chronology of important events in American psychology is at:
http://www.cwu.edu/~warren/today.html

Full-text versions of classic psychological papers can be found at:
http://psychclassics.yorku.ca/

This site contains many links to sites related to the history of psychology:
http://elvers.stjoe.udayton.edu/history/welcome.htm

STATISTICAL REASONING: AN INTRODUCTION

Statistical thinking will one day be as necessary for efficient citizenship as the ability to read and write. (H. G. WELLS)

The purpose of this appendix is to give you some idea why an understanding of statistics is crucial to the conduct and interpretation of psychological research. We also give some attention to how statistical reasoning is used in psychological research, even though we can hardly hope to turn you into an expert statistician from reading this one section. This appendix serves as a review for those of you who have already taken statistics. Students new to statistics may need to read the section several times very carefully, since there is quite a bit of new information. You may be aware by now that if you were to complete graduate work for the Ph.D. in psychology, you would probably be required to take a minimum of three courses in statistics.

Many aspects of the world we live in can be treated in terms of probabilities. We do not always know with complete certainty that events will occur but only that they will happen some proportion of the time or with a certain probability. A common example is weather forecasting. Meteorologists say there is an 80 percent chance of rain or a 20 percent chance of snow, given certain prior conditions. Even when the prior conditions are known, it is impossible to predict perfectly the future weather. Much of human behavior is probabilistic in the same sense. **Inferential statistics** are useful in helping psychologists estimate the probability of whether differences in groups of observations between two conditions have been produced by random, or chance, factors. **Descriptive statistics** help psychologists summarize or describe observations. We first examine descriptive statistics and then turn to inferential statistics.

▼ DESCRIPTIVE STATISTICS: TELLING IT LIKE IT IS

When we conduct an experiment and measure an independent variable, we typically produce a large array of numbers. What are we to do with them? First, we need to create a system and organize them. We do not have to look at the whole array of numbers produced by subjects in the different conditions of the experiment; instead, we can look at a briefer version. By summarizing the data, we may see general trends that are otherwise hidden by the large array of numbers. Descriptive statistics provide this organizing and summarizing function. The two main types are measures of **central tendency** (the typical score) and measures of **dispersion** (the spread of the data).

Let us take a hypothetical experimental situation. A drug company has sponsored a test of the effects of LSD on the behavior of rats, so we decide to see how the drug affects the rats' running speed. Forty food-deprived rats have been trained to run a straight-alley maze for a food reward. We randomly assign them to two groups. To one group, we administer LSD by injection and observe the effect on the speed with which they run the alley for food 30 minutes after the injection. The other group is tested in a similar manner 30 minutes after receiving an injection of a placebo. The following are the running times for the 20 control subjects in seconds: 13, 11, 14, 18, 12, 14, 10, 13, 13, 16, 15, 9, 12, 20, 11, 13, 12, 17, 15, and 14. The running times for the subjects receiving the LSD injections

▼ **FIGURE B.1**

Histograms representing scores for 20 subjects in the control and experimental conditions of the hypothetical LSD experiment.

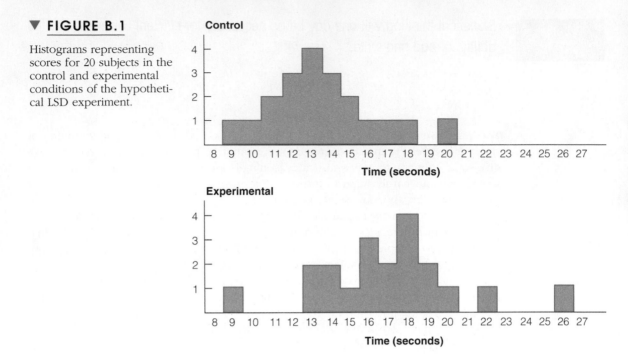

are 17, 15, 16, 20, 14, 19, 14, 13, 18, 18, 26, 17, 19, 13, 16, 22, 18, 16, 18, and 9. Now that we have the running times, what do we do with them? One thing we might want is a graphical representation of the numbers, as in the two **histograms** shown in Figure B.1. Here, the running times in seconds appear along the abscissa (*X*-axis), and the frequency with which each time occurred in the two conditions is displayed along the ordinate (*Y*-axis). Running times for the control subjects are given in the top histogram; those for the experimental subjects are represented in the bottom one. Another way to represent the same information is to use a **frequency polygon.** Its construction is equivalent to that of the histogram; you can visualize this type of graph by connecting the midpoints of the bars in the histogram. Idealized frequency polygons appear later in the appendix (in Figure B.2). In both conditions in Figure B.1, the greatest number of scores occurs in the middle; they tend to tail off toward the ends. This is more obvious for the control than for the experimental subjects. Also, the times for the experimental group tend to be greater than those for the control group. Both the histogram and the frequency polygon are types of **frequency distributions.** They help systematize the data somewhat, but there are more efficient summary descriptions.

Central Tendency

The most common summary description of data is some measure of central tendency, which, as the term implies, indicates the center of the distribution of scores. By far the most typical measure of central tendency in psychological research is the **arithmetic mean.** The mean ($\bar{X}$) is simply the sum of all the scores (ΣX) divided by the number of scores (*n*), or $\bar{X} = \Sigma X/n$. It is what most people think of as the average of a set of numbers, although the term *average* technically applies to any measure of central tendency. The sums of the running times for the experimental and control conditions of our hypothetical experiment were 338 and 272 seconds, respectively. Since there were 20 observations in each condition, the means are 16.9 seconds for the experimental condition and 13.6 for the control.

The mean is the most useful measure of central tendency, and almost all inferential statistics, which we come to later, are based on it. Therefore, this statistic is used whenever possible. However, another measure of central tendency is sometimes used: the **median**. It is the score above which half of the distribution lies and below which the other half lies. The median, then, is the midpoint of the distribution. When the number of scores (n) in the distribution is odd, such as 27, the median is the fourteenth score from the bottom or top, since that score divides the distribution into two groups of thirteen scores. When the number of scores is an even number, the median is the arithmetic mean of the two middle scores, if the scores are not tied. So the median of the scores 66, 70, 72, 76, 80, and 96 is (72 + 76)/2, or 74. When, as often happens, the two middle scores are tied, as in the distribution of scores from the hypothetical LSD experiment, the convention is to designate the median as the appropriate proportion of the distance between the *limits* of the particular score, where the limits are a half score above and below the tied score. This should become clear with an example. Consider the distributions of scores from our experiment. If you arrange the 20 control running times from lowest to highest, you will discover that the eighth, ninth, tenth, and eleventh scores are all 13. Under such conditions, the tenth score is considered the median. It is considered to lie three-quarters of the distance between the limits of 12.5 and 13.5. So the median would be 12.5 + 0.75, or 13.25, for the control subjects. By the same reasoning (and you should try it yourself), we find that the median for the experimental subjects is 17.

Why is the median used? The primary reason is that it has the (desirable) property of being insensitive to extreme scores. In the distribution of scores of 66, 70, 72, 76, 80, and 96, the median of the distribution would remain exactly the same if the lowest score were 1 rather than 66, or the highest score were 1,223 rather than 96. The mean, on the other hand, would differ widely with these other scores. Often this benefit can be extremely useful in summarizing data from the real world. In our LSD experiment, suppose that one of the rats given LSD had stopped halfway down the alley to examine a particularly interesting feature of the runway before continuing on its way to the goal box, and thus its time to complete the runway was 45 minutes, or 2,700 seconds. If this score replaced the 26-second score in the original distribution, the mean would go from 16.9 seconds to 150.6, or from 3.30 seconds greater than the control mean to 137.0 seconds greater. This would be only because of one very deviant score: in such cases, researchers frequently use the median score rather than the mean to represent the central tendency. Using the mean can give an unrepresentative estimate of central tendency because of the great influence of the one score. However, using the median can limit severely any statistical tests that can be applied to the data.

Measures of Dispersion

Measures of central tendency indicate the center of the scores, whereas measures of dispersion indicate how the scores are spread out about the center. In deciding on a measure of dispersion, we want to provide a number that reflects the amount of spread that

▼ **TABLE B.1**

Calculation of the Mean Deviations and Absolute Mean Deviations from Two Sets of Scores. The Sum of the Deviations (Differences) in Calculating the Mean Deviation Is Zero, which Is Why It Is Necessary to Use the Absolute Mean Deviation.

Control Group			Experimental Group		
X	$(X - \bar{X})$	$|X - \bar{X}|$	X	$(X - \bar{X})$	$|X - \bar{X}|$
9	−4.60	4.60	9	−7.90	7.90
10	−3.60	3.60	13	−3.90	3.90
11	−2.60	2.60	13	−3.90	3.90
11	−2.60	2.60	14	−2.90	2.90
12	−1.60	1.60	14	−2.90	2.90
12	−1.60	1.60	15	−1.90	1.90
12	−1.60	1.60	16	−0.90	0.90
13	−0.60	0.60	16	−0.90	0.90
13	−0.60	0.60	16	−0.90	0.90
13	−0.60	0.60	17	+0.10	0.10
13	−0.60	0.60	17	+0.10	0.10
14	+0.40	0.40	18	+1.10	1.10
14	+0.40	0.40	18	+1.10	1.10
14	+0.40	0.40	18	+1.10	1.10
15	+1.40	1.40	18	+1.10	1.10
15	+1.40	1.40	19	+2.10	2.10
16	+2.40	2.40	19	+2.10	2.10
17	+3.40	3.40	20	+3.10	3.10
18	+4.40	4.40	22	+5.10	5.10
20	+6.40	6.40	26	+9.10	9.10
$\Sigma X = 272$	Total = 0.0	Total = 41.20	$\Sigma X = 338$	Total = 0.00	Total = 52.20

$\bar{X} = 13.60$

Absolute mean deviation = $\dfrac{41.20}{20}$ = 2.06

$\bar{X} = 16.90$

Absolute mean deviation = $\dfrac{52.20}{20}$ = 2.61

the scores exhibit around some central-tendency measure, usually the mean. One such measure that would be appropriate is the mean deviation. This is calculated by taking the difference between the mean and every score in a distribution, summing these differences, and then dividing by the number of scores. However, it is actually necessary to take the mean absolute difference (that is, to ignore the sign of the difference: whether the score is greater or less than the mean). The reason is that the sum of the deviations of scores about the mean is always zero, a defining characteristic of the mean (see Table B.1). Thus, the mean deviation must be the **absolute mean deviation.** The mean deviations for our hypothetical experimental conditions in the LSD experiment are calculated in Table B.1. The symbol | | indicates the absolute value of a number: $|-6| = 6$.

The absolute mean deviation of a set of scores is an adequate measure of dispersion and is based on the same logic involved in finding the mean of a distribution. However, the standard deviation and variance (defined later) are preferred to the mean deviation, because they have mathematical properties that make them much more useful in more advanced statistical computations. The logic behind their calculation is quite similar to that of the mean deviation, which is why we have considered the mean deviation here. In calculating the mean deviation, we had to take the absolute value of the difference of each score from the mean, so that these differences would not add up to zero. Instead of taking the absolute difference, we could have gotten rid of the troublesome negative numbers by squaring the differences. This is exactly what is done in calculating the variance and standard deviation of a distribution.

The **variance** of a distribution is defined as *the sum of the squared deviations from the mean, divided by the number of scores.* In other words, the difference between each score and the mean is taken and squared; then, all these values are summed and divided by the number of scores. The following is the formula for the variance:

$$s^2 = \frac{\Sigma(X - \bar{X})^2}{n} \tag{B.1}$$

where s^2 represents the variance, X the individual scores, $\bar{X}$ the mean, and n the number of scores or observations. Although the variance is a useful number, it describes dispersion in squared units—squared running times in this example—which is often not very useful. To get back to the original unit of measurement, all we have to do is take the square root of the variance. The **standard deviation** results from taking the *square root of the variance* and is represented by s (some texts denote it by sd). Since s is the original unit of measurement, it and the mean are presented together to describe a distribution of scores. As seen later, the variance is used primarily to calculate other statistics, such as F, which is an inferential statistic.

$$s = \sqrt{\frac{\Sigma(X - \bar{X})^2}{n}} \tag{B.2}$$

Calculation of the standard deviations for the control and experimental conditions from the LSD experiment by the mean-deviation method is illustrated in Table B.2.

The formulas for the variance and standard deviation of a distribution given in Equations B.1 and B.2 are rather cumbersome; in practice, the equivalent computational formulas are used. The standard-deviation computational formula is

$$s = \sqrt{\frac{\Sigma X^2}{n} - \bar{X}^2} \tag{B.3}$$

where ΣX^2 is the sum of the squares of all the scores, $\bar{X}$ is the mean of the distribution, and n is the number of scores. Similarly, the computational formula for variance is

$$s^2 = \frac{\Sigma X^2}{n} - \bar{X}^2 \tag{B.4}$$

The value in each case is the same as that obtained when the definitional formula is used.

In describing an array of data, psychologists typically present two descriptive statistics, the mean and the standard deviation. Although there are other measures of central tendency and dispersion, these are most useful for descriptive purposes. Variance is used extensively, as we shall see, in inferential statistics.

A Note on Calculation

Throughout this appendix, we illustrate statistical procedures with detailed calculations, as is done in Table B.2. We do this in the hopes that the logic behind the calculations will become clear. However, it is entirely possible that you will never have to

▼ **TABLE B.2**

Calculation of the Standard Deviation, S, for the Control and Experimental Conditions by the Mean-deviation Method.

	Control Group			Experimental Group	
X	$(X - \bar{X})$	$(X - \bar{X})^2$	X	$(X - \bar{X})$	$(X - \bar{X})^2$
9	−4.60	21.16	9	−7.90	62.41
10	−3.60	12.96	13	−3.90	15.21
11	−2.60	6.76	13	−3.90	15.21
11	−2.60	6.76	14	−2.90	8.41
12	−1.60	2.56	14	−2.90	8.41
12	−1.60	2.56	15	−1.90	3.61
12	−1.60	2.56	16	−0.90	0.81
13	−0.60	0.36	16	−0.90	0.81
13	−0.60	0.36	16	−0.90	0.81
13	−0.60	0.36	17	+0.10	0.01
13	−0.60	0.36	17	+0.10	0.01
14	+0.40	0.16	18	+1.10	1.21
14	+0.40	0.16	18	+1.10	1.21
14	+0.40	0.16	18	+1.10	1.21
15	+1.40	1.96	18	+1.10	1.21
15	+1.40	1.96	19	+2.10	4.41
16	+2.40	5.76	19	+2.10	4.41
17	+3.40	11.56	20	+3.10	9.61
18	+4.40	19.36	22	+5.10	26.01
20	+6.40	40.96	26	+9.10	82.81
$\Sigma X = 272$	Total = 0.00	$\Sigma(X - \bar{X}) = 138.80$	$\Sigma X = 338$	Total = 0.00	$\Sigma(X - \bar{X})^2 = 247.80$
$\bar{X} = 13.60$			$\bar{X} = 16.90$		

$$s = \sqrt{\frac{\Sigma(X - \bar{X})^2}{n}}$$

$$s = \sqrt{\frac{138.80}{20}}$$

$$s = 2.63$$

$$s = \sqrt{\frac{\Sigma(X - \bar{X})^2}{n}}$$

$$s = \sqrt{\frac{247.80}{20}}$$

$$s = 3.52$$

work through a statistical procedure step by step. Many calculators and computers will calculate statistics for you. Often, all that you need to do is enter the data into the calculator or computer; with a few additional commands, the results will be determined. Computers are popular for statistical analyses, because they are fast and do not make mistakes unless you enter the data incorrectly or select the wrong program.

The Normal Distribution

The graphs of the scores of the hypothetical LSD experiment in Figure B.1 show that the scores pile up in the middle but tail off toward the extreme ends (tails) of the distribution of scores. Although these numbers are hypothetical, this sort of distribution has a property that occurs for most measures of behavior. That is, for most phenomena that are measured, scores cluster in the center of the distribution. This configuration is called the **normal curve,** an example of which is presented in Figure B.2 (the curve

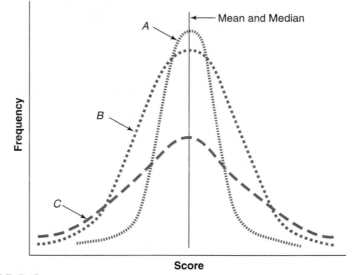

▼ FIGURE B.2

Three examples of the normal curve that differ in variability. *C* has the greatest variability and *A* the least. The normal curve is a symmetrical distribution in which the mean and median have the same value.

labeled *B*). When put on a graph, psychological data typically are most numerous in the middle of the set of scores; they decline in frequency with distance from the middle in a roughly symmetrical way. A score 10 points below the center of the distribution occurs about as frequently as a score 10 points above the center.

The three curves shown in Figure B.2 are all symmetrical. In such distributions of scores, the mean and median of the distribution both fall at the same point or score. Curves with the same mean and median may differ in their variability, as do the curves in Figure B.2. The tall, thin curve labeled *A* would have a smaller standard deviation than the other two. Similarly, the broad, flat curve (*C*) would have a greater standard deviation than the other two.

The normal curve has a very useful property. It turns out that a specific proportion of scores falls under each part of the normal curve. This feature is illustrated in Figure B.3. On each side of the normal curve in Figure B.3, there is a point at which the curve slightly reverses its direction; it starts bending outward more. This is called the **inflection point.** The inflection point in the curve is always one standard deviation from the mean. In fact, the normal curve has the useful property that specific proportions of the distribution of scores it represents are contained within specific areas of the curve itself. About 68 percent of all scores are contained within one standard deviation of the mean (34 percent on each side). Similarly, almost 96 percent of the scores are contained within two standard deviations of the mean, and 99.74 percent of the scores are within three standard deviations. The percentage in each area is shown in Figure B.3.

This property of normal curves is extremely useful: If we know an individual's score and the mean and the standard deviation in the distribution of scores, we also

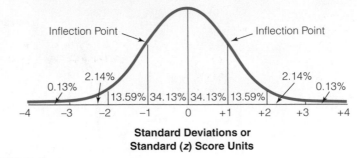

Inflection Point

Inflection Point

0.13%

2.14%

13.59% | 34.13% | 34.13% | 13.59%

2.14%

0.13%

−4　−3　−2　−1　0　+1　+2　+3　+4

**Standard Deviations or
Standard (z) Score Units**

▼ **FIGURE B.3**

Proportions of scores in specific areas under the normal curve. The inflection points are one standard deviation from the mean.

know the person's relative rank. For example, most IQ tests are devised so that the population mean is 100 and the standard deviation is 15. If a person has an IQ of 115, we know that he or she has scored higher than 84 percent of all people on the test (50 percent of the people below the mean and 34 percent above). Similarly, a person with an IQ of 130 has scored higher than almost 98 percent of all people, and a person with an IQ of 145 has scored higher than 99.87 percent of the population.

Many distributions of scores in psychological data are, or at least are assumed to be, normal. It is common to compare scores across normal distributions with different means and variances in terms of **standard scores,** or **z scores.** This is simply the difference between an individual score and the mean, expressed in units of standard deviations. So an IQ of 115 translates to a z score of 1.00, that is, [115 − 100]/15, and an IQ of 78 translates to a z score of −1.47, that is, [78 − 100]/15. Standard scores are useful since they allow comparison of the relative ranks of scores for people across distributions in which the means and standard deviations vary greatly. Grades in courses should be calculated in terms of z scores if the means and standard deviations of the scores vary widely from one test to the next. Thus, a person's eventual rank in the class is calculated more faithfully by finding the mean of the z scores than by finding the mean of the raw scores of the tests.

When it is said that data in some experiment or other are *normally distributed,* it means that if they are graphed, they will tend to form a normal distribution. Thus, *normal,* as it is used in psychological research, usually refers to a type of distribution, not to a value judgment as to the goodness or badness of the scores.

Correlation Coefficient

In Chapter 2, we describe correlational research. The purpose of correlational research is to see how two or more attributes of an organism vary together. The strength and direction of a correlation is determined by the calculation of a correlation coefficient. We will consider just one: **Pearson product-moment correlation coefficient,** or **Pearson r.** Shown in Box B.1 is the calculation formula for r, using the hypothetical data relating head size to memory performance discussed in Chapter 2.

Box B.1

Computing
Pearson r

Let us call one set of numbers in Table B.3. X scores and the other set Y scores. For example, head sizes might be X scores and words recalled Y scores. The formula for computing Pearson r from the raw scores in panels (a), (b), or (c) of Table 2.1 is

$$= \frac{n\sum XY - (\sum X)(\sum Y)}{\sqrt{\left[n\sum X^2 - (\sum X)^2\right]\left[n\sum Y^2 - (\sum Y)^2\right]}} \qquad (B.5)$$

The n refers to the number of subjects on which observations are taken (here, 10); the terms $\sum X$ and $\sum Y$ are the totals of the X and Y scores, respectively; $\sum X^2$ and $\sum Y^2$ are the sum of all the X (or Y) values after each is squared; and the $(\sum X)^2$ and $(\sum Y)^2$ are the total of all the X or Y values with the entire total or sum squared. This leaves the value $\sum XY$, or the sum of the cross-products.

▼ **TABLE B.3**

Calculation of Pearson r for the Data in the First (a) Column of Table 2.1, by the Raw-Score Formula (Equation B.5).

	X			Y		
Subject Number	Head Size (cm)	X^2	Words Recalled	Y^2		$X \cdot Y$
1	50.8	2580.64	17	289		863.60
2	63.5	4032.25	21	441		1330.50
3	45.7	2088.49	16	256		731.20
4	25.4	645.16	11	121		279.40
5	29.2	852.64	9	81		262.80
6	49.5	2450.25	15	225		742.50
7	38.1	1451.61	13	169		495.30
8	30.5	930.25	12	144		366.00
9	35.6	1267.36	14	196		498.40
10	58.4	3410.56	23	529		1343.20
$n = 10$	$\sum X = 426.70$	$\sum X^2 = 19{,}709.21$	$\sum Y = 151$	$\sum Y^2 = 2451$		$\sum XY = 6915.90$

$$r = \frac{n\sum XY - (\sum X)(\sum Y)}{\sqrt{\left[n\sum X^2 - (\sum X)^2\right]\left[n\sum Y^2 - (\sum Y)^2 2\right]}}$$

$$r = \frac{10(6915.90) - (426.70)(151)}{\sqrt{\left[(10)(19.709.21) - (426.70)^2\right]\left[(10)(2451) - (151)^2\right]}}$$

$$r = \frac{69{,}159.00 - 64{,}431.70}{\sqrt{[197{,}092.10 - 182{,}072.89][24{,}510 - 22{,}801]}}$$

$$r = 4727.30\sqrt{[15{,}019.21][1709]} = \frac{4727.30}{\sqrt{25{,}667{,}829.89}}$$

$$r = \frac{4727.30}{5066.34}$$

$$r = +0.93$$

continued

Box B.1
continued

This is obtained very simply by multiplying each X value by its corresponding Y and then summing these products. You may see other formulas for calculation of Pearson r besides the raw-score formula in equation B.5, but these will be equivalent (in general) to the one presented here. An illustration of how Pearson r is calculated using this raw-score formula is presented in Table B.3 using the data from the (a) column of Table 2.1 (Chapter 2, page 37). You should try to work out the values for Pearson r for the (b) and (c) panels yourself, to make certain you understand how to calculate the values and to gain an intuitive feel for the concept of correlation. The values of r are given below the appropriate columns in Table 2.1.

▼ INFERENTIAL STATISTICS

Descriptive statistics lead to a summary of the results of the LSD experiment as the following: The mean running time for the control group was 13.6 seconds, with a standard deviation of 2.63, whereas the experimental subjects injected with LSD had a mean of 16.9 seconds and a standard deviation of 3.52. Should we take the 3.3-second difference between the mean running times seriously? Perhaps it is owing merely to chance factors, such as measurement error or the fact that a few rats in the control group had a particularly good day and thus felt like running a bit faster. How large must the difference be for us to conclude that it is unlikely to have occurred by chance alone? Inferential statistics are used to answer this question.

The procedure is not too complicated. We choose an appropriate statistical test for the experimental situation, perform a few straightforward computations on a calculator (or computer), and then consult a special table. The table informs us of the probability that the difference we have found between our conditions is a result of random factors. If it is sufficiently unlikely to have occurred by chance, we conclude that the difference is statistically significant. But, although the actual computational procedures are often quite simple, you need to understand the logic behind them so that you will appreciate how statistical inferences are made.

Sampling

A **population** is a complete set of measurements (or individuals or objects) having some common observable characteristic. Examples of populations are all U.S. citizens of voting age and all albino rats that have had injections of LSD. It is impossible to study the entire population in each case. If we could measure the entire population of rats for running speed after either an injection of LSD or an injection of a chemically inert substance, then we would better know what the effects of LSD were, since we would have measured the entire population. (Any difference could still, of course, be attributable to measurement error.) But since it is almost always impractical to measure an entire population, we must *sample* from it. A **sample** is a subset of a population; this is almost always what we are examining when we compare experimental conditions. We make statistical inferences, then we draw a conclusion that is based on only a sample of observations about an entire population. We really want to know about the effects of LSD and the inert substance on rats in general, and we hope to draw this conclusion from a sample of, say, 20 rats in each condition. Box B.2 contains some of the parameters used with population measures and the statistics used with sample data.

Samples should always be as representative as possible of the population under study. One way of accomplishing this is through **random sampling,** by which members are picked from the population by some completely arbitrary means. (Random sampling is often carried out by using a random-numbers table, such as the one in Table H in Appendix C). Technically, we can only generalize to the population from which we have sampled, although if taken literally, this would make experimental research hardly worth doing. If we received 50 rats from a supply house for our hypothetical experiment, selected a sample of 40, and randomly assigned them to the two conditions of the experiment, would our conclusions then be true only of the population of 50 rats? Perhaps technically, but no one would care about the result if this were so, and no one would have wasted the time doing the experiment. We would at least want to assume that the results are characteristic of that strain of rats. In practice, psychologists assume that their results generalize more widely than the limited population from which they sampled for their experiment. We consider the problem of generality of results and the basis of this assumption more fully in Chapters 10 and 14.

Box B.2
Statistical
Notation

Characteristics of a population of scores are called **parameters,** whereas characteristics of a sample of scores drawn from a large population are **statistics.** The mean of an entire population of scores is a parameter, and the mean of a sample is a statistic. To maintain these distinctions, different symbols are used for population parameters and sample statistics. Some of the most frequent symbols are listed here. Some have been explained; the others are discussed in the next few pages.

N = number of scores in a population

n = number of scores in a sample

μ = population mean (μ is pronounced "mu")

$\bar{X}$ = sample mean

σ^2= population variance (σ is pronounced "sigma")

s^2 = sample variance $\dfrac{\Sigma(X - \bar{X})^2}{n}$

$\hat{s}^2$ = unbiased estimate of population variance $\dfrac{\Sigma(X - \bar{X})^2}{n-1}$

σ = population standard deviation

s = sample standard deviation

$\hat{s}$ = sample standard deviation based on the unbiased variance estimate

$\sigma_{\bar{x}}$ = standard error of the mean $\dfrac{\sigma}{\sqrt{N}}$

$\hat{s}_{\bar{x}}$= estimated standard error of the mean, $\dfrac{\hat{s}}{\sqrt{n}}$

The Distribution of Sample Means

One way we could ask about the reliability of our hypothetical experiment would be to perform it repeatedly with new groups of rats. Of course, it would be very unlikely for us to get exactly the same mean running times for the experimental and control conditions in these replications. The means in seconds for the experimental and control conditions in four replications might be 17.9 and 12.5, 16.0 and 13.4, 16.6 and 14.5, and 15.4 and 15.1. Since the experimental rats that receive the LSD always run more slowly than the control rats, this would increase our confidence in the original finding, although the difference is rather small in the last replication. If we repeated the experiment like this and plotted the distribution of the sample means obtained in the two conditions, these distributions would be normal and would have all the characteristics of a normal distribution, such as a certain proportion of the scores falling under a portion of the curve. This useful outcome would also occur if we found the difference between the two means in each experiment and plotted these differences. Because the differences are normally distributed, we can determine how often a particular mean difference will occur. This ability provides a great deal of information, and it is the basis of inferential statistics.

To give you a better idea of the concept of the **distribution of sample means,** let us borrow an example from a class demonstration by Horowitz (1974, pp. 179–182). Horowitz manufactured a population of 1,000 normally distributed scores so that the mean and standard deviation of the entire population would be known. This is almost never the case in actual research situations, of course. His 1,000 scores ranged from 0 to 100 with a mean of 50 and a standard deviation of 15.8. The scores were listed on 1,000 slips of paper and placed in a container. Horowitz had 96 students take samples of 10 slips from the container and calculate the mean. On each draw from the container, a slip was taken out, its number was noted, and then the slip was replaced. The slips were then mixed up somewhat in the container, and another slip was drawn, and so on. After each student calculated the mean of the 10 scores in her or his sample, Horowitz collected all 96 and plotted the distribution of sample means, which is represented in Table B.4. The intervals between which means might fall are shown on the left; the number of means falling within each interval is shown on the right. The distribution is almost perfectly symmetrical, with almost as many scores in any interval a certain distance below the true mean of the population (50) as above it. Also, the mean of the 96 sample means (49.99) is quite close to the actual mean of the population (50). But the main thing that Table B.4 shows is the great variability among the sample means. Although each sample of 10 was presumably random and not biased in any way, one sample had a mean of 37.8, while another had a mean of 62.3. Obviously, these are very disparate means, even though they were sampled from the same population. If you were doing an experiment and found two very different sample means, and you were trying to decide whether they came from the same underlying distribution or two different distributions, you might think that such a large difference would indicate that they came from different distributions. In other words, you would think that the experimental treatment produced scores significantly different (from a different distribution) from the control scores. Usually this is a good rule—the larger the difference between means in the conditions, the more likely the means are to be reliably different—but as we have seen here, even random sampling from a known distribution can produce sample means that differ greatly from each other and from the true population mean, which is known in this case. Keep this lesson in mind while pondering small differences between means. Is

▼ **TABLE B.4**

The Distribution of Sample Means for the 96 Samples Taken by Students in Horowitz's Class. Each Sample Mean Was Based on 10 Observations. After *Elements of Statistics for Psychology and Education* **(Table 8.1), By L. M. Horowitz, 1974, New York: Mcgraw-Hill.**

Interval	Frequency	
62.0–63.9	1	
60.0–61.9	1	
58.0–59.9	3	
56.0–57.9	7	
54.0–55.9	9	
52.0–53.9	12	
50.0–51.9	15	Mean of sample means = 49.99
48.0–49.9	15	Standard deviation (s) of
46.0–47.9	13	sample means = 5.01
44.0–45.9	9	
42.0–43.9	6	
40.0–41.9	3	
38.0–39.9	1	
36.0–37.9	1	
	96 samples	

the 3.3-second difference between experimental and control means in our hypothetical LSD experiment really reliable?

The Standard Error of the Mean The **standard error of the mean** is the standard deviation of a distribution of sample means. In the data in Table B.4, it is 5.01. The standard error of the mean gives us some idea of the amount of variability in the distribution of sample means, or how likely it is that the value of any particular sample mean is in error. Large standard errors indicate great variability, whereas small ones tell us that any particular sample mean is likely to be quite close to the actual population mean. Thus, the standard error of the mean is a very useful number.

You might be wondering why we bother to tell you about the standard error of the mean if, in order to calculate it, you must repeat an experiment numerous times to get the distribution of sample means and then calculate its standard deviation. Fortunately, you do not have to repeat it. The formula for finding the standard error of the mean (represented by $\sigma_{\bar{x}}$) is simply the standard deviation of the population (σ) divided by the square root of the number of observations $(\sqrt{N})$.

$$\sigma_{\bar{x}} = \frac{\sigma}{\sqrt{N}} \tag{B.6}$$

Now, if you are still with us, you might well be thinking, "Terrific. What good does this do me, since the standard deviation of the population, the numerator in Equation B.6, is never known?" That has occurred to statisticians, too, so they have devised a method for estimating the standard deviation of the population from the standard deviation of a sample. If you look back at Equation B.2, where the formula for the standard deviation

▼ TABLE B.5

The Distribution of Sample Means for the 96 Samples Taken by Students when Sample Size (N) is 50. The Distribution Is Again Normal, as in Table B.4, but when Each Sample Is Based on a Larger Sample Size, as It Is Here, the Variability of the Distribution (Represented by the Standard Error of the Mean) is Much Smaller. After *Elements of Statistics for Psychology and Education* (Table 8.2), By L. M. Horowitz, 1974, New York: Mcgraw-Hill.

Interval	Frequency	
55.0–55.9	1	
54.0–54.9	3	
53.0–53.9	5	
52.0–52.9	9	
51.0–51.9	13	
50.0–50.9	17	
49.0–49.9	16	Mean of sample means-=-49.95
48.0–48.9	14	Standard deviation ($\hat{s}$) of sample means-=-2.23
47.0–47.9	9	
46.0–46.9	6	
45.0–45.9	2	
44.0–44.9	1	
	96 samples	

of a sample (s) appears, and simply replace the n in the denominator by $n - 1$, then you have the formula for getting an unbiased estimate of σ, the standard deviation of the population. The equation for finding the standard error of distribution of sample means (called the standard error of the mean, or $\hat{s}_{\bar{x}}$) is

$$\text{Estimated } \sigma_{\bar{x}} = \hat{s}_{\bar{x}} = \frac{\hat{s}}{\sqrt{n}} \tag{B.7}$$

Obviously, we want the standard error of the mean to be as small as possible, since it represents the error we have in assuming that our sample mean represents the population mean. Equations B.6 and B.7 tell us how to do this: Increase the size of the sample, n, which increases the denominator in the equations. The greater n, the sample size, is, the smaller will be the standard error of the mean, $\hat{s}_{\bar{x}}$. This should be no surprise. If the population involves 1,000 scores, the sample mean should be closer to the population mean if there are 500 observations in the sample than if there are only 10.

Horowitz drove this point home to the 96 students in his class by having them repeat the exercise of drawing slips from the population of 1,000 scores and calculating the mean again; but this time, he had them sample 50 slips, rather than only 10. The resulting distribution of sample means is given in Table B.5. This time, with larger samples, there is much less variability in the sample means the students obtained. They are much closer to the actual population mean of 50. The standard deviation of the distribution of sample means, or the standard error of the mean, is 2.23, as opposed to 5.01 when the sample size was only 10. If $n = 100$ in a sample from the 1,000 scores, the standard error of the mean would be 1.59; with a sample of 500, it would be 0.71; and with 1,000 scores in a sample, it would be only 0.50. (These were calculated from Equation B.6, since the standard deviation, σ, is known for the entire population.) The reason we might not get the population mean even with a sample of 1,000 is that the sampling was done with replacement; that is, after a slip was drawn, it was returned to the container; thus, it might have been drawn more than once, while some slips were never drawn.

The lesson to be learned is that we should always try to maximize the number of observations—the sample size—in experimental conditions, so that the statistics obtained will be as close as possible to the population parameters.

Testing Hypotheses

Scientists set up experiments to test hypotheses. The conventional statistical logic for testing hypotheses runs something like this. An experimenter arranges conditions, such as the experimental (LSD) and control (placebo) in our experiment with rats, to test an **experimental hypothesis.** The experimental hypothesis in this case is that LSD will have some effect on running speed. This is tested by pitting it against the **null hypothesis,** which maintains that the two conditions do not differ in their effects on running speed. Stated another way, the experimental hypothesis is that the samples of running speeds come from two different underlying populations (that is, populations with different distributions); the null hypothesis is that the two samples come from the same distribution.

A critical assumption is that it is impossible to prove the alternative hypothesis conclusively, since there is always some chance that the two samples come from the same population, no matter how different they appear. What inferential statistics allow us to do, though, is to determine how confident we can be in rejecting the null hypothesis. The alternative hypothesis is thus tested indirectly; if we can be quite confident in rejecting the null hypothesis, then we assume that the alternative hypothesis is correct and that there is a real difference between scores in the different conditions. Psychologists have agreed, by convention, that if calculations from a statistical test show that there is less than a 0.05 probability (a 5 percent chance) that the null hypothesis is correct, we can reject it and accept the alternative hypothesis.

We will describe the concept of probability briefly in this context. Consider the following problem: What is the probability that if we randomly draw a card from a deck of 52 cards, it will be a spade? Since there are 13 spades in a deck, the probability of drawing a spade is 13 divided by 52, or 1/4, or 0.25. In general, if there are r ways that an event can occur and a total of N possibilities, then the probability of the event is r/N. What is the probability that a fair coin will come up heads when flipped? There are two ways a coin can come up, so $N = 2$. One of them is heads, so $r = 1$. So the probability of heads is 1/2, or 0.50.

Now we can more precisely describe what the conventional level of 0.05 for statistical significance means. If the null hypothesis were actually true, a researcher would obtain such a large difference between conditions five times or less in 100. If the chances are this slight in making an error by rejecting the null hypothesis, then it is deemed safe to do so and to opt for the alternative hypothesis. The 0.05 criterion is referred to as the 0.05 **level of confidence,** since a mistake will be made only five times in 100. When the null hypothesis is rejected, researchers conclude that the results are statistically significant. In other words, the researchers can be quite confident that the difference obtained between the conditions is trustworthy and that if the experiment were repeated, the same outcome would result.

The logic of pitting an experimental hypothesis against the null hypothesis has come under attack in recent years for several reasons. Some argue that it gives a misleading idea as to how scientists operate. For one thing, not many researchers around the world lose any sleep over the null hypothesis. In general, experiments are set up to test our theories; what is of primary concern is how the results of the experiments can be interpreted or accounted for in the light of our theories. Of special interest is the case in which important experimental results seem irreconcilable with the major theories of a phenomenon. So experiments are important because of what they tell us about our theories and ideas—this is why we designed them in the first place—and not about whether the null hypothesis is rejected. But the null hypothesis testing logic is widely used as an introduction, however oversimplified, to the way scientific inference proceeds. Thus, we present it here. Do not be misled, though, into thinking that psychologists spend their days dreaming up experimental hypotheses to pit against null hypotheses. This is so in part, but the processes of scientific inference are fortunately much more varied and complicated than the logic of using the null hypothesis would lead us to believe (see Chapter 1).

Testing Hypotheses: Parameters Known The logic of testing hypotheses against the null hypothesis can be aptly illustrated in cases in which the parameters of a population are known and we wish to determine whether a particular sample comes from the population. Such cases are quite unusual in actual research, since population parameters are rarely known.

Suppose you were interested in whether the members of your experimental psychology class were reliably above the national mean in intelligence as measured by IQ tests (or reliably below, as the case may be). We know the population parameters in this case. The mean is 100, and the standard deviation is 15. You could test your class easily enough by giving them the short form of some intelligence test, such as the Wechsler Adult Intelligence Scale developed for group testing. Suppose you randomly sampled 25 people from your class of 100 and found the mean IQ of the sample to be 108, with a standard deviation of 5.

How do we go about testing the experimental hypothesis that the class is reliably brighter than the population as a whole? First, let us consider the hypotheses. The experimental hypothesis is that the students are brighter than people in the nation as a whole, or that the IQ scores of the students sampled come from a different population than randomly selected people. The null hypothesis is that no reliable difference exists between our sample and the national mean, or that the students in the class are a sample from the same national population. If the null hypothesis were actually the case, the difference between the sample mean of 108 and the population parameter mean (μ) of 100 would be due to random factors. This is not implausible, because we have seen from our discussion of the sample distribution of means how much a sample mean can differ from a population parameter, even when the sample is selected in an unbiased manner. Remember Horowitz's classroom demonstration, the results of which are portrayed in Tables B.4 and B.5.

The normal curve, the distribution of sample means, and z scores can be used to help us determine how likely it is that the null hypothesis is false. When unbiased samples are taken from a larger population, the means of these samples are normally distributed. With normal distributions, we can specify what proportion of the distribution falls under each part of the curve, as seen in Figure B.3. Finally, also remember that

z scores are the calculation of any score in a normal distribution in terms of standard deviation units from the mean.

All this is by way of review. Now, how does this help us? What we do in testing the hypothesis that the sample is actually from a population with a mean IQ greater than the population at large is to treat the sample mean as an individual score (in terms of our earlier discussion) and calculate a z score on the basis of the deviation of the sample mean from the population mean. In this case, we know the population mean is 100 and the class mean of the randomly selected students is 108. To calculate the z score, we also need to know the standard error of the mean: the standard deviation of the distribution of sample means. So the equation for the z score here is

$$z = \frac{\bar{X} - \mu}{\sigma_{\bar{X}}} \tag{B.8}$$

The standard error of the mean ($\sigma_{\bar{x}}$) is found by dividing the standard deviation of the population, σ (which we know in the case of IQ scores is 15) by $\sqrt{n}$, which is the sample size of the class, or $\sqrt{25}$. (This reasoning follows from Equation B.6.) The σ is thus $15 / \sqrt{25}$, or 3. Therefore, z is 108 − 100/3, or 2.67.

A z score of 2.67 allows us to reject the null hypothesis with reasonable confidence and conclude, in favor of the alternative hypothesis, that the class is actually superior to the population at large in terms of IQ. We establish this by asking this question: How likely is a z score of 2.67 to occur when a sample mean is drawn from a larger population, when the mean of the population is actually 100? The answer is that it will occur only 0.0038 of the time, or 38 times in 10,000. (We will come to how this was calculated in the next paragraph.) The custom in rejecting the null hypothesis is that if it could occur only one time in 20 by chance, we would reject it, so the difference in the class sample mean is significantly different from the mean of the population.

To explain how this rather remarkable conclusion is reached, we need to refer again to the special property of the normal curve, which is that a certain proportion of cases falls under each part of the curve. Figure B.3 shows that a z score of ±2.00 is highly improbable. Greater scores in either direction occur only 2.15 percent of the time. In other words, the probability of such an occurrence is 0.0215. This is also below the 5 percent or 0.05 level of significance (or level of confidence), so any mean score two or more standard deviations from the population mean is considered, using the logic we have outlined here, to be reliably (significantly) different from the population mean. In fact, the critical z value for rejecting the null hypothesis at the 0.05 level of confidence is ±1.96. Table A in Appendix C presents (1) z scores from zero to four, with (2) the amount of area between the mean and z, and (3) most important, the amount of area beyond z. The amount of area beyond z is the probability of finding a score that distant from the mean on the basis of chance alone. Once again, when this probability falls below 0.05, as it does with z scores of +1.96 (or more), we reject the null hypothesis. With a z of 2.67, as in our IQ example, the probability of such a rare occurrence is only 0.0038.

The statistical problem we have just considered—comparing a sample mean to a population parameter to see whether the sample comes from that population—is rather artificial, since population parameters are rarely known. But this example does exhibit characteristics of most common statistical tests. In all tests, some computations are performed on the data or raw scores gathered from an experiment; a value is found, as in the z score just calculated; and then this value is compared with a distribution of values so that we can determine the likelihood that such a value could be obtained if the null hypothesis were in fact true. This distribution tells us, then, with what probability our result can be attributed to random variation. If the probability is less than five cases in 100 ($p < .05$), then by convention we say that the null hypothesis can be rejected. This probability is sometimes called the **alpha (α) level.** As mentioned, some psychologists prefer values of 0.01 or even 0.001 (1 in 100 or 1,000, respectively), so that they can be more certain that the rejection of the null hypothesis is made correctly.

Our z-score test can also serve to introduce you very briefly to some other important statistical concepts. First, let us consider two types of errors that can be made by applying statistical tests to experimental data, according to the null hypothesis testing logic. A **type I error** is rejection of the null hypothesis when it is actually true, and the probability that this error is being made is indexed by the alpha level. If the alpha level is $p = .05$, then we shall mistakenly reject the null hypothesis in five cases in 100. This illustrates the probabilistic nature of inferential statistics; we are not absolutely certain that a null hypothesis can be rejected—only reasonably certain. Thus, the lower the α level or p level we employ in determining statistical significance, the less chance we have of making a type I error. However, this increases the probability of a **type II error,** which occurs when we *fail* to reject the null hypothesis when it is actually *false*. Thus, by setting α levels at different points, we systematically decrease and increase the two types of errors. They trade off against one another. The two types of errors are described in Table B.6.

Scientists are generally conservative in such matters, so the α level is usually kept fairly small, at such points as 0.05 or 0.01 (rather than, say, 0.10 or 0.15). Thus, we minimize the error of rejecting the null hypothesis when it is true, or claiming a difference in our results when it is not there. As a consequence, though, we increase the probability of type II errors. A *conservative* statistical test minimizes type I errors, whereas more *liberal* statistical tests increase the probability of type I error but decrease that of a type II error.

Unfortunately, we can never know for sure in our experimental situations whether we are committing type I or type II errors. We find this out primarily through experimental replications of our results. However, we can also find this out by calculating the

▼ **TABLE B.6**

The Nature of Type I and Type II Errors. A Type I Error Occurs when the Experimenter Falsely Rejects a True Null Hypothesis. The Probability of this Occurring Is Determined by the α Level. A Type II Error Occurs when the Experimenter Does Not Reject a False Null Hypothesis. When the Null Hypothesis Is False and Rejected, the Experimenter Has Made a Correct Decision, which Is Determined by the Power of the Experiment.

	Actual State of Affairs in the Population	
Decision of Experimenter	The independent variable *had no* effect; the null hypothesis is true.	The independent variable *had* an effect; the null hypothesis is false.
Reject null hypothesis	**Type I error**—a false decision that an effect exists, which occurs with probability α.	*Correct decision*—this is determined by the power of the experiment.
Do not reject null hypothesis	*Correct decision*	**Type II error**—a failure to detect that the treatment had an effect.

power of a statistical test. The power of a statistical test is the probability of rejecting the null hypothesis when it is actually false; obviously, we always want to maximize the power of our statistical tests. This is not the place to describe how the power of tests is calculated, but we can note the two main factors that influence power. Look back to the z score formula in Equation B.8. Whatever would make the z score larger would increase the power of the statistical test, or the likelihood of rejecting the null hypothesis. The value μ, the population mean, is fixed. Thus, only two changes in the values of Equation B.8 can affect z. One is the difference between the sample mean and the population mean $(\bar{X} - \mu)$ and the other is n, the size of the sample. If the discrepancy between μ and $\bar{X}$ is increased (or in other cases, if the difference between sample means in an experimental comparison is increased), the probability of rejecting the null hypothesis is also increased.

But there is nothing we can do about the size of the difference between means; it is fixed. What we can do to increase the power of our statistical tests is to increase the sample size. The reason for this, in brief, is that with larger samples, we can be more confident that our sample means represent the means of the populations from which they are drawn, and thus we can be more confident that any difference between a sample mean and a population mean (or between two sample means) is reliable. Sample size can have a great effect on the power of a test, as shown in Table B.7. Presented there are the z scores and p values for our difference between a sample mean of 108 IQ points and the population mean of 100, as the sample size varies. Obviously, as the sample size varies, so will our conclusion as to whether the sample comes from a national population or a more restricted, high-IQ population. If we assume that the null hypothesis is actually false here, then by increasing sample size, we decrease the probability of a type II error, or increase the power of the test we are using.

One final issue to be considered is specification of directionality of statistical tests. According to conventional logic involved in testing an alternative hypothesis against the null hypothesis, the alternative hypothesis may be **directional** or **nondirectional**. If an experiment has an experimental and a control group, a nondirectional alternative hypothesis would simply be that the two groups would differ in performance on the dependent variable. But a directional hypothesis would state in addition the predicted direction of the difference; for example, the experimental group might be predicted to do better than the control.

This distinction is important, because if the alternative hypothesis is directional, a **one-tailed** (or one-sided) **statistical test** is used, but if the alternative hypothesis is nondirectional, a **two-tailed** (two-sided) **test** is used. One versus two "tails" refers to whether in looking up a p level associated with some determined value of the statistical test (say, $z = 1.69$), we consider one or both tails of the distribution (see Figure B.4).

This should be clearer with reference to our earlier example. We took a sample ($n = 25$) of students, determined that the mean IQ of the sample was 108, and calculated a $z = +2.67$ in testing to see whether this was different from the mean population IQ of 100. If we had no prior expectation of how the sample IQ should deviate from the normal population—if we thought it could be either greater or lower—this would have been a nondirectional hypothesis. In fact, we did expect the sample IQ to be greater than 100, so we were testing a directional hypothesis and thus used a one-tailed test. This means that we looked up the resulting z score in only one tail of the normal distribution: that greater than zero. A $z = +2.67$ leads to a one-tailed p value of 0.0038. If the hypothesis were nondirectional, then we would have no *a priori* right to expect the

▼ TABLE B.7

How Varying Sample Size (n) Affects the Power of a Statistical Test, or How Likely it is that the Null Hypothesis Can Be Rejected when the Test Is Used. The Example Is From the z Score (Calculated in the Text) on a Mean Sample IQ of 108, where

$$z = \frac{\bar{X} - \mu}{\sigma_{\bar{x}}}$$

if the Mean Difference Remains the Same but n Increases, z Increases because

$$\sigma_{\bar{x}} = \frac{\sigma}{\sqrt{n}}$$

n	$\bar{X} - \mu$	$\sigma_{\bar{X}}$	z	p*
2	8	13.14	0.61	.2709
5	8	6.70	1.19	.1170
7	8	5.67	1.41	.0793
10	8	4.74	1.69	.0455[†]
12	8	4.33	1.85	.0322[†]
15	8	3.88	2.06	.0197[†]
17	8	3.64	2.20	.0139[†]
20	8	3.35	2.38	.0087[†]
25	8	3.00	2.67	.0038[†]
50	8	2.12	3.77	.0001[†]
75	8	1.73	4.62	<.00003[†]
100	8	1.50	5.33	<.00003[†]

*p values are one tailed.

[†]All these values meet the conventional level of statistical significance, $p < .05$ (one tailed).

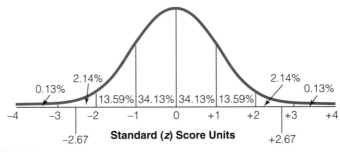

▼ FIGURE B.4

This is the standard normal distribution that is presented in Figure B.3. There are two sides, or tails, to the distribution; positive and negative. If an experimenter simply asserts that there should be a difference between an experimental and a control condition but does not specify the direction of the difference, this is called a nondirectional hypothesis. If $z = 2.67$ is found, it is necessary to look up the probability that this will occur in both the positive and negative tails of the distribution and add the two, since the experimenter has not specified whether the difference should be positive or negative. When the experimenter has specified the direction or difference, one need only look up the probability in one tail. Since the distribution is symmetrical, the probability that the null hypothesis can be rejected is half as great with a one-tailed as with a two-tailed test. The less certain one is about the outcome of an experiment, the greater the difference between the conditions must be for it to be decided that it is not due to chance.

resultant z score to be greater instead of less than zero. The z could fall in the positive or negative tail. Since the difference could have occurred in either direction, we use a two-tailed test. In practice, since the two tails of the distribution are symmetrical, we simply double the p level for the one-tailed test. In our example, if the hypothesis had been nondirectional, p would equal 2×0.0038, or 0.0076, still well below 0.05.

Two-tailed tests are more conservative and less powerful than one-tailed tests; it is harder to reject the null hypothesis. If we are uncertain about the outcome of an experiment, we need a greater value of the statistic to allow us to declare a difference. In practice, most investigators prefer to use the more conservative two-tailed test, with sufficient power ensured by fairly large sample sizes.

Tests for Differences between Two Groups

There is a bewildering variety of statistical tests for almost every purpose. At present, we are interested in discussing tests that assess the reliability of a difference between two groups or conditions. How do we pick an appropriate test from all those available? There is no hard-and-fast rule. Tests vary in the assumptions they make, their power, and the types of situation for which they are appropriate. Perhaps the most popular test for the difference between two means in psychological research is the **t test**. Since the t test provides the same estimate of reliability as does the simple analysis of variance (to be discussed soon), we will first concentrate on two other tests, the **Mann-Whitney U test** and the **Wilcoxon signed-ranks test.** These tests also are useful in introducing yet another type of statistical test.

The Mann-Whitney and Wilcoxon tests are **nonparametric tests,** as opposed to **parametric tests.** Parametric statistical tests make assumptions about the underlying population parameters of the samples on which the tests are performed. Common assumptions of parametric tests hold that the variances of the underlying populations being compared are equivalent and that the underlying distributions are normal. If these assumptions are not met, then the test may be inappropriate. But how can we ever know whether the assumptions underlying the test are met, since we do not know the population parameters? Usually we cannot know, except by estimating population parameters from sample statistics. However, if we turn to nonparametric statistics, the problem does not arise, because these tests make no assumptions about the underlying population parameters. Since the parameters cannot be known anyway, this provides an important reason for using nonparametric tests. Another reason is simplicity: These tests generally are very easy to calculate and can often even be done by hand. However, nonparametric tests are usually less powerful than parametric tests employed in the same situation; that is, they are less likely to provide a rejection of the null hypothesis.

The Mann-Whitney U test is used when we wish to compare two samples to decide whether they come from the same or different underlying populations. It is used when the two samples are composed of different subjects, or in **between-subjects designs.** The underlying rationale for the Mann-Whitney test is not discussed here. In general, the logic is the same as in other statistical tests in which a value is computed from the test and compared with a distribution of values to determine whether the null hypothesis should be rejected. The way in which the Mann-Whitney test is applied to actual data is outlined in Box B.3, testing the reliability of the difference between the two samples in our hypothetical LSD experiment.

Box B.3

Calculation of a Mann-Whitney U Test on Hypothetical Experimental Data from Figure B.1

Step 1: Rank all the numbers for *both* groups together, beginning with the smallest number. Assign it the lowest rank.

Control (Placebo) Latency (sec)	Rank	Experimental (LSD) Latency (sec)	Rank
9	1.5	9	1.5
10	3.0	13	11.5
11	4.5	13	11.5
11	4.5	14	17.0
12	7.0	14	17.0
12	7.0	15	21.0
12	7.0	16	24.5
13	11.5	16	24.5
13	11.5	16	24.5
13	11.5	17	28.0
13	11.5	17	28.0
14	17.0	18	32.0
14	17.0	18	32.0
14	17.0	18	32.0
15	21.0	18	32.0
15	21.0	19	35.5
16	24.5	19	35.5
17	28.0	20	37.5
18	32.0	22	39.0
20	37.5	26	40.0
	Σ rank$_1$ 295.5		Σ rank$_2$ 524.5

Note: When scores are tied, assign the mean value of the tied ranks to each. Thus, for both 9-second times in this example, the rank 1.5 is assigned (the mean of 1 and 2).

Step 2: The equations for finding U and U' are as follows, where n_1 is the size of the smaller sample, n_2 is the size of the larger, ΣR_1 is the sum of the ranks of the smaller sample, and ΣR_2 is the sum of the ranks of the larger sample. Obviously, the sample subscripts are important only if the sample sizes are unequal, which is not the case here.

$$U = n_1 n_2 + \frac{n_1(n_1+1)}{2} - \Sigma R_1$$

$$U = (20)(20) + \frac{(20)(21)}{2} - 295.5 \tag{B.9}$$

$$U = 400 + 210 - 295.5$$

$$U = 314.5$$

$$U' = n_1 n_2 + \frac{n_2(n_2+1)}{2} - \Sigma R_2$$

$$U' = (20)(20) + \frac{(20)(21)}{2} - 524.5 \tag{B.10}$$

$$U' = 85.5$$

continued

Box B.3
continued

> Actually, it is necessary to compute only U or U', because the other can be found according to the equations
>
> $$U = n_1 n_2 - U'$$
>
> or
>
> $$U' = n_1 n_2 - U$$
>
> *Step 3:* Take U or U', whichever value is smaller, and look in Table B in Appendix C to see whether the difference between the two groups is reliable. The values in Table B are recorded according to different sample sizes. In this case, both sample sizes are 20, so the critical value from the table is 88. For the difference between the two groups to be judged reliable, the U or U' from the experiment must be *less than* the appropriate value in Table B. Since 85.5 is less than 88, we can conclude that the difference between the two groups is reliable at the .001 level of confidence.
>
> *Note:* Table B is appropriate only for situations in which the sizes of the two samples are between 8 and 21. For other cases, you should consult an advanced text.

The Wilcoxon signed-ranks test is also used in testing for the difference between two samples, but in this case, the design must be a **related measures design.** In other words, either the same subjects must serve in both the experimental and control groups (a within-subjects design) or the subjects must be matched in some way. Of course, precautions must be taken in within-subjects designs to ensure that some variable such as practice or fatigue is not confounded with the variable of interest (see Chapter 3). But as long as the experiment has been done well, the Wilcoxon signed-ranks test is an appropriate tool for analysis of the results.

Before considering the signed-ranks test, we will examine its simpler cousin, the **sign test,** which is also appropriate in the same situations. The sign test is the essence of simplicity. Suppose we have 26 subjects serving in both conditions of an experiment in which we are predicting that when subjects are in the experimental condition, they will do better than when they are in the control condition. Now suppose that 19 subjects actually do better in the experimental condition than in the control, while the reverse is true for the other 7. Is this difference reliable? The sign test allows us to answer this question without more information about what the actual scores were. In terms of the null hypothesis, we might expect 13 subjects to perform better in the experimental condition and 13 in the control. The sign test allows us to compute the exact probability that the null hypothesis is false when there are 19 cases in the predicted direction but also seven reversals, or exceptions. It turns out that the null hypothesis can be rejected in this case with a 0.014 confidence level (one tailed). With a nondirectional prediction, p equals 0.028 (two tailed). Once again, we cannot delve into the details of how this is computed, but in Table C in Appendix C, we present the α levels (one tailed) for cases of sample sizes from 3 to 42, when there are x number of exceptions to the predicted hypothesis. So, for example, when there are 16 subjects in the experiment (remember, in both conditions) and 13 show the predicted pattern of results while 3 exhibit reversals, we can reject the null hypothesis at the 0.011 level of confidence (one tailed).

The sign test uses very little of the information from an experiment: just whether the subjects performed better or worse in one condition than in another. For the sign test, it does not matter whether the difference in performance is great or small; the direction of the difference is all that matters. The sign test therefore wastes much of the information gathered in an experiment and is not a very powerful statistical test. The Wilcoxon signed-ranks test is like the sign test in that it is used in situations where the same (or matched) subjects are employed in two conditions and the direction of the difference is taken into account. However, in the Wilcoxon signed-ranks test, the size of the difference is taken into account, too. For this reason, it is also called the sized sign test. An example of how the Wilcoxon signed-ranks test is used is given in Box B.4.

Box B.4

Calculation of the Wilcoxon Signed-Ranks Test

Imagine an experiment testing whether Professor Humboldt von Widget's memory course, "How to Constipate Your Mind by Remembering Everything," really works. First, a group of 30 subjects is presented with 50 words to be remembered. Then the subjects are randomly separated into two groups, and a check indicates that the groups do not differ reliably in the mean number of words recalled. The experimental group is given Professor von Widget's three-week course, whereas the control group is not. Then all 30 subjects are tested again on another 50-word list. The controls show no improvement from one list to another. The question we ask here is whether the experimental subjects' memories were reliably improved. (*Note:* We could—and should—also compare the experimental subjects' performance on the second test with that of the controls. The Mann-Whitney test is appropriate for this comparison. Do you know why?) We employ the Wilcoxon signed-ranks test to assess whether the experimental subjects improved reliably from the first test to the second.

Step 1: Place the data in a table (such as the one shown later in this box) in which both scores for each subject (before and after the memory course) are paired together. Find and record the difference between the pairs.

Step 2: Rank the values of the differences according to size, beginning with the smallest. *Ignore the sign.* Use the absolute values of the numbers. For tied ranks, assign each the mean value of the ranks. (See the right-hand column of the table here.)

Step 3: Add the ranks for all the difference values that are negative (5.5 + 2.5 + 8.5 + 5.5 = 22.0) and positive (14 + 15 + 2.5 + 8.5 + 8.5 + 2.5+13 + 2.5 + 11.5 + 8.5 + 11.5 = 98.0). These are the signed-rank values.

Step 4: Take the signed-rank value that is smallest (22 in this case), and go to Table D in Appendix C. Look up the number of pairs of observations (listed as *n* on the left). There are 15 in this case. Then look at the number under the desired level of significance. Since the direction of the outcome was predicted in this case (we expected the memory course to help rather than hurt recall of words), let us choose the value under the .025 level of significance for a one-

continued

Box B.4
continued

tailed test. This value is 25. If the smaller of the two values from the experiment is *below* the appropriate value in the table, then the result is reliable. Since 22 is below 25, we can conclude that Professor von Widget's course really did help memory for words.

Note: Remember that the controls showed no improvement in performance from one test to the other. This is a crucial bit of information, for otherwise we could not rule out two plausible competing hypotheses. One is that the improvement on the second list was simply owing to practice on the first, and the other is that the second list was easier than the first. Actually, if Professor von Widget's course were as effective as numerous memory courses currently on the market, results from an actual experiment would show (and have shown) more spectacular improvement than the hypothetical results here. Memory-improvement courses, all of which embody the same few principles, really work for objective materials, such as word lists.

	Mean Number of Words Recalled			
Subject	Before	After	Difference	Rank
1	11	17	+6	14.0
2	18	16	−2	5.5
3	9	21	+12	15.0
4	15	16	+1	2.5
5	14	17	+3	8.5
6	12	15	+3	8.5
7	17	16	−1	2.5
8	16	17	+1	2.5
9	15	20	+5	13.0
10	19	16	−3	8.5
11	12	13	+1	2.5
12	16	14	−2	5.5
13	10	14	+4	11.5
14	17	20	+3	8.5
15	6	10	+4	11.5
	$\bar{X} = 13.80$	$\bar{X} = 16.07$		

t Test

In Boxes B.5 and B.6, we present the corresponding *t* tests for the analyses presented in the previous two boxes. The *t* test is a parametric test; this means that we assume that the underlying distributions are roughly normal in shape. Furthermore, the *t* test and other parametric tests were designed to be used on data that are at least interval in nature. The *U* test and the sign test require only ordinal data. The *t* tests are essentially based on *z* scores having to do with the standard error of the difference between means. Thus, even if the computational formulas appear unusual at first, the underlying logic is the same as that discussed earlier in this appendix.

Box B.5

Calculation of a Between-Subjects t Test

These are hypothetical experimental data previously discussed (see Box B.3). The calculation formula is

$$t = \frac{\bar{X}_1 - \bar{X}_2}{\sqrt{\left[\dfrac{\sum X_1^2 - \dfrac{(\sum X_1)^2}{N_1} + \sum X_2^2 - \dfrac{(\sum X_2)^2}{N_2}}{N_2 + N_2 - 2}\right]\left[\dfrac{1}{N_1} + \dfrac{1}{N_2}\right]}} \qquad (B.11)$$

$\bar{X}_1$ = mean of group 1
$\bar{X}_2$ = mean of group 2
N_1 = number of scores in group 1
N_2 = number of scores in group 2

$\sum X_1^2$ = sum of squared scores in group 1
$\sum X_2^2$ = sum of squared scores in group 2
$(\sum X_1)^2$ = square of group 1 sum
$(\sum X_2)^2$ = square of group 2 sum

Control (Placebo)				Experimental (LSD)			
X	X^2	X	X^2	X	X^2	X	X^2
9	81	13	169	9	81	17	289
10	100	14	196	13	169	18	324
11	121	14	196	13	169	18	324
11	121	14	196	14	196	18	324
12	144	15	225	14	196	18	324
12	144	15	225	15	225	19	361
12	144	16	256	16	256	19	361
13	169	17	289	16	356	20	400
13	169	18	324	16	356	22	484
13	169	20	400	17	289	26	676
$\sum X = 272$			$\sum X^2 = 3838$	$\sum X = 338$			$\sum X^2 = 5960$
$\bar{X} = 13.60$				$\bar{X} = 16.90$			

Step 1: After calculating $\sum X$, $\sum X^2$, and $\bar{X}$ for each group (by the way, there is no need to rank order our data), we need to calculate $(\sum\sum X)^2/N$ for each group: $(272)^2/20 = 3699.20$ and $(338)^2/20 = 5712.20$. Then we need to determine $6X2 - (\sum X)^2/N$ for each group. We get $3838 - 3699.2 = 138.8$ and $5960 - 5712.2 = 247.8$.

Step 2: Now we add the two group figures we obtained in the last step ($247.8 + 138.8$) and divide this sum by $N_1 + N_2 - 2$, to get $386.6/38 = 10.17$.

Step 3: The quotient obtained in Step 2 (10.17) is multiplied by $[(1/N_1 + 1/N_2)]$ to get $(10.17)(2/20) = 1.02$.

Step 4: We now take the square root of the product obtained in Step 3 to get $\sqrt{1.02} = 1.01$.

Step 5: We find the absolute difference between the mean scores of the two groups (by subtracting one from the other and ignoring the sign): $16.90 - 13.60 = 3.30$.

continued

Box B.5

continued

Step 6: t = the difference between means (Step 5) divided by the results of Step 4: 3.30/1.01 = 3.27. So, our *t* = 3.27. To evaluate this, we look in the tabled values of *t* in Table E in Appendix C. We enter this table with the number of **degrees of freedom** (*df*) in our experiment, which means the number of scores that are free to vary. For a between-subjects t, the degrees of freedom are $N_1 + N_2 - 2$—in this case, *df* = 38. For *p* = .05 and *df* = 38, the critical value of t is 2.04 in our table (always take the next lowest *df* to calculate the critical value). Since our obtained *t* exceeds the critical value, we can reject the hypothesis that our two groups have the same running scores; that is, we can say that LSD had an effect on the behavior of our subjects.

Box B.6

Calculation of a
Within-Subjects
t-Test

The hypothetical data come from Professor von Widget's experiment (see Box B.4). The computational formula for the within-subjects *t* test is

$$t = \sqrt{\frac{N-1}{\left[N\Sigma D^2 / (\Sigma D)^2\right] - 1}}$$ (B.12)

where *N* = number of subjects and *D* = difference in the scores of a given subject (or matched subject pair) in the two conditions.

Mean Number of Words Recalled				
Subject	Before	After	Difference	D^2
1	11	17	+6	36
2	18	16	−2	4
3	9	21	+12	144
4	15	16	+1	1
5	14	17	+3	9
6	12	15	+3	9
7	17	16	−1	1
8	16	17	+1	1
9	15	20	+5	25
10	19	16	−3	9
11	12	13	+1	1
12	16	14	−2	4
13	10	14	+4	16
14	17	20	+3	9
15	6	10	+4	16
	$\bar{X} = 13.80$	$\bar{X} = 16.07$	$\Sigma D = 35$	$\Sigma D^2 = 285$
			$(\Sigma D)^2 = 1,225$	

Step 1: After you arrange the scores for each subject in pairs, as shown in this table, record the difference between each pair, then square each of these difference scores.

Step 2: Add the difference scores across subjects, which yields ΣD, then square this sum. $\Sigma D = 35$; $(\Sigma D)^2 = 1,225$.

continued

Step 3: Calculate the sum of the squared difference scores to get $\Sigma D^2 = 285$.

Step 4: Multiply ΣD^2 (Step 3) by the number of subjects: $285 \times 15 = 4.275$.

Step 5: Divide the product found in Step 5 by $(\Sigma D)^2$: $4.275/1.225 = 3.49$. Then subtract 1 from the result: $3.49 - 1 = 2.49$.

Step 6: Divide the number of subjects less 1 $(N - 1)$ by the result of Step 5: $14/2.49 = 5.62$.

Step 7: t is $\sqrt{5.62}$, or 2.37.

Step 8: To evaluate t, compare it with the critical value shown in statistical Table E in Appendix C. Enter the table with $N - 1$ df. For this study, $df = 14$. With $df = 14$, the critical value of t is 2.145 for $p = .05$. Since the obtained t exceeds the critical value, we can conclude that von Widget's course really did affect word recall.

Magnitude of Effect

In summary, calculating a statistic such as z or t allows us to determine whether the results are due to chance factors. Determining the α level of a difference, as in Box B.5, tells us that the difference is significant statistically, and we can reject the null hypothesis. It is an interesting characteristic of t (and the F test that we discuss next) that the value of t needed to reject the null hypothesis decreases as the degrees of freedom increase. This means that the power of t increases with sample size just as does z (see Table B.2). It is also the case, as the formula for the independent groups t in Box B.5 indicates, that as we hold the difference between means constant, increasing the sample size (n) will increase the value of t by making the denominator smaller. This, too, will allow us to have more power and reject more null hypotheses. In some cases, then, it is possible that very small differences between means will be statistically significant. Usually when we do an experiment, we want substantial differences between means—a big effect of the independent variable. With a very powerful experiment, however, we can detect differences between means that are exceptionally small. In the latter instance, we may not know whether the difference is owing to a powerful independent variable or a very powerful statistical test.

How do we know when we have a powerful independent variable? To determine the **magnitude of effect** of the independent variable, we need a way of showing the degree to which belonging in a particular group predicts the behavior. In the example in Box B.5, we would like to have a calculation that would allow us some idea whether a rat had received a placebo or LSD. The information we need is a correlation coefficient, because we want to predict what happened to a rat in much the same way we would want to predict a memory score based on head size, as in Box B.1. After we have conducted a t test, we can then calculate a correlation to assess the magnitude of the effect. The correlation coefficient that would be appropriate here is r_{pb}, which is called the **point biserial** correlation. The formula is

(B.13)

$$r_{pb} = \sqrt{t^2 / (t^2 + df)}$$

The value of r_{pb} can be between 0 and 1.00. By convention, values up to 0.3 are considered to be small, a value from 0.31 to 0.5 is moderate, and values over 0.5 are appreciable (Thompson & Buchanan, 1979). For the data in Box B.5, $t = 3.27$ and $df = 38$, which by formula B.6 yields $r_{pb} = 0.47$. This would be deemed a moderate effect. The same formula for r_{pb} could be used for the results in Box B.13. Why don't you determine what it is?

The most important additional measure of effect size that you need to know is **eta (η),** which is used to determine how wrong the null hypothesis is after conducting an F test. To anticipate the discussion in the next section, the F test in its simplest form is much like the t test, except that there are more than two levels of the independent variable (say, several dosages of LSD). More complicated experiments that have two or more independent variables, each with several levels, can also be analyzed with the F test. As with r_{pb}, η is a correlation between the scores on the dependent variable and group membership. The larger the value of η, the better we can predict group membership on the basis of a participant's score, which means a larger effect size.

In an analysis of variance, we calculate the ratio of two variances (this will become clear momentarily), and significance is related to two degrees of freedom: one df for the numerator (n) and one for the denominator (d) of the F ratio. So, the formula for η is:

$$\eta = \sqrt{df_n \times F / (df_n \times F) + df_d} \qquad (B.14)$$

Measures of magnitude of effect have another important use, which is also related to the fact that rejecting the null hypothesis is dependent on sample size. Suppose we conduct an experiment and discover that the value of t is not large enough to reject the null hypothesis even though the difference between means is not zero (that is, they differ). One reason that the t value is small could be a sample size too small to detect a statistically significant difference between the means. In this case, a prudent researcher would calculate the appropriate measure of magnitude of effect, such as r_{pb}. If the coefficient yields a moderate or appreciable value, then it might be wise to increase the sample size in the experiment in order to reject the null hypothesis. Getting statistically significant results is important, but it is really only "half the battle." Significant results that are very small are not particularly exciting. Appreciable effects that are not statistically significant probably mean that you are on to something, and an increase in statistical power is warranted.

There are other measures of magnitude of effect, but we will not present them. The logic is the same regardless of the statistical test: The inferential statistics tell us how sure we may be that the null hypothesis is wrong. On the other hand, the correlation coefficients, such as r_{pb}, measure the magnitude of the effect of the independent variable—the degree to which the null hypothesis is wrong (Thompson & Buchanan, 1979).

The Analysis of Variance

Most psychological research has progressed beyond the stage at which only two conditions, an experimental and a control, are compared with each other. Rather than varying only the presence or absence of some independent variable, researchers often systematically vary the magnitude of the independent variable. In our example of the effects of LSD on running speed of rats, it may be quite useful to vary the amount of LSD administered to the rats. Perhaps effects are different at low dosages than at high ones. We could not determine this from the two-group design in which one group received LSD in some amount and the other did not. To evaluate the results of such an experiment with multiple groups, we must employ the **analysis of variance,** in particular the **simple analysis of variance.** Simple analysis of variance is used when one factor or independent variable (such as the amount of LSD) is varied systematically. Thus, it is also called one-factor analysis of variance. Often, researchers are interested in more complex situations. They may be interested in varying two or more factors simultaneously. In such two-factor or multifactor experimental designs, the analysis of variance is also appropriate, but it is more complicated. In this section, we introduce you to the logic of simple and two-factor analysis of variance (abbreviated ANOVA). However, in our examples and discussion, we stick to the case of between-subjects experimental designs. Calculations for within-subjects designs are different.

At the heart of the analysis-of-variance procedure is a comparison of variance estimates. We have already discussed the concept of variance and its estimation from one particular sample of observations. You should refer back to the section on measures of dispersion if the concept of variance is hazy to you at this point. Recall that the equation for the unbiased estimate of the population variance is

$$\hat{s}^2 = \frac{\sum(X - \bar{X})^2}{n - 1} \tag{B.15}$$

and that when the deviation of scores from the mean is large, the variance will be great. Similarly, when the deviations from the mean are small, the variance will be small.

In the analysis of variance, two independent estimates of variance are obtained. One is based on the variability *between* the different experimental groups: how much the means of the different groups vary from one another. Actually, the variance is computed as to how much the individual group means differ from the overall mean of all scores in the experiment. The greater the difference among the means of the groups, the greater will be the **between-groups variance.**

The other estimate of variance is the **within-groups variance.** This is the concept that we have already discussed in considering estimates of variance from individual samples; now we are concerned with finding an estimate of within-groups variance that is representative of all the individual groups, so we take the mean of the variances of these groups. The within-groups variance gives us an estimate of how much subjects in the groups differ from one another (or the mean of the group). In short, two variance estimates are obtained: one for the variance within groups and one for the variance between groups. Now, what good does this do?

The basic logic of testing to see whether the scores of the different groups or conditions are reliably different is as follows. The null hypothesis is that all the subjects in the various conditions are drawn from the same underlying population; the experimental variable has no effect. If the null hypothesis is true and all the scores in the different groups come from the same population, then the between-groups variance should be the same as the within-groups variance. The means from the different groups should vary from one another no more nor less than do the scores within the groups. For us to be able to reject the null hypothesis, then, the means of the different groups must vary from one another more than the scores vary within the groups. The greater the variance (differences) between the groups of the experiment, the more likely the independent variable is to have had an effect, especially if the within-groups variance is low.

The person who originated this logic was the eminent British statistician R. A. Fisher; the test is referred to as an **F test** in his honor. The *F* test is simply a ratio of the between-groups variance estimate to the within-groups variance estimate:

$$F = \frac{\text{Between-groups variance}}{\text{Within-groups variance}} \tag{B.16}$$

According to the logic we have just outlined, the *F* ratio under the null hypothesis should be 1.00, because the between-groups variance should be the same as the within-groups variance. The greater the between-groups variance is than the within-groups variance and, consequently, the greater the *F* ratio is than 1.00, the more confident we can be in rejecting the null hypothesis. Exactly how much greater the *F* ratio must be than 1.00 depends on the degrees of freedom in the experiment or how free the measures are to vary. This depends both on the number of groups or conditions in the experiment and on the number of observations in each group. The greater the number of degrees of freedom, the smaller need be the value of the *F* ratio to be judged a significant effect, as you can see from examining Table F in Appendix C. You should follow the computational example in Box B.7 carefully to gain a feel for the analysis of variance.

Box B.7
Computing
Simple Analysis
of Variance

Imagine that you just performed an experiment testing the effects of LSD on the running speeds of rats, but you administered three levels of LSD rather than only two, as in our earlier example. Ten rats received no LSD, 10 others received a small amount, and yet a third group of 10 received a great amount. Thus, the experiment employs a between-subjects design, in which the amount of LSD (none, small, large) is the independent variable and running time is the dependent variable. First, calculate the sum of the scores (ΣX) and the sum of the squared values of the scores (ΣX^2).

	Amount of LSD		
	None	Small	Large
	13	17	26
	11	15	20
	14	16	29
	18	20	31
	12	13	17
	14	19	25
	10	18	26
	13	17	23
	16	19	25
	12	21	27
ΣX	133	175	249
$\bar{X}$	13.30	17.50	24.90
ΣX^2	1819	3115	6351

continued

Box B.7
continued

A basic quantity in calculation of analysis of variance is the *sum of squares,* which is an abbreviated form of the term *sum of squared deviations from the mean.* If you look back to Equation B.1, which defines the variance of a sample, you will see that the sum of squares is the numerator. There are actually three sums of squares of interest. First is the total sum of squares (SS_{total}), which is defined as the sum of the squared deviations of the individual scores from the grand mean, or the mean of all the scores in all groups in the experiment. Second is the sum of squares between groups ($SS_{between}$), which is the sum of the squared deviations of the group means from the grand mean. Third, the sum of squares within groups (SS_{within}) is the mean of the sum of the squared deviations in the individual scores within groups or conditions from the group means. It turns out that $SS_{total} = SS_{between} + SS_{within}$, so that in practice only two sums of squares need be calculated; the third can be found by subtraction.

These sums of squares could be calculated by taking the deviations from the appropriate means, squaring them, and then finding the sum, but such a method would take much time and labor. Fortunately, computational formulas allow the calculations to be done more easily, especially if the values of ΣX and ΣX^2 have been found for each group, as in the present data. The formula for finding the total sum of squares is

$$SS_{total} = \Sigma\Sigma X^2 - \frac{T^2}{N} \tag{B.17}$$

where $\Sigma\Sigma X^2$ means that each score within each group is squared (X^2) and all these squared values are added together, so ΣX^2. There are two separate summation signs, one for summing the squared values within groups and one for then summing these ΣX^2 across the different groups. The T is for the total of all scores; N here is the total number of scores in the experiment. So SS_{total} in our example is calculated in the following way:

$$SS_{total} = \Sigma\Sigma X^2 - \frac{T^2}{N}$$

$$SS_{total} = 1819 + 3115 + 6351 - \frac{(133 + 175 + 249)^2}{30}$$

$$SS_{total} = 11{,}285 - \frac{310{,}249}{30}$$

$$SS_{total} = 11{,}285 - 10{,}341.63$$

$$SS_{total} = 943.37$$

The between-groups sum of squares is calculated with the following formula:

$$SS_{between} = \Sigma \frac{(\Sigma X)^2}{n} - \frac{T^2}{N} \tag{B.18}$$

continued

Box B.7
continued

The first part of the formula means that the sum of the values for each group is squared and then divided by the number of observations on which it is based, or $(\Sigma X)^2/n$; then, these values are summed across groups, so $\Sigma(\Sigma X)^2/n$. The second part of the formula is the same as for the SS_{total}:

$$SS_{between} = \frac{\Sigma(\Sigma X)^2}{n} - \frac{T^2}{N}$$

$$SS_{between} = \frac{17,689}{10} + \frac{30,625}{10} + \frac{62,001}{10} = 11,031.50$$

$$SS_{between} = 11,031.50 - 10,341.63$$

$$SS_{between} = 689.87$$

The sum of squares within groups can be found by subtracting $SS_{between}$ from SS_{total}, so $SS_{within} = 943.37 - 689.87 = 253.50$ But as a check, it is also worthwhile to compute it directly. This is done by computing an SS_{total}, as in Equation B.16, for each group and summing all these sums of squares for the individual groups. Unless you have made an error, this quantity should equal SS_{within} obtained by subtraction.

After we have obtained the various sums of squares, it is convenient to construct an analysis-of-variance table, such as the one that follows. In the far left column appears the source of variance, or source. Keep in mind that there are two primary sources of variance we are interested in comparing: between groups and within groups.

In the next column are the number of degrees of freedom (df). These can be thought of as the number of scores that are free to vary, given that the total is fixed. For the degrees of freedom between groups, if the overall total is fixed, all groups are free to vary except one. So the between-groups df is the number of groups minus one. In our example, then, it is $3 - 1 = 2$. The within-groups df is equal to the total number of scores minus the number of groups, because there is one score in each group that cannot vary if the group total is fixed. So within-groups df is $30 - 3 = 27$. The total df equals between-groups df plus within-groups df.

The third column holds the sum of squares (SS), which have already been calculated. The fourth column is for the mean squares (MS), which are found by dividing the SS for each row by the df. Each mean square is an estimate of the population variance, if the null hypothesis is true. But if the independent variable had an effect, the between-groups mean square should be larger than the within-groups mean square.

As already discussed in the text, these two values are compared by computing an F ratio, which is found by dividing the $MS_{between}$ by the MS_{within}. Once the F value is calculated, it is necessary to determine whether the value reaches an acceptable level of statistical significance. By looking in Table F in Appendix C, we can see that for 2 and 26 degrees of freedom (the closest we can get to 2 and 27), an F value of 9.12 is needed for the .001 level of significance. Our F value surpasses 9.12, so we can conclude that the groups varied reliably in running speed because of variation in the independent variable, the amount of LSD injected.

continued

Box B.7
continued

Source	df	SS	MS	F	p
Between groups	2	689.87	344.94	36.73	<.001
Within groups	27	253.50	9.39		
Total	29	943.37			

Note: If you compute analyses of variance with the aid of a calculator, you must guard against errors. If you ever come up with a negative sum of squares within groups (by subtracting $SS_{between}$ from SS_{total}), you will know you have made an error. You cannot have a negative sum of squares. You should compute SS_{within} both by subtraction and directly, anyway, as a check. One common error is to confuse ΣX^2 (square each number and then sum the squares) with $(\Sigma X)^2$, which is the square of the total (ΣX) of the scores.

If the simple analysis of variance indicates that there is reliable variation among the conditions of an experiment, this still does not tell us all we would like to know. In particular, it is still of great interest to know which of the individual conditions vary among themselves. This is especially important in cases where independent-variable manipulation is qualitative in nature. **Quantitative variation** of an independent variable refers to the case in which the quantity of an independent variable is manipulated (for example, the amount of LSD), whereas with **qualitative variation,** conditions vary but not in some easily specified quantitative manner. An example of qualitative variation is an instructional manipulation in which the different conditions vary in the instructions that are given at the beginning of the experiment. In such cases, it is not enough simply to say that the conditions vary reliably from one another. It is of interest to know which particular conditions differ. To answer this question, we need to perform tests, after the simple analysis of variance. In these follow-up tests, the conditions of the experiments are taken two at a time and compared so that we can see which pairs are reliably different. A great variety of statistical tests can be used for this purpose. We could perform analyses of variance on groups taken as pairs, which is equivalent to performing *t* tests, but usually other tests are performed. These include the Newman-Keuls test, the Scheffé test, Duncan's multiple-range test, Tukey's HSD (Honestly Significant Differences) test, and Dunnett's test. These vary in their assumptions and their power. You should consult statistical texts when you need to use a follow-up test.

Multifactor Analysis of Variance A frustrating aspect to the study of behavior is the fact that there are rarely any simple or one-factor explanations. Even the simplest behaviors studied in laboratory situations turn out to be affected by multiple factors. To discover these multiple determinants of behavior and how they interact, we must perform experiments in which more than one factor is varied simultaneously. The appropriate procedure for analyzing results of such experiments is **multifactor analysis of variance.** This may involve analysis of experiments in which any number of factors are concerned, but in practice, it is rare to find more than four variables of interest manipulated simultaneously. With two factors, the analysis is referred to as a two-way ANOVA; where there are three factors, it is a three-way ANOVA; and so on.

The importance of such complex designs involving more than one factor is the fact that they allow us to assess how different factors may interact to produce an experimental result. Recall that an interaction occurs when the effect of one experimental variable is affected by the level of the other experimental variable (see Chapter 3). If we performed a 2 × 2 experiment (this refers to two different factors with two different levels of each factor) on interpersonal attraction involving sex of the subject (male versus female) and sex of the experimental confederate whom the subject was to evaluate, we might discover an interaction effect. If the distance the subject stands from the confederate were one of the dependent variables, then we might find that male subjects tend to stand closer to female confederates and female subjects closer to male confederates. This is an example of an interaction. There is no simple generalization as to how close male or female subjects will stand to a confederate in an experiment; it depends on the sex of the confederate.

When performing a complex analysis of variance, we find out the separate effects of each factor in the experiment (called **main effects**) and how the variables affect one another (called **interaction effects,** or simply interactions). If women tended to stand closer to the confederate than did men, regardless of sex of the confederate, this would be a main effect of sex of subject on interpersonal distance. And, again, an interaction would be the different effect of sex of subject, depending on sex of the confederate.

We cannot devote space to explaining completely how these complex analyses of variance are performed. Briefly, the $SS_{between}$ is found as it is in the simple or one-way analysis of variance, but it is further decomposed into the main effects of the independent variables and their interactions. Then, mean squares are computed on the basis of these sums of squares by dividing by the appropriate number of degrees of freedom, and F ratios are obtained as before. An example is shown in Box B.8.

The analysis of variance is a parametric statistical test; thus, assumptions are built into the test about the population parameters underlying the samples. The two most important assumptions in the type of analysis of variance we are considering (the fixed-effects model) state that the observations in each condition are normally distributed and

Box B.8

Calculation of a 2 × 2 ANOVA on the Data from a Memory Experiment

This experiment had 40 subjects. They were divided into four groups of 10, each group representing a different condition. Two groups were given high-imagery words to learn, or words that refer to concrete objects that are easily visualized (for example, *elephant, chair, automobile*). The other two groups received low-imagery words, or ones that are abstract and hard to form images of (such as *beauty, democracy, truth*). The two groups that received each type of word differed in the learning instructions they were given. One group of subjects in each of the two imagery conditions was told to repeat each word until they saw the next word appear on the screen. These subjects were in the rote rehearsal condition. Subjects in the elaborative rehearsal condition were instructed to create mental images or meaningful associations between the words as they were learning them. Thus, the experiment represents a 2 × 2 factorial design, with one factor being the type of material studied (high- or low-imagery words) and the other being the instructions subjects were given (rote- or elaborative-rehearsal instructions). The design is between subjects, since a different group of subjects participated in each of the four conditions. The number of words recalled by each subject appears in the following table. Then the steps involved in the analysis of variance, which allow us to analyze appropriately the results of the experiment, are outlined.

continued

Box B.8

continued

	High-Imagery Words		Low-Imagery Words	
Rote Rehearsal	Elaborative Rehearsal	Rote Rehearsal	Elaborative Rehearsal	
5	8	4	7
7	8	1	6
6	9	5	3
4	7	6	3
4	10	4	5
9	10	3	6
7	8	4	2
5	9	4	4
5	8	5	5
6	9	3	4
$\Sigma X = 58$	86	39	45
$\bar{X} = 5.8$	8.6	3.9	4.5
$\Sigma X^2 = 358$	748	169	225
$\Sigma\Sigma X^2 = (358 + \cdots + 225) = 1500$		$\Sigma\Sigma X = 228$	

Step 1: Square the grand sum ($\Sigma\Sigma X = 228$) and divide by the total number of scores (40): $(\Sigma\Sigma X)^2/N = (288)^2/40 = 1299.6$ This is the correction term.

Step 2: SS Total $= \Sigma\Sigma X^2 - (\Sigma\Sigma X)^2/N$. Subtract the results of Step 1 from 1500: $1500 - 1299.6 = 200.4$.

Step 3: SS imagery. Get the sum of all scores in each imagery condition, square each sum, then divide each sum by the number of scores yielding each sum, add the two quotients, and then subtract the results of Step 1 from the last sum.

$$SS\text{ imagery} = (58+86)^2/20 + (39+45)^2/20 - \text{Step 1}$$
$$= \frac{144^2 + 84^2}{20} - 1299.6$$
$$= 1389.6 - 1299.6$$
$$= 90$$

Step 4: SS Rehearsal. This is calculated in the same manner as Step 3, except that you base your calculations on the grand sum of each type of rehearsal.

$$SS\text{ Rehearsal} = \frac{(86+45)^2 + (58+39)^2}{20} - \text{Step 1}$$
$$= 1328.5 - 1299.6$$
$$= 28.9$$

Step 5: SS Imagery $\times$ Rehearsal. Square each group sum and add the squares.

continued

Box B.8

continued

Then divide each sum by the number of scores in each sum. From the last result, subtract Step 1, the *SS* Imagery (Step 3), and *SS* Rehearsal (Step 4).

$$SSI \times R = \frac{58^2 + 86^2 + 39^2 + 45^2}{20} - \text{Step 1} - \text{Step 3} - \text{Step 4}$$

$$= 14306 / 10 - 1299.6 - 90 - 28.9$$

$$= 12.1$$

Step 6: SS Error. Subtract each treatment *SS* from *SS* Total.

$$SS \text{ Error} = 200.4 - 90 - 28.9 - 12.1$$
$$= 69.4$$

Step 7: Determining degrees of freedom.

$$df \text{ Total} = \text{Number of measures less one } (40 - 1) = 39$$
$$df \text{ Imagery} = \text{Number of levels of imagery less one } (2 - 1) = 1$$
$$df \text{ Rehearsal} = \text{Number of levels of rehearsal less one } (2 - 1) = 1$$
$$df \, I \times R = df \text{ imagery} \times df \text{ rehearsal } (1 \times 1) = 1$$
$$df \text{ Error} = df \text{ total} - df \text{ imagery} - df \text{ rehearsal} - df \, I \times R$$
$$(39 - 1 - 1 - 1) = 36$$

Summary Table of a 2 × 2 ANOVA					
Source	SS	df	MS	F	p
Imagery	90.0	1	90.0	46.6	<.05
Rehearsal	28.9	1	28.9	15.0	<.05
Imagery × Rehearsal	12.1	1	12.1	6.3	<.05
Error	69.4	36	1.9		

Step 8: Summary table. Calculate mean squares (*MS*) by dividing *SS* by the number of *df*. Then calculate the F ratios by dividing the treatment *MS* by the *MS* Error.

Step 9: To determine the significance of the *F* ratio, enter statistical Table F in Appendix C with the *df* for the numerator (in this case it is always 1) and with the *df* for the denominator (*df* Error), which is 36, for any effect in which you are interested. We can conclude that the type of words and type of rehearsal both influenced recall. But we should note that the effects of word type were dependent on the type of rehearsal (that is, we obtained an interaction). Elaborative rehearsal produced better recall than rote rehearsal, but the effect was larger on high-imagery words than on low-imagery words.

that the within-groups variances of the different conditions are equivalent. This latter assumption is called the **homogeneity of variance** assumption. It is assumed that manipulation of the independent variables should affect the variance between groups but not the variance within groups. Statisticians have shown that the analysis of variance is a **robust statistical test,** or one in which violations of its assumptions are unlikely to lead to erroneous conclusions. Most investigators do not even check for violations of the assumptions, but even if they do and they find that the assumptions are violated, the best solution is simply to employ a more conservative level of confidence (say, 0.01 instead of 0.05). The fact that a manipulation has influenced the variance of the different experimental conditions may be quite interesting in its own right, because it indicates that the subjects in the condition with the high variance were differentially influenced by the treatment. Understanding this fact may be a clue to understanding behavior in the situation.

χ^2 Test for Independence

Table B.8 shows data like that in Table 2.1, which illustrates the frequencies with which men and women selected majors in five departments at a small college. The null hypothesis holds that the choice of major is independent of (not contingent on) a person's sex. If the two variables are independent, we should see roughly equivalent relative frequencies in each of the cells of Table B.8. However, the frequencies are different, and we can use the **chi-squared (χ^2) test for independence** to determine whether sex is related to choice of major.

The formula for determining χ^2 is as follows:

$$\chi^2 = \Sigma(O - E)^2/E \qquad (B.19)$$

where O refers to the observed frequencies (the ones shown in each cell of Table B.8), and E refers to the expected frequencies for each cell. As shown in Box B.9, where χ^2 is calculated, the expected frequencies are calculated by multiplying together the row and column total for a particular cell and then dividing that multiplicand by the total number of frequencies in the table. So, for women selecting a major in history, the expected frequencies would be $(154 \times 115)/378$, which equals 46.85. The complete calculation is shown in Box B.9.

▼ **TABLE B.8**

A 2 × 5 Contingency Table Showing the Frequencies with which Men and Women Selected Majors in Five Departments at a Small College. The Relative Frequencies (%) of Men and Women in Each Major Are Shown in Parentheses.

Gender	Major Program					Row Total
	History	Psychology	English	Biology	Economics	
Women	37(32.2%)	24(64.9%)	41(66.1%)	31(38.8%)	21(25%)	154
Men	78(67.8%)	13(35.1%)	21(33.9%)	49(61.2%)	63(72%)	224
Column Total	115	37	62	80	84	378

Box B.9

Calculation of χ^2 for the Data in Table B.8

Step 1: Calculate the expected frequencies for each cell.

Women (W) × History (H)	$(115 \times 154)/378 = 46.85$
W × Psychology (P)	$(37 \times 154)/378 = 15.07$
W × English (En)	$(62 \times 154)/378 = 25.26$
W × Biology (B)	$(80 \times 154)/378 = 32.59$
W × Economics (Ec)	$(84 \times 154)/378 = 34.22$
Men (M) × H	$(115 \times 224)/378 = 68.15$
M × P	$(37 \times 224)/378 = 21.90$
M × En	$(62 \times 224)/378 = 36.74$
M × B	$(80 \times 224)/378 = 47.41$
M × Ec	$(84 \times 224)/378 = 49.78$

Step 2: Subtract the expected frequencies from the observed, square each difference, and divide that difference by the expected frequency for that cell.

W × H	$(37 - 46.85)^2/46.85 = 97.02/46.85 = 2.07$
W × P	$(24 - 15.07)^2/15.07 = 79.74/15.07 = 5.29$
W × En	$(41 - 25.26)^2/25.25 = 247.75/25.26 = 9.81$
W × B	$(31 - 32.59)^2/32.59 = 2.53/32.59 = 0.08$
W × EC	$(21 - 34.22)^2/34.22 = 174.77/34.22 = 5.11$
M × H	$(78 - 68.15)^2/68.15 = 97.02/68.15 = 1.42$
M × P	$(13 - 21.9)^2/21.9 = 79.21/21.9 = 3.62$
M × En	$(21 - 36.74)^2/36.74 = 247.75/36.74 = 6.74$
M × B	$(49 - 47.41)^2/47.41 = 2.53/47.41 = 0.05$
M × EC	$(63 - 49.78)^2/49.78 = 174.77/49.78 = 3.51$

Step 3: Sum the numbers from Step 2 to obtain χ^2.

$\chi^2 = 2.07 + 5.29 + 9.81 + 0.08 + 5.11 + 1.42 + 3.62 + 6.74 + 0.05 + 3.51 = 37.7$

Step 4: Check the significance of χ^2 in Table G of Appendix C. The degrees of freedom for this statistic are the number of rows less one times the number of columns less one. In this case the degrees of freedom are $(2 - 1) \times (5 - 1) = 4$. To be significant at $p < .05$, a χ^2 with four degrees of freedom must be equal to or greater than 9.49. Because our $\chi^2 = 37.7$, it exceeds the critical value. We have a significant statistic and can reject the null hypothesis that sex and choice of major are independent.

▼ MISUSES OF STATISTICS

Statistics are used so often that it seems possible to bolster any argument with them. They are employed by politicians, economists, advertisers, psychologists, and many others to support various views, so it is little wonder that people have gained the impression that statistics can be bent to any purpose. But adage has it that "statistics don't lie, statisticians do." Actually, there is probably little to fear from statisticians themselves, because their sophistication permits them to differentiate a true argument from a false one based on statistics. Nonetheless, statistics can be misused to create a false impression. You should be aware of some common misuses, so that you will not be misled by them.

Use of Small or Biased Samples

Many television commercials implicitly mislead us with small or biased samples. Viewers see a woman who is asked to test two brands of detergent on her family's greasy and grass-stained clothes. She is pitting her usual product, BAF, against new Super Crud Remover (SCR). BAF goes into one washer, SCR goes into the other, and later the woman is shown exclaiming over the better job that SCR did. Announcer: "Are you convinced?" Woman: "Why, yes. I will always use Super Crud Remover from now on. It really gets the crud off my clothes." Even making the unlikely assumption that the whole demonstration was not rigged, observers should know better than to be convinced by such a small sample (one case). If the "experiment" were repeated honestly with a hundred consumers, would all of them pick SCR? The advertiser tries to leave us with the impression that because this one woman prefers the product, everyone (the population) will. But we should be careful about assuming something to be true of the population at large from a sample of one.

Another problem is that a sample of individuals surveyed for such an ad might be deliberately biased. Advertisers are always surveying groups that are likely to be predisposed in their favor anyway, such as people who already own the product. Advertisers ask consumers, "How well do you like your Bass-o-matic?" and then show a small sample of interviews that went well from the manufacturer's point of view. It would be more convincing to sample people who had never used the product and to test the product against its main rivals. Since more advertising claims on television must now be based on facts, this type of commercial is becoming more widely used. In one interesting ad, owners of one type of luxury car are asked to test it against a competitor car. Here is a case in which the sample tested is expected to be biased *against* the new product in favor of the old product, so if a preference is found for the new product, it seems to argue much more strongly for the new product.

Whenever you hear about preferences that people have exhibited, ask two questions about the sample: (1) How large was it? (2) How were people chosen to be in it?

The Exaggerated Graph A common way to show or hide differences in graphs is to exaggerate the results being plotted. This involves changing the scale on the graph in order to show off a difference, or (more rarely) to hide a difference. Suppose that the number of murders in a city increased from 72 to 80 to 91 over three years. The next year, the mayor is running for reelection and is eager to show that the city has been safe for the last three years under her administration. So her campaign workers draw up the graph shown on the left side of Figure B.5. By making the scale on the Y-axis very long, they create the impression that the murder rate is fairly steady. In the same year, the city police are arguing that they need higher staffing levels. They want to show that the city is becoming more unsafe, so they depict the murder rate as increasing steeply by changing the scale, as in the right-hand graph of Figure B.5.

The facts are shown accurately in both groups. However, the left graph gives the impression that the murder rate is increasing very gradually, hardly worth worrying about. (Hasn't the mayor done a good job leading the city?) The right graph, on the other hand, creates the impression that the murder rate is increasing dramatically. (Don't we need more police?)

These graphing techniques are common. In fact, exaggerated scales are used in some of the graphs in this book to show patterns of results more clearly. You should

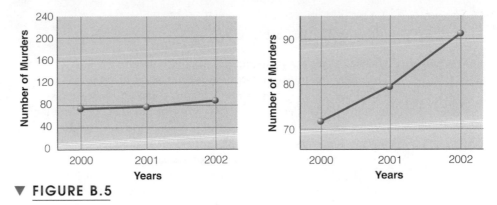

▼ **FIGURE B.5**

Variation in Scales. The graph at the left seems to show the murder rate to be increasing only slightly, whereas the one at the right shows the rate going up dramatically. Yet both graphs actually show the murder rate accurately—the difference is the scale on the Y-axis. It is important to examine a graph carefully and note the scale of measurement, since scale changes can make small differences look large and vice versa.

always look carefully at the scale in a graph. With experimental data, it is more important to determine whether a difference is statistically reliable than to determine whether the difference appears large when graphed.

Absent or Inappropriate Comparisons

A common ploy used in advertising is to say that some product has x percent more of something good or y percent less of something bad. "Buy the new Thunderbolt, since it gives 27 percent better gas mileage." This sounds convincing until you stop to ask yourself, "Twenty-seven percent better than what?" A missing comparison here makes the statistic completely meaningless. Perhaps the Thunderbolt gets 27 percent better mileage than a two-ton tank, which is hardly an argument for buying it.

Even when a specific comparison is made, it is often still inappropriate. The claim is frequently made in advertising that a product is better than last year's model. "Buy the new, improved, Thunderbolt. It gets 27 percent better mileage than last year's model." Of course, it could still be a real dog, even if it's better than last year's dog. What the consumer would really like is a comparison of the mileage efficiency of the new Thunderbolt with other new cars in roughly the same class, as is now provided by government testing.

Another problem in making comparisons is the lack of information on the reliability of differences. In one commercial, two cars of the same make and year were filled with one gallon of gas and test-driven at a constant speed around a track. The difference in the test was the type of gasoline used. One car stopped before the other, and the viewers were supposed to conclude that the sponsor's gasoline was superior to the other brand. But only after a long series of comparisons could a researcher statistically test for a reliable difference between the two types of gas. This is the same problem that occurs in the case of comparing two detergents—the sample of observations is too small.

In general, watch to make sure that in statements involving a comparison, the object of comparison is described and is appropriate. There should also be some statement about whether any differences are statistically reliable.

The Gambler's Fallacy

Statistical tests are based on probability theory: the theory of expectations about the likelihood of random events. It is interesting to note that people's perceptions of the randomness of events do not agree in some important respects with ideas from probability theory. People often draw conclusions that seem irrational when judged by the logic of probability theory. There is much interesting research on this phenomenon (for example, Tversky & Kahneman, 1971, 1974). Here, we will examine one of the most common mistakes in judgments of probability.

Imagine that a person flips a coin 1,000 times. If it is a fair coin, it should come up heads about 500 times and tails about 500 times. The probability of its coming up heads over a large number of trials is 0.50, but, of course, even a fair coin will probably not come up heads exactly 500 times in 1,000 flips: It might come up 490 or 505. Yet the result is fairly close. Now, what if the person is betting on whether the coin will come up heads or tails? If the situation is truly random, a gambler has a probability of 0.50 of winning on any particular trial. Imagine that on five trials in a row, the gambler bets five dollars that the coin will come up heads, and each time it comes up tails. Of course, the fact that the coin comes up tails five times in a row is unusual, and the chances of such an event are quite low (0.03). The gambler notes this odd occurrence. On the next bet, he doubles his bet to ten dollars and again bets on heads. Now he is more certain that the coin will come up heads.

The logic the gambler uses is as follows. "The coin is a fair coin. On the average, it will come up heads half the time and tails half the time. The coin has just come up tails five times in a row. Therefore, it is due to come up heads to even things up, because on the average it will come up heads half the time. So I should bet on heads and even increase my bet." More generally, the logic is: "If the game is truly random and I am losing, then I should keep playing, because my luck is bound to change for the better." This kind of logic keeps gambling casinos at Las Vegas and Atlantic City humming and wipes out the fortunes of otherwise intelligent people.

The fallacy of the argument is in applying the laws of probability—such as a fair coin coming up heads half the time—that hold only over tremendously large numbers of events. The laws cannot be applied to small runs. What the gambler overlooks is that the flips of the coin are independent events; what happened on previous flips does not influence what happens next. If the coin came up tails five times in a row, this does not increase the probability of heads on the next throw. It is still 0.50. The coin does not have a memory for previous trials, as the gambler seems to assume implicitly. The gambler should not feel any more certain on the sixth trial than he or she did on the first five. The probability of heads showing has not changed.

In some sense, the gambler's mistake is natural. There is a ring of truth to the argument, and it is based on true laws of probability. Over a very large series of throws, a fair coin will come up heads 50 percent of the time. The error comes in applying to a small series what is true over a very large series of events. The laws do not apply to small series of random events as well. With, say, 10 million coin flips, heads will come up almost exactly 50 percent of the time. But if a gambler takes a small series of the larger number, say, five flips, heads could come up either zero or five times with a probability of 0.06. These outcomes (all heads or all tails) are not terribly likely, but they are not vanishingly small, either.

▼ SUMMARY

1. Understanding some elementary principles about statistics is crucial to the conduct of psychological research. There are two branches of statistics, descriptive and inferential.

2. Descriptive statistics are used to summarize and organize raw data. There are graphical methods for doing this, such as histograms and frequency polygons. However, the primary summary measures are those of central tendency of a distribution and dispersion of a distribution.

3. The primary measure of central tendency is the mean of the distribution, or what is usually called the average of the scores. The median (the middlemost score) is sometimes used, especially for distributions with extreme scores. The primary measures of dispersion are the standard deviation and variance. The standard deviation is used more often in descriptive statistics, and the variance is used primarily in inferential statistics. Most distributions in psychology are assumed to be normal, which means that the mean and median fall in the same place; that the distribution is symmetrical; and that a certain proportion of scores falls under each part of the normal curve.

4. Inferential statistics allow us to make inferences about the reliability of differences among conditions. We want to infer from a sample of scores what the case is for the populations involved. A great variety of tests are used in inferential statistics. A similar logic is applied in all. An alternative hypothesis is tested against the null hypothesis, which holds that there are no differences among groups in the experiment. Computations are performed that give rise to a value. This value is then compared with a distribution of values in a table that informs us what level of confidence we can have in rejecting the null hypothesis.

5. We use a z-score test for comparing a sample with a known population to see whether the sample comes from the same population. To determine whether two groups, an experimental and a control, differ from one another, we use the t test or Mann-Whitney U test, which apply when two independent groups of subjects are employed, and the sign test, t test, and Wilcoxon signed-ranks test, which apply when the measures in the two conditions are related (either by using a within-subjects design or by matching subjects). The Mann-Whitney and Wilcoxon tests are nonparametric statistical tests, since they do not make any assumptions about the population parameters underlying the sample observations that are actually used. To determine how wrong the null hypothesis is, a measure of the magnitude of effect of the independent variable is calculated. This measure is usually in the form of a correlation coefficient. A sizable magnitude of effect without statistical significance suggests that a larger sample size may be needed to reject the null hypothesis.

6. The analysis of variance is the important statistical procedure used in making comparisons among more than two groups. The simple analysis of variance is used in testing for reliability when one independent variable is manipulated. More-complicated multifactor analyses are used when two or more independent variables are manipulated simultaneously. These multifactor designs are especially important in that they allow us to assess the interaction of factors that determine behavior.

7. Disraeli said that "there are three kinds of lies—lies, damned lies, and statistics." Some ways in which statistics can be misused include drawing conclusions from small or biased samples; exaggerating the scales on graphs for effect; making inappropriate comparisons; and assuming that the laws of probability that hold for huge samples of observations can be generalized to small samples (as in the gambler's fallacy). Statistics themselves do not lie, but they can be used to give misleading impressions.

▼ KEY TERMS

absolute mean deviation
alpha (α) level
analysis of variance
arithmetic mean
between-groups variance
between-subjects design
central tendency
chi-squared (χ^2) test for independence
degrees of freedom
descriptive statistics
directional test
dispersion
distribution of sample means
eta (η)
experimental hypothesis
F test
frequency distributions
frequency polygon
histograms
homogeneity of variance
inferential statistics
inflection point
interaction effects
level of confidence
magnitude of effect
main effects
Mann-Whitney U test
median
multifactor analysis of variance
nondirectional test
nonparametric tests

normal curve
null hypothesis
one-tailed statistical test
parameters
parametric tests
Pearson product-moment correlation coefficient
Pearson r
point biserial
population
power of a statistical test
qualitative variation
quantitative variation
random sampling
related measures design
robust statistical test
sample
sign test
simple analysis of variance
standard deviation
standard error of the mean
standard scores
statistics
t test
two-tailed test
type I error
type II error
variance
Wilcoxon signed-ranks test
within-groups variance
z scores

 WEB CONNECTIONS

Explore the step-by step presentation of:

Central Tendency and Variability

Z Scores

Standard Error

Hypothesis Testing

Correlation

***t*-Test for One Sample**

***t*-Test for Between Groups and Related Groups**

on the Cengage Learning Psychology Resource Center, Statistics and Research Methods activities at:

http://academic.cengage.com/psychology/workshops

A complete statistics book with analysis and demonstration package can be found at:

http://www.ruf.rice.edu/~lane/rvls.html

This site contains statistical analysis programs for nearly any applied statistical problem:

http://members.aol.com/johnp71/javastat.html

APPENDIX C

STATISTICAL TABLES

▼ TABLE A

Proportions of Area Under the Normal Curve

How to use Table A: The values in Table A represent the proportion of areas in the standard normal curve, which has a mean of 0, a standard deviation of 1.00, and a total area equal to 1.00. To use Table A, the raw score must first be transformed into a z score. Column A represents this z score; Column B represents the distance between the mean of the standard-normal distribution (0) and the z score; and Column C represents the proportion of area beyond a given z.

Column A gives the positive z score.

Column B gives the area between the mean and z. Since the curve is symmetrical, areas for negative z scores are the same as those for positive ones.

Column C gives the area that is beyond z.

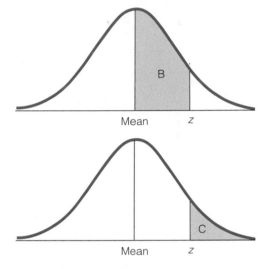

(A)	(B)	(C)	(A)	(B)	(C)	(A)	(B)	(C)
z	Area between Mean and z	Area beyond z	z	Area between Mean and z	Area beyond z	z	Area between Mean and z	Area beyond z
0.00	.0000	.5000	0.14	.0557	.4443	0.28	.1103	.3897
0.01	.0040	.4960	0.15	.0596	.4404	0.29	.1141	.3859
0.02	.0080	.4920	0.16	.0636	.4364	0.30	.1179	.3821
0.03	.0120	.4880	0.17	.0675	.4325	0.31	.1217	.3783
0.04	.0160	.4840	0.18	.0714	.4286	0.32	.1255	.3745
0.05	.0199	.4801	0.19	.0753	.4247	0.33	.1293	.3707
0.06	.0239	.4761	0.20	.0793	.4207	0.34	.1331	.3669
0.07	.0279	.4721	0.21	.0832	.4168	0.35	.1368	.3632
0.08	.0319	.4681	0.22	.0871	.4129	0.36	.1406	.3594
0.09	.0359	.4641	0.23	.0910	.4090	0.37	.1443	.3557
0.10	.0398	.4602	0.24	.0948	.4052	0.38	.1480	.3520
0.11	.0438	.4562	0.25	.0987	.4013	0.39	.1517	.3483
0.12	.0478	.4522	0.26	.1026	.3974	0.40	.1554	.3446
0.13	.0517	.4483	0.27	.1064	.3936	0.41	.1591	.3409

Continued at top of next column. ↑

Continued at top of next column. ↑

Continued at top of next page. →

▼ **TABLE A**

Continued

(A)	(B)	(C)	(A)	(B)	(C)	(A)	(B)	(C)
z	Area between Mean and z	Area beyond z	z	Area between Mean and z	Area beyond z	z	Area between Mean and z	Area beyond z
0.42	.1628	.3372	0.87	.3078	.1922	1.32	.4066	.0934
0.43	.1664	.3336	0.88	.3106	.1894	1.33	.4082	.0918
0.44	.1700	.3300	0.89	.3133	.1867	1.34	.4099	.0901
0.45	.1736	.3264	0.90	.3159	.1841	1.35	.4115	.0885
0.46	.1772	.3228	0.91	.3186	.1814	1.36	.4131	.0869
0.47	.1808	.3192	0.92	.3212	.1788	1.37	.4147	.0853
0.48	.1844	.3156	0.93	.3238	.1762	1.38	.4162	.0838
0.49	.1879	.3121	0.94	.3264	.1736	1.39	.4177	.0823
0.50	.1915	.3085	0.95	.3289	.1711	1.40	.4192	.0808
0.51	.1950	.3050	0.96	.3315	.1685	1.41	.4207	.0793
0.52	.1985	.3015	0.97	.3340	.1660	1.42	.4222	.0778
0.53	.2019	.2981	0.98	.3365	.1635	1.43	.4236	.0764
0.54	.2054	.2946	0.99	.3389	.1611	1.44	.4251	.0749
0.55	.2088	.2912	1.00	.3413	.1587	1.45	.4265	.0735
0.56	.2123	.2877	1.01	.3438	.1562	1.46	.4279	.0721
0.57	.2157	.2843	1.02	.3461	.1539	1.47	.4292	.0708
0.58	.2190	.2810	1.03	.3485	.1515	1.48	.4306	.0694
0.59	.2224	.2776	1.04	.3508	.1492	1.49	.4319	.0681
0.60	.2257	.2743	1.05	.3531	.1469	1.50	.4332	.0668
0.61	.2291	.2709	1.06	.3554	.1446	1.51	.4345	.0655
0.62	.2324	.2676	1.07	.3577	.1423	1.52	.4357	.0643
0.63	.2357	.2643	1.08	.3599	.1401	1.53	.4370	.0630
0.64	.2389	.2611	1.09	.3621	.1379	1.54	.4382	.0618
0.65	.2422	.2578	1.10	.3643	.1357	1.55	.4394	.0606
0.66	.2454	.2546	1.11	.3665	.1335	1.56	.4406	.0594
0.67	.2486	.2514	1.12	.3686	.1314	1.57	.4418	.0582
0.68	.2517	.2483	1.13	.3708	.1292	1.58	.4429	.0571
0.69	.2549	.2451	1.14	.3729	.1271	1.59	.4441	.0559
0.70	.2580	.2420	1.15	.3749	.1251	1.60	.4452	.0548
0.71	.2611	.2389	1.16	.3770	.1230	1.61	.4463	.0537
0.72	.2642	.2358	1.17	.3790	.1210	1.62	.4474	.0526
0.73	.2673	.2327	1.18	.3810	.1190	1.63	.4484	.0516
0.74	.2704	.2296	1.19	.3830	.1170	1.64	.4495	.0505
0.75	.2734	.2266	1.20	.3849	.1151	1.65	.4505	.0495
0.76	.2764	.2236	1.21	.3869	.1131	1.66	.4515	.0485
0.77	.2794	.2206	1.22	.3888	.1112	1.67	.4525	.0475
0.78	.2823	.2177	1.23	.3907	.1093	1.68	.4535	.0465
0.79	.2852	.2148	1.24	.3925	.1075	1.69	.4545	.0455
0.80	.2881	.2119	1.25	.3944	.1056	1.70	.4554	.0446
0.81	.2910	.2090	1.26	.3962	.1038	1.71	.4564	.0436
0.82	.2939	.2061	1.27	.3980	.1020	1.72	.4573	.0427
0.83	.2967	.2033	1.28	.3997	.1003	1.73	.4582	.0418
0.84	.2995	.2005	1.29	.4015	.0985	1.74	.4591	.0409
0.85	.3023	.1977	1.30	.4032	.0968	1.75	.4599	.0401
0.86	.3051	.1949	1.31	.4049	.0951	1.76	.4608	.0392

Continued at top of next column. ↑   Continued at top of next column. ↑   Continued at top of next page. →

▼ TABLE A
Continued

(A) z	(B) Area between Mean and z	(C) Area beyond z	(A) z	(B) Area between Mean and z	(C) Area beyond z	(A) z	(B) Area between Mean and z	(C) Area beyond z
1.77	.4616	.0384	2.22	.4868	.0132	2.67	.4962	.0038
1.78	.4625	.0375	2.23	.4871	.0129	2.68	.4963	.0037
1.79	.4633	.0367	2.24	.4875	.0125	2.69	.4964	.0036
1.80	.4641	.0359	2.25	.4878	.0122	2.70	.4965	.0035
1.81	.4649	.0351	2.26	.4881	.0119	2.71	.4966	.0034
1.82	.4656	.0344	2.27	.4884	.0116	2.72	.4967	.0033
1.83	.4664	.0336	2.28	.4887	.0113	2.73	.4968	.0032
1.84	.4671	.0329	2.29	.4890	.0110	2.74	.4969	.0031
1.85	.4678	.0322	2.30	.4893	.0107	2.75	.4970	.0030
1.86	.4686	.0314	2.31	.4896	.0104	2.76	.4971	.0029
1.87	.4693	.0307	2.32	.4898	.0102	2.77	.4972	.0028
1.88	.4699	.0301	2.33	.4901	.0099	2.78	.4973	.0027
1.89	.4706	.0294	2.34	.4904	.0096	2.79	.4974	.0026
1.90	.4713	.0287	2.35	.4906	.0094	2.80	.4974	.0026
1.91	.4719	.0281	2.36	.4909	.0091	2.81	.4975	.0025
1.92	.4726	.0274	2.37	.4911	.0089	2.82	.4976	.0024
1.93	.4732	.0268	2.38	.4913	.0087	2.83	.4977	.0023
1.94	.4738	.0262	2.39	.4916	.0084	2.84	.4977	.0023
1.95	.4744	.0256	2.40	.4918	.0082	2.85	.4978	.0022
1.96	.4750	.0250	2.41	.4920	.0080	2.86	.4979	.0021
1.97	.4756	.0244	2.42	.4922	.0078	2.87	.4979	.0021
1.98	.4761	.0239	2.43	.4925	.0075	2.88	.4980	.0020
1.99	.4767	.0233	2.44	.4927	.0073	2.89	.4981	.0019
2.00	.4772	.0228	2.45	.4929	.0071	2.90	.4981	.0019
2.01	.4778	.0222	2.46	.4931	.0069	2.91	.4982	.0018
2.02	.4783	.0217	2.47	.4932	.0068	2.92	.4982	.0018
2.03	.4788	.0212	2.48	.4934	.0066	2.93	.4983	.0017
2.04	.4793	.0207	2.49	.4936	.0064	2.94	.4984	.0016
2.05	.4798	.0202	2.50	.4938	.0062	2.95	.4984	.0016
2.06	.4803	.0197	2.51	.4940	.0060	2.96	.4985	.0015
2.07	.4808	.0192	2.52	.4941	.0059	2.97	.4985	.0015
2.08	.4812	.0188	2.53	.4943	.0057	2.98	.4986	.0014
2.09	.4817	.0183	2.54	.4945	.0055	2.99	.4986	.0014
2.10	.4821	.0179	2.55	.4946	.0054	3.00	.4987	.0013
2.11	.4826	.0174	2.56	.4948	.0052	3.01	.4987	.0013
2.12	.4830	.0170	2.57	.4949	.0051	3.02	.4987	.0013
2.13	.4834	.0166	2.58	.4951	.0049	3.03	.4988	.0012
2.14	.4838	.0162	2.59	.4952	.0048	3.04	.4988	.0012
2.15	.4842	.0158	2.60	.4953	.0047	3.05	.4989	.0011
2.16	.4846	.0154	2.61	.4955	.0045	3.06	.4989	.0011
2.17	.4850	.0150	2.62	.4956	.0044	3.07	.4989	.0011
2.18	.4854	.0146	2.63	.4957	.0043	3.08	.4990	.0010
2.19	.4857	.0143	2.64	.4959	.0041	3.09	.4990	.0010
2.20	.4861	.0139	2.65	.4960	.0040	3.10	.4990	.0010
2.21	.4864	.0136	2.66	.4961	.0039	3.11	.4991	.0009

Continued at top of next column. ↑   *Continued at top of next column.* ↑   *Continued at top of next page.* →

▼ **TABLE A**

Continued

(A)	(B)	(C)	(A)	(B)	(C)	(A)	(B)	(C)
z	Area between Mean and z	Area beyond z	z	Area between Mean and z	Area beyond z	z	Area between Mean and z	Area beyond z
3.12	.4991	.0009	3.20	.4993	.0007	3.40	.4997	.0003
3.13	.4991	.0009	3.21	.4993	.0007	3.45	.4997	.0003
3.14	.4992	.0008	3.22	.4994	.0006	3.50	.4998	.0002
3.15	.4992	.0008	3.23	.4994	.0006	3.60	.4998	.0002
3.16	.4992	.0008	3.24	.4994	.0006	3.70	.4999	.0001
3.17	.4992	.0008	3.25	.4994	.0006	3.80	.4999	.0001
3.18	.4993	.0007	3.30	.4995	.0005	3.90	.49995	.00005
3.19	.4993	.0007	3.35	.4996	.0004	4.00	.49997	.00003

Continued at top of next column. ↑   *Continued at top of next column.* ↑

▼ **TABLE B**

Critical Values of the *U* Statistic of the Mann-Whitney Test
To use these tables, first decide what level significance you want with either a one- or a two-tailed test. For example, if you want $p = .05$, two-tailed, use (c). Then locate the number of cases or measures (*n*) in both groups in the particular subtable you have chosen. The *U* value you have calculated must be *less* than that at the appropriate place in the table. For example, if you had 18 subjects in each group of an experiment, and calculated $U = 90$, then you could conclude that the null hypothesis can be rejected, because the critical *U* value with groups of these sizes is 99 [see subtable (c)].

(*a*) Critical Values of *U* for a One-Tailed Test at .001 or for a Two-Tailed Test at .002											
n_1/n_2	9	10	11	12	13	14	15	16	17	18	19	20
1												
2												
3										0	0	0	0
4		0	0	0	1	1	1	2	2	3	3	3
5	1	1	2	2	3	3	4	5	5	6	7	7
6	2	3	4	4	5	6	7	8	9	10	11	12
7	3	5	6	7	8	9	10	11	13	14	15	16
8	5	6	8	9	11	12	14	15	17	18	20	21
9	7	8	10	12	14	15	17	19	21	23	25	26
10	8	10	12	14	17	19	21	23	25	27	29	32
11	10	12	15	17	20	22	24	27	29	32	34	37
12	12	14	17	20	23	25	28	31	34	37	40	42
13	14	17	20	23	26	29	32	35	38	42	45	48
14	15	19	22	25	29	32	36	39	43	46	50	54
15	17	21	24	28	32	36	40	43	47	51	55	59
16	19	23	27	31	35	39	43	48	52	56	60	65
17	21	25	29	34	38	43	47	52	57	61	66	70
18	23	27	32	37	42	46	51	56	61	66	71	76
19	25	29	34	40	45	50	55	60	66	71	77	82
20	26	32	37	42	48	54	59	65	70	76	82	88

Continued

▼ TABLE B

Continued

(b) Critical Values of *U* for a One-Tailed Test at .01 or for a Two-Tailed Test at .02

n_1/n_2	9	10	11	12	13	14	15	16	17	18	19	20
1												
2					0	0	0	0	0	0	1	1
3	1	1	1	2	2	2	3	3	4	4	4	5
4	3	3	4	5	5	6	7	7	8	9	9	10
5	5	6	7	8	9	10	11	12	13	14	15	16
6	7	8	9	11	12	13	15	16	18	19	20	22
7	9	11	12	14	16	17	19	21	23	24	26	28
8	11	13	15	17	20	22	24	26	28	30	32	34
9	14	16	18	21	23	26	28	31	33	36	38	40
10	16	19	22	24	27	30	33	36	38	41	44	47
11	18	22	25	28	31	34	37	41	44	47	50	53
12	21	24	28	31	35	38	42	46	49	53	56	60
13	23	27	31	35	39	43	47	51	55	59	63	67
14	26	30	34	38	43	47	51	56	60	65	69	73
15	28	33	37	42	47	51	56	61	66	70	75	80
16	31	36	41	46	51	56	61	66	71	76	82	87
17	33	38	44	49	55	60	66	71	77	82	88	93
18	36	41	47	53	59	65	70	76	82	88	94	100
19	38	44	50	56	63	69	75	82	88	94	101	107
20	40	47	53	60	67	73	80	87	93	100	107	114

(c) Critical Values of *U* for a One-Tailed Test at .025 or for a Two-Tailed Test at .05

n_1/n_2	9	10	11	12	13	14	15	16	17	18	19	20
1												
2	0	0	1	1	1	1	1	1	2	2	2	2
3	2	3	3	4	4	5	5	6	6	7	7	8
4	4	5	6	7	8	9	10	11	11	12	13	13
5	7	8	9	11	12	13	14	15	17	18	19	20
6	10	11	13	14	16	17	19	21	22	24	25	27
7	12	14	16	18	20	22	24	26	28	30	32	34
8	15	17	19	22	24	26	29	31	34	36	38	41
9	17	20	23	26	28	31	34	37	39	42	45	48
10	20	23	26	29	33	36	39	42	45	48	52	55
11	23	26	30	33	37	40	44	47	51	55	58	62
12	26	29	33	37	41	45	49	53	57	61	65	69
13	28	33	37	41	45	50	54	59	63	67	72	76
14	31	36	40	45	50	55	59	64	67	74	78	83
15	34	39	44	49	54	59	64	70	75	80	85	90
16	37	42	47	53	59	64	70	75	81	86	92	98
17	39	45	51	57	63	67	75	81	87	93	99	105
18	42	48	55	61	67	74	80	86	93	99	106	112
19	45	52	58	65	72	78	85	92	99	106	113	119
20	48	55	62	69	76	83	90	98	105	112	119	127

Continued

▼ **TABLE B**

Continued

	(d) Critical Values of U for a One-Tailed Test at .05 or for a Two-Tailed Test at .10											
n_1/n_2	9	10	11	12	13	14	15	16	17	18	19	20
1											0	0
2	1	1	1	2	2	2	3	3	3	4	4	4
3	3	4	5	5	6	7	7	8	9	9	10	11
4	6	7	8	9	10	11	12	14	15	16	17	18
5	9	11	12	13	15	16	18	19	20	22	23	25
6	12	14	16	17	19	21	23	25	26	28	30	32
7	15	17	19	21	24	26	28	30	33	35	37	39
8	18	20	23	26	28	31	33	36	39	41	44	47
9	21	24	27	30	33	36	39	42	45	48	51	54
10	24	27	31	34	37	41	44	48	51	55	58	62
11	27	31	34	38	42	46	50	54	57	61	65	69
12	30	34	38	42	47	51	55	60	64	68	72	77
13	33	37	42	47	51	56	61	65	70	75	80	84
14	36	41	46	51	56	61	66	71	77	82	87	92
15	39	44	50	55	61	66	72	77	83	88	94	100
16	42	48	54	60	65	71	77	83	89	95	101	107
17	45	51	57	64	70	77	83	89	96	102	109	115
18	48	55	61	68	75	82	88	95	102	109	116	123
19	51	58	65	72	80	87	94	101	109	116	123	130
20	54	62	69	77	84	92	100	107	115	123	130	138

Source: Adapted from "Extended Tables for the Mann-Whitney Statistic," by D. Aube, 1953, *Bulletin of the Institute of Educational Research at Indiana University 1, No. 2,* Tables 1, 3, 5, and 7. Taken from *Nonparametric Statistics for the Behavioral Sciences,* by S. Siegel, 1956, New York: McGraw-Hill Book Company. Reprinted by permission of the Institute of Educational Research and McGraw-Hill Book Company.

▼ **TABLE C**

Distribution for the Sign Test

Alpha levels of the sign test for pairs of observations ranging from 3 to 42. An *x* denotes the number of exceptions (the number of times the difference between conditions is in the unexpected direction), while the *p* level indicates the probability that that number of exceptions could occur by chance. If there are 28 paired observations and 20 are ordered in the expected direction, with 8 exceptions, the probability that this could occur by chance is .018.

x p	x p	x p	x p	x p	x p
n = 3	*n* = 6	*n* = 8	*n* = 10	*n* = 12	*n* = 14
0 .125	0 .016	0 .004	0 .001	1 .003	1 .001
	1 .109	1 .035	1 .011	2 .019	2 .006
n = 4	2 .344	2 .145	2 .055	3 .073	3 .029
0 .062			3 .172	4 .194	4 .090
1 .312	*n* = 7	*n* = 9			5 .212
	0 .008	0 .002	*n* = 11	*n* = 13	
n = 5	1 .062	1 .020	0 .000	1 .002	*n* = 15
0 .031	2 .227	2 .090	1 .006	2 .011	1 .000
1 .188		3 .254	2 .033	3 .016	2 .004
			3 .113	4 .133	3 .018
			4 .274		4 .059
					5 .151

Continued

▼ TABLE C

Continued

x	p	x	p	x	p	x	p	x	p	x	p
n = 16		**n = 21**		**n = 26**		**n = 31**		**n = 35**		**n = 39**	
2	.002	4	.004	6	.005	7	.002	9	.003	11	.005
3	.011	5	.013	7	.014	8	.005	10	.008	12	.012
4	.038	6	.039	8	.038	9	.015	11	.020	13	.027
5	.105	7	.095	9	.084	10	.035	12	.045	14	.054
6	.227	8	.192	10	.163	11	.075	13	.088	15	.100
						12	.141	14	.155	16	.168
n = 17		**n = 22**		**n = 27**							
2	.001	4	.002	6	.003	**n = 32**		**n = 36**		**n = 40**	
3	.006	5	.008	7	.010	8	.004	9	.002	11	.003
4	.025	6	.026	8	.026	9	.010	10	.006	12	.008
5	.072	7	.067	9	.061	10	.025	11	.014	13	.019
6	.166	8	.143	10	.124	11	.055	12	.033	14	.040
				11	.221	12	.108	13	.066	15	.077
n = 18		**n = 23**				13	.189	14	.121	16	.134
3	.004	4	.001	**n = 28**				15	.203		
4	.015	5	.005	6	.002	**n = 33**				**n = 41**	
5	.048	6	.017	7	.006	8	.002	**n = 37**		11	.002
6	.119	7	.047	8	.018	9	.007	10	.004	12	.006
7	.240	8	.105	9	.044	10	.018	11	.010	13	.014
		9	.202	10	.092	11	.040	12	.024	14	.030
n = 19				11	.172	12	.081	13	.049	15	.059
3	.002	**n = 24**				13	.148	14	.094	16	.106
4	.010	5	.008	**n = 29**				15	.162	17	.174
5	.032	6	.011	7	.004	**n = 34**					
6	.084	7	.032	8	.012	9	.005	**n = 38**		**n = 42**	
7	.180	8	.076	9	.031	10	.012	10	.003	12	.004
		9	.154	10	.068	11	.029	11	.007	13	.010
n = 20				11	.132	12	.061	12	.017	14	.022
3	.001	**n = 25**				13	.115	13	.036	15	.044
4	.006	5	.002	**n = 30**		14	.196	14	.072	16	.082
5	.021	6	.007	7	.003			15	.128	17	.140
6	.058	7	.022	8	.008						
7	.132	8	.051	9	.021						
		9	.115	10	.049						
		10	.212	11	.100						
				12	.181						

▼ TABLE D

Critical Values of Wilcoxon's *T* Statistic for the Matched-pairs Signed-ranks Test

To use this table, first locate the number of *pairs* of scores in the *n* column. The critical values for several levels of significance are listed in the columns to the right. For example, if *n* were 15 and the computed value 19, it would be concluded that since 19 is less than 20, the difference between conditions is significant beyond the .02 level of significance for a two-tailed test.

	Level of Significance for One-Tailed Test		
	.025	.01	.005
	Level of Significance for Two-Tailed Test		
n	.05	.02	.01
6	1	—	—
7	2	0	—
8	4	2	0
9	6	3	2
10	8	5	3
11	11	7	5
12	14	10	7
13	17	13	10
14	21	16	13
15	25	20	16
16	30	24	19
17	35	28	23
18	40	33	28
19	46	38	32
20	52	43	37
21	59	49	43
22	66	56	49
23	73	62	55
24	81	69	61
25	90	77	68

Note: n is the number of matched pairs.

Source: Adapted from *Some Rapid Approximate Statistical Procedures (Rev. ed.),* by F. Wilcoxon, 1964, New York: American Cyanamid Company. Taken from *Nonparametric Statistics for the Behavioral Sciences,* by S. Siegel, 1956, New York: McGraw-Hill Book Company. Reprinted by permission of the American Cyanamid Company and McGraw-Hill Book Company.

▼ TABLE E

Critical Values of *t*

To find the appropriate value of *t*, read across the row that contains the number of degrees of freedom in your experiment. The columns are determined by the level of significance you have chosen, and the cell entries are the critical values for each *df* at each probability level. The value of *t* you obtain must be *equal to* or *greater than* that in the table in order to be significant. For example, with *df* = 15 and *p* = .05 (two-tailed test), your *t* must be greater than or equal to 2.131.

	Level of Significance for a One-Tailed Test							
	.25	.10	.05	.025	.01	.005	.0025	.001
	Level of Significance for a Two-Tailed Test							
df	.50	.20	.10	.05	.02	.01	.005	.002
1	1.000	3.078	6.314	12.706	31.821	63.657	127.321	318.309
2	0.816	1.886	2.920	4.303	6.965	9.925	14.089	22.327
3	0.765	1.638	2.353	3.182	4.541	5.841	7.453	10.214
4	0.741	1.533	2.132	2.776	3.747	4.604	5.598	7.173
5	0.727	1.476	2.015	2.571	3.365	4.032	4.773	5.893
6	0.718	1.440	1.943	2.447	3.143	3.707	4.317	5.208
7	0.711	1.415	1.895	2.365	2.998	3.499	4.029	4.785
8	0.706	1.397	1.880	2.306	2.896	3.366	3.833	4.501
9	0.703	1.383	1.833	2.262	2.821	3.256	3.690	4.297
10	0.700	1.372	1.812	2.228	2.764	3.169	3.581	4.144
11	0.697	1.363	1.796	2.201	2.718	3.106	3.497	4.025
12	0.695	1.356	1.782	2.179	2.681	3.055	3.428	3.930
13	0.694	1.350	1.771	2.160	2.650	3.012	3.372	3.852
14	0.692	1.345	1.761	2.145	2.624	2.977	3.326	3.787
15	0.691	1.341	1.753	2.131	2.602	2.947	3.286	3.733
16	0.690	1.337	1.746	2.120	2.583	2.921	3.252	3.686
17	0.689	1.333	1.740	2.110	2.567	2.898	3.223	3.646
18	0.688	1.330	1.734	2.101	2.552	2.878	3.197	3.610
19	0.688	1.328	1.729	2.093	2.539	2.861	3.174	3.579
20	0.687	1.325	1.725	2.086	2.528	2.845	3.153	3.552
21	0.686	1.323	1.721	2.080	2.518	2.831	3.135	3.527
22	0.686	1.321	1.717	2.074	2.508	2.819	3.119	3.505
23	0.685	1.319	1.714	2.069	2.500	2.807	3.104	3.485
24	0.685	1.318	1.711	2.064	2.492	2.797	3.090	3.467
25	0.684	1.316	1.708	2.060	2.485	2.787	3.078	3.450
26	0.684	1.315	1.706	2.056	2.479	2.779	3.067	3.435
27	0.684	1.314	1.703	2.052	2.473	2.771	3.057	3.421
28	0.683	1.313	1.701	2.048	2.467	2.763	3.047	3.408
29	0.683	1.311	1.699	2.045	2.462	2.756	3.038	3.396
30	0.683	1.310	1.697	2.042	2.457	2.750	3.030	3.385
35	0.682	1.306	1.690	2.030	2.438	2.724	2.996	3.340
40	0.681	1.303	1.684	2.021	2.423	2.704	2.971	3.307
45	0.680	1.301	1.679	2.014	2.412	2.690	2.952	3.281
50	0.679	1.299	1.676	2.009	2.403	2.678	2.937	3.261
55	0.679	1.297	1.673	2.004	2.396	2.668	2.925	3.245
60	0.679	1.296	1.671	2.000	2.390	2.668	2.915	3.232
70	0.678	1.294	1.667	1.994	2.381	2.648	2.899	3.211

Continued

▼ **TABLE E**
Continued

	Level of Significance for a One-Tailed Test							
	.25	.10	.05	.025	.01	.005	.0025	.001
	Level of Significance for a Two-Tailed Test							
df	.50	.20	.10	.05	.02	.01	.005	.002
80	0.678	1.292	1.664	1.990	2.374	2.639	2.877	3.195
90	0.677	1.291	1.662	1.987	2.368	2.632	2.878	3.183
100	0.677	1.290	1.660	1.984	2.364	2.626	2.871	3.174
∞	.674	1.282	1.645	1.960	2.326	2.576	2.807	3.090

Source: Table E is taken from "Extended Tables of the Percentage Points of Student's *t*-Distribution," by E.T. Federighi, 1959, *Journal of the American Statistical Association, 54*, 683–688. It is reproduced by permission of the American Statistical Association.

▼ **TABLE F**

Critical Values of the *F* Distribution
Find the location of appropriate values in the table by looking up the degrees of freedom in the numerator and denominator of the *F* ratio. After you have decided on the level of significance desired, the obtained *F* ratio must be *greater* than that in the table. For example, with $p = .05$ and 9 *df* in the numerator and 28 in the denominator, your *F* value must be greater than 2.24 to be reliable.

df for Denominator	α	df for Numerator								
		1	2	3	4	5	6	7	8	9
3	.25	2.02	2.28	2.36	2.39	2.41	2.42	2.43	2.44	2.44
	.10	5.54	5.46	5.39	5.34	5.31	5.28	5.27	5.25	5.24
	.05	10.1	9.55	9.28	9.12	9.01	8.94	8.89	8.85	8.81
	.025	17.4	16.0	15.4	15.1	14.9	14.7	14.6	14.5	14.5
	.01	34.1	30.8	29.5	28.7	28.2	27.9	27.7	27.5	27.4
	.001	167	148	141	137	135	133	132	131	130
4	.25	1.81	2.00	2.05	2.06	2.07	2.08	2.08	2.08	2.08
	.10	4.54	4.32	4.19	4.11	4.05	4.01	3.98	3.95	3.94
	.05	7.71	6.94	6.59	6.39	6.26	6.16	6.09	6.04	6.00
	.025	12.2	10.6	9.98	9.60	9.36	9.20	9.07	8.98	8.90
	.01	21.2	18.0	16.7	16.0	15.5	15.2	15.0	14.8	14.7
	.001	74.1	61.2	56.2	53.4	51.7	50.5	49.7	49.0	48.5
5	.25	1.69	1.85	1.88	1.89	1.89	1.89	1.89	1.89	1.89
	.10	4.06	3.78	3.62	3.52	3.45	3.40	3.37	3.34	3.32
	.05	6.61	5.79	5.41	5.19	5.05	4.95	4.88	4.82	4.77
	.025	10.0	8.43	7.76	7.39	7.15	6.98	6.85	6.76	6.68
	.01	16.3	13.3	12.1	11.4	11.0	10.7	10.5	10.3	10.2
	.001	47.2	37.1	33.2	31.1	29.8	28.8	28.2	27.6	27.2

Continued

▼ **TABLE F**

Continued

df for Denominator	α	\multicolumn{9}{c}{df for Numerator}
		1	2	3	4	5	6	7	8	9
6	.25	1.62	1.76	1.78	1.79	1.79	1.78	1.78	1.78	1.77
	.10	3.78	3.46	3.29	3.18	3.11	3.05	3.01	2.98	2.96
	.05	5.99	5.14	4.76	4.53	4.39	4.28	4.21	4.15	4.10
	.025	8.81	7.26	6.60	6.23	5.99	5.82	5.70	5.60	5.52
	.01	13.8	10.9	9.78	9.15	8.75	8.47	8.26	8.10	7.98
	.001	35.5	27.0	23.7	21.9	20.8	20.0	19.5	19.0	18.7
7	.25	1.57	1.70	1.72	1.72	1.71	1.71	1.70	1.70	1.69
	.10	3.59	3.26	3.07	2.96	2.88	2.83	2.78	2.75	2.72
	.05	5.59	4.74	4.35	4.12	3.97	3.87	3.79	3.73	3.68
	.025	8.07	6.54	5.89	5.52	5.29	5.12	4.99	4.90	4.82
	.01	12.2	9.55	8.45	7.85	7.46	7.19	6.99	6.84	6.72
	.001	29.2	21.7	18.8	17.2	16.2	15.5	15.0	14.6	14.3
8	.25	1.54	1.66	1.67	1.66	1.66	1.65	1.64	1.64	1.63
	.10	3.46	3.11	2.92	2.81	2.73	2.67	2.62	2.59	2.56
	.05	5.32	4.46	4.07	3.84	3.69	3.58	3.50	3.44	3.39
	.025	7.57	6.06	5.42	5.05	4.82	4.65	4.53	4.43	4.36
	.01	11.3	8.65	7.59	7.01	6.63	6.37	6.18	6.03	5.91
	.001	25.4	18.5	15.8	14.4	13.5	12.9	12.4	12.0	11.8
9	.25	1.51	1.62	1.63	1.63	1.62	1.61	1.60	1.60	1.59
	.10	3.36	3.01	2.81	2.69	2.61	2.55	2.51	2.47	2.44
	.05	5.12	4.26	3.86	3.63	3.48	3.37	3.29	3.23	3.18
	.025	7.21	5.71	5.08	4.72	4.48	4.32	4.20	4.10	4.03
	.01	10.6	8.02	6.99	6.42	6.06	5.80	5.61	5.47	5.35
	.001	22.9	16.4	13.9	12.6	11.7	11.1	10.7	10.4	10.1
10	.25	1.49	1.60	1.60	1.59	1.59	1.58	1.57	1.56	1.56
	.10	3.29	2.92	2.73	2.61	2.52	2.46	2.41	2.38	2.35
	.05	4.96	4.10	3.71	3.48	3.33	3.22	3.14	3.07	3.02
	.025	6.94	5.46	4.83	4.47	4.24	4.07	3.95	3.85	3.78
	.01	10.0	7.56	6.55	5.99	5.64	5.39	5.20	5.06	4.94
	.001	21.0	14.9	12.6	11.3	10.5	9.92	9.52	9.20	8.96
11	.25	1.47	1.58	1.58	1.57	1.56	1.55	1.54	1.53	1.53
	.10	3.23	2.86	2.66	2.54	2.45	2.39	2.34	2.30	2.27
	.05	4.84	3.98	3.59	3.36	3.20	3.09	3.01	2.95	2.90
	.025	6.72	5.26	4.63	4.28	4.04	3.88	3.76	3.66	3.59
	.01	9.65	7.21	6.22	5.67	5.32	5.07	4.89	4.74	4.63
	.001	19.7	13.8	11.6	10.4	9.58	9.05	8.66	8.35	8.12
12	.25	1.46	1.56	1.56	1.55	1.54	1.53	1.52	1.51	1.51
	.10	3.18	2.81	2.61	2.48	2.39	2.33	2.28	2.24	2.21
	.05	4.75	3.89	3.49	3.26	3.11	3.00	2.91	2.85	2.80
	.025	6.55	5.10	4.47	4.12	3.89	3.73	3.61	3.51	3.44
	.01	9.33	6.93	5.95	5.41	5.06	4.82	4.64	4.50	4.39
	.001	18.6	13.0	10.8	9.63	8.89	8.38	8.00	7.71	7.48
	.25	1.45	1.55	1.55	1.53	1.52	1.51	1.50	1.49	1.49
	.10	3.14	2.76	2.56	2.43	2.35	2.28	2.23	2.20	2.16
	.05	4.67	3.81	3.41	3.18	3.03	2.92	2.83	2.77	2.71

Continued

▼ **TABLE F**

Continued

df for Denominator	α	\multicolumn{9}{c}{df for Numerator}
		1	2	3	4	5	6	7	8	9
13	.025	6.41	4.97	4.35	4.00	3.77	3.60	3.48	3.39	3.31
	.01	9.07	6.70	5.74	5.21	4.86	4.62	4.44	4.30	4.19
	.001	17.8	12.3	10.2	9.07	8.35	7.86	7.49	7.21	6.98
	.25	1.44	1.53	1.53	1.52	1.51	1.50	1.49	1.48	1.47
	.10	3.10	2.73	2.52	2.39	2.31	2.24	2.19	2.15	2.12
	.05	4.60	3.74	3.34	3.11	2.96	2.85	2.76	2.70	2.65
14	.025	6.30	4.86	4.24	3.89	3.66	3.50	3.38	3.29	3.21
	.01	8.86	6.51	5.56	5.04	4.69	4.46	4.28	4.14	4.03
	.001	17.1	11.8	9.73	8.62	7.92	7.43	7.08	6.80	6.58
	.25	1.43	1.52	1.52	1.51	1.49	1.48	1.47	1.46	1.46
	.10	3.07	2.70	2.49	2.36	2.27	2.21	2.16	2.12	2.09
	.05	4.54	3.68	3.29	3.06	2.90	2.79	2.71	2.64	2.59
15	.025	6.20	4.77	4.15	3.80	3.58	3.41	3.29	3.20	3.12
	.01	8.68	6.36	5.42	4.89	4.56	4.32	4.14	4.00	3.89
	.001	16.6	11.3	9.34	8.25	7.57	7.09	6.74	6.47	6.26
	.25	1.42	1.51	1.51	1.50	1.48	1.47	1.46	1.45	1.44
	.10	3.05	2.67	2.46	2.33	2.24	2.18	2.13	2.09	2.06
	.05	4.49	3.63	3.24	3.01	2.85	2.74	2.66	2.59	2.54
16	.025	6.12	4.69	4.08	3.73	3.50	3.34	3.22	3.12	3.05
	.01	8.53	6.23	5.29	4.77	4.44	4.20	4.03	3.89	3.78
	.001	16.1	11.00	9.00	7.94	7.27	6.81	6.46	6.19	5.98
	.25	1.42	1.51	1.50	1.49	1.47	1.46	1.45	1.44	1.43
	.10	3.03	2.64	2.44	2.31	2.22	2.15	2.10	2.06	2.03
	.05	4.45	3.59	3.20	2.96	2.81	2.70	2.61	2.55	2.49
17	.025	6.04	4.62	4.01	3.66	3.44	3.28	3.16	3.06	2.98
	.01	8.40	6.11	5.18	4.67	4.34	4.10	3.93	3.79	3.68
	.001	15.7	10.7	8.73	7.68	7.02	6.56	6.22	5.96	5.75
	.25	1.41	1.50	1.49	1.48	1.46	1.45	1.44	1.43	1.42
	.10	3.01	2.62	2.42	2.29	2.20	2.13	2.08	2.04	2.00
	.05	4.41	3.55	3.16	2.93	2.77	2.66	2.58	2.51	2.46
18	.025	5.98	4.56	3.95	3.61	3.38	3.22	3.10	3.01	2.93
	.01	8.29	6.01	5.09	4.58	4.25	4.01	3.84	3.71	3.60
	.001	15.4	10.4	8.49	7.46	6.81	6.35	6.02	5.76	5.56
	.25	1.41	1.49	1.49	1.47	1.46	1.44	1.43	1.42	1.41
	.10	2.99	2.61	2.40	2.27	2.18	2.11	2.06	2.02	1.98
19	.05	4.38	3.52	3.13	2.90	2.74	2.63	2.54	2.48	2.42
	.025	5.92	4.51	3.90	3.56	3.33	3.17	3.05	2.96	2.88
	.01	8.18	5.93	5.01	4.50	4.17	3.94	3.77	3.63	3.52
	.001	15.1	10.2	8.28	7.26	6.62	6.18	5.85	5.59	5.39
	.25	1.40	1.49	1.48	1.47	1.45	1.44	1.43	1.42	1.41
	.10	2.97	2.59	2.38	2.25	2.16	2.09	2.04	2.00	1.96
20	.05	4.35	3.49	3.10	2.87	2.71	2.60	2.51	2.45	2.39
	.025	5.87	4.46	3.86	3.51	3.29	3.13	3.01	2.91	2.84
	.01	8.10	5.85	4.94	4.43	4.10	3.87	3.70	3.56	3.46
	.001	14.8	9.95	8.10	7.10	6.46	6.02	5.69	5.44	5.24

Continued

▼ **TABLE F**

Continued

df for Denominator	α	1	2	3	4	5	6	7	8	9
					df for Numerator					
	.25	1.40	1.48	1.47	1.45	1.44	1.42	1.41	1.40	1.39
	.10	2.95	2.56	2.35	2.22	2.13	2.06	2.01	1.97	1.93
22	.05	4.30	3.44	3.05	2.82	2.66	2.55	2.46	2.40	2.34
	.025	5.79	4.38	3.78	3.44	3.22	3.05	2.93	2.84	2.76
	.01	7.95	5.72	4.82	4.31	3.99	3.76	3.59	3.45	3.35
	.001	14.4	9.61	7.80	6.81	6.19	5.76	5.44	5.19	4.99
	.25	1.39	1.47	1.46	1.44	1.43	1.41	1.40	1.39	1.38
	.10	2.93	2.54	2.33	2.19	2.10	2.04	1.98	1.94	1.91
24	.05	4.26	3.40	3.01	2.78	2.62	2.51	2.42	2.36	2.30
	.025	5.72	4.32	3.72	3.38	3.15	2.99	2.87	2.78	2.70
	.01	7.82	5.61	4.72	4.22	3.90	3.67	3.50	3.36	3.26
	.001	14.0	9.34	7.55	6.59	5.98	5.55	5.23	4.99	4.80
	.25	1.38	1.46	1.45	1.44	1.42	1.41	1.39	1.38	1.37
	.10	2.91	2.52	2.31	2.17	2.08	2.01	1.96	1.92	1.88
26	.05	4.23	3.37	2.98	2.74	2.59	2.47	2.39	2.32	2.27
	.025	5.66	4.27	3.67	3.33	3.10	2.94	2.82	2.73	2.65
	.01	7.72	5.53	4.64	4.14	3.82	3.59	3.42	3.29	3.18
	.001	13.7	9.12	7.36	6.41	5.80	5.38	5.07	4.83	4.64
	.25	1.38	1.46	1.45	1.43	1.41	1.40	1.39	1.38	1.37
	.10	2.89	2.50	2.29	2.16	2.06	2.00	1.94	1.90	1.87
28	.05	4.20	3.34	2.95	2.71	2.56	2.45	2.36	2.29	2.24
	.025	5.61	4.22	3.63	3.29	3.06	2.90	2.78	2.69	2.61
	.01	7.64	5.45	4.57	4.07	3.75	3.53	3.36	3.23	3.12
	.001	13.5	8.93	7.19	6.25	5.66	5.24	4.93	4.69	4.50
	.25	1.38	1.45	1.44	1.42	1.41	1.39	1.38	1.37	1.36
	.10	2.88	2.49	2.28	2.14	2.05	1.98	1.93	1.88	1.85
30	.05	4.17	3.32	2.92	2.69	2.53	2.42	2.33	2.27	2.21
	.025	5.57	4.18	3.59	3.25	3.03	2.87	2.75	2.65	2.57
	.01	7.56	5.39	4.51	4.02	3.70	3.47	3.30	3.17	3.07
	.001	13.3	8.77	7.05	6.12	5.53	5.12	4.82	4.58	4.39
	.25	1.36	1.44	1.42	1.40	1.39	1.37	1.36	1.35	1.34
	.10	2.84	2.44	2.23	2.09	2.00	1.93	1.87	1.83	1.79
40	.05	4.08	3.23	2.84	2.61	2.45	2.34	2.25	2.18	2.12
	.025	5.42	4.05	3.46	3.13	2.90	2.74	2.62	2.53	2.45
	.01	7.31	5.18	4.31	3.83	3.51	3.29	3.12	2.99	2.89
	.001	12.6	8.25	6.60	5.70	5.13	4.73	4.44	4.21	4.02
	.25	1.35	1.42	1.41	1.38	1.37	1.35	1.33	1.32	1.31
	.10	2.79	2.39	2.18	2.04	1.95	1.87	1.82	1.77	1.74
60	.05	4.00	3.15	2.76	2.53	2.37	2.25	2.17	2.10	2.04
	.025	5.29	3.93	3.34	3.01	2.79	2.63	2.51	2.41	2.33
	.01	7.08	4.98	4.13	3.65	3.34	3.12	2.95	2.82	2.72
	.001	12.0	7.76	6.17	5.31	4.76	4.37	4.09	3.87	3.69
	.25	1.34	1.40	1.39	1.37	1.35	1.33	1.31	1.30	1.29
	.10	2.75	2.35	2.13	1.99	1.90	1.82	1.77	1.72	1.68
120	.05	3.92	3.07	2.68	2.45	2.29	2.17	2.09	2.02	1.96
	.025	5.15	3.80	3.23	2.89	2.67	2.52	2.39	2.30	2.22

Continued

▼ **TABLE F**

Continued

df for Denominator	α	\multicolumn{9}{c}{df for Numerator}
		1	2	3	4	5	6	7	8	9
	.01	6.85	4.79	3.95	3.48	3.17	2.96	2.79	2.66	2.56
	.001	11.4	7.32	5.79	4.95	4.42	4.04	3.77	3.55	3.38
	.25	1.32	1.39	1.37	1.35	1.33	1.31	1.29	1.28	1.27
	.10	2.71	2.30	2.08	1.94	1.85	1.77	1.72	1.67	1.63
∞	.05	3.84	3.00	2.60	2.37	2.21	2.10	2.01	1.94	1.88
	.025	5.02	3.69	3.12	2.79	2.57	2.41	2.29	2.19	2.11
	.01	6.63	4.61	3.78	3.32	3.02	2.80	2.64	2.51	2.41
	.001	10.8	6.91	5.42	4.62	4.10	3.74	3.47	3.27	3.10

Source: Adapted and abridged from *Biometrika Tables for Statisticians, 2nd ed., vol. 1* (Table 18), edited by E. S. Pearson and H. O. Hartley, 1958, New York: Cambridge University Press. With permission of the *Biometrika* trustees.

▼ **TABLE G**

Critical Values of the χ^2 Distribution
Find the critical value by entering the table with the number of degrees of freedom [(# Rows − 1) (# Columns − 1)]. A significant χ^2 must equal or exceed the value for a given significance level. For example, with $p = .05$ and $df = 9$, χ^2 must be greater than or equal to 16.92.

df	p = .10	p = .05	p = .01
1	2.71	3.84	6.63
2	4.62	5.99	9.21
3	6.25	7.82	11.35
4	7.78	9.49	13.28
5	9.24	11.07	15.09
6	10.64	12.59	16.81
7	12.02	14.07	18.48
8	13.36	15.51	20.09
9	14.68	16.92	21.66
10	15.99	18.31	23.21
11	17.28	19.68	24.72
12	18.55	21.03	26.21
13	19.81	22.36	27.69
14	21.06	23.69	29.14
15	22.31	25.00	30.58
16	23.54	26.30	32.00
17	24.77	27.59	33.41
18	25.99	28.87	34.81
19	27.20	30.14	36.19
20	28.41	31.41	37.56
21	29.62	32.67	38.92
22	30.81	33.93	40.29
23	32.01	35.17	41.64
24	33.20	36.42	42.98
25	34.38	37.65	44.32

Source: Abridged from table in *Fundamental Statistics for the Behavioral Sciences* (3rd ed.), by D. C. Howell, 1995, Belmont, CA: Duxbury.

▼ TABLE H

Random Numbers

	1	2	3	4	5	6	7	8	9
1	32942	95416	42339	59045	26693	49057	87496	20624	14819
2	07410	99859	83828	21409	29094	65114	36701	25762	12827
3	59981	68155	45673	76210	58219	45738	29550	24736	09574
4	46251	25437	69654	99716	11563	08803	86027	51867	12116
5	65558	51904	93123	27887	53138	21488	09095	78777	71240
6	99187	19258	86421	16401	19397	83297	40111	49326	81686
7	35641	00301	16096	34775	21562	97983	45040	19200	16383
8	14031	00936	81518	48440	02218	04756	19506	60695	88494
9	60677	15076	92554	26042	23472	69869	62877	19584	39576
10	66314	05212	67859	89356	20056	30648	87349	20389	53805
11	20416	87410	75646	64176	82752	63606	37011	57346	69512
12	28701	56992	70423	62415	40807	98086	58850	28968	45297
13	74579	33844	33426	07570	00728	07079	19322	56325	84819
14	62615	52342	82968	75540	80045	53069	20665	21282	07768
15	93945	06293	22879	08161	01442	75071	21427	94842	26210
16	75689	76131	96837	67450	44511	50424	82848	41975	71663
17	02921	16919	35424	93209	52133	87327	95897	65171	20376
18	14295	34969	14216	03191	61647	30296	66667	10101	63203
19	05303	91109	82403	40312	62191	67023	90073	83205	71344
20	57071	90357	12901	08899	91039	67251	28701	03846	94589
21	78471	57741	13599	84390	32146	00871	09354	22745	65806
22	89242	79337	59293	47481	07740	43345	25716	70020	54005
23	14955	59592	97035	80430	87220	06392	79028	57123	52872
24	42446	41880	37415	47472	04513	49494	08860	08038	43624
25	18534	22346	54556	17558	73689	14894	05030	19561	56517
26	39284	33737	42512	86411	23753	29690	26096	81361	93099
27	33922	37329	89911	55876	28379	81031	22058	21487	54613
28	78355	54013	50774	30666	61205	42574	47773	36027	27174
29	08845	99145	94316	88974	29828	97069	90327	61842	29604
30	01769	71825	55957	98271	02784	66731	40311	88495	18821
31	17639	38284	59478	90409	21997	56199	30068	82800	69692
32	05851	58653	99949	63505	40409	85551	90729	64938	52403
33	42396	40112	11469	03476	03328	84238	26570	51790	42122
34	13318	14192	98167	75631	74141	22369	36757	89117	54998
35	60571	54786	26281	01855	30706	66578	32019	65884	58485
36	09531	81853	59334	70929	03544	18510	89541	13555	21168
37	72865	16829	86542	00396	20363	13010	69645	49608	54738
38	56324	31093	77924	28622	83543	28912	15059	80192	83964
39	78192	21626	91399	07235	07104	73652	64425	85149	75409
40	64666	34767	97298	92708	01994	53188	78476	07804	62404
41	82201	75694	02808	65983	74373	66693	13094	74183	73020
42	15360	73776	40914	85190	54278	99054	62944	47351	89098
43	68142	67957	70896	37983	20487	95350	16371	03426	13895
44	19138	31200	30616	14639	44406	44236	57360	81644	94761
45	28155	03521	36415	78452	92359	81091	56513	88321	97910
46	87971	29031	51780	27376	81056	86155	55488	50590	74514
47	58147	68841	53625	02059	75223	16783	19272	61994	71090
48	18875	52809	70594	41649	32935	26430	82096	01605	65846
49	75109	56474	74111	31966	29969	70093	98901	84550	25769
50	35983	03742	76822	12073	59463	84420	15868	99505	11426
51	12651	61644	11769	75109	86996	97669	25757	32535	07122

Continued

▼ **TABLE H**

Continued

	1	2	3	4	5	6	7	8	9
52	81769	74436	02630	72310	45049	18029	07469	42341	98173
53	36737	98863	77240	76251	00654	64688	09343	70278	67331
54	82861	54371	76610	94934	72748	44124	05610	53750	95938
55	21325	15732	24127	37431	09723	63529	73977	95218	96074
56	74146	47887	62463	23045	41490	07954	22597	60012	98866
57	90759	64410	54179	66075	61051	75385	51378	08360	95946
58	55683	98078	02238	91540	21219	17720	87817	41705	95785
59	79686	17969	76061	83748	55920	83612	41540	86492	06447
60	70333	00201	86201	69716	78185	62154	77930	67663	29529
61	14042	53536	07779	04157	41172	36473	42123	43929	50533
62	59911	08256	06596	48416	69770	68797	56080	14223	59199
63	62368	62623	62742	14891	39247	52242	98832	69533	91174
64	57529	97751	54976	48957	74599	08759	78494	52785	68526
65	15469	90574	78033	66885	13936	42117	71831	22961	94225
66	18625	23674	53850	32827	81647	80820	00420	63555	74489
67	74626	68394	88562	70745	23701	45630	65891	58220	35442
68	11119	16519	27384	90199	79210	76965	99546	30323	31664
69	41101	17336	48951	53674	17880	45260	08575	49321	36191
70	32123	91576	84221	78902	82010	30847	62329	63898	23268
71	26091	68409	69704	82267	14751	13151	93115	01437	56945
72	67680	79790	48462	59278	44185	29616	76531	19589	83139
73	15184	19260	14073	07026	25264	08388	27182	22557	61501
74	58010	45039	57181	10238	36874	28546	37444	80824	63981
75	56425	53996	86245	32623	78858	08143	60377	42925	42815
76	82630	84066	13592	60642	17904	99718	63432	88642	37858
77	14927	40909	23900	48761	44860	92467	31742	87142	03607
78	23740	22505	07489	85986	74420	21744	97711	36648	35620
79	32990	97446	03711	63824	07953	85965	87089	11687	92414
80	05310	24058	91946	78437	34365	82469	12430	84754	19354
81	21839	39937	27534	88913	49055	19218	47712	67677	51889
82	08833	42549	93981	94051	28382	83725	72643	64233	97252
83	58336	11139	47479	00931	91560	95372	97642	33856	54825
84	62032	91144	75478	47431	52726	30289	42411	91886	51818
85	45171	30557	53116	04118	58301	24375	65609	85810	18620
86	91611	62656	60128	35609	63698	78356	50682	22505	01692
87	55472	63819	86314	49174	93582	73604	78614	78849	23096
88	18573	09729	74091	53994	10970	86557	65661	41854	26037
89	60866	02955	90288	82136	83644	94455	06560	78029	98768
90	45043	55608	82767	60890	74646	79485	13619	98868	40857
91	17831	09737	79473	75945	28394	79334	70577	38048	03607
92	40137	03981	07585	18128	11178	32601	27994	05641	22600
93	77776	31343	14576	97706	16039	47517	43300	59080	80392
94	69605	44104	40103	95635	05635	81673	68657	09559	23510
95	19916	52934	26499	09821	87331	80993	61299	36979	73599
96	02606	58552	07678	56619	65325	30705	99582	53390	46357
97	65183	73160	87131	35530	47946	09854	18080	02321	05809
98	10740	98914	44916	11322	89717	88189	30143	52687	19420
99	98642	89822	71691	51573	83666	61642	46683	33761	47542
100	60139	25601	93663	25547	02654	94829	48672	28736	84994

REFERENCES

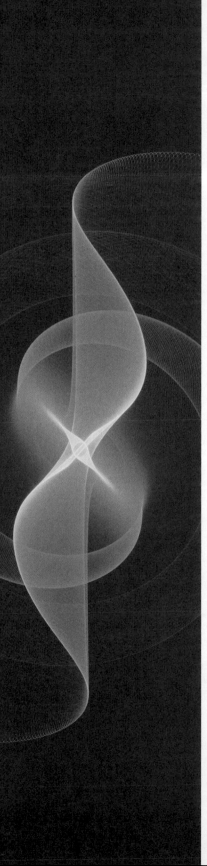

Adams, J. A. (1972). Research and the future of engineering psychology. *American Psychologist, 27,* 615–622.

Adamson, R. E. (1952). Functional fixedness as related to problem solving: A repetition of three experiments. *Journal of Experimental Psychology, 44,* 288–291.

Adler, R. (2001). Psychoneuroimmunology. *Current Directions in Psychological Science, 10,* 94–98.

Ader, R., & Cohen, N. (1982). Behaviorally conditioned immunosuppression and murine systemic lupus erythematosus. *Science, 215,* 1534–1536.

Adler, S. A., Gerhardstein, P., & Rovee-Collier, C. (1998). Levels-of-processing effects in infant memory? *Child Development, 69,* 280–294.

Ahn, W., & Graham, L. M. (1999). The impact of necessity and sufficiency in the Wason four-card selection task. *Psychological Science, 10,* 237–242.

American Psychological Association. (1987). *Case-book on ethical issues.* Washington, DC: Author.

American Psychological Association. (2001). *Publication manual of the American Psychological Association* (5th Ed.). Washington DC: Author.

American Psychological Association. (2002). *Ethical principles of psychologists and code of conduct 2002.* Retrieved March 21, 2003, from http://www.apa.org/ethics/code2002.html.

American Psychological Association. (2003a). *Guidelines for ethical conduct in the care and use of animals.* Retrieved March 21, 2003, from http://www.apa.org/science/anguide.html.

American Psychological Association. (2003b). *Research with animals in psychology.* Retrieved March 21, 2003, from http://www.apa.org/science/animal2.html.

Amodio, D. M., Harmon-Jones, E., & Devine, P. (2003). Individual differences in the activation and control of affective race bias as assessed by startle eye-blink response and self-report. *Journal of Personality & Social Psychology, 84,* 738–753.

Amsel, A. (1994). Précis of frustration theory: An analysis of dispositional learning and memory. *Psychonomic Bulletin & Review, 1,* 280–296.

Angell, J. R. (1907). The province of functional psychology. *Psychological Review, 14,* 61–91.

Arnold, D. H., Fisher, P. H., Doctoroff, G. L., & Dobbs, J. (2002). Accelerating math development in Head Start classrooms. *Journal of Educational Psychology, 94,* 762-770.

Asch, S. E. (1951).   Effect of group pressure upon the modification and distortion of judgment. In H. Guetzknow (Ed.), *Groups, leadership, and men* (pp. 117-190). Pittsburgh: Carnegie.

Asch, S. E. (1956).   Studies of independence and conformity: I.A minority of one against a unanimous majority. *Psychological Monographs, 70,* 9 (Whole No. 416).

Asch, S. E. (1958).   Effects of group pressure upon the modification and distortion of judgments. In E. E. Maccoby, T. M. Newcomb, & E. L. Hartley (Eds.), *Readings in social psychology* (3rd ed., pp. 174-183). New York: Holt.

Baker, T. (2006, November).   Dr. Ambati is youngest volunteer surgeon in flying eye hospital's history. *MSG Science/Medical News.* Medical College of Georgia. Retrieved July 20, 2007, from http://www.mcg.edu/news/2006NewsRel/Ambati091806.html.

Balota, D. A., & Cortese, M. J. (2000).   Theories in cognitive psychology. In A. Kazdin (Ed.), *The encyclopedia of psychology.* Washington, DC: American Psychological Association.

Barber, T. X. (1976).   *Pitfalls in human research: Ten pivotal points.* New York: Pergamon.

Barber, T. X., & Silver, M. J. (1968).   Fact, fiction, and the experimenter bias effect. *Psychological Bulletin Monograph Supplement, 70* (6, pt. 2), 1-29.

Barker, R. G. (1968).   *Ecological psychology.* Stanford, CA: Stanford University Press.

Barker, R. G., & Wright, H. F. (1951).   *One boy's day.* New York: Harper and Row.

Baron, R. A., & Bell, P. A. (1976).   Aggression and heat: The influence of ambient temperature, negative affect, and a cooling drink on physical aggression. *Journal of Personality and Social Psychology, 33,* 245-255.

Bartoshuk, L. M. (2000).   Comparing sensory experiences across individuals: Recent psychophysical advances illuminate genetic variation in taste perception. *Chemical Senses, 25,* 447-460.

Bateson, J. E. G., & Hui, M. K. (1992).   The ecological validity of photographic slides and videotapes in simulating the service setting. *Journal of Consumer Research, 19,* 271-281.

Baumrind, D. (1964).   Some thoughts on ethics of research: After reading Milgram's "Behavioral study of obedience." *American Psychologist, 19,* 421-423.

Beck, S. B. (1963).   Eyelid conditioning as a function of CS intensity, UCS intensity, and Manifest Anxiety Scale score. *Journal of Experimental Psychology, 66,* 429-438.

Bem, D. J. (2004).   Writing the empirical journal article. In J. M. Darley, M. P. Zanna, & H. L. Roediger III (Eds.), *The Compleat Academic* (pp. 185-219). Washington DC: American Psychological Association.

Benjamin, L. T. (1997).   *A history of psychology: Original sources and contemporary research.* New York, McGraw-Hill.

Bevan, W. (1980).   On getting in bed with a lion. *American Psychologist, 35,* 779-789.

Bhalla, M., & Proffitt, D. R. (1999).   Visual-motor recalibration in geographical slant perception. *Journal of Experimental Psychology: Human Perception and Performance, 25,* 1076-1096.

Blaney, R. H. (1986).   Affect and memory: A review. *Psychological Bulletin, 99,* 229-246.

Blass, T. (1999).   The Milgram paradigm after 35 years: Some things we now know about obedience to authority. *Journal of Applied Social Psychology, 29,* 955-978.

Blass, T. (2002).   *Obedience to authority: Current perspectives on the Milgram paradigm.* Mahwah, NJ: Lawrence Erlbaum Associates.

Blaxton, T. A. (1989).   Investigating dissociations among memory measures: Support for a transfer appropriate processing framework. *Journal of Experimental Psychology: Learning, Memory, and Cognition, 15,* 657-668.

Blough, D. S. (1958).   A method for obtaining psychophysical thresholds from pigeons. *Journal of the Experimental Analysis of Behavior, 1,* 31-43.

Blough, D. S. (1961).   Experiments in animal psychophysics. *Scientific American, 205,* 32.

Blum, D. (2002).   *Love at Goon Park: Harry Harlow and the science of affection* (pp. 113-290). New York: Berkley.

Boneau, C. A. (1998).   Hermann Ebbinghaus: On the road to progress or down the garden path? In M. Wertheimer (Ed.), *Portraits of pioneers in psychology,* (Vol. 3, pp. 51-64). Washington, DC: American Psychological Association.

Boring, E. G. (1950).   A history of experimental psychology. New York: Appleton-Century-Crofts.

Boroditsky, L. (2000).   Metaphoric structuring: Understanding time through spatial metaphors. *Cognition, 75,* 1-28.

Boroditsky, L., & Ramscar, M. (2002).   The roles of body and mind in abstract thought. *Psychological Science, 13,* 185-189.

Bornstein, M. H., & Sigman, M. D. (1986).   Continuity in mental development from infancy. *Child Development, 57,* 251-274.

Bowd, A. D. (1980).   Ethical reservations about psychological research with animals. *Psychological Record, 30,* 201-210.

Bower, G. (1961).   A contrast effect in differential conditioning. *Journal of Experimental Psychology, 62,* 196-199.

Bramel, D., & Friend, R. (1981).   Hawthorne, the myth of the docile worker, and class bias in psychology. *American Psychologist, 36,* 867-878.

Brannigan, A., & Zwerman, W. (2001).   The real "Hawthorne effect." *Society,* Jan/Feb, 55-60.

Breitmayer, B. J., & Ramey, C. T. (1986).   Biological nonoptimality and quality of postnatal environment as codeterminants of intellectual development. *Child Development, 57,* 1151-1165.

Brickner, M. A., Harkins, S. G., & Ostrom, T. M. (1986). Effects of personal involvement: Thought-provoking implications for social loafing. *Journal of Personality and Social Psychology, 51,* 763–769.

Bridgeman, B., McCamley-Jenkins, L., & Ervin, N. (2000). *Predictions of freshman grade-point average from the revised and recentered SAT1: Reasoning test.* (College Board Research Report No. 2000-1). New York: College Entrance Examination Board.

Bridgman, P. W. (1945). Some general principles of operational analysis. *Psychological Review, 52,* 246–249.

Broad, W., & Wade, M. (1982). *Betrayers of the truth: Fraud and deceit in the halls of science.* New York: Simon and Schuster.

Broadbent, D. E. (1971). *Decision and stress.* New York: Academic Press.

Bronzaft, A. L. (1993). Architects, engineers and planners as anti-noise advocates. *Journal of Architectural and Planning Research, 10,* 146–159.

Brown, J. (1958). Some tests of the decay theory of immediate memory. *Quarterly Journal of Experimental Psychology, 10,* 12–21.

Brown, R. (1962). Models of attitude change. In R. Brown, E. Galanter, E. H. Hess, & G. Mandler (Eds.), *New directions in psychology* (Vol. 1, pp. 1–85). New York: Holt, Rinehart, and Winston.

Brown, R., & Kulik, J. (1977). Flashbulb memories. *Cognition, 5,* 73–79.

Bryant, R. A., & Barnier, A. J. (1999). Eliciting autobiographical pseudomemories: The relevance of hypnosis, hypnotizability, and attributions. *International Journal of Clinical & Experimental Hypnosis, 47,* 267–283.

Buckner, R. L., & Tulving, E. (1995). Neuroimaging studies of memory: Theory and recent PET findings. In F. Boller & J. Grafman (Eds.), Handbook of neuropsychology (Vol. 10, pp. 439–466). Amsterdam: Elsevier.

Bulgren, J. A., Deshler, D. D., Schumaker, J. B., & Lenz, B. K. (2000). The use and effectiveness of analogical instruction in diverse secondary content classrooms. *Journal of Educational Psychology, 92,* 426–441.

Bullinger, H. J., & Dangelmaier, M. (2003). Virtual prototyping and testing of in-vehicle interfaces. *Ergonomics, 46,* 1-3, 41–51.

Bushman, B. J., & Huesmann, L. R. (2006). Short-term and long-term effects of violent media on aggression in children and adults. *Archives of Pediatrics and Adolescent Medicine, 160,* 348–352.

Bushman, B. J., Ridge, R. D., Da, E., Key, C. W., & Busath, G. L. (2007). When God sanctions killing. *Psychological Science, 18,* 204–207.

Buss, D. M., & Schmitt, D. P. (1993). Sexual strategies theory: An evolutionary perspective on human mating. *Psychological Review, 100,* 204–232.

Butters, N., & Cermak, L. S. (1986). A case study of the forgetting of autobiographical knowledge: Implications for the study of retrograde amnesia. In D. Rubin (Ed.), *Autobiographical memory* (pp. 253–272). New York: Cambridge University Press.

Calhoun, J. B. (1962). Population density and social pathology. *Scientific American, 206,* 139–148.

Calhoun, J. B. (1966). The role of space in animal sociology. *Journal of Social Issues, 22,* 46–58.

Calhoun, J. B. (1971). Space and the strategy of life. In A. H. Esser (Ed.), *Behavior and environment. The use of space by animals and men* (pp. 329–387). New-York: Plenum.

Campbell, D. T., & Erlebacher, A. (1970a). How regression artifacts in quasi-experimental evaluations can mistakenly make compensatory education look harmful. In J. Helmuth (Ed.), *Compensatory education: A national debate: Vol. 3, Disadvantaged child.* (pp. 185–210). New York: Brunner/Mazel.

Campbell, D. T., & Erlbacher, A. (1970b). Reply to the replies. In J. Helmuth (Ed.), *Compensatory education: A national debate: Vol. 3, Disadvantaged child* (pp. 221–225). New York: Brunner/Mazel.

Campbell, D. T., & Stanley, J. C. (1966). *Experimental and quasi-experimental designs for research.* Chicago: Rand McNally.

Capaldi, E. J. (1964). Effect of N-length, number of different N-lengths, and number of reinforcements on resistance to extinction. *Journal of Experimental Psychology, 68,* 230–239.

Capaldi, E. J. (1994). The sequential view: From rapidly fading stimulus traces to the organization of memory and the abstract concept of number. *Psychonomic Bulletin & Review, 1,* 156–181.

Carnevale, P. J., & Probst, T. M. (1998). Social values and social conflict in creative problem-solving and categorization. *Journal of Personality and Social Psychology, 74,* 1300–1309.

Carter, L. F. (1941). Intensity of conditioned stimulus and rate of conditioning. *Journal of Experimental Psychology, 28,* 481–490.

Cermak, L. S., & Craik, F. I. M. (Eds.). (1979). *Levels of processing in human memory.* Hillsdale, NJ: Erlbaum.

Cermak, L. S., & Reale, L. (1978). Depth of processing and retention of words by alcoholic Korsakoff patients. *Journal of Experimental Psychology: Human Learning and Memory, 4,* 165–174.

Cheesman, J., & Merikle, P. M. (1984). Priming with and without awareness. *Perception & Psychophysics, 36,* 387–395.

Cheesman, J., & Merikle, P. M. (1986). Distinguishing conscious from unconscious perception. *Canadian Journal of Psychology, 40,* 343–367.

Chekroun, P., & Brauer, M. (2002). The bystander effect and social control behavior: The effect of the presence of others on people's reactions to norm violations. *European Journal of Social Psychology, 32,* 853–866.

Childress, M. E., Hart, S. G., & Bortolussi, M. R. (1982). The reliability and validity of flight task workload ratings. *Proceedings of the Human Factors Society, 26,* 319-323.

Chomsky, N. (1959). A review of Skinner's Verbal Behavior. *Language, 35,* 26-58.

Churchland, P. M., & Churchland, P. S. (1990). Could a machine think? *Scientific American,* (January) 32-37.

Cicirelli, V. G. (1970). The relevance of the regression artifact problem to the Westinghouse-Ohio evaluation of Head Start. A reply to Campbell and Eriebacher. In J. Helmuth (Ed.), *Compensatory education: A national debate: Vol. 3, Disadvantaged child* (pp. 211-215). New York: Brunner/Mazel.

Cicirelli, V., & Granger, R. (1969, June). *The impact of Head Start: An evaluation of the effects of Head Start on children's cognitive and affective development.* A report presented to the Office of Economic Opportunity pursuant to Contract B89-4356. Westinghouse Learning Corporation, Ohio University. (Distributed by Clearinghouse for Federal Scientific and Technical Information, U.S. Department of Commerce, National Bureau of Standards, Institute of Applied Technology, PB 184-328.)

Clark, H. H. (1973). The language-as-fixed effect fallacy: A critique of language statistics in psychological research. *Journal of Verbal Learning and Verbal Behavior, 12,* 335-359.

Clark, W. C. (1969). Sensory-decision theory analysis of the placebo effect on the criterion for pain and thermal sensitivity (d'). *Journal of Abnormal Psychology, 74,* 363-371.

Clark, W. C., & Yang, J. C. (1974). Acupunctural analgesia: Evaluation by signal detection theory. *Science, 184,* 1096-1098.

Cohen, S., Glass, D. C., & Singer, J. E. (1973). Apartment noise, auditory discrimination and reading ability in children. *Journal of Experimental Social Psychology, 9,* 407-422.

Colom, R., Jung, R. E., & Haier, R. J. (2006). Finding the g-factor in brain structure using the method of correlated vectors. *Intelligence, 34,* 561-570.

Cook, T. D., & Campbell, D. T. (1979). *Quasi-experimentation: Design and analysis issues for field-settings.* Chicago: Rand McNally.

Coren, S., Ward, L. M., & Enns, J. T. (1994). *Sensation and perception.* Fort Worth: Harcourt Brace.

Cornsweet, T. N. (1962). The staircase method in psychophysics. *American Journal of Psychology, 75,* 485-491.

Correll, J., Park, B., Judd, C. M., & Wittenbrink, B. (2002). The police officer's dilemma: Using ethnicity to disambiguate potentially threatening individuals. *Journal of Personality & Social Psychology, 83,* 1314-1329.

Corrigan, P. W., Holmens, E. P., Luchins, D., Buican, B., Basit, A., & Parks, J. J. (1994). Staff burnout in a psychiatric hospital: A cross-lagged panel design. *Journal of Organizational Behavior, 15,* 65-74.

Cowey, A. (1995). Blindsight in monkeys. *Nature, 373,* 247-249.

Cox, J. R., & Griggs, R. A. (1982). The effects of experience on performance in Wason's selection task. *Memory & Cognition, 10,* 496-502.

Craik, F. I. M. (1977). Age differences in human memory. In J. E. Birren & W. Schaie (Eds.), *Handbook of the psychology of aging.* New York: Van Nostrand Reinhold.

Craik, F. I. M., & Lockhart, R. S. (1972). Levels of processing: A framework for memory research. *Journal of Verbal Learning and Verbal Behavior, 11,* 671-684.

Craik, F. I. M., & Tulving, E. (1975). Depth of processing and the retention of words in episodic memory. *Journal of Experimental Psychology: General, 104,* 671-684.

Cutler, B. L., & Penrod, S. D. (1989). Forensically relevant moderators of the relation between eyewitness identification accuracy and confidence. *Journal of Applied Psychology, 74,* 650-652.

D'Amato, M. R. (1970). *Experimental psychology: Methodology, psychophysics, and learning.* New York: McGraw-Hill.

Darley, J. M., & Latané, B. (1968). Bystander intervention in emergencies: Diffusion of responsibility. *Journal of Personality and Social Psychology, 8,* 377-383.

DeGreene, K. B. (Ed.). (1970). *Systems psychology.* New York: McGraw-Hill.

Devine, P. G., & Elliot, A. J. (1995). Are racial stereotypes really fading? The Princeton trilogy revisited. *Personality and Social Psychology Bulletin, 21,* 1139-1150.

Dewar, R. E., Kline, D. W., & Swanson, H. A. (1994). Age differences in the comprehension of traffic sign symbols. *Transportation Research Board 73rd Annual Meeting* (Paper No. 940979). Washington, DC: Transportation Research Board.

Dewey, J. (1896). The reflex arc concept in psychology. *Psychological Review, 3,* 357-370.

Doll, R. (1955). Etiology of lung cancer. *Advances in Cancer Research, 3,* 1-50.

Donders, F. C. (1868/1969). Over de snelheidvan psychische processes. (On the speed of mental processes.) (w. Koster, Trans.). In W.G. Koster, *Attention and performance II* (pp. 412-431). Amsterdam: North Holland.

Duncan, J. (2003). Intelligence tests predict brain response to demanding task events. *Nature Neuroscience, 6,* 207-208.

Duncan, J., Seitz, R. J., Kolodny, J., Bor, D., Herzog, H., Ahmed, A., et al. (2000). A neural basis for general intelligence. *Science, 289,* 457-460.

Duncker, K. (1945). On problem solving. *Psychological Monographs, 58,* 1-112. (Whole No. 270).

Dunn, J. (1998). Implicit memory and amnesia. In K. Kirsner & C. Speelman (Eds.), *Implicit and explicit mental processes* (pp. 99-117). Mahwah, NJ: Erlbaum.

Dweck, C. S. (1999). *Self-theories: Their role in motivation, personality, and development.* Philadelphia: Psychology Press.

Dweck, C. S., & Bempechat, J. (1983). Children's theories of intelligence: Consequences for learning. In S. G. Paris, G. M. Olson, & H. W. Stevenson (Eds.), *Learning and motivation in the classroom* (pp. 239-256). Hillsdale, NJ: Erlbaum.

Dweck, C. S., & Elliott, E. S. (1983). Achievement motivation. In E. M. Hetherington (Ed.), *Handbook of child psychology: Vol. 4, Socialization, personality, and development.* New York: Wiley.

Dweck, C., Mangels, J., & Good, C. (2004). Motivational effects on attention, cognition, and performance. In D. Y. Dai & R. J. Sternberg (Eds.), *Motivation, emotion, and cognition: Integrative perspectives on intellectual functioning and development* (pp. 41-55). Mahwah, NJ: Erlbaum.

Eagly, A. H., & Wood, W. (1999). The origins of sex differences in human behavior: Evolved dispositions versus social roles. *American Psychologist, 54,* 408-423.

Ebbinghaus, H. (1885/1913). *Memory: A contribution to experimental psychology.* New York: Columbia University Press. (Reprinted by Dover, 1964)

Edwards, A. C. (2003). Response to the spiritual intelligence debate: Are some conceptual distinctions needed here? *International Journal for the Psychology of Religion, 13,* 49-52.

Eibl-Eibesfeldt, I. (1970). *Ethology: The biology of behavior.* New York: Holt, Rinehart & Winston.

Eibl-Eibesfeldt, I. (1972). Similarities and differences between cultures in expressive movements. In R. A. Hinde (Ed.), *Non-verbal communication* (pp. 297-312). Cambridge: Cambridge University Press.

Ellsworth, J., & Ames, L. (1998). *Critical perspectives on Project Head Start: Revisioning the hope and challenge.* Albany, NY: State University of New York Press.

Elmes, D. G., Chapman, P. F., & Selig, C. W. (1984). Role of mood and connotation in the spacing effect. *Bulletin of the Psychonomic Society, 22,* 186-188.

Elmes, D. G., Kantowitz, B. H., & Roediger, H. L. (1992). *Research methods in psychology* (4th Ed.). St. Paul: West.

Elmes, D. G., Kantowitz, B. H., & Roediger, H. L. (2006). *Research methods in psychology* (8th Ed.). Belmont, CA: Wadsworth Thomson Learning.

Emmons, R. A. (2000). Is spirituality an intelligence? Motivation, cognition, and the psychology of ultimate concern. *International Journal for the Psychology of Religion, 10,* 3-26.

Engle, R. W. (2002). Working memory capacity as executive attention. *Current Directions in Psychology, 11,* 19-23.

Engle, R., Tuholski, S. W., Laughlin, J. E., & Conway, A. R. A. (1999). Working memory, short-term memory, and general fluid intelligence: A latent-variable approach. *Journal of Experimental Psychology: General, 128,* 309-331.

Ericsson, K. A., & Simon, H. A. (1979). Verbal reports as data. *Psychological Review, 87,* 215-251.

Ericsson, K. A., Krampe, R., & Tesch-Romer, C. (1993). The role of deliberate practice in the acquisition of expert performance. *Psychological Review, 100,* 363-406.

Eriksen, C. W. (1960). Discrimination and learning without awareness: A methodological survey and evaluation. *Psychological Review, 67,* 279-300.

Eron, L. D. (1982). Parent-child interaction, television violence, and aggression in children. *American Psychologist, 37,* 197-211.

Eron, L. D., Huesmann, L. R., Lefkowitz, M. M., & Walder, L. O. (1972). Does television violence cause aggression? *American Psychologist, 27,* 253-263.

Evans, G. W., Palsane, M. N., Lepore, S. J., & Martin, J. (1989). Residential density and psychological health: The mediating effects of social support. *Journal of Personality and Social Psychology, 57,* 994-999.

Evans, G. W., & Wener, R. E. (2007). Crowding and personal space invasion on the train: Please don't make me sit in the middle. *Journal of Environmental Psychology, 27,* 90-94.

Evans, J. W., & Schiller, J. (1970). How preoccupation with possible regression artifacts can lead to a faulty strategy for the evaluation of social action programs: A reply to Campbell and Erlebacher. In J. Helmuth (Ed.), *Compensatory education: A national debate: Vol. 3, Disadvantaged child* (pp. 216-220). New York: Brunner/Mazel.

Eveland, W. P., Seo, M., & Marton, K. (2002). Learning from the news in campaign 2000: An experimental comparison of TV news, newspapers, and online news. *Media Psychology, 4,* 353-378.

Eysenck, H. J., & Eaves, L. J. (1981). *The cause and effects of smoking.* New York: Gage.

Farah, M. J. (1990). *Visual agnosia.* Cambridge, MA: The MIT Press.

Farmer, C. M. (1995). *Effectiveness estimates for center high mounted stop lamps: A six-year study.* Arlington, VA: Insurance Institute for Highway Safety.

Fechner, G. (1860/1966). *Elements of psychophysics* (Vol. 1, H. E. Adler, D. H. Howes, & E. G. Boring, Trans.). New York: Holt, Rinehart, and Winston.

Feingold, B. F. (1975). Hyperkinesis and learning disabilities linked to artificial food flavors and colors. *American Journal of Nursing, 75,* 797-803.

Festinger, L. (1957). *A theory of cognitive dissonance.* Stanford, CA: Stanford University Press.

Festinger, L., Riecken, H. W., & Schachter, S. (1956). *When prophecy fails.* Minneapolis: University of Minnesota Press.

Ficken, M. S., Rusch, K. M., Taylor, S. J., & Powers, D. R. (2000). Blue-throated hummingbird song: A pinnacle of nonoscine vocalizations. *Auk, 117,* 120-128.

Fischhoff, B., Slovic, P., & Lichtenstein, S. (1977). Knowing with certainty: The appropriateness of extreme confidence. *Journal of Experimental Psychology: Human Perception and Performance, 3,* 522-564.

Fisher, R. P., & Craik, F. I. M. (1977). Interaction between encoding and retrieval operations in cued recall. *Journal of Experimental Psychology: Human Learning and Memory, 3,* 701-711.

Fishman, D. B., & Neigher, W. D. (1982). American psychology in the eighties: Who will buy? *American Psychologist, 37,* 533-546.

Fossey, D. (1972). Living with mountain gorillas. In T. B. Allen (Ed.), *The marvels of animal behavior.* Washington, DC: National Geographic Society.

Fostervold, K. I., Buckmann, E., & Lie, I. (2001). VDU-screen filters: Remedy or the ubiquitous Hawthorne effect? *International Journal of Industrial Ergonomics, 27,* 107-118.

Fraser, S. (Ed.). (1995). *The bell curve wars: Race, intelligence and the future of America.* New York: Basic Books.

Freedman, J. L., & Landauer, T. K. (1966). Retrieval of long-term memory: "Tip-of-the-tongue" phenomenon. *Psychonomic Science, 4,* 309-310.

Friend, R., Rafferty, Y., & Bramel, D. (1990). A puzzling misinterpretation of the Asch "conformity" study. *European Journal of Social Psychology, 20,* 29-44.

Frost, R., Katz, L., & Bentin, S. (1987). Strategies for visual word recognition and orthographical depth: A multilingual comparison. *Journal of Experimental Psychology: Human Perception and Performance, 13,* 104-115.

Furnham, A. (2001). Remembering stories as a function of the medium of presentation. *Psychological Reports, 89,* 483-486.

Furumoto, L. (1991). From "paired associates" to a psychology of self: The intellectual odyssey of Mary Whiton Calkins. In G. A. Kimble, M. Werthheimer, & C. L. White (Eds.), *Portraits of pioneers in psychology.* Hillsdale, NJ: Erlbaum.

Gabbert, F., Memon, A., & Allan, K. (2003). Memory conformity: Can eyewitnesses influence each other's memories for an event? *Applied Cognitive Psychology, 17,* 533-543.

Gabrenya, W. K., Latané, B., & Wang, Y. (1983). Social loafing in cross-cultural perspective: Chinese on Taiwan. *Journal of Cross-Cultural Psychology, 14,* 368-384.

Gabrieli, J. D. E., Keane, M. M., Zarella, M. M., & Poldrack, R. A. (1997). Preservation of implicit memory for new associations in global amnesia. *Psychological Science, 8,* 326-329.

Galle, O. R., Grove, W. R., & McPherson, J. M. (1972). Population density and pathology: What are the relations for man? *Science, 176,* 23-30.

Galton, F., Sir. (1869/1979). *Hereditary genius: An inquiry into its laws and consequences.* London: Julian Friedman Publishers.

Gardiner, J. M., Java, R. I., & Richardson-Klavehn, A. (1996). How level of processing really influences awareness in recognition memory. *Canadian Journal of Experimental Psychology, 50,* 114-122.

Gardner, H. (1983). *Frames of mind: The theory of multiple intelligences.* New York: Basic Books.

Gardner, H. (1998a). Are there additional intelligences? The case for naturalist, spiritual, and existential intelligences. In J. Kane (Ed.), *Education, information, and transformation.* Englewood Cliffs, NJ: Prentice Hall.

Gardner, H. (1998b). *Extraordinary minds: Portraits of 4 exceptional individuals and an examination of our own extraordinariness.* New York: Basic Books.

Gardner, H. (2000a). *Intelligence reframed: Multiple intelligences for the 21st century.* New York: Basic Books.

Gardner, H. (2000b). A case against spiritual intelligence. *International Journal for the Psychology of Religion, 10,* 27-34.

Gardner, H. (2007). *Five minds for the future* (pp. 1-20). Boston: Harvard Business School Press.

Garner, W. R. (1974). *The processing of information and structure.* Hillsdale, NJ: Erlbaum.

Garner, W. R., Hake, H. W., & Eriksen, C. W. (1956). Operationism and the concept of perception. *Psychological Review, 63,* 149-159.

Geher, G., Bauman, K. P., Hubbard, S. E. K., & Legare, J. R. (2002). Self and other obedience estimates: Biases and moderators. *Journal of Social Psychology, 142,* 677-689.

Gentner, D., Loewenstein, J., & Thompson, L. (2003). Learning and transfer: A general role for analogical encoding. *Journal of Educational Psychology, 95,* 393-405.

German, T. P., & Defeyter, M. A. (2000). Immunity to functional fixedness in young children. *Psychonomic Bulletin & Review, 2000,* 707-712.

Gibson, J. J. (1979). *The ecological approach to perception.* Boston: Houghton Mifflin.

Gick, M. L., & Holyoak, K. J. (1980). Analogical problem solving. *Cognitive Psychology, 12,* 306-355.

Gick, M. L., & Holyoak, K. J. (1983). Schema induction and analogical transfer. *Cognitive Psychology, 15,* 1-38.

Gigerenzer, G. (1993). The superego, the ego, and the id in statistical reasoning. In G. Keren & C. Lewids (Eds.), *A handbook for data analysis in the behavioral sciences: Methodological issues.* (pp. 311-339). Mahwah, NJ: Erlbaum.

Ginsburg, H. J., & Miller, S. M. (1982). Sex differences in children's risk-taking behavior. *Child Development, 53,* 426-428.

Glaser, M. O., & Glaser, W. R. (1982). Time course analysis of the Stroop phenomenon. *Journal of Experimental Psychology: Human Perception and Performance, 8,* 875-894.

Glucksberg, S. (1966). *Symbolic processes.* Dubuque, IA: William C. Brown.

Glucksberg, S., & Danks, J. H. (1967). Functional fixedness: Stimulus equivalence mediated by semantic-acoustic similarity. *Journal of Experimental Psychology, 74,* 400-405.

Glucksberg, S., & Danks, J. H. (1968).   Effects of discriminative labels and nonsense labels upon availability of novel function. *Journal of Verbal Learning and Verbal Behavior, 7,* 72–76.

Glucksberg, S., & Weisberg, R. W. (1966).   Verbal behavior and problem solving: Some effects of labelling in a functional fixedness problem. *Journal of Experimental Psychology, 71,* 659–664.

Goodman, M. J., Tijerina, L., Bents, F. D., & Wierwille, W. W. (1999).   Using cellular telephones in vehicles: Safe or unsafe? *Transportation Human Factors, 1,* 3–42.

Graf, P., & Schacter, D. L. (1985).   Implicit and explicit memory for new associations in normal and amnesic subjects. *Journal of Experimental Psychology: Learning, Memory and Cognition, 11,* 501–518.

Grant, D. A., & Schneider, D. E. (1948).   Intensity of the conditional stimulus and strength of conditioning: I. The conditioned eyelid response to light. *Journal of Experimental Psychology, 38,* 690–696.

Green, B. G., Shaffer, G. S., & Gilmore, M. M. (1993). A semantically-labeled magnitude scale of oral sensation with apparent ratio properties. *Chemical Senses, 18,* 683–702.

Green, D. M., & Swets, J. A. (1966).   *Signal detection theory and psychophysics.* New York: Wiley.

Greenough, W. T. (1992).   Animal rights replies distort(ed) and misinform(ed). *Psychological Science, 3,* 142.

Greenwald, A. G. (1992).   New look 3: Unconscious cognition reclaimed. *American Psychologist, 47,* 766–779.

Gregory, R. L. (1970).   *The intelligent eye.* New York: McGraw-Hill.

Grice, G. R. (1966).   Dependence of empirical laws upon the source of experimental variation. *Psychological Bulletin, 66,* 488–498.

Grice, G. R., & Hunter, J. J. (1964).   Stimulus intensity effects depend upon the type of experimental design. *Psychological Review, 71,* 247–256.

Guilford, J. P. (1967).   *The nature of human intelligence.* New York: McGraw-Hill.

Hadamard, J. (1945).   *The psychology of invention in the mathematical field.* Princeton, NJ: Princeton University Press.

Hahn, G., Charlin, V. L., Sussman, S., Dent, C. W., Manzi, J., Stacy, A., Flay, B., Hansen, W. B., & Burton, D. (1990).   Adolescent's first and most recent use situations of smokeless tobacco and cigarettes: Similarities and differences. *Addictive Behavior, 15,* 439–448.

Haier, R. J., Jung, R. E., Yeo, R. A., Head, K., & Alkire, M. T. (2004).   Structural brain variation and general intelligence. *NeuroImage, 23,* 425–433.

Haines, M. M., Stansfeld, S. A., Head, J., & Job, R. F. S. (2002).   Multilevel modelling of aircraft noise on performance tests in schools around Heathrow Airport London. *Journal of Epidemiology and Community Health, 56,* 139–144.

Hanowski, R. J., Kantowitz, B. H., & Kantowitz, S. C. (1996).   Driver memory for in-vehicle advanced traveller information system messages. *13th Biennial Symposium on Night Visibility and Driver Behavior.* Washington, DC: National Research Council.

Hanson, N. R. (1958).   *Patterns of discovery.* Cambridge: Cambridge University Press.

Hardy, J. D., Wolff, H. G., & Goodell, H. (1952).   *Pain reactions and sensations.* Baltimore: Williams & Wilkins.

Harre, R. (1983). *Great scientific experiments.* Oxford: Oxford University Press.

Harlow, H. F. (1958).   The nature of love. *American Psychologist, 13,* 673–685.

Hart, B. M., Allen, K. E., Buell, J. S., Harris, F. R., & Wolf, M. M. (1964).   Effects of social reinforcement on operant crying. *Journal of Experimental Child Psychology, 1,* 145–153.

Hart, J. T. (1965).   Memory and the feeling-of-knowing experience. *Journal of Educational Psychology, 56,* 208–216.

Hart, S. G., Hauser, J. R., & Leser, P. T. (1984).   Inflight evaluation of four measures of pilot workload. *Proceedings of the Human Factors Society, 28,* 945–949.

Hauser, L. (1997).   Searle's Chinese box: Debunking the Chinese room argument. *Minds and Machines, 7,* 199–226.

Hebb, D. O., & Donderi, D. C. (1987).   *Textbook of psychology* (4th Ed.). Hillsdale, NJ: Erlbaum.

Helmholtz, H. von (1962).   *Treatise on physiological optics* (Vol. 3), J. P. C. Southall, Ed. New York: Dover.

Herman, L. M., & Kantowitz, B. H. (1970).   The psychological refractory period effect: Only half the double stimulation story? *Psychological Bulletin, 73,* 74–86.

Herrnstein, R. J. (1962).   Placebo effect in the rat. *Science, 138,* 677–678.

Herrnstein, R. J., & Murray, C. (1994).   *The bell curve.* New York: The Free Press.

Hetherington, E. M., & Parke, R. D. (1986).   *Child psychology: A contemporary viewpoint* (pp. 429–480). New York: McGraw-Hill.

Hilts, P. J. (1995).   *Memory's ghost. The nature of memory and the strange tale of Mr. M.* New York: Simon & Schuster.

Holland, P. W. (1993).   Which comes first, cause or effect? In G. Keren & C. Lewids (Eds.), *A handbook for data analysis in the behavioral sciences: Methodological issues* (pp. 273–282). Mahwah, NJ: Erlbaum.

Holyoak, K. J. (1990).   Problem solving. In D. N. Osherson & E. E. Smith (Eds.), *Thinking: An invitation to cognitive science* (Vol. 3, pp. 117–146). Cambridge: MIT Press.

Holyoak, K. J., & Thagard, P. (1989).   Analogical mapping by constraint satisfaction. *Cognitive Science, 13,* 295–355.

Holyoak, K. J., & Thagard, P. (1997).   The analogical mind. *American Psychologist, 52,* 35–44.

Horowitz, L. M. (1974).   *Elements of statistics for psychology and education.* New York: McGraw-Hill.

Howard, D. V., & Wiggs, C. L. (1993).   Aging and learning: Insights from implicit and explicit tests. In J. Cerella,

W. J. Hoyer, J. Rybash, & M. Commons (Eds.), *Adult age differences: Limits on loss.* New York: Academic Press.

Howell, D. C. (2008). *Fundamental statistics for the behavioral sciences* (6th Ed., Ch. 9). Belmont, CA: Wadsworth.

Howell, W. C. (1994). Human factors and the challenges of the future. *Psychological Science, 5,* 1–7.

Huesmann, L. R., Eron, L. D., Lefkowitz, M. M., & Walder, L. O. (1973). Television violence and aggression: The causal effect remains. *American Psychologist, 28,* 617–620.

Huesmann, L. R., Moise-Titus, J., Podolski, C. L., Eron, L. D. (2003). Longitudinal relations between children's exposure to TV violence and their aggressive and violent behavior in young adulthood: 1977–1992. *Developmental Psychology, 39,* 2001–221.

Huesmann, L. R., & Taylor, L. D. (2006). The role of media violence in violent behavior. *Annual Review of Public Health, 27,* 393–415.

Huff, D. (1954). *How to lie with statistics.* New York: Norton.

Hull, C. L. (1943). *Principles of behavior.* New York: Appleton-Century-Crofts.

Hunt, E., & Lansman, M. (1975). Cognitive theory applied to individual differences. In W. K. Estes (Ed.), *Handbook of learning and cognitive process* (Vol. 1, pp. 81–110). Hillsdale, NJ: Erlbaum.

Hunt, E., Streissguth, A., Kerr, B., & Olson, H. (1995). Mothers' alcohol consumption during pregnancy: Effects on spatial-visual reasoning in 14-year-old children. *Psychological Science, 6,* 339–342.

Huxley, A. (1946). *Science, liberty and peace.* New York: Harper.

Hyde, T. S., & Jenkins, J. J. (1969). Differential effects of incidental tasks on the organization of recall of a list of highly associated words. *Journal of Experimental Psychology, 82,* 472–481.

Hygge, S., Evans, G., & Bullinger, M. (2002). A prospective study of some effects of aircraft noise on cognitive performance in school children. *Psychological Science, 13,* 469–474.

Hyman, R. (1964). *The nature of psychological inquiry.* Englewood Cliffs, NJ: Prentice-Hall.

Intraub, H., & Nicklos, H. (1985). Levels of processing and picture memory: The physical superiority effect. *Journal of Experimental Psychology: Learning, Memory, and Cognition, 11,* 284–298.

Irwin, M. R., & Miller, A. H. (2007). Depressive disorders and immunity: 20 years of progress and discovery. *Brain, Behavior, and Immunity, 21,* 374–383.

Iwanaga, M., & Ito, T. (2002). Disturbance effect of music on processing of verbal and spatial memories. *Perceptual and Motor Skills, 94,* 1251–1258.

Jacob, T., Tennenbaum, D., Seilhamer, R. A., Bargiel, K., & Sharon, T. (1994). Reactivity effects during naturalistic observation of distressed and nondistressed families. *Journal of Family Psychology, 8,* 354–363.

Jacobs, J. (1961). *Death and life of great American cities.* New York: Random House.

Jacobson, E. (1978). *You must relax* (5th Ed.). New York: McGraw-Hill.

Jacoby, L. L., & Dallas, M. (1981). On the relationship between autobiographical memory and perceptual learning. *Journal of Experimental Psychology: General, 3,* 306–340.

Jacoby, L. L., & Witherspoon, D. (1982). Remembering without awareness. *Canadian Journal of Psychology, 32,* 300–324.

Jagacinski, R. J., & Flach, J. M. (2003). *Control theory for humans: Quantitative approaches to modeling performance.* Mahwah, NJ, Erlbaum.

James, W. (1890). *Principles of psychology.* New York: Holt.

Jenkins, J. (1979). Four points to remember: A tetrahedral model of memory experiments. In L. S. Cermak & F. I. M. Craik (Eds.), *Levels of processing in human memory* (pp. 429–446). Hillsdale, NJ: Erlbaum.

Jennings, J. R., & Coles, M. G. H. (1991a). Introduction. In J. R. Jennings & M. G. H. Coles (Eds.), *Handbook of cognitive psychophysiology.* New York: Wiley.

Jennings, J. R., & Coles, M. G. H. (Eds.). (1991b). *Handbook of cognitive psychophysiology.* New York: Wiley.

Jensen, A. R. (1969). How much can we boost I.Q. and scholastic achievement? *Harvard Educational Review, 39,* 1–123.

Jones, D. (1999). The cognitive psychology of auditory distraction: The 1997 BPS Bradbent Lecture. *British Journal of Psychology, 90,* 167–187.

Kahneman, D. (1973). *Attention and effort.* Englewood Cliffs, NJ: Prentice-Hall.

Kahng, S. W., Boscoe, J. H., & Byrne, S. (2003). The use of an escape contingency and a token economy to increase food acceptance. *Journal of Applied Behavior Analysis, 36,* 349–353.

Kamin, L. J. (1969). Predictability, surprise, attention, and conditioning. In B. A. Campbell & R. M. Church (Eds.), *Punishment and aversive behavior* (pp. 279–296). New York: Appleton-Century-Crofts.

Kangas, J., & Bradway, K. (1971). Intelligence at middle age: A thirty-eight year follow-up. *Developmental Psychology, 5,* 333–337.

Kantowitz, B. H. (1972). Response force as an indicant of conflict in double stimulation. *Journal of Experimental Psychology, 110,* 302–309.

Kantowitz, B. H. (1982). Interfacing human information processing and engineering psychology. In W. C. Howell & E. A. Fleishman (Eds.), *Human Performance and Productivity* (pp. 31–81). Hillsdale, NJ: Erlbaum.

Kantowitz, B. H. (1985). Stages and channels in human information processing: A limited analysis of theory and methodology. *Journal of Mathematical Psychology, 29,* 135–174.

Kantowitz, B. H. (1987).   Premises and promises of psychophysiology. *Contemporary Psychology, 32,* 1002–1004.

Kantowitz, B. H. (1989a).   Interfacing human and machine intelligence. In P. A. Hancock & M. H. Chignell (Eds.), *Intelligent interfaces: Theory, research and design* (pp. 49–67). Amsterdam: Elsevier.

Kantowitz, B. H. (1989b).   The role of human information processing models in system development. *Proceedings of the Human Factors Society 33rd Annual Meeting,* 1059–1063. Santa Monica, CA: Human Factors Society.

Kantowitz, B. H. (1995).   Simulator evaluation of heavy-vehicle driver workload. *Proceedings of the Human Factors and Ergonomics Society 39th Annual Meeting* (Vol. 2, pp. 1107–1111). Santa Monica, CA: Human Factors and Ergonomics Society.

Kantowitz, B. H. (1998).   Computational models for transportation human factors. *Proceedings of the Human Factors and Ergonomics Society 42nd Annual Meeting, 2,* 1220–1221.

Kantowitz, B. H. (2001).   Using microworlds to design intelligent interfaces that minimize driver distraction. *Proceedings of the First International Driving Symposium on Human Factors in Driver Assessment, Training and Vehicle Design,* 42–57. Aspen, CO.

Kantowitz, B. H., & Campbell, J. L. (1996).   Pilot workload and flightdeck automation. In R. Parasuraman & M. Mouloua (Eds.), *Human performance in automated systems* (pp. 117–136). Human workload in aviation.

Kantowitz, B. H., & Casper, P. A. (1988).   Human workload in aviation. In E. Wiener & D. Nagel (Eds.), *Human factors in aviation* (pp. 157–186). New York: Academic Press.

Kantowitz, B. H., & Fujita, Y. (1990).   Cognitive theory, identifiability and human reliability analysis (HRA). *Reliability Engineering and System Safety, 29,* 317–328.

Kantowitz, B. H., Hart, S. G., & Bortolussi, M. R. (1983).   Measuring pilot workload in a moving-base simulator: I. Asynchronous secondary choice-reaction task. *Proceedings of the Human Factors Society, 27,* 319–322.

Kantowitz, B. H., & Knight, J. L. (1976).   Testing tapping timesharing: Auditory secondary task. *Acta Psychologica, 40,* 343–362.

Kantowitz, B. H., & Sanders, M. S. (1972).   Partial advance information and stimulus dimensionality. *Journal of Experimental Psychology, 92,* 412–418.

Kantowitz, B. H., & Simsek, O. (2000).   Secondary task measures of driver workload. In P. Hancock Desmond (Eds.), *Stress, workload, and fatigue.* (pp. 395–408). Mahwah, NJ: Erlbaum.

Kantowitz, B. H., & Sorkin, R. D. (1983).   *Human factors: Understanding people-system relationships.* New York: Wiley.

Kaufman, L. (1974).   *Sight and mind.* New York: Oxford.

Kawai, N., & Imada, H. (1996).   Between- and within-subject effects of US duration on conditioned suppression in rats: Contrast makes otherwise unnoticed duration stand out. *Learning and Motivation, 27,* 92–111.

Kazdin, A. E. (2001).   *Behavior modification in applied settings.* Belmont, CA: Wadsworth/Thomson Learning.

Keisler, A., & Willingham, C. T. (2007).   Non-declarative sequence learning does not show savings in relearing. *Human Movement Science, 26,* 247–256.

Keith-Spiegel, P., & Koocher, G. P. (2005).   The IRB paradox: Could the protectors also encourage deceit? *Ethics & Behavior, 15,* 339–349.

Kelman, H. (1966).   Deception in social research. *Transaction, 3,* 20–24.

Keppel, G., & Underwood, B. J. (1962).   Proactive inhibition in short term retention of single items. *Journal of Verbal Learning and Verbal Behavior, 1,* 153–161.

Kihlstrom, J. F., Barnhardt, T. M., & Tataryn, D. J. (1992).   The psychological unconscious: Found, lost, regained. *American Psychologist, 47,* 788–791.

King, D. J. (1968).   Retention of connected meaningful material as a function of presentation and recall. *Journal of Experimental Psychology, 77,* 676–683.

Kinsey, A., Pomeroy, W., & Martin, C. (1953).   *Sexual behavior in the human female.* Philadelphia: Saunders.

Kintsch, W., & Kozminsky, E. (1977).   Summarizing stories after reading and listening. *Journal of Educational Psychology, 69,* 491–499.

Kluger, A. N., & Tikochinsky, J. (2001).   The error of accepting the "theoretical" null hypothesis: The rise, fall, and resurrection of commonsense hypotheses in psychology. *Psychological Bulletin, 127* (3), 408–423.

Kolodner, J. L. (1997).   Educational implications of analogy: A view from case-based reasoning. *American Psychologist, 52,* 57–66.

Koriat, A., & Levy-Sadot, R. (2001).   The combined contributions of the cue-familiarity and accessibility heuristics to feelings of knowing. *Journal of Experimental Psychology: Learning, Memory, & Cognition, 27,* 34–53.

Koestler, A. (1964).   *The act of creation.* New York: Dell.

Köhler, W. (1927).   *The mentality of apes.* London: Routledge and Kegan Paul.

Kohn, A. (1986).   *False prophets.* New York: Basil Blackwell.

Koocher, G. P. (1977).   Bathroom behavior and human dignity. *Journal of Personality and Social Psychology, 35,* 120–121.

Kravitz, D. A., & Martin, B. (1986).   Ringelmann rediscovered: The original article. *Journal of Personality and Social Psychology, 50,* 936–941.

Kuhn, T. S. (1970).   Logic of discovery or psychology of research. In I. Lakatos & A. Musgrave (Eds.), *Criticism and the growth of knowledge* (pp. 1–23). New York: Cambridge University Press.

Kulpe, O. (1893).   Grundriss der Psychologie. Auf experimenteller basis dargestellt [An outline of psychology from an experimental perspective]. Leipzig: Englemann.

Kwilecki, S. (2000). Spiritual intelligence as a theory of individual religion: A case application. *International Journal for the Psychology of Religion, 10,* 35–46.

Lane, D. M., & Robertson, L. (1979). The generality of the levels of processing hypothesis: An application to memory for chess positions. *Memory & Cognition, 7,* 253–256.

Latané, B. (1981). The psychology of social impact. *American Psychologist, 36,* 343–356.

Latané, B., & Darley, J. M. (1970). *The unresponsive bystander: Why doesn't he help?* New York: Appleton-Century-Crofts.

Latané, B., Williams, K., & Harkins, S. (1979). Many hands make light the work: Causes and consequences of social loafing. *Journal of Personality and Social Psychology, 37,* 822–832.

Lee, Y-S. (2002). Levels of processing and phonological priming in Chinese character completion tests. *Journal of Psycholinguistic Research, 31,* 349–362.

Lester, B. M., & Brazelton, T. B. (1982). Cross-cultural assessment of neonatal behavior. In D. A. Wagner & H. W. Stevenson (Eds.), *Cultural perspectives on child development.* San Francisco: Freeman.

Levy, S. R., Plaks, J. E., Hong, Y., Chiu, C., & Dweck, C. S. (2001). Static versus dynamic theories and the perception of groups: Different routes to different destinations. *Personality and Social Psychology Review, 5,* 156–168.

Lewin, K. (1948). *Resolving social conflicts.* New York: Harper.

Lichtenstein, S., & Fischhoff, B. (1977). Do those who know more also know more about how much they know? *Organizational Behavior and Human Performance, 20,* 159–183.

Locke, J. (1659/1959). *An essay concerning human understanding.* New York: Dover.

Lockhart, R. S., & Craik, F. I. M. (1990). Levels of processing: A retrospective comment on a framework for memory research. *Canadian Journal of Psychology, 44,* 87–112.

Loft, S., Sanderson, P., Neal, A., & Mooij, M. (2007). Modeling and predicting mental workload in en route air traffic control: Critical review and broader implications. *Human Factors, 49,* 376–399.

Loftus, E. F., & Klinger, M. R. (1992). Is the unconscious smart or dumb? *American Psychologist, 47,* 761–765.

LoLordo, V. M. (2001). Learned helplessness and depression. In M. E. Carroll & B. J. Overmier (Eds.), *Animal research and human health: Advancing human welfare through behavioral science* (pp. 63–77). Washington, DC: American Psychological Association.

Long, G. M., & Garvey, P. M. (1988). The effects of target wavelength on dynamic visual acuity under photopic and scotopic viewing. *Human Factors, 30,* 3–14.

Lovelace, E. A., & Twohig, P. T. (1990). Healthy older adult's perception of their memory function and use of mnemonics. *Bulletin of the Psychonomic Society, 28,* 115–118.

Lowe, D. G., & Mitterer, J. O. (1982). Selective and divided attention in a Stroop task. *Canadian Journal of Psychology, 36,* 684–700.

Luminet, O., Curci, A., Marsh, E. J., Wessel, I., Constantin, T., Gencoz, F., & Yogo, M. (2004). The cognitive, emotional, and social impacts of the September 11th attacks: Group differences in memory for the reception context and its determinants. *The Journal of General Psychology, 131,* 197–224.

MacLeod, C. M. (1988). Forgotten but not gone: Savings for pictures and words in long term memory. *Journal of Experimental Psychology: Learning, Memory, and Cognition, 14,* 195–212.

Madigan, S. (1983). Picture memory. In J. C. Yuille (Ed.), *Imagery, memory, and cognition: Essays in honor of Allan Paivio* (pp. 65–89). Hillsdale, NJ: Erlbaum.

Malone, T. B. (1986). The centered high-mounted brake light: A human factors success story. *Human Factors Society Bulletin, 29.*

Mann, T. (1994). Informed consent for psychological research: Do subjects comprehend consent forms and understand their legal rights? *Psychological Science, 5,* 140–143.

Mantzicopoulos, P. (2003). Flunking kindergarten after Head Start: An inquiry into the contribution of contextual and individual variables. *Journal of Educational Psychology, 95,* 268–278.

Marcel, A. J. (1983). Conscious and unconscious perception: Experiments on visual masking and word recognition. *Cognitive Psychology, 15,* 197–237.

Marks, L. E. (1974). *Sensory processes: The new psychophysics.* New York: Academic Press.

Maril, A., Simons, J. S., Mitchell, J. P., Schwwartz, B. L., & Schacter, D. L. (2003). Feeling-of-knowing in episodic memory: An event-related fMRI study. *Neuroimage, 18,* 827–836.

Marriott, P. (1949). Size of working groups and output. *Occupational Psychology, 23,* 47–57.

Marshall, J. E., & Heslin, R. (1975). Boys and girls together: Sexual composition and the effect of density and group size on cohesiveness. *Journal of Personality and Social Psychology, 31,* 952–961.

Martell, R. F., & Willis, C. E. (1993). Effects of observers' performance expectations on behavior ratings of work groups: Memory or response bias? *Organizational Behavior and Human Decision Processes, 56,* 91–109.

Massaro, D. W. (1975). *Experimental psychology and information processing.* Chicago: Rand McNally.

Mayer, R. E. (1983). *Thinking, problem solving, cognition.* New York: Freeman.

McCall, R. B. (1990). *Fundamentals of statistics for the behavioral sciences* (5th Ed.). San Diego: Harcourt Brace.

McConahay, J. B., Hardee, B. B., & Batts, V. (1981). Has racism declined in America? It depends on who is asking and what is asked. *Journal of Conflict Resolution, 25*, 563-579.

McDaniel, M. A., Friedman, A., & Bourne, L. E. (1978). Remembering the levels of information in words. *Memory & Cognition, 6*, 156-164.

McDermott, K. B., & Buckner, R. L. (2002). Functional neuroimaging studies of memory retrieval. In L. R. Squire & D. L. Schacter (Ed.), *Neuropsychology of Memory* (3rd Ed.) (pp. 166-173). New York: Guilford Press.

McDougall, D., Hawkins, J., Brady, M., & Jenkins, A. (2006). Recent innovations in the changing criterion design: Implications for research and practice in special education. *The Journal of Special Education, 40*, 2-15.

McDougall, D., & Smith, D. (2006). Recent innovation in small-*n* designs for research and practice in professional school counseling. *Professional School Counseling, 9*, 392-400.

Meade, M. L., & Roediger, H. L., III (2002). Explorations in the social contagion of memory. *Memory & Cognition, 30*, 995-1009.

Medawar, P. B. (1969). *Induction and intuition in scientific thought.* London: Methuen.

Merikle, P. M., & Reingold, E. M. (1992). Measuring unconscious perceptual processes. In R. F. Bornstein & T. S. Pittman (Eds.), *Perception without awareness: Cognitive, clinical & social perspectives* (pp. 55-80). New York: Guilford Press.

Merikle, P. M., Smilek, D., & Eastwood, J. D. (2001). Perception without awareness: Perspectives from cognitive psychology. *Cognition, 79*, 114-134.

Metcalfe, J. (1986). Premonitions of insight predict impending error. *Journal of Experimental Psychology: Learning, Memory, and Cognition, 12*, 623-634.

Middlemist, R. D., Knowles, E. S., & Matter, C. F. (1977). What to do and what to report: A reply to Koocher. *Journal of Personality and Social Psychology, 35*, 122-124.

Milgram, S. (1963). Behavioral study of obedience. *Journal of Abnormal and Social Psychology, 67*, 371-378.

Milgram, S. (1964a). Group pressure and actions against a person. *Journal of Abnormal and Social Psychology, 69*, 137-143.

Milgram, S. (1964b). Issues in the study of obedience: A reply to Baumrind. *American Psychologist, 19*, 848-852.

Milgram, S. (1965). Some conditions of obedience and disobedience to authority. *Human Relations, 18*, 57-76.

Milgram, S. (1974). *Obedience to authority: An experimental view.* New York: Harper & Row.

Miller, A. G., Collins, B. E., & Brief, D. E. (1995). Perspectives on obedience to authority: The legacy of the Milgram experiments. *Journal of Social Issues, 51*, 1-19.

Miller, D. B. (1977). Roles of naturalistic observation in comparative psychology. *American Psychologist, 32*, 211-219.

Miller, J., & Ulrich, R. (1998). Locus of the effect of the number of alternative responses: Evidence from the lateralized readiness potential. *Journal of Experimental Psychology: Human Perception & Performance, 24* (4), 1215-1231.

Miller, J. O., Franz, V., & Ulrich, R. (1999). Effects of stimulus intensity on response force in simple, go-no-go, and choice RT. *Perception and Psychophysics, 67*, 107-119.

Miller, N. E. (1959). Liberalization of basic S-R concepts: Extensions to conflict behavior, motivation and social learning. In S. Koch (Ed.), *Psychology: A study of a science* (Vol. 2, pp. 196-292). New York: McGraw Hill.

Miller, N. E. (1985). The value of behavioral research on animals. *American Psychologist, 40*, 423-440.

Mitchell, C. J., & Lovibond, P. F. (2002). Backward and forward blocking in human electrodermal conditioning: Blocking requires an assumption of outcome additivity. *Quarterly Journal of Experimental Psychology, 55B*, 311-329.

Mook, D. G. (1983). In defense of external invalidity. *American Psychologist, 38*, 379-387.

Moriarty, T. (1975). Crime, commitment, and the responsive bystander: Two field studies. *Journal of Personality and Social Psychology, 31*, 370-376.

Morris, C. D., Bransford, J. D., & Franks, J. J. (1977). Levels of processing versus transfer appropriate processing. *Journal of Verbal Learning and Verbal Behavior, 16*, 519-533.

Mortimer, R. G. (1993). The high mounted brake lamp: A cause without a theory. *Proceedings of the Human Factors and Ergonomics Society 37th Annual Meeting* (pp. 955-959). Santa Monica, CA: Human Factors and Ergonomics Society.

Moscovitch, M. (1982). Multiple dissociations of functions in the amnesic syndrome. In L. Cermak (Ed.), *Human memory and amnesia.* Hillsdale, NJ: Erlbaum.

Moy, P., Xenos, M. A., & Hess, V. K. (2005). Priming effects of late-night comedy. *International Journal of Public Opinion Research, 18*, 198-210.

Murphy, M. D., & Brown, A. L. (1975). Incidental learning in preschool children as a function of level of cognitive analysis. *Journal of Experimental Child Psychology, 19*, 509-523.

National Advisory Mental Health Council Behavioral Science Task Force. (1995). Basic behavioral science research for mental health: A national investment (executive summary). *Psychological Science, 6*, 192-202.

National Safety Council. (1999). *Injury facts, 1999 Edition.* Itasca, IL: Author.

Natsoulas, T. (1967). What are perceptual reports about? *Psychological Bulletin, 67*, 249-272.

Navon, D., & Miller, J. (2002).   Queuing or sharing? A critical evaluation of the single-bottleneck notion. *Cognitive Psychology, 44,* 193-251.

Nelson, T. O. (1977).   Repetition and levels of processing. *Journal of Verbal Learning and Verbal Behavior, 16,* 151-171.

Ng, C. F. (2000).   Effects of building construction noise on residents: A quasi-experiment. *Journal of Environmental Psychology, 20,* 375-385.

Neisser, U., & Harsch, N. (1992).   Phantom flashbulbs: False recollections of hearing the news about Challenger. In E. Winograd & U. Neisser (Eds.), *Affect and accuracy in recall* (pp. 9-31). New York: Cambridge University Press.

Niedzwienska, A. (2003).   Distortion of autobiographical memories. *Applied Cognitive Psychology, 17,* 81-91.

Nisbett, R. (1995).   Race, IQ, and scientism. In S. Fraser (Ed.), *The bell curve wars: Race, intelligence and the future of America* (pp. 36-57). New York: Basic Books.

Nisbett, R. E., & Wilson, T. D. (1977).   Telling more than we can know: Verbal reports on mental processes. *Psychological Review, 84,* 231-259.

Nissani, M. (1990).   A cognitive interpretation of Stanley Milgram's observations on obedience to authority. *American Psychologist, 45,* 1384-1385.

Norman, J. (2002).   Two visual systems and two theories of perception: An attempt to reconcile the constructivist and ecological approaches. *Behavioral and Brain Sciences, 25,* 73-144.

Notterman, J. M., & Mintz, D. E. (1965).   *Dynamics of response.* New York: Wiley.

Novick, L. R. (1990).   Representational transfer in problem solving. *Psychological Science, 1,* 128-132.

Oltmanns, T. F., Martin, M., Neale, J. M., & Davison, G. C. (2006).   *Case studies in abnormal psychology* (7th Ed., pp. 1-14). New York, Wiley.

Olton, R. M., & Johnson, D. M. (1976).   Mechanisms of incubation in creative problem solving. *American Journal of Psychology, 89,* 617-630.

Orne, M. T. (1962).   On the social psychology of the psychological experiment: With particular reference to demand characteristics and their implications. *American Psychologist, 17,* 776-783.

Orne, M. T. (1969).   Demand characteristics and the concept of quasi-controls. In R. Rosnow & R. L. Rosenthal (Eds.), *Artifact in behavioral research* (pp. 147-179). New York: Academic Press.

Orne, M. T., & Evans, T. J. (1965).   Social control in the psychological experiment: Antisocial behavior and hypnosis. *Journal of Personality and Social Psychology, 1,* 189-200.

Pachella, R. G. (1974).   The interpretation of reaction time in information-processing research. In B. H. Kantowitz (Ed.), *Human information processing—Tutorials in performance and cognition* (pp. 41-82). Hillsdale, NJ: Erlbaum.

Padilla, A. M. (1971).   Analysis of incentive and behavioral contrast in the rat. *Journal of Comparative and Physiological Psychology, 45,* 464-470.

Paillard, J., Michel, F., & Stelmach, G. (1983).   Localization without content: A tactile analogue of "blind-sight." *Archives of Neurology, 40,* 548-551.

Paivio, A. (1969).   Mental imagery in associative learning and memory. *Psychological Review, 76,* 241-263.

Papini, M. R., Thomas, B. L., & McVicar, D. G. (2002).   Between-subject PREE and within-subject PREE in spaced-trial extinction with pigeons. *Learning and Motivation, 33,* 485-509.

Parr, W. V., Heatherbell, D., & White, K. G. (2002).   Demystifying wine expertise: Olfactory threshold, perceptual skill and semantic memory in expert and novice wine judges. *Chemical Senses, 27,* 475-755.

Parsons, H. M. (1970).   Life and death. *Human Factors, 12,* 1-6.

Parsons, H. M. (1974).   What happened at Hawthorne? *Science, 183,* 922-931.

Pashler, H. (1989).   Dissociations and dependencies between speed and accuracy: Evidence for a two-component theory of divided attention in simple tasks. *Cognitive Psychology, 21,* 469-514.

Pavlov, I. P. (1963).   *Lectures on conditioned reflexes.* New York: International Publishers.

Payne, B. K. (2001).   Prejudice and perception: The role of automatic and controlled process in misperceiving a weapon. *Journal of Personality & Social Psychology, 81,* 181-192.

Payne, B. K., Lambert, A. J., & Jacoby, L. L. (2002).   Best laid plans: Effects of goals on accessibility bias and cognitive control in race-based misperceptions of weapons. *Journal of Experimental Social Psychology, 38,* 384-396.

Pedhazur, E. J., & Pedhazur Schmelkin, L. (1991).   *Measurement, design, and analysis: An integrated approach.* Hillsdale, NJ: Erlbaum.

Peirce, C. S. (1877).   The fixation of belief. *Popular Science Monthly, 12,* 1-15. Reprinted in E. C. Moore (Ed.). (1972). *Charles Sanders Peirce: The essential writings.* New York: Harper & Row.

Perfect, T. J., & Hollins, T. S. (1999).   Feeling-of-knowing judgments do not predict subsequent recognition performance for eyewitness memory. *Journal of Experimental Psychology: Applied, 5,* 250-264.

Peterson, L. R., & Peterson, M. J. (1959).   Short term retention of individual items. *Journal of Experimental Psychology, 58,* 193-198.

Piaget, J. (1932).   *The language and thought of the child* (2nd Ed.). London: Routledge & Kegan Paul.

Piaget, J., & Inhelder, B. (1969).   *The psychology of the child.* London: Routledge & Kegan Paul.

Pickren, W. E., & Dewsbury, D. A. (2002).   *Evolving perspectives on the history of psychology.* Washington, DC: American Psychological Association.

Piliavin, I. M., Rodin, J., & Piliavin, J. A. (1969).   Good samaritanism: An underground phenomenon? *Journal of Personality and Social Psychology, 13,* 289-299.

Plant, E. A., Peruche, B. M., & Butz, D. A. (2005).   Eliminating automatic racial bias: Making race non-diagnostic for responses to criminal suspects. *Journal of Experimental Social Psychology, 41,* 141-156.

Plous, S. (1991).   An attitude survey of animal rights activists. *Psychological Science, 2,* 194-196.

Plous, S. (1996a).   Attitudes towards the use of animals in psychological research and education. *American Psychologist, 51,* 1167-1180.

Plous, S. (1996b).   Attitudes towards the use of animals in psychological research and education: Results from a national survey of psychology majors. *Psychological Science, 7,* 352-358.

Poincaré, H. (1929).   *The foundations of science.* New York: Science House, Inc.

Popper, K. R. (1961).   *The logic of scientific discovery.* New York: Basic Books.

Posner, M. I. (1973).   *Cognition: An introduction.* Glenview, IL: Scott, Foresman.

Posner, M. I. (1993).   Attention before and during the decade of the brain. In D. Meyer & S. Kornblum (Eds.), *Attention and performance XIV* (pp. 340-351). Cambridge: MIT Press.

Posner, M. I., & Raichle, M. E. (1994).   Images of mind. New York: Scientific American Library.

Proctor, R. W., & Capaldi, E. J. (2001).   Empirical evaluation and justification of methodologies in psychological science. *Psychological Bulletin 127* (3), 759-777.

Prescott, J., & Wilkie, J. (2007).   Pain tolerance selectively increased by a sweet-smelling odor. *Psychological Science, 18,* 308-311.

Proffitt, D. R. (2006).   Embodied perception and the economy of action. *Perspectives on Psychological Science, 1,* 110-122.

Proffitt, D. R., Bhalla, M., Gossweiller, R., & Midgett, J. (1995).   Perceiving geographical slant. *Psychonomic Bulletin & Review, 2,* 409-428.

Pytte, C. L., Rusch, K. M., & Ficken, M. S. (2003).   Regulation of vocal amplitude by the blue-throated hummingbird, *Lampornis clemenciae. Animal Behavior, 66,* 703-710.

Queller, S., & Smith, E. R. (2002).   Subtyping versus bookkeeping in stereotype learning and change: Connectionist simulations and empirical findings. *Journal of Personality and Social Psychology, 82,* 300-313.

Rapoport, A. (1975).   Towards a redefinition of density. *Environment and Behavior, 7,* 133-158.

Reed, M. P., & Green, P. A. (1999).   Comparison of driving performance on-road and in a low-cost simulator using a concurrent telephone dialling task. *Ergonomics, 42* (8), 1015-1037.

Reed, S. B., Kirsch, I., Wickless, C., Moffitt, K. H., & Taren, P. (1996).   Reporting biases in hyponosis: Suggestion or compliance? *Journal of Abnormal Psychology, 105,* 142-145.

Rescorla, R. (1999).   Within-subject partial reinforcement extinction effect in autoshaping. *Quarterly Journal of Experimental Psychology, 52B,* 75-87.

Rescorla, R. A. (1967).   Pavlovian conditioning and its proper control procedures. *Psychological Review, 74,* 71-80.

Rescorla, R. A. (1988).   Pavlovian conditioning: It's not what you think it is. *American Psychologist, 43,* 151-160.

Rieber, R. W., & Salzinger, K. (1998).   *Psychology: Theoritical-historical perspectives* (2nd Ed.) Washington, DC: American Psychological Association.

Ringelmann, M. (1913).   Recherches sur les moteurs animes: Travail de l'homme. *Annales de l'Institut National Agronomique,* 2e series-tome XII, 1-40.

Roberts, C. (1971).   Debate I. Animal experimentation and evolution. *American Scholar, 40,* 497-503.

Roberts, S., & Pashler, H. (2000).   How persuasive is a good fit? A comment on theory testing. *Psychological Review, 107,* 358-367.

Rodgers, J. L., & Rowe, D. C. (2002).   Theory development should begin (but not end) with good empirical fits. A comment on Roberts and Pashler (2000). *Psychological Review, 109* (3), 599-603.

Roediger, H. L. (1990).   Implicit memory: Retention without remembering. *American Psychologist, 45,* 1043-1056.

Roediger, H. L., III, Marsh, E. J., & Lee, S. C. (2002).   Varieties of memory. In H. Pashler & D. Medin (Eds.), *Steven's handbook of experimental psychology* (3rd Ed.), *Vol 2: Memory and cognitive processes* (pp. 1-41). New York: Wiley.

Roediger, H. L., III, & McDermott, K. B. (1993).   Implicit memory in normal human subjects. In F. Boller & J. Grafman (Eds.), *Handbook of neuropsychology* (Vol. 8, pp. 63-131). Amsterdam: Elsevier.

Roediger, H. L., III, Meade, M. L., & Bergman, E. T. (2001).   Social contagion of memory. *Psychonomic Bulletin & Review, 8,* 365-371.

Roediger, H. L., III, Weldon, M. S., Stadler, M. A., & Riegler, G. H. (1992).   Direct comparison of word stems and world fragments in implicit and explicit retention tests. *Journal of Experimental Psychology: Learning, Memory, and Cognition, 18,* 1251-1269.

Roediger, H. L., III. (2007).   Twelve tips for authors. *Observer, 20,* 39-41.

Roediger, H. L., III. (2008).   Relativity of remembering: Why the laws of memory vanished. *Annual Review of Psychology, 59,* 225-254.

Rollin, B. E. (1985).   The moral status of research animals in psychology. *American Psychologist, 40,* 920-926.

Rose, T. L. (1978).   The functional relationship between artificial food colors and hyperactivity. *Journal of Applied Behavior Analysis, 11,* 439-446.

Rosenthal, R. (1966).   Experimenter effects in behavioral research. New York: Appleton-Century-Crofts.

Rosenthal, R. (1969). Interpersonal expectations: Effects of the experimenter's hypothesis. In R. Rosental & R. L. Rosnow (Eds.), *Artifact in behavioral research* (pp. 183–277). New York: Academic Press.

Rosenthal, R. (2002). Covert communication in classrooms, clinics, courtrooms, and cubicles. *American Psychologist, 57,* 839–849.

Rosenthal, R., & Fode, K. (1963). The effects of experimenter bias on the performance of the albino rat. *Behavioral Science, 8,* 183–189.

Ross, E. A. (1908). *Social psychology.* New York: MacMillan.

Ross, M. (1989). Relation of implicit theories to the construction of personal histories. *Psychological Review, 96,* 341–357.

Rovee-Coller, C. (1993). The capacity for long-term memory in infancy. *Current Directions in Psychological Science, 2,* 130–135.

Rowan, A. N., & Lowe, F. M. (1995). *The animal research controversy: Protest, process, & public policy.* North Grafton, MA: Tufts University Center for Animals and Public Policy.

Rowland, L. W. (1939). Will hypnotized persons try to harm themselves or others? *Journal of Abnormal Social Psychology, 34,* 114–117.

Saegert, S., Mackintosh, E., & West, S. (1975). Two studies of crowding in urban public spaces. *Environment and Behavior, 7,* 159–184.

Salmon, W. C. (1988). Rational prediction. In A. Grünbaum & W. C. Slamon (Eds.), *The limitations of deductivism* (pp. 47–60) Berkley: University of California Press.

Salvucci, D. D., Mandalia, H. M., Kuge, N., & Yamamura, T. (2007). Lane-change detection using a computational driver model. *Human Factors, 49,* 532–542.

Scarborough, D. L. (1972). Stimulus modality effects on forgetting in short term memory. *Journal of Experimental Psychology, 95,* 285–289.

Schacter, D. L. (1983). Feeling of knowing in episodic memory. *Journal of Experimental Psychology, 9,* 39–54.

Schacter, D. L. (1987). Implicit memory: History and current status. *Journal of Experimental Psychology: Learning, Memory, and Cognition, 13,* 501–518.

Schacter, D. L. (1990). Introduction to implicit memory: Multiple perspectives. *Bulletin of the Psychonomic Society, 28,* 338–340.

Schaie, K. W. (1977). Quasi-experimental designs in the psychology of aging. In J. E. Birren & K. W. Schaie (Eds.), *Handbook of psychology and aging.* New York: Van Nostrand.

Schmolck, H., Buffalo, E. A., & Squire, L. R. (2000). Memory distortions develop over time: Recollections of the O. J. Simpson trial verdict after 15 and 32 months. *Psychological Science, 11,* 39–45.

Schreibman, L., O'Neill, R. E., & Koegel, R. L. (1983). Behavioral training for siblings of autistic children. *Journal of Applied Behavior Analysis, 16,* 129–138.

Schultz, D. P., & Schultz, S. E. (1987). *A history of modern psychology* (4th Ed.). New York: Academic Press.

Scialfa, C. T., Garvey, P. M., Gish, K. W., Deering, L. M., Leibowitz, H. W., & Goebel, C. C. (1988). Relationships among measures of static and dynamic visual sensitivity. *Human Factors, 30,* 677–688.

Searle, J. R. (1980). Minds, brains, and programs. *Behavioral and Brain Sciences, 3,* 417–458.

Searle, J. R. (1990). Is the brain's mind a computer program? *Scientific American,* (January) 26–31.

Seidenberg, M. S., & McClelland, J. L. (1989). A distributed, developmental model of word recognition and naming. *Psychological Review, 96,* 523–568.

Sergent, C., & Dehaene, S. (2004). Is consciousness a gradual phenomenon? Evidence for an all-or-none bifurcation during the attentional blink. *Psychological Science, 15,* 720–729.

Sherif, M. (1935). A study of some social factors in perception. *Archives of Psychology,* 187.

Shimamura, A. P. (1986). Priming effects in amnesia: Evidence for a dissociable memory function. *Quarterly Journal of Experimental Psychology, 38A,* 619–644.

Shweder, R. A., & Sullivan, M. A. (1993). Cultural psychology: Who needs it? In L. W. Porter & M. R. Rosenzweig (Eds.), *Annual review of psychology* (Vol. 44, pp. 497–523). Palo Alto, CA: Annual Reviews.

Sidman, M. (1960). *Tactics of scientific research.* New York: Basic Books.

Silveira, T. (1971). *Incubation: The effect of interruption timing and length on problem solution and quality of problem processing.* Unpublished doctoral dissertation, University of Oregon.

Singer, P. (1995). Animal experimentation: Philosophical perspectives. In W. T. Reich (Ed.), *Encyclopedia of bioethics,* (Vol. 1, pp. 147–153). New York: Free Press.

Skinner, B. F. (1957). *Verbal behavior.* New York: Appleton-Century-Crofts.

Skinner, B. F. (1959). The flight from the laboratory (pp. 242–257). *Cumulative Record,* New York: Appleton-Century-Crofts.

Slaughter-Defoe, D. T., & Rubin, H. H. (2001). A longitudinal case study of Head Start eligible children: Implications for urban education. *Educational Psychologist, 36,* 31–44.

Smith, A. D., & Winograd, E. (1978). Adult age differences in remembering faces. *Developmental Psychology, 14,* 443–444.

Smith, E. R., & Miller, F. D. (1978). Limits on perceptions of cognitive processes: A reply to Nisbett and Wilson. *Psychological Review, 85,* 355–362.

Smith, S. M. (1995). Getting into and out of mental ruts: A theory of fixation, incubation, and insight. In R. J. Sternberg & J. E. Davidson (Eds.), *The Nature of Insight* (pp. 229–251).

Smith, S. M., & Blankenship, S. E. (1989). Incubation effects. *Bulletin of the Psychonomic Society, 27,* 311–314.

Smith, S. M., & Blankenship, S. E. (1991). Incubation and the persistence of fixation in problem-solving. *American Journal of Psychology, 104,* 61–87.

Snellgrove, L. (1981). Knowledge of results. In L.T. Benjamin & K. D. Lowman (Eds.), *Activities handbook for the teaching of psychology* (p. 66). Washington, DC: American Psychological Association.

Spence, K. W. (1948). The postulates and methods of "behaviorism." *Psychological Review, 55,* 67-78.

Spencer, S. J., Steele, C. M., & Quinn, D. M. (1999). Stereotype threat and woman's math performance. *Journal of Experimental Social Psychology, 35,* 4-28.

Spencer, R. M., & Weisberg, R. W. (1986). Context-dependent effects on analogical transfer. *Memory & Cognition, 14,* 442-449.

Stanley, A. (1990, May 8). Pre-med student, 12, goes for record. *Roanoke Times & World-News, 1,* 10.

Steele, C. M., & Aronson, J. (1995). Stereotype threat and the intellectual test performance of African Americans. *Journal of Personality & Social Psychology, 69,* 797-811.

Steinhauser, M., Maier, M., & Hubner, R. (2007). Cognitive control under stress. *Psychological Science, 18,* 540-545.

Sternberg, R. J. (1988). *The triarchic mind: A new theory of human intelligence.* New York: Viking.

Sternberg, R. J. (1992). How to win acceptances by psychological journals: 21 tips for better writing. *APS Observer,* (September) 12-18.

Sternberg, R. J. (1993). *The psychologist's companion* (3rd Ed.). New York: Cambridge University Press.

Sternberg, R. J. (1995). For whom the bell curve tolls: A review of the bell curve. *Psychological Science, 6,* 257-261.

Sternberg, R. J. (1997). Intelligence and lifelong learning: What's new and how can we use it? *American Psychologist, 52,* 1134-1139.

Sternberg, R. J., Grigorenko, E. L., & Kalmar, D. A. (2001). The role of theory in unified psychology. *Journal of Theoretical and Philosophical Psychology, 21* (2), 100-117.

Sternberg, R. J., & Salter, W. (1982). Conceptions of intelligence. In R. J. Sternberg (Ed.), *Handbook of human intelligence* (pp. 3-28). Cambridge: Cambridge University Press.

Sternberg, S. (2001). Separate modifiability, mental modules, and the use of pure and composite measures to reveal them. *Acta Psychologica, 106,* 147-246.

Stevens, S. S. (1961). The psychophysics of sensory functions. In W. A. Rosenblith, *Sensory communication* (pp. 1-33). Cambridge: MIT Press.

Stokols, D., & Altman, I., (Eds.). (1987). *Handbook of environmental psychology* (Vol. 1). New York: Wiley.

Strayer, D. L., & Drews, F. A. (2007). Cell-phone-induced driver distraction. *Current Directions in Psychological Science, 16,* 128-131.

Strayer, D. L., Drews, F. A., & Johnston, W. A. (2003). Cell phone-induced failures of visual attention during simulated driving. *Journal of Experimental Psychology: Applied, 95,* 23-32.

Strayer, D. L., & Johnston, W. A. (2001). Driven to distractions: Dual-task studies of simulated driving and conversing on a cellular telephone. *Psychological Science, 12* (5), 462-466.

Stroop, J. R. (1935). Studies of interference in serial verbal reactions. *Journal of Experimental Psychology, 18,* 643-662.

Sussman, S., Hahn, G., Dent, C. W., Stacy, A. W., Burton, D., & Flay, B. R. (1993). Naturalistic observation of adolescent tobacco use. *International Journal of Addictions, 28,* 803-811.

Svartdal, F. (2000). Persistence during extinction: Conventional and reversed PREE under multiple schedules. *Learning and Motivation, 31,* 21-40.

Svartdal, F. (2003). Extinction after partial reinforcement: Predicted versus judged persistence. *Scandinavian Journal of Psychology, 44,* 55-64.

Swazey, J. P., Anderson, M. S., & Lewis, K. S. (1993). Ethical problems in academic research. *American Scientist, 81,* 542-553.

Swets, J. A., Dawes, R. M., & Monahan, J. (2000). Psychological science can improve diagnostic decisions. *Psychological Science in the Public Interest, 1* (1), 1-26.

Swinnen, S. P., Schmidt, R. A., Nicholson, D. E., & Shapiro, D. C. (1990). Information feedback for skill acquisition: Instantaneous knowledge of results degrades learning. *Journal of Experimental Psychology: Learning, Memory, and Cognition, 16,* 706-716.

Talarico, J. M., & Rubin, D. C. (2003). Confidence, not consistency, characterizes flashbulb memories. *Psychological Science, 14,* 455-461.

Telford, C. W. (1931). The refractory phase of voluntary and associative responses. *Journal of Experimental Psychology, 14,* 35-36.

Theeuwes, J., & Alferdinck, J. W. A. M. (1995). Rear light arrangements for cars equipped with a center high-mounted stop lamp. *Human Factors, 37,* 371-380.

Theios, J. (1973). Reaction time measurements in the study of memory processes. In G. H. Bower (Ed.), *The psychology of learning and motivation* (Vol. 7, pp. 44-85). New York: Academic Press.

Thompson, J. B., & Buchanan, W. (1979). *Analyzing psychological data.* New York: Scribner's.

Thompson, K. M., Graham, J. D., & Zellner, J. W. (2001). *Risk-benefit analysis methods for vehicle safety devices.* 17th International Technical Conference on the Enhanced Safety of Vehicles, Amsterdam, Netherlands.

Thompson, K. M., Segui-Gomez, M., & Graham, J. D. (2002). Validating benefit and cost estimates: The case of airbag regulation. *Risk Analysis, 22* (4), 803-811.

Thorndike, E. L. (1898). Animal intelligence: An experimental study of the associative processes in animals. *Psychological Review Monograph Supplement, 2.*

Thorndike, E. L. (1932). *The fundamentals of learning.* New York: Teachers College, Columbia University.

Tombu, M., & Joliceur, P. (2003). A central capacity sharing model of dual-task performance. *Journal of Experimental Psychology: Human Perception and Performance, 29* (1), 3–18.

Tulving, E. (1992). Ebbinghaus, Hermann. In L. R. Squire (Ed.), *Encyclopedia of learning and memory* (pp. 151–154). New York: Macmillan.

Tulving, E., & Pearlstone, Z. (1966). Availability versus accessibility of information in memory for words. *Journal of Verbal Learning and Verbal Behavior, 5,* 381–391.

Turing, A. M. (1950). Computing machinery and intelligence. *Mind, 59,* 433–460.

Tversky, B., & Marsh, E. J. (2000). Biased retellings of events yield biased memories. *Cognitive Psychology, 40,* 1–38.

Ueda, T., Nawa, Y., Yukawa, E., Taketani, F., & Hara, Y. (2006). Change in dynamic visual acuity by pupil dilation. *Human Factors, 48,* 651–655.

Ulrich, R., & Mattes, S. (1996). Does immediate arousal enhance response force in simple reaction time? *Quarterly Journal of Experimental Psychology, Section A: Human Experimental Psychology, 49,* 972–990.

Ulrich, R., Mattes, S., & Miller, J. (1999). Donder's assumption of pure insertion: An evaluation on the basis of response dynamics. *Acta Psychologica, 102,* 43–75.

Underwood, B. J. (1975). Individual differences as a crucible in theory construction. *American Psychologist, 30,* 128–134.

van Wolkenten, H., Davis, J. M., Gong, M. L., & de Waal, F. B. M. (2006). Coping with acute crowding by *Cebus paella. International Journal of Primatology, 27,* 1241–1256.

Velten, E. A. (1968). A laboratory task for the induction of mood states. *Behavior Research and Therapy, 6,* 473–478.

Walden, P. (2004). Survey procedures, content, and dataset overview. In D. Romer, K. Kenski, P. Waldman, C. Adasiewicz, & K. H. Jamieson (Eds.), *Capturing campaign dynamics: The national Annenberg Election Survey* (pp. 12–33). New York: Oxford University Press.

Warrington, E. K., & Weiskrantz, L. (1970). Amnesic syndrome: Consolidation or retrieval? *Nature, 228,* 628–630.

Wason, P. C. (1968). Reasoning about a rule. *Quarterly Journal of Experimental Psychology, 20,* 273–281.

Watson, J. B. (1913). Psychology as the behaviorist views it. *Psychological Review, 20,* 158–177.

Watson, J. B. (1919). *Psychology from the standpoint of a behaviorist.* Philadelphia: Lippincott.

Watson, J. B. (1925). *Behaviorism.* New York: Norton.

Waugh, N. C., & Norman, D. A. (1965). Primary memory. *Psychological Review, 72,* 89–104.

Webb, E. J., Campbell, D. T., Schwartz, R. D., & Sechrest, L. (1966). *Unobtrusive measures: Nonreactive research in the social sciences.* Chicago: Rand McNally.

Weiskrantz, L. (1986). *Blindsight: A case study and implications.* Oxford: Clarendon Press.

Weiskrantz, L. (1997). *Consciousness lost and found: A neuropsychological explanation* (pp. 40–42). New York: Oxford.

Weiskrantz, L. (2002). Prime-sight and blindsight. *Cognition and Consciousness, 11,* 568–581.

Weiskrantz, L., Cowey, A., & LeMare, C. (1998). Learning from the pupil: A spatial visual channel in the absence of V1 in monkey and human. *Brain, 121,* 1065–1072.

Weizenbaum, J. (1976). *Computer power and human reason.* San Francisco: W. H. Freeman.

Weldon, M. S., & Roediger, H. L. (1987). Altering retrieval demands reverses the picture superiority effect. *Memory & Cognition, 15,* 269–280.

Welker, R. L. (1976). Acquisition of a free-operant-appetitive response in pigeons as a function of prior experience with response-independent food. *Learning and Motivation, 7,* 394–405.

Wesp, R., Cichello, P., Gracia, E. B., & Davis, K. (2004). Observing and engaging in purposeful actions with objects influences estimates of their size. *Perception & Psychophysics, 66,* 1261–1267.

White, R. J. (1971). Debate II. Antivivisection: The reluctant hydra. *American Scholar, 40,* 503–512.

Wickelgren, W. A. (1977). Learning and memory. Englewood Cliffs, NJ: Prentice-Hall.

Wickström, G., & Bendix, T. (2000). The "Hawthorne effect"—what did the original Hawthorne studies actually show? *Scandanarian Journal of Work Environment Health, 26* (4), 363–367.

Willerman, L., Schultz, R., Rutledge, J. N., & Bigler, E. D. (1991). In vivo brain size and intelligence. *Intelligence, 15,* 223–228.

Williams, K. D., Nida, S. A., Baca, L. D., & Latané, B. (1989). Social loafing and swimming: Effects of identifiability of individual and relay performance of intercollegiate swimmers. *Basic and Applied Social Psychology, 10,* 73–82.

Williams, K., Harkins, S., & Latané, B. (1981). Identifiability as a deterrent to social loafing: Two cheering experiments. *Journal of Personality and Social Psychology, 40,* 303–311.

Witt, J. K., & Proffitt, D. (2005). See the ball, hit the ball: Apparent ball size is correlated with batting average. *Psychological Science, 16,* 937–938.

Wolf, M. M., & Risley, T. R. (1971). Reinforcement: Applied research. In R. Glaser (Ed.), *The nature of reinforcement* (pp. 310–325). New York: Academic Press.

Wolters, G., & Goudsmit, J. J. (2005). Flashbulb and event memory of September 11, 2001: Consistency, confidence, and age effects. *Psychological Reports, 96,* 605–619.

Wood, J. M., Garth, D., Grounds, G., McKay, P., & Mulvahil, A. (2003). Pupil dilation does affect some aspects of daytime driving performance. *British Journal of Ophthalmology, 87,* 1387–1390.

Woodworth, R. S., & Schlosberg, H. (1954). *Experimental psychology* (Rev. Ed., pp. 396–397, 485–486). New York: Henry Holt and Company.

Wundt, W. (1874). *Principles of physiological psychology.* Leipzig: Englemann.

Yeager, K. (1996). R&D and the dimensions of value. *EPRI Journal, 21,* 16-25.

Young, P. C. (1952). Antisocial uses of hypnosis. In L. M. LeCron (Ed.), *Experimental hypnosis.* New York: Macmillan.

Young, P. T. (1928). Precautions in animal experimentation. *Psychological Bulletin, 25,* 487–489.

Zajonc, R. B. (1962). Response suppression in perceptual defense. *Journal of Experimental Psychology, 64,* 206-214.

Zimbardo, P. G. (2007). *The Lucifer effect: Understanding how good people turn evil.* New York: Random House.

Zimmer, H. D., & Engelkamp, J. (1999). Levels-of-processing effects in subject-performed tasks. *Memory & Cognition, 27,* 907–914.

Zuckerman, M. (1995). Good and bad humors: Biochemical bases of personality and its disorders. *Psychological Science, 6,* 325-332.

GLOSSARY

A _priori_ method according to Peirce, a way of fixing belief according to the reasonableness of the event

AB design a frequently used design in therapy in which a therapy (B) is instituted after measuring a particular behavior (A); a poor research design

ABA design _see_ Reversal design

ABAB design a completed reversal design often used in therapy such that the therapeutic procedure (B) is reintroduced

ABBA design intrasubject counterbalancing in which treatments or conditions A and B are administered in the ABBA or BAAB order

Abscissa the horizontal axis (or _X_-axis) in a graph

Absolute mean deviation the absolute value of deviations of scores about the mean

Absolute threshold in psychophysics, a hypothetical barrier that incoming stimuli must cross before they can be perceived

Abstract short summary at the beginning of a journal article that informs the reader about what was done (method) and results

Affections emotional reactions, such as hatred, joy, and love

Afterimage that which arises after looking at a visual stimulus, usually for several seconds. _See_ Positive afterimage; Negative afterimage

AI (artificial intelligence) the notion that computer programs can execute actions thought to require intelligence when done by people

Alpha level _see_ Significance level

Alpha waves high-amplitude, slow-brain waves seen during relaxed wakefulness

Alternating treatments design a small-_n_ design in which there are more than two levels of the independent variable

Amnesia a memory disorder, usually caused by some injury to the brain, characterized by either total or partial memory loss

Analogy understanding one concept in terms of another

Analysis of variance a statistical test appropriate for analyzing reliability from experiments with any number of levels on one or more independent variables

Analytical approach attempts to predict events on the basis of a theory or model

Anthropomorphizing   attributing human characteristics or emotions, such as happiness, to animals

APA format   the journal article format specified by the American Psychological Association (APA); the *Publication Manual of APA* is currently in its fifth edition

Aphasic   a person who has a disorder of language; usually associated with damage to the left hemisphere of the brain

Apparatus   a subsection of the method portion of a technical paper that describes any special equipment used in the research to test participants

Applied research   research aimed at solving a practical problem

Arithmetic mean   usually called the mean, it is a measure of central tendency that is the sum of the scores divided by the number of scores

Asymmetrical transfer   *see* Carryover effect

Auditory oddball task   a monitoring task in which the observer counts the less frequent of two distinct auditory stimuli

Author   the person or persons responsible for a technical paper; a literature search via an author's name can be profitable source of additional references

Autobiographical memory   memory for one's own life

Autokinetic phenomenon   the perception by a person in a dark room that a single, stationary spot of light appears to move

Awareness   an issue in perception as to whether an individual can respond perceptually to an event in the absence of conscious awareness

Balanced Latin square   a counterbalancing scheme in which each condition is preceded and followed equally often by every other condition

Baseline   a measurement used as the basis for comparison, usually when no treatment is given

Basic research   research aimed at increasing fundamental understanding

Behaviorism   the school of psychology, originated by John Watson, that directed psychologists' attention to the study of overt behavior, not mind or mental events

Beta (β)   a statistic in signal detection theory related to the criterion adopted by the observer

Beta waves   low-amplitude, fast brain waves seen during attention to cognitive tasks

Between-groups variance   a measure of the dispersion among groups in an experiment

Between-subjects design   an experimental design in which each subject is tested under only one level of each independent variable

Bit   the basic unit of information measured in binary digits

Blind   experiment in which subjects do not know whether or not they are in the treatment condition

Blindsight   according to Weiskrantz, the effect of certain kinds of brain damage in which the subject has an inability to recognize objects but retains the ability to detect the presence and movement of objects

Blocking   a previously learned conditioned stimulus blocks learning to a new conditioned stimulus presented in a compound with it because the new one is redundant

Bottom-up processing   cognitive processes involving feature extraction that begin with sensory stimulation

Boundary conditions   the necessary conditions to produce a phenomenon, or the conditions required to obtain the phenomenon

Brown-Peterson technique   a way of studying short-term memory that involves first presenting a to-be-remembered item and then presenting material that limits rehearsal for a retention interval prior to a retention test

Bystander intervention (bystander effect)   the more people who observe a crisis and who are potential helpers, the less likely any one bystander is to help the victim

Capacity sharing   a class of attention models that postulate a common resource needed for mental operations

Carryover effect   the relatively permanent effect that testing subjects in one condition has on their later behavior in another condition

Case study   the intensive investigation of a particular instance, or case, of some behavior; does not allow inferences of cause and effect but is merely descriptive

Categorized list   words used in memory experiments that are related by being members of the same category; for example, articles of furniture: chair, bed, sofa, table

Cause   we infer a cause from experimental results when we see an effect produced by the varied factor

Ceiling effect   *see* Scale attenuation effects

Central bottleneck   a class of attention models that postulate sequential processing of one task at a time

Central tendency   the center of a distribution of scores; descriptive statistics indicating the center of a distribution of scores (*see* Mean, Median)

Changing-criterion design   a small-n design in which the criterion to obtain some outcome changes systematically over time

Chinese room   a thought experiment developed by Searle that supposedly shows that artificial intelligence is impossible

Chi-squared (χ^2) test for independence   a statistical test often used to determine the significance of the relationship between the variables in contingency research

Choice-reaction task   a secondary task involving more than one stimulus and more than one response that is used to measure the attentional demands of a primary task

Choice-reaction time   *see* Donders B reaction

Chronological age   the physical age of an individual

Classical conditioning   a basic form of learning, in which stimuli initially incapable of evoking certain responses acquire the ability to do so through repeated pairing with other stimuli (unconditioned stimuli) that are able to elicit such responses; also called respondent conditioning

Cognitive psychology   the study of how people acquire, store, and use information

Cohort   the people who are equivalent in age to a person being examined in a study of development

Cohort effects   a potential confounding when age is a variable, attributable to the effects of the people living at a time when a given individual is developing

Computerized literature search   a method of searching databases in a library or on the Web using a computer

Conceptual replication   the attempt to demonstrate an experimental phenomenon with an entirely new paradigm or set of experimental conditions (*see* Converging operations)

Conceptually driven processing   *see* Top-down processing

Conditioned response (CR)   the learned response to a conditioned stimulus

Conditioned stimulus (CS)   an originally neutral stimulus that, through repeated pairings with an unconditioned stimulus, acquires the ability to elicit the response originally produced only by the unconditioned stimulus

Confidentiality   the researcher's guideline stating that information obtained about subjects should remain confidential unless otherwise agreed

Confirmation bias   the tendency to seek out information that confirms rather than disconfirms one's hypothesis

Conformity   bringing behavior into agreement with social norms

Confounding   the simultaneous variation of a second variable with an independent variable of interest so that any effect on the dependent variable cannot be attributed with certainty to the independent variable; inherent in correlational research

Construct validity   when several measures fit sensibly together and converge on (and can be explained by) an underlying psychological concept

Contingency   the relationship between a response and its outcome in operant conditioning or the conditioned stimulus–unconditioned stimulus relationship in classical conditioning

Contingency research   a relational research design in which the frequencies of all combinations of two variables are assessed to determine the relationship between them

Continuous reinforcement   a schedule of reinforcement in which a reward follows every time the appropriate behavior is emitted

Control condition   an experimental condition, usually with no treatment, used as a baseline

Control group   a group of participants given no experimental treatment

Control variable   a potential independent variable that is held constant in an experiment

Converging operations   a set of related lines of investigation that all bolster a common conclusion

Correlation coefficient   a number that can vary from -1.00 to $+1.00$ and that indicates the degree of relation between two variables

Correlational research   allows the experimenter to determine simultaneously the degree and direction of a relationship with a single statistic

Counterbalancing   a term describing any technique used to vary systematically the order of conditions in an experiment to distribute the effects of time of testing (e.g., practice and fatigue), so they are not confounded with conditions

Criterion   in signal detection the level set by the decision process to determine whether to say "yes" or "no" to whether a stimulus is present

Criterion validity   *see* Predictive validity

Critical experiment   a key experiment that purports to distinguish among competing theories

Cross-lagged-panel correlation procedure   involves several correlations that help determine the direction of possible causality among variables

Crossover interaction   the reversal of the effect of one independent variable on a dependent variable at a certain level of a second independent variable

Cross-sectional design   design using a large sample of the population of various ages at one time for testing purposes (*contrast with* Longitudinal design)

Cross-sequential design   an experiment that combines the cross-sectional and longitudinal procedures

d′   a statistic in signal detection theory related to the sensitivity of the observer

Data   the scores obtained on a dependent variable

Data-driven processing   *see* Bottom-up processing

Debriefing   when subjects are told all details of an experiment after they have participated; an ethical obligation of the researcher

Deception   a research technique in which the participant is misled about some aspect of the project; may be unethical

Decision threshold   the stimulus that elicits a response resulting from both the criterion and the strength of the stimulus (*see* Beta, d')

Deduction   reasoning from the general to the particular

Degrees of freedom   the number of values free to vary if the total number of values and their sum are fixed

Delimiting observations   especially in naturalistic observation, the necessity to limit or choose the classes of behaviors to be observed

Demand characteristics   those cues available to subjects in an experiment that may enable them to determine the purpose of the experiment or what is expected by the experimenter

Density   a primary independent variable in crowding research, which is usually defined as the number of people per unit area

Dependent variable   the variable measured and recorded by the experimenter

Descriptive statistics   methods of organizing and summarizing data

Design   the framework of an experiment—the independent, dependent, subject, and control variables

Determinism   the philosophical belief that all events derive from causes

Deviant-case analysis   investigation of similar cases that differ in outcome in an attempt to specify the reasons for the different outcomes

Difference   a basic property of all measurement scales such that objects or their attributes can be categorized as different from each other

Difference threshold   the average point at which two stimuli are judged to be different

Differential carryover effects   a problem in within-subject experimental designs when exposure to earlier conditions alters behavior on later conditions

Diffusion ($I = N^{-t}$)   the power law showing that impact (I) of other people decreases as a function of the number (N) of other people

Diffusion of responsibility   the tendency for individuals to assume less responsibility to act in a group situation

Direct approach to perception   Gibson's idea that we directly pick up and use the information afforded by the environment

Direct replication   the repetition of an experiment as identically as possible to the first performance, to determine whether the same results will be obtained

Direct scaling   a scaling technique in which the observer responds directly in psychological scale units

Directional test   *see* One-tailed test

Discriminative stimulus (S^D)   a stimulus that indicates whether or not a response will be reinforced

Discussion   a section of a technical paper in which the author draws theoretical conclusions by examining, interpreting, and qualifying the results

Dispersion   the amount of spread in a distribution of scores

Distributed-criterion design   a small-n design in which the criteria for outcomes are distributed among two or more behaviors (*see* Changing-criterion design)

Distribution of sample means   a distribution of sample means taken from a population that approximates a normal distribution

Dizygotic   developing from two different fertilized eggs

Dolorimeter   a device similar to a hair dryer that can present a focused radiant heat to the skin

Donders A reaction   a reaction time task in which one stimulus is linked with one response

Donders B reaction   a reaction time task in which there are two or more responses, each linked to its own stimulus

Donders C reaction   a reaction time task in which there are two stimuli but only one response

Double-blind experiment   an experimental technique in which neither the subject nor the experimenter knows which subjects are in which treatment conditions

Double dissociation of function   a technique in which opposite behaviors are elicited by two different tasks from different areas of functioning (*see* Converging operations)

Dualism   the idea that the mind and the body are separate entities

Dynamic perimetry   a procedure, used to measure the visual field, in which a small visual target is gradually brought into the field of vision

Dynamic visual acuity   ability to perceive detail in moving objects

Einstellung   *see* Set

Electroencephalogram (EEG)   a recording of the electrical activity of the brain that is done by electrodes placed on the scalp

Emmert's law   the size of an afterimage is proportional to the viewing distance

Empirical   relying on or derived from observation or experiment

Empirical approach   in contrast to the analytical approach, attempts to achieve predictive power on the basis of empirical regularities

Empirical theory of perception   the argument that perceptions are determined entirely by past experience

Episodic memory   memories that are autobiographical and personally dated

Equal interval   a property of measurement scales such that a one-unit change is equivalent throughout the range of the scale

Eta (n)   a measure of magnitude of effect for the *F* test

Ethical issues   a variety of problems concerning the treatment of research participants, such as deception, informed consent, and the humane treatment of animal subjects

Ethogram   a relatively complete inventory of species-specific behaviors shown by one species

Ethology   the study of naturally occurring behavior

Event-related potential (ERP)   a type of brain wave that is measured shortly after a specific evoking stimulus (*see* N100, N400, P200, and P300)

Ex post facto   literally, "from after the fact"; describes conditions in an experiment that are determined not prior to the experiment but only after some manipulation has occurred naturally

Experiment   the systematic manipulation of some factors in the environment to observe the effect of this manipulation on behavior

Experimental control   the holding constant of extraneous variables in an experiment so that any effect on the dependent variable can be attributed to manipulation of the independent variable

Experimental error   any variation in the dependent variable that is not caused by the independent variable

Experimental extinction   when the reinforcer of an instrumental response is no longer given after the response

Experimental hypothesis   the research hypothesis that specifies the effects of the independent variables (*contrast with* Null hypothesis)

Experimental reliability   the extent to which the experimental results can be replicated or will be obtained again if the experiment is repeated

Experimenter bias   the effect that an experimenter may unknowingly exert on results of an experiment, usually in a direction favoring the experimenter's hypothesis

Experimenter effects   artifactual results due to the presence of an experimenter

Explanation   statements that make a set of events intelligible

Explicit memory test   a memory test that requires a person to try consciously to remember specific events

Extraneous variables   control variables, also known as nuisance variables

F test   a ratio of two variances that is the basis of the analysis of variance

Face validity   the condition in which a measuring instrument intuitively seems to measure what it is supposed to measure

Factorial design   an experimental design in which each level of every independent variable occurs with all levels of the other independent variables

False alarm   the incorrect reporting of the presence of a signal on a trial in which only noise occurs

Falsifiability view   the assertion by Popper that negative results of a test are more informative than positive results

Fatigue effect   a form of carryover effect in which behavior decreases over the course of an experiment

Fechner's law   the logarithmic relation, developed by Fechner, of sensation to stimulus intensity: $\psi = k \log(s)$

Field research   research conducted in natural settings where subjects typically do not know that they are in an experiment

Figures   graphical presentations of data in the results sections of a research report

Flashbulb memory   one's vivid memory for hearing the news of a surprising event

Floor effect   *see* Scale attenuation effects

fMRI   functional magnetic resonance imaging is a tool for measuring blood flow in the brain, a correlate of neural activity

Forced-choice recognition test   a test in which the participant must select between two or more statements; often used to control response styles

Fraud   the deliberate distortion of research results, which includes fabricating data, altering data, and deliberately not reporting results thought to be inappropriate to one's interests

Free recall   test in which subjects retrieve to-be-remembered items without the aid of external retrieval cues; they can recall in any order so recall is *free* in that sense

Freedom to withdraw   experimenters' ethical obligation to allow their subjects to discontinue participation in the research project

Frequency distribution   a set of scores arranged in order along a distribution, indicating the number of times each score occurs

Frequency polygon   a line graph of a frequency distribution

Functional fixedness   the inability to use an object in a new context if it has already served a different function

Functionalism   the school of psychology concerned with the function of psychological processes

General practice effects   the tendency for performance to improve with repetition

Generality of results   the issue of whether a particular experimental result will be obtained under different circumstances, such as with a different subject population or in a different experimental setting

Generalization   formation of broad propositions derived from individual facts

Gestalt psychology   the school of psychology emphasizing whole patterns as important in perception, rather than the artificial analysis of experience into parts (as in structuralism)

Graphemic   the letter level of perceptual analysis

Hallucination   a report of an experience in the absence of any apparent stimulation

Hawthorne effect   the condition in which performance in an experiment is affected by the knowledge of participants that they are in an experiment (*see* Demand characteristics)

Heterogeneous   dissimilar; varying from others

Higher-order interaction   interaction effects involving more than two independent variables in multifactor experiments

Histogram   a frequency distribution in which the height of bars in the graph indicates the frequency of a class of scores; also called a bar graph

History effects   a possible confound in research that inadvertently takes place between measurements because of historical changes in the participant

Hit   the correct detection of a signal that has been presented

Homogeneity of variance   the analysis of variance assumes that the within-groups variances of the different conditions are equivalent

Homogeneous   similar; of the same kind as others

Human factors   the discipline that tries to optimize the relationship between technology and the human

Hypothesis   a testable statement that offers a predicted relationship between dependent and independent variables

Ideas   thoughts

Illumination   an intermediate stage in problem solving in which the individual gains insight or discovers a potential solution to a problem

Illusion   a mistake or distorted perception

Images   a component of conscious experience involving seeing "in the mind's eye"

Imitation game   *see* Turing test

Impact ($I = N^t$)   the power law showing that the impact (I) of others increases with the number (N) of other people

Implicit attitude measures   tests that measure a person's attitudes (e.g., about race) without their awareness of what is being measured

Implicit memory test   a "memory" test that does not require a person to explicitly remember specific experiences but that spontaneously exhibits the effects of those experiences

Incubation   during problem solving, a time when a person turns to other matters after failing to solve the problem. The problem is said to incubate, much as eggs do while a hen sits on them, and can be solved more quickly later

Independent variable   the variable manipulated by the experimenter

Indirect approach to perception   the idea that perception results from the interpretation of sensations

Indirect scaling   the psychological scale is built up indirectly by putting successive just-noticeable difference units in a row

Induction   reasoning from the particular to the general

Inferential statistics   procedures for determining the reliability and generality of a particular experimental finding

Inflection point   the point in a normal curve in which the tail starts to spread; one standard deviation away from the mean

Information   facts; data from the external world; also a unit of measurement in information theory

Informed consent   potential participants' decision whether to participate in an experiment

Insight   the time of illumination in problem solving; when an idea is "hatched"; sometimes accompanied by an "aha" experience

Institutional Animal Care and Use Committee (IACUC)   a committee that oversees the protection of animal subjects in nearly every United States institution that conducts research

Institutional Review Board (IRB)   a board that oversees the protection of human participants in nearly every United States institution that conducts research

Instrumental conditioning   conditioning in which a subject learns to make a response that leads to a reward or prevents a punishment; in contrast to classical conditioning, no eliciting stimulus is presented

Intelligence   mental age (as determined by a test) divided by chronological age times 100

Interaction   an experimental result that occurs when the levels of one independent variable are differentially affected by the levels of other independent variables

Interpolated task   a task used to fill the interval between the study of material and its recall in memory experiments

Interval of uncertainty   the difference between the higher and lower thresholds in a calculation of the difference threshold

Interval scale   a measurement scale that possess the properties of difference, magnitude, and equal intervals

Intervening variables   abstract concepts that link independent variables to dependent variables

Introduction   the portion of a technical paper that specifies the problem to be studied and tells why it is important

Introspection   a method used by structural psychologists to look within and examine their own consciousness

Just-noticeable difference (JND)   coined by Fechner, the internal sensation evoked by one difference threshold and the basic unit defining an internal psychological scale

Labeled magnitude scale   a ratio psychophysical scale that pairs numbers bounded by 0 and 100 with verbal labels that range from "nothing" to "the strongest sensation imaginable"

Landolt C   a way of measuring visual acuity, in which the gap of the C is varied and the observer determines when the gap is no longer visible

Large-*n* design   an experiment involving a large number of subjects; usually analyzed by complex statistical procedures

Latency   amount of time needed to complete a task

Law of effect   the principle that reinforcement of a response leads to the response being more likely to occur in the future

Level   the value of an independent variable

Level of confidence   *see* Significance level

Levels of processing   a framework for studying memory that predicts that semantic or "deeper" encoding tasks will produce better memory for the material than perceptual or "shallow" encoding tasks

Literature search   a method of searching databases in a library or on the Web using a computer

Longitudinal design   the repeated testing of one group of people as they age (*contrast with* Cross-sectional design)

Long-term memory   retrieval of memories that have disappeared from consciousness after their initial perception

Magnitude   a property of measurement scales having to do with the fact that scale values can be ordered on the basis of magnitude: if A > B and B > C, then A > C

Magnitude of effect   a calculation, such as r_{pb}, that reveals the magnitude of the effect of the independent variable—how wrong the null hypothesis is

Magnitude estimation   observers assign numbers to the attributes of stimuli usually without restriction except that the numbers be assigned proportional to the judged magnitude (a ratio scale)

Main effect   the condition in which the effect of one independent variable is the same at all levels of another independent variable

Mann-Whitney *U* test   a nonparametric test to determine the difference between two samples

Mapping   in problem solving, the set of correspondences between a source and target problem; how the two problems "map" onto each other

Masking   the technique of presenting a jumbled visual stimulus immediately after a target stimulus in order to stop the visual persistence of the target

Matching   attempting to make different groups of subjects equivalent based upon subject characteristics or scores on tests

Matched groups design   an experimental design in which subjects are matched on some variable assumed to be correlated with the dependent variable and then randomly assigned to conditions

Materials   a subsection of the methods section that describes any written or videotaped sketches, questionnaires, surveys, and so forth that were used to test subjects

Measurement   the systematic assignment of numbers or names to objects or attributes of objects

Measurement scales   in order of increasing informativeness nominal, ordinal, interval, and ratio

Median   a measure of central tendency; the middle score of a distribution, or the one that divides a distribution in half

Mediator   a variable that provides the causal link between two variables; an underlying causal mechanism

Mental age   the intellectual age of an individual as gauged by an IQ test in contrast to the chronological age

Mental workload   an intervening variable, similar to attention, that modulates the tuning between the demands of the environment and the capability of the organism

Method   a section of a technical paper that describes in detail the operations performed by the experimenter

Method of authority   a method of fixing belief in which an authority's word is taken on faith (*contrast with* Empirical)

Method of limits a psychophysical procedure for determining thresholds in which ascending and descending sequences of stimuli are presented

Method of tenacity a method of fixing belief involving a steadfast adherence to a particular belief, regardless of contrary arguments or data (*contrast with* Empirical)

Mixed design an experimental design containing both within- and between-subject independent variables

Modality effects different effects on retention often produced by visual and auditory presentation; auditory presentation usually produces better memory for the last few items in a series than does visual presentation

Monitoring task a form of dichotic listening in which observers are not required to verbalize a message as it is presented

Monotonic relationship the relationship between two variables in which an increase on one variable is accompanied by a consistent increase or decrease on the other variable

Monozygotic developing from the same fertilized egg

Mozart effect the finding that listening to Mozart compositions leads to increased performance on visual-spatial tests

Multifactor analysis of variance an analysis of variance of experiments that have more than one independent variable

Multiple intelligences the theory that intelligence is actually composed of seven different intelligences

Multiple-baseline design a small-n design in which different behaviors (or different people) receive baseline periods of varying lengths prior to the introduction of the independent variable

N100 a negative component of the event-related potential occurring about 100 ms after stimulus onset that indexes basic analysis of the stimulus

N400 a negative component of the event-related potential occurring about 400 ms after stimulus onset that is supposed to index surprise or incongruity

Nativistic theory of perception the theory that genetic "wired-in" mechanisms account for perceptual capabilities (*see* Empirical theory of perception)

Naturalistic observation the description of naturally occurring events without intervention on the part of the investigator

Nature theory the theory that genetic differences underlie individual differences

Negative afterimage is opposite in brightness and complementary in color to the visual stimulus (*contrast with* Positive afterimage)

Negative contrast effect a decrease in behavior when reinforcement magnitude is decreased such that the behavior is less than when it has always been followed by a small magnitude

Negative correlation an observed relationship between two variables in which a change in one variable is accompanied by a change in the opposite direction in the second variable

Negative reinforcing stimulus a stimulus that, when removed, increases the likelihood of the response that removed it

Noise a complex sound composed of many different frequencies

Nominal scale a measurement scale that possesses the property of difference

Nondirectional test *see* Two-tailed test

Nonparametric tests statistical tests that do not make assumptions about the underlying population distribution; usually used when the data are not at the interval/ratio level

Nonsense syllables for example, consonant-vowel-consonant trigams (e.g., YUN) that do not have meaning in the English language

Normal curve a distribution producing a symmetric, bell-shaped curve

Normal line of regard the line of vision that individuals normally adopt when engaged in a particular task (e.g., driving an automobile)

Null contingency a reinforcement contingency in which there is no relation between a response and reinforcing stimuli

Null hypothesis the prediction that the independent variable will have no effect on the dependent variable

Null result an experimental outcome in which the dependent variable is not influenced by the independent variable

Nurture view the belief that experiential factors influence how an organism develops

Obedience conformity to a direct order or command

Objective measures dependent variables such as reaction time that can be easily verified (*contrast with* Subjective measures)

Objective threshold according to Cheesman and Merikle, the stimulus energy level that elicits truly random behavior (*compare with* Subjective threshold)

Observation the careful watching and recording of a phenomenon

One-tailed test a test that places the rejection area at one end of a distribution

Operant conditioning   *see* Instrumental conditioning

Operational definition   a definition of a concept in terms of the operations that must be performed to demonstrate the concept

Operationism   the position that concepts are defined by the operations used to measure and produce them, but ignores the fact that at least two sets of observations are needed for a complete definition

Ordinal scale   a measurement scale the possess the properties of difference and magnitude

Ordinate   the vertical axis (or *Y*-axis) in a graph

Organization   structures of existing knowledge; one characteristic of a good theory

P200 and P300   positive components of the event-related potential occurring 200 and 300 ms, respectively, after stimulus onset that index attention to the stimulus

Paired-associate recall   a memory task in which a pair of words is given (e.g., mongoose–elephant); later the first word is provided and the task is to recall the second word

Parallel forms   two alternative forms of a test

Parallel-distributed processing (PDP)   uses computer models to simulate cognition; model consists of a network of simple processing units that fall in distinct layers, with all of the processing units within a layer connected to all of the processing units in adjacent layers

Parameters   statistics that describe characteristics of populations

Parametric tests   statistical tests that assume a normal distribution of scores and interval or ratio level of measurement

Parsimony   using the smallest number of statements in a theory

Partial reinforcement   a schedule of reinforcement in which a reward follows a desired response only on some occasions

Partial reinforcement extinction effect (PREE)   the greater resistance to extinction exhibited for responses learned under partial rather than continuous schedules of reinforcement

Participant observation   an observation technique in which the observer participates with those being observed; for example, living with gorillas in the wild

Pearson *r*   a parametric measure of correlation between two variables

Perception   the awareness process typically viewed as more complex than sensation and usually involving an interpretation of sensation

Perceptual defense   an unwillingness to report perceiving unpleasant material, in contrast to an inability to perceive such material

Personal equation   differences in reaction time first noticed by eighteenth-century astronomers

Personal space   the physical area surrounding a person within which a person will experience discomfort if another person enters; measured by noting the person's defensive reactions

Phenomenological experience   a person's awareness of his or her own state of mind

Pheromones   odors given off by a person (or animal) that are related to sexual receptivity

Phonemic (phonological)   the sound level of the perceptual analysis of words

Photopic vision   vision controlled by the cones in the retina, typically in day viewing conditions

Placebo effect   the improvement often shown in drug-effectiveness studies when patients believe they have received a drug, although they have actually received an inert substance

Plagiarism   the uncredited use of another person's words, data, or ideas

Point biserial *r*   a correlation coefficient often used in two-group experiments to determine the magnitude of effect of the independent variable

Point of subjective equality   the mean of the upper and lower threshold in a determination of the difference threshold

Population   the total set of potential observations (from which a sample can be drawn)

Positive afterimage   is similar in brightness and color to the original visual stimulus

Positive contrast effect   rarely found improvements in behavior when reinforcement magnitude is increased and the behavior is compared with that which has always been followed by a large magnitude of reinforcement

Positive correlation   an observed relationship between two variables in which a change in one variable is accompanied by a change in the same direction in the second variable

Positive reinforcing stimulus   a stimulus that, when presented, increases the likelihood of the response that produced it

Power (of a statistical test)   the probability that a test will reject the null hypothesis when it is in fact false

Practice effect   a carryover effect in an experiment such that behavior improves during the experiment because of practice and not because of the independent variable

Precision   the quality of being exactly specified

Prediction   statement of a future outcome before data are collected

Predictive validity   the ability of a test score to predict behavior on some criterion measure; also called criterion validity (e.g., if a law school entrance exam correctly predicts success as a lawyer)

Preparation   the initial stage in problem solving in which an individual becomes immersed in thinking about the facts and considerations surrounding a given problem

Primacy effect   the better retention of information occurring at the beginning of a list, relative to information in the middle

Primary task   the most important task in a set of concurrent tasks

Prime   prior experience that may not facilitate (prime) behavior

Prime sight   the afterimages perceived by patient D.B. to visual stimuli for which he claimed to be blind

Priming   facilitation of a response because of a previous experience; for example, prior presentation of a word speeds later reading of the same word

Proactive interference   forgetting that is produced by prior learning

Problem   a vague question that is too general to be tested without additional refinement (*see* Hypothesis)

Procedure   a subsection of the method section of a technical paper that explains what happened to the participants/subjects and contains enough information that someone else could replicate the study (repeat the study exactly as it was originally conducted)

Protection from harm   ethical researchers' commitment to protect their subjects from any harm

Pseudoconditioning   a temporary elevation in the amplitude of the conditioned response that is not due to association between the conditioned stimulus and the unconditioned stimulus

Psychological refractory period   in choice reactions with a delay between stimuli, the period in which reaction time of the second response is delayed

Psychoneuroimmunology   an interdisciplinary field that examines the relationships among behavior, neural, endocrine, and immune processes

Psychophysical methods   such as the method of limits that were started by Fechner and include modern methods such as signal detection

Psychophysics   the study of how changes in physical stimuli are translated into psychological experience

Psychophysiology   using physical measures to infer psychological processes (*contrast with* Psychophysics)

Punishment   a stimulus that, when presented, decreases the likelihood of the action that produced it

Pure insertion   the assumption that a mental module can be added or deleted without altering the processing duration of other modules

Qualitative variation   manipulation of an independent variable along a dimension that is not easily quantified, such as providing people different types of instructions in an experiment

Quality-adjusted life year (QALY)   a statistically adjusted estimate of the benefit of new technology

Quantitative variation   manipulation of an independent variable along a measurable dimension, such as the number of food pellets given a rat as reinforcement

Quasi-experiment   an experiment in which the independent variable occurs naturally and is not under direct control of the experimenter

Quasi-experimental designs   an experiment in which the independent variable occurs naturally and is not under direct control of the experimenter

Quasi-independent variable   an independent variable that is selected or measured rather than manipulated directly

Random assignment   a procedure that ensures each subject has an equal chance of being assigned to experimental treatments

Random sample   an unbiased sample in which each unit of the population has an equal chance of being selected

Random selection   a procedure that ensures each member of a population has an equal chance of being a participant in an experiment

Random-groups design   the random assignment of subjects to conditions in a between-subjects design

Randomization   a statistical sample procedure where every element has an equal probability of being selected

Range-bound changing criterion   a variation of the changing-criterion design, in which the criteria for outcomes have a range specified by an upper and lower bound

Ratio scale   a measurement scale that possesses the properties of difference magnitude, equal intervals, and a meaningful zero point

Reaction-time experiment   an experiment in which time is the dependent measure; usually speeded reactions are measured in these experiments

Reactivity   a participant's unplanned reaction to the researcher or research setting that may confound the results of the research

Recall   a measure of retention in which reproduction of material is required

Receiver-operating characteristic (ROC)   *see* ROC function

Recency effect   the better retention of information at the end of a list, relative to information in the middle

Recognition   a measure of retention in which familiarity of information is judged

References   found at the end of a technical paper; only articles cited in the text are included in the reference section

Regression artifacts   an artifact in the measurement of change on a variable when groups of subjects who scored at the extremes on the variable are tested again (*see* Regression to the mean)

Regression to the mean   the tendency for extreme measures on some variable to be closer to the group mean when remeasured, owing to unreliability of measurement

Related measures design   one in which several measures are taken either on the same subject or on subjects matched on important dimensions

Relational research   research that tries to determine how two or more variables are related

Reliability   the repeatability of an experimental result; an estimation from inferential statistics of the likelihood that a finding is repeatable; also, the consistency of a test or measuring instrument determined by computing a correlation between scores obtained by subjects taking the test twice (test–retest reliability), by their taking two different parallel forms of the test, or by scores obtained on each half of the test (split-half reliability)

Reliability of results   refers to the repeatability of an experimental result; inferential statistics provide an estimate of how likely it is that a finding is repeatable; also refers to the consistency of a test or measuring instrument determined by computing a correlation between scores obtained by participants taking the test twice (test–retest reliability) or taking two different parallel forms of the test (parallel test reliability), or by examining scores obtained on two halves of the test (split-half reliability)

Removing harmful consequences   ethical researchers' attempts to remove any harmful consequences that their subjects may have incurred

Replication   the repetition of an earlier experiment to duplicate (and perhaps extend) its findings (*also see* Systematic replication)

Representativeness   an issue concerning whether the variables in an experiment allow extensions to more general situations

Reproducibility   *see* Reliability

Respondent conditioning   *see* Classical conditioning

Restriction of range   when the sample does not represent the full range of possible values for a given variable or factor; it reduces the degree of an observed correlation or relationship between two variables

Results   a section of a technical paper that describes that data obtained in the research and provides statistical analyses conducted on the data

Retrieval cue   information presented at the time of a memory test to aid recall

Retroactive interference   the forgetting of material produced by learning of subsequent material

Reversal (ABA) design   a small-n design in which a subject's behavior is measured under a baseline (A) condition, then an experimental treatment is applied during the B phase and any changes in behavior are observed; finally, the original baseline (A) conditions are reinstituted to ensure that the experimental treatment was responsible for any observed change during the B phase

Robust tests   powerful statistical tests

ROC function (receiver operating characteristic)   a plot graphing hits against false alarms

Running head   the heading that appears at the top of the page of a published article

Sample   observations selected from a population

Sample generalization   a representativeness issue concerning whether the sample used in an experiment is representative of other samples

Sampling   in statistics the selection of subjects or items for experiments

Savings method   Memory can be measured as a reduction (savings) in the number of trials needed to relearn previously studied material

Savings score   the difference between the number of trials in original learning (OL) of a list and its relearning (RL) divided by the number of trials in original learning, with this ratio multiplied by 100

Scale-attenuation effects   difficulties in interpreting results when performance on the dependent variable is either nearly perfect (a ceiling effect) or nearly lacking altogether (a floor effect)

Scientific method   the formulation and testing of hypotheses by systematic observation and experiment; the formulation and testing of theories by induction and deduction

Scotoma   a region of blindness in the visual field caused by a physical defect in the visual system

Scotopic vision   night vision that is controlled by the rods in the retina

Secondary task   an extra task on which performance is an index of attention

Self-correcting   a procedure that automatically detects and repairs errors

Semantic   meaningful analysis of words

Sensation   the basic and elemental intake of stimulus information

Separate modifiability   a form of independence that occurs when one mental module can be changed without modifying another module

Serial position   the order in which information appears when studied for a later memory test

Serial position curve   the graphical representation of retention as a function of the input position of the information; usually, memory is better for the first items (primacy effect) and the last items (recency effect) than for those in the middle; this typical finding is referred to as the serial position effect

Serial recall   a memory test in which subjects try to recall material in the exact order in which it was presented; recalling a telephone number exemplifies a serial recall task

Set   the effect of expectancy of cognition; for example, if the people solve problems in one particular way, they will often approach new problems in the same set way, even when the original strategy is no longer effective; *also called* Einstellung, from the original German experiment

Shape constancy   an object's shape appears constant despite changes in retinal sensations

Shaping   a technique for conditioning a desired response by rewarding successive approximations to that response

Short-term memory   recovery of information shortly after it has been perceived and before it has left conscious awareness

Sign test   a nonparametric test used to determine differences between two sets of scores obtained in a related measures design

Significance level   the probability that an experimental finding is due to chance, or random fluctuation, operating in the data

Simple (one-factor) analysis   an analysis of variance for an experiment that has one independent variable with more than two levels

Simple reaction   *see* Donders A reaction

Simulating control participants   experimental participants who are told to simulate the behavior of how they expect others will act (e.g., people told to simulate hyponosis)

Simultaneous contrast   changes in instrumental behavior that result from the subject's experiencing two or more contrasting magnitudes of reinforcement

Single-blind experiment   an experiment in which subjects were not aware of their assigned treatment conditions

Skewed distribution   a nonsymmetrical distribution

Small-n design   research design using a small number of subjects

Social facilitation   the increase in individual effort produced by the presence of other people and when individual performance is measured

Social loafing   the decrease in individual effort that sometimes occurs when other people are present and when group performance is measured

Social norms   society's standards for behavior

Social pathology   the breakdown of ordinary social interaction often observed in animals subjected to extreme crowding

Social psychology   the psychological study of how society affects the individual

Speciesism   a term used to describe the view that animal life is qualitatively different from human life

Speed–accuracy trade-off   in reaction time experiments, the ability of the responder to substitute changes in the percentage of correct responses for changes in speed of responding

Split-half reliability   the determination of reliability of a test by dividing the test items into two arbitrary groups and correlating the scores obtained on the two halves of the test

Split-litter technique   the random assignment of animals from the same litter to different groups; a type of matched groups design

Stability   when a dependent measure yields the same score in repeated experiments given the same subject, same levels of the independent variable, and so forth

Staircase method   a newer method of limits procedure that concentrates stimulus presentations around the threshold

Standard deviation   a descriptive measure of dispersion; square root of the sum of squared deviations of each score from the mean, divided by the number of scores

Standard error of the mean   the standard deviation of the distribution of sample means

Statistical prediction rules   based on predictor variables and diagnostic information that can be consulted during detection decisions

Statistical reliability   rejecting the null hypothesis on the basis of a statistical test that yields an alpha level of less than .05

Statistics   numbers used for description or inference

Stevens' law   the principle, stated by Stevens, that sensation grows as a power of stimulus intensity: $\psi = S^n$

Stimulus error   an error of introspection in which the observer reported seeing an object (e.g., a table) rather than the elements that made up the experience (e.g., color, pattern)

Stimulus onset asynchrony   the time interval between two stimuli in a choice-reaction time task

Stress   a psychological state of an organism when there is a disparity between its ability to cope with demands of the environment and the level of such demands

Strong AI   the view that machines can possess intelligence of the sort possessed by humans

Strong inference   Platt's view that scientific progress comes about through a series of tests of alternative theoretical outcomes

Stroop effect   difficulty in naming the color of an object when the color conflicts with the name of the object (when the word blue is printed in red ink)

Structural consistency (problem solving)   when mapped elements in the source and target problems play similar roles

Structuralism   the school of psychology, originated by Wundt, in which the primary task of psychology was considered to be the analysis of the structure of conscious experience through introspection

Subject (participant)   A person participating in the research

Subject representativeness   the determination of generality of results across different subject populations

Subject variable   a characteristic of people that can be measured or described but cannot be varied experimentally (e.g., height, weight, sex, and IQ)

Subjective measures   introspective reports given on rating scales that usually cannot be objectively verified

Subjective report   verbal report of a person's perceived mental state

Subjective threshold   the stimulus energy level that yields claims of unawareness but behavior indicating perception of the event (*see* Objective threshold)

Subtractive method   a technique originated by Donders to estimate the amount of time required for various mental operations by subtracting one component from another

Survey research   the technique of obtaining a limited amount of information from a large number of people, usually through random sampling

Synergism   another term for interaction in which the joint effects of two variables combine in a way that is not a simple function of their individual effects

Systematic replication   the repetition of an experiment while varying numerous factors considered to be irrelevant to the phenomenon to see if it will survive these changes

t **test**   a parametric statistical test for determining the significance of the difference between two groups, or between two treatments

Tables   a nongraphical way of summarizing data in a technical paper; summary values of the dependent variable are presented under headings describing the levels of the independent variable

Target   the test item in a priming task; of interest is whether prior experience facilitates (primes) a decision about the target

Tachistoscope   a device that allows very rapid presentation of visual stimuli

Testability   ability of a theory to be examined locally and empirically

Test–retest reliability   the practice of giving the same test twice in succession over a short interval to see if the scores are stable or reliable; generally expressed as a correlation between scores on the tests

Tetrahedral model of memory experiments   Jenkins's four-part analysis of memory experiments into type of subjects, orienting tasks, type of test, and type of materials

Theory   a set of related statements that explain a variety of occurrences

Theory of signal detection   posits that sensory impressions and decision processes together determine the detection of signals

Thought   cognition

Threshold   *see* Absolute threshold and Difference threshold

Time-lag design   a quasi-experimental design similar to the cross-sectional design in which people of different ages are compared at different times so that their age at the time of testing is the same

Title   provides an idea of the contents of an article or technical paper and usually states only the dependent and independent variables

Tonal agnosia   an inability to appreciate melody in music and speech; usually associated with damage to the right hemisphere of the brain

Top-down processing   cognitive processes that begin with knowledge of concepts (*contrast with* Bottom-up processing)

Transfer-appropriate processing   the principle that whether encoding activities promote memory will depend on the type of test used to assess memory performance

Trials to criterion   the number of study and test trials needed to recall material perfectly

True zero   the absence of a physical property (zero weight in grams) as opposed to an arbitrary zero, such as zero degrees centigrade

Truncated range   a problem in interpreting low correlations; the amount of dispersion (or range) of scores on one variable may be small, thus leading to the low correlation found

Turing test   the test devised by Turing in which a machine gives answers indistinguishable from those of humans; supposedly supports the strong AI position

Two-tailed test   a test that places the rejection area at both ends of a distribution

Type I error   the probability that the null hypothesis is rejected when it is in fact true; equals the significance level

Type II error   the failure to reject the null hypothesis when it is in fact false

Unconditioned response (UCR)   a response made to an unconditioned stimulus

Unconditioned stimulus (UCS)   a stimulus that can elicit a response in the absence of conditioning

Unconscious inference   Helmholtz's view that perception involves inferences about sensations and that the observer is unaware of making the inferences

Unobtrusive measures   measures taken from the results of behavior, not from the behavior itself (*see* Nonreactive)

Unobtrusive observations   *see* Nonreactive

Validity   whether a procedure or observation is sound or genuine

Variable   something that can be measured or manipulated

Variable representativeness   the determination of generality of results across different manipulations of an independent variable or different dependent variables

Variance   a measure of dispersion; the standard deviation squared

Verbal report   a subject's description of his or her phenomenological experience, often very difficult to verify

Verification   the final stage in problem solving that involves careful checking of a potential solution

Visual mask   used in computer tasks to block visual afterimages

Wason card selection task   a reasoning task in which subjects often choose options that confirm (rather than disconfirm) their hypotheses

Weak AI   the view that computer programs can be used to test theories of human intelligence

Weber's law   a formula developed by Weber that states that the smallest perceptible difference (the just-noticeable difference) between two stimuli (for example, weights) can be stated as a ratio between the stimuli that is independent of their magnitude, $\Delta I / I = K$

What-if experiment   an experiment performed to see what might happen rather than to test a specific hypothesis

Wilcoxon signed-ranks test   a nonparametric test used to determine differences between two sets of scores obtained in a related measures design

Within-group variance   a measure of the dispersion among subjects in the same group in an experiment

Within-subjects design   an experimental design in which each subject is tested under more than one level of the independent variable

Word-fragment completion task   an implicit memory test in which the subject has to fill in the missing letters of a fragmented word

Workload   the amount of attention-demanding effort imposed on a person

χ^2 test for independence   a statistical test often used to determine whether the data in a contingency table are statistically significant

Yes/no recognition test   a memory test on which subjects decide whether each item was studied or not (by saying yes it was or no it was not)

z score   a standard score in which the difference between an individual score and the mean is expressed in units of standard deviations

NAME INDEX

SUBJECT INDEX

Questions for Critical Readers

Introduction
1. What is the author's goal?
2. What hypothesis will be tested in the experiment?
3. If I had to design an experiment to test this hypothesis, what would I do?

Method
4(a). Is my proposed method better than the author's?
4(b). Does the author's method actually test the hypothesis?
4(c). What are the independent, dependent, and control variables?
5. Using the subjects, apparatus or materials, and procedures described by the author, what results would I predict for this experiment?

Results
6. Did the author get unexpected results?
7(a). How would I interpret these results?
7(b). What applications and implications would I draw from my interpretation of the results?
7(c). Can I think of another explanation for these results?

Discussion
8(a). Does my interpretation or the author's better represent the data?
8(b). Do I or does the author offer the more-cogent discussion of the applications and implications of the results?

A Summary of the Information in each Section of a Research Report

Section	Information
Title	*Experiments:* State independent and dependent variables—"The effects of X on Y." *Other studies:* State the relationships examined—"The relation between X and Y."
Abstract	In less than 960 characters, state what was done to whom and summarize the most important results.
Introduction	State what you plan to do and why (you may have to review results from related research). Predicted results may be appropriate.
Method	Present enough information to allow someone else to repeat your study exactly the way you did it. For clarity use subheadings (*Subjects, Apparatus,* etc.) and make sure that dependent, independent, subject, and control variables are specified.
Results	Summarize important results in tables or figures. Direct the reader to data that seem most relevant to the purpose of the research.
Discussion	State how the results relate to the hypotheses or predictions stated in the introduction. Inferences and theoretical statements are appropriate.
References	In APA format, list only those references that were cited in your report.